AF361281

BEYOND HUMAN

Decentring the Anthropocene in Spanish Ecocriticism

Beyond Human

Decentring the Anthropocene in Spanish Ecocriticism

EDITED BY MARYANNE L. LEONE AND SHANNA LINO

UNIVERSITY OF TORONTO PRESS
Toronto Buffalo London

© University of Toronto Press 2023
Toronto Buffalo London
utorontopress.com
Printed in the USA

ISBN 978-1-4875-4832-2 (cloth)   ISBN 978-1-4875-4833-9 (EPUB)
                                   ISBN 978-1-4875-4835-3 (PDF)

Toronto Iberic

Library and Archives Canada Cataloguing in Publication

Title: Beyond human : decentring the anthropocene in Spanish
    ecocriticism / edited by Maryanne L. Leone and Shanna Lino.
Names: Leone, Maryanne L., editor. | Lino, Shanna, editor.
Series: Toronto Iberic.
Description: Series statement: Toronto Iberic | Includes
    bibliographical references and index.
Identifiers: Canadiana (print) 20230446574 | Canadiana (ebook)
    20230446639 | ISBN 9781487548322 (hardcover) |
    ISBN 9781487548353 (PDF) | ISBN 9781487548339 (EPUB)
Subjects: LCSH: Ecocriticism – Spain. | LCSH: Spanish literature –
    History and criticism. | LCSH: Ecology in literature.
Classification: LCC PN98.E36 B49 2023 | DDC 860.9/3553 – dc23

Cover design: Val Cooke
Cover image: Marta Zafra

We wish to acknowledge the land on which the University of Toronto Press
operates. This land is the traditional territory of the Wendat, the Anishnaabeg,
the Haudenosaunee, the Métis, and the Mississaugas of the Credit First Nation.

This book has been published with the help of funding from the
Assumption University D'Amour College of Liberal Arts and Sciences, the
Glendon College Research Grant, York University's Faculty of Liberal Arts &
Professional Studies, and a Social Sciences and Humanities Research
Council Exchange Knowledge Mobilization Grant.

University of Toronto Press acknowledges the financial support of the
Government of Canada, the Canada Council for the Arts, and the Ontario Arts
Council, an agency of the Government of Ontario, for its publishing activities.

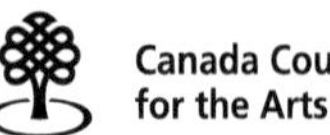

Funded by the   Financé par le
Government gouvernement
of Canada   du Canada

Canadä

To those who seek refuge and with whom we are entangled.

Contents

Part Two: Anthropocene, Capitalocene, Chthulucene

Part Three: Disruptive Agentic Paradigms

Part Four: Medium as Activism Igniter

Maps and Illustrations

Map

Illustrations

Foreword

LUIS I. PRÁDANOS

During the last few years, Maryanne L. Leone and Shanna Lino have organized a number of vibrant conference panels related to Spanish ecocriticism. By doing so, they have facilitated and promoted the development of this rapidly emerging field while establishing a solid network of innovative Spanish literary and cultural scholars interested in learning from and contributing to ongoing global environmental humanities debates. The fruit of this collaborative multi-year effort is this delightful edited volume.

Beyond Human starts with a thorough, incisive, overarching, and theoretically sophisticated introduction that stands alone as a useful overview of both the current state of Spanish ecocriticism and its future directions. Leone and Lino's introduction explicitly points to the many temporal, theoretical, conceptual, and spatial connections among chapters that make the volume a coherent contribution, which is an unusual achievement for a multi-authored academic volume. One of the threads that weaves most chapters together entails an uncompromised critique of the anthropocentric cultural paradigm that – during the last few hundred years – has been transforming differences into hierarchies and inequalities, as well as its recent neoliberal toxic narratives and imaginaries that exacerbate ongoing processes of exploitation and extinction. As Leone and Lino elegantly put it, "If every act is political, so too is it ecological." This claim – and the volume in general – aligns with the political ecology reminder that socioecological problems should always be considered issues of power.

This volume provides ecocritical readings from different historical periods. Historicizing the ecocrisis may be the main contribution of this book as it is filling a significant gap within this emerging field. Most Spanish ecocritical collective interventions to date – such as *Ethics of Life: Contemporary Iberian Debates* (edited by Kata Beilin and William

Viestenz, 2016), *Environmental Cultural Studies through Time: The Luso-Hispanic World* (special issue of *Hispanic Issues On Line*, vol. 24, 2019, edited by Kata Beilin, Kathleen Conolly, and Micah McKay), or "Ecología y estudios culturales ibéricos contemporáneos" (special section in *Arizona Journal of Hispanic Cultural Studies*, vol. 23, 2019, edited by myself) – have focused on contemporary literary and cultural manifestations. For this reason, the chapters that explicitly explore non-contemporary periods are especially welcome, as they provide ecocritical approaches, for example, to Baroque comedies and treatises, pastoral romance, and Enlightenment essays. This cultural historical angle permeates most essays within the volume, such as the post-humanist approach to Regenerationism in Óscar Iván Useche's chapter or the brilliant ecocritical approach to naturalism in Michael L. Martínez's contribution.

Beyond Human is well balanced as it features both junior and senior literary and cultural scholars. Similarly, the book includes established environmental cultural researchers as well as a number of scholars who have only recently embraced ecocriticism and the environmental humanities. Although literary studies dominate the book, its scope is diverse, including ecocritical analysis of novels, poems, dramas, and essays. The volume also features a few examples of visual cultural manifestations, ranging from graphic novels to TV shows. As a whole, the book covers a wide variety of topics relevant to the environmental humanities debate (water, waste, non-human agency and multispecies collaborations, humour and horror, critiques of the Anthropocene, ecofeminism, etc.), showing the theoretical sophistication, thematic heterogeneity, and philosophical nuance surrounding Spanish ecocriticism.

This is a much-needed volume that contributes to expanding and enriching the already vibrant debate within Spanish ecocriticism. At this point, and adding this excellent book to the significant number of essays and books dealing with Spanish environmental cultural studies that have proliferated during the last few years, we can affirm without hesitation that Spanish ecocriticism is a highly visible, relevant, and energizing force within Spanish literary and cultural studies. From now on, scholars in our field have no excuse for ignoring the biophysical context in which cultures are always embedded.

Acknowledgments

Unknowingly, the seeds for this book were planted years ago. Our colliding and mutually enlivening research on cultural representations of forced migration, gender-based oppression, and other forms of systemic subjugation – including nationalism and ableism – organically brought forth our sustained inquiry into refuge in the context of ecological crisis. The partnership that developed has been among the most fruitful undertakings of our careers and for that we are grateful, to each other and to those without whom this publication would not have been possible. We hope that those who read *Beyond Human* – whose focus on Spanish cultural production through the ages aims to fill a gap in the environmental humanities – will find it to be a worthwhile and engaging tome for its unique probing of ecocritical concerns, responses, and innovative proposals. This collection is the culmination of the efforts of many, whose steadfast commitment to us and to our project are a challenge to summarize.

First and foremost, we thank our fellow Hispanists and feminists, especially Nina L. Molinaro, Debra Faszer-McMahon, Victoria L. Ketz, Dawn Smith-Sherwood, Carmen Flys Junquera, and Luis (Iñaki) Prádanos, who have championed our work through a multitude of conferences (EASLCE, KFLC, MACHL, NeMLA) and have bolstered our critical voices through the publication of important monographs in our field. It has been an honour to learn from you. We are likewise very grateful to the contributors of this volume for their adhesion to this project; their willingness to continually explore, discuss, draft, and revise speaks not only to their generosity, but also to their belief in the power of collaboration and critique to inspire change. Thank you for entrusting us with your outstanding essays.

We would like to recognize Assumption University (the D'Amour College of Liberal Arts and Sciences) and York University (the Faculty of Liberal Arts & Professional Studies and Glendon College) for their funding through faculty development grants, research leaves and course releases, conference stipends, and publication support. We extend our appreciation to colleagues at our respective institutions who have provided incalculable guidance to our careers as faculty and researchers, including those in Assumption's Department of Modern and Classical Languages and Cultures, and Vivienne Anthony at the Emmanuel d'Alzon Library, as well as those who have counselled us as women in academia, namely Dona Kercher, Ellen Anderson, Michol Hoffman, Maria João Maciel Jorge, Susan Ehrlich, and Sheila Embleton. We are thankful as well to our editor at the University of Toronto Press, Mark Thompson, for his interest in this project for Toronto Iberic, his patience, and his gracious stewardship.

Special thanks must also be extended to our earliest supporters and mentors at the universities where we completed our graduate studies. At the University of Kansas, we acknowledge Robert C. Spires, in memoriam (1936–2013), for the foundation in Spanish literary studies and for cultivating a special bond among his students, who aim to carry on his exemplary professional ethics and dedication to the field, and we recognize the KU graduate program in Spanish community, whose camaraderie and care for one another throughout the years is unparalleled. From the University of Toronto, we are indebted to the wisdom imparted and opportunities granted by Stephen Rupp; the synergy and *cariño* extended by Berenice Villagómez, Rita M. Palacios, and Sean Hutchman; and particularly to Robert A. Davidson for modelling courage, forgiveness, and a contagious enthusiasm for envisioning new paths and motivating others to do the same.

We must express our gratitude to our families. To Antonio, for your unabating flexibility, dependable encouragement, and steady partnership, I (Maryanne) am immensely grateful. Thank you, Santi; your sense of humour grounds me and your adventure seeking encourages me to imagine new possibilities. To Daniel C. and Maryanne V. Leone, you inspire me in your unwavering dedication to your family, communities, and careers. I am grateful to José, for your creative, critical spirit, and to Marisol, always in my heart, for your lifelong enjoyment of literature and writing, as well as to both for our Spanish home. Appreciation is also felt for Luna and Hayley, for their companionship, playfulness, and insistence that I take a break. And, to my sisters Stephanie and Susan, my extended family, and my nurturing friends, on whom I can count, always, thank you.

To Kevin, without whom this endeavour would have been inconceivable, thank you for your unceasing selflessness, the sincerity of your companionship, and the bounty of your patience. Thank you also to Fiona and Daphne for your curiosity, wit, and reminders to keep it real. To Connie Lino and in loving memory of Manuel Lino, I (Shanna) am grateful for your passion, perseverance, and unconditional confidence in me. And finally, my gratitude goes to Carmen Fernandes, Nando Fernandes, Julie Taylor Fernandes, Soraya Silva, and Betsy Frazer, as well as to Rosanna Granato, Maxine Britto, and Lisa McFarland for, together, forming the netting that has allowed so many worthwhile risks to be taken and dreams to be pursued.

BEYOND HUMAN

Historicizing the Ecocrisis: Beyond-Human Experiences in Spanish Natureculture

MARYANNE L. LEONE AND SHANNA LINO

In December 2019, Spain's world-renowned Museo del Prado collaborated with the World Wildlife Fund (WWF) in a powerful advertising campaign titled "+1,5°C Lo Cambia Todo" ("+1.5°C Changes Everything") designed to coincide with the 2019 UN Climate Change Summit (COP25) in Madrid. The WWF selected four masterpieces from the museum's permanent collection to be altered in ways that envisioned the damaging consequences of a rapidly warming climate: rising sea levels, mass extinction, extreme drought, and the turmoil experienced by human climate refugees.[1] The doctored images were exhibited on billboards across Madrid's city centre and were shared through an accompanying digital engagement campaign, #LoCambiaTodo, whose purpose was to raise awareness of the devastating effects of which climate scientists warn if global temperatures rise by so much as 1.5°C. The partnership between the conservation and art organizations evinces the inseparability of nature from culture, whose enmeshment is fundamental to contemporary ecocritical thought. Further, this manifest entwinement between human and beyond-human entities – animal, ambient, and aesthetic-discursive – lays bare not only the relationality between artistic creation and ecological health, but also the *sine qua non* of decentring human exceptionalism as the environmental humanities reflect upon, advocate for, and materially participate in radically shifting towards systems of knowledge, policy, and practice that might ensure our planet's survival.

In Donna Haraway's contemplations about the naming and dating of the Anthropocene, the ecofeminist and history-of-consciousness scholar argues that the greatest outrage of this geological boundary is "the destruction of places and times of refuge for people and other critters" and that "our job is to make the Anthropocene as short/thin as possible and to cultivate with each other in every way imaginable epochs to come that can replenish refuge" ("Anthropocene" 159). Indeed, the four reimagined El Prado paintings call dramatic attention to "the wiping out of most of the refugia from which diverse species assemblages (with or without people) can be reconstituted after major events" (Tsing qtd. in Haraway, "Anthropocene" 159), all the while manifesting the power of art to focus human awareness on the beyond-human interconnectedness that characterizes the urgent need to recover sites of refuge. To this end, the artivist campaign showcases discourse in the process of transforming historical reality to direct not only human *apprehension*, but also concrete *action* that can materially address our current planetary challenges.

The four remastered paintings expose naturecultural interconnections that do not assure happy endings, socially, ecologically, or scientifically; rather, in the non-teleological meeting between human and non-human subjects, these encounters demand response and respect and, in turn, flatten the mundane differences between previously conceived Great Divides: animal/human, nature/culture, organic/technical, and wild/domestic (Haraway, *Species* 15). For example, in the post-apocalyptic alteration of *Felipe IV a caballo* (*Philip IV on Horseback*, c. 1635–6), by Spanish Baroque painter Diego Velázquez, the human and equine subjects no longer appear dominant and regal, elevated from within the El Pardo forest of Madrid and overlooking the Sierra de Guadarrama; instead, the open-mouthed, wide-eyed monarch and mane-drenched, air-gasping horse, while still equally centred on the canvas, are now mostly submerged in flood waters. No refugia are evident for the king, his horse, or the inundated ecosystem below, and so the deluge of all entities is inextricably experienced. Another El Prado work altered for the campaign is Early Netherlandish painter Joachim Patinir's *Landscape with Charon Crossing the Styx* (c. 1515–24): whereas in the original masterpiece the flowing blue-green waters of the Styx dominate the central vertical axis that separates heaven from hell in accordance with the biblical narrative, in the re-envisioned account, the entire canvas is dominated by the amber and russet colours of the infernal fires and desiccated texture of the sere terrain. As with Velázquez's naturalist painting, the modified version of Patinir's *weltlandschaft* ("world landscape") emphasizes the embeddedness of beyond-human subjects destined to lose all refugia and urges immediate action and accountability.

The other two paintings similarly point to the naturecultural developments that result from the greatest ecological emergencies of our time. In the remastered version of Joaquín Sorolla's *Niños en la playa* (*Boys at the Beach*, 1909), the pinkish flesh of children playing in what were previously the purplish summer hues of the Valencian coast's waters now appears strangled by algae and among dead fish in the grey and synaesthetically pungent Mediterranean Sea. The ecological displacement and death experienced by the aquatic creatures and maritime vegetation – which materially entangle with the entrapped human bodies – are likewise ineluctable for the human climate refugees that replace Francisco de Goya's lady and servant in the re-envisioning of his 1777 tapestry cartoon *El quitasol* (*The Parasol*). In the remastered pictorial text, rather than seeking protection from the sun for her delicate, noble skin, the contemporary protagonist yearns for warmth and shelter from wind, which the refugee camp's sea of plastic cannot adequately provide. Through the four actuated masterpieces, the human and more-than-human actors "become who they are *in the dance of relating*" (Haraway, *Species* 25; original emphasis): vegetal, animal, human, atmospheric, aquatic, terrestrial, and discursive entities disclose the historical and contemporary material interconnectivity of all structures on our planet.

Beyond Human: Decentring the Anthropocene in Spanish Ecocriticism draws a historical arc from sixteenth-century to present-day Spain and inserts itself into a growing corpus of international ecocritical thought that acknowledges the material historicity of more-than-human nature. As a transnational and pluriform critical lens that took root in the 1990s, ecocriticism has increasingly complexified the dismantlement of status quo planetary structures. If important volumes from that decade and the aughts confirm the humanities' irrevocable ecological turn and environmental criticism's methodological diversity (Buell; Glotfelty and Fromm; Harrington and Tallamadge; Kerridge and Sammells), subsequent noteworthy collections expand the field's generic and disciplinary limits, crucially bridging ecocriticism with critical gender, class, and race theories (Adamson et al.; Armbruster and Wallace; Gaard and Murphy; Nishime and Williams). And it is from the mid teens of the twenty-first century onwards that scholarship has notably furthered the cogency of post-disciplinary ecocritical pathways, obviating previous inertial categorizations of so-called environmental literature. Broadening geographic and discursive frames, Serpil Opperman has shown that the field is open to transglobal dialogues and advocates for the integrating of older voices with present ones as a means to realize less anthropogenic ecological visions. Scott Slovic, Swarnalatha Rangarajan, and Vidya Sarveswaran have taken on the task of articulating the socioecological plight of the world's poor while contributing to a growing corpus that effectively dismantles the perception of environmentalism as irrelevant, elitist, or epistemologically and institutionally centred in the US and UK, building upon the groundbreaking work of Joan Martinez-Alier, Rob Nixon, and Graham Huggan and Helen Tiffin, who theorize the disproportionate impact of environmental calamities on the globe's impoverished citizens.

Particularly pertinent to our study is the advancement of the material and feminist dimensions of ecocriticism, which offer new non-phallocentric and non-anthropocentric practices that call attention to women's active roles in environmental, social, and interspecies justice, thereby developing additional insights into the study of matter both in texts and as texts (Estok, Gaard, Iovino, Oppermann). By attending to the intersectionalities between the ecological sciences, queer and postcolonial theory, environmental philosophy and politics, (radical) economics, and new materialisms, contemporary ecocritics engage in the evaluation of far more than a static nature represented within supposedly separated cultural manifestations; they interrogate instead a naturecultural performativity via diffractive practices that illuminate the intra-actions between the human and the non-human (Barad, Haraway, Latour). Activating the notion of diffraction as difference with other beings that is neither reflective nor reproductive, *Beyond Human* takes account of "the fullness of matter's implication in its *ongoing historicity*" (Barad 129; emphasis added); our chapters revisit existing and familiar discursive practices and query the historical anthropocentric and anthropogenic ideologies that perpetuate human and non-human suffering within the epochally defining temporal frame of the Anthropocene. Our collection expands upon articulations of enmeshment of more-than-human entities in terms of *place* – spatial complexes, webs, networks, and ecosystems – to assess likewise entanglements of *time* – geological, historical, synchronous, and asynchronous – and draws linkages for the evaluation of ecological acts, including those that may not have been recognized as such: seventeenth-century royal medical advice to listen to birdsong, post-1898 technological innovation to redefine national identity, and late twentieth-century historical fiction on post-civil-war freedom fighting.

Dialoguing with an expanding body of environmental humanities research that probes the role of culture in exposing, informing, and transforming the ethical dimensions of our pressing global ecological problems, *Beyond Human* explores key questions relating to ecological equity, justice, and responsibility within and beyond Spain. With these aims in mind, this book extends the historical range and breadth of textual genres considered for their material relevance, uniquely tracing the anthropocentric, anthropogenic, and anthropocenic formation of Spanish cultural identity, as well as its chronicled resistance to that tendency. In this way, *Beyond Human* complements important collections that – recently and crucially – have begun to examine the relational material semiotics of naturecultures to make visible the economic growth hegemony in post-capitalist Spain.

Ecocultural Hispanists engage in animal studies and rights (Beilin, Beusterien), ecopolitical activism and artivism (Feinberg and Larson, Flys Junquera and Raquejo Grado, Seguín, Trevathan, Ugarte), and human–non-human enmeshment (Ares-López, Viestenz). They critique biotechnological responses to ecological crises (Beilin) as well as agro-industrial food systems and genetic modification (Marí, Beilin). Environmental humanists studying Spain examine consumer and post-industrial pollution (Feinberg and Larson) and, through the cultural archaeology of trash, expose the Spanish impulse to discard and hide waste since the country's transition to democracy (Amago). Ecocritics focused on this contemporary period champion communitarian creativity and advocate integrating an ecological ethos into Iberian cultural studies (Beilin and Ares-López, Prádanos).[2] As with these noteworthy studies, *Beyond Human* analyses intentionally crafted ecocritical texts and movements, and yet also (re)reads literary, filmic, and documentary works whose ecocritical significance may have been less deliberate but whose material implications are nevertheless significant. Therefore, drawing connections across all four of its parts, this book illuminates the way ecological consciousness, anthropocentrality, and non-human nature have distinctly steered critical moments in Spain's historical and cultural development and continually reconceptualized the country's ecosocial identity.

The questions in the present collection are largely informed by two pivotal 2019 essays that assert the imperative to expand Iberian naturecultural studies. In "Culturas de naturaleza y naturalezas-culturas. Hacia una redefinición de los estudios culturales desde el Antropoceno" (*Arizona Journal of Hispanic Cultural Studies*, vol. 23), *Beyond Human* contributor Daniel Ares-López deftly articulates the value of materialist, performative, and relational conceptual frameworks – with a particular focus on the Francoist period – for Iberian cultural critics who aim to explain historical transformations of the twentieth century from the perspective of the Anthropocene. In the introduction that Kata Beilin and Ares-López write for *Hispanic Issues On Line* (vol. 24), the ecocritics advocate in a pan-Hispanic context a material-semiotic application to colonial and transatlantic studies. Our book asks: What would it mean to extend the narratological tracing of Spain's socioecological present beyond the limits of the twentieth century? What can we learn from Spanish naturecultural discursive practices that date back to the *Siglo de Oro*, that forecast post-human interrelationality into future centuries, or that shift beyond-human considerations laterally through fantastical settings that facilitate the reconceptualization of limits on both the human and the discursive? To answer these questions, essays in *Beyond Human* engage with ecofeminism and ethics of care (Frost, Leone, Viestenz), postcolonial ecocriticism (Gasior, Ketz), trans-corporeality (González-Rodríguez and Brito-Vera, Lino), animal and plant studies (Ares-López, Beusterien, Colbert), post-humanism (Almanza-Gálvez, Martín Galván), and environmental tourism and economics (Marek, C. Martínez, M. Martínez, McKay, Useche) to collectively make two bold assertions: (1) Spanish cultural studies must expose the material historicity that spatio-temporally entangles today's ecological crises and ecosocial injustices with previous, future, and contemporaneous entities; and (2) to do so will require the simultaneous decentring of the human and of the Anthropocene as an ecocritical framework.

Therefore, this book acknowledges that humans have exercised and continue to execute a profound geological agency on the planet's biosphere, and at the same time aims to decentre the human so as to illuminate the webbed – spatial, temporal, ontological, and material – agencies of biotic and abiotic life forms. Still, to shift the emphasis towards more-than-human enmeshment, we recognize the need to engage with dominant human-centred perspectives in social, cultural, political, economic, and scientific models that have emanated from Western societies such as Spain. The centring of the human could not be more apparent than in the prefix of the term that has come to describe the current period of ecological crisis. The Anthropocene framework gained currency within and beyond scientific scholarship after atmospheric chemist Paul J. Crutzen and marine scientist Eugene F. Stoermer proposed the naming of a new geological epoch due to humans' profound impact on the earth's climate and biodiversity from population growth, urbanization, fossil fuel use, land fertilization, and other activities (17).[3] Noting the arbitrariness of pinpointing the start of the Anthropocene, they nonetheless associate the development of greenhouse gases with the invention of the steam engine during the eighteenth century. Subsequent studies have disputed whether the epoch commenced with the Industrial Revolution, proposing other pivotal moments of human activity that more likely became the driving force for geological transformation, including human use of fire, the development of agricultural land cultivation, European expansionism and colonization, the production of synthetic chemicals following World War II, and global economic growth. Nonetheless, all involve histories of technology that trace natural-resource use for human expansion (Baer; McNeill and Engelke; Parikka). Irrespective of the exact moment in anthropological development that will come to denote the beginning of this epoch, Crutzen and Stoermer have called on scientists to devise "a world-wide accepted strategy leading to sustainability of ecosystems against human induced stresses" (18). Their influential designation has drawn critical attention to the irreversible impact of anthropogenic activities on the ecosphere and has contributed to productive discussions in the sciences, arts, and humanities.

Along with growing popular use of the term *Anthropocene*, debate has developed about the limitations of the concept for addressing the paradigms that have led to current ecological crises. While some argue for its utility, others propose that by focusing squarely on the human, the Anthropocene maintains the Cartesian separation from nature that has provided the underlying rationale for humans' irresponsible treatment of the non-human. Critics also hold that the Anthropocene inaccurately attributes responsibility for earth changes to all peoples regardless of sharp differences in resource use and power within global political, economic, and social systems (Haraway, *Staying*; Moore, "Rise"; Plumwood). Another argument against the framework is that the often-singular focus on climate change tends to ignore animals even though the hierarchization of humans, then livestock, and then pets before all others has been integral to the Anthropocene's emergence (Tønnessen and Oma ix). Despite the theoretical limitations, which environmental historian Jason W. Moore has characterized as a flawed "Green Arithmetic" of Society + Nature = History, thus simply perpetuating the dichotomous thinking that has created our present-day environmental crises, the Anthropocene thesis was a "courageous proposal" because it catalysed the recognition of "humanity as a geological agent," which was a crucial first step in acknowledging the entwinement of human and natural history ("Introduction" 3–4).

Beyond Human: Decentring the Anthropocene in Spanish Ecocriticism both exposes anthropocenic logic and brings forth resistant voices that consider nature and the human not in binary opposition but rather as constitutive of an integrated ecological system on earth.[4] We interrogate Spanish culture throughout the centuries that posits nature as passive or subordinate, or that denies "non-human claims to the earth and to elements of mind, reason and ethical consideration" (Plumwood 4). Ecophilosopher Val Plumwood alerts us to the notion of background-ing, that is, the fundamental need to recognize the hegemonic presenta-tion of nature as an inert surface on which humans masterfully act and to which no moral obligation is owed, similar to androcentric perspec-tives on women and to colonial views on Indigenous peoples (104–9). Many of our contributors consider texts in which nature has been stud-ied previously as this type of background and activate its agency within cultural studies practices to reveal it non-teleologically. In this way, we join theorists such as Stacy Alaimo, Haraway, and Plumwood, who suggest that the connoted antagonism demands terminological alternatives to refer to a biodiversity that is other-than-human. To make clear our book's commitment to decentring the human, any conceptualization in the cultural expressions of a nature that is separate from the human realm is made explicit by a preceding qualifier, such as *non-human*, *beyond-human*, or *more-than-human*. As a counter-paradigm to backgrounding, therefore, we propose models of environmental and human interpenetration that recognize the relationality, uniqueness, and necessity of all life forms in the complex biosphere.

Shifting away from an anthropocenic, binary perspective, *Beyond Human* argues that theoretical alternatives for understanding human-influenced changes to the earth's climate and biodiversity better decentre humans and support an ecosocial understanding of more-than-human matter. Moore's contention that the Capitalocene more accurately historicizes the twenty-first-century ecological crisis by pointing to capitalism as its primary cause and locating capitalism's roots in colonialism, particularly beginning with fifteenth-century imperial Spain, highlights the value of studying contemporary environmental concerns through ecocritical readings of Iberian texts from the early modern period onwards.[5] Rather than viewing all humans as one monolithic actor, the Capitalocene differentiates humans' planetary impact due to imperialist, patriarchal, racist, and consumerist structures and emphasizes the presence of a *"capitalist world-ecology*: a civilization that joins the accumulation of capital, the pursuit of power, and the production of nature as an organic whole" (Moore, "Rise" 97; original emphasis).[6] Haraway also speaks of the Capitalocene to emphasize the extractivist, extinction-generating human practices that have facilitated wealth accumulation and displaced peoples, animals, plants, and other organisms. All species, from humans to bacteria, in inter-/intra-action have effected change on the planet. However, human activities of a consequential "scale, rate/speed, synchronicity, and complexity," as well as "systematically linked patterns that threaten major system collapse after major system collapse after major system collapse," mark this moment as "an inflection point" (Haraway, "Anthropocene" 159). While the Anthropocene argument focuses primarily on the impact of human activity on the earth, the Capitalocene paradigm calls attention as well to the dependence of capitalism upon non-human nature and the influence and response of the more-than-human environment to capitalism.

To ignore the ecohistorical relevance of capital is to fail to see human and non-human life in a complexly integrated and mutually influencing web. Conceptually and practically, capitalism relies on the reformulation of nature as raw materials and on the association of many humans with an undervalued nature in order to produce Cheap Labour and Cheap Nature that serve not only economic objectives but also the amassment of power (Moore, "Rise").[7] As anthropologist Anna Lowenhaupt Tsing points out, because value created outside capitalism is converted into capitalist assets and because economic diversity is needed for capitalism to succeed, "sites of instability and refusal of capitalist governance" exist in which people and non-human entities move in and out of the capitalist organizing system (301). These "pericapitalist" activities, places, and moments intimate the kinds of non-instrumental valuations of the human and the more-than-human that Plumwood advocates to counter capitalist ideologies of extraction. As this book shows, Spanish cultural works from the early modern era to the present day articulate, some intentionally and others unintentionally, that the so-called productive work requiring cheap goods and cheap bodies literally and figuratively have displaced, enslaved, and reshaped human societies and non-human matter in a culture based on ideologies of extraction that has accelerated human-induced changes to the non-human environment (Moore, "Rise" 84–5, 91, 98–9). The depleted refuges represented in the Prado-WWF campaign and in other texts analysed by our contributors suggest not only that the capitalist world-ecology has disrupted water supplies, increased global temperatures, and created life-ending toxicity, but also that the Cheap Nature on which capitalism depends is being increasingly diminished. The essays in *Beyond Human* engage directly with debates surrounding the Anthropocene and Capitalocene to understand capitalist development's necro-environmental impact and pericapitalist dynamics in Spain, from colonialism in the Canary Islands and the imperial court of Philip II in Madrid to present-day and future devastation throughout the country. For example, the landscape as a wild foe in need of taming to further so-called human progress and comfort is a recurring theme in Spain's national and economic histories. Whereas Enlightenment development transformed seemingly barren lands into agricultural canvases, at the turn of the twentieth century wetlands along the Valencian coast were converted to rice fields, and in the last twenty years swathes of agricultural and undeveloped land have suburbanized exponentially, ever deepening the country's ecological and carbon footprints.

Spain faces environmental concerns shared by countries worldwide, the greatest being the rising atmospheric temperature caused by carbon emissions, with its coastal borders and semi-arid climate presenting particular vulnerabilities. Spain's fresh water has reduced by 20 per cent in the last twenty-five years, and fertilizers and pesticides contaminate Spain's increasingly limited freshwater reserves, leading to competition among the country's autonomous regions for hydric distribution. At the same time, more suburbanization, golf courses, and areas of irrigation populate the landscape. Spain's mushrooming agro-industry, which produces 30 per cent of the continent's fresh produce (up to 80 per cent in the winter months) and has led certain regions to be referred to as Europe's orchard, is predicated upon monocrops harvested with cheap migrant labour within an astonishing 32,000 hectares of greenhouses. This sea of plastic in the south-eastern province of Almería is the human construction on earth that is the most visible from space, even more prominent than the Great Wall of China or the Egyptian pyramids. Its extension is so vast that the 430 square kilometres of white plastic, which reflects the sunlight back into the atmosphere in what is known as the albedo effect, has actually caused the average temperature of the region to decrease by 0.3°C per decade since 1970 (Campra and Millstein). Local politicians and the exponentially enriched agro-industrial corporations seek to greenwash this fact as evidence of the ecological and climatic benefits that the hydroponic greenhouses provide.[8] Yet studies reveal a higher incidence of miscarriage in the female partners of sprayers and an increase in depression, neurological disorders (such as headaches, tremors, and paraesthesia), and suicide rates among the (mostly migrant) labourers due to pesticide and herbicide exposure (Parrón, "Clinical" and "Increased Risk"). This physiological and psychological toxicity, together with the chemical, human, and nanoplastic waste that runs off into the Mediterranean Sea, makes Southern Spain's "mar de plástico" ("plastic sea") a definitive example of the ways in which (non-human) nature, (racialized) bodies, and (imported) labour are cheapened – extracted, abused, and consumed to sustain capitalocenic dynamics.[9] That the semi-arid region is now flushed with 60,000 cubic metres per day of desalinated water produced by a local plant, and that entire industries have developed in the surrounding area to produce the massive amounts of short-lived plastic required by the greenhouses, is incontrovertible evidence of Spain's unique anthropogenic impact on the earth's surface.

While Almería's microclimate is cooling artificially, increases in global ocean temperatures mean that marine biodiversity is diminishing and, even though the Spanish government has been aggressively combating illegal fishing operations outside its territorial waters, fishing levels currently surpass by 24 per cent the level recommended for maintaining ecological balance (Planelles). On land, Spain's illegal dumps – a residual effect of capitalist accumulation – have caught the attention of the European Union's Court of Justice, which condemned the country in 2015 for failing to close sixty-two sites in six provinces despite prior warnings ("Commission Refers Spain"). As Spanish ecologist Francisco Segura notes, the country needs to radically alter its waste-management practices, shifting away from an overdependence on dumping and incineration to focus instead on reduction, reuse, and recycling (Planelles). Among the most detrimental anthropogenic activities for which Spain is known, however, is the mass-scale tourism-related construction along the country's coasts, which has led to flooding, contamination, and the disruption of large ecosystems. In a report jointly issued in 2018 by Greenpeace and Spain's Sustainability Observatory, titled *A Toda Costa* (*At All Co(a)sts*), researchers point out that 80 per cent of the coastline's natural resources have been degraded by urban development and that in the last thirty years, the built surface area of Spain's coasts has doubled from 240,000 hectares (2 per cent) to 530,000 (13.1 per cent). In the report's conclusion, its writers press for the immediate cessation of coastal urban development, a sector in which employment is currently growing by 7 per cent annually, whereas the country's overall economic growth across all industries is only approximately 2.6 per cent; a major reduction in consumption of finite natural resources; and a significant review of the outdated "Ley de Costas," which was established in 1988 and is utterly inadequate for present-day ecosystemic protection. Nevertheless, with its call to implement economic development alternatives based on conservation that would be more economically profitable than the degradation of ecosystems and their services (152), *A Toda Costa* ultimately appeals to its readers' anthropocentric and capital-driven motivations for saving Spain's coastline.

In light of Spain's participation in the global trend of fostering green growth rather than addressing the country's role in spurring the Anthropocene's principal root cause – consumerism – local degrowth movements and scholarship are increasingly promoting alternatives to techno-optimism.[10] As a confederation of more than three hundred Spanish ecological organizations, Ecologistas en Acción (Ecologists in Action) critiques the neoliberal fallacy of an environmental sustainability that does not question growth and instead advocates for widespread degrowth, including the detouristification of the Spanish economy and of Iberian politics. Ecofeminists such as economist Amaia Pérez Orozco and anthropologist, social educator, and agricultural engineer Yayo Herrero López advocate alternative economic models that account for both the planet's ecological limits and the care provision – most often by women – that is required for sustaining life.[11] Characterizing as ecocidal any economic, political, or social models that do not consider the environmental limits of a biosphere that makes all life possible, Herrero argues that ecological and social justice, as well as viable economies, are possible only within a framework of sustainability that recognizes both human ecodependency and inter-human dependency (2–5). What is more, recognition alone of these dependencies is insufficient; rather, a truly just sustainability requires the implementation of a revolutionary, reimagined ecological economic system that emphasizes reciprocal care, the meeting of human needs, and respect for the earth's limits: "Cuando no tienes la conciencia del límite, que es un problema que tenemos como cultura … lo que acabas es generando un sistema de derechos que se construyen a costa de otras personas" ("When you are not conscious of limits, which is a cultural problem that we have, you end up generating a system of rights built upon the backs of others"; Herrero 21; our trans.). The Capitalocene's growth economy relies on a myth of unlimited resources, continually increasing consumption, and measurements that ignore unmonetized work or insufficiently value costs, including gendered, racialized, and class-based extractivist exchanges of work and care that, ultimately, are ecologically detrimental to all. Instead of techno-optimism – the notion that scientific and technological innovations will resolve environmental crises within current global hegemonic structures – ecological economists favour "biomimetic" activity, which consists of necessity-based resource use, renewable energy sources, and the sustaining of diverse plant and animal species in order to imitate as much as possible the environment's closed production-consumption-regeneration cycles, diversity, and local circulation (Herrero 11). From this ecologically mindful perspective, sustainability of life and social interdependence replace the individualistic "lógica androcéntrica de acumulación" ("androcentric logic of accumulation") that has fomented ecosocial precarity with structural socio-economic changes that address the heterogeneous experiences of gender and income inequality among humans and the exploitation of non-human nature (Pérez Orozco 30).

Although broad-based support for degrowth remains elusive in Spain, a cultural shift in favour of alternatives to expansive economic goals and growth-fuelled consumption culture has strengthened since 2007. That year marked the collapse of the country's real-estate market following two decades of expansion buoyed by excessive housing construction, infrastructure development (high-speed trains, airports, and roads), speculative investment, and overzealous lending that left almost five million people without work (26 per cent of the working-age population), tens of thousands evicted or facing foreclosures for mortgage default, and farmland converted into ghost towns

(Herrero 11; Méndez Gutiérrez del Valle and Plaza Tabasco; "Sueños Rotos"). Simply put, what in the last decade and a half has come to be known as "La Crisis" exposed the fallacy that growth economics might yield either human well-being or environmental health, giving new ecological and economic meaning to the term in Spain.

In *Postgrowth Imaginaries: New Ecologies and Counterhegemonic Culture in Post-2008 Spain*, US-based Spanish ecocritic Luis I. Prádanos argues that if a primary objective of the environmental humanities is to evince the links between culture and ecology while mobilizing ecological awareness, cultural critics must focus on texts that conceive of and enact "radically different postgrowth cultural imaginaries able to open the floor to new political possibilities" so as to overcome "the cruel optimism inherent in the current crisis of political imagination fostered by our toxic epistemological, material, and affective attachment to economic growth" (20). *Beyond Human* responds to this call not only with imagined alternatives for the present and future, but also by historicizing the dominant Spanish cultural imaginary that adheres to the neoliberal fantasy of perpetual growth and environmental stability in the Capitalocene. Our contributors show that texts have been engaging with these critical environmental concerns for five hundred years, even if unwittingly, and in many cases have provided glimpses of alternate paradigms. Dealing with periods of Spanish colonialism, nation-building, and capitalist development, our contributors identify ecocentric imaginaries that are attentive to Indigenous and feminist world views and critical of techno-optimistic promotions of growth, and that promote interspecies prosperity that is unlinked from monetary wealth.

Dismantling the non-human–human dichotomy and nature-culture divide in ways that decentre the human is critical in order to imagine alternative socio-economic policies and ecocultural structures that promote the ecological health of the planet. No one kind of being occupies the centre of the ecosphere and, likewise, no one agency reigns. While we maintain that anthropogenic activity has substantially altered the environment, often in ways that threaten the lives of all earth beings, to decentre the Anthropocene means to replace the centralization of human impact on and control of non-human nature with a broader affirmation of agentic capacities, which have histories of their own and participate pluriformly in the ecological web. With this objective in mind, this book performatively situates the human within a relational ontology with the more-than-human and participates in discursive practices whose bodily materiality accounts for the "ongoing reconfigurings of the world" (Barad 133–5). Our work is congruent with post-humanist theorist Rosi Braidotti's dismantling of the humanist, Cartesian conception of attributive agential intentionality and exemplifies how intra-agency occurs in ongoing acts of boundary crossing and exclusions among matter. Through Alaimo's trans-corporeality, *Beyond Human* underscores the permeability of bodies by other bodies of all kinds (e.g., plants, animals, machines, [wet]landscapes, monsters, futuristic and hybrid beings, and natural resources, but also discourse, narratives, and artistic expression) and articulates the foreclosure of the dominant conception of nature as an inert background against which humans act to prompt an environmental ethos predicated on co-constitution. Within this material appreciation of existence, humans are not exterior to or even *in* nature but "of the world in its differential becoming," in a conceptualization that intermeshes nature and culture (Barad 147). In this ontology of co-becoming, our book's naturecultural studies decentre the Anthropocene, not only through the Capitalocene's expression of the systemic causes of planetary stress, but also by advancing Haraway's Chthulucene, whose focus on multispecies assemblages among biotic and abiotic beings builds on empathy and kindness. Therefore, through ecomaterialist studies of Iberian cultures, the essays in this collection subvert narratives of human exceptionalism and disclose stories of historical and spatial entanglements to foster the realization of shared habitats and ontological mappings.

Beyond Human's contributors theorize sympoiesis, or "making-with," in works that connect halting ecological destruction to engendering ecojustice (Haraway, *Staying* 58). In the context of the 2008 global financial crisis and the Spain-specific, corruption-fuelled real-estate bubble and bust, surviving the vulnerability of the Capitalocene requires unconditional hospitality and unconventional kinships (Viestenz, Leone). Cultivating spherological immunity (Viestenz) is a promising avenue for confronting what Estok calls ecophobia, the fear of and contempt for the natural environment that allows for humans' ecologically harmful practices. *Beyond Human*'s contributors critically examine texts that reinforce human–non-human hierarchies (Useche, Frost, Martín Galván, Lino, Ketz) and prioritize humans' aesthetic and recreational pleasures (Beusterien, Ares-López). Other works upend these divisions more explicitly through new-materialist and naturecultural imperatives as conditions required for non-humans to thrive (Ares-López, Colbert, González-Rodríguez and Brito-Vera, Viestenz, Leone, McKay). Finally, feminist and postcolonial ecocriticism calls attention to the mastery narratives of patriarchal institutions that have disrupted ecosystems (Frost, Ketz, Leone, M. Martínez) and models an ethics of care that involves dialogical responsibility and more-than-human agency (Leone).

With critiques of works from the Golden Age to the twenty-first century and from a wide range of genres – *comedia*, pastoral romance and naturalist fiction, royal treatises, agricultural reports, painting, scientific and satirical essays, post-Transition historical and contemporary narrative, horror fiction and film, young adult and speculative literature, poetry and graphic novels, cartoons, and television series – *Beyond Human* (re)reads Renaissance classics, literature about the Spanish-American and Spanish Civil Wars, and contemporary cultural production as necessarily ecologically bound. This book examines the interrelations between Iberian cultural practices, historical developments, and ecological processes, which until recently remained insufficiently theorized. By standardizing ecosocial analysis and by widening avenues for ecopedagogical approaches to econaturalist, ecodystopian, ecolonial, ecohorror, and ecopostcolonial texts, our collection participates in the transformation of our discipline and draws an arc towards a more equitable and sustainable ecocentric future.

The essays in *Beyond Human* are presented in four parts that reflect our book's aims: (1) to acknowledge the material historicity of more-than-human nature, (2) to decentre anthropocenic agentivity, (3) to model the enmeshment and trans-corporeality of all entities – material and discursive, and (4) to promote ecosocial engagement through/with culture. The collection's first part, "Tracing Environmental Culture in Spain," identifies historical, political, economic, and ideological roots and practices from the sixteenth to the twentieth centuries that have contributed to the contemporary ecocrisis. In the first essay, "Lope's *Los guanches de Tenerife y conquista de Gran Canaria*: An Ecolonialist Reading," Bonnie L. Gasior's assessment of this 1618 work as an example of Golden Age literary environmental critique examines the ways in which Lope de Vega's *comedia* about colonial excursions to the Canary Islands may have reflected Indigenous world views and early modern precursors to present-day ecocritical postures that seek to dissolve dichotomies such as Spain/colony and human/nature. Lope's dramatization of the encounter between the Guanche people and the colonists is a window to a critical moment in Spanish history in which ecological postures such as those espoused by the Indigenous people of Tenerife clashed with the enterprising drive of the colonial project.

Drawing on ornithology, in "Birdsong and the Earth's Polyrhythm: The Life of a Caged Blue Rock Thrush in Early Modern Spain," John Beusterien reads a seventeenth-century treatise on caged birdsong, the first in Europe, as a prelude to present-day (dis)connections with the environment. His nominal biogeography of Juan Bautista Jamarro's *Conocimiento de las diez aves menores de jaula, su canto, enfermedad, cura y cría* (1604) considers the interest in bird species for the curative potential of their song and analyses the impact of their capture on the earth's polyrhythm and on humans' embodied spatial understanding of themselves in a holistic cross-species system. Reflecting on his teaching, Beusterien shows that an early modern anthropocentric manual on practices that attempt to dominate non-human nature offers ecopedagogical opportunities to animate awareness of material interconnections in everyday surroundings.

Connecting issues surrounding water and land control from the Greco-Roman period to the Renaissance, as well as the Francoist dictatorship, early Spanish democracy, and the present moment, Margaret Marek's "Water Grabbing and the Dammed Esla: The Enchanted Waters of Jorge de Montemayor and the Riaño Reservoir" analyses the historical drowning of towns in the Riaño Valley in correlation with the literary representation of trauma as experienced by Montemayor's lovesick shepherds in the pastoral romance *La Diana* (1559) through the parallelism of fallacy. In both cases, idyllic waterscapes are appropriated and rendered artificial in an attempt to engineer oblivion, under either the ruse of touristic development or the promise of purge and renewal. In response to environmental and emotional losses, present-day herders and eco-activists are working to revive transhumance as a co-beneficial practice in Spain's *dehesas* ("meadows") that supports degrowth economics, while *riañenses* ("Riaño inhabitants") organize to maintain the memory of the ecocidal embankment and to remove the dam(m/n)ed waters from the Valley.

Complementing Marek's study of a misconceived irrigational public work, Daniel Frost focuses on the Spanish Enlightenment's assault on beyond-human nature in the name of cultivating rural Spain in his comparative reading of the *Informe sobre la Ley Agraria* (1797) by minister of justice Gaspar Melchior de Jovellanos and two paintings by Francisco de Goya: *El aquelarre* (*The Witches' Sabbath*) and *Baile en las orillas del Manzanares* (*Dance on the Banks of the Manzanares*, 1776–7). His chapter, "Of Witches and Land Reform in Enlightenment Spain," exposes the ambivalence of government policies that may have been socially progressive on the one hand – by providing greater access to land for the average labourer, for example – but were patriarchal and ecologically uncritical on the other. By examining reformist binary conceptions of nature/culture, reason/superstition, and unfruitful/productive, Frost presents a case study of the eighteenth-century, androcentric perspective on human progress that theorists such as Carolyn Merchant and Plumwood have identified as an underlying framework for ecological crises.

The final essay in this part turns to the incipient field of plant cognition and to scholarship on animal cognition in order to elucidate the plight of Republican soldiers who sought refuge in the mountains during and in the aftermath of the Spanish Civil War (1936–9). Through a reading of floral and faunal non-humans as conscious beings, Olga Colbert's "Plant, Animal, and Human Consciousness in Julio Llamazares's *Luna de lobos*" reveals a cosmovision of an interconnected system of humans with plant and non-human animal life, as well as with soil, minerals, and the Leonese landscape, that resists politically motivated, capitalism-induced, and technologically driven disappearances. The chapter also posits a metonymic congruence between the soldiers' transformation into werewolves, state persecution, and breaking points in nature beyond which the repercussions of anthropogenic activity can no longer be reversed unless through supernatural intervention.

The chapters in *Beyond Human*'s second part, "Anthropocene, Capitalocene, Chthulucene," interrogate the anthropocentric, -genic, and -cenic interrelationality of nation-(re)building, economic manipulation, and systemic buttressing of violence, precarity, and excess through texts that foreground the post-imperial, modern, and futuristic dismantlement of human limits. In "Leonardo Torres Quevedo's Automata and the Consolidation of Technological Regenerationism," Óscar Iván Useche exposes the ambivalence of turn-of-the-century automation that prioritized innovation and the economy over the environment while redefining Spain's national identity amid traditionalist preferences following the Spanish-American War of 1898. Useche delineates the Regenerationist forces and (pre-)capitalist practices that would eventually culminate in contemporary ecological subjugation and reveals that while Torres Quevedo may have sought to approach the relationship between technology and human consciousness in a more nuanced fashion than his predecessors or contemporaries – querying vitalism, mechanical determinism, and Cartesian theory – ultimately, his automation theories remained human-centred, all in the name of so-called progress.

Nevertheless, Iberian cultural history is not devoid of successful examples of mutually beneficial, beyond-human entanglements. Michael L. Martínez's piece discusses early twentieth-century Valencian *tancats* as an example of pre-capitalist fishing practices based on the co-preservation of human and aquatic species, and William Viestenz's contribution explores a forward-thinking recognition of post-immunological sympoiesis whereby wounding leads to both human and animal co-survival. Like Useche's focus on Regenerationist automation, M. Martínez's study is attentive to the anxieties relating to Spain's political and economic restructuring following the country's 1898 military defeat. At the same time, "The Spectre of Capitalism: Reading the Anthropocene in Vicente Blasco Ibáñez's *Cañas y barro*" enmeshes naturalist and contemporary discursive practices that critique not only human-nature dualism but also – via Moore – the Capitalocene framework as a point of ecocritical departure. In so doing, this chapter evinces the power with which Spanish naturalism's ecological tropes, metaphor, and narrative patterns are equipped to confront our current socio-environmental crises, in ways that other disciplines are not.

For his part, Viestenz grounds his chapter, "Jesús Carrasco's *Intemperie*: The Literature of Post-Immunological Modernity," in unconditional hospitality and spherological immunity in order to read multispecies assemblages as models for survival despite the ever-increasing vulnerability of human and other-than-human populations in the Chthulucene. Asserting that *Intemperie*'s portrayal of environmental devastation, mass rural depopulation, and economic scarcity points to the systemic origins of capitalist crisis, Viestenz argues that the text manifests a possible corrective to a world in the process of ruination. Specifically, the novel mediates the intersection of politics and the body through a sustained representation of kin-making that acknowledges and values the interrelationality of life forms and objects, humans and other creatures, within the precarious conditions of the current geological era.

Juan Carlos Martín Galván's chapter extends this part's critique of unrestrained economic growth by analysing transhumanism in Rosa Montero's novel *Los tiempos del odio* to show that anthropocentric essentialism not only aggravates our environmental crises but, moreover, fosters enmity among humans and between human and non-human others. "Transhumanism and Necropolitics in Rosa Montero's *Times of Hatred*" engages with Achille Mbembe's notion of necropolitics to highlight multiple systems of violence that inflict death upon citizens of democratic states and contends that, ultimately, the novel challenges anthropocentric thinking in order to posit non-human agency and alternative post-human ontologies capable of bridging the conspicuous gap that divides human and non-human species.

Linking with both Viestenz's exploration of beyond-human precarity and Martín Galván's exposé of human hubris that is decentred by blurring the limits between life and death, Micah McKay provides an innovative approach to Spanish ecocritical cultural studies with his discussion of trash in terms of its political potential of salvage and ability to create, therefore, a political solidarity in the midst of ecological devastation. In "The Salvage Poetics of Ben Clark's *Basura*," McKay applies Tsing's theorization of the relationship between salvage and capitalism to analyse the ragpicker metaphor, which mediates the possibility of cultivating life and meaning in a world full of garbage.

As chapters in the second part show, the Capitalocene argument catalyses our awareness of the problematic historical and systemic organization of nature at the service of economic growth, whereas the Chthulucene elaborates a promising, hopeful response to its extinguishing effects. The authors in the third part, "Disruptive Agentic Paradigms," concentrate on models through which to counter a dominant and domineering neoliberal economics that coterminously emboldens patriarchy, speciesism, and human-centredness. Dismantling anthropocenic frameworks of past, present, future, and fantastical realms, these chapters foreground the materialist frameworks of natureculture, agentivity, and trans-corporeality to evince an ontology of interconnected human and more-than-human existence. Situated in the economic, environmental, and social precarity of Spain's post-Crisis period, Maryanne L. Leone's chapter articulates an ecofeminist ethics of care and reveals the trans-corporeal agentic potential of human and non-human entities, such as animals, water, air, and discarded objects, that call attention to ecological interconnectivity to spur dialogical responsibility. "Ecofeminist Materialism and Entanglements of Care in Sara Mesa's *Un incendio invisible*" examines these dynamics as models for replacing hegemonic centralism in intimate relation to the marginalization of women, elders, ethnic minorities, and gender-nonconforming people.

In their analysis of twenty-first-century crime television, María Luz González-Rodríguez and María Concepción Brito-Vera probe contemporary human unease on the Canarian archipelago, where island volcanic and organic matter, more-than-human assemblages, and trans-corporeal agency continually make themselves known, exhuming human bodies and activating a beyond-human "aquapelagic" ecoconsciousness that, in relation with Gasior's chapter in part one, recalls a counter- or pre-*godo* ("Spanish mainlander") equilibrium. Foregrounding porosity, "Trans-Corporeal Matter Narratives in *Hierro*" challenges continentalist and islander perceptions of isolation to emphasize the relationality of the island's environment, cultures, and peoples in the actualization of *herreñidad* ("El Hierro identity").

An evaluation of Spanish ecohistoricity reveals that imperialism and modern dictatorial regimes, both marked by extreme androcentricity, relied heavily on a human-exceptionalist prioritization of suffering, which this book examines both as manifested through the caging of birds for the purpose of human healing in Beusterien's chapter and through taurine exploitation for human entertainment in Daniel

Ares-López's "*¡El toro no entiende de toreo!* Taurine Naturecultures, Wenceslao Fernández Flórez's Anti-Taurine Essays, and the Emergence of Post-Humanist Views of Animals in Spain." Suffering imposed by humans on beyond-human species is an element that tests the nature-culture paradigm. Yet, in his study of *tauromaquia* as a material-semiotic assemblage rather than as a sociocultural institution, Ares-López's analysis of the mid-twentieth-century comic anti-taurine essays, written during the tradition's zenith in Spain, unmasks the human relegation of bovids as an enactment of masculinity that presupposes the brutality of bullfighting as an emblematic Spanish practice, thus precluding the interactive and adaptive capacity of biotic organisms.

Extending the consumptive materializations of animal lives through fantastical imaginations of hybrid beings, Shanna Lino engages with Catalan author Albert Sánchez Piñol's agentic exploration of humanity's ecologically catastrophic and cyclically self-annihilating practices. "Ecohorror as Critique of Anthropogenic (Self-)Destruction in Albert Sánchez Piñol's *Cold Skin*" builds upon ecogothic queries of the uncanny and abject and a growing corpus of criticism that identifies the catalysing potential of monster fiction to illuminate ways in which the 2002 novel and its English-language cinematic adaptation by Xavier Gens (*Cold Skin*, 2017) dismantle verticality, blur the nature-culture divide, and promote beyond-human hybridity. Positioning the significance of these texts within an appraisal of recurring human exceptionalism, Lino presents a clear case for how ecohorror and the ecogothic enable us to more clearly perceive ecophobic tendencies and to embrace non-human agentism as a step to activism.

This book's fourth and final part, "Medium as Activism Igniter," emphasizes the materiality of discursivity through the study of three limit-obfuscating genres that explicitly bridge cultural production with activism and harness the power of text and image to generate alternative ecosocial, -political, and -economic models. Each chapter illuminates the discursive disruption of human and cultural limits, whether by exploring fantastical spheres and creatures, by reversing the course of time, or by satirically exposing our dystopian ecological present. In "Monstrous Humanity: An Ecopostcolonial Reading of Laura Gallego García's Trilogy *Guardianes de la Ciudadela*," Victoria L. Ketz asserts the potency of young adult fiction to promote ecojustice among the genre's readers. As she shows, attitudes towards the environment and non-human species in these works expose and challenge the ideologies surrounding speciesism, racism, sexism, and imperialism, all reflections of the cultural values of the contemporary historical moment. For a young adult audience in the process of determining its own set of individual moral, ethical, religious, and political beliefs amid psychological and physiological changes, stories that model inter-connectivity with non-human creatures, in this case monsters, can be particularly influential in cultivating ecocitizens who will embrace the other as they address the multitude of global environmental problems faced by our world.

With "*La cuenta atrás*: An Ecodystopian Graphic Novel on Spain's Greatest Ecological Disaster," Carla Almanza-Gálvez contends that graphic fiction is likewise an ideal vehicle for ecocultural analysis and civic engagement. She examines the visual and formal properties of *La cuenta atrás*, a graphic novel by Galician comics and television-series writer Carlos Portela and Catalan comic-book artist and illustrator Sergi San Julián, which inverts the temporal directionality of human action in a synecdochical town that is manipulated by its government's misrepresentation of the ecological devastation caused by massive oil pollution. The visual text not only makes patent the embeddedness of the environment with our collectively uncertain and dystopian future, but also productively reimagines the implications of an iconic disaster similar to that of the 2002 *Prestige* oil spill so as to give prominence to the roles that ecosystems, non-human species, and collective volunteer actions play in sustaining human society.

Also probing the visual form's particular adeptness at distilling complex arguments that are critical of global capitalism and commodification, Christine M. Martínez's chapter demonstrates that Spanish cartoonists have persistently and fervently advocated accessible modes of ecological thinking through image. In "Drawing Ecological Thought: Anthropomorphism and Satire as Critique of Capitalism in the Twenty-First-Century Spanish Comic," she reads Brieva's, El Roto's, and Ramón's graphic satire for its ability to displace hegemonic narratives by attending to the intricacies of ecological networks and material flows that engage non-human forms eco-ethically.

Whether it originated in a wet market or a laboratory, the COVID-19 pandemic has made clear that despite the material porosity of all entities on our planet, exposure is not uniformly experienced. The disproportionate impact of the health crisis on disadvantaged communities is intimately linked to the neoliberal and capitalist, eco-unconscious structures of societies that marginalize the world's poorest, as well as its elders, racialized populations, ethnic minorities, and displaced peoples. Global competition for vaccines and international reluctance to implement policies that acknowledge that world health requires planetary health evince widespread environmental racism. Such destructive hegemonic practices ignore what several Indigenous epistemologies understand, and what, for example, Anishinaabe philosophy refers to as *mino-mnaamodzawin*: living well *with* the planet (McGregor). Ironically, a century ago, another deadly influenza pandemic became known as the Spanish flu, not because its epidemiological origin could be traced to that country, but because in the post–World War I era, the news agencies of neutral Spain were freer to report on the escalating death toll than their counterparts in other Western nations concerned about maintaining morale. The discursive framing of biotic and abiotic intra-actions was as materially real then as it was in the early days of the COVID-19 crisis, when morale-boosting reports claimed pandemic-related environmental benefits of remote work, whose viability is itself inequitably distributed. In actuality, techno-optimistic responses to the health crisis have exponentially exacerbated carbon emissions and waste through increases in biomedical packaging and the explosion of the delivery economy.

Beyond Human: Decentring the Anthropocene in Spanish Ecocriticism links the ecopolitical processes that have relied on the control and contamination of water, the organization of and extraction from land for (agro-)industrial production, the domestication of plant life and wildlife for human pleasure, and the subjugation of Indigenous peoples to buttress royal and colonial power or national and cultural identity with historically evolving ecocentric critiques of expansionist economics and global consumerism. If every act is political, so too is it ecological. We argue that in the case of Spain, this ecotemporal entanglement manifests as the eco(un)consciousness of canonical and contemporary works/acts whose historical specificity – as products of the Renaissance, Enlightenment, Regenerationist, naturalist, or Francoist periods, or from the post-dictatorial or post-2008 eras – is not antonymous with their condition as anthropocenic texts or as materially discursive agents. The following chapters evince this interrelationality.

NOTES

 1 The four original paintings, along with their remastered equivalents, may
   be seen in a 2019 *Artnet* news report by Caroline Elbaor.
 2 The volumes that offer the most convincing proposals, and from which
   the majority of these cited examples hail, are Katarzyna Beilin and William
   Viestenz's 2016 *Ethics of Life: Contemporary Iberian Debates*, and special
   sections and issues such as those edited in 2019 by Luis I. Prádanos for the
   Arizona Journal of Hispanic Cultural Studies (introduced in his "Ecología")
   and by Kata Beilin et al. for *Hispanic Issues On Line* (*Environmental Cultural
   Studies through Time: The Luso-Hispanic World*).

3 Although Crutzen and Stoermer mention precursors to the Anthropocene, such as late nineteenth-century geologist Antonio Stoppani's reference to an *Anthropozoic era*, applied philosopher Clive Hamilton and global ecologist Jacques Grinevald argue that these earlier notions are too distant from the contemporary understanding of the earth's non-linear evolution.

4 While there is no question that ecocritical action must resist "anthropocentric logic," many scholars propose that the theoretical framework of the Anthropocene is an avenue to do so precisely because it acknowledges and aims to dismantle our anthropocentrism in the anthropocenic period in which anthropogenic activity has altered the ecosystem. For clarity, we understand *anthropogenic* to describe the results of human activity on non-human nature and *anthropocentric* and *anthropocentrism* to denote human-centred values congruent with the notion that humans are the most significant earth being. By contrast, we employ *anthropocenic* to refer to the geological epoch described above.

5 In his book titled *Facing the Anthropocene: Fossil Capitalism and the Crisis of the Earth System*, ecosocialist activist Ian Angus supports the Anthropocene concept because of its established currency among earth scientists, social scientists, humanists, and the broader public, and expresses concern that the use of the *Capitalocene* term will imperil the unity needed to address climate change (Baer 434–5).

6 Moore's emphasis on the significance of Genoese merchants' union with Iberian monarchs in the creation of the transatlantic trade that constituted early capitalism supports the applicability of this ecocritical paradigm specifically for the Spanish context ("Rise" 86).

7 With Raj Patel, Moore expands on the notion of cheap resources that propel capitalism (i.e., nature and labour) to also include cheap money, care, food, energy, and lives, which together form a violent, frontier-expanding strategy that is aggressive to life making.

8 An example of this kind of greenwashing rhetoric can be read in a recent article in the *Diario Digital de Actualidad Hortofrutícola*, which boasts that the climatic cooling resulting from the reflection of sunlight by Almería's greenhouses is fuelling exciting climate-action research in the United States related to whitening rooftops and roads in order to not only lower summer temperatures, but also to reduce energy consumption and pollution ("La NASA recuerda").

9 Ecologistas en Acción has condemned the unregulated production, use, and improper disposal of the plastic required for Almería's greenhouses and has highlighted the work of University of Granada medical researcher Nicolás Olea, who has demonstrated a ubiquity of nanoplastic toxicity among Spaniards that is leading to serious adverse endocrine disruption in the country's children and young people.

10 The 1972 report *The Limits to Growth*, prepared for the then recently formed
   Club of Rome, a group of renowned scientists, economists, business
   leaders, and politicians interested in global environmental, economic,
   political, and social concerns brought attention to the impossibility
   of continued material growth and economic expansion due to finite
   resources. The report's prediction of widespread collapse within one
   hundred years both provoked scepticism and galvanized environmentalist
   activism (Meadows et al.; Prats et al. 4).

11 Herrero López is currently vice president of FUHEM, a not-for-profit
   foundation focused on educational responses to the ecosocial issues of
   social justice, democracy, and environmental sustainability, and formerly
   served as FUHEM's general director and as a coordinator for Ecologistas
   en Acción.

WORKS CITED AND CONSULTED

Adamson, Joni, et al., editors. *Environmental Justice Reader: Politics, Poetics and
   Pedagogy*. U of Arizona P, 2002.

Alaimo, Stacy. *Bodily Natures: Science, Environment, and the Material Self*.
   Indiana UP, 2010.

Amago, Samuel. *Basura: Cultures of Waste in Contemporary Spain*. U of
   Virginia P, 2021.

Angus, Ian. *Facing the Anthropocene: Fossil Capitalism and the Crisis of the Earth
   System*. Monthly Review Press, 2016.

Ares-López, Daniel. "Culturas de naturaleza y naturalezas-culturas. Hacia
   una redefinición de los estudios culturales desde el Antropoceno." *Arizona
   Journal of Hispanic Cultural Studies*, vol. 23, 2019, pp. 215–34. *Project MUSE*,
   https://doi.org/10.1353/hcs.2019.0004.

Armbruster, Karla, and Kathleen R. Wallace, editors. *Beyond Nature Writing:
   Expanding the Boundaries of Ecocriticism*. UP of Virginia, 2001.

*A Toda Costa: Análisis de la evolución y estado de conservación de los bienes y servicios
   que proporcionan las costas*. Greenpeace España, 2018, https://es.greenpeace
   .org/es/sala-de-prensa/informes/a-toda-costa-informe-ampliado/.

Baer, Hans. "Anthropocene or Capitalocene? Two Political Ecological
   Perspectives." *Human Ecology*, vol. 45, no. 3, 2017, pp. 433–5. *Springer Link*,
   https://doi.org/10.1007/s10745-017-9895-4.

Barad, Karen. "Posthumanist Performativity: Toward an Understanding of
   How Matter Comes to Matter." *Material Feminisms*, edited by Stacy Alaimo
   and Susan Hekman, Indiana UP, 2008, pp. 120–54.

Beilin, Katarzyna Olga. *In Search of an Alternative Biopolitics: Anti-Bullfighting,
   Animality, and the Environment in Contemporary Spain*. Ohio State UP, 2015.

Beilin, Kata, and Daniel Ares-López. "Environmental Cultural Studies as a Transdisciplinary Field: Latin American and Iberian Studies." *Hispanic Issues On Line*, vol. 24, 2019, https://conservancy.umn.edu/bitstream /handle/11299/212979/hiol_24_intro_beilin_and_ares-lopez.pdf?sequence =1&isAllowed=y.

Beilin, Kata, et al., editors. *Environmental Cultural Studies through Time: The Luso-Hispanic World*, special issue of *Hispanic Issues On Line*, vol. 24, 2019, https://cla.umn.edu/hispanic-issues/online/environmental-cultural -studies-through-time-luso-hispanic-world.

Beilin, Katarzyna Olga, and William Viestenz, editors. *Ethics of Life: Contemporary Iberian Debates*. Vanderbilt UP, 2016.

Beusterien, John. *Canines in Cervantes and Velázquez: An Animal Studies Reading of Early Modern Spain*. Ashgate, 2013.

Braidotti, Rosi. *The Posthuman*. Polity, 2013.

Buell, Lawrence. *The Future of Environmental Criticism: Environmental Crisis and Literary Imagination*. Blackwell, 2005.

Campra, Pablo, and Dev Millstein. "Mesoscale Climatic Simulation of Surface Air Temperature Cooling by Highly Reflective Greenhouses in SE Spain." *Environmental Science & Technology*, vol. 47, no. 21, 2013, pp. 12,284–90. *ACS Publications*, https://doi.org/10.1021/es402093q.

"Commission Refers Spain to Court over Illegal Landfills." *European Commission*, 16 July 2015, https://ec.europa.eu/commission/presscorner /detail/en/IP_15_5354.

Crutzen, Paul J., and Eugene F. Stoermer. "The 'Anthropocene.'" *Global Change Newsletter*, no. 41, 2000, pp. 17–18.

Ecologistas en Acción (Grupo Almería). "Comenzamos una serie de acciones contra el plástico agrícola," *Ecologistas en Acción*, 19 Mar. 2021, https:// www.ecologistasenaccion.org/166550/comenzamos-una-serie-de-acciones -contra-el-plastico-agricola/.

Elbaor, Caroline. "The Prado Is 'Updating' Its Most Cherished Masterpieces to Illustrate the Dystopian Chaos Unleashed by Climate Change." *Artnet*, 4 Dec. 2019, https://news.artnet.com/art-world/museo-del-prado-wwf -painting-masterpieces-climate-change-1721970.

Estok, Simon C. *The Ecophobia Hypothesis*. Routledge, 2018.

FUHEM – Educación + Ecosocial. FUHEM, https://www.fuhem.es/. Accessed 16 Jan. 2023.

Gaard, Greta, and Patrick D. Murphy, editors. *Ecofeminist Literary Criticism: Theory, Interpretation, Pedagogy*. U of Illinois P, 1998.

Gaard, Greta, et al., editors. *International Perspectives in Feminist Ecocriticism*. Routledge, 2013.

Glotfelty, Cheryll, and Harold Fromm, editors. *The Ecocriticism Reader: Landmarks in Literary Ecology*. U of Georgia P, 1996.

Hamilton, Clive, and Jacques Grinevald. "Was the Anthropocene Anticipated?" *The Anthropocene Review*, vol. 2, no. 1, 2015, pp. 59–72. *SAGE Journals*, https://doi.org/10.1177/2053019614567155.

Haraway, Donna. "Anthropocene, Capitalocene, Plantationocene, Chthulucene: Making Kin." *Environmental Humanities*, vol. 6, no. 1, 2015, pp. 159–65. *Duke UP*, https://doi.org/10.1215/22011919-3615934.

Haraway, Donna J. *Staying with the Trouble: Making Kin in the Chthulucene.* Duke UP, 2016.

Haraway, Donna J. *When Species Meet*. U of Minnesota P, 2008.

Harrington, Henry, and John Tallamadge, editors. *Reading under the Sign of Nature: New Essays in Ecocriticism*. U of Utah P, 2000.

Herrero, Yayo. "Ecologismo: Una cuestión de límites." Interview by Dara Medina Chirono. *Encrucijadas: Revista Crítica de Ciencias Sociales*, vol. 11, June 2016, e1101, https://recyt.fecyt.es/index.php/encrucijadas/article/view/79005.

Huggan, Graham, and Helen Tiffin. *Postcolonial Ecocriticism: Literature, Animals, Environment*. Routledge, 2010.

Iovino, Serenella, and Serpil Oppermann. *Material Ecocriticism*. Indiana UP, 2014.

Kerridge, Richard, and Neil Sammells, editors. *Writing the Environment: Ecocriticism and Literature*. Zed Books, 1998.

Latour, Bruno. "Agency at the Time of the Anthropocene." *New Literary History*, vol. 45, no. 1, winter 2014, pp. 1–18. *Project MUSE*, https://doi.org/10.1353/nlh.2014.0003.

Latour, Bruno. *We Have Never Been Modern*. Harvard UP, 1993.

Martinez-Alier, Joan. *The Environmentalism of the Poor: A Study of Ecological Conflicts and Valuation*. Edward Elgar Publishing, 2002.

McGregor, Deborah. "Mino-Mnaamodzawin: Achieving Indigenous Environmental Justice in Canada." *Environment and Society*, vol. 9, no. 1, 2018, pp. 7–24. *Berghahn Journals*, https://doi.org/10.3167/ares.2018.090102.

McNeill, J.R., and Peter Engelke. *The Great Acceleration: An Environmental History of the Anthropocene since 1945*. The Belknap Press of Harvard UP, 2014.

Meadows, Donella M., et al. *The Limits to Growth*. Universe Books, 1972, https://www.clubofrome.org/publication/the-limits-to-growth/.

Méndez Gutiérrez del Valle, Ricardo, and Julio Plaza Tabasco. "Crisis inmobiliaria y desahucios hipotecarios en España: Una perspectiva geográfica." *Boletín de la Asociación Geógrafos Españoles*, no. 71, 2016, pp. 99–127, https://doi.org/10.21138/bage.2276.

Moore, Jason W. "Introduction. Anthropocene or Capitalocene? Nature, History, and the Crisis of Capitalism." *Anthropocene or Capitalocene? Nature,*

History, and the Crisis of Capitalism, edited by Jason W. Moore, PM Press, 2016, pp. 1–11.

Moore, Jason W. "The Rise of Cheap Nature." *Anthropocene or Capitalocene? Nature, History, and the Crisis of Capitalism*, edited by Jason W. Moore, PM Press, 2016, pp. 78–115.

"La NASA recuerda que los invernaderos bajan cada 10 años 0'3 °C la temperatura del Poniente, mientras sube 0'5 °C en la región." Horto Info, 16 Sept. 2022, https://hortoinfo.es/nasa-invernaderos-bajan-temperatura -almeria/.

Nishime, Leilani, and Kim D. Hester Williams, editors. *Racial Ecologies*. U of Washington P, 2018.

Nixon, Rob. *Slow Violence and the Environmentalism of the Poor*. Harvard UP, 2011.

Oppermann, Serpil, editor. *New International Voices in Ecocriticism*. Lexington Books, 2014.

Parikka, Jussi. "Anthropocene." *Posthuman Glossary*, edited by Rosi Braidotti and Maria Hlavajova, Bloomsbury, 2018, pp. 51–3.

Parrón, T., et al. "Clinical and Biochemical Changes in Greenhouse Sprayers Chronically Exposed to Pesticides." *Human & Experimental Toxicology*, vol. 15, no. 12, Dec. 1996, pp. 957–63. *SAGE Journals*, https://doi.org/10.1177 /096032719601501203.

Parrón, T., et al. "Increased Risk of Suicide with Exposure to Pesticides in an intensive Agricultural Area. A 12-Year Retrospective Study." *Forensic Science International*, vol. 79, no. 1, May 1996, pp. 53–63. *ScienceDirect*, https:// doi.org/10.1016/0379-0738(96)01895-6.

Patel, Raj, and Jason W. Moore. *A History of the World in Seven Cheap Things: A Guide to Capitalism, Nature, and the Future of the Planet*. U of California P, 2017.

Pérez Orozco, Amaia. "Amenaza tormenta: La crisis de los cuidados y la reorganización del sistema económico." *Revista de Economía Crítica*, no. 5, 2006, pp. 7–37.

Planelles, Manuel. "España vulnerable ante el reto medioambiental." *El País*, 6 June 2016, https://elpais.com/elpais/2016/06/02/ciencia/1464880153 _418408.html.

Plumwood, Val. *Environmental Culture: The Ecological Crisis of Reason*. Routledge, 2002.

Prádanos, Luis I. "Ecología y estudios culturales ibéricos en el siglo XXI." *Arizona Journal of Hispanic Cultural Studies*, vol. 23, 2019, pp. 133–44. *Project MUSE*, https://doi.org/10.1353/hcs.2019.0013.

Prádanos, Luis I. *Postgrowth Imaginaries: New Ecologies and Counterhegemonic Culture in Post-2008 Spain*. Liverpool UP, 2018.

Prats, Fernando, et al. *The Critical Crossroads: On the Ecosocial Crisis and the Change of Historical Epoch*. Translated by Jean Byrne, Foro Transiciones, 2016.

Slovic, Scott, et al., editors. *Ecocriticism of the Global South*. Lexington Books, 2015.

"Sueños Rotos: El impacto de la crisis de la vivienda española en los grupos vulnerables." *Human Rights Watch*, 27 May 2014, https://www.hrw.org/es/report/2014/05/27/suenos-rotos/el-impacto-de-la-crisis-de-la-vivienda-espanola-en-los-grupos#.

Tønnessen, Morten, and Kristen Armstrong Oma. "Introduction." *Thinking about Animals in the Age of the Anthropocene*, edited by Morten Tønnessen et al. Lexington Books, 2016, pp. vi–xix.

Tsing, Anna Lowenhaupt. *The Mushroom at the End of the World: On the Possibility of Life in Capitalist Ruins*. Princeton UP, 2015. *ProQuest Ebook Central*, http://ebookcentral.proquest.com/lib/york/detail.action?docID=2028320.

PART ONE

Tracing Environmental Culture in Spain

Lope's *Los guanches de Tenerife y conquista de Gran Canaria*: An Ecolonialist Reading

BONNIE L. GASIOR

In 1618, Lope de Vega (1562–1635) published this eponymous play loosely based on the series of incursions on the Canary Islands that culminated in 1496.[1] At the end of the fifteenth century – to put this in context – Columbus was only on his second of four voyages, making the takeover of the island of Tenerife a contemporaneous, albeit lesser-known, extension of Spanish imperialism closer to the peninsula.[2] In comparison, by the time Lope dramatized the event, Spain already had well over a century of colonizing experience under its proverbial belt, giving its culturati ample time to apperceive the politics of conquest.[3] Although this fictionalized version of the military event is yet another example of a recountal from the Spanish point of view, with all of the partiality it implies, this essay proposes that Lope recasts the (hi)story, as per his title, in a way that puts the Guanches, the island's autochthonous inhabitants, front and centre.[4] Although neither Lope nor his works have been associated with environmentalism, some inductive reasoning might cast a (sympathetic) light on an ecocritical reading of the play.

In his 1609 *Arte nuevo de hacer comedias en este tiempo* (*The New Art of Writing Plays*), Lope presents an at-the-time-controversial argument to the Academy of Madrid: with a nod to the title of his three hundred-plus "versessay," he prescribes new *comedia* rules. His premise is that change is good, that the evolution of theatre is inevitable, and that the early seventeenth-century theatregoer deserves consideration in the

My neologism uniting "ecology" on one hand and "colonialism" on the other emphasizes the inescapability yet vulnerability of nature in recorded New World literary contexts.

reformulation. At the heart of this matter, then, were human beings, specifically the masses, who comprised the majority of the paying audience:

> Y escribo por el arte que inventaron
> los que el vulgar aplauso pretendieron,
> porque, como las paga el vulgo, es justo
> hablarle en necio para darle gusto
>
> (I write in accordance with the art invented by
> those who aspired to the commoners' applause,
> and since commoners are our customers, it is only fair
> to speak his language to appease him; 45–8)[5]

While Lope's argument may seem reasonable to a twenty-first-century reader familiar with quasi-social justice issues, his critics, including rival Miguel de Cervantes (1547–1616), insinuated that Lope promoted theatre reform for personal gain (i.e., to increase ticket sales). Nevertheless, Lope prevailed and continued with bravado to put into effect the recommendations he set forth. To this day, Lope is considered the people's playwright of early modern Spain, and his acknowledgment of the *vulgo* ("the masses") suggests a favouring of the marginalized. In three of his more canonical plays – *Fuenteovejuna* (1618), *El perro del hortelano* (*Dog in a Manger*, 1618), and *La dama boba* (*The Lady Simpleton*, 1613) – for example, Lope protects the town by not revealing the murderer of the Comendador, satirizes what Margaret Wilson calls "aristocratic depravity" (279), and ensures that Finea, the simpleton in question, comes out ahead, respectively. In that sense, then, Lope's plays had a relatability factor that the *vulgo* surely relished. In the context of *Los guanches*, perhaps we can look to Cervantes, ironically, whose *Quixote* character Sansón Carrasco clarifies that while a historian must record events exactly as they transpired, "el poeta puede contar o cantar las cosas, no como fueron, sino como debían ser" ("a poet can tell or sing things, not as they were, but as they should have been"; II, 49). It is in this spirit that I read the play as a sort of apologetic history. Although Lope does not modify the eventual outcome – the Guanches indeed are conquered and cultural syncretism is looming by act 3 – he does afford the Aboriginals a powerful, interrogating voice, what A. Robert Lauer calls a "decentring strategy" that aligns itself with the island's greatest commodity: its natural and human resources (34).[6]

The play's allegory manifests as opportunistic Spaniards on one hand and exploited native islanders on the other. Lope develops the contrast between the soldiers and the Guanches in a way that not only adopts a Lascasian attitude towards conquest, but also transcends it by using his Indigenous characters as mouthpieces to question the legitimacy of conquest itself.[7] By underscoring connections to the natural world, particularly when musing Spanish prerogative, the Guanche collective voice anticipates (self-)preservation efforts of more modern times. In addition, the symbiosis recalls another shift from centre, what ecocritics Fiona Becket and Terry Gifford call "decentring of the human subject," whereby humanity's and nature's survival are co-dependent (8).[8] Although terms such as *Anthropocene* and *ecocriticism* are anachronistic in an early modern context, Lope's dramatic piece prefigures many of the issues they denote, raise, and problematize today.

Pioneering ecocritic Lawrence Buell defines ecocriticism as the "study of the relationship between literature and environment conducted in a spirit of commitment to environmental praxis" (20). This responsibility intensifies by default when Indigenous cultures, whose existences are in play and at stake, drive the plot. On one hand, for example, Lope portrays the Guanches as childlike, artless, and barbarous, in a move that again echoes Las Casas; on the other, he underscores their sensibility as they repeatedly call into question the bellicose endeavours of the Spanish by invoking nature as a way to underscore risk to the land. By frequently stressing the deep connection between the more-than-human natural world and the Guanche people, Lope implicates his compatriots' controversial, nation-expanding enterprise as ecologically and culturally devastating.[9]

The environmental history of conquest as recorded in New World accounts has garnered attention from scholars only in the last half century, despite its latent protagonism in most Atlantic-world travel literature. While historians such as Alfred W. Crosby explore the consequences of ecosystem clash (*Columbian Exchange*), and Mark A. Burkholder and Lyman L. Johnson likewise cite disease and abuse as enablers of empire in their seminal *Colonial Latin America*, ecolonialist readings of Spanish colonial texts, which serve to dismantle and destabilize human-nature dichotomies and therefore better contextualize those repercussions as a multi-directional interrelationship, have only recently emerged. Part excoriation against colonialism, part climate-change manifesto, Raj Patel and Jason W. Moore's *A History of the World in Seven Cheap Things*, for example, traces the broad abuses of nature at moments of economic catastrophe to claim that "[h]istory is made not through the separation of humans from nature but through their evolving, diverse configurations" (20). Patel and Moore identify forced Indigenous and African labour as the lynchpin in subsequent

Iberian-controlled systems of production (46), such as the colonial encomienda system, the ultimate, toxic human-nature relationship.[10] The authors demand an urgent reconsideration of our collective, longstanding disregard for our "[w]orld-ecology" (38), "how humans make environments and environments make humans" (38), in order to prevent the exhaustion of planetary life resources. Consequently, (re)reading texts that traditionally have marginalized or overlooked non-human nature's role in human enterprise will not only enrich existing scholarship, but also give way to new understandings of – if not underscore cautionary tales between – human and non-human inhabitants of the earth, as is the case with the Spaniards, the Guanches, and the island of Tenerife as portrayed in Lope's play.

From an anthropological perspective, the origins of the Guanches and their language have been shrouded in mystery.[11] As John Mercer points out, "Unluckily, no written record has been left by the island people of life, seen from their viewpoint, in the aftermath of the 1478–96 conquests" (213), which would have assisted scholars trying to understand contact zone occurrences.[12] Despite this void, writers have documented numerous descriptions of the Guanches that corroborate their demeanour, way of life, and culture. For example, in 1892, nineteenth-century ethnographic tendencies aside, Charles Edwards offers a benevolent if not compassionate view by qualifying the Guanches as "a people who knew nothing of money, who had but to scratch the soil to make it bring forth fruit, and under a climate of proverbial sweetness, it may be imagined that ambition did not greatly abound. The poor lived in peace and plenty, each under the shade of his own fig tree, and the monarchs of their respective kingdoms did their best for the common weal" (170). The romanticization of the Guanches, while wholly subjective, nevertheless corroborates general historic opinion. For example, Antonio de Viana's epic poem *Antigüedades de las islas afortunadas de la Gran Canaria* (*Antiquities from the Fortunate Canary Islands*), from which Lope's dramatization of Spanish and Guanche history originates, celebrates Guanche culture and underscores the Indigenous group's indecent treatment. Lambasting a previous depiction by Alonso de Espinosa (*Los guanches de Tenerife*, 1594) in his preambulatory "Al discreto y piadoso lector" ("To the Discreet and Pious Reader"), Viana cites "las injurias que a mi patria hizo el extranjero a título de celebrarla, agravió a los antiguos naturales en muchas varias opiniones que afirma, obscureciendo su clara descendencia, y afeando la compostura de sus costumbres y república" ("how the foreigner insulted my country under the pretext of celebrating it, offending the native inhabitants with several of his claims, shrouding their clear lineage, and faulting their customs and republic"; 3). Mercer puts Viana's bemoaning into perspective: "The reader may have noticed that the alternation of Canary magnanimity and European treachery is recorded in the annals of the *invaders* – so the contrast is unlikely to have been overemphasized" (202; emphasis in original).[13] Viana retorts by establishing not only the Guanches' admirable physical abilities but also their extraordinary character and disposition:

> Tenían todos por la mayor parte
> magnánimo valor, altivo espíritu
> valientes fuerzas, ligereza y brío
> dispuesto talle, cuerpo giganteo
> rostros alegres, graves y apacibles
> agudo entendimiento, gran memoria
> trato noble, honesto y agradable
>
> (Most were of
> magnanimous courage, proud spirit
> valiant strength, agility, and verve
> of sizable stature with
> happy, serious, and friendly faces
> sharp wit, impressive memory
> and noble, honest, and agreeable manners; 24)

Lope's decision to base his play on Viana's poem and not a recorded historical account suggests that he, too, was sympathetic to the Guanches' plight. We only need to examine a few scenes of the *comedia* to recognize Lope's own appreciation for – and probable dismay at – the obliteration of Guanche society that valued, depended on, and was defined by non-human nature. The Guanches' voice resounds throughout the plot, in contrast with Bencomo's self-depiction as a king whose first order of business each day is to check on his livestock rather than marvelling at or from – as would most others – his golden palace (1023–4). The islanders' words, therefore, figure as much more than mere plot mechanisms; they reinforce the interconnectedness between ethics and ecology to yield a counterhistorical – if not contrite – account of regrettable acts.

When juxtaposed with the inherent bellicosity of conquests as political exploits, the *comedia* at once establishes the Guanches' connection with the non-human natural world and infers, by association, a disregard for such relationships by non-Indigenous groups. As self-described human ecologist Joseph W. Meeker asserts, "Human behavior has generally been guided by presumed metaphysical principles which have neglected to recognize that man is a species of animal whose welfare depends upon successful integration with the plants, animals and land that make up the environment" (163).[14] By failing to consider the vital interconnectedness between oneself and more-than-human nature, humans are and will continue to be unprepared to rebound from Mother Nature wronged, the repercussions of which are ever-present in 2021. Literary ecologist William Rueckert sees our misguided exploits as further aggravating our precarious situation: "[M]an's tragic flaw is his anthropocentric (as opposed to biocentric) vision, and his compulsion to conquer, humanize, domesticate, violate, and exploit every natural thing" (113). Lope explores this premise throughout the play in an act-ending Guanche remark that also serves to decry Spanish materialism:

> Si buscáis, cristianos fuertes,
> oro, perlas, piedras, plata,
> no lo hallaréis escondido
> si no en nuestras entrañas;
>
> (If you seek, mighty Christians,
> gold, pearls, precious stones, silver,
> you will not find them hidden
> but rather in our hearts; 2930–3)

Moreover, such affirmations substantiate human–non-human entwinement, which, when considered collectively, demonstrate the legitimacy of historical revisionism.

The myriad conquests that the Spaniards realized against Indigenous groups during the colonial period share the same unsettling yet typical discursive markings. With violence as the common denominator, inscribed on the former are superiority and rationality; on the latter, savagery and simplicity. Lope's play, in that sense, reveals its kinship with its chronicle cousins. One of the few studies on the play, Javier Lorenzo's "Lope's Imperial Geography: Cosmography, Gender, and Dietetics in *Los guanches de Tenerife y conquista de Canaria*," fleshes out these inscriptions to yield a gendered spectacle, which aligns with ecofeminists Cathleen McGuire and Colleen McGuire's assertion that "the domination of women and the domination of nature are fundamentally connected" (201n). Lorenzo argues that "[i]n Lope's play, the political desire for control and possession of the colonial space is articulated through images of penetration and ingestion ... rendering the colonial subject a feminized object of desire to be metaphorically and literally consumed" (2), an observation that aligns with my previous analysis of "Feminising the Conquest" (Gasior 19). Nevertheless, I read the play as more nuanced and in a way that upholds but ultimately challenges the colonial binary, as well as the opposition of human and non-human nature that runs parallel to it.[15] Indeed, the nature-steeped imagery that forms part of Guanche ideology could be read as part of an ecological manifesto that ultimately problematizes conquests in general and early modern Spanish incursions in particular to explore the broader eco-centric underpinnings and implications in the dramatic work.[16] If Lope sets a stage in which the natural world is depicted as inseparable from those who live in it (Buell uses the term "continuum"; 19), then just as the Spanish cite religion to justify their imperialistic tendencies, the Guanches invoke their oneness with nature to ultimately destabilize the official account of the Spanish military feat. By affording the Guanches this textual agency, Lope hints that their subjugation is a crime against nature, both literally and figuratively.

The play opens with a troop of Spaniards making landfall and her-alding, "Bárbara es esta nación" ("This nation is uncivilized"; line 21), which subsequently calls for the yoking of the Guanches (36–7).[17] The evaluation serves to qualify the conquest as "justa, heroica y santa" ("just, heroic, holy"; 43), thereby reinforcing and justifying its evange-lizing aims.[18] The Spaniards figuratively stake their claim, hedge their bets, and establish their mission as conveniently necessary. The imposi-tion of order over the Other as a pretext to eventually appropriate the island and its inhabitants attests to the assertion by American historian Lynn White, Jr., that "[e]specially in its Western form, Christianity is the most anthropocentric religion the world has seen" (9). The Spanish, tone-setting appraisal stands in stark contrast to the first words of Dácil, King Bencomo's daughter, whose nature-infused discourse serves to accentuate the Guanches' connection with the beyond-human natural world, in contrast with its undervaluation by the Spanish.[19] She muses over a "verde ribera" ("green bank"; 116), "fresca laguna" ("refreshing lagoon"; 118), "fuente bella" ("beautiful spring"; 119), "árboles fron-dosos" ("lush trees"; 131), "jilguerillos y canarios" ("goldfinches and canaries"; 128), and "blanca nieve" ("pure snow"; 137), which consti-tute the overall "armonía y concierto" ("harmony and order"; 126) on Tenerife. She waxes hyperbolic as she gazes at the sky – "[J]urarías que alma tiene" ("You would swear it had a soul"; 164) – personifying the embodiment of the Guanches' world view and reinforcing biophilia. In act 2 (1020–50), Bencomo echoes Dácil's sentiments. It bears mention-ing that while these sorts of *locus amoenus* descriptions abound in plays of the time, coming from the mouths of marginalized Aboriginal char-acters, they assume more explicit, critical dimensions that transcend *comedia* convention to at once underscore the Guanches' palpable relationship with the earth as well as presage its imperiled status. The subjugation of Indigenous peoples on the brink of colonization, then, by default signals the subjugation of all nature – human and non-human – making Lope's play a harbinger of the ecological crises afflicting the world today.[20]

Bencomo, although proud of his daughter's appreciation of the surrounding flora and fauna, reminds her that another incursion by the Spaniards is immanent as Castillo, a Spanish captain, arrives exhausted at the edge of a lake: "[D]os veces se han atrevido … / y dos veces de su espada nos habemos resistido" ("They have tried twice … / and twice we have resisted their sword"; 178–81). Castillo's thirst, which manifests as both literal (he shows signs of dehydration) and metaphorical (he is dressed in full armour, heralding the next military operation), is exacerbated and temporarily quenched by the alluring Dácil, who represents a potential sexual conquest within the larger imperialistic undertaking. Indeed, this scene substantiates how beholding women's Aboriginal bodies has a satiating effect, as Castillo infers:

> [L]o que a un hombre que ver puede
> frutas de tierras extrañas,
> que viéndolas tan hermosas,
> bien las desea comer
>
> (When a man sees
> fruits from strange lands
> their beauty
> whets his appetite; 757–60)

Rather than respond coyly, Dácil instead dissents actively, thus anticipating the other resisting, Indigenous voices throughout the play: "Tenéisnos por hechiceras" ("You take us for sorceresses"; 767). Furthermore, this association of the Guanche women with kindred practices underscores their misconstrued affinity with nature. The Spain-colony dichotomy Lope establishes to comply with theatrical convention thus is rendered problematic by default, as the collective Indigenous voices throughout the *comedia* represent a constant reminder of its fallibility.

Dácil's encounter with Castillo at the lake is additionally noteworthy because rather than find her engaged in idle pursuits such as bathing or swimming that are common to *comedia* storylines – which would privilege his gaze on her Indigenous (likely unclothed) body and encourage voyeuristic activities – she instead secretly ascends to and observes him from an overhanging tree branch. Castillo discovers her only thanks to the reflection she casts upon the water, a moment that exemplifies the human–non-human contours Lope explores. By placing Dácil in a position of (visual) privilege normally reserved for Spanish males, the scene functions as a tone-setting synecdoche that parallels and prefigures the Guanches' propensity to probe Spanish prerogative as an assault on nature and, by association, their culture.[21] Furthermore, the role inversion recalls what ecocritic Donna Haraway termed *natureculture* in *The Companion Species Manifesto* and which anthropologist Nicholas Malone and conservation biologist Kathryn Ovenden summarize as "a synthesis of nature and culture that recognizes their inseparability in ecological relationships that are both biophysically and socially formed" (1). In this scene, Dácil is physically and symbolically one with the thicket, and her purview endows nature with the same linguistic and visual advantage, ultimately soldering the purported nature-culture divide.

As the two characters gingerly engage in conversation, Dácil's responses to Castillo's questions further reinforce the Guanches' unity with their environs:

> CASTILLO: ¿Quién eres?
> DÁCIL: Esto.
> CASTILLO: ¿Qué es esto?
> DÁCIL: Lo que ves.
>
> (CASTILLO: Who are you?
> DÁCIL: This.
> CASTILLO: What is this?
> DÁCIL: What you see; 662–5)

Although lacking parentheticals, Dácil's response infers a gesticulation of her surroundings, of which she unwaveringly sees herself as an extension. The fact that Castillo's question would normally elicit a response that involved a name, yet Dácil offers him a suggestive demonstrative pronoun, signals a more comprehensive and nature-bound understanding of her identity. Their dialogue eventually assumes amorous undertones – another popular *comedia* convention – as a love-struck Dácil repeats four times "lindo español" ("charming Spaniard"; 667, 669, 677, 702), and an ingratiated Castillo compares himself, ironically, to a "tímido conejo" ("timid rabbit"; 684) before Dácil's arresting beauty. The first act, then, serves to anticipate the conquest of Castillo over Dácil as an allegory of the larger, political, territorial conquest that intensifies in acts 2 and 3. More importantly, though, it posits Lope's predilection for the Guanche ecological perspective, as Dácil's vantage point and reply in tandem demonstrate.

In act 2, the Guanches increasingly question Spanish presence on the island by astutely portraying themselves as objects of Spanish ambition and prerogative. Bencomo's first words immediately decry the Spaniards' colonizing intentions, qualifying their objective to dominate the Guanche people and land as lunacy: "Pues, ¿qué me quieren a mí / estos españoles locos?" ("So, what do these crazy Spaniards / want from me?"; 1010–11). The king's warranted anxiety manifests in several ways, the first of which involves a series of nature metaphors posed as thought-provoking questions to criticize his counterparts' acquisition aims:

> Pues si toda mi riqueza
> es dos limpios caracoles,
> ¿A qué vienen españoles
> a conquistar mi pobreza?
>
> (So, if all my riches
> amount to two fine seashells,
> What are the Spaniards after?
> My poverty?; 1051–4)

He continues:

> ¿Voy a buscar a los españoles yo?
> ¿Qué pájaro me llevó
> por encima de la mar?
> ¿Tengo yo rayos y truenos
> como ellos? ¿Formo yo acaso
> fuego con que un hombre abraso
> de que todos vienen llenos?
> ¿Traigo yo picos agudos,
> sino estos dardos tostados,
> y algunos ramos cortados,
> ya de sus hojas desnudos?
>
> (Do I seek out Spaniards to conquer?
> What bird carried me
> over the sea?
> Do I, perchance, have lightning and thunder
> like them? Do I make fire

that burns a man
like they do?
I have no sharp spears,
other than these flaming darts,
and a few sticks; 1059–70)[22]

From a colonial perspective, the imagery in Bencomo's utterance emphasizes the modesty and inherent dignity of Guanche culture and, at the same time, it condemns opposing Spanish brutality and opportunism. In addition, from an ecolonial point of view, when presented through a powerful string of interrogatives, the collectivity of the images debilitates Spanish culture by semantically transforming boats into birds and guns into thunder. Once again, Haraway's notion of natureculture suggests that Spanish and Guanche cultures are portrayed in tension precisely because, for the Guanche people, nature and culture are inseparable.

Although Bencomo acknowledges that militarily his people are no match for the steel-wielding Spaniards, Lope insinuates that the Guanches are morally superior and affords the King, the ultimate representative of the Other, a counter-discourse that challenges the integrity of the political enterprise.[23] Tinguaro's statement further fans those flames of discontent when he affirms that the Spaniards "no saben luchar, correr, dar saltos, / jugar un árbol, esgrimir un pino, / tirar un arco, derribar un toro" ("do not know how to fight, run, jump, / engage a shrub, sword fight a pine tree, / shoot an arrow, take down a bull"; 262–4). Both characters insinuate that in fact, the Spanish, not the Guanches, are uncultured because they are unable to engage skilfully with non-human nature. Siley, a Guanche captain and ally of Bencomo, delivers the final discursive blow by voicing his own assessment of the situation with ironic, derisive undertones. He refers to the Spanish ships as "cargadas de hechicerías" ("sorcery-laden"; 1667), implies that Spanish reasoning emanates from "negras bocas" ("evil mouths"; 1673), and alludes to the depositing of souls from men to Guanche women through "enredos … invenciones y marañas" ("tricks … lies and artifices"; 1701–2), "a escondidas de los hombres / dando a las mujeres almas" ("behind Guanche men's backs / giving women souls"; 1707–8).[24] These references to witchcraft, deception, and violence that hint at the Spaniards' aberrant behaviour are typically those not associated with Indigenous discourse of the early modern period but rather originate from its European counterpart to characterize Indigenous groups of non-Christianized lands. By appropriating the colonizer's own terminology to disgrace Spanish behaviour, Siley demonstrates not only the wisdom to critique the invaders in a way they would understand but also recasts – and recalls – Dácil's previous sorcery comment to Castillo, which now resounds with irony. As a result, such discourse at once subverts hegemonic order and furthers early modern ecocriticism's anti-binary aims.

A more-than-human nature constitutes the cornerstone of Guanche discourse in act 3, as evinced by the agrarian-related words of the first eight verses: "ganado" ("livestock"; 2011), "ordeñar" ("to milk"; 2012), "ribera" ("river bank"; 2014), "monte" ("mountain"; 2018), "prado" ("meadow"; 2018). When contrasted to the previous battle scene, the pastoral imagery intensifies the polarity between different expressions of agency, from the relentless Spaniards on one hand and more pacific and nature-bound Guanches on the other. The Guanches' attitude demonstrates that, in an ecolonialist context, agency is not merely a question of activity versus passivity but rather a manifestation of subjectivity. In this act's culminating scene, Lope initially portrays the Guanches as innocent and infantile when they fail to recognize that a statue of the Virgin of Candelaria carrying a child holding a bird – a clear portent of Christian-Guanche religious syncretism – is merely an inanimate object, not a flesh-and-blood human.[25] While the Guanche men mind the statue, Dácil coerces Castillo, the only Spaniard to remain on the island due to a battle injury, into a marriage proposal and then designates another insensate object, a boulder, to bear witness to his promise and their union.[26] A delighted Castillo welcomes what he perceives as Dácil's naïveté, interpreting her strategy as potentially advantageous to him should he decide to renege.[27]

In the subsequent scene, Captain Castillo, who coincidentally has spent over a year on the island, expectedly undergoes a physical, Cabeza-de-Vaca-esque transformation worthy of note.[28] His own compatriots fail to recognize their former leader, mistaking him for a Guanche, as Captain Trujillo's evaluation of him – "Bárbaro, fiero, arrogante" ("Barbarous, wild, arrogant") – exemplifies (2672). Castillo's appearance renders him not only an extension of his surroundings but also and more importantly, a powerful, subversive figure that embodies the natureculture synthesis with which the Spanish must now contend. Because this scene is not based on a historical account but instead operates as a plot device, it favours Lope's ostensibly ecocritical agenda by implying that Castillo has gained wisdom from the Guanches. Castillo's outward appearance, not to mention his retort to Trujillo – "¿Cuando la española gente / suele proceder tan mal?" ("Since when do the Spanish people / behave so poorly?"; 2650–1) – implies not only discord but also cultural estrangement. Castillo's use of the third person indicates he no longer sees himself as a Spaniard, as his previous comment and acknowledgment of Dácil attest: "[Q]ue viviendo amor en mí / puse la patria en olvido" ("Love made me forget / about my country"; 2714–15). Forsooth, Castillo has meshed with Dácil's "esto" from act 1.

Although the concluding verses augur the anticipated re-establishment of *comedia* order – Guanche men celebrate the absorption of kingdoms, Spanish soldiers' interests turn to land exploitation (gold, silver, pearls), and Castillo reappears in a stage direction "ya muy galán" ("handsomely"), signalling his cultural reintegration – the echo of Indigenous voices throughout the play linger and persist. Dácil, for one, vehemently objects not only to the attitude of the men in general but to Castillo's in particular, as he has opportunely forgotten his matrimonial promise. She subsequently solicits testimony from the boulder before a dismissive Castillo, at which moment smaller pieces dislodge to reveal the Angel Michael holding the image of the Virgen of Candelaria.[29] This occurrence at once signals the settling of Christianity but more importantly, holds Castillo accountable. Reframing Dácil's misperceived ingenuity as naturecultural wisdom in utter rebuke of Castillo's haughtiness complements Merediz's claim that Lope admonished colonial rapacity (192n). While for many scholars this geological phenomenon figures at worst a coincidence or at best some divine occurrence, in fact, it upholds an ecocritical agenda. According to ecofeminist Karen Barad, to consider a performative understanding of natureculture practices is one way to redefine representation and to disrupt binary thinking that instead "takes account of the fact that knowing does not come from standing at a distance and representing but rather from a direct material engagement with the world" (49). Barad drives home her point by specifying the how and who of performative acts: "Importantly, what is at issue is precisely the nature of these enactments … And humans are not the only ones engaged in performative enactments" (49). The boulder, then, cannot be interpreted in this context as a mere plot-advancing object but rather a meaning-generating subject. Furthermore, when considered alongside the agency of the insentient statue, thanks largely to the Judeo-Christian tradition's acceptance and promotion of miracles, the boulder activity – comparable to human speech – assumes similar connotations and associations.

In sum, Lope's play engages ecopolitical thought in ways that anticipate more modern ecosocial issues, like those relating to twentieth-century Latin American Indigenous groups often at the mercy of land developers, tribal tourism, and global warming.[30] If, as environmental humanist Dana Phillips affirms, "Nature is thoroughly implicated in culture, and culture is thoroughly implicated in nature" (577–8), then we have a great deal to learn from this interdependence, as the plethora of images of more-than-human nature throughout the play demonstrates. While such words individually do not necessarily signal an ecocritical moment, when considered collectively and given their repeatedly entwined association with the Guanches throughout the play, they create a formidable ecopoetics. As a result, they enable Lope to bow to convention and reinforce one duality (Spanish/Guanche) while ultimately challenging another (human/non-human nature). At times, they even acquire symbolic relevance: by the third act, nature assumes darker hues with the milking of cows at dusk (2012), references to shadowy caves (2055), and black dust (2256), all of which portend a metaphorical eclipse of the natural world. By this third act, then, Lope views the stakes of conquest in a way that disrupts traditional colonial narratives by transcending the long-standing civilization-barbarism binary and, instead, heralding ecolonialism.[31]

Today, Lope's *comedia* comes full circle and stands as an enduring reminder of the short- and long-term effects of predation of land and people. Mercer outlines the years after the conquest as ones marked by land misappropriation, misallocations, and malfeasance (214–16). He furthermore cites deforestation and the disappearance of streams in the sixteenth century as ecological tragedies, hence explaining the island's current condition as "dry, windswept and barren valleys and mountains" (219). Tenerife, therefore, serves as cautionary tale of climate change for the twenty-first century – Vakoch asserts that "we can learn much from those who have traveled through boundaries of nature and culture" (8) – and Lope's play thus reads as a vindication of a noteworthy yet understated moment in Guanche history.

Renowned Spanish philologist Ramón Menéndez Pidal described Lope as someone who, "hasta el fin de su vida[,] colocó la naturaleza por cima del arte" ("throughout his life preferred nature over art"; 26–7). Early modernist Alexander Samson, furthermore, reminds us of Lope's own horticultural activity throughout his lifetime and of how he often invoked gardens – microcosms of the greater natural world – as political metaphors with allegorical possibilities (126). These symbolic grounds reach their maximum expression in a play like *Los guanches*, as Tenerife comes to be understood as the ultimate arable, conquered perhaps, but not without disruption and resistance by the Guanches, who value the natural world in a holistic way that decentres the human.[32] The repeated non-human images that Lope invokes represent more than coincidental floral and faunal descriptions or mere sites of untapped economic potential. Rather, they act as a network of metaphors of the native islanders and as a tangible manifestation of their ethos.[33] In this way, Lope establishes a connection that portends emerging ecocentric anxieties and, more importantly, problematizes the (jeopardized) symbiosis and inextricable link between the environment and Indigenous peoples. The countless references to the more-than-human natural world and their meaningful connection to the Guanches – at once prized and in peril – expose Spanish immorality and legitimize Guanche interrogation in a sort of green audit of Tenerife. If "Belardo" in Lope's *romance* "Hortelano era Belardo" ("Belardo Was a Gardener"), was, as critics agree, an autobiographical reference, then Lope identifies as not only a writer but also a horticulturist. By definition, these growers figure as some of the staunchest defenders of beyond-human nature who not only understand but also revere the delicate equilibrium in which humans and non-human entities coexist. For this reason, Lope's famous moniker as "El monstruo de la naturaleza" ("monster of nature") could now indeed take on new meaning as we contemplate the possibilities of what could be read as a case of Spanish early modern literary environmental activism.[34]

NOTES

1 In her critical edition, Eyda M. Merediz calls the play a "drama histórico" ("historical drama"; 11).

2 As Alfred Crosby points out, "The Guanches deserve more attention than they have received. They were, with the possible exception of the Arawaks of the West Indies, the first people to be driven over the cliff of extinction by modern imperialism" (*Ecological Imperialism* 80).

3 Felipe Fernández-Armesto makes reference to the zeitgeist of the late fifteenth century: "Evidently the attitude the Spaniards later adopted towards the Indians of the New World and the question of their juridical standing were not dissimilar from those they evinced towards the Canary Islands: the implicit doctrine that the monarchs' title to the unconquered islands gave them the right to wage war upon the inhabitants, was also present, *mutatis mutandis*, in the great Alexandrine Bulls on the conquest of the New World and in the *Requerimiento*" (126).

4 Although Lope wrote many more plays in his lifetime than any of his contemporaries, *Los guanches* has only recently garnered critical attention. Therefore, the reading proposed is doubly significant: "A growing number of scholars are clearly interested in expanding the purview of ecocritical practice by widening the canon of texts for ecocritical investigation and placing environmental criticism in a more productive relation with other, perhaps suspiciously humanistic, theoretical perspectives and critical practices" (Rosendale and Slovic xvii).

5 All translations are my own. Page numbers correspond to the Spanish original.

6 Lauer explains that these strategies "partially destabilize or challenge the official ideological component of these dramas" (34).

7 Bartolomé de las Casas (1484–1566), although considered a resolute defender of New World Indigenous peoples, did not oppose conquest but rather the violence that characterized it in his *La Brevísima relación de la destrucción de las Indias* (*Brief Account of the Destruction of the Indies*, 1552).

8 Louise Westling points out that literary environmentalism is merely two decades old, yet rich traditions of it have been represented in all major cultures (2).

9 A brief history of the Canary Islands as it relates to Spain is important in understanding the contentious relationship between the islanders and their mainland counterparts, the origins of which date back to 1402. In 1494, Alonso Fernández de Lugo led an offensive on Tenerife that would prove disastrous, as some 2,000 Spaniards perished. The actual name of the battle site turned town – La Matanza ("the Slaughter") – is a tragic reminder of their defeat. The persistence of the Spanish finally paid off, though, and after years of failed attempts, they finally took over the island in 1496 and all but exterminated the Guanche people in the process. The Guanches' fate was thus sealed by the end of the century. Today, Spanish mainlanders' ecologically and culturally destructive attitudes are captured in the Canarian term *godo*, which, as contributors to this collection María Luz González-Rodríguez and María Concepción Brito-Vera point out, Canary Islanders employ to denounce Spaniards from the Peninsula for their persistent (post)colonial marginalization of the islands' peoples and rhythms in the name of profit-driven exploitation.

10 This and any form of slavery views the Other as subhuman to justify its acquisitive practices: "The rise of capitalism gave us the idea not only that society was relatively independent of the web of life but also that most women, Indigenous Peoples, slaves, and colonized peoples everywhere were not fully human and thus not members of society" (Patel and Moore 24). The Guanches' ecological alliance reinforces this (mis)perception, which in turn fuels the colonial agenda. As ecocritics Catrin Gersdorf and Sylvia Mayer claim, historical and ideological misappropriations of nature have long been justification for systems of cultural and social oppression (12). See also "Cartesian revolution" (Patel and Moore 54).

11 Scientific and linguistic publications on the Guanche people abound, yet uncertainty about their linguistic roots and controversy surrounding their origins – popular European myth portrays them as tall with blond hair and blue eyes – persists today. See, for example, Bynon; Fregel et al.; Maca-Meyer et al.; Rodríguez-Varela et al.; Zurita et al.

12 See Pratt 4.

13 Although born in Tenerife in 1578, Viana is not a direct Guanche descendent.

14 Laroche and Munroe point out our connections to nature at the most basic of levels: "From the microbiome within our guts, to the air we breathe, to the food we process and digest, we are linked in ways that exceed our wilful selves and that have collateral effects (both negative and positive) for those with whom we share this planet" (xvii).

15 Feminist ecocritic Douglas A. Vakoch asserts that ecofeminist literary criticism at once "reveals the oppressiveness of patriarchal, dualistic thinking" and "*emancipatory* strategies employed by ecofeminist literary critics as antidotes" (10; emphasis in original).

16 I have argued in my ecofeminist reading that Lope espouses a female poetics of incursion with Lascasian undertones in a lyrical rewriting of the fifteenth-century takeover of the island by Spanish *conquistadores* (Gasior).

17 This metaphor not only serves to underline inferiority and disorder, it also reduces humans to animals with the reference to yokes, ropes used to bind and control beasts of burden. Furthermore, Alonso's eventual questions insinuate savagery and foretell Spanish dominion:

¿Es tu Rey hombre grave?
¿Castiga, premia, en qué entiende?
¿Tenéis leyes? ¿Hay ciudades?
¿Cómo os gobernáis aquí?

(Is your King a serious man?
Does he punish and reward accordingly?
Do you have laws and cities?
How do you govern here?; 971–4)

18 See Moisés Castillo's brilliant *Indios en escena: La representación del amerindio en el teatro del Siglo de Oro* (*Amerindians on Stage: The Representation of the Amerindian in the Golden Age Theatre*).

19 Mercer clarifies that "'Ben Como' was the name of the leader of Taoro" (200).

20 In her ecopostcolonial analysis of Laura Gallego García's monster trilogy, *Beyond Human* contributor Victoria L. Ketz likewise assesses the colonial and anthropocentric hierarchizing of human and non-human life at the expense of ecological equilibrium in ways that, as Luis I. Prádanos has stated, impose on all beings a universal definition of the good life that is neither desirable nor viable for most (53). Whereas in Lope the Spanish colonial subjugation of the Guanche people shows utter disregard for

the Indigenous world views of Tenerife's original inhabitants and their symbiosis with the natural environment, in Gallego's young adult literature, the ruling class carefully constructs a cultural narrative around the social fantasy of human superiority over other species, thereby perpetuating colonial dynamics that include the dispossession of common rights and of collective knowledge.

21 Merediz sees Dácil as another example of agency by Indigenous women in the Spanish early modern period: "El personaje de Dácil es muy interesante porque constituye una recreación literaria de figuras históricas femeninas somo [*sic*] La Malinche y Malitzín y Pocahontas que facilitan las conquistas europeas" ("Dácil is very interesting because she constitutes a literary recreation of female historical figures such as La Malinche and Malitzín and Pocahontas who facilitated European conquests"; 41n).

22 Fernández-Armesto repines, "The conquest, moreover, took a heavy toll, throughout the archipelago, in deaths, deportations, enslavements, and 'cultural shock', and may have caused a demographic cataclysm similar to that which befell the conquered peoples of the New World" (11). On a different note, Bencomo rounds out his interrogation with two verses that are reminiscent of Sor Juana later on that same century in "Hombres necios" ("Foolish Men"): "¿En qué fuego oculto fundo / la muerte, engaño y traición?" ("In what hidden fire do I fuse / death, deceit and treason?"; 1073–4).

23 Nevertheless, Crosby refers to the Guanches as "disunited": they lived across seven islands, lacked seafaring skills, spoke different languages, and were recruitable for Spanish pursuits (*Ecological Imperialism* 87). Their defensive disadvantage, according to White, was notable in light of "the technological superiority of Europe" (7).

24 This idea of soul consignment permeates act 2 and figures a way for Lope to reframe conquest, as did Las Casas, as a more peaceful venture grounded in religion. The neoplatonic idea of men (Laurencio) giving women (Finea) souls, a metaphor for love, is also a theme in another of Lope's plays, *La dama boba*.

25 Crosby calls this the "cultural disorientation or reorientation of the Guanches" (around 1400, when the Virgin Mary appeared to shepherds): "She left behind an image of herself, the statue ever after called Our Lady of Candelaria, which was involved in a number of miracles in the Canaries until its destruction in a flood in the nineteenth century" (*Ecological Imperialism* 88). Curiously, Sir Clements Markham, in his translation of Espinosa, confirms that the Virgin appeared for the first time around 1400. See pp. 45–8 for details, many of which the play reflects.

26 Dácil's world view is merely different from, not inferior to, Castillo's, as Manes upholds: "In contrast, for animistic cultures, those that see the

natural world as inspirited, not just people, but also animals, plants, and even 'inert' entities such as stones and rivers are perceived as being articulate and at times intelligible subjects, able to communicate and interact with humans for good or ill. In addition to human language, there is also the language of birds, the wind, earthworms, wolves, and waterfalls – a world of autonomous speakers whose intents (especially for hunter-gatherer peoples) one ignores at one's peril" (18).

27 Toward the end of act 3, Dácil – the parentheticals clarify that she speaks and is alone – delivers a sonnet that furthermore celebrates not only her shrewdness but also her awareness of Castillo's fickleness.

28 Álvar Nuñez Cabeza de Vaca (1490–1559) was a Spanish conquistador who shipwrecked along with four others along the coast of Florida in 1528. After eight years of wandering the New World lands, his altered appearance complicated his rescue: he retells in his 1542 *Naufragios* that only when he spoke Spanish did his compatriots give credence to his identity.

29 The splintering of the rock is related to geophony, naturally occurring, non-biological sounds from a habitat. In a literary ecocritical sense, the event could be considered a form of non-verbal speech.

30 See, for example, Anderson et al.; Kronik and Verner; Mowforth et al.; and Zeppel (particularly ch. 3).

31 This idea anticipates Patel and Moore's term "reparation ecology" (43).

32 This defiance manifests historically when the Guanches were exported to nearby Madeira as slaves in the late fifteenth century. Patel and Moore confirm that the Guanches' opposition resulted in stronger control of their living conditions in 1473 (29).

33 A recent article on *La voz del despertar* asserts in its title that "[l]a biodiversidad del planeta es preservada en un 80% por los pueblos indígenas" ("80 per cent of earth's biodiversity is preserved by Indigenous people"). In order to make this determination, a research group from the University of Barcelona cohabitated with and studied three Indigenous groups in the Congo, Borneo, and the Amazons, respectively, for a year and a half between the years 2011 and 2015. In a similar vein, Alexander Zaitchik makes a case for Indigenous groups rather than environmentalists to lead the charge of protecting now jeopardized ecosystems.

34 A special note of thanks to Mindy Badía and Yolanda Gamboa for their invaluable comments on an earlier version of this essay; to Margaret Marek for her solidarity and comic relief during the revisions phase; and to my graduate research assistant, Jaclyn Taylor, whose help with formatting proved invaluable. I am also deeply indebted to Shanna Lino and Maryanne L. Leone for their superb suggestions that bolstered the theoretical framework of my reading.

WORKS CITED AND CONSULTED

Anderson, E.N., et. al. *Political Ecology in a Yucatec Maya Community*. U of Arizona P, 2005.

Barad, Karen. *Meeting the Universe Halfway: Quantum Physics and the Entanglement of Matter and Meaning*. Duke UP, 2007.

Becket, Fiona, and Terry Gifford. *Culture, Creativity and Environment: New Environmentalist Criticism*. Rodopi, 2007.

"La biodiversidad del planeta es preservada en un 80% por los pueblos indígenas." *La voz del despertar*, 12 May 2019, https://www.lavozdeldespertar .com/?p=5982&fbclid=IwAR1im4PDvffAE0QvVWMk0b4V1wfwBnIAQpfMJ 8J4RAZ1gU4doM_8i8rQmrY.

Buell, Lawrence. *Writing for an Endangered World: Literature, Culture, and Environment in the US and Beyond*. The Belknap Press of Harvard UP, 2001.

Burkholder, Mark A., and Lyman L. Johnson. *Colonial Latin America*. Oxford UP, 1990.

Bynon, James. "The Contribution of Linguistics to History in the Field of Berber Studies." *Language and History in Africa*, edited by David Dalby, Africana Publishing, 1970, pp. 64–77.

Castillo, Moisés. *Indios en escena: La representación del amerindio en el teatro del Siglo de Oro*. Purdue UP, 2009.

Cervantes, Miguel de. *Segunda parte del ingenioso hidalgo Don Quijote de la Mancha*. Edited by John Jay Allen, Cátedra, 1994.

Crosby, Alfred W. *The Columbian Exchange: Biological and Cultural Consequences of 1492*. Greenwood, 1972.

Crosby, Alfred W. *Ecological Imperialism: The Biological Expansion of Europe, 900–1900*. Cambridge UP, 1986.

Edwards, Charles. "The Guanches of Tenerife." *Littell's Living Age*, vol. 194, July–September 1892, pp. 165–76. *HathiTrust Digital Library*, https:// hdl.handle.net/2027/uiug.30112055313941.

Espinosa, Friar Alonso de. *The Guanches of Tenerife: The Holy Image of Our Lady of Candelaria and the Spanish Conquest and Settlement*. Translated by Sir Clements Markham, Hakluyt Society, 1907.

Fernández-Armesto, Felipe. *The Canary Islands after the Conquest: The Making of a Colonial Society in the Early Sixteenth Century*. Clarendon, 1982.

Fregel, Rosa, et al. "The Maternal Aborigine Colonization of La Palma (Canary Islands)." *European Journal of Human Genetics*, vol. 17, no. 10, October 2009, pp. 1314–24. *Nature*, https://doi.org/10.1038/ejhg.2009.46.

Gasior, Bonnie. "Feminising the Conquest: Lope de Vega's Female Poetics of Incursion in *Los guanches de Tenerife y conquista de Gran Canaria*." *Acta Universitatis Carolinae – Philosophica et Historica 3. Studia Historica LVIII*.

Cultural Conquests 1500–2000, edited by Tim Kirk and Luda Klusakova, Karolinum, 2008, pp. 19–29.

Gersdorf, Catrin, and Sylvia Mayer. "Nature in Literary and Cultural Studies: Defining the Subject of Ecocriticism – An Introduction." Nature in Literary and Cultural Studies: Transatlantic Conversations on Ecocriticism, edited by Catrin Gersdorf and Sylvia Mayer, Rodopi, 2006, pp. 9–21.

Glotfelty, Cheryll, and Harold Fromm, editors. *The Ecocriticism Reader: Landmarks in Literary Ecology.* U of Georgia P, 1996.

Haraway, Donna J. *The Companion Species Manifesto.* Prickly Paradigm, 2003.

Kronik, Jakob, and Dorte Verner. *Indigenous Peoples and Climate Change in Latin America and the Caribbean.* World Bank Publications, 2010.

Laroche, Rebecca, and Jennifer Munroe. *Shakespeare and Ecofeminist Theory.* Bloomsbury, 2017.

Lauer, A. Robert. "The Iberian Encounter of America in the Spanish Theater of the Golden Age." *Pacific Coast Philology*, vol. 28, no. 1, 1993, pp. 32–42. *JSTOR*, https://doi.org/10.2307/1316421.

Lorenzo, Javier. "Lope's Imperial Geography: Cosmography, Gender, and Dietetics in *Los guanches de Tenerife y conquista de Canaria.*" *Bulletin of the Comediantes*, vol. 64, no. 1, 2012, pp. 1–18. *Project MUSE*, https://doi.org /10.1353/boc.2012.0017.

Maca-Meyer, Nicole, et al. "Ancient mtDNA Analysis and the Origin of the Guanches." *European Journal of Human Genetics*, vol. 12, no. 2, February 2004, pp. 155–62. *Nature*, https://doi.org/10.1038/sj.ejhg.5201075.

Malone, Nicholas, and Kathryn Ovenden. "Natureculture." *The International Encyclopedia of Primatology*, edited by Agustín Fuentes et al., Wiley, 2016, https://doi.org/10.1002/9781119179313.wbprim0135.

Manes, Christopher. "Nature and Silence." Glotfelty and Fromm, pp. 15–29.

McGuire, Cathleen, and Colleen McGuire. "Grass-Roots Ecofeminism." *Ecofeminist Literary Criticism: Theory, Interpretation, Pedagogy*, edited by Greta Gaard and Patrick D. Murphy, U of Illinois P, 1998, pp. 186–202.

Meeker, Joseph W. "The Comic Mode." Glotfelty and Fromm, pp. 155–69.

Menéndez Pidal, Ramón. *De Cervantes y Lope de Vega.* Espasa-Calpe, 1958.

Mercer, John. *The Canary Islanders: Their Prehistory, Conquest, and Survival.* Collings, 1980.

Merediz, Eyda M. "Estudio crítico Introducción." *Comedia la famosa de Los guanches de Tenerife y conquista de Canaria*, edited by Eyda M. Merediz, Juan de la Cuesta, 2003, pp. 9–25.

Mowforth, Martin, et al. *Tourism and Responsibility: Perspectives from Latin America and the Caribbean.* Routledge, 2008.

Patel, Raj, and Jason W. Moore. *A History of the World in Seven Cheap Things: A Guide to Capitalism, Nature, and the Future of the Planet.* U of California P, 2017.

Phillips, Dana. "Ecocriticism, Literary Theory, and the Truth of Ecology." *New Literary History*, vol. 30, no. 3, Summer 1999, pp. 577–602. *Project MUSE*, https://doi.org/10.1353/nlh.1999.0040.

Prádanos, Luis I. *Postgrowth Imaginaries: New Ecologies and Counterhegemonic Culture in Post-2008 Spain*. Liverpool UP, 2018.

Pratt, Mary Louise. *Imperial Eyes: Travel Writing and Transculturation*. Routledge, 1991.

Rodríguez-Varela, Ricardo, et al. "Genomic Analyses of Pre-European Conquest Human Remains from the Canary Islands Reveal Close Affinity to Modern North Africans." *Current Biology*, vol. 27, no. 21, 2017, pp. 3396–402. *Cell Press*, https://doi.org/10.1016/j.cub.2017.09.059.

Rosendale, Steven, and Scott Slovic. "Introduction: Extending Ecocriticism." The Greening of Literary Scholarship: Literature, Theory, and the Environment, edited by Steven Rosendale, University of Iowa Press, 2002, pp. xv–xxx. *JSTOR*, https://doi.org/10.2307/j.ctt20q1x4v.5.

Rueckert, William. "The Remorseless Inevitableness of Things." Glotfelty and Fromm, pp. 105–23.

Samson, Alexander. "Outdoor Pursuits: Spanish Gardens, the *huerto* and Lope de Vega's *Novelas a Marcia Leonarda*." *Locus amoenus: Gardens and Horticulture in the Renaissance*, edited by Alexander Samson, Wiley-Blackwell, 2012, pp. 124–50.

Vakoch, Douglas A. "Introduction: A Different Story." *Feminist Ecocriticism: Environment, Women, and Literature*, edited by Douglas A. Vakoch. Lexington Books, 2012, pp. 1–13.

Vega, Lope de. *El arte de hacer comedias en este tiempo (1609)*. Edited by Enrique García Santo-Tomas, Cátedra, 2009.

Vega, Lope de. *Los guanches de Tenerife y conquista de Gran Canaria*. Edited by Eyda M. Merediz, Juan de la Cuesta, 2003.

Viana, Antonio de. *Antigüedades de las islas afortunadas de la Gran Canaria*. Edited by J.R.M., Tipografía de la Laguna, 1905.

Westling, Louise. "Introduction." *The Cambridge Companion to Literature and the Environment*, edited by Louise Westling, Cambridge UP, 2014, pp. 1–13.

White, Lynn, Jr. "The Historical Roots of Our Ecological Crisis." Glotfelty and Fromm, pp. 3–14.

Wilson, Margaret. "Lope as Satirist: Two Themes in *El perro del hortelano*." *Hispanic Review*, vol. 40, no. 3, Summer 1972, pp. 271–82. *JSTOR*, https://doi.org/10.2307/471793.

Zaitchik, Alexander. "How Conservation Became Colonialism." *Foreign Policy*, 16 July 2018, https://foreignpolicy.com/2018/07/16/how-conservation-became-colonialism-environment-indigenous-people-ecuador-mining/.

Zeppel, Heather. *Indigenous Ecotourism: Sustainable Development and Management*. Cabi, 2006.

Zurita, Ada I., et al. "Y-chromosome STR Haplotypes in the Canary Islands Population (Spain)." *Forensic Science International*, vol. 148, nos. 2–3, March 2005, pp. 233–8. *ScienceDirect*, https://doi.org/10.1016/j.forsciint.2004.05.004.

Chapter Two

Birdsong and the Earth's Polyrhythm: The Life of a Caged Blue Rock Thrush in Early Modern Spain

JOHN BEUSTERIEN

a caged bird stands on the grave of dreams
his shadow shouts on a nightmare scream

Maya Angelou, "Caged Bird"

In the Fall of 2019, I taught in Seville, Spain, and each day on my way to class I passed by a small shop that sold live caged songbirds. When I went to get my hair cut, the barber near my school also had a caged bird and, as he cut, I asked him about the singing above my head. The barber explained that he had decorated the barbershop with all sorts of antiques from shops of a bygone era and that caged songbirds were a standard. In fact, he told me, caged birds were still found in many barbershops in the towns around Seville and when men go to get their hair cut, they bring their songbird with them. The barber described to me what he considered to be a typical barbershop scene: a barber and his clients discuss their songbirds and often one man, considered the judge, declares which bird sings most beautifully.

This experience led me to think about the history of caged birds and to ask when people first began to collect live caged songbirds in Spain. *Conocimiento de las diez aves menores de jaula, su canto, enfermedad, cura y cría* (*Concerning Ten Small Caged Songbirds, Their Song, Sickness, Care, and Breeding*, 1604), is the earliest European treatise about caged birds and one of the first books on ornithology ever published.[1] Ornithologies

---

A special thanks to Amelia Gillespie for the research help and collaboration. Thanks to Corinne Griffin for the permission to use a recording of her birdsong performance. Thanks also to Jacob Baum, Ross Forman, Timothy Foster, Charles Greer, Martha Otis, Maryanne L. Leone, Shanna Lino, and Carolyn Nadeau.

are examinations of birds as empirical objects and three – written by Conrad Gesner, Antonio Valli da Todi, and Ulisse Aldrovandi – predate *Conocimiento de las diez aves menores de jaula*.[2] Nonetheless, *Conocimiento de las diez aves menores de jaula* is the first European treatise about caged songbirds that examines birds in an empirical way.[3]

The following study examines the early modern ornithologist Juan Baustista Jamarro and, instead of locating his treatise within the field of the history of science, it examines the text from a humanities perspective and shows how one can read Jamarro's treatise to hear birdsong. Juan Bautista Jamarro was a surgeon, dentist, and bloodletter from Naples who served as personal physician to King Philip II of Spain.[4] He was also renowned in early modern Spain for his ability to understand birdsong, which Juan de Arce Solorceno, a poet from Philip II's court, compared to great feats by the gods from classical Rome.[5]

Conocimiento de las diez aves menores de jaula makes clear that the practice of keeping caged songbirds was already commonplace over four hundred years ago.[6] Because they are such an important sign of the earth's ecological future, the disappearance of birds, like insects and ice caps, is a harbinger of climate change triggered by human activity.[7] Influenced by the Anthropocene, scholars are increasingly reading books and other cultural artefacts from the Spanish-speaking world through the lens of environmental cultural studies (Beilin et al.). This essay contributes to the field of environmental cultural studies and, more broadly, the environmental humanities by explaining the ecocritical importance of a text about songbirds and by underscoring the detriment to their song when separated from their natural habitat in cages.

The first part of the chapter explains the need to listen to birdsong within the bird's original habitat in order to be sensitive to the earth's polyrhythm. The chapter then tells the life story of the newly named Filipo, a blue rock thrush (*Monticola solitarius*), one of the birds described in *Conocimiento de las diez aves menores de jaula*. It argues that Filipo's life in a cage separated him from the earth's polyrhythm. The chapter concludes by describing how student performances of the birdsongs from Jamarro's text can lead toward a greater sensitivity of the earth's polyrhythm.

The Earth's Polyrhythm

Birdsong cannot come from within a cage because it must be experienced in conjunction with earth's natural rhythms, whether those of other birds, animals, trees, stones, the sun, clouds, or even of a certain smell in the air. Australian philosopher Elizabeth Grosz notes that a planetary rhythm "runs through all of life and connects the living in its various forms to the non-organic forces and qualities of materiality itself" (19).[8] Grosz is especially interested in the connection between planetary rhythm and birdsong. She points out that recognizing connections between human music and birdsong is one way to better appreciate planetary rhythm. She explains that birdsong – like human music – is commonly learned rather than innate. Likewise, birdsongs can be spontaneously modified, either by adding new learned elements or by modifying existing ones. The range of improvisational skills for birds depends on when they acquire new sounds and calls. Like humans, the younger the bird, the more particularly susceptible they are to learning new songs (38). Grosz concludes by underscoring the importance of birdsong in connection to the different rhythms that constitute living habitats across the planet, writing that "rhythm is what connects the most elementary and primitive bodily structures of even the most simple organisms to the implacable movements of the universe itself" (19).

David G. Haskell, a professor of biology and poet, reaches similar conclusions about birdsong when he explains that listening to birdsong helps to better appreciate the planetary rhythm, which he defines as the interconnectivity of beings on earth. He writes that when heard in the bird's natural habitat, "bird and human minds connect, [and] a new language is born." The new language "weaves many species into a communicative whole, a web of listening and speech. Language-learning is indeed for everyone. It unites us." He continues: "Every species has its own tempo of sound-making through the year, tuned to the particularities of food plants and insects, refined by local weather. In these sounds we learn that there are not just four seasons, but dozens or hundreds." Birdsong helps unveil the entire world as a system of cross-species kinships, and, for Haskell, birdsong is one of the rhythms that best opens a sensibility to earth's other rhythms. This sensibility to rhythm can lead to an appreciation of how humanity's rhythm fits into the design of the planet: "In attending to the sounds of bird species, our senses learn the language of belonging. Over time, this embodied knowledge of place tells us what is changing, what is gained, and what is lost." The recognition of the connection between birdsong and other rhythms of a specific natural habitat illuminates an embodied spatial knowledge, specifically, humanity's place on the planet.

Embodied knowledge is acquired slowly. It is not an explosive idea that comes to the brain in a flash but becomes part of the body's routine through repetition. Musicologist Rachel Mundy has coined the term "animanities" to define the interdisciplinary work that she conducts, combining biological and musical analyses of bird song in a way that decentres the anthropocentric way that music has been studied heretofore. Mundy expresses an animanities methodology in "Why Listen to Animals":

> Listening to birds taught me to hear spatially, using my ears to locate birds I couldn't see through walls or foliage. I learned to recognize the songs and calls of various species, and tried to understand those sounds as symbols of a rich invisible world … I learned to hear sentience, selfhood, and meaning in sound too. Before seeing them, I could hear a deer stamp his foot in the scrub; I'd hear the local hawk's chicks begging for food; and I'd hear the alarm calls of thrushes warning me that something they considered dangerous, probably another pedestrian, was on the path ahead.

For Mundy, the aural experience of birdsong interconnects with a wider interspecies soundscape. Birdsong enables her to hear spatially, connecting soundscape to earthscape and catalyzing an awareness of the heightened sentience of different species. According to Mundy, one may acquire the knowledge of natural space through the commonplace listening to birds, an experience that she describes as transcendent. Indeed, Mundy credits the transcendence of routine listening for the development of her powerful voice, which is predicated on a human-bird connection and forges a new language within the earth's polyrhythm. In short, birdsong inspires Mundy to more keenly recognize a structuring vibration that undoes human exceptionalism and forces the reckoning of birdsong with other contingencies of the lifeworld.

The Biogeography of Filipo, the Blue Rock Thrush (c. 1594–c. 1598)

The transcendent interspecies experience described above notwithstanding, if Mundy were to listen to a bird sing from within a cage, she would not perceive the ways in which the song interconnects with the earth's polyrhythm. When a bird is caged, its rhythm no longer connects with the different species, forces, and landscapes with which it forms a communicative whole. In this context, birdsong cannot be appreciated as the language and music that connects the living to non-organic forces or materiality in the ways that have informed Grosz's philosophical, Haskell's biological, or Mundy's musicological practices. In the following section, I describe the biogeography of a blue rock thrush, whom I name "Filipo," in order to signal a common cultural practice that regrettably and tragically separated birdsong from the earth's polyrhythm.

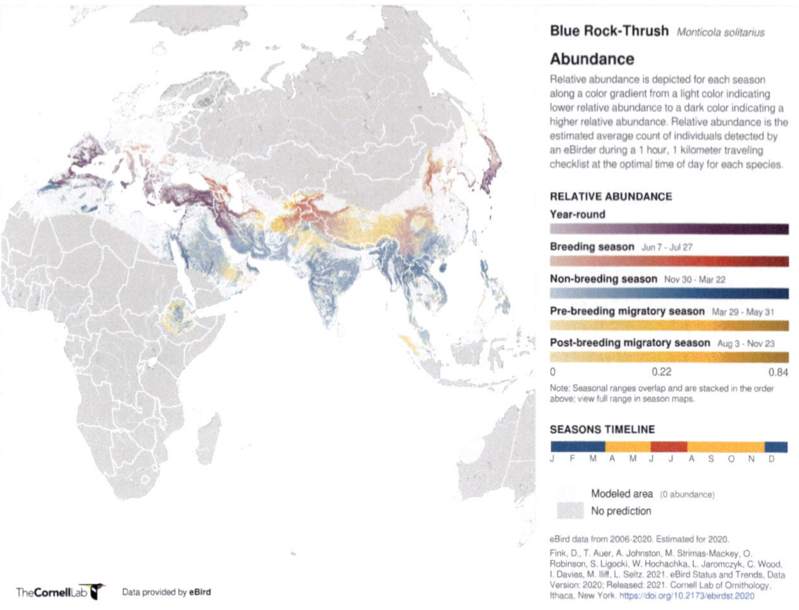

Map 2.1. Geographic range of the blue rock thrush (*Monticola solitarius*)

Notes: This material uses data from the eBird Status and Trends Project at the Cornell Lab of Ornithology, eBird.org. Any opinions, findings, and conclusions or recommendations expressed in this material are those of the author and do not necessarily reflect the views of the Cornell Lab of Ornithology.

Source: Cornell Lab of Ornithology.

As the study of the distribution of species and ecosystems, biogeography traces animals in their geographical range in the wild. Biogeographers generally study species in ecosystems in geological terms. A biogeography of the blue rock thrush maps its habitat (map 2.1). The bird is found across an immense land-mass that extends from Northern Africa and Southern Europe to China and Indonesia. The biogeography also maps the places where the birds generally take residence (in the mountains) and those where they breed. In Spain, the blue rock thrush is considered sedentary and a partial migrant because it does not travel long distances, but simply moves from the mountains to lower altitudes for breeding once a year from late April to mid July ("Blue Rock-Thrush").

I believe that biogeography needs to reach beyond the sciences and that scholars in the humanities are uniquely equipped to provide contributions to this field.[9] In the context of the Anthropocene, in which humanity has come to determine animal habitats, the study of the human institutions that affect the lives of animals has taken on added urgency. Humanities scholars can shed light on the formation of the cultural institution of caging songbirds, as well as other practices that take birds out of natural habitats. The humanities can also study the life histories of individual birds (versus an entire species) in order to enhance human compassion, to inspire greater appreciation of avian intelligence, and to shore up support for conservation efforts.[10] Finally, a nominal biogeography of the individual specimen of a songbird can underscore the importance of understanding the earth's polyrhythm.

This chapter is the first nominal biogeography of the unnamed blue rock thrush described in Jamarro's caged songbird treatise. I have chosen to give this bird, who probably lived from about 1594 to 1598, the name Filipo because the critic who writes a nominal biogeography must choose to give a name to the animal individual that, until the present, had never been deemed worthy of a proper name (Beusterien, "What's in a Name?"). During the reign of Philip II, powerful men deemed certain animals as worthy of proper names. Conquistadors often gave names to their fighting dogs, and Gonzalo Argote de Molina published the names of Philip II's hunting dogs (Beusterien, *Transoceanic Animals* 223). But no one in the historical record ever thought to name any of Philip II's caged songbirds. I choose "Filipo" in order to turn attention away from the standard historical biography that focuses on the male human ruler. In writing about Filipo the blue rock thrush, rather than Philip the king, the biogeography refocuses history towards an animal.

This nominal biogeography inverts the masculinist colonial practice of naming a domestic animal by making the story about a bird, not the human king. In choosing the name Filipo, I am inspired by Spanish playwrights from the period who also used the name for one of their most popular and intriguing type characters, a former Black captive who turns saint and who is also described as a king, a soldier, and a warrior.[11] Plays about the character Filipo simultaneously evoke the Spanish king Philip and the Black dramatic character who has escaped a life in captivity. The choice of Filipo, then, for the blue rock thrush pushes the bounds of how to think about the history of captivity because it calls attention to the history of both racism and speciesism. Indeed, the metaphor that Maya Angelou uses in her poem "Caged Bird," as well as the first of seven autobiographical volumes, *I Know Why the Caged Bird Sings*, in which the caged bird symbolizes a chained enslaved person, likewise makes readers consider not only the history of racism, but also the practice of caging birds.[12]

Filipo the blue rock thrush sang for human pleasure and his physical suffering was irrelevant to the king. The last entry in Jamarro's treatise is devoted to the blue rock thrush, a songbird commonly caged in early seventeenth-century Spain.[13] The title page of the tenth entry contains a woodcut and description of the bird (fig. 2.1). Beyond never naming the blue rock thrush, Juan Bautista Jamarro's *Conocimiento de las diez aves menores de jaula* never imagines Filipo's life in the wild. Placed in a cage, his song – which up until that point had formed a part of an integrated ecological system – was supposed to please the ailing king. I imagine that in 1594, Filipo's mother laid three to five eggs in a hidden rock cavity in the mountainous cliffs of the Alicante region in Spain. The tempo of Filipo's song would have depended on the rhythms of the lives of reptiles, insects, berries, and seeds. During most of the year, the blue rock thrush eats mainly insects, but supplements these in the summer and spring breeding season with small reptiles and in the fall and winter with fruit and berries. The rhythm of Filipo's song also would have depended on the mountainous landscape. Generally solitary, the blue rock thrush prefers to nest in crevices among rocks at high elevation, often under an overhang or in a crevice, perching itself on top of the overhang to sing. For the purposes of mating, the male blue rock thrush descends to lower elevations such as the grasslands to sing.

While the circumstances of his birth are speculative, we know that Filipo ended his life not in the wild but in a cage. Jamarro used his expertise as a surgeon and bloodletter to care for King Philip II during his dying days. While drawing blood was a practice in vogue in the period for nearly all cures, including old age, the king loved to listen to songbirds and he sorely missed their sounds when he was away from them.[14] Therefore, along with bloodletting, Jamarro considered birdsong an essential remedy for the ailing monarch.[15]

During the king's final days, Jamarro wrote his treatise on songbirds in order to describe the ten most important species that had been placed in King Philip II's private quarters in the Escorial. The surgeon's descriptions explain each bird's origins, what to do if the bird is sick, the upkeep of the cage, and what to feed each. The published version of Jamarro's birdsong treatise contains a woodcut image of each bird species: nightingale, common linnet, European goldfinch, canary, European calandra-lark, citril finch, European serin, Eurasian siskin, European greenfinch, and blue rock thrush.[16]

The main focus of the entry for each bird is a description of his song. Jamarro wrote over fifty onomatopoeias, trying to capture a graphic rendering of birdsongs that today are encoded by sonograms in a fixed repertoire of signals. For instance, according to Jamarro, if the European goldfinch song is to be "música bien concertado y acabada y que dure" ("properly arranged and accomplished and lasting"), it should be as follows: "chim, belín, ruchá, cha cha, ruchá, chibalí, chibalí, chibalá, chibalá, balá, ruchá chau chau, chau" (*Conocimiento* 48, 23). Jamarro also provides non-standard variants. One variation on the standard song of the European goldfinch is "tupilí, tupilí, tupilí, tupilí, colio" (23).

The accuracy of the details included in the woodcut images of all ten birds is remarkable. No colour, however, is provided since the images were printed with black ink on white paper. Contrary to most songbirds, which have unremarkable colour features, Filipo's bright blue hue would have made him unique in Philip's collection.[17] In contrast with female blue rock thrushes, who are generally light brown (fig. 2.1), the male blue rock thrush is generally an extraordinary blue (fig. 2.2). Filipo would have spent most of the time in the wild alone. Jamarro was familiar with the solitary nature of the blue rock thrush and, in fact, calls the species *solitario*.[18] The last entry of the treatise is likewise titled "De Solitario."[19] *Solitario* refers to the standard species name in the early modern period, like today, and the denomination of a *solitario* ("solitary") bird variety still refers more generally to a variety of species that does not flock together. Interestingly, aside from *solitario*, Jamarro also points to an alternative species name, one commonly used to distinguish the bird by underscoring its colour: "Algunos dicen que estos pájaros son turqueses en España" ("Some say that in Spain these birds are called turquoises"; *Conocimiento* 48). The use of this term (literally a Turkish stone) indicates that people made a semantic connection between the colour of the bird and the Ottoman Empire. Therefore, the name for the caged bird would also have alluded indirectly to the situation of Turkish captives, the paradigmatic Spanish enemy of the period, and, in turn, to Spaniards held captive by the Turks.

Indeed, in his short comic play *La gran sultana*, Miguel de Cervantes (1547–1616) refers in an off-handed and ironic way to the early modern conflation between captive birds and people when he creates Madrigal, a human character who is a Spanish captive in the Ottoman Empire and who claims to understand birdsong (Beusterien, "Madrigal"). The contemporaneous intertextual reference from Miguel de Cervantes thereby relates the captivity of humans to that of birds and, in turn, substantiates an ecocritical reading of Filipo's caging as an example of anthropocentric imperial domination.[20]

Jamarro chose what he considers the top ten songbirds for his treatise. He writes that he listed the nightingale first and the blue rock thrush last

64   John Beusterien

Fig. 2.1. Woodcut of "Del solitario," from *Conocimiento de las diez aves menores de jaula*, by Juan Bautista Jamarro

Source: Photograph by John Beusterien. Public domain.

Fig. 2.2. Blue rock thrush (*Monticola solitarius*)

Sources: Cornell Lab of Ornithology. Photograph by Pedro Marques.

because he considered them to be the two best singers of the ten. While the nightingale holds "el primer lugar entre las aves" ("first place among the songbirds"), the song of the blue rock thrush is "concertadísima, y muy perfecta, con vueltas muy perfectas y acabadas" ("masterfully put together with fine turns of phrase and finishes"; *Conocimiento* 1–2, 48). He concludes by stating that the nightingale's song is equally beautiful as that of the blue rock thrush, but that he prefers to not take sides in the debate over which of the two sings more perfectly.

The surgeon was not interested in the bird's natural rhythm. The entries about each species concern what is best for the bird only insofar as it relates to providing the maximum output of birdsong for the king's benefit and pleasure. Ignoring what the bird would have eaten in the wild, the Neapolitan bloodletter provides dietary advice so the bird will remain healthy for singing. He provides a different recipe for feeding the blue rock thrush depending on whether he is sick or in good health. If the bird is faring well, Jamarro states that the royal cooks in the Escorial should prepare "corazones de cordero picados y revueltos con la pasta y huevos cocidos" ("diced lamb hearts mixed into a paste to which is added hard-boiled (chicken) eggs"; *Conocimiento* 47). Furthermore, "la comida no se le echa en el comedero, sino pegarle la pasta de los huevos a la jaula y ellos la pican allí" ("the food paste from the crushed eggs should not be put in a bowl, but rather stuck to the cage so that the bird can peck it off"; 48–9).[21] Jamarro also provides advice on the proper age to hunt the blue rock thrush so that its song will be the most true.[22] He explains that it must be hunted when it is an adult with an already-established song. Fledglings should not be hunted and caged because they will simply imitate other caged birds (50). Moreover, the court surgeon provides tricks that can be employed to manipulate the bird into singing more often. He states that a mirror be placed in the cage, commenting that "es propio de este pájaro el mirarse" ("it is normal for this species to look at its reflection"; 48).[23] Birdsong by males intensifies during breeding season and, in the presence of the mirror image of a bird, Filipo would have sung to possibly express fear and anger or joy and triumph at a potential rival.

While Jamarro may have been interested in maintaining a healthy songbird, his descriptions of the bird's eating, hunting, and mirror remain anthropogenic practices geared toward keeping captive birds singing. Nevertheless, the attempts to manipulate Filipo to sing for human pleasure ultimately fail. Jamarro writes that when the blue rock thrush "siente gente, no canta de pura tristeza" ("feels the presence of a human, he does not sing out of pure sadness"; *Conocimiento* 48). Since birds experience stress in cages, I suspect that Filipo would have expressed anger and tried to leave his cage constantly.[24] Jamarro writes that blue rock thrushes generally "de coraje se mueren" ("die out of rage"; 47). I am guessing that Filipo died at the age of four in 1598, probably within a year of having arrived at the Escorial and the same year as the death of King Philip II. The caging of a songbird, supposedly salubrious to the king, most likely turned out to be death-inducing for the bird.

Jamarro's treatise describes the human institution of caging songbirds, a cultural practice that interrupted the natural unfolding of each bird's rhythms. Since Filipo the blue rock thrush was hunted, captured, and brought to a cage in the king's palace, his birdsong did not take place in the rocky parts of mountains where the species nests, or in the lowlands where it forages and breeds. Taking into account the meaning of birdsong as described by Grosz, Haskell, and Mundy, Philip II may have heard sounds coming from Filipo's cage, but he did not truly hear the blue rock thrush's birdsong because he was in a cage in the Escorial, disassociated from the complex interconnectivity of planetary rhythms.

Reading Jamarro So as to Listen to Birdsong from outside the Cage

There are many ways that educators who focus on culture and literature can study the environment, particularly birdsong. For example, a class might study Indigenous knowledge systems in pre-Columbian Mesoamerica for the importance of birds and birdsong.[25] Spanish literature professors might also show the ecocritical importance of birdsong by revisiting canonical literary texts like the poetry of the Christian mystic and Carmelite friar Juan de Yepes y Álvarez (San Juan de la Cruz), whose verses explore the theme of the solitary bird's song.[26]

While texts like Jamarro's *Conocimiento de las diez aves menores de jaula* have not generally been taught in classes devoted to Spanish literature or culture, the critical reading of an underappreciated book like a bird treatise encourages an appreciation of birdsong. For instance, at the "Animal/Language: An Interdisciplinary Conference" hosted by Texas Tech University in 2019, students from my class performed Jamarro's birdsong onomatopoeias found in the treatise. I instructed two undergraduate and three graduate students from my Spanish classes to interrupt my talk and to read one of the birdsongs that Jamarro transcribes in the treatise. Corinne Griffin, an undergraduate student in drama and beginning-level Spanish, performed the words "xa, xa, chiui chiui, tan, tan, tan, tan quió, chi, chi, tim, tim, chim, cho, cho, ió, hi, hi" (15). Corinne gave me permission to record and reproduce her performance for this chapter ("By Corinne Griffin"). She repeated the phrase five times and read the words as if she were a bird, inflecting each syllable with a change of tone and volume and making sonic breaks between each word. Corinne's fifteen-second performance of the birdsong jolted the audience into disorientation. What were the strange sounds from her mouth? Was this human song, language, or birdsong?

The birdsong performances by my students made the audience aware of an early modern Spanish text that described the practice of listening to birdsong from cages. The student performance also refocused how the audience understood the use of birds as spectacles for human pleasure more generally. In the early modern period, aside from possessing collections of caged songbirds, elites watched live birds as part of dramatic performances, they collected works of art made out of bird feathers, they kept live exotic birds in menageries, and they collected and caged talking parrots.[27] Instead of watching a bird, the audience watched students perform birdsong. Letting birds loose from their cages has long been a sign of creativity and the students' live performance of the transcribed birdsong constituted a lyrical moment that figuratively let birds loose.[28] The sounds did not make sense in any human language nor were they recognizable as birdsong. They were sounds on the edge of meaning that decentred the cultural practice of extracting and crafting birds for performance and spectacles for human pleasure.

Taken at face value, Jamarro's treatise describes an unnamed blue rock thrush caged by humans. The surgeon described birds as empirical objects of study whose songs were supposed to please a Spanish king in the monastery-palace complex of the Escorial. The text set an unfortunate precedent for the anthropogenic cultural practice still common today in Spain. Teachers of early modern Spanish texts, nonetheless, can read the bird treatise in a way that redirects the author's human-centric focus. They can point out how the unnamed blue rock thrush was an individual. They can provide the bird a name and comment on his sadness, rage, and death as reactions to being caged by humans. They can also have students dramatically interpret the written birdsong from Jamarro's treatise.

I used the student performances to upend a text that describes caged songbirds for human pleasure and as a way to inspire the listening of birdsong. I suggest that teachers go outside with their class to listen, for, as Canadian poet Don McKay writes about birdsong: "If we listened for an evening we would learn to hear" (qtd. in Mason 131). In the context of human-bound animal extinctions and resurrections, birdsong can be a slow and repeated experience of engaged listening that might help disavow distractive technology, including its bird-metaphorical social platform Twitter.

In guiding students on a path toward the earth's polyrhythm, *Conocimiento de las diez aves menores de jaula* can be a springboard to discover the earth as a living body and to understand better what French philosopher Luce Irigaray means when she writes that animals do not belong to the human nor in the human space, but in a space appropriate to their lives (Štuva). Ultimately, students can read the early modern Spanish bird treatise in order to more closely understand birdsong as part of an ever changing, melodious conjunction of tones that sound with other rhythms like those of the sun and darkness, of a tree, of the air, the stoop outside the window, the sky, or even of a nest in a hidden crevice on the coast of Alicante.

NOTES

1 All translations into English of titles and quotations are my own.

2 While the Englishmen Francis Willughby (1635–72) and John Ray (1627–1705) are sometimes considered the first modern ornithologists, Jamarro's treatise predates both. Other books of ornithology that precede Willughby and Ray include *Historia Animalium* (1555) by Conrad Gesner (1516–65), *Il Canto degl'Augelli* (1601) by Antonio Valli da Todi, and a number of books on ornithology published between 1599 and 1603 by Ulisse Aldrovandi (1522–1605). For more on early modern bird management and the development of ornithological science, see Birkhead and van Balen.

3 The first European treatise dedicated to caged birds, *Conocimiento de las diez aves menores de jaula*, was later republished in 1775 and included fourteen, rather than ten, caged birds. The first caged bird treatise in Italy was *Uccelliera overo discorso della natura e proprieta di diversi uccelii* (1622) by Giovanni Pietro Olina (1585–1645). The first treatise in England was *Manual of Cage-Birds: British and Foreign* (1847).

4 Evidence of Jamarro's work as King Philip II's personal physician is found in the manuscript version of Jamarro's *Tratado de la dentadura, sus enfermedades y remedios*, a manual on toothaches and their remedies. In the prologue to this treatise, Jamarro writes, "Los días pasados … presenté a Vuestra Alteza un tratado de la manera como se han de criar los pájaros que se tienen por recreación y conocer y remediar sus enfermedades" ("These last days … I presented to your Royal Highness a treatise on how to breed birds that are kept for entertainment so you can identify them and cure their illnesses"). The prologue of the dentist manual proves that Jamarro wrote the treatise on caged birds in 1597, seven years before the

Spanish Royal Printing Press published it. It is noteworthy that Jamarro's dentist manual, which merits greater attention among historians of dentistry, is one of the earliest treatises of its kind. Jamarro's life history shows the connection between dentistry, surgery, and the practice of drawing blood. Jamarro also wrote a manual on bloodletting, *Indicación de la sangría* (Valladolid, 1604), of which no known copies survive.

5 Solorceno wrote a sonnet that leads off *Conocimiento de las diez aves menores de jaula*, in which he deifies Jamarro by writing that just as Minerva invented the art of weaving, and Hephaestus the art of iron crafting, so Jamarro comprehended birdsong.

6 The ubiquity of this practice is described in Jamarro's treatise and, indeed, he promises a second treatise on caged birds in which he will discuss ten more common species (he lists each species). Jamarro writes, "[O]tras muchas aves, que por la prolijidad dejo; y esto no fue por falta del conocimiento de ellas, ni de su cría, sino por entender, que estos que van en este mi tratado son los mejores y más comunes, de cuyo canto más gustan los aficionados a estos pajarillos. Y siendo, como espero será este mi libro bien recibido, me dará ánimo para que diga en otro de la naturaleza, cría y diversidad de los demás que en este mi libro dejo de decir" ("I have omitted all sorts of other birds because there are too many to fill a single volume. I know about a great number of other birds and about their breeding, but I have decided to only include the best and most common songbirds in this treatise because these birds song give the most pleasure to those who enjoy birdsong. If it is the case that my book is well received – and I expect it will be – then I will write an additional treatise that describes the characteristics, breeding, and diversity of all those birds that I left out of this one"; *Conocimiento* 49–50).

7 For the connection between the decline of insects and birds, see Sánchez-Bayo and Wyckhuys.

8 Grosz's theory about planetary rhythm is influenced by the description of birdsong by French philosophers Gilles Deleuze and Félix Guattari in *A Thousand Plateaus: Capitalism and Schizophrenia* (312–16). Deleuze and Guattari discuss birdsong in relation to repetition as a productive power that courses through all things and they explain the structuring vibration of rhythm as a tenuous gathering of materiality that includes animals and the environment.

9 For a humanities biogeography of an elephant, rhinoceros, armadillo, lion, and bull, see Beusterien, *Transoceanic Animals*.

10 For a study of the importance of the conservation of birds, see Dooren.

11 Plays with the character of the Black protagonist Filipo include *El prodigio de Etiopia* by Lope de Vega, *Virtudes vencen señales* by Luis Vélez de Guevara, and *El negro más prodigioso* by Juan Bautista Diamante, among others. See Beusterien, *Eye*.

12 Maya Angelou borrows the title *I Know Why the Caged Bird Sings* from the
   nineteenth-century poem "Sympathy" by Paul Laurence Dunbar.

13 One contemporary author of an emblem bird book writes that "el canto
   del pájaro solitario es muy suave y apacible a los que son aficionados a
   enjaular pájaros" ("the song of the blue rock thrush is sweet and pleasant
   to those who are fond of caging birds"; Marcuello 50r).

14 King Philip writes that when he was living away from his home in Lisbon
   in 1582, he nostalgically remembered listening to nightingales: "y de lo
   que más soledad he tenido es del cantar de los ruiseñores, que hogaño
   no los he oído, como esta casa es lejos del campo" ("and that which has
   made me feel the loneliest is that this year I have not heard the song of
   nightingales because my home here is far from the countryside"; qtd. in
   Escudero 463).

15 Relevantly, Jamarro's connection to birdsong and one's health is borne
   out in a recent study that argues that listening to birds eases depression,
   anxiety, and stress (Cox et al.).

16 The binomial Latin (L) name of each species of the ten birds followed
   by the name that Jamarro gives in sixteenth-century Spanish (S)
   and Neapolitan Italian (N) for each bird are: nightingale (L: *Luscinia
   megarhynchos*; S: *ruiseñor*; N: *ruxio nuello*); common linnet (L: *Carduelis
   cannabina*; S: *pardillo*; N: *capesusco*), European goldfinch (L: *Carduelis
   carduelis*; S: *gilguero*; N: *cardillo*), canary (L: *Serinus canaria*; S: *canario*; N:
   canarii), European calandra-lark (L: *Melanocorypha calandra*; S: *calandria*),
   citril finch (L: *Cardulis citronella*; S: *pinchón*; N: *froncillo*), European serin
   (L: *Serinus serinus*; S: *verdecillo*; N: *reguecillo*), Eurasian siskin (L: *Carduelis
   spinus*; S: *lugano*; N: *lecora*), European greenfinch (L: *Carduelis chloris*;
   S: *verderón*; N: *furgoro*), and blue rock thrush (L: *Monticola solitarius*;
   S: *solitario*; N: *solitario*).

17 Following English naturalist Charles Darwin, ornithologists typically note
   that birds either have striking colours or sing beautifully, but that the most
   decoratively coloured birds do not sing because sexual selection developed
   only one of the two traits. As the founder of modern evolutionary studies
   notes, "[B]right colours and the power of song seem to replace each other.
   We can perceive that the plumage did not vary in brightness, or if bright
   colours were dangerous to the species, other means would have to be
   employed to charm the females; and the voice being rendered melodious
   would offer one such means" (Darwin 53).

18 Today, the species is commonly called the *roquero solitario* in Spanish
   (compare with *passero solitario* [lone sparrow] in Italian and *melro azul* [blue
   blackbird] in Portuguese). In his treatise, Jamarro states that the species
   of the bird is called *solitario* in both Neapolitan and Spanish and, 150
   years later, the Swedish zoologist Carl Linnaeus formalized the binomial

nomenclature, coining the name *Monticola solitarius* (literally, "solitary mountain dweller") for the blue rock thrush.

19 In general, ornithologists in the early modern period like Conrad Gessner confused the blue rock thrush with other solitary species like the alpine accentor and the rufous-tailed rock thrush (Lewis 547).

20 The theme of captivity is ecocritically explored as well in Bonnie L. Gasior's chapter in this volume about a Lope de Vega play contemporaneous with Jamarro's writing and Cervantes's comic drama that centres on the colonial conquest of the Guanches of Tenerife. The problematization of human and non-human extermination as an imperial practice, which Gasior reads in the Golden Age playwright's representation of the Guanches' inseparability from the island's ecology, is notably absent in the ornithological treatise published during Philip II's court twenty years prior.

21 Martínez Montiño's 1611 cookbook contains 506 recipes for human meals and uses the word "pasta" to refer to a paste or mash often made from marzipan (Nadeau).

22 Evidence of hunting live birds with nets is found in *Venationes Ferarum, Auium, Piscium. Pugnae bestiariorum: & mutuae bestiarum* (*Hunts of Wild Animals, Birds and Fishes*), which widely circulated throughout sixteenth- and seventeenth-century Europe. *Venationes Ferarum* provides images of the ways birds were typically hunted, including ducks, storks, ostriches, partridges, and blackbirds. One image shows how the blue rock thrush may have been hunted: two birds are bound by a cord to the ground to serve as bait for other birds, and a branch is covered with glue so that a bird that lands nearby gets its feet stuck and cannot fly away.

23 The placement of mirrors in the cages of birds can also be found in sixteenth-century English poetry. In John Skelton's *Speak Parrot*, the parrot describes a mirror placed in his cage: "a mirror of glass, that I may toot therein" ("toot" means "to look at something searchingly").

24 For scientific studies on the mental turmoil experienced by parrots, see Bradshaw et al. For the mental anguish of songbirds in cages, see Hoek and Ten Cate.

25 The study of Indigenous knowledge systems can help students understand and appreciate the earth's polyrhythm. For an analysis of the relationship of birdsong and Indigenous knowledge systems (the aesthetics of sound and culture among the Kaluli people of Papaua New Guinea), see Feld. For studies on the relationship between birds and Indigenous knowledge systems in pre-Columbian Mesoamerica, see Malamud and Norton. Ecocritic Randy Malamud and historian Marcy Norton explain the importance, for instance, of the study of birds with respect to the Mesoamerican belief systems of *tonalismo* and *nagualismo* – a spirituality

attuned to the rhythms of the ecosystem in which birds form divine counterparts to humans. Regarding the quetzal bird, Norton notes that its "gleaming green feathers" were indispensable in the "instantiation of divinity" (69).

26 Aside from the Biblical Psalms, the theme of solitude and the solitary bird can be found in Spanish poetry from the fifteenth century, such as in the work of Mayor de la Cueva (1476–1556; Boase 158). P.J. Lewis, professor of French literature, points to a number of literary and religious writers that connected the trope of the solitary bird with the theme of solitude. In the sixteenth century authors seem to have taken a specific interest in the Spanish blue rock thrush, particularly with respect to the theme of solitude as found in mysticism (Lewis; Sánchez Costa). As Lewis points out, the appearance of the theme of the lonely bird in the work of Christian mystics like San Juan may have also been inspired by mystical Sufism (544). I especially appreciate Lewis's connection between San Juan and Sufism because of the value of birdsong in Sufist texts like those of Yunus Emre (1238–1320), who describes birdsong as a guide: "Night goes, day arrives … / Look to the right and to left, don't just go off on any path: / Listen to the voice of the birds: See how / once that bird was an egg on the ground in a nest: / A powerful voice …" (Emre 135). Also, showing the posterior influence of San Juan, Johannes Ludovicus, a Christian mystic and Carmelite, published *Passer solitarius: h.e. vita et functiones animae contemplativae* (1634) which focuses on contemplative life and solitude (Lewis 544).

27 For live birds in early modern plays, see Ruano de la Haza and Allen (509). For feather art or mosaics, see Russo et al.; Kern. For live birds in menageries of elites, see Haag; Martínez Arranz; Lopezosa Aparacio. For parrots, see Jordan Gschwend (330); Boehrer (57).

28 One early modern author writes that freeing birds connects to artistic creation. Giorgio Vasari (1511–74), writer of *Lives of the Most Excellent Painters, Sculptors, and Architects* (1550), states that when Leonardo da Vinci (1452–1519) regularly walked by markets where caged songbirds were sold, "he would pay the price asked, take them from their cages, and let them fly off into the air … In return he was so favoured by nature that to whatever he turned his mind or thoughts the results were always inspired and perfect" (Dennis).

WORKS CITED AND CONSULTED

Angelou, Maya. "Caged Bird." 1983. *Poetry Foundation*, https://www .poetryfoundation.org/poems/48989/caged-bird.

Beilin, Kata, et al., editors. *Environmental Cultural Studies through Time: The Luso-Hispanic World*, special issue of *Hispanic Issues On Line*, vol. 24, 2019,

https://cla.umn.edu/hispanic-issues/online/environmental-cultural
-studies-through-time-luso-hispanic-world.

Beusterien, John. *An Eye on Race: Perspectives from Theater in Imperial Spain.*
Bucknell UP, 2006.

Beusterien, John. "Madrigal in Miguel de Cervantes's *La gran sultana*: An
Animal Studies Approach." *Romance Notes*, vol. 60, no. 3, 2020, pp. 437–49.
Project MUSE, https://doi.org/10.1353/rmc.2020.0043.

Beusterien, John. *Transoceanic Animals as Spectacle in Early Modern Spain.*
Amsterdam UP, 2020.

Beusterien, John. "What's in a Name? Animals and Humanities Biogeography."
Companion to Spanish Environmental Cultural Studies, edited by Luis I.
Prádanos, Tamesis, 2023, pp. 119–24.

"Bird Watching Alicante -Blue Rock Thrush-." *Refugio Marnes*, https://www
.refugiomarnes.com/en/activities/birding-species/bird-watching-alicante
/. Accessed 27 Jan. 2023.

Birkhead, T.R., and S. van Balen. "Bird-Keeping and the Development of
Ornithological Science." *Archives of Natural History*, vol. 35, no. 2, 2008,
pp. 281–305. *Edinburgh University Press*, https://doi.org/10.3366
/E0260954108000399.

"Blue Rock-Thrush (*Monticola solitarius*)." *The IUCN Red List of Threatened
Species*, 2016, e.T22708286A87933903, https://doi.org/10.2305/IUCN
.UK.2016-3.RLTS.T22708286A87933903.en.

Boase, Roger. *Secrets of Pinar's Game: Court Ladies and Courtly Verse in Fifteenth-
Century Spain.* Brill, 2017.

Boehrer, Bruce Thomas. *Parrot Culture: Our 2,500-Year-Long Fascination with the
World's Most Talkative Bird.* U of Pennsylvania P, 2004.

Bradshaw, G.A., et al. "Avian Affective Dysregulation: Psychiatric Models
and Treatment for Parrots in Captivity." 30th Annual Association of Avian
Veterinarians Conference, 10–13 August 2009, Milwaukee. *Kerulos Center for
Nonviolence*, https://kerulos.org/wp-content/uploads/2018/07
/Bradshaw_Yenkosky_McCarthy_910_FINAL_8.13.09_AAV-TABLES
.pdf.

"By Corinne Griffin." *YouTube*, uploaded by John Druzbik, 14 Mar. 2023,
https://www.youtube.com/watch?v=92vX2Q2i0XU&ab_channel
=JohnDruzbik.

Cox, Daniel T.C., et al. "Doses of Neighborhood Nature: The Benefits for
Mental Health of Living with Nature." *BioScience*, vol. 67, no. 2, 2017, pp. 147–55.
Oxford Academic, https://doi.org/10.1093/biosci/biw173.

Darwin, Charles. *The Descent of Man, and Selection in Relation to Sex.* Vol. 2,
D. Appleton, 1871.

Deleuze, Gilles, and Félix Guattari. *A Thousand Plateaus: Capitalism and
Schizophrenia.* Translated by Brian Massumi, U of Minnesota P, 1987.

Dennis, Jerry. "A History of Captive Birds." *Michigan Quarterly Review*, vol. 53, no. 3, summer 2014, http://hdl.handle.net/2027/spo.act2080.0053.301.

Dooren, Thom van. *Flight Ways: Life and Loss at the Edge of Extinction*. Columbia UP, 2014.

Emre, Yunus, and Nesimi. *The Two Great Turkish Sufi Poets: Their Lives and Selection of Their Poems*. Translated by Paul Smith, New Humanity Books / Book Heaven, 2014.

Escudero, José Antonio. *Felipe II: El rey en el despacho*. Complutense, 2002.

Feld, Steven. *Sound and Sentiment: Birds, Weeping, Poetics, and Song in Kaluli Expression*. 3rd ed., Duke UP, 2012.

Grosz, Elizabeth. *Chaos, Territory, Art: Deleuze and the Framing of the Earth*. Columbia UP, 2008.

Haag, Sabine, editor. *Echt tierisch! Die Menagerie des Fürsten (An Exhibition of the Kunsthistorisches Museum Vienna)*. KHM-Museumsverband, 2015.

Haskell, David G. "The Voices of Birds and the Language of Belonging." *Emergence Magazine*, 26 May 2019, https://emergencemagazine.org/essay/the-voices-of-birds-and-the-language-of-belonging/.

Hoek, Caroline S. Van, and Carel ten Cate. "Abnormal Behavior in Caged Birds Kept as Pets." *Journal of Applied Animal Welfare Science*, vol. 1, no. 1, 1998, pp. 51–64. *Taylor & Francis Online*, https://doi.org/10.1207/s15327604jaws0101_5.

Jamarro, Juan Bautista. *Conocimiento de las diez aves menores de jaula, su canto, enfermedad, cura y cría*. Imprenta Real, 1604.

Jamarro, Juan Bautista. *Tratado de la dentadura, sus enfermedades y remedios*. 10 June 1597. *Biblioteca Digital Hispánica*, http://bdh.bne.es/bnesearch/detalle/bdh0000125692. Accessed 30 Jan. 2023.

Jordan Gschwend, Annemarie. *A cidade global: Lisboa no Renascimento / The Global City: Lisbon in the Renaissance*, Museu Nacional de Arte Antiga, 2017.

Kern, Margit. "Cultured Materiality in Early Modern Art: Feather Mosaics in Sixteenth-Century Collections." *The Nomadic Object: The Challenge of World for Early Modern Religious Art*, edited by Christine Göttler and Mia M. Mochizuiki, Brill, 2018, pp. 319–42.

Lewis, Paul J. "*Passer solitarius*: Tribulations of a Lonely Bird in Poetry and Natural History, from Petrarch to Buffon." *Solitudo: Spaces, Places, and Times of Solitude in Late Medieval and Early Modern Cultures*, edited by Karl A.E. Enenkel and Christine Göttler, Brill, 2018, pp. 531–60.

Lopezosa Aparacio, Concepción. "La imagen de la ambición: El Real Gallinero en los altos del Prado." *Homenaje a Julian Gállego*, special issue of *Anales de Historia del Arte*, 2008, pp. 213–28.

Malamud, Randy. *Poetic Animals and Animal Souls*. Palgrave Macmillan, 2003.

Manual of Cage-Birds, British and Foreign. Oxford UP, 1847.

Marcuello, Francisco. *Primera parte de la historia natural y moral de las aves*. Juan de Lanaja y Quartanet, 1617.

Martínez Arranz, Raúl. *Collecting the New World: America and the Development of Museums in Early Spain*. 2011. New York U, MA thesis.

Mason, Travis V. *Ornithologies of Desire: Ecocritical Essays, Avian Poetics, and Don McKay*. Wilfrid Laurier UP, 2013.

Mundy, Rachel. "Why Listen to Animals?" *Society for Literature, Science, and the Arts*, 12 Oct. 2018, https://www.litsciarts.org/2018/10/12/why-listen-to-animals/?fbclid=IwAR0z-Z-Qtbg8BQSyoFA4CyIsgiiYblHSaJWCx8Lf6Jgk3YpygUAh4cb3nKo.

Nadeau, Carolyn. Personal email communication with author. 10 Mar. 2020.

Norton, Marcy. "Going to the Birds: Animals as Things and Beings in Early Modernity." *Early Modern Things: Objects and Their Histories, 1500–1800*, edited by Paula Findlen, Routledge, 2013, pp. 53–83.

Ruano de la Haza, J.M., and John J. Allen. *Los teatros comerciales del siglo XVII y la escenificación de la comedia*. Castalia, 1994.

Russo, Alessandra, et al., editors. *Images Take Flight: Feather Art in Mexico and Europe, 1400–1700*. Hirmer Verlag, 2015.

Sánchez-Bayo, Francisco, and Kris A.G. Wyckhuys. "Worldwide Decline of the Entomofauna: A Review of Its Drivers." *Biological Conservation*, vol. 232, 2019, pp. 8–27. *ScienceDirect*, https://doi.org/10.1016/j.biocon.2019.01.020.

Sánchez Costa, Enrique. "El pájaro solitario sanjuanista: Una aproximación." *Rilce: Revista Filología Hispánica*, vol. 24, no. 2, 2008, pp. 407–19. *Universidad de Navarra*, https://doi.org/10.15581/008.24.26333.

Skelton, John. *Speak, Parrot*. 1568. *The Ex-Classics Web Site*, https://www.exclassics.com/skelton/skel063.htm.

Straet, Jan van der. *Venationes Ferarum, Auium, Piscium.Pugnae bestiariorum: & mutuae bestiarum*. Poem captions by C. Kiliano. Biblioteca Nacional, R/30769.

Štuva, Sara. "Breathing with Animals: Irigaray's Contribution to Animal Ethics." *Breathing with Luce Irigaray*, edited by Lenart Škof and Emily A. Holmes, Bloomsbury, 2013, pp. 130–48.

Water Grabbing and the Dammed Esla: The Enchanted Waters of Jorge de Montemayor and the Riaño Reservoir

MARGARET MAREK

The floodgates closed on the last day of 1987, just before European Union legislation would deem the enterprise environmentally unviable. Residents had been displaced, a medieval church relocated, and the Esla dammed. Leonese painter Luis Prado Allende's stark photograph *Primeras aguas en el pantano de Riaño* (*The First Waters of the Riaño Reservoir*) documents this scene: in the foreground, a few stray cattle stand in water not yet knee-deep; wild grasses peek out over the surface. High above, intrusive pilings support the roadway. The Picos de Europa stand in the background. Since then, the remains of nine historic villages (Riaño, Anciles, Burón, Éscaro, Huelde, Pedrosa del Rey, La Puerta, Salio, and Vegacerneja) lie irrevocably submerged beneath the Riaño Reservoir.[1] It is difficult to reconcile pre- and post-*pantano* landscapes. A recent travel piece by journalist Andrea Cubillas is accompanied by an interactive graphic that, with a drag of the mouse, juxtaposes two corresponding views, the original village of Riaño and the new Riaño, which overlooks the reservoir ("Destrucción").[2] To the naïve visitor these superficially idyllic waters evoke the healing *locus amoenus* of Jorge de Montemayor's *La Diana* (1559).[3] Beneath their surface, however, rests a "cuna de muerte" ("cradle of death"; Carbajal Vega).[4]

It would be unconscionable to equate the prodigious trauma suffered by the former inhabitants of the submerged villages with the conflicted romantic relationships characteristic of the psychologically undeveloped shepherds of the Spanish pastoral book. However, the comparison unearths a pervasive pattern of Iberian water grabbing both literary – observable in *La Diana*, in sorceress Felicia's ministrations of enchanted water to remedy lovesickness – and literal – in the Riaño Reservoir, itself reflected in both the propagandistic literature of its proponents and its billing as a touristic destination.[5] Both Montemayor's text and the discourse surrounding the Riaño Reservoir deliberately employ copious, reiterative interplay between the seemingly binary oppositions of natural/artificial and truthfulness/artifice, a process that undergirds the human predilection to dominate nature. This essay examines the overarching water (grabbing) cycle – appropriation of nature, followed by environmental and emotional trauma, leading to engineered oblivion – in the sixteenth and twentieth centuries, when possible locating its origins in the classical world, and acknowledges its culmination in the climate disaster of the present day.

Location, Location, Location: The Banks of the Esla

Critic Werner Krauss notes that the *libro de pastores* ("pastoral book") is plottable geographically and – though without mention of Riaño – identifies *La Diana* with the mountains of León (367). In the *Argumento deste libro* ("Plot of This Book"), Montemayor reveals the origins of his title character: "En los campos de la principal y antigua ciudad de León, riberas del río Ezla, hubo una pastora llamada Diana, cuya hermosura fue extremadísima sobre todas las de su tiempo" ("In the fields of the old and illustrious city of León, on the banks of the Esla River, there lived a shepherdess named Diana, whose beauty exceeded that of any other in her time"; 108).[6] Following literary historians and critics Alonso Cortés and Marcelino Menéndez Pelayo, critic and editor Asunción Rallo explicitly links Montemayor's shepherdess to Valencia de Don Juan.[7] This village lies a mere 106 kilometres by road, 76 as the crow flies, from the new Riaño. Prefiguratively, the literary water grabbing of *La Diana* occurs in close geographical proximity to the Riaño Reservoir.

Despite the intervening four hundred years, the two additionally occupy an unexpected temporal proximity. In 1579, a mere twenty years following the publication of the novel, construction began on another infamous Spanish dam, the Tibi in Alicante, locating water domination within early modern Iberia. Considered "el hito más monumental de la ingeniería española renacentista" ("the greatest engineering achievement of Renaissance Spain"; "Así es"), the Tibi, standing at an impressive height of 46 metres, reigned as the world's tallest dam for nearly three hundred years ("Visitamos"). Analogous in form and function, the state-of-the-art Tibi and Riaño respectively exemplify imperial and nationalistic prowess. The Tibi was carried out under the auspices of Felipe II to increase irrigation on a grand scale ("Así es"). In the twentieth century, Riaño's disparate proponents, which included Alfonso XIII, dictators Primo de Rivera and Franco, and the socialist governments of Indalecio Prieto and Felipe González, were seduced by this "gran plan hidrológico para hacer regable el país y producir energía eléctrica" ("great hydrologic plan to make the nation irrigable and to produce electricity"; MUSAC and FCAYC 6–7).

Staunch insistence on historic betterment achieved through the domination of water reverberates today, and both dams are actively promoted as touristic sites.[8] The ecological costs of the Tibi were left untallied, but financial costs, spanning fourteen years and after several delays, reached "la suma de '58,23 libras, 17 sueldos y 4 dineros,' según los documentos de la época" ("the sum of '58.23 pounds, 17 solidi and 4 dinars,' according to documents from the time"; "Así es"). The Riaño, which experienced even more protracted delays, presents a convoluted timeline. Initial plans were drawn up in the 1902 "Plan general de riegos y pantanos" ("General Plan for Irrigation and Reservoirs") and refined in 1934 (Bernardo). Construction began in 1965, residents were displaced beginning in 1985, and the floodgates closed in 1987.[9]

Waterworks: From Fountains to the Dammed Esla

Spain has a long damming history. The Riaño, neither the first, the last, nor the largest, is likely the most contested, so much so that in 1984 activist cavers from the group Espeleología de León rappelled down the face of the dam to paint "demolición" ("demolition") in massive red block letters.[10] Apprehending the impact of water control, whether literary or literal, necessitates a return to the source. Journalist Antonio Villareal counts 1,225 dams in Spain, more than half of which date from the Franco regime. The 1970s was the most prolific decade, topping out at 212, followed by 187 in the 1980s, 186 in the first decade of the 2000s, and an additional 45 in the last decade. In a worldwide ranking by the number of dams, Spain takes seventh place (Villareal). Yet many of Spain's approximately 1,800 rivers lie dry for much of the year, including the Tajo, the Duero, the Guadiana, and the Guadalquivir, which empty into the Atlantic, and the Ebro, which empties into the Mediterranean. Of these, only the Guadalquivir, and to a lesser extent the Ebro, is navigable. The Esla, of interest to the present study, flows north to south from the Cantabrian Mountains into the Duero, forming the latter's largest tributary.

The shepherds of *La Diana* graze their flocks along the same banks "del caudaloso Ezla … por la orilla de sus cristalinas aguas" ("of the roaring Esla … along the shores of its crystalline waters"; 161). Montemayor's epithet is repeated in the carefully orchestrated promotional videography produced by the Confederación Hidrográfica del Duero (CHD): "[S]obre todo regula *el caudaloso Esla* que juega un papel de primer orden en la red hidrográfica del Duero" ("More than anything it regulates the *roaring Esla*, which plays a vital role in the hydrographic network of the Douro"; "Embalse de Riaño" 00:03:23–30; my emphasis).[11] Despite this hydraulic intervention meant to stabilize water levels, the Esla has increasingly experienced concerning arid periods, such as those of 2017 and 2019 ("Climatología"). However, in December of 2019 León sustained more flood damage than any other province, totalling more than three million euros (Rabanillo). Spain perennially alternates between drought and deluge, and so depends on reservoirs for irrigation, hydroelectricity, and flood mitigation. Climate change only exacerbates these already taxing conditions.

To exert control over water, Greco-Roman hydraulic engineering produced aqueducts, dams, reservoirs, baths, and fountains. Civil engineer Juan Carlos Castillo Barranco counts seventy-three remains of or references to dams in Hispania, dating from the first and fourth centuries CE. Of these, one reservoir dam, the Arévalo (Ávila), and one diversion dam, the Río Frío (Segovia), manage the flow of the Duero (66). For classical archaeologist Andrew Wilson, Roman water control constituted "a powerful political tool for rulers and elites ... asserting control over the resources necessary to construct them, and sometimes over nature itself" (1). The Spanish term *fuente* refers to both architectural fountains and natural springs, an equivalence that presumes human exploitation of water. The definition elaborated by lexicographer Sebastián de Covarrubias Horozco, contemporary to Montemayor, distinguishes between waters that flow perennially and those that flow seasonally, a contrast that, though here referring to natural springs, inevitably recalls the persistent, periodic fluctuations that characterize Spain's rivers, including the Esla: "Fuente perenal, la que siempre corre, a diferencia de las que en cierto tiempo del año se secan" ("Perennial stream, one which always flows, as opposed to those that dry up at certain times of the year"; 933). He highlights the fundamental essence and symbolism of water: "Hay muchos lugares que su nombre empieza por fuente y la razón es porque donde no hay agua no puede haber habitación, y así las ciudades y lugares grandes se edificaron cerca de ríos, y los menores pueblos donde hubiese fuentes" ("There are many place names that begin with *fuente* and the reason is that where there is no water there can be no inhabitancy, and so cities and large settlements were established near rivers, and small towns where there were springs"; 933). Covarrubias notes the importance of water to the founding of early human settlements, such as those of the Riaño Valley, emphasizing the power associated with possession and domination of water so evident in subsequent discourse about the Riaño Reservoir. Surprisingly, though, despite his explicit assertion of human reliance on water control, Covarrubias's definition excludes architectural fountains.

As in the Iberian Peninsula, both springs and fountains abound in Montemayor's novel. In contrast to the seemingly natural "fuente de los alisos" ("spring of the alders"), Felicia's palace boasts numerous artificial, architectural fountains. Each more decorated than the last, these structures contain nymphs wrought of speckled marble, silver, and gold; bronze lions; jasper columns; and laurel trees sculpted in gold and enamelled in green (258–9, 275–6). These intricate figures partici-pate in a culture of Greco-Roman public fountain statuary, which com-monly included human figures, nymphs, and animals such as dogs, lions, and dolphins, who spouted water from their mouths, breasts, or genitals (Aristodemou, "Fountain Figures" 199). These commonalities typify the widespread fabrication, temporally and geographically, of ostentatious water features, bearing testament to the ongoing human desire and ability to dominate water and to substantiate this control in the form of a visual, physical, aesthetically pleasing structure, a practice continued by the Riaño Reservoir.

Trauma, Displacement, and Inundation: An Open Wound

In 1975, ten years into the dam's construction, the *ABC* newspaper sent reporter Francisco del Brío and photographer Ángel Carchenilla to the Riaño Valley to cover the project:

> En los nueve pueblos afectados vivían 3.100 personas, había 2.000 casas de vecindad, 30.000 fincas rústicas, cuatro cines, un campamento juvenil, un Parador Nacional de Turismo, tres hoteles, 300 empresas industriales, minas de mercurio, flúor, antimonio y carbón, varios palacios, un insti-tuto de Segunda Enseñanza, 20 escuelas, 3.000 reses de vacuno y 5.000 de ganado lanar.

> (In the nine villages affected there lived 3,100 people, there were 2,000 houses in the surrounding area, 30,000 rural properties, four movie thea-tres, a youth camp, a national touristic parador, three hotels, 300 industrial companies, mercury, fluoride, antimony, and coal mines, several palaces, a high school, 20 elementary-middle schools, 3,000 head of cattle and 5,000 wool sheep)[12]

After the election of socialist Felipe González in 1982, many believed that the project would be abandoned, yet its completion came to signify the socialist government's disregard for human and ecological loss, just as the Porma dam completed twenty years prior represented the developmentalist drives of the fascist agenda (Ruiz).

The very waters of the reservoir render the ecological damage to the Riaño Valley invisible, irreparable, and incalculable. Disingenuously and artificially recast by touristic publicity as the "fiordos leoneses" ("Leonese fjords"), the valley retains no trace of the native ecosystems. The human loss has been well documented. Huelde, the closest to the site of the dam, was the first to go. Many residents relocated to Palencia and León, but many others stayed.[13] For Rosa Villadares, the ringing of church bells remains a trigger, thirty years later:

> En esta época vivíamos a toque de campana. Si traían las actas de ocupación, sonaba; para formar barricada, sonaba; si venían a cortar los árboles, sonaba; si había que dormir en el Ayuntamiento, sonaba. Te acostabas esperando que al día siguiente no tocasen las campanas porque no traían nada bueno ... Y al final llegó la maquinaría. Pero esta vez ya no la veíamos desde la ventana sino desde la calle, viendo cómo nos tiraban la casa.

> (In those days we lived by the tolling of the bell. If they brought occupation orders, it rang; if we needed to form a barricade, it rang; if they came to cut the trees, it rang; if we had to sleep in the town hall, it rang. You went to bed hoping that the next day the bells wouldn't ring, because they never brought anything good ... And at the end the bulldozers came. But this time we weren't watching them from the window, but from the street, seeing as how they threw us out of the house; qtd. in Cubillas, "Riaño")

These glimpses, which constitute a mere fraction of the total loss incurred by residents of the Riaño Valley at the hands of the government, mirror the overarching human disregard for the natural world.

The magnitude of this trauma is further compounded by the harm to non-human life, which remains largely uncatalogued.[14] In the words of Riaño resident Manuel Álvarez: "No éramos capaces de sacar las vacas de la zona. Las echábamos al pasto y se daban la vuelta situándose al pie de lo que había su cuadra. Bramaban preguntándose dónde estaba la cuadra donde ellas dormían. Lo mismo que mi perro que siempre estaba al lado de los escombros. Tenía que ir hasta allí para darle de comer porque si no se me moría" ("We couldn't keep the cows out. We took them to graze, but they kept coming back, standing around where their pen used to be, mooing, and wondering what had become of the shelter where they used to sleep. And my dog, too. He wouldn't come away from the debris. I had to go all the way out there to feed him, or he would have died"; qtd. in Cubillas, "Destrucción"). These losses, human and non-human, are pooled in the waters of the Riaño Reservoir.

The "Región" exhibition, presented in 2017 by the Museo de Arte Contemporáneo de Castilla y León (MUSAC) and the Fundación Cerezales Antonino y Cinia (FCAYC), displayed documents such as Franco's signature of approval to begin construction, newspaper accounts, radio and television broadcasts, engineering plans and aerial photographs, personal effects, domestic items, and artistic installations.[15] Exhibit 21 is a grouping of the keys to demolished homes. Exhibit 24, Miguel Carracedo's "Conjunto fotográfico de los pueblos afectados por el pantano de Riaño" ("Photographic Collection of the Towns Affected by the Riaño Reservoir"), displays photos taken between 1983 and 1987, each of a house subsequently demolished (MUSAC and FCAYC 57).[16] These 302 matted and framed photographs, colour-coded by village, substantiate the loss and trauma of those who mourn for their submerged histories.[17] Whatever attraction the present-day artificial *pantano* might yield for tourists, the evicted residents' wounds are intensified periodically by endemic conditions of drought.[18] At these times, the remains of the demolished villages resurface, along with the historic Roman settlements lying beneath them.[19] The brand-new village of Riaño, fashioned on heretofore unspoiled mountain peaks, adds a tertiary layer of ecological and human distress.

Both types of trauma see a forerunner in Montemayor's shepherds, whose lovesickness must be mitigated by death or supernatural recourse.[20] Optimally suited for ecocritical analysis given the pastoral book's generic association with transhumant herding, Montemayor's *La Diana* – whose notoriously complex plot divides prolifically, like a river, into numerous branches and sub-branches that take their own respective twists and turns, rendering a succinct summary impossible – follows four main sets of lovers led by nymphs Dórida, Polydora, and Cinthia on a pilgrimage to the temple of the goddess Diana.[21] As chastity is required, the title character, in love with Sireno but married at her parents' behest to Delio, is barred from access to the magical remedy proffered by "la sabia Felicia, cuyo oficio es dar remedio a pasiones enamoradas" ("the sorceress Felicia, whose calling is to heal the passions of love"; 192). Diana is loved by both Sireno and Sylvano, although the latter, after drinking Felicia's enchanted water, falls in love with Selvagia, herself formerly in love with Alanio and enmeshed in a love triangle. However, the lovesickness suffered by Sireno and Belisa is more dire.

Belisa's tale is quite intricate. At the hands of necromancer Alfeo, she seems to have witnessed the murder of her beloved Arsileo by his father and unintentional romantic rival, Arsenio. At the end of Book IV, Cinthia explains to Belisa that desire for the beloved originates in the memory, "como de una fuente donde nace el principio del deseo" ("like a fountain whence rises the origin of desire"; 302). This passage evokes Covarrubias's definition of "fuente" as "source," including the metaphorical seat of desire, the artistic, foundational, and the fluvial source: "[F]uentes suelen ser origen y principio de ríos, allegándose a su corriente las de otros manantiales, por alusión decimos acudir a la fuente cuando recurrimos al principio de lo que vamos tratando y averiguando" ("Because springs are usually the origin and source of rivers, adding to their own current those of other streams, by extension we say consult the source when we seek the earliest reference to the item under discussion"; 933). The image of the beloved was thought to physically imprint itself upon the lover's *memoria*, the hindmost chamber of the brain. With time, though, the source – in every sense of the word – becomes attenuated: "[C]omo la memoria sea una cosa que cuanto más va, más pierde su fuerza y vigor, olvidándose de lo que le entregaron los ojos ... De la misma manera que a los ríos se les acabaría su corriente, si dejasen de manar las fuentes adonde nacen" ("Just as the memory loses its force and strength over time, forgetting that which the eyes have entrusted to it ... In the same way that rivers' currents would dry up if their sources stopped flowing"; 302). As the mountain spring branches off into smaller streams, time dilutes desire. This association in turn suggests the erasure produced by the notorious Lethe, but as Belisa's trauma has been engineered by Alfeo – Arsileo is indeed alive and well and his father is not in love with Belisa – she will not need to forget him by partaking of Felicia's enchanted water.[22]

In contrast, Sireno requires Felicia's machinations. After a year-long absence from the realm that intimates the seasonal migration of the flock from winter to summer pastures, he returns a changed man, "los ojos hechos fuentes, el rostro mudado" ("his eyes turned to fountains, his face altered"), having learned of Diana's marriage (111). Just as Riaño's waters obscure an idyllic past, Sireno's tears blur his vision. In keeping with Greco-Roman and Arabic medical writers' prescriptions of lush natural settings for sufferers of lovesickness, the pristine valley affords respite. Simultaneously, this setting provokes suffering: "'¡Ay memoria mía, enemiga de mi descanso! ... que en este prado vi a mi señora, ... junto a aquella clara fuente, cercada de altos y verdes alisos'" ("'Oh memory, enemy of my respite! ... in this meadow I saw my lady, ... beside that clear stream bordered by tall green alders'"; 112). The valley mnemonically retrieves

Diana's image.[23] Clearly, the imprudent directive to just add water, whether the enchanting water of the *pantano* or the enchanted water of Felicia, does not produce erasure of either the environmental or the personal trauma.

By means of the same physiological process that imprints Diana's image upon Sireno's memory, Felicia's palace memorializes a seemingly interminable and spatially impossible series of mythological and historical figures, inscribed on a massive octagonal column. An inner chamber commemorates a catalogue of celebrated Spanish noblewomen, in whose honour Orpheus will sing. The decoration, increasingly elaborate, features walls of gold and floors set with precious stones. Felicia's memory theatre has been carefully curated to mesmerize the viewer: "En tan grande admiración puso a los pastores y pastoras las cosas que allí veían, que no sabían qué decir, porque la riqueza de la casa era tan grande, las figuras que allí estaban, tan naturales, el artificio de la cuadra, y la orden que las damas que allí retratadas tenían, que no les parecía poderse imaginar en el mundo cosa más perfecta" ("The things they saw there so amazed the shepherds and shepherdesses that they did not know what to say, because the richness of the hall was so great, the figures there so lifelike, because of the artistry of the room and the arrangement of the ladies depicted there, that they could not seem to imagine a more perfect place in the world"; 275).[24] The Riaño Reservoir, another artificially engineered environment, too, will appear exquisitely natural.

Competing (Love) Interests: Land and Water Grabbing

Along both the literary and the literal banks of the Esla, water is subject to control. The enchanted water of Felicia's palace, which lies within Diana's temple, is not available to everyone. Those permitted to enter demonstrate no sympathy for the married shepherdess, seeing her exclusion as a matter of course, as indicated by the plaque above the entrance:

> Quien entra, mire bien cómo ha vivido,
> y el don de castidad, si l'ha guardado,
> y la que quiere bien o l'ha querido
> mire s'a causa d'otro s'ha mudado.
> Y si la fe primera no ha perdido,
> y aquel primero amor ha conservado,
> entrar puede'n el templo de Diana,
> cuya virtud y gracia es sobrehumana.

(May those who enter think carefully about the way they have lived
and the virtue of chastity, whether they have kept it,
and those who love well or have loved well
may they consider whether they have ever abandoned
    this love for the love of another.
And if they have not lost faith,
and have kept that first love constant,
they may enter the temple of Diana
whose virtue and grace are beyond human capacity; 260)

Yet Diana has lost neither her first love for Sireno nor her virtue, which remains intact within the bounds of marriage. By this logic, therefore, Diana ought rightfully to gain admittance. Just as civil authorities forcibly impose the inundation on the former residents of the Riaño Valley, Felica unjustly blocks Diana's access to the healing enchanted water.

Like their respective Greco-Roman and early modern architectural precursors, both Felicia's palace and the Riaño Reservoir denote the inscription of political ambitions on environmental constructs.[25] Throughout the Roman Empire, rulers and wealthy patrons commissioned opulent, monumental fountain structures (Aristodemou, "Introduction II" 10), which, coupled with their mundane function to supply water, showcased imperial grandeur (Aristodemou and Tassios, "Preface" iii). Classical architectural historian Brenda Longfellow notes that the monumental fountain, which "spoke to the prestige of all involved in its construction: the patron, the city in which it was built, and the gods and emperors to whom it was dedicated," visibly conferred glory on the benefactor (1). Critic Benjamin Nelson unveils a parallel motive in the elaboration of Felicia's palace: "Montemayor uses his literary edifice to praise Charles V and liken him to Caesar" (251).[26] Finally, for Ruiz, just as the Tibi Dam memorializes Felipe II, the Porma and Riaño Reservoirs "significan la soberbia del poder frente al pueblo, las raíces, sus casas, sus tierras, sus pueblos" ("signify the hubris of power versus the people, their roots, their houses, their land, their towns"). The link between water control and political ostentation, then, operates in all three of the temporal snapshots considered by this study.

While we may not typically attribute environmental harm to either classical or early modern land use – and much less to the literary *locus amoenus* in either period – science writer Mohi Kumar supplies this corrective: "Humans have been altering landscapes planetwide for thousands of years: since at least 1000 B.C.E., by which time people in regions across the globe had abandoned foraging in favor of continually producing crops." Archaeobotanists Dorian Q. Fuller et al. concur:

"Unlike Pleistocene hunter-gatherers, farming societies have transformed the surface of the earth, its atmospheric composition (increasing greenhouse gases), and impacted the genomes and geographies of many other species, especially domesticated ones" (61). In the case of Iberia, for centuries Merino flocks traversed the Peninsula, land suited poorly for agriculture but ideally for pasture. These herds grazed in the mountain passes during the mild summer and migrated hundreds of miles to the plains, where they spent the remainder of the year.[27] One of Spain's most important scientific developments, the Merino breed is inextricably woven into Spain's political, social, cultural, and environmental identity.[28] It stands to reason, then, that Merino flock owners historically received special dispensation from the crown (which itself owned lucrative flocks) and enjoyed reprieve from military duty and certain taxes, as well as the right of way for sheep to travel across agricultural lands, which created tensions between competing herders and growers.

As in Montemayor's novel, transhumance found a fecund environment in the unsubmerged Riaño Valley, where, as in so much of *la montaña de León*, nearly every family had at least some tie to transhumant Merino herding. Today very few, if any, practise transhumance in the traditional way. Ecologists and herders alike maintain that the *dehesa* ecosystem, grassy plains interspersed with Encina oak, depends upon the migrations, both for survival and for the prevention of brush fires. Movements such as Made in Slow attempt to restore and preserve this cultural and economic heritage transparently and sustainably (Díaz).

Damning Evidence: The Unsustainable Effects on the Esla

The Riaño Reservoir obliterated forest and native species and razed traditional crops, pastures, and touristic sites (Pastor). In addition, the reservoir did away with some of the most bountiful Leonese fishing preserves: "Hoy el valle de Riaño está prácticamente muerto" ("Today the Riaño Valley is nearly dead"; Bernardo). The justification for Riaño, the alleged irrigation of 83,000 hectares of unused Leonese lands, was deemed artifice by locals and ecologists alike, who argued that a surplus of the very crops intended to be irrigated by the reservoir had led the European Union to disincentivize their cultivation.[29] To add insult to injury, the *pantano* irrigates only about 39 per cent of the projected capacity (Bernardo).[30] The human and ecological sacrifice was for naught.

The Riaño Vive movement seeks not only to educate about the nefarious demolition of the Riaño Valley, and about other regions that have suffered a similar fate, but to reclaim the valley. In the words of founder and president Alfonso González Matorra: "RIAÑO VIVE, lucha y luchará por ello mientras las aguas de los ríos fluyan montaña abajo, por que [sic] sabemos lo que se esconde bajo esas aguas ahora, entrampadas" ("RIAÑO LIVES, fights, and will continue to fight for Riaño as long as the rivers flow down from these mountains, because we know about the deception now hidden beneath these waters"; original emphasis). He rails against the lasting human, economic, and environmental costs that outweigh any marginal benefits attributed to the creation of reservoirs, especially to Riaño. The movement's goal is simple: "[que] se mantenga vivo el recuerdo del valle y para que la gente no se acostumbre a ver el pantano como algo normal" ("to keep the memory of the valley alive and to keep people from getting used to viewing the reservoir as a something ordinary"; qtd. in Carnero, "El embalse de Riaño"). Another group, La Plataforma por la Recuperación del Valle de Riaño, formed in 2007 by concerned locals, environmentalists, and other activists, also calls for the draining of the reservoir. At a minimum, they demand the planting of one tree per hectare of subsidized irrigation lands, as required by European Union regulations since 2010, which for the Riaño Valley would translate to millions of trees.[31] Riaño is an environmental failure on every count. With climate change, the water levels of the reservoir drop every year. Furthermore, the dam's electrical output could be achieved by a mere 49 hectares of solar panels (Pastor). Both groups' active social media presence attests that the *pantano*'s enchanting waters have not obliterated the memory of the submerged valley, despite the newfound touristic popularity of the so-called "fiordos leoneses."

Like the reservoir, Felicia's enchanted water, a short-lived remedy, fails to meet its objective (El Saffar 184).[32] Sireno's artificially achieved indifference to Diana soon falters: "Pasados contentamientos, / ¿qué queréis?; / dejadme, no me canséis" ("Former delights, / what do you want?; / leave me alone, stop tormenting me"; 349). Sylvano, too, once again appears susceptible to Diana. Both former suitors remember the lovelorn times with fondness, prompting Selvagia's jealousy: "A todos pareció muy bien lo que Sylvano decía, aunque Selvagia no estaba muy bien en ello, mas por no dar a entender celos donde tan gran amor conocía, calló por entonces" ("To the others everything that Sylvano said seemed very fitting, and although Selvagia was not pleased, so as not to intimate jealousy where she felt such great love, at that moment she remained quiet"; 353). These passages call into question the efficacy of Felicia's remedy, which simply does not hold water. Critical analyses of Montemayor's novel illustrate the dual renewing and destructive properties of water, unintentionally evoking the *pantano*. T. Anthony Perry sees wishful, symbolic potential: "The liquid potion signifies a desire to purge and renew; water washes away, liquefies the hardened configurations of our destinies, restores the feeling of infinite possibility" (232). In other words, Felicia's cure is simply too good to be true.[33] Comparably, Riaño's proponents highlight the biodiversity of the region, without acknowledging the prior wilful destruction of local ecosystems. Commentary on Felicia's enchanted water underscores the drastic and, at one time inconceivable, changes wrought by the waters of the *pantano*, changes that continue to herald its deadly origins.[34] As with the waters of a dam, these currents continue to circle back around.

Tourism Euros/Pesetas/*Reales*: It's a Question of Marketing

Montemayor's shepherds, traditionally viewed by critics as pilgrims, are early modern Iberian (medical) tourists.[35] By saving the nymphs from the three *salvajes* ("wild men"), noble female warrior Felismena pays their entrance fee to Diana's temple, and thereby Felicia's palace. Sireno, Sylvano, and Belisa are Leonese, but Selvagia comes from the west (Lusitania), and Felismena from southern Spain (the fictional Vandalia). As they travel with nymphs Dórida, Cinthia, and Polidora to Felicia's palace, they follow in the footsteps of visitors to Greco-Roman nymphaea: "Nymphs, because of their association with springs, are often healing deities. Healing gods as a rule are close to a water source, preferably one that is heated or has interesting mineral properties" (Larson 5). In this case, appearances are deceiving. In Riaño's enticing but deleterious waters, which shroud the ecological and emotional damage accrued by inundation of the valley, today's tourists can jet ski, for example, an activity flagrantly damaging to the environment.

Like the phoenix rising from its ashes, some see a new incarnation of the submerged lands. Travel writer Irene González extols the new Riaño and the reservoir as "el paraíso de los Fiordos Leoneses" ("The Paradise of the Leonese Fjords"). At the time of this writing, the area has just begun to host European bison, a species that inhabited the Cantabrian mountain range for twelve thousand years before dying out on the continent in 1919 (Carnero, "Bisonte europeo"). Nature lovers can sign up for guided excursions to learn to identify moths, mushrooms, and wild flowers in the idyllic surroundings of the new Riaño, voted best village in summer 2019 ("Riaño, elegido 'Mejor pueblo de España'"). To compound matters, the Ayuntamiento de Riaño ("Riaño town council") has designated the nearby Anciles Valley, which terminates in the

Riaño Reservoir, both a tourist attraction and a research centre for water buffalo, European bison, and Pottoka horses, objectives that are mutually incompatible in many ways. Journalist José María Campos cites tourism official Pelayo García, who cryptically notes that the water buffalo, not native to the area, "habían llegado a este paraje por una situación de emergencia" ("had arrived due to an emergency situation"). Leonese environmental journalist María Carnero's editorial lauds the reintroduction of the bison and the recent Change.org campaign urging the Ministerio de Transición Ecológica ("Ministry of Ecological Transformation") to protect this species. However, she warns that Fernando Morán, mayor of Riaño and director of the Centro de Conservación del Bisonte Europeo en España ("Centre for the Conservation of European Buffalo in Spain"), is already drafting provisions for hunting them in the area (Carnero, "Bisonte europeo"). While the conservation and study of wildlife appears altruistic, these measures in fact constitute Riaño's shallow attempts to recast itself as a panacea of the disparate ills of past ecological and human damage. The new village depends financially on present-day tourism, itself artfully garbed in environmental sustainability.[36]

Like the Riaño Reservoir, Felicia's enchanted water has its detractors. In chapter 6 of the first volume of *Don Quixote*, Cervantes raises the question during the examination of Alonso Quijano's library, which contains more than one hundred large, costly, nicely bound volumes: "Y pues comenzamos por *La Diana* de Montemayor, soy de parecer que no se queme, sino que se le quite todo aquello que trata de la sabia Felicia y de la agua encantada, y casi todos los versos mayores, y quédesele enhorabuena la prosa, y la honra de ser primero en semejantes libros" ("And beginning with Montemayor's *La Diana*, I am of the opinion that it not be burned, but that everything having to do with the sorceress Felicia and the enchanted water be removed, and almost all of the longer lines of poetry, and preserve it for the felicity of its prose and the honour of being the first of these kind of books"; 66). The priest, an incompetent inquisitor who lacks the ability to discern worthy from unworthy texts, consigns most of the books to the fire. Of the *libros de pastores* mentioned, he damns five and saves five, including Cervantes's *La Galatea*. Attempting to unequivocally interpret Cervantes's often contradictory views is rather like trying to flatten a Möbius strip. However, though not wholly effective as a remedy for lovesickness, Felicia's enchanted water suits the purposes of the narrative, both ostensibly providing closure and calling that closure into question. Felicia's enchanted water is in the eye of the beholder.

Ambiguity similarly characterizes discourse about Riaño. The CHD acclaims the ecosystem that has been artificially fashioned by the reservoir:

> En 1994 esta zona fue declarada por la Junta de Castilla y León parque regional por haberse conservado en ella ecosistemas propios de la región eurosiberiana que tiene como expresión más significativa extensas áreas de bosque atlántico caracterizadas por robledales y hayedos con unas poblaciones de fauna entre las que destacan el oso pardo y el urogallo.

> (In 1994 this area was declared a regional park by the Junta de Castilla y León for its conservation of ecosystems native to the Euro-Siberian zone whose flora is most known for its extensive Atlantic forests of oak and beech, and whose most distinguished fauna include the black bear and the wood grouse; "Embalse de Riaño" 00:03:45–00:04:17)

This and other texts exhort tourists to visit this enchanting and unnatural natural environment. The commercialization of the *pantano* attempts to stem the flow of the trauma by replacing it with an aesthetically pleasing engineered landscape, much as in Montemayor's novel, where Felicia transplants Sylvano's love from Diana onto Selvagia. However, Felicia's and the *pantano*'s enchanting waters ultimately prove ineffective.

Conclusion

As critic Juan Bautista Avalle-Arce remarks of the *libro de pastores*: "Todo momento histórico se ve apuntalado por una serie de aspiraciones, represiones, mitos expresados o implícitos que, estudiados colectivamente, en el plano intelectual nos dan la radiografía ideológica del período" ("Every moment in history is marked by a series of aspirations, repressions, and blatant or tacit myths, which when studied collectively give us, in an intellectual sense, an ideological X-ray of the period"; 14). From the evidence presented here, such an X-ray relevantly depicts human land consumption and abuse. Sumptuous, environmentally themed programming notwithstanding, the "fiordos leoneses" remain as artificial as Felicia's palace. In both settings, the traveller is encouraged to partake of these forgetful enchanted waters, thereby reproducing the cycle that includes the appropriation of idyllic landscape, subsequent acute trauma, and, finally, an engineered oblivion of questionable effectiveness. Perhaps the most apt X-ray of the present day can be found in "+ 1,5°C Lo Cambia Todo," which digitally despoils four world masterpieces to illustrate the effects of climate change. The alterations to Velázquez's *Felipe IV a caballo* (1635–6) and Patinir's *Landscape with Charon Crossing the Styx* (c. 1515–24) best serve the purposes of the present study, both temporally and thematically. The former paints the monarch astride his mount, neck-deep in waters that, having filled in the surrounding mountainous countryside, closely resemble the *pantano*. The latter echoes the *pantano* during the formidable drought of 2017.[37] Charon's boat lies aground in the desiccated riverbed. As intended, their effect is, frankly, terrifying.[38] As our species appears to be largely unmoved by environmental destruction, the hope is that we may be better dissuaded by the (implied, suggestive) obliteration of renowned, human paintings. As in Montemayor's novel, in these early modern works we descry a long arc of environmental destruction. While we persistently locate this destruction narrowly, within the twentieth and twenty-first centuries, the pattern predominates irrespective of historical period.

NOTES

1 I refer to these villages of the north-western province of León collectively as the Riaño Valley. Some writers conflate Riaño, the largest of the villages, with the others, referring collectively to "Riaño," which is also the name of the reservoir. I refer to the new village as the new Riaño.

2 Also included are a map tracing the flow of the Esla before and after the reservoir, an eight-minute video containing photographs of each of the nine villages, footage of the razing of the church clock tower, and excerpts from interviews with former residents (Cubillas, "Destrucción"). To get a sense of the heyday of the Riaño Valley, see the *Diario de Valderrueda*'s recent commemoration of Riaño, "La Suiza Española" ("The Spanish Switzerland"), prior to the construction of the reservoir. This piece features ten color photographs taken in the 1920s and 1930s by prominent German photographer Otto Wunderlish, compelling in their depiction of landscape and scenes of daily life and work ("Así era Riaño").

3 In the summers of 2014 and 2016, I was fortunate to spend time with Argimiro Rodríguez Villaroel and his family, both in the *montaña de León* ("Leonese mountains") and in the *dehesa extremeña* ("Extremaduran grasslands"). This family's shepherding roots go back to the 1700s, if not earlier. None of my work on transhumant Merino herding would be possible without their extraordinary hospitality – especially that of María Fernández Villarroel, who shepherded me all over the province, including on a visit to the *pantano*. All remaining errors are my own. I humbly dedicate this piece to all who were displaced by the Riaño Reservoir.

4 The full comment, a reaction on social media to Riaño's winning the title
  of "Mejor pueblo de España" ("Best Village in Spain") in July of 2019,
  reads as follows: "Cuidado que hay pueblos de montaña en España mucho
  mejores y más bonitos que Riaño, cuna de muerte" ("Careful, there are
  much better and prettier Spanish mountain towns than Riaño, that cradle
  of death"). See also "Riaño, elegido 'Mejor pueblo de España.'"

5 This connection between literal and literary is further fortified when we
  consider that the nearby Embalse de Porma, completed in 1967, now bears
  the name of the engineer who created it, well-known postmodern writer
  Juan Benet (1927–93). Benet's novel *Volverás a Región* (*You Will Return to
  Region*, 1967) presumedly is set in León.

6 All references to *La Diana* come from Asunción Rallo's edition. All
  translations into English of this work and of other texts are my own.

7 "Recuérdese que es en Valencia de Don Juan donde los reyes Felipe III y
  Margarita, en su viaje a León en 1603, conocen a Diana, 'decantada belleza,
  cuyo nombre propio era Ana, siendo ya entonces al parecer de algunos
  sessenta años,' según el testimonio de P. Sepúlveda. También Lope de Vega
  en su *Dorotea* (acto I, escena segunda) afirma: 'La Diana de Montemayor
  fue una dama natural de Valencia de Don Juan, junto a León, y Ezla su río,
  y ellos serán eternos por su pluma'" ("Remember that it is in Valencia de
  Don Juan where King Felipe III and Margarita, on their trip to León in 1603,
  meet Diana, that 'celebrated beauty, whose real name was Ana, who at that
  time was apparently about sixty years of age,' according to the testimony of
  P. Sepúlveda. Lope de Vega also affirms in the *Dorotea* [act 1, scene 2] that
  'Montemayor's Diana was a lady from Valencia de Don Juan, near León, on
  the Esla River, places to which his pen will grant eternal fame'"; 109n5).

8 The CHD pitches the Riaño Reservoir simultaneously as a recreational
  and ecological paradise. Similarly, hikers can be seen climbing to the crest
  of the Tibi ("Visitamos"). However, this two-minute production, which
  provides close-up and aerial footage of the Tibi, contains a problematic
  factual error, in that it dates the beginning of the dam's construction to
  1680. The Tibi draws on its historical precedence: "El pantano más antiguo
  de Europa en funcionamiento, construido a finales del siglo XVI en Tibi
  (Alicante), constituye uno de los ejes centrales de un ambicioso proyecto
  para impulsar turísticamente el interior de una provincia conocida,
  fundamentalmente, por su oferta de sol y playa" ("The oldest working
  European reservoir, built at the end of the sixteenth century in Tibi
  [Alicante], is at the heart of an ambitious plan to promote inland tourism
  in a province that is known primarily for its sunny seashore"; "Así es").

9 As journalist Ángela Bernardo notes, the three hundred million pesetas
  budgeted for the Riaño Dam did not include expropriations, exceeding
  1,600 million.

10 See Leonese journalist Ana Gaitero's review of the documentary *Mi valle*,
which re-examines the Riaño Reservoir in 2015. Similarly, activist Ramiro
Pinto Prieto documents the painting of phrases such as "Riaño: ¿Guernika
del PSOE?" ("Riaño: Guernika of the Spanish Socialist Workers' Party?")
on local buildings.

11 Like Diana's, visiting shepherdess Selvagia's village is plotted with
precision: "En el valeroso e inexpugnable reino de los Lusitanos hay dos
caudalosos ríos que, cansados de regar la mayor parte de nuestra España,
no muy lejos el uno del otro entran en el mar océano" ("In the valiant and
impregnable kingdom of the Lusitani there are two roaring rivers, which,
exhausted from irrigating most of our Spain, not very far away from one
another empty into the ocean"; 138–9). One of these is the Duero.

12 Ángel Carchenilla's photograph of del Brío's conversation with eight
Riaño residents accompanies the article. Both the article and the photo are
republished in the Revista Comarcal blog (Del Brío). Six of the shepherds
pictured wear *madreñas*, wooden clogs typically worn – even today – in the
mountains of León, especially by herders. Historically, these villages are
predominantly associated with transhumant Merino flocks.

13 Jánovas, in the Province of Huesca, Aragón, offered a precedent. The
village was demolished but the dam was never built.

14 The TVE Informe Semanal video "Réquiem por una Comarca" contains
interviews with (yet undisplaced) residents and footage of the valley.

15 The *Región (Los relatos). Cambio del paisaje y políticas del agua (Region (The
Narratives). Changes in Landscape and the Politics of Water)* exhibition (named
for Benet's novel) was on display from 2 December 2017 until 27 May
2018 (MUSAC and FCAYC). See also the website of writer, activist, and
Riaño protestor Pinto Prieto, who has collected photographs, newspaper
clippings, and pamphlets related to the protests and news coverage of the
construction of the Riaño Reservoir.

16 In the words of Víctor del Río, "[F]orman un impresionante mosaico en
uno de los muros del MUSAC" ("They form an impressive mosaic on
one of the walls of the MUSAC"). This exhibition employs mnemotechnic
principles, an effect paralleled in Montemayor's novel, where the
shepherds are transfixed by the memory theatre that constitutes Felicia's
palace.

17 This collective anguish is additionally encapsulated in song: "Canto a
mi tierra pequeña / tierra que me vió [sic] nacer, / y aunque mi tierra no
exista / yo la llevo aquí en mi ser. // Riaño, Riaño / lanza tus penas al
viento / que escuche el lamento / que quiebra tu voz. / Deja que aquellos
que un día / forjaron tu ruina / contemplen su error" ("I sing to my
little homeland / homeland that saw my birth, / and even though my
homeland doesn't exist / I carry it here in my soul. // Riaño, Riaño / cast

your sorrows to the wind / may it listen to the lament / that makes your voice break. / Let those who one day fashioned your ruin / contemplate their error"; De Pablo). I owe a debt to Bernardo's childhood recollection of these lyrics.

18   As Cubillas writes in 2017:

> Hay heridas imposibles de curar, que no cicatrizan. Heridas que permanecen abiertas durante toda la vida, que no se olvidan. Heridas que en Riaño duelen desde hace 30 años. Porque sí, han podido pasar 10.950 días, pero la herida del pantano está aún hoy viva como el primer día, cómo aquel fatídico 7 de julio de 1987 cuando las raíces de nueve pueblos se despegaron, para siempre, de la tierra.

> (There are some wounds that are impossible to remedy, that never heal. Wounds that remain open for your whole life, that are never forgotten. Wounds that have been hurting in Riaño for thirty years. Because yes, 10,950 days have passed, but the wound of the reservoir is as deep today as it was on the first day, that fateful 7 July 1987, when the roots of nine villages were forever eradicated from the land; "Riaño") This article includes the video and transcripts of interviews with former residents of the Riaño Valley.

19   A 2012 drought permitted the archaeological excavation of the Cueva del Oso (normally underwater) by Ana Neira and Federico Bernaldo de Quirós, of the University of León, who unearthed a series of medieval coins (MUSAC and FCAYC 33).

20   Montemayor's highly influential novel spawned myriad progeny. The *libro de pastores*, devoured voraciously by the early modern Spanish reading public, is replete with technical herding terms such as *almagre, apero, borrego, cabaña, mesta*, and *rediles*. I develop these ideas more fully in my article "Mammoth Woolly Migrations: Transhumance, Extinction, and the Cervantine Shepherd." For all their glitter, Montemayor's are working shepherds. Given the prominence of the enchanted water as a remedy for lovesickness, however, *La Diana* is uniquely rich for an analysis of early modern Iberian water control.

21   The complicated love story between non-shepherd nobles Felismena and Felis, who hail from Vandalia (thought to represent Seville), is primary to the novel, but not relevant to the present analysis.

22   For critic Bruno Damiani, the Esla "in its function, by plan or coincidence, brings to mind Dante's River Elsa whose water dulls the mind" (59). Two literal Iberian rivers have been associated with this mythological Greek river of oblivion: previously warring Phoenicians and Greeks referred to

the present-day Guadalete, in Cádiz, as the Lethe to memorialize their mutual desire to forget their differences; and like the Lethe, the waters of the Limia, in northern Portugal, were once rumoured by the Romans to cause memory loss.

23 I study the topic of the arts of memory and their relation to lovesickness extensively in *Impressions of Melancholy: Memory and Lovesickness in the Spanish Pastoral Book*.

24 In his review Ruiz notes the deliberate even-handedness of the MUSAC and FCAYC exhibition, which "expone con pretendida objetividad la transformación del territorio producida por las grandes obras hidráulicas … Y digo pretendida objetividad porque el sentimiento del visitante vira hacia un lado cuando ve esas fotogénicas láminas de agua pero imagina todo lo que hay allá abajo hundido" ("exposes with intended objectivity the transformation of the land produced by the great hydraulic works … And I say intended objectivity, because visitors' emotions are swayed to one side when they see those picturesque colour plates of the water but imagine everything that is submerged beneath").

25 See the analyses of Felicia's palace by Juan Bautista Avalle-Arce, Frederick de Armas, and Benjamin Nelson, among others.

26 Especially telling when one takes into account the Riaño Reservoir, Nelson, citing Américo Castro, argues that Montemayor's setting of *La Diana* in Spain "reflects … 'el integralismo hispánico,' or rather, the desire of a Spaniard to live on his own soil and be identified with it" (245).

27 Migration patterns take many forms; this one is the most archetypal.

28 Julius Klein and Carla Rahn Phillips and William Phillips, Jr., study the Mesta and the Merino wool trade in early modern Spain. The comprehensive work of Manuel Rodríguez Pascual focuses on transhumant Merino shepherds and flocks.

29 To no avail, Guillermo Hernández, mayor of Riaño from 1983 to 1987, provided an alternative model that would have avoided the demolition of the villages and lessened the ecological impact, by instead creating three or four smaller reservoirs in the area (Cubillas, "Riaño").

30 The CHD artfully sidesteps the issue, stating that the reservoir has the capacity to irrigate about 80,000 hectares, without confirming its actual yield of irrigation:

> [El Esla] aporta cerca de 5.300 hectómetros cúbicos de agua parte de los cuales se almacena en el Embalse de Riaño, que es el más grande de todos cuantos ha construido el Estado en esta cuenca. Este embalse tiene una capacidad superior a los 650 hectómetros cúbicos de agua que son suficientes para garantizar el riego de 80.000 hectáreas ubicadas fundamentalmente en la Provincia de León.

([The Esla] supplies nearly 5,300 cubic hectometres of water, part of which is stored in the Riaño Reservoir, which is the largest of all that the State has constructed in this basin. This reservoir has a capacity of greater than the 650 cubic hectometres sufficient to guarantee the irrigation of 80,000 hectares located primarily in the Province of León; "Embalse de Riaño" 00:02:42–00:03:15)

31 That this is a seemingly impossible number of trees is precisely the point. Coincidentally, the preponderance of plants and trees is a staple of the pastoral. As Rallo notes, several critics have commented upon the abundant references to the alder in *La Diana*: M. Debax counts twenty-five mentions of this tree, while for Menéndez Pelayo, the place name, "la fuente de los alisos" ("the fountain of the alders") is repeated "hasta la saciedad" ("ad nauseum"; qtd. in Montemayor 112n16). Damiani finds this beautiful natural setting injurious to the shepherds who frequent it (60).

32 For El Saffar, "[t]he lack of ending, along with the implied erosion of Sireno and Sylvano's indifference to Diana, suggest Montemayor's awareness of the unsatisfactory nature of the solution offered by the Sabia [Wise] Felicia" (185). Perhaps a similar feeling of dissatisfaction leads Gaspar Gil Polo to reunite Sireno and Diana in *La Diana enamorada* (1564).

33 Critics have long expressed doubts about the use of the enchanted water. Perry asserts that "it is naïve to believe that Montemayor was taken in by Felicia's wizardry" (232). For de Armas, "[w]hen the shepherds return to their natural environment [after drinking the enchanted water], they have changed in ways otherwise inconceivable" (333).

34 Damiani compares Felicia's cure to Psalm 137: "[T]he anguish is intensified by the memory of a love that once was. Thus, like men and women banished from a happy land, they languish in a way that suggests suffering of biblical exiles: 'By the rivers of Babylon, there we sat down, yea, we wept, when we remembered Zion'" (60). Once again, this language replicates descriptions of the trauma suffered by the former residents of the Riaño Valley.

35 See Damiani; de Armas; Nelson. For Nelson, Felicia's palace is modelled after the Roman Septizodium, whose ruins constituted a popular pilgrimage site featured in early modern travel guides (250).

36 At the time of this writing, one can reserve a 4x4 Safari tour of the Anciles Valley through Sendas de Arnua for about seventy euros ("Safari en el Valle de Anciles").

37 Aerial video footage attests to the alarming reduction of the reservoir to only 22 per cent of capacity: "Riaño resurje [sic] de sus cenizas … Cada día el pantano baja 30 centímetros … Y las imágenes son espectaculares" ("Riaño resurges from its ashes … Every day the reservoir drops 30

centimetres … And the images are spectacular"; "Pantano de Riaño, verano 2017").

38 This collaboration between the Museo del Prado and the World Wildlife Fund was designed to coincide with the UN Climate Change Conference in December 2019 in Madrid. For a discussion of this project and to view the original paintings alongside their respective catastrophic re-imaginings, see artist and curator Caroline Elbaor. The remaining altered paintings include Sorolla's *Niños en la playa* (1909) and Goya's *El quitasol* (1777): "The altered works were installed on billboards in Madrid and shared online using the hashtag #LoCambiaTodo as a way to expand and continue political and social conversations through art" (Lasane). As Maryanne L. Leone and Shanna Lino explore in their introduction to this collection, the joint initiative's dystopian recreations contest human-centred inhabitation of the planet earth and, in so doing, participate in a natureculturally informed dislodging of anthropocentric conventions and perspectives.

WORKS CITED AND CONSULTED

Aristodemou, Georgia A. "Fountain Figures from the Greek Provinces: Monumentality in Fountain Structures of Roman Greece as Revealed through Their Sculptural Display Programs and Their Patrons." Aristodemou and Tassios, pp. 193–217.

Aristodemou, Georgia A. "Introduction II." Aristodemou and Tassios, pp. 10–12.

Aristodemou, Georgia A., and Theodosios P. Tassios, editors. *Great Waterworks in Roman Greece: Aqueducts and Monumental Fountains: Function in Context.* Archaeopress, 2018.

Aristodemou, Georgia A., and Theodosios P. Tassios. "Preface." Aristodemou and Tassios, pp. iii–iv.

"Así era Riaño (León) hace casi 100 años …" *Diario de Valderrueda*, 6 Oct. 2018, https://www.diariodevalderrueda.es/texto-diario/mostrar/706470/asi-riano-hace-casi-100-anos.

"Así es el pantano más antiguo de Europa." *ABC*, 24 Jan. 2016, https://www.abc.es/espana/comunidad-valenciana/alicante/abci-pantano-mas-antiguo-europa-201601241803_noticia.html.

Avalle-Arce, Juan Bautista. *La novela pastoril española.* 2nd ed., Istmo, 1974.

Bernardo, Ángela. "Riaño, el Jánovas que sí ocurrió." *Hipertextual*, 1 Nov. 2015, https://www.hipertextual.com/2015/11/riano-pantano-janovas-salvados.

Campos, José María. "Riaño trabaja en convertir Anciles en un paraje de estudio del bisonte cántabrico." *Diario de León*, 5 Apr. 2020, https://www.diariodeleon.es/articulo/provincia/riano-trabaja-convertir-anciles-paraje-estudio-bisonte-cantabrico/202004050132192001950.html.

Carbajal Vega, Santiago. Comment on "Riaño, elegido 'Mejor pueblo de
   España' en el concurso de la Cadena SER." *Cadena SER*, 26 July 2019, https://
   cadenaser.com/emisora/2019/07/26/radio_leon/1564132638_213923.html
   ?fbclid=IwAR3AAr9zxbdSdKcKE1l1cIKHA2svPBQoPY0Kf9k0FeCLSAcFm2
   -N1tXQzq4.

Carnero, María. "Bisonte europeo, ¿nacer para morir?" *Diario de León*, 26 June
   2020, https://www.diariodeleon.es/opinion/maria-carnero/bisonte
   -europeo-nacer-morir/202006261106212025230.html.

Carnero, María. "El embalse de Riaño figura entre los 'delitos' ambientales
   más traumáticos." *Diario de León*, 11 Mar. 2015, https://www.diariodeleon
   .es/articulo/provincia/embalse-riano-figura-lsquo-delitos-rsquo
   -ambientales-mas-traumaticos/201503110400001499321.html.

Castillo Barranco, Juan Carlos, and Miguel Arenillas Parra. "Las presas
   romanas en España. Propuesta de inventario." *Revista de Obras Públicas*,
   no. 3.475, Mar. 2007, pp. 65–80, https://www.seprem.es/st_hp_f
   /ICongresoHistoria/LAS_PRESAS_ROMANAS_EN_ESPANA-PROPUESTA
   _DE_INVENTARIO.pdf.

Cervantes Saavedra, Miguel de. *Don Quijote de la Mancha*. Edited by Francisco
   Rico, RAE, 2015.

"La climatología causó en 2019 daños en 73.755 hectáreas de cultivos de
   León." *Diario de León*, 20 Jan. 2020, https://www.diariodeleon.es/articulo
   /provincia/climatologia-causo-2019-danos-73755-hectareas-cultivos
   -leon/202001200236111978515.html.

Covarrubias Horozco, Sebastián de. *Tesoro de la lengua castellana o española*.
   Edited by Ignacio Arellano and Rafael Zafra, U of Navarra, 2006.

Cubillas, Andrea. "La destrucción de todo un valle." *Leonoticias*, 7 July 2017,
   https://www.leonoticias.com/comarcas/destruccion-valle-20170708201445
   -nt.html.

Cubillas, Andrea. "Riaño, una herida que no se olvida." *El Norte de Castilla*,
   8 July 2017, https://www.elnortedecastilla.es/leon/riano-herida-olvida
   -20170707201904-nt.html.

Damiani, Bruno. "Journey to Felicia: *La Diana* as Pilgrimage: A Study in
   Symbolism." *Bibliothèque D'Humanisme et Renaissance*, vol. 44, no. 1, 1983,
   pp. 59–76. *Springer Link*, https://doi.org/10.1007/BF01878307.

De Armas, Frederick A. "Caves of Fame and Wisdom in the Spanish Pastoral
   Novel." *Studies in Philology*, vol. 82, no. 3, 1985, pp. 332–58.

Del Brío, Francisco. "Los pueblos sumergidos de León." *Revista comarcal*,
   8 June 2015, https://noticiascomarcales.blogspot.com/2015/06/los-pueblos
   -sumergidos-de-leon.html.

Del Río, Víctor. "Narración sumergida." *El cultural*, 5 Jan. 2018, https://www
   .elespanol.com/el-cultural/20180105/narracion-sumergida/274973685_0
   .html.

De Pablo, José Manuel. "Riaño." *YouTube*, uploaded by María González, 6 Feb. 2012, https://www.youtube.com/watch?v=c2V-lKQ79sI&list =RDc2V-lKQ79sI&start_radio=1.

Díaz, Alberto. *Made in Slow*. https://www.madeinslow.com/en/. Accessed 1 Feb. 2023.

El Saffar, Ruth. "Structural and Thematic Discontinuity in Montemayor's *Diana*." *MLN*, vol. 86, no. 2, 1971, pp. 182–98. *JSTOR*, https://doi.org /10.2307/2907614.

Elbaor, Caroline. "The Prado Is 'Updating' Its Most Cherished Masterpieces to Illustrate the Dystopian Chaos Unleashed by Climate Change." Artnet, 4 Dec. 2019, https://news.artnet.com/art-world/museo-del-prado-wwf -painting-masterpieces-climate-change-1721970.

"Embalse de Riaño." *YouTube*, uploaded by Confederación Hidrográfica del Duero, 13 Aug. 2015, https://www.youtube.com/watch?v=agKy20KWPPo.

Fuller, Dorian Q., et al. "Comparing Pathways to Agriculture." Archaeology International, vol. 18, no. 1, 2015, pp. 61–6. *UCL Press*, https://doi.org /10.5334/ai.1808.

Gaitero, Ana. "La película de Riaño." *Diario de León*, 6 Nov. 2016, https://www .diariodeleon.es/articulo/afondo/la-pelicula-de-riano/201611060400001637774 .html.

González, Irene. "Navegar entre glaciares por los Fiordos leoneses." *Viajar*, 4 Apr. 2018, https://viajar.elperiodico.com/destinos/navegar-glaciares -fiordos-leoneses.

González Matorra, Alfonso. "Riaño Vive, no vive para el pasado, sino para la eternidad." *iLeón*, 26 Mar. 2016, https://www.ileon.com/el_alma_del _agua/los_nuevos_pantanos_de_leon/062827/riano-vive-no-vive-para-el -pasado-sino-para-la-eternidad.

Klein, Julius. *The Mesta: A Study in Spanish Economic History, 1273–1836*. Kennikat Press, 1964.

Krauss, Werner. "Localización y desplazamientos en la novela pastoril española." *Actas del Segundo Congreso Internacional de Hispanistas: Celebrado en Nijmegen del 20 al 25 de agosto de 1965*, edited by Jaime Sánchez Romeralo and Norbert Poulussen, Nijmegen, 1967, pp. 363–9.

Kumar, Mohi. "Ancient Farmers Irreversibly Altered Earth's Face by 3000 Years Ago." *Science*, 30 Aug. 2019, https://doi.org/10.1126/science .aaz3312.

Larson, Jennifer. *Greek Nymphs: Myth, Cult, Lore*. Oxford UP, 2001.

Lasane, Andrew. "Paintings from Prado Museum Collection Given Climate Change Makeovers." *Colossal*, 8 Dec. 2019, https://www.thisiscolossal .com/2019/12/prado-museum-climate-change/.

Longfellow, Brenda. *Roman Imperialism and Civic Patronage: Form, Meaning, and Ideology in Monumental Fountain Complexes*. Cambridge UP, 2011.

Marek, Margaret. *Impressions of Melancholy: Memory and Lovesickness in the Spanish Pastoral Book*. 2003. Pennsylvania State U, PhD thesis.

Marek, Margaret. "Mammoth Woolly Migrations: Transhumance, Extinction, and the Cervantine Shepherd." *Laberinto*, vol. 10, 2017, pp. 27–51, https://acmrs.asu.edu/sites/default/files/2020-01/v10_Laberinto_Marek_0.pdf.

Montemayor, Jorge de. *La Diana (1559)*. Edited by Asunción Rallo, Cátedra, 1995.

Museo de Arte Contemporáneo de Castilla y León (MUSAC) and Fundación Cerezales Antonino y Cinia (FCAYC). "Región (Los relatos). Cambio del paisaje y políticas del agua." Guía de Sala – MUSAC, 2 Dec. 2017–27 May 2018, https://www.musac.es/FOTOS/VISITAS_GUIADAS/REGION_GUIA%20SALA_MUSAC_CAST_ENG.pdf.

Nelson, Benjamin J. "Pilgrimaging to the Temple of Diana: Jorge de Montemayor, Merida, and the Septizodium." *"Los cielos se agotaron de prodigios": Essays in Honor of Frederick A. de Armas*, edited by Christopher B. Wiemer et al., Juan de la Cuesta, 2018, pp. 245–55.

"Pantano de Riaño, verano 2017." YouTube, uploaded by Leonoticias Diariodigital, 24 Aug. 2017, https://youtu.be/l0cDX5bUrlc.

Pastor, Fernando. "La lucha por vaciar el pantano de Riaño." *Diagonal*, 6 June 2011, https://www.diagonalperiodico.net/global/la-lucha-por-vaciar-pantano-riano.html.

Perry, T. Anthony. "Ideal Love and Human Reality in Montemayor's *La Diana*." *PMLA*, vol. 84, no. 2, 1969, pp. 227–34. *Cambridge Core*, https://doi.org/10.2307/1261279.

Phillips, Carla Rahn, and William D. Phillips, Jr. *Spain's Golden Fleece: Wool Production and the Wool Trade from the Middle Ages to the Nineteenth Century*. Johns Hopkins UP, 1997.

Pinto Prieto, Ramiro. "Lucha por la recuperación de Riaño." https://www.ramiropinto.es/hemeroteca/verdes-riano/recuperacion-de-riano/. Accessed 1 Feb. 2023.

Prado Allende, Luis. *Primeras aguas en el pantano de Riaño*. 1987. "31 de diciembre de 1987, el último día del valle de Riaño," by A. Vega, *iLeón*, 31 Dec. 2017, https://ileon.eldiario.es/actualidad/riano-pantano-presa-provincia-leon-historia-decada-aniversario-agua_1_9470732.html.

Rabanillo, Maite. "Dominio público hidráulico: CHD valora en 3 M€ los daños en las riberas que dejaron las riadas." *Diario de León*, 7 Mar. 2020, https://www.diariodeleon.es/articulo/provincia/chd-valora-3-danos-riberas-dejaron-riadas/202003070233031994315.html?utm_medium=email&utm_source=Newsletter&utm_campaign=200307.

"Réquiem por una Comarca." TVE Informe Semanal, 1985. *YouTube*, uploaded by agustin lasai rodrigez [Riaño Vive], 29 Jan. 2011, https://www.youtube.com/watch?v=GCwbkQlRc-s.

"Riaño, elegido 'Mejor pueblo de España' en el concurso de la Cadena SER." *Cadena SER*, 6 July 2019, https://cadenaser.com/emisora/2019/07/26 /radio_leon/1564132638_213923.html?fbclid=IwAR3AAr9zxbdSdKcKE1l1c IKHA2svPBQoPY0Kf9k0FeCLSAcFm2-N1tXQzq4.

Rodríguez Pascual, Manuel. *La trashumancia: Cultura, cañadas y viajes*. 5th ed., Edilesa, 2004.

Ruiz, Rafa. "30 años del embalse de Riaño, 50 años de Porma: la soberbia del poder." *El Asombrario & Co.*, 16 Jan. 2018, https://elasombrario.publico.es /embalses-riano-porma-soberbia-poder/.

"Safari en el Valle de Anciles." *Sendas de Arnua*, https://www.sendasdearnua .com/safari-valle-de-anciles-experiencia/. Accessed 19 Apr. 2023.

Villareal, Antonio. "Españoles, tenemos un exceso de pantanos: Ha llegado la hora de destruir estos 15." *El confidencial*, 27 Apr. 2018, https://www .elconfidencial.com/tecnologia/ciencia/2018-04-27/exceso-pantanos -demolicion-naturaleza-cauce_1555632/.

"Visitamos el pantano en funcionamiento más antiguo de Europa." *Viajestic*, 26 Jan. 2016, https://www.lasexta.com/viajestic/escapadas/visitamos -pantano-funcionamiento-mas-antiguo-europa_2016012657ea44910cf2a a7f694ab223.html#:~:text=El%20embalse%20de%20Tibi%20se,que%20 todav%C3%ADa%20sigue%20en%20funcionamiento.&text=Se%20 encuentra%20en%20Tibi%2C%20Alicante,m%C3%A1s%20antiguo%20 de%20toda%20Europa.

Wilson, Andrew. "Water, Power and Culture in the Roman and Byzantine Worlds: An Introduction." *Water History*, vol. 4, 2012, pp. 1–9. *Springer Link*, https://doi.org/10.1007/s12685-012-0050-2.

Of Witches and Land Reform in Enlightenment Spain

DANIEL FROST

Introduction

Early in the summer of 1808, on the way home from exile in Mallorca, former Minister of Grace and Justice Gaspar Melchor de Jovellanos travelled through northern Spain to Asturias. Crossing the high plains of Soria, he remarked on the "famosos campos y praderas de Barahona" ("famous fields and plains of Barahona"), where witches were said to have gathered "cuando se creó que las había" ("back when people still believed in them"; Jovellanos, "De vuelta" 129).[1] Jovellanos had been imprisoned in 1801 for promoting liberal ideas, questioning royal and ecclesiastical entitlements, and proclaiming agricultural reform as a path to economic freedom and prosperity, ideas that he articulated in the *Informe de la Sociedad Económica de Madrid al Real y Supremo Consejo de Castilla en el expediente de ley agaria* (*Report of the Economic Society of Madrid to the Royal and Supreme Council of Castilla on the Agrarian Law Dossier*, 1795), which had drawn the inquisitors' ire.[2] Free at last to return to the institute that he had founded to teach exact sciences to his countrymen in Gijón, he journeyed across the peninsula, pen in hand, resuming his longtime habit of describing the landscapes through which he passed. His penchant for description reflects both an admiration for the land and a tendency to categorize what he saw according to a rationalist view of nature inseparable from the economy (Caso González 20; see also Phillips 98–9). That tension would continue to influence him as he took up his occupation in Gijón.

Ten years earlier, in 1798, Spanish romantic painter Franscisco de Goya depicted a landscape analogous to the fields of Barahona in the background of his painting *El aquelarre* (*The Witches' Sabbath*), where desolate peaks rise in the twilight behind a circle of peasant women paying tribute to a towering black goat. The devilish figure, its horns entwined with laurel, holds its front legs outstretched as if directing a ritual as the women offer up a tribute of infants, some alive, some dead, more of them strewn on the barren ground.[3] Grotesque to the point of caricature, Goya's image evokes a scene that is very much in line with a vision of rural Spain that Jovellanos depicts in other works such as the *Elogio de Carlos Tercero* (*Eulogy for Carlos III*, 1788), but opposed to the vision of a reformed landscape that he presents in the *Informe*. Goya's raw, unfinished lands, plunged in shadow and presided over by superstitious peasants, correlate to landscapes that, in Jovellanos's *Elogio*, have not yet received the light of reform: "¡Volved los ojos a aquellas tristes épocas en que España vivió entregada a la superstición, y a la ignorancia!" ("Look back to those dismal times of a Spain enslaved to superstition and ignorance!"), writes Jovellanos, "¡Qué espectáculo de horror y de lástima!" ("What a horrible and disgraceful spectacle!"; *Elogio* 12). If only the light of reason were to reach such lands, he implies, Spain might finally emerge from the benighted state into which it had been plunged by the end of the Austrian dynasty in the seventeenth century.

Jovellanos's texts do not dialogue directly with Goya's painting, but a pattern of imagery common to both indicates a tension between reason and superstition, wilderness and agriculture, rural traditions and enlightened reform that characterize the transition from Old Spain to a new regime.[4] A distinguishing feature of that pattern is the association of superstition and backwardness with lands that have not been cultivated as opposed to civilization and happiness in lands that have been brought under control. Compare, for instance, the witches of Goya's *El aquelarre* with the colourful citizens in his *Baile en las orillas del Manzanares* (*Dance on the Banks of the Manzanares*, 1776–7), who are enjoying the day on a riverbank outside Madrid, away from the city but not far from the Pontones bridge in the middle ground and the dome of San Francisco in the distance, reminders of a prevailing urban sensibility. Similarly, in the *Informe*, Jovellanos imagines a simple, happy, and productive rural society at home in a well-cultivated landscape: "salgan nuestros labradores de los poblados á los campos, contraigan la sencillez é inocencia de costumbres que se respira en ellos, no conozcan otro placer, otra diversión que sus fiestas y romerías, sus danzas y meriendas; ... y entonces el candor y la alegría serán inseparables de su carácter y constituirán su felicidad" ("when our laborers move from the towns to the countryside, and adopt the simplicity and innocence of its atmosphere; and come to know no pleasure greater than the village festivals and *romerías*, its dances and picnics, ... frankness and joy will infuse their character, and they will know true happiness"; §430).[5] The beckoning *campos* recall both Goya's riverbank and the fields of Horace's second Epode, tended by the happy few (*beatus ille*) who live away from town and court. In Jovellanos's eighteenth-century reimagining, Horace's Golden Age is not lost to the past but a promise of the future, where candour, contentment, innocence, and tranquillity characterize a restored rural condition.

Beatific as they may appear, however, Jovellanos's and Goya's neoclassical landscapes belie the processes that produced them, processes that linked – and continue to link – cultivation with domination. The writings of Jovellanos and like-minded reformers in eighteenth-century Spain advance a perspective that pits *el hombre,* a sexist term meant to represent humans equipped with reason and science, against nature, which is considered a non-human realm of geographical features, plants, and beasts subject to human improvement. That nature is often represented as female and ripe for development, thereby entangling land reform efforts within a broader culture of men's domination of women. In the *Informe,* Jovellanos identifies dominion over nature as the basis of all human activity and culture. God, Jovellanos maintains, "le entregó [al hombre] el dominio de la tierra, colocándole en ella, y condenándole a vivir del producto de su trabajo; al mismo tiempo que le dio el derecho de enseñorearla, le impuso la pensión de cultivarla … A este sagrado interés debe el hombre su conservación, y el mundo su cultura" ("placed him [man] on the earth and made him its master, condemning him to live off the fruit of his labor. Thus, upon granting man the right to rule over nature, the Creator imposed upon him the duty of cultivating it … To this sacred interest man owes his conservation and the world its cultivation"; §21). An insistence on *man* as a metonym for humanity and nature as realm to be taken reinforces a male-centred perspective long advanced by the Church and upheld in Spanish society through primogeniture (*mayorazgos*). Deplore as he may the *mayorazgos* as misguided economic policy, Jovellanos does not debate the principle on which they rest, namely that the will of God is to assure "la subsistencia del hombre niño sobre el amor paterno, del hombre viejo sobre el reconocimiento filial; y del hombre robusto sobre la necesidad del trabajo" ("the child's [subsistence] … based upon fatherly love; the elderly's … founded upon filial care; and that of the robust man … founded on the need to work"; §187). Invoking the highest patriarchal and Judeo-Christian authority, Jovellanos asserts men's God-given right to possess the land as a principle of culture itself.

The relationship between cultivation, gender, and control that lies unquestioned at the heart of the *Informe* bears attention in light of ecocriticism, which points to the age of reason as a turning point in Western ideas of humankind's place within nature. Ecofeminist historian Carolyn Merchant argues that concepts of order, progress, property, and commerce that emerged with a scientific revolution engendered mainly by men tended to characterize nature as an adversary to be conquered, "a disorderly and chaotic realm to be subdued and controlled" (*Death* 127). Such images crop up in Jovellanos's work, and to some extent in Goya's as well, in his assertions that a main purpose of government is to remove unproductive and disorderly figures from the land to free human agriculture from "estorbos que retardan su progreso" ("hurdles that impede or slow its progress"; *Informe* §19). Affirming control of nature as a path to progress, Jovellanos's work casts progress as what ecofeminist philosopher Val Plumwood has called "the adjunct to reason, the side opposing nature in the West's dominant cultural narrative of reason progressively mastering nature that justifies maximizing rational control of the earth" ("Nature as Agency" 5). This essay examines the development of such mastering narratives in Jovellanos's work, narratives that exalt reason and reform in ways that help to expose what ecofeminist scholar Karen Warren calls "the nature of connections between the domination of women (and other oppressed humans) and the domination of nature" (x). A closer reading of agriculture in Jovellanos's works and the anthropocentric culture in which they take shape reveals the limits of his vision, exposing some of the oppressive structures inherent in the Spanish Enlightenment's struggle to impose a human consciousness on the land.[6]

An Admirable Spectacle

Jovellanos's most widely read text is undoubtedly the *Informe*, which posits an adversarial relationship between nature and agriculture in Spain, detailing a number of legal and physical obstacles (*estorbos*) to agricultural prosperity (§6). The report, officially prepared by the Sociedad de Amigos del País ("Society of Friends of the Country") but authored and delivered by Jovellanos, rests on the principle that agriculture is the chief source of individual wealth and public revenue (§303).[7] Recalling physiocratic principles from an exchange of agrarian ideas around Europe (Corredera 276; Frost 184n40), the report makes numerous recommendations to the Crown for how best to facilitate the spread of agriculture on Spanish soil.

Although grounded in a concern for the land, Jovellanos's reformist discourse inextricably binds nature to human power and influence (Phillips 105). The primary aim of the *Informe* is to uproot privileges granted to nobility, municipalities, the church, and livestock owners, whose interests hinder common farmers' (*labradores*) ability to work the land (§332). By proposing avenues to a free market and private land ownership, Jovellanos articulates a position socially progressive enough to run afoul of the monarchist establishment, but does so at the expense of the natural environment. Indeed, in many cases, the difficulties that the report lists come from "estorbos físicos, o derivados de la naturaleza" ("physical obstacles, or those derived from nature") that impede cultivation or obstruct the free circulation and consumption of agricultural products (§367). In either case, Jovellanos casts the farmer's work as a struggle with a recalcitrant foe: "el oficio de labrador es luchar a todas horas con la naturaleza, que de suyo nada produce sino maleza, y que solo da frutos sazonados a fuerza de trabajo y cultivo" ("the work of every farmer is a constant struggle against nature, which when unattended produces nothing but weeds and brush, and must be labored on and cultivated in order to bear fruit"; §363). In nature, Jovellanos finds value only in *frutos sazonados*, goods coaxed from the land through human effort. The natural landscape itself seems to produce nothing valuable; whatever ecosystems exist among the *maleza* mean nothing to him. Even the term *maleza*, which refers both to weeds (also known as *malas hierbas*) and, more broadly, to dense groups of bushes or trees, derives from the same root as *maldad* (from Lat. *malitia*, "evil" or "bad"), suggesting a generalized antipathy towards vegetation that interferes with agricultural production.[8]

In presenting the *maleza* as an obstacle to human prosperity, Jovellanos ascribes an unruly agency to nature that agriculture must overcome. Certain obstacles, in fact, are so formidable that they may be conquered only by the combined force of many: "La necesidad de vencer esta especie de estorbos, que acaso fue la primera á despertar en los hombres la idea de un interés común, y á reunir los pueblos para promoverle, forma todavía uno de los primeros objetos, y señala una de las primeras obligaciones de toda Sociedad política" ("The need to overcome this kind of impediment, which was perhaps what first awakened in men the idea of a shared or common interest, and therefore what induced them to live in groups or villages, is still one of the most basic objects and chief obligations of all political societies"; §363). The passage attributes the origins of society to the combined efforts of men, who, in Jovellanos's gendered portrayal of human agency, band together to subdue nature. Such is the root of all political association, he maintains, grounded in a perception that non-human nature must be altered to promote human interests. Government, by his reasoning, develops as an outgrowth of society's principal objective to prevail over nature, and the agents of that conquest are, determinedly, men.

The role of government extends only so far, however. Evoking common interest, Jovellanos recalls the economic philosophies of classical economists like Adam Smith, whom he cites (§8n2, §219n1), that theorize the role of self-interest in economic relations on the presumption that the best social benefit can usually be accomplished when individuals act reasonably to benefit themselves. For Jovellanos, agriculture serves its producers' interests above all, and, as for Smith, the government need have little direct role to play in bringing food to the table: "El oficio de las leyes no debe ser excitar ni dirigir, sino solamente proteger el interés de sus agentes, naturalmente activo y bien dirigido á su objeto" ("the role of laws with regard to the ownership of land and labor should not be to excite or to direct, but to protect their agents' interest, which is naturally active and well suited to its object"; §24). The government's role, in short, is to clear the way for self-interest to lead "naturally" to its end, even if that end involves disrupting natural ecologies of which humans themselves are part. Inured to the irony, Jovellanos argues throughout the *Informe* for the government to remove legal impediments to the economic exploitation of nature.

Nature, however, gets in his way. Calling attention to Spain's rugged and varied topography, for example, Jovellanos cites irrigation as one of three major areas of concern (along with road networks and ports). He maintains that the government's obligation should be to provide resources so that whoever wishes to cultivate lands without water may have access to it, however monumental the task (§370). He envisions feats of engineering to turn deep, swiftly flowing rivers into manageable sources of irrigation, fortifying their banks, excavating canals, building locks, levelling hills or tunnelling through them so that water may be carried to "tierras sedientas" ("thirsty lands"; §370).[9] Agricultural historians have pointed out how agrarian practices such as those favoured by Jovellanos, designed to force productivity in adverse conditions, posed significant damage to local ecologies, whether by enabling vast monocultures (such as the olive groves of Andalucía), subject to disease and fire, or causing ruderalization of nearby lands (Naredo 56). Indeed, as José Naredo and Fernando Parra argue, enforced agriculture, based on Enlightenment systems that evolved through the nineteenth century and into contemporary times, reduces and degrades biological diversity, landscape quality, and ecological stability significantly more than traditional agricultural practices, which tend to be generally better adapted to local ecosystems (327).[10] Not foreseeing such environmental impacts, however, Jovellanos advocates extending agricultural systems to every corner of the realm, bringing as much land as possible under human control.

A focus of Jovellanos's interest is the nation's *despoblados* and *baldíos*, depopulated areas of the countryside that remained largely uncultivated. Among the historical, political, and geographical reasons that Jovellanos gives for why the lands lay fallow, he especially impugns the Mesta, the society of Castilian sheep and cattle raisers whose members enjoyed broad legal privileges (*fueros*) and whose herds were allowed almost unfettered access to pastureland around the Spain's central plain (§39–§45). Such privileges made Mesta members the de facto holders of the land, for which they paid minimal rents and across which their enormous flocks passed seasonally without regard for private ownership or the impact of transhumance on the vegetation in their path.[11] Jovellanos considers such privileges unjust and ineffective agricultural policy, calling instead for the *enajenación*, or enclosure, of Spain's pasturelands (§48). The call for enclosure remains one of his most daring and enduring, proposing a fundamental change in the way that the land was to be managed, cultivated, and owned in Spain. Jovellanos reasons that delivering corporate property to private owners would put much more land up for cultivation, freeing it from privileges and entail, attracting capital investment, and incorporating it more completely into a market economy.

Historian Vicent Llombart points out that despite the boldness of the *Informe*'s recommendations for the time, the ideas it contained were hardly new, representing more of a culmination of Spanish Enlightenment thought than a break from it (142–3). Proposals to incorporate uncultivated lands into a nationwide market recall earlier, smaller-scale attempts by ministers of Carlos III to cultivate the deserted countryside for what they considered the good of the nation. In 1767, jurist and politician Pablo de Olavide undertook plans devised by treasury minister Pedro Rodríguez de Campomanes and the reformist Pedro Pablo Abarca, count of Aranda, then president of the Council of Castile, to build settlements in the Sierra Morena, a notoriously remote and unpopulated region on the route between Madrid and Seville. The mountains between Castilla-La Mancha and Andalucía had long obstructed traffic between the two cities, jeopardizing economic exchange and, especially, the movement of riches from the American colonies to the capital. For Miguel de Ondeano, Olavide's successor, the difficulty of the passage represented a shadow in the enlightened realm, a "feo borrón" ("ugly smudge") that resisted cultivation and darkened the regime's "resplandor" ("shining splendour"; qtd. in Avilés Fernández). Ondeano describes the repopulation plan as a means to prepare wild, rugged, and overgrown lands for the production of primary goods for national consumption (15). Like Jovellanos, Ondeano casts undeveloped areas as dangerous and unproductive – or, perhaps better, dangerous for being unproductive – and therefore in imminent need of reform.

The reformers' disdain for the unworked, uncultivated areas implies a separation from nature that Plumwood considers the (misguided) basis for human agents to assert dominion over the earth. Considering themselves "outside of and apart from a plastic, passive, and 'dead' nature which lacks any agency or meaning," planners such as the architects of the Sierra Morena plan recall Plumwood's "colonizing" reformers, who presume themselves justified in claiming lands – and in many cases, their inhabitants – for their own purposes ("Nature as Agency" 11–12). The 1767 *Real Cédula* (*Royal Decree*) that authorized new settlements in the Sierra Morena reflects the colonizing perspective on which the plan was based. Unlike Spain's Atlantic colonies, the new settlements did not incorporate lands seized from Indigenous communities, but rather developed interior lands where very few people lived, deeming them empty and worthless for comprising only *maleza*.[12] Here again is the tendency to designate lands as "unused, underused, or empty," the hallmark of what Plumwood sees as a European colonial ideology that "reduces the land to a passive and neutral surface for the inscription of human projects" ("Decolonizing" 53, 69). The *Real Cédula* reflects the dimension of just such a project in Spain, outlining in meticulous detail how the new settlements were to be sited, designed, divided, and maintained, including instructions for how the plots granted to each settler were to be enclosed and cultivated, how houses were to be built and community infrastructure (mills, irrigation, municipal offices, workshops) distributed. Once the lands were deemed fit for human occupation, each household would be furnished a pickaxe, hoe, hatchet, hammer, plough, field knife and other tools of the sort at the superintendent's expense, to aid in keeping nature in order or at bay (*Real Cédula* 3–7).

The hammers and ploughs granted to settlers, along with the livestock, fertilizers and seeds, represented the tools of colonization, the means to inscribe the enlightened reformers' idealized plans on the land.[13] Those plans depended on making the land productive for market, displacing local flora and fauna in favour of agricultural systems that would produce goods both for the settlers and the nation. Hence, much of the colonization effort was designed to secure the lines of communication to the capital Madrid, building new roads through rough territory and stationing new agricultural colonies regularly along the route as a way to eliminate the dangers of banditry and isolation, improve cultivation, and smooth the way for goods moving between cities. Military engineer Carlos LeMaur's famous road through the Despeñaperros pass was central to the project, replacing what had been, in Ondeano's words, "un camino de horror, espanto, y miedo" ("a horrible, dreadful, fearful route"; qtd. in Avilés Fernández) with what royal emissary Antonio Ponz describes as a "sumptuous" new thoroughfare (Ponz 85).[14] Ponz's description indicates how the new settlements had brought what many believed to be wild, desolate lands under control, turning a once unproductive wilderness, "donde antes nada se cogía, … abrigo de lobos y ladrones" ("where before nothing was picked … a shelter for wolves and thieves"), into the image of a productive, civilized, colonized, and enlightenment landscape (85).

The *Nuevas Poblaciones* bear the stamp of Carlos III's enlightened despotism and his determination to bring intellectual, social, and economic reform to the land itself. In praise of that system in the *Elogio*, Jovellanos lauds the Crown's attention to agricultural colonies, the redistribution of communal lands, and other reforms that he would later recommend in the *Informe* as part of the tangled relationship between land, culture, and reform under Carlos III (*Elogio* 7–8). A panegyric rather than a report, the *Elogio* is unequivocal in its praise of the ideals of enlightened leadership, framing the Crown's embrace of economic principles in agricultural terms. Jovellanos declares that just leadership grows out of the sovereign's ability to shed light – the light of reason, manifested in "útiles verdades" ("useful truths") or "conocimientos útiles" ("useful knowledge") – across the cultural landscape (14, 22). He represents the light of reason and reform through an agrarian metaphor, affirming that Carlos "sembró en la Nación las semillas de luz" ("sowed in the Nation the seeds of light") destined to enlighten his subjects. The ability to cultivate the seeds of enlightenment, Jovellanos declares, is the deceased sovereign's greatest triumph:

> Sin tu protección, sin tu generosidad, sin el ardiente amor que profesas a tus pueblos, estas preciosas semillas hubieran perecido. Caídas en una tierra estéril, la cizaña de la contradicción las hubiera sofocado en su seno. Tú has hecho respetar las tiernas plantas que germinaron: tú vas ya a recoger su fruto; y este fruto de ilustración y de verdad será la prenda más cierta de la felicidad de tu pueblo.

> (Without your protection, your generosity, and the ardent love that you profess for your peoples, these precious seeds would have perished. Had they fallen in a barren land, the weeds of contradiction would have choked them in the womb. You have instilled respect for the tender plants that germinated: now, you may reap their fruit, and the fruit of enlightenment and truth will be the surest sign of your people's happiness; *Elogio* 49)

The passage brings cultivation to the very language of power; dense with agricultural references, it depicts the past as a sterile ground on which seeds of reason, the "precious" source of human happiness, cannot take root until cultivated by a gardener king whose love for his human subjects turns nature to the nation's ends. The entanglement of natural imagery with reformist discourse in the passage does not loosen the binary between nature and culture, as ecocritical philosophers Donna Haraway, Karen Barad, and others seek to do, so much as bind it more tightly, affirming the ascendancy of reason, in the form of enlightenment, over the non-human natural realm.[15] For Jovellanos, the fruit of reason is truth itself, propagated in a discourse that posits controlling nature as the basis of an epistemology that values human industry and happiness above all.

Extending the metaphor, Jovellanos glorifies Carlos's attempts to regenerate Spanish culture through an embrace of exact sciences, whose aim is to "desembaraz[ar] los senderos de la sabiduría" ("clear the paths of knowledge"; *Elogio* 50) by studying "los más escondidos misterios de la Naturaleza" ("Nature's most hidden secrets"; 29). The passage represents nature as a dense and obscure reality that must be tamed, understood, penetrated by observation, then brought under control by reason and planning. Through an enlightened understanding of nature and a reasoned application of practical principles, Jovellanos contends, *estorbos* such as the sterility of Spanish culture can be remedied and nature finally reduced to "un sistema de orden y de unidad antes desconocido" ("a system of order and unity never before seen"; 52). Properly examined and applied, he suggests, enlightened systems of agriculture, colonization, livestock farming, industry, commerce, and other such related *ciencias útiles* can bring all of nature into line with human culture.

Thus Jovellanos's reformed countryside is a vision of enlightenment, a rural space improved by modern methods from "[lo] estéril e ingrato que era" ("the sterile and unfavourable place it was") into "un jardín continuado y lleno de amenidad y abundancia" ("a continuous garden, endlessly pleasing and abundant"; *Informe* §365; my trans.). With his *Informe*, he exhorts the ministers of Carlos IV to expand his predecessors' agrarian reforms, hoping, like Olavide, to triumph over the *estorbos físicos* in the land (§368). Returning to the *despoblados, baldíos,* and *dehesas* that had so concerned reformers before him, Jovellanos proposes to reduce all of Spain's land to serve human interests. The report culminates in a vision of human labour's victory over nature, which brings not just a completed system of exploitation but also a sense of beauty to the landscape:

> Sin duda que a ella [la lucha con la naturaleza] debe la naturaleza grandes mejoras. A doquiera que se vuelva la vista se ve hermoseada y

perfeccionada por la mano del hombre. Por todas partes descuajados los bosques, ahuyentadas las fieras, secos los lagos, acanalados los ríos, refrenados los mares, cultivada toda la superficie de la tierra y llena de alquerías y aldeas y de bellas y magníficas poblaciones, se ofrecen en admirable espectáculo los monumentos de la industria humana y los esfuerzos del interés común para proteger y facilitar el interés individual.

(Who can doubt that nature has been greatly improved by men's struggle with it. Wherever one looks, nature is beautified and perfected by the hand of man. Everywhere the forests are cleared, the beasts driven away, the lakes dry, the rivers channelized, the seas held back, the whole surface of the earth cultivated and full of farmsteads and villages and beautiful and magnificent towns; the admirable spectacle is a monument to human industry and to efforts made in the common interest to protect and facilitate individual interest; *Informe* §407; my trans.)

The appeal of the scene, for Jovellanos, is the degree to which the land has been adapted to human production and consumption: thinned forests and channelled rivers facilitate the movement of goods, a land free of predators is safer for farmers and their herds, and ports sheltered from the open ocean safeguard the nation's shipping capacity. The hardships of nature overcome, beauty is utility in Jovellanos's evaluation of the land (Phillips 103). Everywhere he looks, nature, like a painting, has been beautified by *la mano del hombre*, incorporated into a gendered discourse that justifies manipulating the land for commercial ends.

For historical geographer Luis Urteaga, the passage exemplifies the "antropocentrismo profano" ("profane anthropocentrism") of the Spanish Enlightenment, an optimism born not of faith in divine works but in "una firme creencia en el poder del hombre" ("a firm belief in the power of man"; 31). The image seems prescient against a contemporary Spanish landscape of housing colonies, industrial parks, hydroelectric dams, seaports, highways, and deforested plains, and Merchant argues that such scenes evince the fundamental shift away from conceptions of the earth as a living organism and nurturing mother, prevalent before the Scientific Revolution, to a more modern view of nature as a machine to be perfected (*Death* 2–3). Cultural theorist Raymond Williams has likewise observed that the supreme confidence to adapt nature to human designs was the real invention of eighteenth-century reformism (124). Williams affirms that the specialization of the land into a prospect – that is, a commanding, human-centred view of nature, advanced in writing and painting as well by methods for moving the earth (machines, irrigation systems, industrialized agriculture) – involved a conceptual distancing from the land by its reformist observers, who were pleased, like Jovellanos, by systems of agricultural exploitation that extended into the realm of semiotics and aesthetics (124–7). Jovellanos's image of a countryside perfected by human industry makes the land into a landscape, a discursive artifice that represents nature as though it were devoid of any meaningful agency beyond its relation to human faculties. It is just such a view, which disentangles humanity from the materiality of nature, that Haraway, Barad and others have sought to dismantle as a way to distinguish a wider web of interdependence among the human and non-human agents of nature.

Jovellanos himself seems to understand that organizing Spain's lands for production depends as much on cultivating a *view* of nature as it does on managing the land. Portraying nature as a realm opposed to human activity, he implores the Crown to array human industry and intellect against it:

> Instruya Vuestra Alteza a la clase propietaria en aquellos útiles conocimientos sobre que se apoya la prosperidad de los Estados, y perfeccione en la clase laboriosa el instrumento de su instrucción para que pueda derivar alguna luz de las investigaciones de los sabios. Por último, luche Vuestra Alteza con la naturaleza, y si puede decirse así, oblíguela a ayudar a los esfuerzos del interés individual, o por lo menos a no frustrarlos.

> (Your Highness, instruct the proprietary class in that useful knowledge on which the prosperity of States rests, and perfect the means by which the labouring class may be taught to derive some light from the investigations of the learned. Lastly, Your Highness, struggle against nature, and if it can be said so, compel it to serve individual interests, or at least not to frustrate them; *Informe* §434; my trans.)

The passage furthers a view of human separation from nature as a pretext for domination, the basis of a consciousness that would "compel" nature to conform to the landowners' economic interests. It is an apotheosis of Plumwood's anthropocentric culture: nature's agency and independence are overcome in the struggle to make the landscape coincide with human interests, considered the source of all value ("Decolonizing" 59). Jovellanos may presume the benefits to be universally applicable in service of the common good, but the agricultural agency he articulates is decidedly gendered: prosperity, after all, rests on applied science and institutionalized instruction – all of which were accessible almost exclusively to men, and all of which rendered nature subservient to men's designs.

Jovellanos's manufactured landscape is an admirable spectacle indeed, a panorama whose magnificence and beauty represents the completion of an agricultural project that submits nature to production and consumption in an anthropocentric and androcentric culture. The "admirable espectáculo" both proclaims and legitimizes humankind's separation from nature: gone are the beasts from the fields, nature's *estorbos* overcome, and everywhere production abounds.[16] It is a vision that suggests what French cultural theorist Guy Debord has called the "total justification" of the Spectacle, a projection of power that makes what is only a particular image of existence appear universal and that forces other "directly lived" aspects of reality out of the illusion (12–13). Never mind that the scene *directly* entails the disruption of native soils, watersheds, forests, and ecosystems; nature has been tamed, reimagined according to the expectations of a masculinized human culture. "Acaso no hay una señal menos equívoca de los progresos de [una] civilización, que ... el ejemplo de lo que pueden sobre la naturaleza el arte y el ingenio" ("There is perhaps no surer sign of a civilization's progress than ... the example of what art and ingenuity can achieve over nature"), Jovellanos writes (*Informe* §365; my trans.). For him, the combination of art and ingenuity becomes the measure of a society's progress, able to turn nature from a set of obstacles into a source of human prosperity. Fusing the productive and the visually pleasing into a continuous system separate from nature, Jovellanos describes a spectacle powerful enough to make all of the land a garden.

Witches in the Shadows

Like most gardens, however, Jovellanos's "jardín continuado" scarcely keeps nature at bay (§365). Merchant has observed how Enlightenment agricultural schemes troubled human relationships with the wild, casting unfinished lands as an *other* to be mastered in an effort to "recover Eden" – a prevailing Western narrative that both prompts and justifies "turning wilderness into garden [and] 'female' nature into civilized society" (*Reinventing* 2–3). That trouble lingers in Jovellanos's texts; hopeful as his vision of agriculture may be, his finished lands are haunted by the memory of witches in Barahona and the circle of rural women whose customs Goya portrays as demonic and profane, or at least, ridiculously freakish. Probing the limits of reforms like the ones Jovellanos proposes, Merchant relates the persistence of witches to the larger project of subduing nature, in which "disorderly women" come to be associated with the unruliness of the wild; the witch, she argues, emerges as a symbol of nature's potential for violence, associated with storms, illness, crop failure, and, as killers of infants, threats to human reproduction (*Death* 127). Gathering in the shadows as the light of reason spreads across the landscape, witches like Goya's, frightful women in the wilderness, represent so many more *estorbos* to be overcome by Enlightenment cultural reform.[17]

An indication of the link between wild, unfinished nature and the disruptive feminine in Jovellanos's Spain rises in the background of Goya's *El aquelarre*, where the bleak, moonlit mountains show no signs of cultivation. The women gathered on this plain are hardly the *labradores* that Jovellanos had envisioned amid the manufactured agricultural landscapes of the *Informe*, delighting in their dances and picnics (*Informe* § 429). Instead, they conjure a sense of dread lurking in the *maleza*. Jovellanos himself acknowledges the difficulty of bringing nature under control. While he exhorts students at the opening of the Real Instituto Asturiano to study agriculture – "aquella arte … que más ennoblece y perfecciona la naturaleza" ("that art … that most ennobles and perfects nature"; "Oración" 324) – he acknowledges that the light of reason has extended only so far: "a la luz de esta antorcha se fueron disipando poco a poco los seres monstruosos, los errores groseros y las fábulas absurdas que había forjado el interés combinado con la ignorancia" ("little by little, the light of this torch has driven away the monstrous beings, the crude errors, and the absurd fables forged by selfishness and ignorance"), but beyond the torchlight there remain "países ignorados y desiertos, pueblos condenados a oscuridad e infortunio" ("remote and deserted regions, communities condemned to darkness and misfortune"; Jovellanos, "Discurso" 326).[18] In the reformer's mind, where reason fails to reach is a realm of superstition, error, ignorance, and myth. It is also, significantly, a wilderness.

Jovellanos's monsters, like the witches of Goya's painting or the fields of Barahona, need not exist to be real. Spanish anthropologist Julio Caro Baroja observes that anxieties around witchcraft arise in relation to social structures as much as they do to metaphysical or religious concepts (24–5). Thus while a resurgence of interest in witches in Jovellanos's time may be seen as a way to mock the obscurantism of the *ancien régime* in an age of reason (see Andioc; Helman, *Jovellanos* 157–81 and "Younger Moratín"), their recurrence also suggests the persistence of customs, beliefs, and relationships to space, especially in regions that have resisted incorporation into androcentric colonizing systems. Merchant's reasoning extends Caro Baroja's point, determining that representations of witches become prevalent when "a new experimental method designed to constrain nature and probe into her secrets would improve and 'civilize' society" (*Death* 148). The civilizing efforts of

Jovellanos and his contemporaries suggest just such a method, what Merchant describes as "new managerial modes of order and power" (148), employed to increase agriculture, and by extension, to incorporate the rural realm into an idealized scheme of innocent pastimes and *felicidad*. In a context in which only the productive is considered valuable, figures that trouble it must be flushed out of the darkness to be overcome, confined to art hung on landowners' walls or reduced to a memory on the Sorian plain.

The witches of Goya and Jovellanos serve mainly a symbolic function, important less as human figures than for the practices, beliefs, and fears with which they are associated. In fact, women of all stripes hampered the reformists' plans. The founding decree of the Sierra Morena project stipulates that the main work of clearing the fields and building the environment for habitation and production be reserved for men; considered unfit for landwork, mothers and children were to be kept in nearby towns and looked after by agents of the Crown until the land had been made habitable (*Real Cédula* 6). Treating women's work of raising children as subordinate to men's efforts to tame nature, the decree demonstrates the open, unquestioned paternalism of the regime.

That paternalism is further sustained in the *Elogio*, the last part of which Jovellanos dedicates to women. After praising the reforms of Carlos III and his ministers, he turns to their counterparts, the "ilustres compañeras" and "señoras asociadas" of the work's full title.[19] What use is knowledge without the benevolence and rectitude of a woman's heart? he asks: "Sí, ilustres compañeras, sí, y os lo aseguro, y la voz del Defensor de los derechos de vuestro sexo no debe seros sospechoso: yo os lo repito: a vosotras toca formar el corazón de los ciudadanos" ("Yes, illustrious female companions, yes, I assure you, and let the voice of your defender be clear: I repeat to you: it is you who must form our citizens' hearts"; *Elogio* 54). With imperious benevolence, Jovellanos assures his female audience that what he considers their natural virtues – simplicity, motivation, compassion, and generosity – are honourably placed in the service of men. A woman's work, he claims, is to prepare their sons and husbands to receive the light of reason and become builders of the nation (55–6). High as the last words of the *Elogio* soar, they ultimately assure the subordination of women to men and the struggle to adapt nature to the nation's ends.

There is almost no mention of women in the *Informe*, and what little there is tends to ally female figures with obstacles to agricultural reform. Jovellanos is dismayed, for example, that labourers do not receive the same fiscal exemptions as sheep and horse breeders, whose profession he considers "hija o criada" ("daughters or maidservants") of agriculture – secondary or subservient to it; even more unjust, then, that the Crown treats livestock breeding as agriculture's "madre y señora" ("mother and lady"; *Informe* §329), unwisely protecting it in the face of reform. In either case, female figures symbolize the government's flawed positions. Elsewhere, in support of an argument for enclosures to protect farmers' fields, Jovellanos alludes to the threat of marauding pests, which includes such dangers as transhumant herds, travellers, "holgazanes y perezosos" ("the lazy and the idle"), and, he adds, women, quoting sixteenth-century agronomist Gabriel Alonso de Herrera's assertion that should women come across an unfenced field of garbanzos they are sure to wreak more havoc than a hailstorm (§25). Whatever pale humour aside, the comment's unabashed misogyny recalls an association of women with "violence, storms … and general chaos" (Merchant, *Death* 3), and serves a reminder of the larger point that women have little role to play in the *Informe's* plans.

Such references punctuate a larger and more problematic association between control of women and agriculture in Jovellanos's work. Citing the long identification of nature, and especially the earth, with a nurturing mother who provided for human needs as a result of their labour, Merchant notes a significant change in depictions of nature as human attitudes became more exploitative in an age of commercialization and technological advance (*Death* 2). Jovellanos's eighteenth-century imagery reflects just such a change. Identifying agriculture as "madre de la inocencia, del honesto trabajo" ("the mother of innocence and honest work"), he characterizes the earth less as a resource to be preserved than one to be exploited through human industry, a source of public wealth that offers up profits ("ventajas") to those who would apply their skills and learning to work the land in their interest (*Informe* §321–2). The learning that Jovellanos promotes relies on applied sciences such as those taught to *alumnos* (male students) in the Real Instituto Asturiano that he directed, disciplines designed to perfect the nation's "instrumentos, máquinas, economía y cálculos" ("instruments, machines, economy and calculations") to advance the study of nature (§343).[20] Specifying what that study entails, Jovellanos represents nature as a body to be explored, its fertility maximized, its "inmensos tesoros" ("immense treasures") discovered and obtained. Perhaps not surprisingly, he calls nature the "gran madre" ("great mother"), a source of reproductive prosperity in an age when women were celebrated as givers of sons (§342).

The earth appears as mother again in Jovellanos's inaugural address at the Instituto Asturiano:

> Fijad vuestra atención en la tierra, en esta madre universal, cuya juventud se renueva con la actual revolución de los cielos, y estudiad a todas horas aquella virtud maravillosa de fomentar las semillas que se confían a su seno, y de asegurar en su reproducción la multiplicación y el consuelo del género humano. Y cuando tan útiles y preciosos dones como presenta a vuestra vista no saciasen vuestros deseos, abrid por fin sus entrañas, y descubriréis nuevas fuentes de riqueza y prosperidad.

> (Focus your attention on the earth, on the universal mother, whose youth is renewed with each turn of the heavens, and dedicate yourself tirelessly to the high virtue of studying of how best to nurture the seeds that have been entrusted to her womb and to ensure through their reproduction the growth and consolation of mankind. And when the useful and precious gifts that she presents do not satisfy your desires, open her womb, and you will discover new sources of wealth and prosperity; "Oración" 324)

It is a provocative image, suggesting the allure of relations with an ever-youthful partner able to nurture future generations through the seeds planted in her womb (with the unsettling vision of a mother's belly opened to reveal what may be productively extracted). "One does not readily slay a mother, dig into her entrails for gold to mutilate her body," Merchant notes, until in an age of increasing commercial exploitation, when the earth comes to be seen no longer as a living, nurturing organism but rather a supply to be mined (*Death* 3). Such imagery, she argues, which traded biological identifications with the earth for depictions of nature as a source of riches, served as "cultural sanctions for the denudation of nature" (2). Similar denuding imagery extended beyond agriculture to a broader vision of scientific practice at the time, including medicine. The image of a female body revealed recalls some of the wax anatomical models that had begun to appear around Europe in Jovellanos's time, figures such as the *Anatomical Venus*, displayed at the Specola museum in Florence beginning in 1775, whose youthful mien and rapturous, swooning expression contrast with her chest and abdomen opened to reveal her organs splayed across the fainting couch on which she lies. For artist and curator Joanna Ebenstein, such models, ostensibly created to teach human anatomy, communicated an "undercurrent of passive eroticism in the inert female body," a fascination that played on notions of voyeurism, desire, and possession related to medical exploration (122). Science and art historian Ludmilla

Jordanova recognizes in such invitations to peel back the layers of the female body "shared metaphors ... of penetration and unveiling, which are equally apt in a sexual and an intellectual context," a perspective that subjects women and their reproductive capabilities to possession and management (55). Jovellanos's exaltation of historical geography folds the earth into just such a context, presenting a feminized model of cultivation to arouse his students' desires.

Jovellanos is not alone in linking agriculture to sex. In a letter to his friend Jovellanos, Francisco de Cabarrús, former minister and member of the Sociedad Matritense de Amigos del País, imbues his commentary on agriculture with an even more rapacious, masculinized eroticism. Commending Jovellanos's "excelente proyecto de ley Agraria" ("excellent project on Agrarian law"; Cabarrús 27), Cabarrús comments that the "especie de resistencia" ("kind of resistance") that nature puts up to the work of the labourer ("opone al trabajo") is hardly an obstacle; quite the contrary, "es más bien incentivo á la actividad que estorbo, y que un poeta compararía con otra especie de blanda resistencia, origen de los mas puros y deliciosos placeres" ("it is more of an incentive than a deterrent, something that a poet might compare with that other sort of mild resistance that produces the purest and most delightful pleasures"; 28). An allusion to amorous poetry barely veils the passage's characterization of farming as an invitation to sex with a mildly resistant partner, one whose agency is little more than an enticement to eventual domination. The implication is clear: for Cabarrús and a prominent circle of eighteenth-century reformers in Spain, the earth has offered herself up for man's taking, and whatever resistance or agency that she may give is expected to be overcome.

Thus the admirable spectacle that Jovellanos regards as man's triumph over nature entails a command over women, as well. His persistently gendered discourse reinforces the association of artistic and economic production with men, indicating a conceptual framework that, as Warren has observed, "sanctions the twin dominations of nature and women" by placing both under the same patriarchal hand (22). To see nature everywhere "beautified and perfected by the hand of man" is to link women and the earth as subordinate figures, impediments to be overcome, bodies to be conquered, even ravished, and exploited for their productiveness (Jovellanos, *Informe* §407).

Jovellanos's *Informe*, emblematic of the range of Enlightenment reforms it represented, thus helped alter the landscape of modern Spain, opening the way for developers to "produce their own nature," as Williams puts it (122), disposing it to the point of view of production and consumption. For Merchant, that vision, as it is fulfilled around Europe, marks a turning point in the treatment of women and the earth, entwining both into a conceptual framework that prefers passivity and control in the spheres of production and reproduction (*Death* 149). It is a vision, ultimately, of what Warren has identified as an oppressive patriarchal conceptual framework, a socially constructed set of beliefs, values, attitudes, and assumptions that serves to explain, justify, and maintain relationships of domination and subordination (20). When the land is identified with women, as Jovellanos and his circle maintain, that oppression extends to the land itself. Jovellanos need disdain neither women nor nature for the framework to hold; indeed, he celebrates both as sources of happiness (*felicidad*) and as makers of men – men who, controlling both, deem themselves sole benefactors of the nation (*Elogio* 56). Turning his gaze from the *vosotras* of the *Elogio* to a land rid of beasts and the fields cleared of witches, he seems pleased by the prospects. "Admirable" as the spectacle may seem, however, figures in the *maleza* reveal it to be ultimately a spectacle of domination.

NOTES

1 Unless otherwise noted, translations from Spanish to English are my own. Enlightenment scholar Edith Helman observes that references to the *campos de Barahona* were something of a metonym for witches' Sabbaths among Spanish enlightenment writers including Moratín, Cean Bermúdez, and Cadalso (*Jovellanos y Goya* 167–8). The entry for *Barahona* in Covarrubias's *Tesoro de la Lengua Castellana* (1611) notes that "en este campo ay fama juntarse los brujos, y sus brujas a sus abominaciones" ("on these fields male and female witches are said to gather to perform their abominations"), although he refutes that reputation: "hablilla es, no ay que darle crédito" ("it is hearsay, not to be believed"; 120).
2 Helman gives a detailed account of the period of persecution that led to Jovellanos's imprisonment in *Jovellanos y Goya* (33–69).
3 *El aquelarre* was one of a six paintings, all related to witches, that the duke and duchess of Alba bought from Goya in 1798 to decorate their summer palace in the countryside outside Madrid (Helman, *Jovellanos y Goya* 168).
4 Jovellanos was an admirer of Goya's work; art historian Janis Tomlinson notes that Goya is mentioned eight times in Jovellanos's diaries between 1793 and 1796 (90). Their paths also crossed at court: Jovellanos's appointment as Minister of Grace and Justice prompted Goya, portraitist of the court of Carlos IV (1708–1808), to paint a well-known portrait of him at his desk, looking wistfully towards the viewer, and it was Jovellanos who engaged Goya to paint the frescoes at the San Antonio de la Florida Chapel (Helman, *Jovellanos y Goya* 55).

5 Unless otherwise noted, English translations of the *Informe* in this text are by Pumarada Cruz. Section numbers in the English version correspond to the Spanish edition.

6 In his chapter for this collection, Óscar Iván Useche examines how such struggles persisted in generations that followed, particularly during the Regenerationist movement post-1898, when technological advancements came to reflect nationwide intellectual anxieties about loss of human control over beyond-human nature.

7 The Sociedad de los Amigos del País was a private association established by Carlos III to "promover la agricultura, industria y oficios" ("promote agriculture, industry, and the trades"; *Gaceta* 444). Not unlike a modern think tank, the Sociedad prepared research and educational initiatives to aid the development of policy.

8 A consultation of the *Nuevo tesoro lexicográfico de la lengua española* (*NTLLE*), an online database containing Spanish dictionaries from the fifteenth to the twentieth centuries, shows that the definition of *maleza* in the *Diccionario de la Real Academia Española* (*DRAE*) varies little between 1780, 1783, and 1791 (which only modernizes the original orthography of 1734): "la copia y abundancia de hierbas silvestres, y espinas que embarazan el paso de algún sitio, y la hacen infructífero" ("the profusion and abundance of wild plants, and thorns that make passage difficult, and render the land unfruitful"); the Spanish term bears scant etymological relationship to the Latin equivalent that the *DRAE* cites: *Silva, nemus vepribus, arbustisque intricatum*. Nuñez de Taboada's definition in 1825 distinguishes between weeds and thickets. Grammarian Vicente Salvá (1846) defines *maleza* as "yerbas malas que perjudican a los sembrados" ("weeds that harm crops"), while the 1787 dictionary of Esteban Terreros y Pando does not include a moral commentary in the definition ("Maleza").

9 Margaret Marek analyses the enduring impact of such water control projects in her chapter for *Beyond Human* on the damming of the Esla River in León, an engineering feat whose disruptions ranged from literary expression of lovesickness in Jorge de Montemayor's sixteenth-century pastoral *La Diana* to the trauma experienced by residents whose villages were submerged in the post-Franco era for the construction of the Riaño Reservoir.

10 Urbanist Ramón Fernández Durán points out the historical difficulties of sustaining centres of population and agricultural activity on Spain's vast interior plain, where water resources were relatively scarce and soils poor compared to "la España húmeda" ("wet Spain"), along the Peninsula's northern coast and its major river valleys (Naredo and Parra 55).

11 Economic researchers Jeffrey Nugent and Nicolás Sánchez dispute claims of the Mesta's inefficiency, arguing instead that the privileges the society

enjoyed helped rather than hindered the allocation of resources in a time of conflict between pastoral and agricultural interests.

12 The Crown issued a *Real Cédula* for the establishment of *Nuevas Poblaciones* ("New Settlements") in the Sierra Morena in 1767, appointing Olavide as the project's superintendent. D. Juan Gaspar de Turriegel was placed in charge of recruiting settlers, most of them from German and Flemish territories, to cultivate lands newly set aside for colonization.

13 Architectural historian Carlos Sambricio examines Olavide's ideas on colonizing in more detail as part of his study of utopian town-planning projects in eighteenth-century Spain.

14 Like Ondeano, Fernándo González Menchaca, the provincial governor of Jaén, laments the high risk and cost of traversing the mountainous regions of northern Andalucía (Ruiz González and Sena Medina 23). Lemaur argues that his plan to excavate and reshape lands in the area are worth the Crown's investment, given the "utilidades inmensas" ("immense utility") of providing agricultural access to what he considers "terreno… bueno y capaz de toda cultura" ("good terrain, suitable for all manner of cultivation") throughout the Sierra Morena (qtd. 25–6).

15 Exploring how "entanglements" of matter, meaning, and agency constitute existence, Barad observes that "to be entangled is not simply to be intertwined with another as in the joining of separate entities, but to lack an independent, self-contained existence" (ix). The comment resonates with Haraway's concept of *natureculture*, which likewise affirms the entanglements of human and non-human existence "against the mistake of, first, taking provisional and local category abstractions like 'nature' and 'culture' for the world and, second, mistaking potent consequences to be pre-existing foundations" (Haraway 6).

16 Environmental historian José Manuel Naredo offers a sobering outline of the long-term ecological repercussions of agrarian reform in Spain, which links modernization to desertification, deforestation, erosion, and species destruction stemming from the advent of industrialized agriculture and continuing to this day.

17 In the *Elogio de Carlos III*, Jovellanos characterizes reforms as a light, or "luz," that "se recoge de todos los ángulos de la tierra [y que] se reúne, se extiende, y muy presto bañará todo nuestro horizonte" ("gathers from every corner of the earth, blending and spreading until soon it will bathe our horizon completely"; 52).

18 Jovellanos encountered such regions himself in his travels around Spain, noting in his diary occasional stops to marvel at remote and barren landscapes, which, Hispanist Ana Rueda observes, provoked his anxiety as a rational thinker (493; see also Phillips 102).

19 The full title reads: *Elogio de Carlos Tercero. Leido á la Real Sociedad de Madrid por el socio d. Gaspar Melchor de Jovellanos, en la Junta plena del sábado 8 de Noviembre de 1788, con asistencia de las señoras asociadas.*
20 Title 1, Chapter 10 of the Real Instituto Asturiano's charter outlines the requirements that *alumnos* must meet to be admitted. Female students (*alumnas*) are not mentioned (Jovellanos, "Ordenanza" 403).

WORKS CITED AND CONSULTED

Andioc, René. "Las reediciones del Auto de fe de Logroño en vida de Moratín." *Anales de la literatura española*, no. 3, 1984, pp. 11–45.

Avilés Fernández, Miguel. "Carlos III y las 'nuevas poblaciones." Introduction. *Carlos III y las "nuevas poblaciones,"* edited by Miguel Avilés Fernández et al., vol. 1, Servicio de Publicaciones de la Universidad de Córdoba, 1988.

Barad, Karen. *Meeting the Universe Halfway: Quantum Physics and the Entanglement of Matter and Meaning.* Duke UP, 2007.

Cabarrús, Francisco. *Cartas del conde de Cabarrús al señor D. Gaspar de Jovellanos, sobre los obstáculos que la naturaleza, la opinión y las leyes oponen a la felicidad pública.* Imprenta de Don Pedro Roca, 1808.

Caro Baroja, Julio. *Las brujas y su mundo.* 3rd ed., Alianza Editorial, 2015. El libro de bolsillo Ciencias sociales 57.

Caso González, José Miguel, et al. *Jovellanos y la naturaleza.* Fundación Foro Jovellanos del Principiado de Asturias, 2006.

Corredera, José. "Labouring Horizons: Passions and Interests in Jovellanos' *Ley Agraria.*" *Dieciocho: Hispanic Enlightenment*, vol. 38, no. 2, 2015, pp. 267–90.

Covarrubias y Orozco, Sebastián de. *Tesoro de la lengua castellana o española.* Luis Sánchez, 1611.

Debord, Guy. *The Society of the Spectacle.* Translated by Donald Nicholson-Smith, Zone Books, 1995.

Ebenstein, Joanna. *The Anatomical Venus: Wax, God, Death and the Ecstatic.* Distributed Art, 2016.

Frost, Daniel. *Cultivating Madrid: Public Space and Middle-Class Culture in the Spanish Capital, 1833–1890.* Bucknell UP, 2008.

Gaceta de Madrid, vol. 50, 12 Dec. 1775, p. 444, https://www.boe.es/datos /pdfs/BOE//1775/050/A00444-00444.pdf.

Haraway, Donna. *The Companion Species Manifesto: Dogs, People, and Significant Otherness.* Prickly Paradigm, 2003.

Helman, Edith. *Jovellanos y Goya.* Taurus, 1970. Persiles 39.

Helman, Edith. "The Younger Moratín and Goya: On Duendes and Brujas." *Hispanic Review*, vol. 27, no. 1, 1959, pp. 103–22. JSTOR, https://doi.org /10.2307/470415.

Jordanova, Ludmilla. *Sexual Visions: Images of Gender in Science and Medicine between the Eighteenth and Twentieth Centuries.* U of Wisconsin P, 1989.

Jovellanos, Gaspar Melchor de. "De vuelta del destierro." *Escritos inéditos de Jovellanos,* edited by Julio Somoza de Montsoriu, Arte y letras, 1891, pp. 89–135. Biblioteca clásica española.

Jovellanos, Gaspar Melchor de. "Discurso sobre el estudio de la Geografía Histórica." *Obras publicadas é inéditas,* vol. 1, pp. 325–9.

Jovellanos, Gaspar Melchor de. *Elogio de Carlos Tercero. Leido á la Real Sociedad de Madrid por el socio d. Gaspar Melchor de Jovellanos, en la Junta plena del sábado 8 de Noviembre de 1788, con asistencia de las señoras asociadas.* Imprenta de Viuda de la Ibarra, 1789.

Jovellanos, Gaspar Melchor de. *Informe de la Sociedad Económica de Madrid al Real y Supremo Consejo de Castilla en el expediente de ley agraria.* Imprenta de Miguel Domingo, 1814. *Hathitrust Digital Library,* https://hdl.handle .net/2027/ucm.5325086968.

Jovellanos, Gaspar Melchor de. *Obras publicadas é inéditas de Don Gaspar Melchor de Jovellanos, colección hecha é ilustrada.* Edited by Cándido Nocedal, Rivadeneyra, 1858–9. 2 vols. Biblioteca de autores espanoles.

Jovellanos, Gaspar Melchor de. "Oración inaugural a la apertura del Real Instituto Asturiano." *Obras publicadas é inéditas,* vol. 1, pp. 318–24.

Jovellanos, Gaspar Melchor de. "Ordenanza para el Real Instituto Asturiano [Instrucción u ordenanza para la nueva escuela de matemáticas, física, química, mineralogía y náutica …]." *Obras publicadas é inéditas,* vol. 2, pp. 399–420.

Llombart, Vicent. "El *Informe de la ley agraria* y su autor, en la historia del pensamiento económico." *Reformas y políticas agrarias en la historia de España (De la Ilustración al primer franquismo),* edited by Ángel García Sanz and Jesús Sanz Fernández, Ministerio de Agricultura, Pesca y Alimentación, Secretaría General Técnica, 1996, pp. 105–59.

"Maleza." *Nuevo tesoro lexicográfico de la lengua española (NTLLE),* 2004, https://apps.rae.es/ntlle/SrvltGUISalirNtlle.

Merchant, Carolyn. *The Death of Nature: Women, Ecology, and the Scientific Revolution.* Harper & Row, 1980.

Merchant, Carolyn. *Reinventing Eden: The Fate of Nature in Western Culture.* Routledge, 2003.

Naredo, José Manuel. "La modernización de la agricultura española y sus repercusiones ecológicas." *Naturaleza transformada: Estudios de historia ambiental en España,* edited by Manuel González de Molina and Joan Martínez Alier, Icaria, 2001, pp. 55–86.

Naredo, José Manuel, and Fernando Parra. *Situación diferencial de los recursos naturales españoles.* Fundación César Manrique, 2002.

Nugent, Jeffrey B., and Nicolás Sánchez. "The Efficiency of the Mesta: A Parable." *Explorations in Economic History*, vol. 26, no. 3, 1989, pp. 261–84. *ScienceDirect*, https://doi.org/10.1016/0014-4983(89)90022-3.

Phillips, Pamela. "Enlightening Nature: An Ecocritical Reading of Eighteenth-Century Spanish Literature." *Hispanic Ecocriticism*, edited by José Manuel Marrero Henríquez, Peter Lang, 2019, pp. 93–112.

Plumwood, Val. "Decolonizing Relationships with Nature." *Decolonizing Nature: Strategies for Conservation in a Post-colonial Era*, edited by William M. Adams and Martin Mulligan, Earthscan, 2001, pp. 51–78.

Plumwood, Val. "Nature as Agency and the Prospects for a Progressive Naturalism." *Capitalism Nature Socialism*, vol. 12, no. 4, 2001, pp. 3–32. *Taylor & Francis Online*, https://doi.org/10.1080/104557501101245225.

Ponz, Antonio. *Viaje de España, en que se da noticia de las cosas más apreciables, y dignas de saberse, que hay en ella*. 3rd ed., vol. 16, viuda de D. Joaquín Ibarra, 1791.

Pumarada Cruz, Yesenia, translator. *Report on the Agrarian Law (1795) and Other Writings*. By Gaspar Melchor de Jovellanos, edited by Gabriel Paquette and Álvaro Caso Bello, Kindle ed., Anthem, 2016.

Real Cédula de su Magestad, que contiene la Instrucción, y fuero de población, que se debe observar en las que se formen de nuevo en la Sierramorena con naturales y estranjeros Católicos. Oficina de Don Antonio Sanz, 1767. HathiTrust Digital Library, https://hdl.handle.net/2027/ucm.5324346026.

Rueda, Ana. "Jovellanos en sus escritos íntimos: El paisaje y la emoción estética de 'lo sublime.'" *Revista de Literatura*, vol. 68, no. 136, 2006, pp. 489–502, https://doi.org/10.3989/revliteratura.2006.v68.i136.17.

Ruiz González, Juan Enrique, and Guillermo Sena Medina. "Carlos Lemaur y el Camino de Despeñaperros." *Carlos III y las "nuevas poblaciones,"* edited by Miguel Avilés Fernández et al., Servicio de Publicaciones de la Universidad, 1988, pp. 23–42.

Sambricio, Carlos. "*Sinapia*: Utopia, Territory and City at the End of the Eighteenth Century." *Views on Eighteenth Century Culture: Design, Books and Ideas*, edited by Leonor Ferrão and Luís Manuel A.V. Bernardo, Cambridge Scholars, 2015, pp. 44–77.

Smith, Adam. Wealth of Nations. [1776]. *Standard EBooks*, https://standarde books.org/ebooks/adam-smith/the-wealth-of-nations.

Tomlinson, Janis A. *Goya in the Twilight of Enlightenment*. Yale UP, 1992.

Urteaga, Luis. "Explotación y conservación de la naturaleza en el pensamiento ilustrado." *Geocrítica*, no. 50, 1984, pp. 7–46.

Warren, Karen J. "Ecological Feminist Philosophies: An Overview of the Issues." *Ecological Feminist Philosophies*, edited by Karen J. Warren, Indiana UP, 1996, pp. ix–xxvi.

Williams, Raymond. *The Country and the City*. Oxford UP, 1973.

Chapter Five

Plant, Animal, and Human Consciousness in Julio Llamazares's *Luna de lobos*

OLGA COLBERT

Luna de lobos, the 1985 novel by Spanish author Julio Llamazares, presents a universe in which humans, plants, and non-human animals live in a highly integrated ecosystem. The novel delineates two seemingly opposite processes: the humanization of nature, resulting in highly conscious plants and animals, and the inverse dehumanization of the novel's human characters. The story follows the survival of four Republican soldiers during and after the Spanish Civil War (1936–9) in the cold mountains of northern Spain. They have been separated from their unit after the destruction of the northern front by Francoist military forces and are forced to hide with little support. For years after the war is lost, these antifascist fighters are hunted down relentlessly by the rural police while their families are watched, harassed, and tortured. Their existence is one of penury and basic survival and they must adapt to their natural environment and make difficult moral choices in order to live another day. While the novel's language includes abundant conventional rhetorical figures to present sentient plants and animals, my analysis will establish correlations between the representation of cognitive functions of plants and animals in *Luna de lobos* and current science. I draw from the emerging field of plant cognition, particularly the work of Daniel Chamovitz, Paco Calvo, and Monica Gagliano, and studies on animal cognition by Frans de Waal, Brian Hare, and Temple Grandin to show that the novel highlights the interconnectedness among all living beings: in the context of a civil war, the soldiers find stronger kinship with non-human animals and plants than with other humans. They begin to share a habitat as well as sensory abilities and circadian rhythms with non-human animals. Consequently, hierarchical notions that situate humans above non-human animals begin to break down. The Republican maquis, as those anti-fascist guerrillas hiding in the mountains were called, also form strong kinship with plants and plant formations, which are capable of feeling sensations and of acting with agency. As borders and hierarchies among living beings dissipate, *Luna de lobos* presents a panpsychic universe, a world in which consciousness may be a fundamental property of reality.

Julio Llamazares's novelistic *oeuvre* shows a strong ecological sensibility. While addressing the plight of humanity, whether empathizing with hard-working coal miners in *Escenas de cine mudo* or defeated soldiers in *Luna de lobos*, his stories depict liminal natural spaces shared with humans, including mining boomtowns in the mountains of León or the villages flooded by dams during Franco's industrialization. Llamazares is concerned with disappearance. In his stories, nature reclaims its place from human civilization and resists its erasure resulting from unchecked technological progress and economic exploitation. The flooding, or burial by water, of Vegamián, Llamazares's birthplace, may well have constituted a foundational trauma for the author, whose characters consistently inhabit worlds on the verge of extinction, like the last inhabitant of an abandoned village in *La lluvia amarilla*, the displaced families from flooded towns in *Distintas formas de mirar el agua*, or the last holdout anti-Francoist soldiers in *Luna de lobos*.

Through similes and prosopopoeia, nature in *Luna de lobos* is shown to possess human-like qualities. It could be argued that this plays into an anthropocentric view of nature's worth as proportional to its humanness, and that the humanization of nature somehow elevates it to human-like value. This is not, however, the way these tropes function in this novel, which engages more deeply with non-human consciousness. Natural elements and processes appear highly animated from the novel's first pages, as the flames from a fire "brotan alegres y amorosas" ("spring up, warm and cheerful") while they rise to the rain's encounter (11, 18).[1] The flames feel emotion while the verb "brotan" indicates that they sprout from the main fire in a way that connects natural elements, plants, and indirectly humans. As with the sentient and purposeful behaviour of the fire, an analysis of flora in *Luna de lobos* reveals a plant consciousness that catalyses interconnectivity among human and (other) non-human beings in the text. My reading of plant and animal animation through cognition science is a twenty-first-century revision of earlier ways of perceiving nature anthropomorphically and androcentrically. It should be noted that most of the research on non-human consciousness included in this essay was completed many years after the publication of Llamazares's novel in 1985, so his strong environmental sensitivity predates the scientific research that confirmed many of his intuitions. In contrast, *The Overstory* (2018), a magnificent novel by Richard Powers that incorporates non-human entities as true characters with agency and a narrative arch, clearly dialogues with current scientific discoveries on non-human consciousness.[2]

The field of plant cognition has achieved some scholarly notoriety in recent years. Daniel Chamovitz, a plant geneticist and author of *What a Plant Knows: A Field Guide to the Senses* (2012), laments the little attention that we pay to plants' sophisticated mechanisms, which allow them to modulate their growth in response to ever-changing conditions. He does not claim that plants are able to think or move in the traditional sense, since they don't have a central nervous system, neurones, or a brain. However, he claims that plants "monitor their visual environment" (9), emit and sense odours (27), know when they are being touched (49), and even perceive sounds (72).

In Llamazares's novel, plants possess a variety of cognitive capabilities: they feel pain, have sentience, and communicate. One of the characters compares his voice to a vegetal moan: "Mi voz apenas era como un gemido vegetal entre las zarzas" ("My voice was nothing but a vegetal whimper among the brambles"), suggesting vegetal sounds as a means of communication (20; my trans.). In *The Hidden Life of Trees*, German forester Peter Wohlleben discusses the work of the Swiss researchers who have proven that plants emit a sharp sound of distress when lacking water: "when trees are really thirsty, they begin to scream" (48).[3] The sound is produced by "vibrations [that] occur in the trunk when the flow of water from the roots to the leaves is interrupted" (48). In their article "Trees: Rendering Ecophysiological Processes Audible," sound artist, researcher, and composer Marcus Maeder and tree scientist Roman Zweifel build on the work of plant physiologists to show that these sounds are ultrasonic and therefore inaudible to the human ear. The experiments deconstruct anthropocentric evaluations of plants as inferior since the inadequacy of the human ear is what prevents it from hearing these sounds.

Reflecting on their 2012 sound installation entitled "Downy Oak: A Prototype of a Spatial Audio Sonification System," Maeder and Zweifel highlight the importance of gathering ecophysiological data as a method to research climate change by determining "increasing temperature and consequently drought stress" in plant life ("Downy Oak" 143). Consequently, being able to listen to the sounds that plants make is useful in preserving the planet's ecosystems. Research at the University of Tel Aviv on tomato and tobacco plants similarly shows that plants stressed by drought "may emit ultrasonic squeals" (Lanese), which can be measured with microphones located ten centimetres away (Vaughan). Therefore, insects may be able to listen to those ultrasonic emittances and make decisions accordingly (Khait et al.). More chilling is the rate of repetition of the sounds: while unstressed plants produced fewer than one sound per hour on average, "drought-stressed tomato plants made 35 sounds an hour, while tobacco plants made 11." This research demonstrates the richness of sensory perception in the vegetal realm, highlighting the artificiality of the boundaries commonly used to separate animals from plants.

In *Luna de lobos*, when plants suffer aggression from humans or elements of nature, such as the wind, they experience pain. The narrative voice employs aggressive language to characterize the wind as a destructive force that not only shakes bushes and trees but violently whips them: "Afuera, el cierzo continúa azotando con violencia los brezos y los robles" ("Outside, the *cierzo* wind continues to violently whip the brambles and the oak trees"; 14; my trans.). As a result of this interaction, the beech trees feel pain as their leaves are severed from their sore branches: "El cierzo … se enredó entre las ramas doloridas de los árboles y desgajó de cuajo las últimas hojas del otoño" ("The cold *cierzo* wind … wraps itself around the trees' sore branches and tears off the last autumn leaves"; 11, 17). On another occasion, plants suffer violence at the hands of humans: Gildo and Juan "golpean con sus gruesas botas la hierba mojada, tratando de ahuyentar el frío" ("stomp their thick boots on the wet grass, trying to shake off the cold"; 14, 21). While the grass is not specifically said to experience pain, the fighters' stomping forcefully upon it suggests that plants must constantly respond sensitively to their surroundings. Chamovitz's fascinating work on plants' reactions to touch and pain has confirmed that plants perceive tactile sensations. He asserts that when a single tomato leaf is wounded, the rest of the leaves on the plant respond, including through the transcription of proteinase inhibitor genes in the intact leaves (68). Jim Whelan of the La Trobe Institute for Agriculture and Food has likewise found that even the slightest touch produces a genetic response in the plant. Ten per cent of a plant's genome changes within thirty minutes of being touched, and its growth is compromised if repeated touching occurs. One reason may be the perception by the plant of a threat, such as when insects land on its leaves. Another explanation for the retarded growth response may be the optimization of sunlight, which also occurs when plants touch one another (La Trobe University).

Beyond a genetic response to touch, the question remains whether plants actually experience pain. Chamovitz opines that plants perceive sensations but do not have subjective experience; therefore, and without a brain, they cannot be said to feel pain (66).[4] He claims, however, that plants are "aware" (137). While awareness is often employed synonymously with consciousness or conscious experience, Chamovitz simply means that plants are aware of sensations, which include "visual environment," "aromas," "touch," and "gravity" (137). In his discussion of pain, Chamovitz uses a broad definition that includes both the physical sensation (intense and unpleasant) and the subjective experience that usually accompanies it, what others call suffering. If a narrower definition of pain were to be applied, however, one that referred only to physical sensations, then the experiments on stressed plants described above would seem to indicate that plants do in fact experience pain.[5] Pertinently, Chamovitz asserts that plants are aware of their past, meaning "they remember past infections and the conditions they've weathered and then modify their current physiology based on these memories" (137–8). This argument contradicts his narrow view of plant consciousness and suggests that plant experience is richer than admitted, even if vegetal entities do not have brains.

Biologists and philosophers within Western academia debate the essential characteristics of consciousness. Contradicting the traditional materialist view, philosopher Paco Calvo asserts that unlike biologists who approach plants as an object, philosophers do so as a subject and ask different types of questions relating, for instance, to agency ("Entrevista").[6] Looking at agency from a cognitive science standpoint, science historian Jessica Riskin, linguists Noam Chomsky and Massimo Piattelli-Palmarini, and physician Fernando Martínez argue that while consciousness is not directly observable, "agency is an observable and measurable trait, which is one of the somatic expressions of consciousness" (Riskin et al.). They define agency as "the engagement by a living entity of a series of calibrated activities, the result of which is a nonrandom situation or occurrence that has the appearance of intentionality" and contend that "all forms of agency require a system of consciousness, understood in this case as a continuous awareness of the living entity's environment." *Luna de lobos*'s treatment of plant consciousness includes an exploration of plant agency such as that expressed in this lively and animated landscape: "la luna se ha asomado" ("the moon peeks out"), "la arcada de agua negra que se comba mansamente" ("the black pool of water swings softly"), and "la senda del rebaño se arrastra" ("the flock's path crawls"; 21; my trans.). The consistent use of prosopopoeia throughout the novel suggests a conscious natural world.

Beyond personification, however, the novel explores subtle but significant shifts between passive and active agency, as well as the interconnections between receptive awareness and intentional behaviour; like humans, plants and natural elements are shown to participate actively in these interspecies dialogues. As Republican resistance fighter Ángel navigates this animated natural space, he hears what seem to be human steps signalling danger: "He escuchado los pasos que se acercan hacia el puente. Un remolino de hierba se abalanza hacia mí y grumos de tierra amarga se meten en mi boca" ("I hear footsteps approaching the bridge. A whirl of grass pounces on me and lumps of bitter earth enter my mouth"; 21–2; my trans.). The first sentence puts the subject in a receptive role, "he escuchado" referring to Ángel's human awareness, while in the second sentence, the active verbs "se alabanza" and "se meten" express the agency of the grass and lumps of soil, respectively, whose behaviour is suggested as intentional. This linguistic choice contrasts the little agency afforded the guerrilleros with the unexpected agency of nature, which runs and enters. As narrator, Ángel repeatedly attributes agency to plants. Later, the Civil Guards open fire on him unexpectedly, and when he is running away, rolling down the hill, branches uprooted by the commotion push him towards safety: "me acompañan y me empujan" ("accompany me and push me forward"; 140; my trans.). As Ángel finds solace in the torn branches, other vegetal beings use their thorns to try to stop his dangerous free fall: "los cardos y las urces se agarran a mi ropa intentando pararme" ("the thistles and heather snatch at my clothes, trying to stop me"; 140, 167). While the thistle and heather shrubs are ultimately unsuccessful in preventing Ángel's fall, their actions show initiative and intention: they push, grab, and enter – acts that are observable to the naked eye – expressing a kind of interspecies caring through which plants and humans participate in a connected ecological spectrum.

The verbs deployed by Llamazares to personify nature indicate an agency and intention that is congruent with Calvo's work in plant neurobiology, an emerging field that "aims to account for the way plants behave purposefully" (Calvo, "What Is It Like" 212) and which has increasingly demonstrated that "the absence of a neocortex does not appear to preclude an organism from experiencing affective states" (Low et al.).[7] Using time-lapse photography, Calvo has shown that plant behaviours are missed by human perception mainly because of the vast difference in the temporal scale of observation between plant and human actions ("Entrevista"). One of Calvo's videos shows a vine altering its trajectory from circular to elliptical when approaching a target, exploiting internal information that guides its best approach to complete the task of finding support for its growth ("On the Possibility"). As with the grass in Llamazares's text, the plant exhibits purposeful behaviour. In her work on the *Mimosa pudica*, evolutionary ecologist Monica Gagliano's claims go beyond plant perception to argue for the possibility of plant memory.[8] The issue of memory in the context of the Spanish Civil War is a significant one, since a main project of the victors was to erase the memory of the preceding regime: "any vestiges of the Second Republic had to be erased, annihilated, and this included social and political dissidence but also any landmarks of that brief democratic period" (Ramblado-Minero 30).[9] By bringing the readers' attention to plant agency and memory, *Luna de lobos* underscores ecocriticism's possibilities for deepening our understanding of the impact of Spain's civil war and its aftermath on Spanish individuals and society.

Therefore, the success of Llamazares's novel in revealing nature's agency with intention lies in its representation of actions that have until recently been unrecognized by humans because the sounds and movements that plants produce are neither observable by the naked human eye nor audible to the unassisted human ear. Expressing this plant agency decentres the human, not only because it identifies behaviours enacted by plants that were previously only equated with human or animal ability, but also because it requires that humans recognize how our own sensory limitations have led us to form anthropocentric world views. Acknowledging vegetal intention and interspecies connections sheds new light on the historical erasure of human limitations that have formed Spain's sociopolitical and environmental postures.

While less studied than collective human perception and thought, plant assemblages offer a fruitful angle from which to analyse plant consciousness. Llamazares describes a beech forest using a communal expression to characterize this grouping of trees, which climb up the mountains "como fantasmagóricos ejércitos de hielo" ("like ghostly armies of ice"; 12, 18). On another occasion, they are described as an army of shadows: "Las hayas … como un fantasmagórico ejército de sombras" ("The beeches … like a ghostly army of shadows"; 107, 129). As an organized grouping – an army – that moves purposefully and expresses intention, the beech trees interconnect seamlessly with the republicans, who, as the civil war ends, are ever less supported by their military organization. In both examples, the vegetal armies exhibit an explicit ghostly quality. By connecting the soldiers to the trees through their shared ghostliness, Llamazares highlights the erasure of the memory of those vanquished by the civil war, for whom there were no public memorials or, in many cases, even private ones.[10] At the same time, the ability of the individual beech trees to work as a team augments any consideration of their agency. According to Calvo, "[P]lants are able to integrate diverse sources of information; to make decisions; and may even be able to perform predictive modelling" ("What Is It Like" 212).[11] Furthermore, representing not only the exclusive "biological interface to the sun," which harnesses solar energy and makes all other life on earth possible, plants also participate in complex underground networks of fungi and plant roots that sustain forests, "all existing in a symbiotic equilibrium transferring nutrients" (Glattfelder 546–7). In sum, the network-like representation of plants in *Luna de lobos* offers an ecological vision of nature that is not only alive but deeply connected to humans, animals, and the rest of the natural world, what mycologist and forest ecologists have termed "the Earth's natural internet" (Stamets 7) or the "Wood Wide Web" (Simard 579).

As with the plants and forests, a variety of animal species populate the story, furthering the entwinement between human and non-human entities in the novel. Dogs are frequently referenced, sometimes as companions, but more often as victims. According to animal behaviourists Temple Grandin and Catherine Johnson, dogs are "genetic wolves who evolved to live and communicate with humans" (*Animals Make Us Human* 25); as such, they occupy a privileged role in human communities and have a unique evolutionary history.[12] As a species, then, dogs have undergone a transformative process inverse to the one experienced by the anti-Francoist fighters in the novel: while friendlier wild wolves have been shown by evolutionary biologists to have approached human settlements and to have eventually remained there, in Llamazares's novel, the guerrilleros who were once part of these communities as teachers, coal mine workers, sons, husbands, and neighbours, are now forced to stay away.[13] Gildo is forced to look at his home from a distance, since his proximity would put his wife and young son in danger (73). Likewise, the war upset Ángel's plan to marry and have a family with Marina and took away his livelihood and identity as a schoolteacher. As will be seen, neither the wolves nor the soldiers are accorded worth in their own right: the wolves are valued anthropocentrically in relation to the townspeople and the Republican soldiers vis-à-vis Francoist supporters.

The transformation of the Republicans from political rivals to enemies who needed to be exterminated is best shown in the chapter that describes the leaflets the government disseminated to facilitate the guerrilleros' capture in exchange for substantial monetary rewards. These "Wanted" signs reveal information pertaining to these men's private lives. Angel's flyer explains his physical appearance (tall, blond), his surname (Suárez Reyero), and that he is a schoolteacher and a member of an Anarchist trade union, and therefore "enemigo del alzamiento nacional" ("enemy of the Glorious National Uprising"; 73, 90).[14] The wording of the leaflet is perversely deceiving, since Ángel, like many other Spaniards, had joined during the Second Republic (1931–6/9), when other political parties and unions were legal. The Law of Political

Responsibilities of 1939 had made those parties illegal retroactively, and ensured that the Republican guerrilleros remained enemies of the state long after the war's conclusion, extending their separation from communities and their dehumanization.

In *Luna de lobos*, the Republican soldiers resist the Francoist's view that devalues them as animals, such as when Ángel pleads to Lina, "Diles que no soy un perro" ("Tell them that I'm not a dog"; 139, 165). This also occurs when Ramiro confronts the town priest, who had denounced his young brother, Juan, to the police: "¡Arrodíllese y rece, hijo de puta! ¡Ahí hay un hombre enterrado, no un perro!" ("Kneel down and pray, you piece of shit. There's a man buried under there, not a dog"; 95, 114). While the novel depicts Francoist attempts to dehumanize in order to eliminate political adversaries, the soldiers reject their dehumanization while also rejecting the domesticity suggested by the dog comparison.[15] Although metaphorical comparisons to dogs aim to dehumanize and encourage the mistreatment of the vanquished Republicans, animal cognition in the novel shows that Llamazares problematizes the traditional hierarchical view of humans' absolute superiority over non-human beings.

Dogs routinely express fear in the novel. When the Republican soldiers find an abandoned and injured dog, who looks at them with terrified eyes, they kill the canine out of mercy, foreshadowing the soldiers' predicament in which their loved ones will suggest that they take their own lives to protect their families from the state's repression (13–14). On other occasions, the dogs' barks communicate sadness: "Un ladrido lejano, triste, como un quejido" ("a sad, distant barking, like a groan"; 12, 18). Ángel's dog Bruna is movingly portrayed as able to infer human feelings. When he returns to his family's home after a long absence, he mentions that "[Bruna] corre hacia mí ... Pero no ladra. En mi propio silencio quizás intuye el peligro" ("she runs towards me ... but she doesn't bark. Perhaps she senses the danger from my silence"; 25, 33). This awareness is in step with what Brian Hare, a pioneer in the field of dog cognition, states as the widely accepted notion that "domestic dogs are unusually skilled at reading human social and communicative behaviour even more so than our nearest primate relatives" (Hare and Tomasello 439). The issue of whether dogs have a theory of mind, that is, the ability to attribute mental states to others, is somewhat controversial. However, cognitive biologists have proven that dogs can adopt human perspectives and follow the researcher's gaze (Veterinärmedizinische Universität Wien). Llamazares's novel portrays dogs as having theory of mind, such as when Bruna is able to read danger into Angel's odd silence.

In the episode in which the protagonist's old dog encounters him after an absence of several months from the farm, the canine companion's diminished eyesight is highlighted and yet her sense of smell – typically dominant in dogs – is not even mentioned: "Bruna, la perra … tarda en reconocerme: está ya casi ciega y yo hacía más de un año que no entraba en esta casa" ("Bruna, the dog … doesn't recognize me at first: she's almost blind, and I haven't been home for more than a year"; 25, 33). Inversely, the human characters begin to rely more and more on the sense of smell, which complements sight as humans' predominant perceptual faculty.[16] Reflecting on animal cognition, primatologist Frans de Waal encourages scientists to understand animals "on their own terms";[17] to properly evaluate animal cognition, de Waal proposes that it be broken into a set of smaller capacities, such as remembering the past and planning for the future, reciprocal altruism, theory of mind, or self-awareness (*Are We Smart Enough* 275, 273). Llamazares's text approximates human and non-human animals by enhancing or flattening their respective senses of smell and sight, while the narrative's consistent comparison between animals and humans serves to expose the fighters' transformation into non-human animals. Furthermore, by providing humans with animal sensory ability, Llamazares subverts the historical anthropocentric undervaluation of plants and non-human animals, due in part to humans' inability to perceive their worth.

Another group of animals consistently mentioned in the novel are sheep, which are caught, killed, and consumed. Their presence exposes the soldiers' duality, on the one hand, as the sheep's predators, which likens the humans to wolves and, on the other, as prey themselves, hunted by the Civil Guards. As both predators (of animals) and prey (of the Nationalists), the soldiers hold a liminal position that further approximates human and non-human animals within one overarching continuum. Both soldiers and sheep are part of a balanced ecosystem. The guerrilleros take from the natural world only what they need, like animals, and pay for it whenever they can, without human plundering. Their defiance of government authority, however, contrasts with the sheep's docility: "El animal camina, dócil y resignado, con el dibujo de la muerte grabado en su mirada" ("It walks behind him, docile and resigned, with the image of death etched on its face"; 34, 44). By characterizing the sheep's passivity upon their impending death as resignation, the narration exposes a human-like quality and conveys the acceptance of their tragic destiny. While the men do not accept their defeat passively, the sheep's predicament foreshadows once again the guerrilleros' future, and at one point, a sheep is shown hanging from a tree "como un extraño fruto ensangrentado" ("like a strange, bloody fruit"; 35, 45).[18] Like sheep and wolves, if caught, anti-Francoist fighters will be killed and perhaps publicly displayed as deterrence to others in the village.

The endless persecution during the civil war and its aftermath takes the maquis away from the domestic animals with whom they interact at the beginning of the story (dogs and sheep) into the world of nocturnal animals whose habitat is located deeper into the woods. The soldiers' transformation into nocturnal beings creates another environment that is apt for the development of non-human kinship. The transmutation of the sun into the moon is shown to be a life-altering experience: "Cuando se olvidan el color y la textura de la luz, cuando la luna se convierte en sol y el sol en un recuerdo, la vista sigue más el dictado de los olores que de las formas, los ojos obedecen al viento antes que a sí mismos" ("When you forget the color and texture of light, when the moon becomes your sun and the sun becomes a memory, your vision is guided more by scent than shapes, and your eyes follow the wind rather than seeking their own direction"; 29, 39). The human body's natural rhythms, built in through evolution to be active in the daytime and to rest at night, are profoundly disrupted here. The guerrilleros endure yet another violation as their circadian rhythms are altered, a process that is equally suffered by the novel's mules, born and raised inside the mines, and coal miners, whose nocturnality is shared with their domesticated non-human animals as well as the text's wild nocturnal fauna. Through these interspecies kinships, Llamazares denounces the anthropocentric hierarchization of living beings, including the ranking of humans according to social class.

The quote above also tracks the development of the soldiers' perceptions and environment: they become attuned to the wind, heavy with scents, and prioritize their sense of smell while diminishing their human dependence on eyesight. Under the light of the moon, their brains' ability to remember the past is compromised, and their growing dependence on the sense of hearing further dethrones eyesight as the men's main perceptual tool: "Cuando la noche lo envuelve todo, permanente e indefinidamente … sólo el instinto puede descubrir los caminos, atravesar las sombras y nombrarlas, descifrar los lenguajes del olor y del sonido" ("When the night wraps around everything, permanently and indefinitely … only instinct can find the right paths, guide you through the shadows and decipher the language of scent and sound"; 29–30, 39). The adverbs "permanently" and "indefinitely" in the quote highlight this shift to a non-human existence, one that reflects the historical reality of the persecution of the *topos* (moles) – as the men and women who hid in the mountains were known – which continued in Spain well into the 1960s. Throughout the text, the chaotic and destabilizing context of the civil war awards the humans the opportunity to realize that their kinship with non-human animals may be indeed stronger and more relevant than that with other humans, putting into question any hierarchical world view that would elevate humans above their non-human counterparts.

On occasion, the novel combines a variety of animals and plant forms into vivid images that show the interconnection among all living beings. When the soldiers are ambushed, a chaotic and bellicose scene portrays stampeding animals with human-like expressiveness, interspersed with people, in a way reminiscent of Picasso's *Guernica*:[19] "Un violento resplandor ilumina el cobertizo. El caballo surge frente a mí, alzándose de bruces, relinchando. Me aplasta contra una de las vacas. Y corro … en medio de las ráfagas. Una vaca se derrumba a mi derecha, acribillada" ("A violent glare fills the barn. The horse rears up in front of me, whinnying. It flattens me against one of the cows. I run through … the bursts of submachine-gun fire. A cow falls flat on the ground"; 106, 127–8). Echoing the imagery and energy of the painting, the horse brays and the cow (bull in the painting) bellows, dispersing in horror under an ominously illuminated sky. In Llamazares's description, the animals' gestures are those donned by humans in the painting, with the horse "alzándose de bruces" reminiscent of the human figures with upswung arms in Picasso. Extending to animals the horrors of the civil war, cows are buried hurriedly in an improvised outdoor pit – a mass grave like those utilized to bury many Spaniards killed in the three-year conflict – and a Civil Guard shoots a cow to finish her off, as if she were a Republican soldier (107–8).

Just beyond this chaos and violence, the beech forest with its "hayas salvadoras" ("saviour beech trees") appears as a haven towards which Ángel runs to save his life (106; my trans.). Llamazares thus furthers the Christian martyrdom allegory initiated while portraying the sheep. This vegetal promised land in which the soldiers seek salvation is not some passive landscape that humans or a higher power manipulate, but rather a forest that possesses agency. Its providential beech trees "cierran sus negras copas a mi espalda" ("close their dark fronds behind my back"), protecting the fighter's back (106, 128). Their active embrace of the soldier with finger-like fronds expounds the biblical trope's ecocritical dimensions. Once in the beech forest, Ángel hides among the brambles and waits motionless for eight or nine hours with his face against the dirt. After the wait becomes unbearable, he starts to leave his position, but the hawthorn "se agarra con rabia a mi ropa arañándome los brazos y la cara" ("claw at my clothing angrily, scratching my arms and face"; 107, 129). The shrub grabs, moves, and acts with intention on another living being and shows emotion: rage. Acting to protect the Republican soldier, the shrub insists that he remain still. By associating the plant's agency not just with humans but with the Republican soldiers specifically, the novel engages in an ecocritical discourse that condemns the Nationalist treatment of Republicans and that demands the latter's ethical treatment by the powers that be, just as the natural world now demands ecological protections from anthropogenic forces.

The previous passages presented a variety of animals, humans, and plants confusedly juxtaposed in a chaotic intermingling of limbs, heads, and screams where the limits among individuals and species are diffuse. Confusion and the erasure of borders are operative as well in the quotes that follow, as a human adopts characteristics of a variety of animals and transforms into a hybrid being. Throughout the text, soldiers routinely emit the sound of owls in order to alert other Republicans to the presence of potentially dangerous humans: "Santiago ha escuchado el grito del búho en el robledal" ("Santiago has heard an owl scream in the oak grove"; 82, 100). By withholding from the reader that the hoots were made by Ángel, the novel blurs the borders between non-human animals and humans. Later on, Ángel reunites with Ramiro by emitting the same sound as a signal. When Ramiro commends the accuracy of Angel's imitation, the latter's response is to further his identification with non-human beings: "Sí, claro … Y corro como el rebeco, y oigo como la liebre, y ataco con la astucia del lobo. Soy ya el mejor animal de todos estos montes" ("Yes, of course … And I can run just like the mountain goat, and I can hear just like a hare, and I attack with the cunning of a wolf. I'm the most skilled animal in all these hills"; 109, 131). Ángel's appreciation for these animals' idiosyncratic skills decentres humans' self-assured superiority. In noting and adopting the most unique skill of each animal, Ángel displays a hybrid quality that diminishes the boundaries between species.

Ecocritic Donna Haraway has argued that biology and evolutionary theory have "reduced the lines between human and animals to a faint trace" (*Simians* 152). A professor of consciousness studies, Haraway emphasizes the interconnectedness among living beings – also highlighted by mycologists – and champions the notion that humans comprise a collection of networks (Kunzru). As a result of the relentless persecution carried out by Franco's repressive apparatus, Ángel has experienced a form of biological evolution in a compressed amount of time that strengthens his kinship to non-human animals in the forest. The destruction of the human-animal dualism sabotages the practices of domination that are systemic in the Western tradition. Ángel evolves, like the animals in that environment, to survive despite the persecution of the repressive state. In this transformation, he is not so much distancing himself from humanity, but from a hierarchical framework that sacrifices or eliminates one group to perpetuate the power of another, as is the case with Republicans and endangered animal species such as the Iberian wolf.

As announced in its title, the wolf has a privileged position in the novel's bestiary. One of ecocriticism's central tenets has been the dethroning of humans as a superior species, separated from non-human animals. Haraway denounces human exceptionalism as the false "premise that humanity alone is not a spatial and temporal web of interspecies dependencies" (*When Species Meet* 11). In Llamazares, this impulse against artificial divisions in the natural world manifests in the rejection of hierarchies among different animal species in a way that is congruent with de Waal's critique of pitting species against one another to see which one is the smartest, since the prevalence of such "*Scala Naturae* assumptions" tends to reject cognitive similarities among different animal groups, such as birds and primates (De Waal and Ferari 201). Likewise, recent work on animal geographies goes beyond the animal-human divide to question artificial categorization among animal species "as food, pets, research subjects, pests that also work to subordinate certain species and reify others" (Gillespie and Collard 9).

Wolves are the animals with whom Republican humans are most closely identified in this novel: they are a threat to the villagers, they kill sheep belonging to others, and they eventually prey on other humans, first by robbing poor peasants in a bus and later by kidnapping the mine's owner for ransom. The eerie announcement that a wolf has arrived in the nearby mountain, howling all night, further transforms the soldiers not only into animals, but into wild beasts who are dangerous to humans. The mention of the wolf's annual arrival prompts the narrator to explain the primitive method used to hunt this species in Riaño, "como los hombres primitivos: acorralándoles" ("like primitive men: corralling them"; 112; my trans.).[20] In this mountain village of León, the wolves are identified with the guerrilleros, likewise hunted by a large group of men who corral them: "El lobo huye, asustado, hacia adelante y cae en la trampa. Le cogen vivo y, durante varios días, le llevan por los pueblos para que la gente le insulte y le escupa antes de matarle" ("The wolf gets scared and runs off straight ahead and falls into the trap. They catch him alive and for several days they parade him around the villages so that everyone can curse him and spit on him before he's killed"; 112, 135).[21] This public shaming was routinely conducted to torture Republican sympathizers, especially women related to Republican soldiers, who were paraded with their heads shaved through their town squares after having force-fed them castor oil.[22] Furthering the text's interspecies association, the reader is told that Ramiro "olfatea la noche como un lobo herido" ("sniffs the night like an injured wolf"), illustrating his enhanced wolf-like perception (12, 18). Finally, during an intimate encounter María tells Ángel, "Hueles como los lobos" ("You smell like a wolf"; 57, 70), to which he responds assertively, "¿Y qué soy?" ("What else would I be?"; 57, 70). The protagonist is both perceived as a non-human by humans and is self-aware of his transformation into a non-human animal.

According to Grandin and Johnson, in contrast to the ubiquitous portrayal of the lone wolf in popular culture, wolves in the wild do not live in packs but in family units, while lone wolves are young adult males looking for a mate (*Animals Make Us Human* 28). The soldiers in *Luna de lobos* initially resemble a pack of wolves and, killed off one by one, eventually a lone wolf. Yet their plight becomes more precarious than that of wolves; the maquis have been separated from their families (packs) and, moreover, have no means by which to seek a mate. Both groups are victims of torture, by the villagers in the wolves' case, and by the Civil Guards in the soldiers'. The relentless persecution by Franco's rural police obliges the fighters to resort to increasingly violent measures for survival: robbery, killing in self-defence, and eventually hijacking the mine's owner to finance their escape to France.

After the men rob a bus – even though somewhat humanely, allowing the poorest riders to keep their money – the references to the moon, and its obvious connection to werewolves, increase. At this point in the narrative, the civil war has ended and the Nationalists have won. Ángel appears "vigilando esa luna que tiembla a mis pies como una trucha muerta" ("keeping watch over the moon that is trembling at my feet like a dead trout") and then recalls his father's instruction to him as a child to notice the moon, "el sol de los muertos" ("the sun of the dead"; 64–5, 80–1). In addition to the full moon, the werewolf figures are constructed in accordance with popular culture: they howl, they perch upon a mountaintop, they develop a menacing persona, and they undergo a physical metamorphosis. The shift from the soldiers' previous association with verisimilar wolves to their portrayal as mythical werewolves upon the war's conclusion acts as a metonym for the country's sociopolitical and ethical deterioration. That the soldiers' moral decline is expressed through their association not with real animals (wolves) but with their subsequent transformation into fantastical creatures (werewolves) decentres any anthropocentric view that hierarchizes humans and suggests, instead, that brutish behaviour cannot be so simply attributed to animality.

Historically, literary critics have distinguished between the "constitutional" werewolf, "a person who, either from a gift inborn or from the use of certain magic arts of which he has learned the secret, is in the habit of changing himself into a wolf from time to time," and a second type, "the involuntary werewolf, whose transformation was unavoidable, owing to the curse or charm of some outside power" (Smith 4–5). The latter is the kind of werewolf we encounter in *Luna de lobos*, forced into metamorphosis by the state's relentless persecution.[23] Brent A. Stypczynski, in his study of the werewolf in modern literature, notes that werewolves "appear during times of social, political, technological and theological change" and "represent our ambivalent feelings regarding points of transition" (*Modern Literary Werewolf* 52). Both the 1930s and the Transition to democracy were times of enormous changes in Spain. While major ideologies (fascism, communism, and democracy) collided worldwide, the civil war's aftermath remained a time of acute suffering for a considerable part of the country's population, which was marginalized, and in some cases obliterated. In the late 1970s and 1980s, ghosts and monsters, including werewolves, proliferated in Spain's literary and cinematic production of the post-Franco years, as critic Jo Labanyi has noted. In her view, "[T]he current postmodern obsession with simulacra may be seen as a return of the past in spectral form" (65). She argues that "Llamazares's werewolves in *Luna de lobos* depend on memory; not their own but that of the collective in the form of the villagers and the Civil Guards who, out of love or terror, keep them alive as ghosts of the past through the stories they tell about them" (76). Shortly after the end of the war, the guerrilla band comes upon a group of lumberjacks, whose youngest member stares at them with admiring fascination, inquiring, "–¿Son ellos, verdad? Los del monte. Lo ha dicho entre feliz y asustado. Como si una manada de lobos hubiera pasado a su lado sin hacerle daño" ("That was them, wasn't it? The men from the hills? He is half contented, half scared, as if a pack of wolves had just passed by without harming him"; 66, 81). Having approached the lumberjacks as humans, the soldiers depart as wolves in the child's eyes, whose uneasy mix of apprehension and admiration captures well the double narrative that circulated about the maquis as dangerous monsters to be feared, on the one hand, and heroes to be admired, on the other. This perceptional tension mirrors the conjoining of fear and awe in human-centred views of so-called wild animals rather than a measured recognition of ecological integration.

A third narrative surrounding the soldiers portrays them as victims of an oppressive state. While kept hostage, the mine's owner summarizes that "[p]ara unos, sois unos simples ladrones y asesinos. Y, para otros, aunque no lo digan, sois unos pobres desgraciados que lo único que hacéis es tratar de salvar la vida" ("[s]ome people think that you're just common thieves and murderers. And others, on the quiet, think of you as poor wretches who are just trying to stay alive"; 81, 99). As expected, the Francoist sympathizer's account omits the heroic narrative; yet he recognizes that the censorship of the soldiers' portrayal as victims of political circumstances reduces the men's identities to that of murderers and thieves. In this repressive context, the soldiers exist only in the townspeople's memory. Significantly, the forest in which the men live is constituted, among other beings, by plants that are capable of memory, as Gagliano's research suggests. Expelled from the human community to which they belonged and at risk of erasure as traces of Spain's Republican past are dismantled, the soldiers have enmeshed with a rich community of non-human entities who perceive, empathize, act, and are, in fact, even capable of remembering.

Francoist oppression also pushes the men deeper into the earth. In a highly introspective passage in which Ángel shares his innermost feelings with the kidnapped mine's owner, he confesses a strong identification with nature: "Siempre, desde niño – le digo –, yo he sentido también la atracción de las montañas. El fuego, el viento, los ríos están vivos, están siempre en movimiento. Las montañas, en cambio, siempre iguales, siempre quietas y en silencio, parecen animales muertos" ("'Ever since I was a boy', I say, 'I've felt attracted to the mountains. The fire, the wind, the rivers, they're all alive, always moving. But the mountains, they're always the same, always peaceful and silent. They're like dead animals'"; 81, 98). Ángel's focusing on the lively qualities of some natural elements (fire, wind, and rivers) while attributing to mountains the quality of immutability reveals the persistence of an anthropocentric vantage point that results from the very limited timescale observation of a human life: while mountains seem relatively stable to the human eye, they are always changing through the processes of erosion, volcanic activity, and tectonic shifts. It is worth noting, nevertheless, that Ángel does not say the mountains are dead, just that they resemble dead animals. Indeed, like animals, mountains decompose, erode, and change, even if at a more geological pace and, similarly, Ángel increasingly integrates with the landscape. In this way, human, animal, and land become inextricably entwined.

There are multiple images of the soldiers buried alive, echoing the ethos of annihilation pursued by the victors of the civil war.

General Emilio Mola famously declared the new regime's intention to "[e]liminar sin escrúpulos ni vacilación a todos los que no piensen como nosotros" ("eliminate without scruples or hesitation all those who do not think as we do"; Preston 18; my trans.).[24] When the Republican maquis seek shelter in a cave that they had previously dug, they describe themselves as "enterrados … en este húmedo agujero" ("buried … in this damp hole"; 40, 51). They hide in a hole in the ground, much like a tomb, from which they only emerge briefly at night. Their physical circumstances approximate those of the unmarked grave in which Juan, Ramiro's seventeen-year-old brother, is buried after being denounced by the town's priest. Towards the end of the novel, when Ángel is the sole survivor, he hides in another confined space appropriately called "un féretro de tierra" ("a dirt coffin") and remarks that for one month, he has been "tumbado como un topo en la fosa que Pedro y yo excavamos en la corte de las cabras" ("stretched out like a mole in this underground tomb that Pedro and I dug out in the pen where we keep the goats"; 146, 173). The references to "casket," "underground tomb," and "mole" stress the soldier's sensation of being buried alive. At the same time, these lexical choices contemplate what the annihilation of the last individual of a living group may look and feel like, therefore portraying the attempted extermination of the Republicans in terms of a species extinction.

The earth, however, is not inert; when it is time to return to his underground hiding place, Ángel says, "[H]a llegado la hora del reencuentro con ese hálito de magmas, de líquenes podridos, que impregna las entrañas de la tierra y el corazón de quien las viola y las habita" ("[T]he time has arrived to come face to face again with the stinking breath of the magma and the rotten lichens that impregnate the entrails of the earth and the heart of those who encroach upon their territory"; 147, 175). As he inhabits the womb of the earth, the reference to the molten natural material from which rocks are formed and to the decomposing plant life suggest both an underworld of death and the rebirth made possible by the breakdown of prior life, in other words, the cycle of life. The quote affirms the agency of the soil and presents the earth as the source of all human and non-human life. Likewise, the passage condemns the earth's plunder (the rape of the earth's womb) by human beings. Occuring at the very end of the novel – after the guards' latest search of Ángel's family home and violent beating of his sister prompts her to ask him to leave – Ángel loses his last refuge: he is doubly expelled from his family's homestead and from the earth's womb.

This expulsion is a precursor of Ángel's forced exile from the nation that rejects him and, consequently, from the landscape that has kept him alive. As the novel ends and Ángel boards a train that will take him towards either safety or death, the text claims that he is filled by yet another natural element, snow: "Sólo hay ya nieve dentro y fuera de mis ojos" ("There's only snow inside and outside of my eyes now"; 153; my trans.).[25] A 1994 Llamazares novel, *Escenas de cine mudo*, uses the same trope in the dedication to the author's deceased mother: "A mi madre, que ya es nieve" ("To my mother, who is already snow"; 5; my trans.). While snow is undoubtedly associated with memory and death in both instances, emphasis here is placed on the interconnection between the living and the dead and between human and non-human nature. On a literal level, the reference implicitly acknowledges that every living being is made out of something that existed before, whether stellar dust, water from clouds, or snow. Indeed, time and again, the novel reveals the interconnectedness of nature, not simply as the recycling of elements (minerals or water), but as alive and possessing a common consciousness. Nature becomes the physical and metaphorical support of a consciousness that, alone, the soldiers are not able to sustain.[26] As the novel concludes, Ángel's consciousness alters and incorporates plant-like qualities. While he never seems to lose the ability to see, smell, or feel cold, he ceases to engage in processes associated with recollecting or regretting the past, or with anticipating or planning for the future. Blending elements of human and vegetal consciousness suggests a survival response that points to the adaptations of human and non-human species to altered environmental conditions.

One could safely conclude that Llamazares's view of the universe in *Luna de lobos* is a panpsychic one. This is hardly surprising, given the consistent ecological concerns of Julio Llamazares's literary production. In the 1930s, prominent scientists like Ernst Schrödinger, Louis de Broglie, and Max Planck proposed that consciousness and reality, the mind and the material, were fundamental components of each other and, in the 1980s, physicist David Bohm developed his theory of the Implicate Order, in which he suggested that space and time might be derived from a deeper level of objective reality whereby everything in the universe is interconnected. In the field of philosophy, panpsychism is a respectable, if counterintuitive, theory of consciousness championed by David Chalmers and Philip Goff that seeks to circumvent what Chalmers calls the hard problem of consciousness, that is, how subjective experience emerges from matter, from the brain. While neuroscience has advanced exponentially in the last few decades, and the brain correlates of many physical functions or experiences have been discovered through functional magnetic resonance imaging and other technology, experts continue to disagree on why or how consciousness occurs. It is not known how brain processes produce a conscious, subjective experience. Chalmers concludes that "where there is simple information processing, there is simple experience, and where there is complex information processing, there is complex experience" (291). Llamazares's novel depicts a complex ecosystem in which plants, humans, and non-human animals are deeply intertwined, sharing different and fluctuating levels of consciousness. The guerrilla fighters are trapped in a present without a future, in which memories of an experience-rich past are a threat to their struggle to survive another day. They live in a natural environment in which plants, by contrast, may be capable of some form of memory. Ángel, Ramiro, Juan, and Gildo represent the end of a Spain that could have been: a progressive, secular society concerned with equality and social justice. This is the project that the Second Republic set forth and that was annihilated by the civil war and Francoism. In this latest state of geological evolution, the Anthropocene, in which humanity has a vast and unprecedented impact on the health and future of the planet, Llamazares not only reminds us of the shared aliveness of all living beings, questioning artificial boundaries and hierarchies, but of nature's ability to reclaim the planet should humans continue to plunder it senselessly in the name of economic advancement and progress.

NOTES

1 Unless otherwise noted, page numbers for the English translation correspond to that of Simon Deefholts and Kathryn Phillips-Miles (Llamazares, *Wolf Moon*).
2 See "Richard Powers & Bill McKibben."
3 While it is tempting to dismiss Wohlleben's reference to screaming in the context of tree cavitation as an example of anthropomorphization of a natural sound, cavitation sounds resemble screams in two important ways: they are distress signals and they have "roughness." Roughness is a quality of sound in which loudness changes very quickly: "The rate at which loudness changes in speech is typically between four and five hertz, or cycles per second … But the rate was much higher with screams, between 30 and 150 hertz" (Choi). According to I. Khait, "Plants begin to emit ultrasonic sounds between 20 and 100 kilohertz" when deprived of water.
4 Neuroscientist Marjorie Woollacott states that the most compelling evidence to support the existence of consciousness without a brain comes from studies of well-documented Near-Death Experiences (NDE), since doctors agree that these patients' brains were non-functioning or even

dead (89). This assertion can be used to support the possibility of plant consciousness.

5 The distinction between the "bottom-up" or "top-down" models of consciousness is fitting here. Woollacott explains: "From the perspective of neuroscience, any input to the brain that comes from other than the usual sensory inputs would be considered top-down" (56). While neuroscientists search for correlates between specific experiences and the brain (bottom-up model), religions like Hinduism and Buddhism uphold the top-down model (55–70).

6 It is worth noting that new materialist approaches in the physical sciences, humanities, social sciences, and the arts see matter as dynamic.

7 The Cambridge Declaration on Consciousness was drafted by a group of cognitive neuroscientists, neuroanatomists, computational neuroscientists, neurophysiologists, and neuropharmacologists of international prominence.

8 In Gagliano's well-known experiments, *Mimosa* plants that were repeatedly dropped but sustained no damage were shown to stop closing their leaves in subsequent falls, which suggests that they were able to use previous experience to adjust future behaviour, that is, to learn (55–71).

9 Another example of this politics of exclusion and erasure practised by Franco's regime can be seen in the promotion of films starring actors with Republican leanings, such as Rosita Díez Gimeno, whose name was stripped from the publicity of her films (Colbert 20).

10 Historian Ian Gibson estimates that there are still 115,000 people buried in mass graves in Spain as a result of the civil war.

11 In contrast, a well-known recent theory on consciousness, Giullio Tononi's Integrated Information Theory (IIT) states that a plant's cell has a higher level of integration than the entire plant, therefore in terms of consciousness a plant would be a society, not an individual, since consciousness requires maximum integration (Mørch).

12 Their connection to human communities is believed to go back 100,000 years, more than any other domesticated animals. Cats, in contrast, have been domesticated for less than 10,000 years (Grandin and Johnson, *Animals Make Us Human* 67).

13 Brian Hare calls this evolutionary process "survival of the friendliest," in contrast to Darwin's "survival of the fittest" ("Survival of the Friendliest" 155). Threat to survival bonds a dog and a girl in the novel that Maryanne L. Leone studies in this collection, in which, she explains, both are victims for whom capitalist growth manifested as real-estate development has resulted in the collapse of municipal infrastructure (electricity, water, garbage disposal) and has lead to mass migration, underscoring the mutually felt impact of environmental toxicity on human and animal

beings. Leone's analysis of the affective communication that develops between the two suggests a similar treatment of canine cognition to that seen in Llamazares's novel.

14 Adolfo Suárez was the first president of the government during Spain's Transition to democracy and one of its architects, together with King Juan Carlos I. I don't think it is coincidental that Ángel, the Republican soldier, is given surnames that recall the Transition to democracy period: Suárez and Reyero (reminiscent of the word *rey* or "king"). In this way, the novel links the democratic regime that was the Second Republic and the new democratic government in the 1970s, even though it was not a republic but a constitutional monarchy. While this novel deals with the 1930s and 1940s, it was published in 1985, at the end of the Transition.

15 In Gregory H. Stanton's *Ten Stages of Genocide*, dehumanization is stage four: "Members of a persecuted group may be compared with animals, parasites, insects or diseases," which makes the group easier to eliminate. On the other hand, Samuel O'Donoghue focuses on the brutalizing power of nature, rather than on Franco's repressive apparatus, as the main cause for the men's dehumanization.

16 For an excellent article on surveillance and the power of sight in this novel, see Susan L. Martín-Márquez's "Vision, Power, and Narrative in *Luna de lobos*."

17 For instance, "elephants were believed to be inept tool users" until more appropriate tests were designed that did not limit them to using their trunks (De Waal, *Are We Smart Enough* 16).

18 During the Jim Crow era in the United States, "strange fruit" referred to Black victims of racial violence hanging from trees after being lynched, as hauntingly evoked by a famous Billie Holliday song of the same title. The lyrics of the first stanza are:

Southern trees bear strange fruit.
Blood on the leaves and blood at the root,
Black bodies swinging in the southern breeze,
Strange fruit hanging from the poplar trees.

19 Picasso's painting is a reaction to the German bombing of the Basque town of Guernica during the Spanish Civil War and a powerful statement against the destruction and senselessness of war.

20 As Margaret Marek's chapter in this collection explores, Riaño, like Vegamián, the birthplace of author Julio Llamazares, was flooded by a dam in the 1980s. Llamazares has written about the ghostliness of these towns that disappeared under water, victims of industrial developmental planning. Their erasure from history echoes the erasure from official

history suffered by the victims of the Republican side during the civil
war. These artificial water reservoirs caused a great deal of population
disruption and trauma as well as environmental damage to the *dehesa*
ecosystem (grassy plains interspersed with Encina oak). In response to the
human and non-human ecosystemic eradication from the affected valleys,
Marek explains, historical and environmental preservation efforts are
presently underway as ecologists and merino shepherds actively seek to
restore traditional transhumant practices all the while contemporary art
curators document and exhibit submerged histories.

21 There is also an identification with Jesus: paraded, insulted, and spat on as
he approaches his crucifixion.

22 In the Middle Ages, wolves were "commonly connected to outlaws, and in
fact even being hanged from the gallows with executed criminals in some
areas of northern Europe, the wolf became seen as an anti-social outsider"
(Stypczynski, *Evolution* 25; also in Smith 27).

23 According to the Ministry of Justice's own statistics, "In July 1939, between
200 and 500 individuals were shot daily in Madrid, 150 in Barcelona, 80 in
Seville, et al. … Seven years later there were concentration camps and 137
labour camps where those unable to justify their political responsibilities
were held" (Blanco Aguinaga).

24 Spanish Civil War historian Paul Preston calls this process a "Spanish
Holocaust" and recalls an episode shortly after the military uprising in
1936 in which a landowner lined up his farm workers and shot dead six
of them to serve as a lesson to the others (29). As Preston concludes, many
landowners considered the landless peasants to be lesser human beings.

25 This is the novel's final sentence.

26 There is a great deal of discussion in the field of artificial intelligence
regarding the feasibility of transferring a human consciousness into a
computer. Futurist Ray Kurzweil is a strong proponent of this.

WORKS CITED AND CONSULTED

Blanco Aguinaga, Carlos. "Literature and Democratization in Spain."
University of Washington, Seattle, WA, 9–11 July 1989. Lecture.
Bohm, David. *Wholeness and the Implicate Order*. Routledge, 1980.
Calvo, Paco. "Entrevista con Paco Calvo." MINT Lab. *YouTube*, uploaded by
Sociedad de Filosofía de la Región de Murcia, 20 Mar. 2018, https://youtu
.be/WBSHDZ26FMg.
Calvo, Paco. "On the Possibility of Plant Sentience." Plenary talk, *The Science
of Consciousness Conference*, Interlaken, Switzerland, 26 June 2019. *YouTube*,
uploaded by The Science of Consciousness (TSC) – Conferences, 9 Aug.
2019, https://youtu.be/9qpUSWk4nPs.

Calvo, Paco. "What Is It Like to Be a Plant?" *Journal of Consciousness Studies*, vol. 23, nos. 9–10, 2017, pp. 205–27.

Chalmers, David J. *The Conscious Mind: In Search of a Fundamental Theory*. Oxford UP, 1996.

Chamovitz, Daniel. *What a Plant Knows: A Field Guide to the Senses*. Oneworld, 2012.

Choi, Charles Q. "Why Is Screaming So Effective? Scientists Explain." *Christian Science Monitor*, 16 July 2015, https://www.csmonitor.com /Science/2015/0716/Why-is-screaming-so-effective-Scientists-explain.

Colbert, Olga. *The Gaze on the Past: Popular Culture and History in Antonio Muñoz Molina's Novels*. Bucknell UP, 2007.

De Waal, Frans. *Are We Smart Enough to Know How Smart Animals Are?* W.W. Norton, 2016.

De Waal, Frans B.M., and Pier Francesco Ferrari. "Towards a Bottom-Up Perspective on Animal and Human Cognition." *Trends in Cognitive Sciences*, vol. 14, no. 5, May 2010, pp. 201–7. *Cell Press*, https://doi.org/10.1016 /j.tics.2010.03.003.

Gagliano, Monica. *Thus Spoke the Plant*. North Atlantic Books, 2018.

Gibson, Ian. "Time to Bury the Dead. An Interview with Ian Gibson." Conducted by Tommy Greene and Eoghan Gilmartin, *Jacobin*, 1 Apr. 2019, https://jacobin.com/2019/04/franco-fascism-poets-federico-garcia-lorca.

Gillespie, Kathryn, and Rosemary-Claire Collard. *Critical Animal Geographies: Politics, Intersections and Hierarchies in a Multispecies World*. Routledge, 2015.

Glattfelder, James B. *Information – Consciousness – Reality. How a New Understanding of the Universe Can Help Answer Age-Old Questions of Existence*. Springer Nature, 2019.

Grandin, Temple, and Catherine Johnson. *Animals in Translation: Using the Mysteries of Autism to Decode Animal Behavior*. Harcourt, 2006.

Grandin, Temple, and Catherine Johnson. *Animals Make Us Human: Creating the Best Life for Animals*. Houghton Mifflin Harcourt, 2009.

Haraway, Donna J. *Simians, Cyborgs, and Women: The Reinvention of Nature*. Routledge, 1991.

Haraway, Donna J. *When Species Meet*. U of Minnesota P, 2008.

Hare, Brian. "Survival of the Friendliest: *Homo sapiens* Evolved via Selection for Prosociality." *Annual Review of Psychology*, vol. 68, Jan. 2017, pp. 155–86. *Annual Reviews*, https://doi.org/10.1146/annurev-psych-010416-044201.

Hare, Brian, and Michael Tomasello. "Human-Like Social Skills in Dogs?" *Trends in Cognitive Sciences*, vol. 9, no. 9, Sept. 2005, pp. 439–44. *Cell Press*, https://doi.org/10.1016/j.tics.2005.07.003.

Khait, I., et al. "Plants Emit Informative Ultrasonic Sounds under Stress." *BioRXiv*, 2 Dec. 2019, https://doi.org/10.1101/507590. Preprint.

Kunzru, Hari. "You Are Cyborg." *WIRED*, 1 Feb. 1997, https://www.wired
.com/1997/02/ffharaway/.

Labanyi, Jo. "History and Hauntology; or, What Does One Do with the Ghosts of
the Past? Reflections on Spanish Film and Fiction of the Post-Franco Period."
*Disremembering the Dictatorship: The Politics of Memory in the Spanish Transition
to Democracy*, edited by Joan Ramon Resina, Rodopi, 2000, pp. 65–81.

Lanese, Nicoletta. "Plants 'Scream' in the Face of Stress." *LiveScience*, 6 Dec.
2019, https://www.livescience.com/plants-squeal-when-stressed.html.

La Trobe University. "Plants Don't Like Touch: Green Thumb Myth Dispelled."
Phys.org News, 17 Dec. 2018, https://phys.org/news/2018-12-dont-green
-thumb-myth-dispelled.html.

Llamazares, Julio. *Escenas de cine mudo*. Seix Barral, 1994.

Llamazares, Julio. *Luna de lobos*. Seix Barral, 1985.

Llamazares, Julio. *Wolf Moon*. Translated by Simon Deefholts and Kathryn
Phillips-Miles, Peter Owen World Series, 2017.

Low, Phillip, et al. *The Cambridge Declaration on Consciousness*. Churchill
College, University of Cambridge, 7 July 2012.

Maeder, Marcus. "Trees". *Immersive Lab*, 2015, https://immersivelab.zhdk
.ch/?page_id=1014.

Maeder, Marcus, and Roman Zweifel. "Downy Oak: Rendering Ecophysiological
Processes in Plants Audible." *Proceedings of the Sound and Music Computing
Conference 2013, SMC 2013, Stockholm, Sweden, 30 July–3 August*, edited by
Roberto Bresin, Logos Verlag, 2013, pp. 142–5. *Zenodo*, https://doi.org
/10.5281/zenodo.850258.

Maeder, Marcus, and Roman Zweifel. "Trees: Rendering Ecophysiological
Processes Audible." Swiss Federal Institute for Forest, Snow, and Landscape
Research WSL, https://www.wsl.ch/en/projects/trees.html. Accessed
5 Feb. 2023.

Martín-Márquez, Susan L. "Vision, Power, and Narrative in *Luna de lobos*: Julio
Llamazares' Spanish Panopticon." *Revista Canadiense de Estudios Hispánicos*,
vol. 19. no. 2, winter 1995, pp. 379–87.

Mørch, Hedda Hassel. "The Integrated Information Theory of Consciousness."
Philosophy Now, no. 121, Aug./Sept. 2017, https://philosophynow.org/issues
/121/The_Integrated_Information_Theory_of_Consciousness.

O'Donoghue, Samuel James Robert. "Nature as Enemy of Man in Julio
Llamazares's *Luna de lobos*." *Forum for Modern Language Studies*, vol. 50, no. 3, July
2014, pp. 356–70. *Oxford Academic*, https://doi.org/10.1093/fmls/cqu023.

Powers, Richard. *The Overstory*. W.W. Norton, 2018.

Preston, Paul. *El holocausto español: Odio y exterminio en la guerra civil y después*.
Translated by Catalina Martínez Muñoz and Eugenia Vázquez Nacarino,
Debate, 2011.

Ramblado-Minero, M. Cinta. "Sites of Memory / Sites of Oblivion in Contemporary Spain." *Revista Canadiense de Estudios Hispánicos*, vol. 36, no. 1, autumn 2011, pp. 29–42.

"Richard Powers & Bill McKibben Discuss The Overstory." *YouTube*, uploaded by JCCSF, 24 Oct. 2019, https://youtu.be/1CVdc_1HaMU.

Riskin, Jessica, et al. "The Consciousness/Agency Duality." Programme. The Science of Consciousness Conference, 13 Apr. 2020, online, https:// consciousness.arizona.edu/events/consciousnessagency-duality.

Simard, Suzanne. "Net Transfer of Carbon between Ectomycorrhizal Tree Species in the Field." Nature, no. 388, 1997, pp. 579–82, https://www .nature.com/articles/41557.

Smith, Kirby Flower. "An Historical Study of the Werewolf in Literature." *PMLA*, vol. 9, no. 1, 1894, pp. 1–42. *JSTOR*, https://doi.org/10.2307/456336.

Stamets, Paul. *Mycelium Running: How Mushrooms Can Save the World*. Ten Speed, 2015.

Stanton, Gregory H. *Ten Stages of Genocide. Genocide Education Project*, https:// genocideeducation.org/wp-content/uploads/2016/03/ten_stages_of _genocide.pdf. Accessed 5 Feb. 2023.

Stypczynski, Brent A. *The Evolution of the Werewolf Archetype in English Literature*. 2008. Kent State U, PhD thesis.

Stypczynski, Brent A. *The Modern Literary Werewolf: A Critical Study of the Mutable Motif*. McFarland, 2013.

Vaughan, Adam. "Recordings Reveal That Plants Make Ultrasonic Sounds When Stressed." *New Scientist*, 5 Dec. 2019, https://www.newscientist .com/article/2226093-recordings-reveal-that-plants-make-ultrasonic-squeals -when-stressed/.

Veterinärmedizinische Universität Wien. "You Spy with Your Little Eye, Dogs Can Adopt the Perspective of Humans." *ScienceDaily*, 7 Apr. 2017, https:// www.sciencedaily.com/releases/2017/04/170407091829.htm.

Wohlleben, Peter. *The Hidden Life of Trees: What They Feel, How They Communicate. Discoveries from a Secret World*. Translated by Jane Billinghurst, Greystone Books, 2016.

Woollacott, Marjorie. *Infinite Awareness: The Awakening of a Scientific Mind*. Rowman & Littlefield, 2015.

PART TWO

Anthropocene, Capitalocene, Chthulucene

Leonardo Torres Quevedo's Automata and the Consolidation of Technological Regenerationism

ÓSCAR IVÁN USECHE

At the outset of the nineteenth century, the symbolic and material refashioning of society prompted by modernization relocated Spain's search for an ancestral national genius in the realities of technological development. Rather than envisioning the reorganization of its traditional values and agrarian economy around the new paradigms of modernization, the country gave prevalence to its industrial and urban growth and urged the secularization of society. These particular circumstances led thinkers and artists to delineate concerns about the centrality of human reason in forging and securing the national future. The ability to generate technological innovation thus became a central consideration in many economic and cultural prospects, revealing some of the sociohistorical forces that, in the name of progress, would culminate in contemporary ecological subjugation.

The profound institutional decomposition that ensued from the loss of the last colonial territories to the war with the United States in 1898 not only cast a shadow over the national morale but also exposed, among other weaknesses, the technological backwardness and isolation of Spain in relation to European powers such as France, Germany, or England.[1] In June 1899, less than one year after the official capitulation to the United States, congressman Eduardo Vicenti alluded to this disparity, suggesting that the country's defeat in the recent war had not been the result of military miscalculations, but the direct consequence of Spain's insufficient development:

Yo no cesaré de repetir que, dejando a un lado un falso patriotismo, debemos inspirarnos en el ejemplo que nos han dado los Estados Unidos. Este pueblo nos ha vencido no sólo por ser más fuerte, sino también por ser más instruido, más educado; de ningún modo por ser más valiente. Ningún yanqui ha presentado a nuestra escuadra o a nuestro ejército su pecho, sino una máquina inventada por algún electricista o algún mecánico. No ha habido lucha. Se nos ha vencido en el laboratorio y en las oficinas, pero no en el mar o en la tierra.

(I won't stop stressing that, if anything, and beyond false feelings of patriotism, we should be inspired by the example that the United States has given us. This country defeated us not only because they are stronger, but also because they are better trained and educated; not because they are more courageous. No American exposed his chest to our armies; we only saw machines invented by an electrician or a technician. There was no fight. Our defeat took place in the lab and in the offices, not at land or at sea; qtd. in Sánchez Ron 175)[2]

Vicenti advocated the promotion of science and technology through educational reform. His assessment responded to a prognosis of national problems that saw the country as a sick body in need of diagnosis and treatment.[3] According to this view, Spain could be rescued from its decline by strengthening its traditional values while embracing modernity's capacity for social transformation. Later grouped under the label of Regenerationism, similar assessments led to strategic plans to reconstitute the country from this state of disarray.[4]

Even though each thinker associated with this intellectual movement interpreted the national decadence in subtly different ways, in general, all concurred that there was an urgency to consolidate a modern and productive industrial society (Fusi 291). As a consequence, they repudiated the institutional structures of the Restoration and rejected the traditional political class, whom they blamed for the country's backwardness and decay. Political, philosophical, and literary reflections framed within this ideological drive have been extensively studied and, recently, cultural critics have also turned their attention to the role of science in the evaluation of the country's problems at that time.[5] One aspect that has not been sufficiently explored, however, is the unique perspective that technology provided on the role of non-human entities or, conversely, on human agency in addressing this historical inflection. Considering technology as yet another important piece in the Regenerationists' efforts to render a prognosis of the country's decline, this essay examines engineering and invention as consequential activities for the nation's moral and economic recuperation. I look at the theoretical and practical work of Spanish engineer, inventor, and entrepreneur Leonardo Torres Quevedo, in particular his approach to automation and machine cognition and his experience devising and constructing automata. Drawing on material ecocriticism and post-human theories,

I argue that his ideas on automatic processes and artificial intelligence upheld the notion of human's mastery throughout the country's push towards modernity. By restoring inventors' and engineers' confidence in their two-pronged mission as defenders of tradition and champions of modernity, his work reaffirmed the metaphysical condition of Spanish national identity while bolstering notions of technological ownership that showed the regenerative capacity of innovation.[6] Even though his projections suggest the ecologically damaging potential of utilitarian approaches to progress, thus anticipating or forerunning current environmental crises, Torres Quevedo's ecocritical shortcomings were inevitable – his interest was that of promoting modernization rather than questioning the anthropocentric footing on which national development was theorized.

Exploring the conceptual possibilities of computing and the practical applications of automation, in his essay "Automática: Complemento de la teoría de las máquinas" ("Automation: Complement to the Theory of Machines," 1914), Torres Quevedo confirms that artefacts, particularly machines, interact with society to produce stories, narratives that, as material ecocritics Serenella Iovino and Serpil Oppermann propose, open new avenues to understand the complex assimilation of modernity (7). As a profoundly religious country, Spain was beset by tensions between spirituality and materialism, which shaped many of the political and economic debates on the role of science and technology in the consolidation of the modern nation. In this context, post-human studies' emphasis on the repercussions of technological development and ecocritical theory's approach to more-than-human materiality offer new perspectives on how engineering and invention could actively participate in the country's attempts to reconcile tradition and progress at the turn of the twentieth century. If, as theologian Elaine Graham suggests, technology intervenes in the shaping of society as a means to materialize specific human ideals, then it is possible to contend that Torres Quevedo's particular vision on artificial cognition aligned with and contributed to the Regenerationists' intellectual endeavour to engineer the country's autochthonous modernity – that is, embracing the materiality of progress while reappraising the traditional social, political, and economic structures that defined and articulated national identity.

Leonardo Torres Quevedo's Socio-technical Imaginaries

By the mid nineteenth century, political critics were already voicing their preoccupation with the shortage of prepared professionals to work on the country's immediate needs. Spain's case was unusual: in other European countries, technological development had been the centre of nationalistic discussions and a cornerstone in matters of national security, economic progress, and social stability. France and England, for example, had urged the advancement of engineering at the service of military interests, either for defence or for expansionist projects. If the extent to which a country was able to design, implement, and use technology to guarantee its national integrity constituted a measure of its development, as Francis Bacon had suggested in the seventeenth century, then Spain's lack of technical capabilities was palpable proof of the country's backwardness. But even in the face of evident underdevelopment, at the turn of the century some figures emerged that were able to produce groundbreaking accomplishments in science and technology and, in that way, modestly contribute to the national modernization. Seldom associated with Regenerationism, scientists, engineers, and educators such as Santiago Ramón y Cajal, Eduardo Hinojosa, and Torres Quevedo, among many others, actively participated in the country's upturn.[7]

In 1895, for example, Torres Quevedo presented a report of his work on mechanical instruments of calculation at the Académie des Sciences in Paris. The text, entitled "Memoria sobre las máquinas algebraicas" ("Report on Algebraic Machines"), describes the challenges he confronted in devising his first algebraic engine, a computer able to solve linear systems of equations and find the real roots of polynomials.[8] In the essay, Torres Quevedo advances a modular architecture for his invention, namely a structure that allowed an uncomplicated expansion of his machine in order to solve more complex problems: "como el número de móviles enlazados y el de ecuaciones de condición, [sic] pueden aumentar cuanto se quiera, deberá decirse que una máquina es un instrumento que enlaza varios móviles e impone mecánicamente ciertas relaciones entre los valores simultáneos de sus desplazamientos" ("Since the number of cogs in the internal mechanism, and the number of conditional equations can be increased as much as one desires, it must be said that a machine is an instrument that links multiple gears and mechanically makes certain calculations among the magnitudes of these wheels' simultaneous movement"; Torres y Quevedo, "Memoria" 204). This algebraic device would come to be one of the first steps in his long and successful career as an inventor, and also a cornerstone in his trajectory as a pioneer of automation and a precursor of computer science.[9] In fact, Torres Quevedo's later work would transcend the practical sphere to delve into the theoretical realms of artificial intelligence and computing: insisting on the impossibility of creating sentient devices, his essays on automation heuristically explore the modular system developed for his calculators and show how it could later be applied to the construction of large-scale automatic systems.

Mostly concerned with the engineering achievements and possible economic revenues of these inventions, in his futuristic vision Torres Quevedo did not account for the environmental impact of his developments. While there is no explicit evidence of this neglectfulness – biographers and historians of science dedicated to his work have not framed the discussion within the more recent critical concerns of environmental studies – his anthropocentrism, within which machines functioned only as extensions of the human spirit, illustrates a common attitude towards technological progress that ended up being ecologically detrimental notwithstanding its positive initial projections. Changes in production patterns or increases in the demand for energy to sustain the scale envisioned here for automatic systems, for example, were overlooked. Torres Quevedo's assessment thereby centred on the ways in which technology altered our understanding of cognition as a distinctive human attribute. This sort of re-evaluation of Descartes's mind-body dualism channelled many of the anxieties that the social transformations of modernization were producing in an otherwise backward country.[10]

It is from this perspective that Torres Quevedo's ideas come to grips with the different economies of signification that emerge at the intersection of technology and imagination amid the turmoil precipitated by the events of 1898. If, as theorist Jeremy Carrette suggests, the material and symbolic impact of critical events – military, technological, or artistic – creates a window of opportunity to re-evaluate our condition as humans and our role in the transformation of the environment, one can argue that by highlighting humans' ability to control their surroundings and (re)shape their future, Torres Quevedo's ingenuity and capacity for invention effectively counteracted the country's pervasive feelings of intellectual and moral failure (Carrette 50). This confidence in Spaniards' ability to hold the reins of their future nonetheless galvanized society into the unrestricted support of capitalist practices that stimulated industrial production regardless of its negative effects on the natural world and on rural communities: pollution, deforestation, and agricultural land abandonment would thus become endemic problems that persist to this day.

Scholarship on Torres Quevedo has mostly focused on making biographical revisions or on exploring his contributions to specific engineering subfields, consistently overlooking the network of ideological projections that structure his work.[11] Here, science and technology scholar Sheila Jasanoff's concept of socio-technical imaginaries comes in handy, for these projections constitute "collectively held, institutionally stabilized, and publicly performed visions of desirable futures, animated by shared understanding of forms of social life and social order attainable through, and supportive of, advances in science and technology" (4). Framed as solutions to the social, economic, and environmental challenges of modernization, many of these imaginaries also transformed intellections of human productivity and social progress – thermodynamics and the theory of evolution are two good examples of such appropriation. Once these structures transcended the theoretical realm and entered cultural imagination, however, many dystopian visions of the future emerged. The notions of mechanizing or automating human processes in order to improve productivity form part of these ambivalent projections: they constituted a promise of a world with better labour conditions as well as a threat to human exceptionalism and to traditional economic and cultural ecosystems.

Equivocal sentiments towards technology would also complicate the ongoing political debate in Spain on the need for a higher-education curriculum that prioritized the practical uses of knowledge. While politicians and educators deemed innovation necessary to increase productivity and dynamize the industrial economy, they also welcomed theorization inasmuch as it helped consolidate the national scientific culture and lessen the country's dependency on foreign technology.[12] Emphasis on the functional aspects of technology to take care of immediate needs had nonetheless concentrated engineers and inventors' efforts in the development and improvement of industrial processes, turning people's relationship with their environment into a utilitarian exchange. In that context, the field of automation gained attention for its practical applications within industry and for its theoretical interest as a site for negotiating antagonistic visions of the national problems: it simultaneously opened the space to design and implement functional artefacts and to generate abstract, original knowledge.

Besides offering ample evidence of the country's complicated process of modernization, the epistemological foundations of the debate on the practicality of knowledge provide a pertinent context to approach Torres Quevedo's contributions to Regenerationism. Within the Spanish socio-technical imaginaries, two philosophical traditions that emerged at the beginning of the nineteenth century are essential to understand how technology intertwined with articulations of national identity, particularly as these contributed to consolidating the traditional dualisms of thinking: abstract and concrete, spiritual and material, theoretical and practical. German *Naturphilosophie*, on the one hand, studied nature to aver and explain the metaphysical character of the national spirit. French positivism, on the other, drew on similar notions to devise concrete mechanisms of social analysis. Analogously, cultural appropriations of technology oscillated between these two contrasting forms of philosophical interpretation. Efforts to develop functional machines that would solve concrete problems, for instance, paralleled those of engineers in conceiving devices with symbolic projections and spiritual potential. Both approaches concurrently devised automatic calculators, industrial looms, and self-acting spinning machines, and manufactured complicated artefacts that replicated leisure or artistic activities, and consequently highlighted the transcendental nature of the human intellect.

Paradoxically, among these technological marvels the most celebrated were not the ones that solved practical problems, increased productivity, or eased domestic taxing activities, but automata, namely mechanized devices coming close to executing tasks which were considered distinctive of the human intellect and dexterity: writing, interpreting music, playing chess, and so forth. As science and technology historian John Tresch explains, "[a]utomatons were potent and paradoxical symbols for this period's clashing world views, whether materialism, traditional Cartesian mind-body dualism, mystical illuminism, or monistic pantheism; they could embody technological control and reduction, as well as channeling supernatural powers that defied clockwork rationality" (91). Since their *mise en scène* nimbly problematized the reaches of rationality and ingenuity, witnessing gadgets perform human actions produced a sort of perplexity in spectators that pushed them to ignore the practical advantages of the technology involved in making the devices possible in the first place. Such an intuitive reaction resembles humans' broader admiration of nature (plants, animals, topography) not for its utility, but simply for its transcendental (spiritual, aesthetic, performative) value.

In his studies on British mathematician Charles Babbage, science historian Simon Schaffer aptly shows how this contradiction articulated the complexity of the nineteenth-century rationalizing imperative. In Babbage's perspective, as Schaffer explains, efforts to rationalize the world heavily relied on the possibility of engineering and mechanizing both physical and intellectual labour (53). To show some of the problematic aspects of this aspiration, Babbage displayed a dancer automaton in his own house in a room contiguous to the one in which he was developing his famous analytical engine, a sophisticated computer built upon the physical assemblage of gears. With the exception of visitors from abroad, guests seldom made it to his workshop, for they became captivated by the dancer and forgot about the other machine. Babbage used this anecdote to "teach his audience about the sinister contrast between foreign seriousness and domestic triviality, between the easy charms of the silver dancer and the demanding challenges of the calculating engine" (58). Babbage's remarks here point to the network of symbolic connections that exists between technology and national representation, as well as to the impact of engineering on reflections about the country's problems and identity.

Towards Technological Regenerationism

The cultural philosophy that supported Regenerationists' projects of social engineering stemmed from similar considerations. Such intellectual programs operated within a dialectical framework that included a reconceptualization of the national character while facilitating the conditions to make the country part of pan-European modernity. Saddled with these competing objectives, their endeavour aimed to strike a balance between the local production of knowledge and the importation of foreign expertise. Torres Quevedo's theorization of automation is inscribed within this duality, becoming much more than just a reflection on human potentiality in relation to material progress. Indeed, his sociotechnical imaginary also entailed an assessment of the local conditions of science and innovation, and, ultimately, a broad reflection on technological ownership, namely the ability of Spain to contribute, with its own intellectual capital, to European modernization.

Beyond its cultural and aesthetic resonances, Regenerationism constituted an intellectual attempt to grapple with the materialistic aspects of progress while revitalizing the idealistic and spiritual character of national identity.[13] Furthermore, once the Spanish-American War confirmed the multiple weaknesses of a backward social structure, a dysfunctional political establishment, and a frail cultural identity, Regenerationists pondered the urgency of institutional refashioning. The defeat not only had military consequences but also moral repercussions – Spain had lost confidence in its own capacity to secure progress. But if the causes for this downfall lay in educational stagnation and the absence of an autochthonous scientific culture, as Vicenti eloquently suggested in his address, then the country's decline could not be blamed entirely on the alleged blind faith in rationality that, according to some conservative sectors, had guided the national agenda. Rather, it could be Óse attributed to more transcendental causes, such as traits of the national identity associated with religiosity and the purported sacredness of tradition. It is in the context of the search for balancing these two perspectives that one can talk of technological Regenerationism.

In *Representations of the Post/Human*, Graham revises the cognitive mechanisms used to conceptualize human and non-human entities. She asserts that even when a conceptualization of a non-human other (monster, animal, cyborg, automaton) may be essential in determining with precision the contours of humanity, historically our understanding of the human condition has stemmed from analysing how society capitalizes on technology to produce or gain control over those non-human others.[14] Material ecocriticism's approach to the interaction between material forms and humans thus sheds light on the importance of vitalism and mechanical determinism as opposing but complementary theories that reframe anthropocentrism in terms of human attributes such as agency or social affiliation. Whereas vitalism (the belief that organic life is different from unanimated objects) locates humans as architects of society, determinism (the belief that every action is the result of physical causes) relies on a rational, technical understanding of reality that sees nature as part of an intricate mechanism.[15] At the beginning of the twentieth century, both approaches formed part of Regenerationists' intellectual quest for solutions to the country's decay. By reframing agency as one of the highest human attributes, modernization could be seen as a positive force. Since human consciousness was situated in a pre-eminent plane, rather than recreating, substituting, or surpassing the human condition, technology offered elements to better understand society and to address its most urgent problems. As it lucidly reaffirms the role and importance of human rationality in advancing modernization, Torres Quevedo's work on the feasibility of creating sentient machines patently embodies the goals of a technological Regenerationism defined within these parameters.

Automation and Spanish Modernization

If one turns again to Jasanoff's idea of technological imaginaries, it is possible to read Torres Quevedo's projects as encoded illustrations of the potential of engineering for boosting the national recovery. His conceptualization of automation, for example, aligns with a post-humanism that sees society's development not as a dystopian teleology but as a moment of collective enthusiasm about the promises of technological mechanization:

> Tuve ocasión de apreciar prácticamente la gran facilidad que dan para estas construcciones [– las máquinas automáticas –] los aparatos electromecánicos, y pensé que se les podría aplicar con éxito. … [M]e parece que [su confiabilidad] será igual ó superior á la que podría ofrecernos [una

persona]. Y esto basta, evidentemente, puesto que [las personas] obtienen resultados á los cuales otorgamos toda nuestra confianza.

(I had the opportunity of testing empirically the advantages that electro-mechanic devices offer to these constructions [– automatic machines –], and I thought it would be feasible to use them for this purpose … I believe that [their reliability] will be similar or superior to that which [a person] could offer. And, evidently, that would be enough since we usually trust [people's] results; Torres y Quevedo, "Automática" 583)

Yet this view was incompatible with the country's morale. Although economic prosperity had produced an apparent shift in the negative associations of science and technology with the destruction of tradition and the desecration of the past, Spain's conflictive regeneration, in turn, had exposed the irreconcilable tension between tradition and modernity (Lenoir 208–9). Not only had scientific discovery and technological development never materialized as social forces, hindering the consolidation of the Spanish modern state, but at the turn of the century they were still perceived as significant threats to the country's foundational values. Rather than presenting an opportunity for reconciling national identity with the multiple transformations of progress, the moral crisis and economic decline that followed the 1898 military defeat questioned the revolutionary possibilities of science and technology. While it was evident that the country needed to transcend its abstract yearning for modernization, the disruptive capacity of this process produced collective distrust and even fear of reason's ascendancy over nature. Automation, however, presented itself as a means to balance these conflictive responses: it could be palpable proof of the advantages of technology and, at the same time, concrete evidence of the irreplaceability of human reason and agency in preserving and controlling the material and natural worlds.

When technological development is analysed through the lens of post-human theory, it becomes clear how some of these contradictory aspects coalesce. In fact, a central strand of post-human thought explores the instrumentalization of technology and its limits within the social realm. As cultural theorist R.L. Rutsky suggests, humans have ended up "technologized" in their attempt to master technology and improve society, meaning that, more than offering tools to gain control over the world, technology has imposed its logic on humanity ("Technologies" 185–6). A post-humanism rooted in these premises offers new explanations of how changes in material conditions, particularly those related to technological development, affect people's roles as agents of social and historical transformation, including the eventual environmental repercussions of such relocations. In other words, post-human theory allows critics to question how humans, no matter the extent to which they are "technologized," can define themselves in relation to non-human agents such as machines or natural forces.

Descartes's ontological distinction between body and mind and its reverberations on Torres Quevedo's conceptualization of automation are useful here to elucidate the anthropocentric underpinnings of technological Regenerationism. Following the principles of Cartesian solipsism, Torres Quevedo understood consciousness as an exclusively human attribute.[16] As a consequence, for him the idea of machine cognition was beyond the bounds of technological possibility. Yet, despite adhering to and even reaffirming this anthropocentrism, his automata were not constricted by Descartes's proposition that non-human entities lacked agency over the external world:

La denominación de autómata se aplica á menudo á una máquina que imita la apariencia y los movimientos de un hombre ó de un animal … Hay otra clase de autómatas que ofrecen un interés mucho más considerable: los que imitan, no los gestos, sino las acciones del hombre, y algunas veces pueden reemplazarle … Se cree que es posible automatizar las operaciones mecánicas, puramente manuales de un obrero, y que, por el contrario, las operaciones que exigen la intervención de las facultades mentales nunca se podrán ejecutar mecánicamente … Intentaré demostrar en esta nota –desde un punto de vista puramente teórico– que siempre es *posible construir un autómata cuyos actos, todos, dependan de ciertas circunstancias más ó menos numerosas, obedeciendo á reglas que se pueden imponer arbitrariamente en el momento de la construcción.*

(The label automaton is often assigned to machines that imitate the appearance and movements of people or animals … There is yet another kind of automata that are much more interesting: the ones that imitate, not the gestures, but people's actions, and on occasion can take their place … It is thought that it is feasible to automate workers' mechanical actions, their physical activities and, conversely, that it won't be possible to mechanically replicate deeds that require the use of mental capacity … I will try to show in this essay – from a purely theoretical perspective – that it is always *possible to build an automaton whose actions, all of them, are conditioned by more or less specific variables and follow rules that can be arbitrarily defined during its construction*; Torres y Quevedo, "Automática" 575–6; emphasis in original)

Although communication with the external world or with other devices can be considered an inherent property of today's automatic machines, in Torres Quevedo's time such a notion constituted a breakthrough in the conceptualization of automation. Expanding on philosophical discussions about the metaphysical essence of reason, in his essay he explains: "[Descartes] pensó sin duda que el autómata, para responder razonablemente, tendría necesidad de hacer él mismo un razonamiento, mientras que en este caso, como en todos los otros, sería su constructor quien pensara por él de antemano" ("Clearly, Descartes was of the opinion that in order to produce an intelligent response, an automaton would need to reason by itself, whereas in our case, as in all cases, it would be the automaton's designer who, beforehand, would do the reasoning for it"; Torres y Quevedo, "Automática" 577). While it was true that automata and other automatic devices might substitute humans in many tasks and be devised to do so with exceptional precision, in the end they would only be able to carry out programs within the parameters of their design.

Iberian historians of science such as Alberto Dou Mas de Xaxás, José García Santesmases, Manuel Garrido, and Francisco González de Posada have seen in this approach to artificial reasoning a precursor of the foundations of modern computing. They have even compared Torres Quevedo's ideas and achievements on machine interaction, informatics, and artificial intelligence to those advanced later in the twentieth century by mathematicians Alan Turing, Norbert Wiener, or John von Neumann.[17] However, Torres Quevedo's accomplishments cannot be inscribed within those conceptual frameworks; rather, I contend, the universal value of his theoretical work lies in the ideas it suggests about the role of reason in addressing social problems. Furthermore, the inventor's tremendous success and the ample recognition that his work gained during the first decades of the twentieth century give him a central role within Spain's socio-technical imaginaries, projections that a century later remain in tension with anthropocentric notions of progress. His main contribution to Regenerationism was therefore that of offering ample evidence, both theoretical and practical, of the insurmountable human intellect and the role engineering and invention, as expressions of that rational capacity, had in the country's regeneration.

In order to dissipate the technological distrust that automation generated, in his essay "Automática: Complemento de la teoría de las máquinas" Torres Quevedo reaffirms this principle of human superiority and shows how it operates on an automatic device. The piece is, in that regard, a pioneering reflection on the theoretical and practical principles of computing, and a study on how to approach the technical problems that emerge in the process of devising a universal machine, that is, a mechanical apparatus able to execute a series of specific tasks without human intervention. Torres Quevedo shows the limitless complexity that an automaton can attain through the superposition of simpler mechanisms, while carefully demonstrating the machine's incapability of doing anything beyond its intended design. For him, its intricacy (including its discerning capabilities) was conditioned by two main factors – energy supply and sensing instruments:

> Los autómatas deberán tener sentidos: termómetros, brújulas, dinamómetros, manómetros … aparatos sensibles a las circunstancias que deben influir en su marcha … Los autómatas deberán tener miembros: las máquinas o los aparatos capaces de ejecutar las operaciones que les sean encomendadas … Los autómatas deberán tener la energía suficiente: los acumuladores, las corrientes de agua, los depósitos de aire comprimido que han de suministrársela a las máquinas destinadas a ejecutar las operaciones necesarias.

> (Automata need senses: thermometers, compasses, dynamometers, manometers … instruments that are sensitive to the circumstances governing their operation … Automata need limbs: mechanisms or devices able to execute the requested tasks … Automata need to be supplied with enough energy: accumulators, water currents, air deposits able to satisfy the demand of the mechanisms in charge of the multiple tasks; Torres y Quevedo, "Automática" 575–6)

Even though Torres Quevedo alludes here to the indispensability of having unrestricted access to natural resources – water, energy, fuel – in the text there is no explicit acknowledgment of the reliance on the environment that such exploitation would generate.[18]

What this delimitation of the machine's capabilities presents, instead, is a philosophical, almost ontological complication. In order to respond to external circumstances and make decisions, the device needed somehow to establish an active interaction with its surroundings:

> Además se necesita – y este es el principal objeto de la Automática – que los autómatas tengan *discernimiento*, que puedan, en cada momento, *teniendo en cuenta las impresiones que reciben, y también, a veces, las que han recibido anteriormente*, ordenar la operación deseada. *Es necesario que los autómatas imiten a los seres vivos, ejecutando sus actos con arreglo a las impresiones que reciban y adaptando su conducta a las circunstancias.*

(In addition, it is necessary – and this is the main goal of Automation – that automata possess the ability to discern, that they process the requested operations instantaneously and *with attention to the measurement of external variables, and, occasionally, values measured in advance. It is essential for automata to imitate living organisms, acting in response to external stimuli and adapting their behaviour to their surroundings*; Torres y Quevedo, "Automática" 576; emphasis in original)

This revision of Descartes's metaphysical distinction between humans and machines (that of agency being a unique and inimitable human attribute), and its extension to the notion of automata, hinges on Torres Quevedo's clear differentiation between reasoning as a self-initiated process and reasoning as a programmed response. Had Torres Quevedo's technological Regenerationism gone a step further so as to allow for the capacity of non-human entities to act on reality, his theory might have decentred the anthropocentrism that remained so embedded in the movement's reconceptualization of the nation. Torres Quevedo's insistence on the more restricted form of reasoning, however, meant that the device executed only that for which its human creator had designed it; the limits of its functionality, consequently, were mostly subjected to mechanical complications (sensors, movement, energy supply), problems for which engineers could always find a solution.

The machine Torres Quevedo envisioned was one able to perform what Spanish scientist Ángel Martín Municio terms "disquisiciones positivas" ("practical analyses"), namely tasks whose complexity is restricted to the limits of human invention (132). His automata were thus nothing but the product of scientific discovery, technological research, and human ingenuity, and as such, the perfect expression of both the material and spiritual possibilities of an anthropocentrically conceived modernization. To demonstrate the feasibility of a functional discerning machine along these theoretical guidelines, Torres Quevedo designed an automatic chess player that evaluated a series of conditions and then made calculated logical decisions to defeat its opponent.[19] Beyond its mechanical accomplishments, the project posed questions about the reaches of artificial reasoning that once again confirmed the impossibility of mimicking human cognition. Furthermore, with its public display, the device also undermined what historian Minsoo Kang describes as "the image of the industrial machine as an irrational, terrifying, destructive, and superhuman entity," a common perception among many thinkers "who felt that the progress of industrialization had taken on a life of its own beyond human interest and control" (243). Indeed, one can argue that the chess player was intended to celebrate the unconditional development of technology as a means to increase humans' control of their surroundings; in other words, as a way of highlighting the anthropocentric character of progress to allay the public's fear that technology would decentre the human. This "story" (understanding the term in Iovino and Opperman's sense) bears a resemblance with Babbage's dancer anecdote in that both not only confirm the eeriness that non-human artefacts generated but also show how that anxiety hinged on automata's ability to mimic unique human qualities. In the case of the chess player, however, there was no direct appreciation of the machine's aesthetic values as a proxy for its utility. Instead, and in contrast to a mechanistic understanding of the material and natural worlds, the valuing of this automaton was ultimately conditioned by its referentiality to the human realm.

In his take on Descartes, in fact, Torres Quevedo addresses this referentiality to clarify in what capacity the automatic devices he was proposing actually possessed discernment:

No hay ninguna diferencia esencial entre la máquina más sencilla y el autómata más complicado; una y otro se reducen á un Sistema material sometido á leyes físicas, que se derivan de su composición; pero cuando estas leyes son complicadas, cuando es necesario un razonamiento importante para deducir de estas leyes las maniobras correspondientes, la máquina que las ejecutase parecería que razonaba por sí misma, y esto es lo que generalmente extravía el juicio de las personas que se ocupan de esta cuestión.

(There is no essential difference between the simplest machine and the most intricate automaton; both can be reduced to Material Systems that are subjected to the physical laws derived from their composition; but when these laws are complex, when significant reasoning is necessary for establishing the procedures that derived from them, it might seem as though the machine executing such calculations is reasoning by itself, and that is precisely what confuses people who study this matter; Torres y Quevedo, "Automática" 577)

If the loss of spirituality in the name of unrestrained materialism was a preoccupation that Spaniards might have had with a future wherein automata or large-scale automation could become ubiquitous, Torres Quevedo offered the promise of a more balanced world wherein machines' capacity for reasoning would be contingent on human initiative. Analogously, society's regeneration depended exclusively on diligent social engineering that, juxtaposing tradition and progress, countenanced human and non-human interaction to honour the rational potential of its members.

Regenerationists' particular way of understanding the country's problems included a vision of the national spirit as a transhistorical entity based on specific religious, geographical, and linguistic traits. As an embodiment of the worst fears of industrial modernization, however, the quest for automation seemed to confirm the unleashed materialism of a society whose essential values had been dislocated, and even replaced by an aberrant reverence for science and technology. Since part of the proposed treatment to alleviate the country's malaise consisted in recovering its transcendental ethos while embracing social and political transformation, a conciliation between spirituality and technology was essential. As an engineer, Torres Quevedo was able to approach the difficult negotiation of these incompatibilities in an original way and incorporate it into his conceptualization of automatic machines (Vaquero Sánchez 301). His efforts to highlight automata's limited discernment, as well as their absolute subordination to human reasoning, thus constituted an attempt to solve some of the tensions surrounding the anthropocentric essence of technological development, a discussion that would continue to intensify beyond the immediate post-1898 period. In line with Regenerationism's rational imperative, Torres Quevedo considered the nation to be ill fated if its members did not embrace the potentials of (human-generated) reasoning and the consequent virtues of social agency, all distinctively human traits that, he maintained, automata would never be able to replicate. In his vision, therefore, engineering and invention prevailed as ideal means to facilitate the country's regeneration and posed no threat of decentring the human.

Yet for turn-of-the-century engineers, machines needed to be much more than just technological extensions of human capacity; they also had to reflect the spiritual aspects of (national) identity. In his speech at Torres Quevedo's swearing-in ceremony as member of the Real Academia de Ciencias in 1901, for example, Francisco de Paula Arrillaga clarified, "Y es que, real y efectivamente, tal espíritu se encuentra incorporado á la materia, por virtud del ordenamiento intencionadamente dirigido á un fin, que el inventor señaló, y persiste en los aparatos y piezas algo de su mente y de su voluntad, dado que sigue la máquina ejecutando lo que aquel ideó y quiso" ("And the point being that, in reality and effectively, due to the purpose and goals that move the inventor, such spirit is constitutive of matter; and since the machine executes what the inventor conceived and desired, parts of his mind and will permeate through its mechanisms and pieces"; 43). Torres Quevedo's conceptualization of automata was indeed an attempt to dissociate technology from scientific materialism, a purported interdependence that had marginalized it from the Regenerationists' efforts to redefine the nation's identity. His reflections on automation, therefore, not only grapple with the question of the role of technology in reshaping different aspects of reality and the pre-eminence of the human intellect, but also, when considering the national character of progress, with the problem of technological ownership. Since the spirit that Torres Quevedo attributed to automata was ultimately human driven, his work resisted the type of entwined network between the material and natural worlds that contemporary material ecocriticism has deemed possible in spaces wherein technology and society coexist (see Clark 111–36). Indeed, at a crucial moment in Spain's self-(re)conception, Torres Quevedo mitigated a national inertia towards rescinding anthropocentrism that would last a century longer.

Conclusion

Understanding engineering and invention not only as useful tools but as active parts in the construction of the national paradigm constitutes one of the most important characteristics of Torres Quevedo's technological Regenerationism. In addition to proposing an alternative reading of the Cartesian debate on the limits of machine cognition, his proposal highlighted the feasibility of creating a functional, discerning automaton that might also be seen as a clear product of Spanish ingenuity. This would be not only a pioneering development in the field of automation, but also an epitome of the nation's creativity and a representation of the discipline, rigour, and application of the Hispanic mind – all traits of the modern national character that Regenerationists wanted to reinforce. In contrast to other inventions, Torres Quevedo's automata were never conceived as commercial products. With the exception of his chess player and a calculating machine that he presented in Paris in 1920 to prove some of his ideas on analytical mechanisms, his automatic devices never left the theoretical realm, working more as philosophical than mathematical or computational artefacts. However, his ideas on discerning machines, automation, and ultimately on the way humans and non-human entities interact are relevant to understanding the links between Regenerationism and technology. Although some critical readings of "Automática: Complemento de la teoría de las máquinas" see his reflections as a pioneering work of computing, cybernetics, and even artificial intelligence, the text's most tangible repercussion is that of highlighting the importance of technological ownership. Only by conceiving automation under these parameters would it then be possible to merge the material and metaphysical aspects of modernization as constitutive parts of the national spirit.

NOTES

1 The idea that Spain somehow failed to join European modernization has been prevalent in historiography and cultural analyses of nineteenth-century Spain. See, for example, studies by Nadal, Glick, López Piñero and Peset Reig, and Tortella Casares. More recent scholarship, following David Ringrose's groundbreaking study *Spain, Europe, and the "Spanish Miracle," 1700–1900*, have challenged the discourse of Spain's failure by situating the particularities of its process of industrialization and scientific development outside an idealized framework set by Germany, England, France, or even the United States. The country's political instability, nonetheless, problematized the adoption of institutional and educational models that would have facilitated a faster and autonomous technological development. See Álvarez Junco; Cruz; Ferris.

2 All translations are my own. Page numbers correspond to the Spanish original.

3 In this regard, the works of Pio Baroja and Santiago Ramón y Cajal are particularly telling. Both writers and physicians approached the country's state of disarray as a pathology associated with notions of degeneration and social and racial decadence. See Sosa-Velasco 18.

4 For detailed accounts on the origins of Regenerationism, see López-Morillas; Harrison; Harrison and Hoyle.

5 See, for example, the works by Sosa-Velasco, Casado de Otaola, and Davis.

6 In this essay, the idea of technological ownership refers to the capacity of generating innovation through the use of local resources and national intellectual capital, that is, ingenuity and originality carried out by Spanish scientists, engineers, and inventors without the assistance of other nations.

7 These key figures exemplify the individual efforts and, in some cases, solitary achievements of scientists, engineers, and educators at the turn of the twentieth century in Spain. Histologist Santiago Ramón y Cajal (1852–1939) achieved world recognition for his cutting-edge research on the nervous system. Ramón y Cajal also dedicated time to reflect upon the problems of the country and wrote extensively on science and scientific education. Eduardo Hinojosa (1852–1919), for his part, was a pioneer legal historian and law professor whose preoccupation with the historical and scientific study of the law led his vision as an educational reformer and public servant at the turn of the century.

8 The report had been previously presented at the Real Academia de Ciencias Exactas, Físicas y Naturales ("Royal Academy of Exact, Physical,

and Natural Sciences") of Madrid in 1893, and included a description of a mechanism able to assign physical magnitudes to different variables in an equation and find solutions by displacing and relocating specific pieces within the device. This machine contributed to the development of automatic calculators, expanding previous achievements of scientists, mathematicians, and inventors such as Babbage (1834), Wetli (1849), Amsler (1854), Coradi (1875), and Kelvin (1876). See González de Posada and González Redondo 799.

9 Torres Quevedo was one of the most prolific and successful Spanish inventors of his time. Francisco González de Posada, one of his biographers, has even proposed the term "ingeniero español universal" ("Spanish universal engineer") to underscore the international and cosmopolitan character of his education and achievements (25ff). His training in engineering offered him a particular insight into the country's problematic modernization and its purported isolation from Europe, a problem he tried to mitigate by giving a transnational projection to his work. His contributions to the development of rigid airships and his incursion in the use of radio waves to remotely control and operate devices gave him renown in Europe and on the other side of the Atlantic. In the United States and Canada, for example, he completed the construction of what would become known as Spanish Aero-Car, a cable carriage to transport passengers over the Niagara River that is still in use. In 1910, with the idea of creating a technical dictionary for Spanish speakers that included the most common terminology used in engineering, he also advocated the establishment of the Unión Hispanoamericana de Bibliografía y Tecnología Científicas ("Hispanic-American Panel of Scientific Bibliography and Technicalities"), whose first mission was to "reunir, catalogar y fomentar las publicaciones científicas en lengua castellana, y cuidar, mantener y perfeccionar el tecnicismo de las ciencias" ("put together, classify, and support scientific publications in Spanish, and protect, preserve, and improve techno-scientific terminology"; "Discurso de Don Leonardo Torres y Quevedo" 17). For more details on this proposal, see José García Santesmases (253).

10 The mind-body dichotomy with which Torres Quevedo engaged in these disquisitions also has been expressed by other thinkers as human-nature opposition. In his chapter for *Beyond Human*, Daniel Frost explores this dynamic in his evaluation of the Enlightenment plans for land reform a century earlier, which framed Spain's progress in terms of taming the natural environment in order to cultivate a productive society. Torres Quevedo's questioning of the boundaries between human reason, intellect, and agency as well as those of automation ultimately maintains a Cartesian dualism that the contemporary post-human vision will transcend. As

Juan Carlos Martín Galván argues in his chapter for this collection on transhumanism and necropolitics in Rosa Montero's fiction, techno-human agency will require an acknowledgment that one's technologically mediated non-humanness (which in Montero manifests as animality) is an inherent part of a subjectivity that resists the human–non-human binary of anthropocentric thinking.

11 See, for example, Rodríguez Alcalde; García Santesmases; González de Posada and González Redondo; Vaquero Sánchez; Garrido.

12 Spain's loss of its last colonies in 1898 revealed, among other problems, profound deficiencies in the national system of higher education. With little or no institutional support, science education had focused on providing essential tools to deal with the country's most urgent needs; military applications and infrastructure, for example, had been prioritized. But even if consistent material development was contingent on the promotion of science both in its theoretical and practical fronts, political reformers and educators could not agree on the necessary measures to remodel curricula. Indeed, the idea that knowledge needed to be useful had hindered the possibility of producing effective educational reforms. See Alberdi 495–504, 525–32.

13 The debate on whether this particular approach to the country's problems can be inscribed within the cultural frame of European modernism has never been settled. For an excellent bibliographical revision of this discussion, see the introduction to *Spain's 1898 Crisis: Regenerationism, Modernism, Postcolonialism*, edited by economic historian Joseph Harrison and Hispanist Alan Hoyle.

14 In Iovino and Oppermann's conceptualization, the term *non-human* denotes a community of expressive presences: not only sentient animals or other biological organisms, but also impersonal agents, ranging from electricity to hurricanes, from metals to bacteria, from nuclear plants to information networks (2–3).

15 See Carrette; Clarke; Graham; Hayles; Jasanoff; Rutsky, *High Technē*.

16 In *Discourse on the Method*, Descartes proposes human reasoning as an exclusive virtue, a metaphysical attribute that makes us different from other living creatures. In his conceptualization, body and mind constitute two separate entities: bodily functions, on the one hand, are complex systems that, with enough dexterity, an engineer could replicate; thinking, on the other hand, is a quality given by God and therefore a trait impossible to recreate without divine intervention. As a result, non-humans (animals, plants, machines) are conditioned by their surroundings but cannot willingly act on them (45–9). Interestingly, just as Torres Quevedo's automata would push the boundaries of non-human mechanical agency at the turn of the twentieth century, contemporary

cognition theory has not only established that consciousness can be non-human but that it can be vegetal, a point that Olga Colbert's chapter in this collection articulates in its analysis of beyond-human sentience and agency, implying that even though plants have not been shown to reason in Cartesian terms, they have been seen to demonstrate intention.

17 While Torres Quevedo's inventions achieved international recognition (see note 9), his essays, memoirs, and scientific papers were mostly published in local journals such as *Revista de Obras Públicas* or *Revista de la Real Academia de Ciencias Exactas, Físicas y Naturales*, whose circulation was limited to Spanish audiences. As a consequence, some of his pioneering ideas on computing and automatic calculation never reached the international scientific community and they could not actively contribute to the later development of cybernetics or artificial intelligence.

18 Although Regenerationists put emphasis on nature and geography, not only as two determining aspects of the Spanish character but also as causes of the country's economic decline, by defending a human-centred logic their movement failed to engage with the ecological implications of their societal reformulation, even while contemplating, as in Torres Quevedo's case, the role of non-human agency in identity. For more on the importance of geography for the Regenerationists, see Hoyle 30–2; Harrison, "Tackling National Decadence" 55–8.

19 The Chess Player is Torres Quevedo's most famous automaton. In 1911, the engineer presented this machine that combined his expertise in mechanical engineering with his ideas on automation. The device proved that with enough information a machine could make decisions and interact with the external world. The Chess Player proposed a fixed game of three pieces – two kings and a rook – and was able to checkmate its opponent in a finite number of moves. See Torres y Quevedo, *Mis inventos* 145–6.

WORK CITED AND CONSULTED

Alberdi, Ramón, et al. *Historia de la educación en España y América*. Coordinated by Buenaventura Delgado Criado. Vol. 3, S.M., 1994.

Álvarez Junco, José. *Mater dolorosa: La idea de España en el siglo XIX*. Taurus, 2003.

Arrillaga, Francisco de Paula. "Discurso del Sr. D. Francisco de Paula Arrillaga." *Discursos leídos ante la Real Academia de Ciencias Exactas, Físicas y Naturales en la recepción pública del Sr. D. Leonardo de Torres y Quevedo el día 19 de mayo de 1901*, Imprenta de Luis Aguado, 1901, pp. 35–54.

Carrette, Jeremy. "Cyborg Politics and Economic Realities: Reflections on Elaine Graham's *Representations of the Post/Human*." *Theology & Sexuality*, vol. 10, no. 2, 2004, pp. 45–55. *Taylor & Francis Online*, https://doi.org/10.1177/135583580401000204.

Casado de Otaola, Santos. *Naturaleza patria: Ciencia y sentimiento de la naturaleza en la España del regeneracionismo.* Marcial Pons Historia, 2010.

Clark, Timothy. *The Value of Ecocriticism.* Cambridge UP, 2019.

Clarke, Bruce. "The Nonhuman." Clarke and Rossini, pp. 141–52.

Clarke, Bruce, and Manuela Rossini, editors. *The Cambridge Companion to Literature and the Posthuman.* Cambridge UP, 2017.

Cruz, Jesús. *The Rise of Middle-Class Culture in Nineteenth-Century Spain.* Louisiana State UP, 2011.

Davis, Ryan A. "Modern Spain, a Myth: Regeneration through Reeducation in Santiago Ramón y Cajal's *Cuentos de vacaciones* (1905)." *Revista de Estudios Hispánicos*, vol. 47, no. 2, 2013, pp. 313–35. *Project MUSE,* https://doi.org /10.1353/rvs.2013.0029.

Descartes, René. *A Discourse on the Method of Correctly Conducting One's Reason and Seeking Truth in the Sciences.* Translated by Ian Maclean, Oxford UP, 2006.

Dou Mas de Xaxás, Alberto. "La inteligencia de las máquinas." *Actas del I simposio "Leonardo Torres Quevedo: Su vida, su tiempo, su obra": 7 al 11 de septiembre de 1987*, edited by Amor González Redondo and Francisco A. González Redondo, Amigos de la Cultura Científica, 1994, pp. 129–44.

Ferris, Kate. *Imagining "America" in Late Nineteenth Century Spain.* Palgrave, 2016.

Fusi, Juan Pablo. "El legado del 98." *Imágenes y ensayos del 98*, edited by Raymond Carr et al., Fundación Cañada Blanch, 1998, pp. 289–302.

García Santesmases, José. *Obra e inventos de Torres Quevedo.* Instituto de España, 1980.

Garrido, Manuel. "Introducción." *Ensayos sobre automática: Su definición y extensión teórica de sus aplicaciones*, by Leonardo Torres Quevedo, KRK, 2008, pp. 13–29.

Glick, Thomas. *Darwin en España.* Ediciones Península, 1982.

González de Posada, Francisco, editor. *Leonardo Torres Quevedo.* Fundación Banco Exterior de España, 1992.

González de Posada, Francisco. *Leonardo Torres Quevedo: Europeo preorteguiano e ingeniero español universal.* Amigos de la Cultura Científica, 1986.

González de Posada, Francisco, and Francisco A. González Redondo. "Leonardo Torres Quevedo (1852–1936): 1ª Parte. Las máquinas algébricas." *La Gaceta de la RSME*, vol. 7, no. 3, 2004, pp. 787–810.

Graham, Elaine L. *Representations of the Post/Human: Monsters, Aliens and Others in Popular Culture.* Rutgers UP, 2002.

Harrison, Joseph. "The Regenerationist Movement in Spain after the Disaster of 1898." *European History Quarterly*, vol. 9, no. 1, 1979, pp. 1–27. *SAGE Journals,* https://doi.org/10.1177/026569147900900102.

Harrison, Joseph. "Tackling National Decadence: Economic Regenerationism in Spain after the Colonial Débâcle." Harrison and Hoyle, pp. 55–67.

Harrison, Joseph, and Alan Hoyle, editors. *Spain's 1898 Crisis: Regenerationism, Modernism, Post-colonialism*. Manchester UP, 2000.

Hayles, Katherine. *How We Became Posthuman: Virtual Bodies in Cybernetics, Literature, and Informatics*. U of Chicago P, 1999.

Hoyle, Alan. "Introduction: The Intellectual Debate." Harrison and Hoyle, pp. 9–51.

Iovino, Serenella, and Serpil Oppermann. "Stories Come to Matter." *Material Ecocriticism*, edited by Serenella Iovino and Serpil Oppermann, Indiana UP, 2014, pp. 1–17.

Jasanoff, Sheila. "Future Imperfect: Science, Technology, and the Imaginations of Modernity." *Dreamscapes of Modernity: Sociotechnical Imaginaries and the Fabrication of Power*, edited by Sheila Jasanoff and Sang-Hyun Kim, U of Chicago P, 2015, pp. 1–33.

Kang, Minsoo. *Sublime Dreams of Living Machines: The Automaton in the European Imagination*. Harvard UP, 2010.

Lenoir, Timothy. "Techno-humanism: Requiem for the Cyborg." *Genesis Redux: Essays in the History and Philosophy of Artificial Life*, edited by Jessica Riskin, U of Chicago P, 2007, pp. 196–220.

López-Morillas, Juan. *Hacia el 98: Literatura, sociedad, ideología*. Ariel, 1972.

López Piñero, José María, and Mariano Peset Reig, editors. *La Ciencia en la España del siglo XIX*. Marcial Pons, 1992.

Martín Municio, Ángel. "Ideas científicas en la época de Torres Quevedo." *Actas del II simposio "Leonardo Torres Quevedo: Su vida, su tiempo, su obra": 12 al 14 de agosto de 1991*, edited by Amor González Redondo and Francisco A. González Redondo, Amigos de la Cultura Científica, 1993, pp. 121–32.

Nadal, Jordi. *El fracaso de la revolución industrial en España, 1814–1913*. Planeta, 1975.

Ringrose, David R. *Spain, Europe, and the "Spanish Miracle," 1700–1900*. Cambridge UP, 1996.

Rodríguez Alcalde, Leopoldo. *Leonardo Torres Quevedo y la cibernética*. Cid, 1966.

Rutsky, R.L. *High Technē: Art and Technology from the Machine Aesthetic to the Posthuman*. U of Minnesota P, 1999. 2 vols.

Rutsky, R.L. "Technologies." Clarke and Rossini, pp. 182–95.

Sánchez Ron, José Manuel. *Cincel, martillo y piedra: Historia de la ciencia en España (siglos XIX y XX)*. Taurus, 2000.

Schaffer, Simon. "Babbage's Dancer and the Impresarios of Mechanism." Cultural Babbage: Technology, Time and Invention, edited by Francis Spufford and Jenny Uglow, Faber and Faber, 1996, pp. 53–80.

Sosa-Velasco, Alfredo Jesús. *Médicos escritores en España, 1885–1955: Santiago Ramón y Cajal, Pío Baroja, Gregorio Marañón y Antonio Vallejo Nágera*. Tamesis, 2010.

Torres y Quevedo, Leonardo. "Automática: Complemento de la teoría de las máquinas." *Revista de Obras Públicas*, vol. 62, no. 2043, 1914, pp. 575–83.

Torres y Quevedo, Leonardo. "Discurso de Don Leonardo Torres y Quevedo." *Discursos leídos ante la Real Academia Española en la recepción pública de Don Leonardo Torres y Quevedo el día 31 de octubre de 1920*, Tipografía de la Revista de Archivos Bibliotecas y Museos, 1920, pp. 3–20.

Torres y Quevedo, Leonardo. "Memoria sobre las máquinas algebraicas." *Revista de Obras Públicas*, vol. 43, nos. 26–33, 1895, pp. 202–5, 209–15, 217–22, 225–7, 233–40, 241–6, 249–54, 257–62.

Torres y Quevedo, Leonardo. *Mis inventos y otras páginas de vulgarización.* Hesperia, 1917.

Tortella Casares, Gabriel. *El desarrollo de la España contemporánea: historia económica de los siglos XIX y XX.* Alianza, 1998.

Tresch, John. "The Machine Awakens: The Science and Politics of the Fantastic Automaton." *French Historical Studies*, vol. 34, no. 1, 2011, pp. 87–123. *Duke UP*, https://doi.org/10.1215/00161071-2010-024.

Vaquero Sánchez, Antonio. "La informática y la automática en la obra de Torres Quevedo." *Actas del IV simposio "Ciencia y técnica en España de 1898 a 1945, Cabrera, Cajal, Torres Quevedo": 3, 4 y 5 de julio de 2002*, edited by Dominga Trujillo et al., Amigos de la Cultura Científica, 2004, pp. 297–308.

Chapter Seven

The Spectre of Capitalism: Reading the Anthropocene in Vicente Blasco Ibáñez's *Cañas y barro*

MICHAEL L. MARTÍNEZ, JR.

Introduction

Literary naturalism in Spain diverged significantly from the tendencies that defined the movement in other European countries such as England and France.[1] Most Spanish novelists rejected the radical determinism that characterized the movement elsewhere. In Spain at the turn of the twentieth century, this rejection reflected the cultural dynamics of the period, specifically, the teachings of the Catholic Church on free will. The deterministic naturalism for which the French novelist Émile Zola was known, for instance, left little room for personal responsibility, since socioeconomic status, heredity, class, and environment inescapably determined the course of one's life. This notion – that factors other than the free actions of the individual determined one's fate – stood in contrast to religious doctrine in Catholic Spain. The Spanish response to this cultural-aesthetic dilemma was best articulated by Emilia Pardo Bazán, who, in *La cuestión palpitante* (1882), advocated that novelists reimagine the theoretical foundations of literary naturalism to better conform to Spain's cultural contours. To be sure, she suggested a reorientation of the novel's focus from "typical persons, places, times, and conflicts to a novelization of the inner individual" (Miller 427). This historical pivot towards the human in Spanish fiction transforms the naturalist novel into a productive site from which to examine the human-nature dualism that defines the Anthropocene.

Indeed, not only in the negotiations with determinism and free will, but in the attempt to make sense of the complex world more broadly, abstract concepts organize our thinking processes, which, in turn, inform everyday behaviours. Often difficult to identify in practice, these cognitive schemes operate on an unconscious level and thereby obtain a certain quality of naturalness or normality, meaning that they appear to be just the way things are, when, in reality, conceptual paradigms are intimately bound with the historical development of material social conditions. Over time, hierarchical schemata are socially constructed in the context of asymmetrical power relationships and, as a result, constantly contested and renegotiated, struggled over and imposed upon. In other words, humanity's grids of intelligibility are shaped by an ongoing relational process between dominant and subordinate groups, crucially defining in this way the boundaries within which thought can take place. Perhaps the most entrenched of these power-centring schemes in the Western cultural tradition is the human-nature dualism, which assumes that everything that is human stands separate and apart from that which is considered nature. The human category and the nature category certainly interact in different ways, but the historical development of the human-nature dualism is such that today nature is characterized as an external ontological object upon which humans, the subject, act.[2] Nature in this way has been transformed into an antagonistic entity, a thing to be dominated, tamed, internalized, or brought within the orbit of the human. Importantly, this binary conceptual framework conditions our behaviour towards the natural environment and underpins the dire socio-environmental situation that threatens the continuity of human life on this planet.

In his pioneering book *Capitalism in the Web of Life: Ecology and the Accumulation of Capital* (2015), the environmental historian Jason W. Moore argues that, while the Anthropocene concept has certainly animated important and timely discussions, the human-nature dualism that structures Anthropocentric discourse diminishes the movement's overall effectiveness. It does this most importantly by framing humanity as a collective, monolithic actor. Indeed, humanity in the Anthropocene is construed as a non-differentiated whole that acts upon nature. It then follows that the totality of human activity has reached such a proportion to merit its own personalized geological epoch: the Anthropocene. And if "[t]he mosaic of human activity in the web of life is reduced to abstract Humanity: a homogenous acting unit," Moore reasons, then critical postures towards "[i]nequality, commodification, imperialism, patriarchy, racial formations, and much more" are thereby excluded from consideration (170). This dehistoricizing process inherent to the Anthropocene's critical apparatus has serious implications for the discourse's emancipatory potential. Most egregiously for Moore is the erasure of the long history of capitalism, which, more than any other force, has conditioned humanity's contemporary relationship with the natural environment. Plainly, capitalism gets a free pass when viewed from the Anthropocene. To confront these shortcomings, Moore has developed a new analytical paradigm that he calls world-ecology. The world-ecological approach decentres the Anthropocene's dualistic foundation, approaches humanity and nature as dialectically co-produced, and construes capitalism as a system of "organizing nature" (Moore 2).

As the present chapter illustrates in part, the literary form of the naturalist novel generally, and the Spanish variety in particular, mobilizes symbolic, imaginative, and affective semiotic currents in a way that renders visible the immense complexity of problems surrounding the human-nature dualism. One such representative naturalist text is *Cañas y barro* (1902) by Vicente Blasco Ibáñez. In perhaps his most important contribution to literary naturalism, the Valencian author explores the destabilizing effects of capitalist modernity within the intergenerational dynamics of the Paloma family. In so doing, the novel brings into sharp relief the ways that capital transforms the relationship between human beings and the natural environment in order to assemble the material conditions necessary for its circulation. As a formal strategy, moreover, Blasco Ibáñez himself also relies on the human-nature dichotomy to construct the narrative, converting the text into an insightful example of how the destruction of ecological systems can be traced back to the conceptual separation of human from nature.[3]

The setting of the novel, what is today the Albufera National Park, serves as the ideal backdrop as the author explores the interplay between humanity, nature, and capitalism. Just south of Valencia on the Mediterranean coast, the Albufera – an area comprising a freshwater lagoon, estuary, forest, rice paddies, and wetlands – teems with biodiversity. The spectre of capitalism looms large in the novel, however, and the forces of capital begin their descent into the region, destined to penetrate, reconfigure, and exploit not only the social relations of production, but also the rich ecology of the region. In depicting the ways that capital organizes both social relations and natural environments, what will emerge from this ecocritical close reading of the text is an insightful critique of the capitalist mode of production by way of an indictment of the socioenvironmentally disastrous changes that capitalism must inherently effect: the destabilization of social relations, the degradation of biodiversity, and the creation of wealth inequalities. The present essay examines *Cañas y barro* from Moore's world-ecological perspective by highlighting the societal and ecological transformations that flow from the human-nature dualism, their representation in the Spanish naturalist novel, and the violence inherent to an economic system that houses a conceptual binary at its core.

Capitalism, the Human-Nature Dualism, and the Paloma Family

Central to the rise of capitalism was the assembly of the material conditions necessary to ensure capital accumulation. Historically, this entailed a series of interrelated processes that included the enclosure of communal lands, the construction of a private-property regime, and the proletarianization of the peasantry. From its imperialist origins to contemporary neocolonialism, an analysis of the long history of capitalism lays bare the astonishing violence that surrounds the installation of these material conditions. But when capital surveils new terrains of accumulation, it goes to work on mental conceptions as well. A key component of the capitalist project is thus to transform the way individuals think about the world around them. The Marxist geographer David Harvey writes that "[c]hanges in mental conceptions have all manner of intended and unintended consequences for acceptable technological and organisational forms, social relations, labour processes, relations to nature, as well as for institutional arrangements" (*Enigma* 121). The contested and always mutable mental conceptions that humans use to organize reality in this way play an important, if underappreciated, role within the logic of capital. Though critics agree that *Cañas y barro* sketches the harsh realities of Valencian daily life to effect social change at the historical moment in which it was written, Blasco Ibáñez's naturalist text is particularly well suited to explore the dialectical relationship between mental conceptions of the natural environment and capital's historical development. The ecological close reading that follows thus reconciles the narrative's original concern for social justice with present-day ecological criticism of the Anthropocene.[4]

The novel's narrative trajectory pivots around the Paloma family. Paloma, the eldest, has been characterized as a "primitive who represents the past and the conservative forces of tradition, a patriarchal figure who is in constant conflict with the modern and its progressive ideas" (Anderson 125). Moreover, his skills as a hunter and fisherman are equalled only by his affection for the Albufera's natural environment. He spends his days "buscándose el sustento en el aire o en el agua, cazando y pescando" ("looking for sustenance in the air or the water, hunting and fishing"), because the Palomas "no servían a nadie" ("didn't serve anybody"; 39).[5] Though he relies solely on the Albufera's natural resources, the elder Paloma nevertheless only appropriates the bare minimum needed for survival. Relatedly, he detests the growing number of *labradores* ("labourers") in the area, whose *tancats*, or "low earthen dikes around small plots at the water's edge" (Hamilton 13), are little by little destroying his beloved freshwater lake. He also nostalgically remembers when a feudal system prevailed in the Albufera and the area's small population could fish and hunt without fear of retribution (Blasco Ibáñez 28).

The Albufera's transition from seigneurial power structures to the capitalist mode of production is textually communicated via Paloma's contentious relationship with his son Tono. Throughout the novel, the family patriarch cruelly insults his son for distancing himself from more traditional ways of living. Beyond the fact that Tono has rejected the hunter-gatherer lifestyle, what is unacceptable for Paloma is that his son is one of those *labradores* that is transforming the physical contours of the Albufera's wetlandscape. Accompanied by his adopted daughter, La Borda, Tono is engaged in the Sisyphean task of building a *tancat*, for he dreams of one day cultivating rice on his own plot of land. It is backbreaking, monotonous, seemingly never-ending work that entails transporting boatloads of mud from one end of the Albufera to the other. Tono's work ethic together with his desire to improve the family's socio-economic status signals a significant change in mental conceptions in the Albufera, one that accompanies the emergence of capitalist relations in the novel.

A closer look at the conceptual frameworks, social relationships, and everyday behaviours exhibited by Paloma and Tono provides an insightful example of the insidiousness of the human-nature dualism in action. To begin with, Blasco Ibáñez formally develops opposing metonymies to build the narrative foundation: the elder Paloma stands in for the pre-capitalist world view, whereas Tono represents incipient capitalism. Issuing from this metonymic structure is a series of character traits that can be traced back to the human-nature binary: each character becomes associated with a specific ecological space of the Albufera, each evinces certain ideas about the essence of property ownership and land management, and each displays certain behaviours concerning the purpose of labour. *Cañas y barro*'s acerbic social criticism derives its potency in large part from the underlying pattern of this totalizing narrative strategy.

Paloma subscribes to a world view that understands humanity as internal to the concept of nature, or, as Moore calls it, "humanity-in-nature" (3). The novel does this in a few ways. First, Paloma undergoes a process of animalization, a common trope of literary naturalism that tends to deemphasize his humanness. To be happy, for instance, all Paloma needs is to live "como un pez del lago o un pájaro de los carrizales, haciendo su nido hoy en una isleta y mañana en un cañar" ("like a fish of the lake or a bird of the reedbeds, making his nest today on an island or tomorrow in a canefield"; 31). Interestingly, the positive connotations that attach to his animalistic characterization diverge from the literary movement's aesthetic more generally, since naturalist writers tended instead to animalize humans in a rather negative light in order to underscore the dehumanizing effects that social class, heredity, and environment have on the individual. As we will see below, however, the positive qualification serves to highlight the contrasting mental conceptions of nature between Paloma and his son Tono. Second, the animalization of Paloma is also manifested by the character's inability to understand socially constructed hierarchies, codes, and rules. For Paloma, modern social constructs are meaningless, because "[p]ara él no existían grandezas humanas: los hombres se dividían en buenos y malos cazadores" ("human grandeur didn't exist for him: humans were divided into good or bad hunters"; 30). Third, he lacks the ability to effectively produce that fundamental marker of human identity – language – and is "cazurro y malhablado" ("slow-witted and foul-mouthed"), frequently speaking in "frases bilingües y retorcidas" ("bilingual and twisted phrases"; 30). Fourth and most importantly, the text also repeatedly insists that Paloma is the progeny of the Albufera, a direct descendent of the natural environment, the offspring of nature: "era insolente con la rudeza de un hijo de la laguna" ("he was insolent with the roughness of a child of the lagoon"), the narrator remarks at one point (29). And unlike his son and those who labour in the rice paddies for paltry wages, "[l]os hijos del lago estaban libres" ("the children of the lake were free"; 36). Understood collectively, the animalization, misanthropy, and tellurian lineage imply that Paloma's world view unifies the two relata of the human-nature dualism, in keeping with pre-capitalist understandings of nature.

Paloma's rejection of the Anthropocene's foundational binary informs additional aspects of his behaviour as well. About the family patriarch, the narrator remarks that "[l]a Albufera era de él y de todos los Pescadores" ("the Albufera was his and all the other fisherman"; 44). This more egalitarian world view suggests that Paloma is guided by a usufructuary understanding of property ownership, the hegemonic pre-capitalist organizational system. The principal marker of the usufructuary system is that public use of land is permitted for all, provided that one does not alter or impair the natural resources in a way that precludes their use for others. The system depends on the responsible use of land and natural resources. The potential consequences of overfishing, overhunting, overuse of water, and deforestation are mitigated through a collective social contract, which is characterized by an understanding that wanton destruction of the natural environment could be potentially fatal to the entire social system. The character's views on property are also closely related to his labour practices: "[Paloma] comía lo suyo, lo que había conquistado durante el día" ("Paloma ate only what was his, what he had caught throughout the day"; 43). To be sure, labour for Paloma means appropriating the Albufera's natural resources at a subsistence level.

Blasco Ibáñez takes great care to differentiate the variegated ecological spaces of the Albufera, and the region's natural environment becomes a crucial point of reference in the author's pursuit of social justice. It's significant, then, that the environmental trope assigned to Paloma is an expanse of the freshwater lake called the *lluent*, or "la verdadera Albufera, el lago libre, con sus bosquecillos de cañas esparcidos a grandes distancias, donde se refugiaban las aves del lago, tan perseguidas por los cazadores de la ciudad" ("the true Albufera, the free lake, with its small copses of reeds spread out at great distances, where the birds of the lake took refuge, so often persecuted by hunters from the city"; 14). Like the birds that are hunted by Valencian city dwellers, Paloma takes refuge in the *lluent* in a futile attempt to insulate himself from the capitalist forces that are bearing down upon El Palmar, the small fishing hamlet that is home to the Paloma family. It furthermore makes sense that, when the narrative is focalized through the perspective of the family patriarch, the lake symbolizes freedom – personified as "el lago libre" – and serves as the symbolic instantiation of his subsistence living, free from the capital-labour relationship that is everywhere encroaching on his idyllic domain (12).

In sharp contrast to his father on all accounts, Tono behaves according to a world view that, like capitalism and the Anthropocene, construes nature as separate from or external to humanity. When focalized through Tono, nature is hostile and must be subjugated, mastered, subdued. The rich ecology of the Albufera is the object. Tono is the subject. And the subject must dominate the object. This dualist cosmovision is powerfully brought to bear through the bellicose discourse employed to describe the construction of the *tancat*. "Su lucha por crear nueva tierra" ("His fight to create new land"), for instance, means that Tono and La Borda "marchaban a sus campos todas las mañanas a continuar la batalla con el lago" ("set off to his land each morning to continue the battle with the lake"; 165). Unlike Paloma, whose ichthyological and ornithological descriptions suggested independence from coercive social forces, Tono's dualistic frame of reference is made explicit through an animalization process that is negatively connoted and thus more in keeping with the standard use of the trope in literary naturalism. For example, one of Paloma's more hurtful barbs is to associate Tono's work with that of a horse. In free indirect style, the narrative at one point suggests that Paloma habitually and publicly ridicules his son by announcing, "¡Caballeros, la gran noticia! … Su hijo olía a caballo. ¡Jí, jí! ¡Un caballo en la isla del Palmar!" ("Gentlemen, the big announcement! … His son smelled like a horse. Ha, ha! A horse on the island of El Palmar!"; 42). Accentuated by the equine imagery, the negatively connoted animalization of the character signals the idea that the human-nature dualism itself tends to corrode the human relata by draining the individual of their species-essence and reducing them to a function of their capacity to labour.

Furthermore, Tono's antagonistic relationship with the Albufera inflects his understanding of work and property ownership. Labour, for Tono, is a means by which to participate in the burgeoning relations of capitalist production that are increasingly coming to dominate life in El Palmar. In a moment of rest from his Herculean task, he imagines the day when he can extract profits from his own plot of arable land: "Había que fijarse en las ventajas del cultivo del arroz: poco trabajo y gran provecho. *Era una verdadera bendición del cielo: nada en el mundo daba más*" ("One had to focus on the advantages of cultivating rice: little work but great profit. *It was all truly a blessing from heaven: nothing in the world gave more*"; 40; emphasis added). That Tono understands the agricultural labour process as a true blessing from heaven coheres with capitalism's understanding of nature as the repository of free gifts, which "capital can use without paying anything" (Harvey, *Marx* 94). From this dualistic framework flows also the type of ownership rights that one enjoys under capitalism. Unlike the usufructuary system of his father, Tono understands the *tancat* through the lens of "exclusionary permanent ownership rights" (Harvey, *Seventeen* 39). The private-property regime constitutes a pillar of the capitalist system, because it bestows upon the owner the right to trade away, alter, or impair commodities with impunity, a crucial precondition of capital accumulation.

The narrative develops Tono's dualistic world view most explicitly through the ecological space that is metonymically associated with him throughout the novel. Given its cultural history in the Western tradition, it is not surprising that the environmental trope that attaches to the character is the wetlands that surround the Albufera's freshwater lake. The environmental humanist Rod Giblett writes that wetlands "have been associated with death and disease, the monstrous and the melancholic, if not the downright mad." Part of the reason for the horror that humans feel around wetlands, marshes, bogs, lagoons, and the like is that they are "neither strictly land nor water" (Giblett 3). Indeed, they are liminal ecological spaces that confound our contemporary predilection for dualistic thought patterns. Exemplified in the text by Tono's *tancat*, the instinctual human response is thus to fill the Albufera's lake in order "to create the dead surface of private property on which agricultural and urban development [can] then take place" (Giblett xi). Significantly, the wetlands in *Cañas y barro* are differentiated from Paloma's *lluent* and portrayed as disease-ridden, pestilent, and extra-human: the stench that emanates from the stagnant "agua muerta" ("dead water") not only emits an "hedor viscoso" ("viscous stench"), but constitutes a miasma that transmits "las malditas tercianas de la Albufera" ("the cursed tertian malaria of the Albufera"), the fever commonly suffered by workers who labour "con agua a la cintura" ("with water up to their waists") in the transitionary ecological space that is the wetlands (100, 119, 7, 9). As a rhetorical strategy, moreover, the depiction of the wetlands as potentially fatal to human life foreshadows the climactic infanticide-suicide that occurs at novel's end.

At an extratextual level, Spain at the turn of the twentieth century was considered a European backwater, a place where cultural and economic progress had stagnated due to the long decline of the Spanish empire. The loss of the last colonial territories after the Disaster of 1898 catalysed Spanish intellectuals to call for modernizing reforms. But since Spain could no longer rely on its colonial possessions to provide the raw materials for increased industrial activity, groups like the Regenerationists and the Generation of '98 advocated for more efficient use of natural resources.[6] The modernization of the national territory was in this way linked to the transformation of the natural environment. Importantly, the process was all underwritten by a concomitant change in mental conceptions that legitimized the human-nature dualism and positioned Enlightenment rationality to "rethink the way Spain used its natural resources and engineer the complete remaking of the countryside in the interest of increased production" (Hamilton 32). As a result, the nature relata was put to work for the human correlative as part of a broader nationalizing process. Though Blasco Ibáñez does not explicitly reference these extratextual modernizing processes, his text does capture the contemporaneous shift in mental conceptions with its portrayal of the Paloma family's divergent conceptualizations of and consequent behaviours towards the natural world.

Coproducing the Socio-environmental Dialectic: Tonet, the *sorteo*, and the Violence of the Human-Nature Dualism

For the residents of El Palmar, the second Sunday of July is the most important day of the year. On that fateful day, the village holds a solemn ceremony called the *sorteo* to decide who will fish which plots of the Albufera throughout the year. The annual raffle for the *redolíns*, or "los puestos de pesca de la Albufera y sus canales" ("the fishing plots of the Albufera and its canals"), is an egalitarian social institution (105). Those who one year win the first plots can in the next year just as easily draw one of the last, less lucrative spaces. The most coveted plots of the Albufera are the first six, called the *Sequióta*, or the canal spaces that lead from the freshwater lake to the ocean (110). To win one of these spaces all but guarantees riches throughout the year. In the narrative present, Tonet, son and grandson to Tono and Paloma, respectively, wins the annual *sorteo*. Some additional context to Tonet's life prior to his stroke of luck will help illustrate the representation of capital's co-production of social relations, human behaviours, and the Albufera's ecological spaces in *Cañas y barro*.

As a child, Tonet at first "siguió con gusto al abuelo en sus expediciones por tierra y agua" ("followed his grandfather with great pleasure on his expeditions over land and water"; 48). He quickly learns to navigate the canals surrounding El Palmar, serves as a guide during the annual hunting expeditions, and becomes a skilled marksman. Paloma is pleased that his grandson is turning into "un verdadero hijo de la Albufera" ("a true child of the Albufera"; 44). Tonet, however, grows tired of the demanding rhythm of subsistence living – collecting the heavy *mornells* each morning, "grandes bolsas de red en cuyo fondo se enroscaban las anguilas" ("large sacks of netting in whose base the eels entangled themselves"), for example, only to return them to the water again under the unforgiving Mediterranean sun (54). To make things worse for young Tonet, Paloma begins acting like a tyrant and, as part of his grandson's education, shifts the majority of daily work to Tonet, who as a result only resists further.

One day, it becomes obvious to Paloma what sort of man Tonet is becoming: "lo que su nieto odiaba ... era el trabajo" ("what his grandson hated ... was work"; 49). After Tonet finally rejects the pre-capitalist lifestyle associated with his grandfather, he begins his descent into alcoholism, and, after a particularly ugly incident at the local tavern, runs off to fight in the Spanish-American War. His return to the Albufera two years later marks the beginning of the present narrative. Upon returning, Tonet at first dedicates himself to the construction of his father's *tancat*, but quickly loses interest, whereupon he turns again to alcohol (100). Tonet's situation is exacerbated finally by the fact that his childhood companion and romantic interest, Neleta, is now married to El Palmar's most powerful resident, the tavern owner Cañamèl. Tonet's victory in the annual *sorteo* sets into motion a series of events that will lead to his eventual suicide in the final pages of the novel.

An ecocritically oriented close reading of the *sorteo* exposes capital's role in reorganizing the dynamics of this socio-environmental practice. For Moore, capitalism does not have an ecology with which it is associated; it is itself an ecology, a way of rearranging both the social relations of production and the natural environment from which capital extracts its free gifts. Because the annual drawing is an institution that likewise organizes social relationships and mediates El Palmar's engagement with the natural environment, the *sorteo* provides the ideal context for exploring these important dimensions of capitalism from the perspective of Moore's world-ecological paradigm.

The *sorteo* is a testament to El Palmar's enduring egalitarian legacy. The freshwater lake belongs to all the community's residents, as evidenced by the internal mechanics of the annual drawing, unlike the burgeoning agricultural system surrounding the area, "donde los hombres han inventado esas porquerías del reparto de la tierra" ("where humans have invented these shameless land repartitions"; 115).[7] While chance indeed decides the economic order of the small fishing hamlet, the year that Tonet wins the *sorteo* the forces of capital have already begun to erode the drawings's egalitarian origins. The first indication that this transformation is underway concerns the introduction of an entrance fee. In a particularly revealing scene, the changing dynamics of the *sorteo* are made evident when an impoverished man speaks out just moments before the drawing, bemoaning the fact that he did not have the money to pay the fee because he drew one of the last *redolíns* the previous year. Paloma characteristically comes to his defence: "él que no pagaba ahora ya pagaría más adelante; y los que tuvieran más que supliesen las faltas de los que nada tenían, pues así había ocurrido siempre … ¡Todos al sorteo!" ("he who couldn't pay now could pay in the future; and the ones who had more could make up the difference for those who didn't have anything, that's how it's always been … Everyone to the drawing!"; 123). Though in this instance Paloma succeeds in defending the sanctity of the *sorteo*, he fails to understand that El Palmar's most important ceremony has already been irrevocably undermined by the logic of capitalism, an ongoing transformation that is formally developed as a function of the tavern owner Cañamèl.

Metonymically associated with advanced capitalism in the novel, Cañamèl has been exploiting the *sorteo* since his arrival to the area. The tavern owner is not allowed to participate in the annual drawing because "no era hijo del pueblo" ("he was not a child of the town"; 117). Yet this does not stop him from mobilizing his surplus capital to take full advantage of the opportunity that the autochthonous ceremony presents. More often than not, the fisherman who draws the first place in the *sorteo* does not possess the fixed capital to maximize the return on his luck, which is when Cañamèl amiably presents his proposition:

> Para explotar la *Sequióta* necesitaba grandes artefactos, varias embarcaciones, marineros a sueldo; y cuando el infeliz, anonadado por su buena suerte, no sabía cómo empezar, se le aproximaba Cañamèl como un ángel bueno. Él tenía lo preciso; ofrecía sus barcos, las mil pesetas de hilo nuevo que se necesitaban para las grandes barreras que debían cerrar el canal y el dinero necesario para adelantar jornales ... De este modo, los sorteos eran casi siempre en beneficio de Cañamèl.

> (In order to exploit the *Sequióta* one needed a great many tools, various watercrafts, salaried sailors; and when the naive one, stunned by his good luck, didn't know how to begin, Cañamèl approached him like a pious angel. He had what they needed; he offered the boats, the thousand pesetas of new fishing thread that was necessary for the large barriers that would close the canal and the money necessary to make advancements on daily wages ... In this way, the drawings were almost always beneficial to Cañamèl; 117)

The asymmetrical power relationship between Cañamèl and El Palmar's lucky resident points to the capital-labour relationship upon which the production of surplus value is predicated. The specific terms of the deal that Cañamèl makes with Tonet dictate that the tavern owner will provide the capital to purchase the means of production, while Tonet and Paloma deliver the necessary labour (128). In true capitalist fashion, Cañamèl is guaranteed a portion of the surplus value created by father and son – "la mitad del producto" ("half of the product") – thereby alienating the workers from the products of their labour (135). Particularly noteworthy in the ecocritical context here is that capital orchestrates the emergence of the capital-labour relationship by exploiting the socio-environmental dialectic embedded within the dynamics of the *sorteo*.

Furthermore, the drawing represents a paradigmatic example of capital's ability to co-opt pre-existing local caches of knowledge and integrate them into the logic of accumulation. When surveilling new terrains, capital does not, so to speak, reinvent the wheel. It dynamically adapts to the social, cultural, epistemological, and environmental specificities that it seeks to exploit. *Cañas y barro* subtly highlights what this appropriation process could look like in practice by relying on formal structures commonly used in the naturalist novel. Indeed, capital's methods for co-opting the *sorteo* are brought into sharp relief by the use of free indirect speech. Speaking through Paloma, the third-person narrator explains that the first residents of El Palmar carefully studied the movements of the local eel population. They found that, at night, the eels would move away from the lake towards the *Sequióta*, whereupon the fishermen would close the dykes, place their nets in the enclosed area, and the eels would simply entangle themselves. This insight into the behaviour of the local eel population initially gave rise to the institution of the *sorteo*, because, for those early inhabitants of El Palmar, an annual drawing was an equitable way of organizing nature in the Albufera. Nevertheless, the arrival of capitalist forces in the region changes everything. Whereas at first the *sorteo* ensured a sustainable equilibrium between the natural environment and the humans who depended on it, the introduction of a figure like Cañamèl fundamentally alters the dynamics of the institution. Cañamèl seizes upon the hamlet's egalitarian social relations and redirects their operationality towards profit extraction. Once a cultural practice that turned the community into stewards of the Albufera's ecology, the *sorteo* becomes transformed into an institution that will exhaust the local eel population in search of surplus value.

Relatedly, capitalism also produces human behaviours that better align with the system's dualist conception of nature. Unlike Tonet, who, instead of enthusiastically working the most lucrative *redolín*, begins to spend more and more time at Cañamèl's tavern, Paloma sets upon the task with gusto: "nunca había trabajado con tanto entusiasmo como al verse dueño de la *Sequióta*" ("never had he worked with such enthusiasm as when he saw himself as the owner of the *Sequióta*"; 161). The transformation that Paloma undergoes in the novel – in particular, his new-found capitalist work ethic – is suggestive of the way that capitalism co-produces human behaviour as a means to extract nature's free gifts. While the dynamics of the *sorteo* have remained largely unaltered – it is still after all a nominally egalitarian institution – what has changed is the structural orientation of the relationships between the individuals participating in the drawing. Now, Cañamèl appropriates a portion of the value embedded in the ecological landscape of the Albufera not for subsistence purposes, but as a strategy for capital accumulation. And because Paloma is engaged in a capital-labour relationship with Cañamèl, the very essence of the labour that he carries out has been fundamentally redirected towards the profit motive. Unbeknownst to the family patriarch, his own human behaviour has in this way been co-produced by the forces of capital, and he has become the very thing that he so detests: one of those *labradores* who are destroying the Albufera's natural ecologies.

Beyond the metamorphosis of Paloma's behaviour, the co-production of the socio-environmental dialectic can be additionally teased out of the novel by exploring the astonishing violence to which capital recurs to establish conditions for accumulation. At a conceptual level, this violence is closely related to a cultural process that constantly negotiates and reconfigures the division between human and nature. Moore substantiates this idea by remarking that "[a]t the heart of modernity's co-productions is the incessant re-working of the boundaries between the human and the extra-human" (17). More specifically, the shifting boundaries of the human-nature dualism not only provide justification for the degradation of the biosphere, as we have seen, but also serve to dehumanize certain groups of people and situate them outside the human relata. To be sure, exclusions from the human category based on race, ethnicity, or gender have historically deprived certain groups of the rights bestowed on those within the human category, leading to all manner of unconscionable acts of cruelty: the conquest of the New World, slavery, genocide, colonialism, neocolonialism, and so on. Not surprisingly, as *Cañas y barro* moves towards its conclusion, the violence that issues from the human-nature dualism is brought into sharp relief in a characteristically violent naturalist *denouement*.

El Palmar is a decidedly patriarchal community and gender roles are sharply defined. Men are expected to hunt and fish, while women are primarily relegated to domestic activities such as childcare. Yet one of the remarkable features of the novel is its subtle depiction of the foundational role that women play in the reproduction of the social order. Indeed, the *sorteo* survives primarily because of the unpaid labour carried out by women, for they sew the enormous amount of netting required to fish the *redolíns*. This is made clear at the end of the summer, when preparations begin to fish the prime canal spaces, and Paloma becomes impatient because "[l]os artefactos que poseía Cañamèl ... no bastaban para la *Sequióta*. Había que comprar mucho hilo, dar trabajo a muchas mujeres de las que tejían red, para explotar cumplidamente el *redolí*" ("the tools that Cañamèl possessed ... were not sufficient for the *Sequióta*. It was necessary to buy a lot of thread, to give work to many of the women who sewed the netting, in order to fully exploit the *redolí*"; 139). While the actions of the male characters are always foregrounded, in the background and year after year, the women of El Palmar deliver the unremunerated labour necessary to produce the fixed capital that is so important for the community's reproduction. This symbolic form of violence issues from the exclusion of women from the paid labour force – long considered an important component of the emergence of the capitalist system – which is conceptually legitimated by a patriarchal definition of the human relata as male and not female.[8] Patriarchal power, like racial and class-based hierarchies, determines who is and who is not considered human.

From this gendered vantage point, a critical analysis of Tono's adopted daughter, La Borda, reveals the symbolic violence involved in the construction of spaces conducive to capitalist accumulation. La Borda is doubly exploited, insofar as the character attends to "los quehaceres del hogar" ("household chores"; 77) and also labours alongside Tono constructing the *tancat* and, with it, the region's broader capitalist landscape. Theoretically speaking, landscapes, like the commodity form itself, conceal unbalanced power relationships, ideologies, and structural violence, even while they leave traces within their materiality of the structures of domination and subordination that contribute to their construction. The historical ascendency of state power is crucial in this regard. The state holds a monopoly on violence and monitors the private-property regime, ensuring that the fruits of a capitalist landscape are unevenly distributed as a function of asymmetrical power relationships. And indeed, in Spain at the turn of the century, gender discrimination was codified into a set of laws that "legally imposed women's subordination to men in all spheres of life," including the *patria potestad* ("legal authority of the nation") clause of the Napoleonic Civil Code of 1889, which dictated that women "did not have equal rights to joint property" (Tsuchiya 212). So, even though La Borda participates in the construction of the built environment upon which capital circulation can take place, she is not entitled to a share of the profits that are extracted from that same landscape. Viewed from the world-ecological prism, then, it is particularly incongruous when the narrator describes La Borda as "aquella expósita infatigable, que valía más que un hombre" ("that indefatigable abandoned child, who was worth more than a man"), revealing in the rhetorical language the socially constructed and constantly mutable essence of conceptual hierarchies like male/female (24).

More closely related to the formal structure of *Cañas y barro*, these gendered negotiations of patriarchal power also play a key role in generating the narrative's climactic moment. As it happens, Tonet is incapable of honouring his end of the contract with Cañamèl and eventually slides back into alcoholism. While drinking in the tavern, he rekindles a secret relationship with Neleta, who serves drinks behind the bar because of her marriage to the owner, and it is implied that they are having sexual relations. Upon Cañamèl's death, Neleta learns that her deceased husband's will forbids her from pursuing romantic relationships for ten years, lest his estate transfer to the family of his first wife. This form of gender discrimination is sanctioned by the state. Cañamèl is perfectly within the letter of the law to proscribe Neleta's activities beyond his own life because in Spain at this time "[w]omen were considered to be minors under the guardianship of their husbands and fathers, who had exclusive authority and proprietary rights over them" (Tsuchiya 212). This means that when Neleta becomes pregnant with Tonet's child, the couple must confront the fact that their love for each other has serious financial implications. Though deterministic circumstances such as patriarchal laws, the natural environment, and heredity certainly play a role, the couple's downfall is ultimately a matter of free will.

The birth of Tonet and Neleta's child takes place the night of the annual *demaná*, a traditional repartitioning ceremony similar to the *sorteo*, but which divides the Albufera into plots for the bird-hunting season. Unlike the *sorteo*, however, citizens from the surrounding towns and cities are allowed to participate, which means that rich Valencians commonly hire El Palmar's residents as guides during the hunting expeditions. Tonet learns that he is to serve as a guide to don Joaquín just as Neleta goes into labour. After the birth of the child, the star-crossed lovers decide to commit infanticide and, under the cover of darkness, Tonet takes the newborn through the canals of the Albufera and cruelly abandons his still-breathing child in the surrounding reeds and mud. The next morning, dreary, disheartened, and ashamed, Tonet takes don Joaquín bird hunting. At one point, when the hunting dog goes to retrieve the carcass of a fallen bird, he brings back, to don Joaquín's horror, the gelatinous body of Tonet's deceased infant son. Unable to confront his guilty conscience, Tonet commits suicide shortly thereafter.

Figuratively understood from an ecocritical perspective, the appearance in the narrative of the Valencian urban middle class is significant. In *Cultivating Nature: The Conservation of a Valencian Working Landscape*, the historian Sarah R. Hamilton writes that, because Spanish modernization relied so heavily on Enlightenment rationality to increase the efficiency of land usage, powerful interest groups from Valencia's growing urban middle class united in response and worked to preserve the pre-industrial cultures that inhabited areas like Paloma's beloved Albufera. She goes on to remark that a faction of the "multifaceted preservation movement" involved in the competing claims over the cultural and physical geography of the Albufera coalesced around "elite sportsmen's enthusiasm for rugged landscapes and game species ... and middle-class demands for outdoor recreation" (30). Against this historical backdrop, the death of Tonet and his infant son signal three developments occurring at both textual and extratextual levels: the end of the Paloma familiar line and by extension the local community's claims to the Albufera; the victory of a new capitalist social order; and the emergence of an exogenous claimant on the cultural and physical geographies of the Albufera, or, the urban middle class of the Valencian capital. The Albufera, once the home of a subsistence community that survived in equilibrium with the natural environment, is transformed into a site of contestation between modernization processes at the national level and Valencia's burgeoning urban middle class, pushing out local claims to the area and silencing working-class voices. Exemplified by the downfall of Tonet, individuals that lack both a capitalist work ethic and personal responsibility have no place in the reconfigured El Palmar: "Cuando se nace pobre, la pereza es el crimen" ("When one is born poor, laziness is a crime"), the narrator intones at one point (288). The deaths of Tonet and his child are in this context symbolic of the end of a past egalitarian age and represent the dawn of a new era of capitalism in the region.

In the wake of the climactic deaths, Tono, Neleta, and La Borda are forced to adapt to the capitalist social order. The death of his son leads Tono to search for and eventually bury Tonet's body in the growing mass of land that is coming to define the Albufera's wetlandscape. While staring at the corpse, Tono realizes the irony of his years-long struggle to build a *tancat*: the father had all along been constructing the tomb of his child (292). Overcome with shame, he decides to keep the crimes of his son a secret, since "[l]a Albufera, madre de todos, guardaría el secreto con tanta fidelidad como él" ("the Albufera, mother of everyone, would keep the secret with as much fidelity as he would"; 286). In so doing, the emergent capitalist landscape of the Albufera conceals the violence that made its construction possible.

Finally, in a moment that demonstrates the author's lack of fidelity to Pardo Bazán's suggestion that the Spanish naturalist novel privilege free will over socio-environmental factors, the text attributes Tonet's personal failings to Neleta. "Ella había sido la tentación" ("She had been the temptation"), the narrator insists: "el impulso que le arrojó [a Tonet] en la sombra; el egoísmo y la codicia con careta del amor que le guiaron hasta el crimen. Por conservar migajas de su fortuna, no vacilaba ella en abandonar un trozo de sus entrañas; y él, esclavo inconsciente, completaba la obra aniquilando su propia carne" ("the impulse that threw Tonet into the darkness; the egoism and greed with a loving countenance that guided him towards the crime. In order to conserve some crumbs of her fortune, she didn't waver in abandoning a piece of her entrails; and he, a thoughtless slave, carried out the act while destroying his own flesh"; 281–2). In recurring to a common patriarchal trope that depicts female characters as witches, sorcerers, or bodies endowed with otherworldly powers, Blasco Ibáñez reveals in a final flourish that the contradictory conclusion to the novel is part and parcel of the Western patriarchal construction of the human-nature dualism that runs throughout.[9]

Conclusions

Viewed from the Anthropocene more than a century after its publication, a close reading of *Cañas y barro* discloses a pair of interrelated lessons that we would do well to integrate into our contemporary understandings of humanity, nature, and the relationship between the two. First, the ideological hegemony of the human-nature dualism plays a key role in the reproduction of the capitalist system and thereby constitutes a formidable obstacle for ongoing projects to transform our relationship to the biosphere. While seemingly a rather philosophical matter best left for scholars, the importance of resituating the conceptual boundary between humanity and nature is in reality a concern for intellectuals and the general public alike. As Blasco Ibáñez lays bare in his naturalist novel, the cognitive schemes that humans use to organize reality are just as important to the logic of capitalism as the material spheres within which capital more noticeably circulates. Moore writes that "[e]fforts to transcend capitalism in any egalitarian and broadly sustainable fashion will be stymied so long as the political imagination is captive to capitalism's either/or organization of reality" (2). An equitable, long-term solution to capital's degradation of the earth's natural resources must confront the role that mental conceptions play in shaping the broadest contours of humanity's relationship to nature.

Second, the epistemological foundation of anthropocentric discourse acts as a significant obstacle to overcoming the growth imperative that governs the capitalist world order. More specifically, the Anthropocene's dehistoricizing posture – or, its construction of humanity as a monolithic actor – negates any green movement's capacity to integrate questions of race, ethnicity, class, or gender into the logic of contestation, effectively erasing the long history of capitalist violence from consideration. Subverting this discursive interplay is of critical importance because the social injustices inherent to the logic of capitalism are legitimized, justified, and perpetuated in large part by the conceptual schemes that the system itself produces. In a mutually reinforcing process, capital loots the free gifts of nature at the same time that it produces wealth inequalities, destabilizes social relations, and commits acts of symbolic and real violence. The goal must then be to delegitimize capital's either/or construction of reality by normalizing the idea that environmental degradation and social injustice are merely two sides of the same coin.

These are all very abstract lessons that do not lend themselves to analysis within the knowledge-formation practices of the sciences. Indeed, they are better suited for the humanities. Encoded within a system of semiotic signs, literature offers an arena within which the conceptual paradigms that define the Anthropocene can be identified and brought to the attention of the public. In this context, an ecocritical approach to the Spanish naturalist novel like the one in this chapter serves a broader historicization process insofar as it defetishizes the perceived normality of the human-nature dualism. In *Cañas y barro*, Blasco Ibáñez deploys ecological tropes, metaphor, and underlying narrative patterns to construct his text and these same formal strategies tend to accentuate the ways that conceptual schemes inform our behaviours. At both textual and extratextual levels, narratives like those of the naturalist variety productively explore the socioenvironmental dialectic and are thus equipped to confront the current crisis in ways that other disciplines are not. When understood through an ecological prism, Paloma, Tono, Tonet, La Borda, Neleta, Cañamèl, and the Albufera convey subtle yet powerful lessons about the possibilities to redirect our present, disastrous course. They do this by underscoring the insidiousness of the human-nature dualism as it operates in practice. The ancient art of storytelling may just be our best bet for confronting socio-environmental crises in the twenty-first century.

NOTES

1 The term *literary naturalism* here and throughout is used to distinguish the literary movement from naturalism in its philosophical, ontological, or methodological usages.
2 See Smith for an outline of the historical development of the human-nature dualism.
3 The twenty-first-century comics that Christine M. Martínez studies in her chapter in this collection present the ecological ramifications of one hundred years of a capitalist culture and economic system that have resulted in an even greater separation between human and non-human nature and the new materialist determination to come back to humans' recognition of their eco-dependent existence.
4 For an extended discussion of literature's role in achieving social justice in the works of Blasco Ibáñez, see Oxford.
5 Unless otherwise noted, all translations are my own. Page numbers correspond to the Spanish original.

6 The Regenerationists' concerns with more efficient (human) uses of the natural environment were likewise congruous with the group's strides to maintaining human–non-human distinctions such as those that Óscar Iván Useche discusses in his chapter in *Beyond Human* on the automata designed by Leonardo Torres Quevedo, for whom the importance of human agency (as an extension of free will) over the non-human remained central to the engineer and inventor's human exceptionalist framework. For additional in-depth analysis of the intellectual climate of the period, see Hamilton, "Creating the National Territory (1874–1936)," in *Cultivating Nature*.

7 This tension between competing land usage interests evokes the extratextual struggle taking place over the Albufera in the first decades of the twentieth century insofar as the city of Valencia actively sought to protect the Albufera "from the ongoing depredations of rice cultivation" (Hamilton 29).

8 See, for instance, Federici.

9 In contrast to the way Neleta is portrayed as furthering capitalism's hold on El Palmar's residents, Daniel Frost's chapter in this collection on the Enlightenment perspective of antagonistic nature interprets painter Francisco Goya's witches as figures who present obstacles to land and cultural reform and thus as impediments to modernization. Depending on one's interpretation of the ethos of Blasco Ibáñez's text vis-à-vis capitalism, insofar as this organizing system is incongruent with the Generation of '98's conception of Spain's identity, the female characters in this novel can be read as positive or negative influences of change in economic structure.

WORKS CITED AND CONSULTED

Anderson, Christopher. "Tío Paloma: The Keeper of the Golden Age Flame in Blasco Ibáñez's *Cañas y barro*." *Romance Notes*, vol. 31, no. 2, winter 1990, 125–31.

Blasco Ibáñez, Vicente. *Cañas y barro*. 1902. Prometeo, 1916.

Federici, Silvia. *Caliban and the Witch: Women, the Body, and Primitive Accumulation*. Autonomedia, 2004.

Giblett, Rod. *Postmodern Wetlands: Culture, History, Ecology*. Edinburgh UP, 1996.

Hamilton, Sarah. *Cultivating Nature: The Conservation of a Valencian Working Landscape*. U of Washington P, 2018.

Harvey, David. *The Enigma of Capital and the Crises of Capitalism*. Oxford UP, 2010.

Harvey, David. *Marx, Capital, and the Madness of Economic Reason*. Oxford UP, 2018.

Harvey, David. *Seventeen Contradictions and the End of Capitalism*. Profile, 2014.

Miller, Stephen. "The Naturalist Novel." *The Cambridge History of Spanish Literature*, edited by David T. Gies. Cambridge UP, 2004, pp. 423–35.

Moore, Jason W. *Capitalism in the Web of Life: Ecology and the Accumulation of Capital*. Verso, 2015.

Oxford, Jeffrey. "Vicente Blasco Ibáñez: From Storyteller to Soldier of the Pen." *Caesura*, vol. 4, no. 2, 2017, pp. 31–44.

Smith, Neil. *Uneven Development: Nature, Capital, and the Production of Space*. U of Georgia P, 1984.

Tsuchiya, Akiko. "Women and Fiction in Post-Franco Spain." *The Cambridge Companion to the Spanish Novel from 1600 to the Present*, edited by Harriet Turner. Cambridge UP, 2003, pp. 212–30.

Chapter Eight

Jesús Carrasco's *Intemperie*: The Literature of Post-Immunological Modernity

WILLIAM VIESTENZ

Jesús Carrasco's debut novel *Intemperie* (2013), set in an unforgiving environment ravished by the annihilating actions of human beings on their ecologies and communities, mines the thematic depths of overexposure. Though situated in the first half of the twentieth century in fairly generic settings, the novel's dramatic evolution invokes in the twenty-first-century reader the violence, suffering, and precarity witnessed during Spain's years of crisis in the late aughts and the 2010s, as well as the ongoing ecocide threatening the conditions of liveability on earth. From this perspective, *Intemperie* can be critically situated within the growing genre of what Iberianist Bécquer Seguín has called the "Spanish crisis novel," a literary form born of the country's Great Recession.

Though Carrasco's novel can be interpreted in the context of the time of its publication and the nationality of its author, its nameless, early twentieth-century setting alludes to the world-making histories of exploitation, power distribution, and resource combustion that bring the modern world writ large to the twenty-first century. Indeed, in a review of the novel, Santos Sanz Villanueva asserts that a "mérito básico" ("basic merit") of the novel is "sobre todo el llevar al límite la descontextualización de la anécdota y practicar sin concesiones la alusión con efectos potenciadores de la densidad de su trágica historia" ("above all its taking to the limit the decontextualization of the anecdote and alluding without concessions, and with stimulating effects, to the density of its tragic history"). By calling the reader's attention away from anecdotal specificity, the novel's environmental devastation, mass rural depopulation, and economic scarcity can be read in reference to the systemic origins of capitalist crisis. This historical arc points to the origins of industrial development and the long entanglement between modernity and ecology. *Intemperie*'s landscape, wracked by severe drought and memories of former agricultural vitality, invokes a form of grief for ecosocial realities that are irretrievably lost and therefore reckons with the finitude of the natural resources that created the conditions of possibility for modernity to unfold. The novel's characters, however, do not become stymied in this grief; instead, *Intemperie* depicts a set of responses to ecocultural loss that calls to mind the environmental humanist Stephanie LeMenager's concept of "petromelancholia," a "productive grieving of oil" that holds up the vanishing object and the pleasures it once sustained in order to account for the damage inflicted and, more importantly, to reconceptualize resource exhaustion and mismanagement as an apt moment for new political futurities and social capacities (102).[1]

With a title that already invokes the theme of overexposure, *Intemperie* is the narration of a young boy who flees his home into the sparse, hostile countryside, trailed by a bailiff whose habitual sexual abuse of the child, enabled by his father's betrayal, led to the decision to seek refuge elsewhere.[2] An elderly goatherd, along with his dog, donkey, and flock of goats, themselves suffering from malnutrition and exposure to extreme drought, take in the boy without demanding an accounting for his past: "me da igual si te has escapado o te has perdido" ("it's all the same to me if you've run away or if you're simply lost"; 25; 36).[3] In terms of future social capacities, *Intemperie* thus inspires an extended meditation on host-guest relationships and the formation of kinship in the absence of the traditional security of family, home, and law. Conditional hospitality, based on a pact of exchange, is rebuffed in the goatherd's sheltering of the boy, of whom no history, identification, or return gift is demanded. This suspension of interrogation coincides with the philosopher Jacques Derrida's notion of unconditional hospitality, which consists in "suspending language, a particular determinate language, and even the address to the other. Shouldn't we also submit to a sort of holding back of the temptation to ask the other who he is, what her name is, where he comes from, etc.?" (135). Instead, Carrasco reconceives hospitality as self-subtraction within a gift economy where a host, through self-privation and giving, harbours otherness without expecting reciprocal benefit.

Carrasco chooses not to reveal the harm that motivates the boy's flight until late in the text, a decision that, in combination with the lack of interior monologue and ambiguity of the spatio-temporal context, is, in his words, a reaction to a digital age in which "cada vez todo es más explícito … el misterio está en constante regresión, y para mí es un valor fundamental en la vida" ("everything is increasingly explicit … mystery is in constant regression, and for me it is a fundamental value in life"; "Jesús Carrasco: La obsesión"). The result is a novel that Roland Barthes would call a writerly text, constituted upon a plurality of meanings requiring active speculation and creation of signification on the part of Carrasco's audience.[4] Through the motif of inner silence, Carrasco thematizes the presence of innate dignity amidst suffering, one of the structural motifs he identifies in the novel.[5] The shepherd's act of hospitality acknowledges an innate respect to those in suffering even if they are strangers with traumas that are illegible and enigmatic.

In this essay, I will argue that in response to the threat of violence and global war, Carrasco's debut novel emphasizes the symbiotic potential of polymorphic assemblages of life. The social capacities and political futurities that the text models are a symptom of, and possible corrective to, a world in the process of ruination.[6] The novel plays on the concept of hosting as not only a gesture of protective enclosure but also a reference to the nature of the biological body, itself a host for other forms of life. I will argue that the text challenges the separated binary of the autonomous body and its environment, as well as that of self and non-self. *Intemperie* thus signals a central dispositive that mediates the intersection of politics and the body in the twentieth century: immunity, with all of its assumptions about self-definition, otherness, and boundary-oriented security. I will approach immunity primarily through the work of the philosopher Peter Sloterdijk to argue that Carrasco's fiction responds to an historical moment in which the spherical immunities of modernity that have allowed for certain ways of life to flourish over the last several centuries, often at the expense of the well-being of other forms of life, have begun to collapse and fold in on themselves, no longer able to maintain protective boundaries from the outside. In his three-part *Spheres-Bubbles-Foams* opus, Sloterdijk describes human beings as innately spherological creatures dependent on immunization from the expectations of harm and intrusion that result from unmediated exposure to the outside. Life and its propagation presuppose the construction of immune-systemic spheres: "The sphere is the interior, disclosed, shared realm inhabited by humans … humans are the beings that establish globes and look out into horizons. Living in spheres means creating the dimension in which humans can be contained. Spheres are immune-systemically effective space creations for ecstatic beings that are operated upon by the outside" (Sloterdijk, *Bubbles* 28). Humanity's reliance on spheres begins with the infantile womb as the protean immune-systemic space, before scaling up to the family, the hearth and *oikos*, the nation state, and, in terms of ecology, the earth itself and its protective atmospheric layers.

Humans are both dependent upon the protections of immunizing, mediating globes, and agents who construct the spheres that are constitutive for the unfolding and flourishing of life. For Sloterdijk, the task of modernity, like all other sphere-making behaviours, is itself engaged with the paradigm of survival: "Peoples, empires, churches and, above all, modern nation states, are not least space-political attempts to recreate fantastic wombs for infantilized mass populations by imaginary and institutional means" (*Bubbles* 68). In Sloterdijk's general immunology, modernity's dominant sphere-making activities are at times imaginary, or composed of the ideologies, myths, and cosmologies that humans use as a mental armour to counter the uncertainty of faith and learned experience of harm, and at other moments institutional, concerning the political, economic, militaristic, and legal measures that ensure the stability and progress of society. Ensconced in the world view of the Capitalocene, this includes reliance on and faith in the market of capital exchange. As Sloterdijk asserts, "[I]ndustrial-scale civilization, the welfare state, the world market and the media sphere: all these large-scale projects aim, in a shelless time, for an imitation of the now impossible, imaginary spheric security" (*Bubbles* 25).

Carrasco's fiction, with its motif of overexposure, asks what kind of life is possible in a shell-less time in which humankind's habitual "attempts to optimize [its] cosmic and immunological status in the face of vague risks of living and acute certainties of death" no longer hold purchase (Sloterdijk, *You Must* 10). How do notions of hospitality, hosting, and kinship evolve as the spherological immunities that traditional state sovereignty once promised are progressively fractured? Twenty-first-century Spain, with the severity of its own spherological collapse in the shape of a burst real-estate bubble, speaks especially to Sloterdijk's critique of the unreliability of modernity's immunological spheres. I will argue that *Intemperie*'s narrative suggests a postmodern immunological politics that challenges viewing the human body as an autopoietic, or, to use Sloterdijk's term, an anthropotechnic, object defined by a constitutive outside that perpetually threatens hostility and irritation. Detailing his concept of anthropotechnics, Sloterdijk asserts that "we must suspend virtually everything that has been said about humans as working beings in order to translate it into the language of practising, or self-forming, and self-enhancing behaviour … It is time to reveal humans as the beings who result from repetition" (*You Must* 4). In a post-immunological modernity, it is even more appropriate to reduce insistence on the autochthonous intentionality of human self-construction and instead to contemplate the various relational entanglements that reveal the human body to be a host infiltrated, surrounded, and, ultimately, partially constructed by other species. The practised repetition that comes to define the shape of anthropo-world-making is not an abstracted process independent of the various agencies embedded within the relational ecologies that encompass human activity. Via multispecies feminist theorist Donna Haraway's work, this chapter will stress that the disturbances brought about by all scales of immuno-spherological failure, from the mass loss of affordable housing, cutbacks to social safety nets through austerity measures, and the seeking of refuge from mass war to the breakdown of ecosystems, open up new conjunctures and a renewed consciousness of the multispecies and other-than-human assemblages that enable the act of living.[7] In response to Sloterdijk's anthropotechnic subject, I will argue that the symbiotic relations of the holobiont, which defines community as including both the host and the array of species in and around it, is a more apt *dispositif* for describing the open ecological frameworks that emerge out of the crises of the Capitalocene. In my analysis of Carrasco's fiction, wounding is one of the primary ways in which a holobiont is formed, as it creates the opening through which otherness is hosted and preserved in the form of a guest. Hosting is itself a form of wounding, as it has privative effects for the one who opens themselves up to harbour otherness, which in turn creates a protective immunity from the hostile outside for the guest seeking shelter, all the while reframing what counts as a discrete, individual subject when entered into unconditional hospitality with humans and other species. The essay will return to the ambivalent and multifaceted semantics of the term *host*, a reference to the fact that the same Indo-European root is the etymological basis for host, guest, and hostility (as well as *hospedaje, huésped, and hostil*).

The opening pages of *Intemperie* give credence to Sloterdijk's suggestion that the human's innate response to dangerous overexposure is to create protective spheres to gain immunity from external operations on the body. The introductory scene, which depicts the runaway boy attempting to evade detection, also emphasizes the contingency of secure enclosure in times of extreme risk and precarity. As a search party including his father and the bailiff follows behind, the boy flees to an olive grove outside his village and takes cover within a self-dug hole covered with twigs. The scene recreates the moment of birth while also pointing towards the repose of death: "Tumbado sobre un costado, su cuerpo en forma de zeta se encajaba en el hoyo sin dejarle apenas espacio para moverse. Los brazos envolviendo las rodillas o sirviendo de almohada, y tan sólo una mínima hornacina para el morral de las previsiones" ("[L]ying on one side, knees drawn up to his chest, with barely enough room to move in that cramped space. His arms either around his knees or serving as a pillow, and only a tiny niche for his knapsack of food"; 1; 9). Carrasco represents in this passage a scene of both rebirth and inhumation, foreshadowing the shallow grave in which the boy places the goatherd's body at the end of the text. Ejected from the secure walls of the family home, the boy inhabits a small, clay space – the biblical material of which the human body is composed – among "olores que lo alejaban de su madre" ("smells that distanced him from his mother"; 2; 10).[8] The boy's childhood passes away towards a new uncertain future that is coming into being. The absence of both family and social structure in the novel ties concretely to the violence that follows from the betrayal of those from whom one expects unconditional immunization from danger, whether in terms of blood relation (the father) or the juridical shielding of the law (the bailiff). Carrasco returns to this connection in an interview from 2013 in relation to the grave economic and political situation of the Spanish state, arguing that the reason violence is not more widespread owes to "la familia. La familia como armazón social oculto o subestructura que está soportando todo eso, esas fricciones" ("the family. The family as a hidden social support or substructure that is supporting all of that, those frictions"; "Jesús Carrasco: La obsesión").[9] The family structure constitutes for Carrasco an immuno-sphere, or a shared realm, that rebuffs operations from the outside – *esas fricciones* that might translate to life-negating violence. However, the womb within which the boy takes shelter is a contingent, precarious *armazón*, subject to the urine that seeps through the twigs when a search party member relieves himself. The refuge is also without an outlet for the child's own waste, which eventually creates an "atmósfera fosforosa" ("sulphurous atmosphere") that transforms "su refugio en una marmita tóxica" ("his refuge into a toxic pot"; 8; 16). Life beyond the immuno-spheres of the social is linked to the abjection of the flesh and therefore also to the reduction of human life to the level of disposability and abandonment to the protections of the law. In this description of the boy's shelter, one is hard-pressed to overlook the toxicity that pervades the living situations of untold others as deregulation and runaway growth jeopardizes the habitability of the earth in late capitalism, ultimately threatening the very possibility of survival in an ever-closer future.

In the boy's self-dug hole, the atmosphere of toxicity, combined with his vulnerability to the abuses of the law, reflects on a microcosmic level any polity that has broken significantly with the social contract and the obligation of the state to preclude a war of all against all. Carrasco's invocation of Spain's *fricciones* in the late aughts and 2010s, with its housing crisis, rampant unemployment, and fracturing of social safety nets, is a backdrop to interpreting in *Intemperie* the absent *armazones* that increase the boy's susceptibility to overexposure. The text alludes to multiple crises: the "besanas lavadas sobre las que ondulaba una costar de barro cocido" ("flattened furrows covered in a crust of baked earth"; 60; 44) recalls an overcooked, post–Great Acceleration climate; the "casas cerradas a cal y canto o puertas derribadas por las que se podía ver el mismo cuadro repetido" ("locked and barred houses or broken-down doors through which the same scene could be seen over and over"; 132; 108) of a village that the boy explores for water connotes the stark landscape of the abandoned towns of Spain's rural depopulation as well as the abandoned developments of the burst housing bubble; or, to use the title of urban design scholar Christopher Marcinkoski's study of Spain's failed housing policies, the cities that never were.[10] It is important to recall that Sloterdijk refers to the state as the womb par excellence that offers imaginary and institutional spherological immunity for "infantilized mass populations" (*Bubbles* 68). In the case of *Intemperie*, the nomadic travelling of the boy and goatherd from one precarious shelter to the next signals a failure of one of the social contract's primary promises, to provide shelter from harm, and the necessity of a new conceptual framework for interpreting violence and globality in the present age.

Catalanist scholar and critical theorist Edgar Illas's research on globalization and the changing conditions of war points the way towards a new possible theorization of post-immunological survival. Illas argues that "global spatiality produces permanent crisis and continuous circulation, unstable boundaries and precarious forms of containment, threatened sovereignties and unlawful interventions, dangerous war zones, and temporary safe zones" (4). Illas's description of a state of global war leads him to put forth survival as the dominant paradigm of the twenty-first century. Nowhere is his proposal and diagnosis of the problem of state sovereignty better represented than in *Intemperie*, especially at the outset as the boy's temporary safe zone and precarious form of containment in the olive grove is a mere prelude to a life fraught with permanent crisis without zones of demarcated jurisdictional power, similar to the unreliable boundaries of the nation state in Illas's analysis.

While I previously asserted that the paradigm of survival impelled the production of modernity's immuno-spherological wombs, Illas reveals that in the new world order one must constantly reassert the right to survival in an infinitely repeating present moment, without the lasting protective enclosures that allow for a rooted way of being oriented towards a far-flung future. In Carrasco's novel, the boy frames overexposure to the *intemperie* as a form of existence on the border of life and death in which one acquires capacities that permit moment-to-moment survival. Bringing to light the novel's indebtedness to the *Bildungsroman*, the boy contemplates that "la intemperie le había empujado mucho más allá de lo que sabía y de lo que no sabía acerca de la vida. Le había llevado hasta el mismo borde de la muerte y allí, en medio de un campo de terror, él había levantado la espada en vez de poner el cuello" ("the elements had pushed him far beyond what he knew and didn't know about life. It had taken him to the very edge of death and there, in the midst of that camp of horrors, he had raised the sword rather than proffered his neck"; 134; 162). Earlier, upon being ambushed by the bailiff and his crew, "el niño no tuvo tiempo de asustarse. Saltaron en él todos los resortes de la supervivencia" ("the boy didn't have time to feel afraid. His survival instincts took over"; 101; 81).[11] By repeatedly invoking the notion of survival as a conscious choice made throughout the text, *Intemperie* stages the paradigmatic mode of existence that Illas locates at the heart of the global war that increasingly defines late capitalism.

In addition to its narration of an ever-present reaffirmation of survival amidst danger, through the *alguacil* the text also acts out an "assemblage of direct violence" that is no longer boundary-oriented by state enclosures, but rather free to roam the *campos de terror* unimpeded (Illas 4). The bailiff appears throughout the novel in zones that exceed the lawful boundaries of his right to authority. As with the tentacular machinations of global war, the bailiff's instruments of violence are not hemmed in by a sovereign limit that immunizes the boy from harm, despite the goatherd's assurance that in the "montes del norte … el alguacil no emprendería un viaje tan largo para buscarlos en un lugar tan alejado de su jurisdicción" ("mountains to the north … the bailiff would not take his pursuit of them into territory so far outside his jurisdiction"; 172; 143). Earlier, the old man, attempting to quell the boy's anxiety, notes, "[L]o único que sé es que el alguacil no tiene jurisdicción aquí" ("All I know is that the bailiff doesn't have jurisdiction here"; 72; 88), which assumes that authority is still bounded by normal sovereign limits that allow for asylum-seeking in other territorial locales. The boy responds in terror: "escuchar el nombre de Satán en labios de otro y sentir cómo la palabra derribaba los muros en que él vivía su oprobio. Verse desnudo frente al viejo y frente al mundo" ("hearing the name of Satan on the lips of another and feeling how that word tore down the walls he had built around his ignominy. Standing naked before the man and the world"; 72; 91–2). The continuous circulation of unbounded threat collapses the material structures and the psychological mechanisms that secure the human subject from external deleterious operations. Subjection to an eternal present rife with threats to survival disallows the ability to recover from previous wounding or to work through trauma, signifying that the past is a continuously haunting presence that is never completely disengaged from the here and now.

The boy's nomadic collaboration with the goatherd and his multispecies companions takes place amid a permanent state of conflict for control over natural resources such as water and food, both quite scarce in the novel's drought-stricken landscape. For Illas, constant intervention for the purposes of survival is typical within a state of global war; these modes include, but are not limited to, "disobedience, the subaltern, exodus, the temporality of the always already, uncreativity, and immanence" (104). The boy's disobedience of the father and of the law, leading to an exodus from the family unit into a shell-less space of uncertainty, is the first stage of a survival intervention in the face of threat. The polyphonic assemblages that he forms with the goatherd and other forms of life – an antipode to the assemblages of direct violence represented by the bailiff – are the second.

In the spaces that open up beyond the immuno-spherological enclosures that separate self from other, family from stranger, and human from non-human, knowledge of other lifeworlds and human–non-human companion relationships grows. Within his makeshift earthbound enclosure, the boy's perception of life becomes more acute as he disrupts the normal operation of lifeworlds that are beyond his everyday sphere of concern: "Durante su encierro reconoció escarabajos, zapateros y, sobre todo, lombrices" ("During his self-imposed imprisonment, he became familiar with his various companions in the hole: beetles, earwigs and, especially, earthworms"; 7; 7). One effect of the boy's overexposure is an increasing awareness of the variegated ways of being and the entangled relationships that other species share below the surface of human perception. A similar reckoning takes place at the end of the story, as the boy attempts to deploy a cast-iron frying pan to dig a grave for the old man. Upon doing so, "a un palmo de profundidad, empezó a encontrar raíces que cruzaban la tierra en todas direcciones, formando un tejido subterráneo en el que la sartén se trababa todo el tiempo" ("a few inches down, however, he encountered roots going in all directions, forming a subterranean fabric in which the frying pan kept getting stuck"; 219; 182). In such an environment of interspecies enmeshment, the materiality of one's own body even becomes more autonomous and disengaged from the mind. In the aforementioned ambush by the bailiff, the boy's "células pensaban por él y entre las opciones posibles no consideraron la de dejarse caer sobre los serones ardientes" ("cells in his body were doing all his thinking for him and, among the various possibilities, they did not once consider that of dropping down onto the burning panniers"; 102; 81–2). Carrasco's representation of the body as a semi-autonomous system that is only partially compliant to the directives of the conscious mind aligns with emergent biological and immunological understandings. As a holobiont, the body is a multispecies system of symbiotic, mutualistic, and, at times, parasitic relationships. Immunological response is more about filtration than siegecraft and involves a constant negotiation about how bodies can co-evolve in tandem over time and in space.

As a counterpoint to the assemblages of direct violence whose non-jurisdictional circulation imposes perpetual risk, survival depends on the formation of assemblages composed of multispecies companionship, which broadens the concept of kinship into an evolving condition not linked strictly to blood ties. When the boy first comes across the goatherd and his companion species, he briefly considers robbing the old man of his knapsack and absconding. The narrator muses that the boy can envision only a solitary life of all-against-all conflict at the outset of his journey; "no sabía nada de lealtades ni del tiempo que pasa entre los seres y los cose con pespuntes cada vez más apretados" ("he knew nothing as yet of loyalties or of the time that passes between man and beast, knitting them together ever more tightly"; 29; 19). Later in the novel, after a period of coexistence, the boy and goatherd merge as two nodes of a single assemblage, as the former is described as an "extensión tónica del viejo, dispuesto para el laboreo que el llano y la intemperie les imponían" ("energetic extension of the old man, prepared for whatever labours the plain and the elements demanded of him"; 85; 67). One could argue that the plot of *Intemperie* is a sustained description of kin-making amongst humans and other creatures within the precarious conditions of what Haraway calls the Chthulucene, an alternative term for the current geological age. Haraway argues that kin-making should be central to the forming of assemblages that acknowledge and value the interrelationality of life forms and objects: "My purpose is to make 'kin' mean something other/ more than entities tied by ancestry or genealogy ... [K]in-making is making persons, not necessarily as individuals or as humans. I was moved in college by Shakespeare's punning between *kin* and *kind* – the kindest were not necessarily kin as family; making kin and making kind ... stretch the imagination and can change the story" (*Staying* 103). The possibility of kinship thus expands beyond the close links of familial ancestry and biology and imbricates humans and non-humans alike. In *Intemperie*, making kin occurs among many species, primarily in the spaces opened up by the privations and wounds of suffering and loss.[12]

Carrasco's novel represents survival as highly dependent on symbiotic multispecies relationships between the humans, dog, goats, and burro, suggesting that the animals are also *extensiones tónicas* of the boy and shepherd.[13] The boy's self-making over the course of the text into a younger version of the old goatherd is the result not of autopoiesis but of a dynamic being-with-others, both human and other-than-human, that creates the conditions of possibility for evolution of the self. The end of the text emphasizes this codependency, as the boy, after the violent murder of the bailiff and his deputy, carries the goatherd's dying body to a clearing. Carrasco paints a scene of companionship, one that features, in Haraway's words, "non-harmonious agencies and ways of living that are accountable both to their disparate inherited histories and to their barely possible but absolutely necessary joint futures" (*Companion* 7). The dog is the natural-cultural result of a history of training and selection to create a form of life attuned to co-living with humans and, in this case, oriented towards herding goats.[14] The beginning of the novel also signals the socially evolved coexistence of humans and dogs that results from inherited histories and shared futures. Fearful that a dog in the search committee might locate his hiding spot, the boy considers that "sólo un perro bien adiestrado podría descubrir su guarida. Un perdiguero o un buen trufero cojo. Quizá un sabueso inglés, uno de esos animales de cortas patas leñosas y orejas lacias que había visto una vez en un periódico llegado de la capital" ("only a well-trained dog could find him in his hiding-place. A gun dog or a truffle hound. Perhaps an English bloodhound, with sturdy legs and floppy ears, like the one he'd seen in a photo in a newspaper brought from the city"; 9–10; 1). The goats, for their part, provide sustenance throughout the text for the human subjects in exchange for their basic needs and securities. The unfolding of all these manners of living occurs through the mutually beneficial formation of various entities into polyphonic assemblages, situated in particular sociopolitical circumstances and inheritors of specific historical processes.[15]

Haraway's articulation of a sympoietic assemblage, a concept that offers an alternative to Sloterdijk's theory of anthropotechnics, helps to illuminate the codependency of the multicreature unit in *Intemperie*. Self-creation, of both humans and animals, is not an abstract process separated out from other intentional actors but is rather made possible only within conjunctions of "diverse kinds of relationalities and with varying degrees of openness to attachments and assemblages with other holobionts" (Haraway, *Staying with the Trouble* 60). The holobiont, or a multispecies aggregation that includes a host and many other symbiotic species, is a critical term in times of disturbance, and relies upon processes that selectively open the discrete body unto the outside world in a calculated silencing of immune defence response. In *Intemperie*, such opening up is not always intentional and often results from collective wounding, which ultimately transforms into a communitarian process. In both scenarios, immunity as a concept broadens to include more than simply the boundary-oriented defence of an autonomous subject from inimical harm. For holobiont bodies, the immune system possesses a filtering function, and its inaction is central to the productive hosting of multispecies, symbiotic assemblages.

Insofar as the novel recalls the *Bildungsroman* genre, *Intemperie* posits self-maturation as a sympoietic phenomenon predicated entirely on multispecies companionship. Shortly after joining the goatherd's coterie, the boy, dehydrated, overexposed to the sun, and psychologically brutalized, suffers through a fever dream in which he loses control over his body as it is invaded by the bites of dogs and infection of microbes: "si la muerte ha de llegar por una mordedura infecciosa o por un desgarro en los ventrículos, es algo que carece de importancia. Tan sólo cuenta la incapacidad para levantar el cuerpo y, aun con las manos medio comidas, destruir la orgía de perros y microbios" ("whether death comes from an infectious bite or a torn ventricle is of no importance. All that matters is his inability to raise his body and, with his only half-eaten hands, stop that orgy of dogs and microbes"; 46–7; 34). The dream depicts the boy's body as a fractured, immuno-suppressed container unable to stave off the depredations of the external world operating upon it and helpless to combat the resulting microbial infections. The trauma refers both to his prior abuse and to his overexposure to the sun, a contingency for which he had not planned prior to fleeing.

Wounding, however, both instigates malignant incursions and invites a hospitable call to care by others, both human and other-than-human. In an effort to awaken the child from his delirium and to care for his dehydration, "el perro le lamía una mano con la misma abrasividad con la que antes le humedecía el rostro y las encías" ("the dog was licking one of the boy's hands as abrasively as it had previously been moistening his face and gums"; 47; 35). The goatherd for his part, brings his face immediately next to the boy's: "el rostro del cabrero, a un palmo del suyo, se interpone entre su cara y el sol como un eclipse de luna" ("the face of the goatherd, only inches from his, interposes itself like a lunar eclipse between him and the sun"; 47; 35). Expanding on the earlier discussion of Derrida and unconditional hospitality, this scene suggests a form of hosting that requires harbouring and safeguarding the other through offering up the self as a form of gift – here the old man offers up his body to overexposure, as a kind of eclipse, to shelter the boy. In essence, the host becomes an immunological shield that compensates for the fractured vulnerability and incursion of harm that haunts the guest, who has fled the *oikos* seeking refuge. This form of immunity, however, demands not self-foreclosure through the mobilization of protective defences, but an opening up to welcoming the non-self. The goatherd's momentary shielding from the sun is part of a general economy of gift giving within the novel's narrative arc as the man shares what little he owns to nurse the boy back to health, without expectation of a return benefit, which would make the exchange more akin to an economic contract with its attendant conditions and reciprocity. While the boy's presence indeed proves beneficial for the old man over the course of the novel, the opening gesture of hospitality is ultimately what brings on the goatherd's demise, as he is beaten by the bailiff and his deputy for not giving up the boy's location and develops wounds that eventually become infected. The animals, too, suffer tremendously at the hands of the bailiff as a result of taking in the boy.

The goatherd's form of unconditional hospitality, centred on wounding and the opening up of the host, is described by the German philosopher Byung-Chul Han, who writes that "the hospitable welcoming of the Other is an inhalation, yet one that does not absorb the Other, but instead harbours and preserves them" (72). Listening, rather than an interrogation of identity, history, and subjectivity – returning also to Derrida – is the centrepiece of unconditional hospitality. In addition, being inhaled by the other as a form of safe harbouring highlights the wound as something that opens one up to the shielding hospitality of otherness. As Han continues, "[T]he wound is the opening through which the Other enters. It is also the ear that keeps itself open for the Other. Someone who is entirely at home with themselves, who locks themselves in their house, is incapable of listening … The wound breaks open that domestic, narcissistic inwardness. Thus it becomes an open door for the Other" (73–4). The boy, as I mentioned earlier, later himself becomes a host who inhales the wounded goatherd, sheltering him in the same motion of self-sacrifice that was offered to him previously, which is how the boy ends up captured by the bailiff after entering the abandoned town to find water and sustenance. The role reversal is not undertaken as a contractual obligation that the boy owes to the man for his original generosity, but is rather an organic modification that is part of the nature of an assemblage and makes it unlike a closed system with defined roles attached to a set cast of actors. As an assemblage, the internal roles played by the man, boy, and other species are contingent and subject to change according to evolving circumstances, which allows for the host, or the body that mediates both internal and external otherness, to suddenly become a guest. This ambivalence recalls the ambiguity of the Indo-European root *ghos-ti*, the root of both *host* and *guest* in addition to a *host* of other terms that would appear to conflict with one another, including *hospital* and *hospice* but also *hostile* and *hostage* (Watkins 31).

That wounding and the breaking open of narcissistic inwardness are the conditions of possibility for the formation of polyphonic assemblages in *Intemperie* suggests a re-evaluation of the intersection of immunity and the political. The idea of hosting has both an ethical and a biological valence, and the model of unconditional harbouring of the guest in *Intemperie* reframes how one thinks about bodies and their immunological closure towards negativity and the non-self. In the construction of communities that allow for ethical and political obligations to take shape, the immunological defences that close off the inside from the outside must be at least partially compromised. Haraway also stresses this point in reference to multispecies companionship: "companion species infect each other all the time. Bodily ethical and political obligations are infectious, or they should be" (*Staying with the Trouble* 115). A post-immunological orientation towards the political encourages a reconsideration of a concept that has been central to understandings of the body, of legal responsibility, and of communication over the last two centuries. Immunity is as much about shielding what inflicts harm – dogs gnawing on one's hands, microbes flooding in through open sores, or the unshielded midday sun – as it is about permitting engagement with symbiotic assemblages of otherness filled with companion relations, such as between the boy, goatherd, burro, goats, and dog, in a dynamic that collapses where one subject ends and another begins.

In the field of immunology, the concept of immunity has already undergone such a revision through the notion of eco-immunity. The physician and philosopher Alfred Tauber details recent developments in epidemiology that challenge seeing immunity in terms of an attack-and-defend paradigm, a provoked response to invasive arrivals from the outside. Instead, Tauber suggests that immunity is a response that also permits tolerance and cooperation and is made up of "the offensive weaponry of immune attack as well as the silence of immune tolerance required to live in a world of others … [W]hen immunity is placed within an ecological framework, i.e., assuming optimal balanced relationships, differentiation of the organism is displaced by integration and coordination that serve as organizing principles." Politically and ethically,

Carrasco's novel extends eco-immunological principles from biology to the formation of community in a Chthulucene besieged by crisis, where economic, ecological, and political devastation inflict wounds on multiple fronts and scales, but also produce new, mutualistic conjunctures of life that arise out of the ruins of spherological collapse.

Though *Intemperie* alludes to new social capacities and political futurities in the crisis-ridden Chthulucene, the vulnerability of life to persistent threat in the novel emphasizes the precarious nature of survival within the auspices of late capitalism. After all, by the end of the text the boy ends up captured; the goatherd dead; most of the goats brutally mauled. Though the boy has taken over the mantle of goat herding left vacant by the old man's death, his future is no less uncertain or fraught with risk. To conclude, it is worth returning to the ambivalent nature of the concept of hosting. While the goatherd invokes an understanding of host that connotes protection and benevolence, the bailiff brings to mind what political theorist Carl Schmitt referred to as the *hostis*, a public enemy who constitutes the possibility of war.[16] Against this oppositional relationship between host and *hostis*, *Intemperie* represents a state of existence in which sovereignty is no longer bounded such that friendship could meaningfully and persistently serve as a counterpoint to enmity and offer dependable immunity from harm. The form of power represented by the bailiff, therefore, is no mere possibility of hostility that would actualize the conditions of the political, in Schmitt's understanding, but is instead the clear and present promise of everimmanent danger and violence. In such circumstances, acquired immunity is contingent, vulnerable to rapidly changing social and political realities, like so many mutated viruses that skirt vaccines meant to quell their propagation. Polyphonic assemblages like the one sketched by Carrasco are constantly endangered, broken apart, and reformed, like the matsutake mushrooms studied by Lowenhaupt Tsing, which emerge from massive deforestation in the Pacific Northwest. As *Intemperie* teaches, life in the Chthulucene demands continual vigilance of the threats that catastrophe portends both for human actors and for the earthworms, goats, dogs, burros, and other life forms that might otherwise pass by unperceived.

NOTES

1 Iberianist Jesse Barker argues that this temporal arc is part of a narrative strategy in which the reality of a coming apocalypse is accentuated by invoking "past times of scarcity or extreme injustice … *Intemperie*'s setting

is recognizably located in early twentieth century rural Spain, but the novel never specifies when or where the story takes place. Its dystopian drought-stricken setting calls to mind the chronic droughts of central and southern Spain, but it also invokes the worldwide water shortages projected for the near future" (182–3). In terms of the petromelancholic, I would not separate so trenchantly the novel's dual temporalities. *Intemperie* approaches the actuality and futurity of crisis by holding up the lost productiveness of modernity as a temporality to be historically excavated and linked to the present. To borrow the environmental humanist Rob Nixon's term, this reveals the drawn-out "slow violence" of ecological devastation.

2 Following Margaret Jull Costa's translation into English, I will refer to the lawman as a *bailiff* in lieu of *sheriff*. This English term corresponds better to the *alguacil* used in Carrasco's novel, which John Margenot very lucidly argues is "no longer used in contemporary Spain to describe an official with civil and criminal jurisdiction" and is thus a purposeful anachronism to situate the "diabolical character much closer to the officer possessed by the devil in Quevedo's *El alguacil endemoniado*" (227n3).

3 Translations of the novel are taken from Margaret Jull Costa's excellent edition and are referenced as the second page number in the parenthetical citations. All others are my own.

4 In *S/Z*, Barthes asserts that the writerly text is valuable because "the goal of literary work (of literature as work) is to make the reader no longer a consumer, but a producer of the text," thereby avoiding that the reader be "plunged into a kind of idleness" (4). In an interview, Carrasco echoes Barthes in asserting that "existe … un terreno intermedio entre el texto y el lector en el que este se apropia de lo escrito y, en cierto modo, lo finaliza" ("an intermediate terrain exists between the text and the reader in which the reader appropriates what is written and, in a certain way, concludes it"; ("'Intemperie' es un 'western' ibérico").

5 Carrasco notes that dignity is not difficult to find; "solo hay que verla, es como la belleza o el arte, y consiste en ser capaz de mantener la postura después de sufrir las inclemencias de la vida … ser capaz de mantener la postura, de ser esa persona que en el metro, cuando alguien está siendo agredido, interviene" ("one only has to see it, it is like beauty or art, and it consists in being capable of maintaining the position after suffering the inclemencies of life … being capable of maintaining the position, of being the person on the metro who, when somebody is being assaulted, intervenes"; "Jesús Carrasco: La obsesión"). The importance of intervention is an additional analytical key for interpreting the novel and features in the work's climax as the goatherd dispatches the bailiff to free the boy from captivity.

6 In this regard I am inspired by anthropologist Anna Lowenhaupt Tsing's study of the matsutake mushroom, which forms assemblages with human history, insects, pine trees, and other species within landscapes that have been disturbed by deforestation, fire, and other ecological change, meaning that "if we want to know what makes places livable we should be studying polyphonic assemblages, gatherings of ways of being" (157).

7 Haraway has also developed the concept of immunity extensively in her work. In "The Biopolitics of Postmodern Bodies," she argues, "[T]he immune system is an elaborate icon for principal systems of symbolic and material 'difference' in late capitalism. Preeminently a twentieth-century object, the immune system is a map drawn to guide recognition and misrecognition of self and other in the dialectics of Western biopolitics. That is, the immune system is a plan for meaningful action to construct and maintain the boundaries for what may count as self and other in the crucial realms of the normal and the pathological" (275).

8 The Book of Job 33:6 is one of many examples: "See, before God I am as you are; I too was formed from a piece of clay" (*New Oxford Annotated Bible* 762).

9 Carrasco repeats this sentiment in an interview with the Spanish national newspaper *ABC*: "El mal y la violencia son el resultado de la fricción entre personajes que habitan un territorio empobrecido. Sucede cuando hay poco pan y muchas bocas" ("Evil and violence are the result of a friction between people that inhabit an impoverished territory. It comes about when there's little bread and many mouths"; "'Intemperie' es un 'western' ibérico").

10 On 31 March 2019, large demonstrations in Madrid took place to call attention to "la España vaciada" ("hollowed-out Spain") to demand measures against the economic and political decisions that have accelerated the emptying of Spain's rural landscape for decades (García). *Intemperie* calls to mind the Castilian landscapes of postwar novelist Miguel Delibes, and it is no coincidence that the autonomous community of Castilla-La Mancha has witnessed both extensive depopulation and development such as that of Ciudad Valdeluz, a largely empty project south of Madrid begun in 2004 but never completed amid the burst real-estate bubble. For more on Spain's failed speculative urbanization, see Marcinkoski. For more on Spain's rural waves of depopulation, see Molino.

11 Similarly, Margenot has analysed *Intemperie*'s "monochromatic desert" setting as a Deleuzian "smooth space forever 'in-between' that is bereft of future and condemned to moral disorder" (226).

12 This human-animal connection might require a communication that encompasses affect and other semiotic cues beyond the normal human

understandings of language, as Maryanne L. Leone suggests in her analysis in this collection of a child and dog's companionship in the precarity of imminent ecological exile. Central to her study and this one is the potential of rebirth and a future communitarianism out of the ruins of capitalist, anthropocenic despoliation.

13 At its outset, the novel invokes the human-canine relationship as one of coevolved companionship, but in this case, the power imbalance is stark. Enveloped in his self-dug enclosure, the boy contemplates that greyhound dogs are the only breed where he lives, "líneas rojas" ("red lines"; 2) blazing down their flanks "como recuerdos de las fustas de los amos. Las mismas que en el secarral sometían a niños, mujeres y perros" ("[as] souvenirs of their masters' whips. The same whips that were used to beat into submission the children, women and dogs of that arid plain"; 10; 2). Symbiosis does not attend to this human-canine companionship as it does within the goatherd's nomadic encampment, and, moreover, the animals', children's, and women's common subjection to the whip show all to be forms of life exposed to death, what Giorgio Agamben calls "bare life." The greyhound is an especially symbolic breed and appears in Dante's *Commedia*, in which Virgil explains that it will one day vanquish the she-wolf, returning "safety to Italia's plains" (8).

14 Haraway proposes the term "natureculture" to refer to the inextricable co-evolution of human and non-human life over time. Humans and other-than-human life do not predate one another, but transform in tandem, enmeshed with one another such that any firm distinction between nature and culture becomes untenable. In *The Companion Species Manifesto*, Haraway asserts that immune systems are a central component of any natureculture, as "they determine where organisms, including people, can live and with whom. The history of the flu is unimaginable without the concept of the co-evolution of humans, pigs, fowl, and viruses" (31).

15 Daniel Ares López's in-depth essay in *Beyond Human* on taurine naturecultures provides a remarkable example of material-semiotic human-animal enmeshment in which the rules of the game, so to speak, seek to protect humans involved in the bullfight from harm – that is, to immunize them – through a spectacle of codependence and violently enforced boundaries.

16 As Near East scholar David Lloyd Dusenbury argues, Schmitt's *Concept of the Political* introduces *hostis* "to aggravate, and not mitigate, the semantics of interwar enmity" (437).

WORKS CITED AND CONSULTED

Agamben, Giorgio. *Homo Sacer: Sovereign Power and Bare Life*. Translated by Daniel Heller-Roazen, Stanford UP, 1998.

Alighieri, Dante. *The Divine Comedy of Dante Alighieri*. Translated by Henry Francis Cary, P.F. Collier, 1909.

Barker, Jesse. *Affect and Belonging in Contemporary Spanish Fiction and Film*. Palgrave Macmillan, 2017.

Barthes, Roland. *S/Z*. Translated by Richard Miller, Blackwell, 2002.

Carrasco, Jesús. *Intemperie*. Seix Barral, 2013.

Carrasco, Jesús. "Jesús Carrasco: '"Intemperie" es un "western" ibérico.'" Interview by Antonio Fontana. *ABC*, 22 Jan. 2013, https://www.abc.es /cultura/cultural/20130122/abci-jesus-carrasco-intemperie-western -201301221058.html?ref=https%3A%2F%2Fwww.google.com%2F.

Carrasco, Jesús. "Jesús Carrasco: La obsesión actual por aprovechar el tiempo me parece atroz." Interview by Mikel López Iturriaga. *El País semanal*, 4 Aug. 2013, https://elpais.com/elpais/2013/08/02/eps/1375442829 _655302.html.

Carrasco, Jesús. *Out in the Open*. Translated by Margaret Jull Costa, Vintage, 2015.

Derrida, Jacques. *Of Hospitality*. Translated by Rachel Bowlby, Stanford UP, 2000.

Dusenbury, David Lloyd. "Carl Schmitt on *Hostis* and *Inimicus*: A Veneer for Bloody-Mindedness." *Ratio Juris*, vol. 28, no. 3, Sept. 2015, pp. 431–9. *Wiley Online Library*, https://doi.org/10.1111/raju.12092.

García, Álvaro. "La manifestación de la 'España vaciada,' en imágenes." *El País*, 31 Mar. 2019, https://elpais.com/elpais/2019/03/31/album/1554029102 _087177.html#foto_gal_2.

Han, Byung-Chul. *The Expulsion of the Other*. Translated by Wieland Hoban, Polity, 2019.

Haraway, Donna. "The Biopolitics of Postmodern Bodies: Constitutions of Self in Immune System Discourse." *Biopolitics: A Reader*, edited by Timothy Campbell and Adam Sitze, Duke UP, 2013, pp. 274–310.

Haraway, Donna. *The Companion Species Manifesto: Dogs, People, and Significant Otherness*. Prickly Paradigm Press, 2003.

Haraway, Donna J. *Staying with the Trouble: Making Kin in the Chthulucene*. Duke UP, 2016.

Illas, Edgar. *The Survival Regime: Global War and the Political*. Routledge, 2019.

LeMenager, Stephanie. *Living Oil: Petroleum Culture in the American Century*. Oxford, 2014.

Lowenhaupt Tsing, Anna. *The Mushroom at the End of the World: On the Possibility of Life in Capitalist Ruins*. Princeton UP, 2015.

Marcinkoski, Christopher. *The City That Never Was*. Princeton Architectural, 2016.

Margenot, John B., III. "Traversing the Intermezzo: Demonic Archetypes in Jesús Carrasco's *Intemperie*." *Symposium*, vol. 71, no. 4, 2017, pp. 218–28. *Taylor & Francis Online*, https://doi.org/10.1080/00397709.2017.1386485.

Molino, Sergio de. *La España vacía: Viaje por un país que nunca fue*. Turner Noema, 2016.

The New Oxford Annotated Bible. Edited by Michael Coogan, 3rd ed., Oxford UP, 2007.

Nixon, Rob. *Slow Violence and the Environmentalism of the Poor*. Harvard UP, 2013.

Sanz Villanueva, Santos. "Parábola de la dignidad." *Mercurio*, no. 149, Mar. 2013, http://mercurio.fundacionjmlara.es/ediciones/2013/mercurio-149/parabola-de-la-dignidad/.

Seguín, Bécquer. "Environmental Apocalypse and the Spanish Crisis Novel." Environmental Cultural Studies through Time: The Luso-Hispanic World, special issue of *Hispanic Issues On Line*, edited by Katarzyna Beilin et al., vol. 24, 2019, pp. 272–88, https://conservancy.umn.edu/bitstream/handle/11299/212955/hiol_24_13_seguin_.pdf?sequence=1&isAllowed=y.

Sloterdijk, Peter. *Bubbles*. Translated by Wieland Hoban, MIT Press, 2011. Vol. 1 of *Spheres*.

Sloterdijk, Peter. *You Must Change Your Life: On Anthropotechnics*. Translated by Wieland Hoban, Polity, 2013.

Tauber, Alfred I. "Philosophy of Immunology." *Stanford Encyclopedia of Philosophy*, Spring 2017 ed., edited by Edward N. Zalta, https://plato.stanford.edu/archives/spr2017/entries/immunology/.

Watkins, Calvert, editor. *The American Heritage Dictionary of Indo-European Roots*. Houghton Mifflin, 2000.

Chapter Nine

Transhumanism and Necropolitics in Rosa Montero's *Times of Hatred*

JUAN CARLOS MARTÍN GALVÁN

This chapter studies Rosa Montero's *Los tiempos del odio* (*Times of Hatred*, (2018) in order to highlight three concomitant anthropocentric practices that, in the novel, function as human niche constructions detrimentally affecting human and non-human natures: transhumanism, advanced capitalism, and necropolitics.[1] I argue that this text underscores how these harmful practices and philosophies, supported by technooptimism, unrestrained economic growth, and so-called progress, aggravate the environmental crisis and foster violence, racism, and enmity among humans as well as between human and non-human others. My analysis focuses on the way Montero's novel examines how contemporary necropolitics dictates humanity's choices and makes them more vulnerable to necropower. I also contend that the text posits alternative post-human ontologies that challenge anthropocentric thinking and recognize non-human agency as well as interconnections among species, which in turn help reassess categorized distinctions diachronically.

To support my discussion, I will rely on Cameroonian philosopher and political theorist Achille Mbembe's groundbreaking work *Necropolitics* (2019), which outlines the corrosive effects of biopower and necropolitics upon the principles of contemporary liberal democracy. Feminist philosopher Rosi Braidotti's approach to the post-human predicament, which advocates for a non-anthropocentric logic towards the construction of a post-human subjectivity, also addresses the influence of biopolitical and necropolitical forces powered by advanced capitalism in determining the fate of human and non-human populations. Similarly, postmodern critic Katherine Hayles' and philosopher David Roden's theoretical developments engaging post-human subjectivities that challenge humanistic dual logic and human exceptionalism will round out the interpretive framework through which I analyse those perspectives that in Montero's novel contest human-centred viewpoints.

Anthropocentrism, Transhumanism, and Post-Humanism

Moral philosopher Gary Steiner indicates that anthropocentric thinking is hierarchical in essence because it proposes that human beings occupy the prime and most central position in the natural world order. Steiner examines the ways in which anthropocentric thinking in Western philosophy, which grants "privileged status" to human beings, considers non-human animals as "inferior to humans in the cosmic order" (1–2). Such human-centred philosophy, which has the tendency to deprive non-human entities of substantial moral worth – claiming that such entities lack rationality, experiences, and values – supports human exceptionalism, an essential trait connected to humanism. Braidotti expands the meaning of the binary logic behind universal humanism, which associates reason, consciousness, or moral behaviour with subjectivity, and which designates otherness as "its negative and specular counterpart" (15). Braidotti's conceptualization of otherness, which refers not only to non-human animals but also to "the sexualized, racialized, and naturalized others, who are reduced to the less than human status of disposable bodies" (15), is central to Montero's text. Roden likewise connects the dual logic of humanism to transhumanism, the latter of which sees "humans as uniquely autonomous or self-fashioning animals" (13). As a philosophical movement, transhumanism aims to profoundly alter the human condition by enhancing the human being's current intellectual and biological capabilities through advanced technologies. Like humanists, transhumanists hold an anthropocentric world view because they grant human beings advantaged status. A transhuman represents an intermediate human, "one augmented and modified on the way to being *posthuman*, the fully technologized successor species to organic *Homo sapiens*" (Graham 9; emphasis in original). The transitional nature of transhumanism is entirely dependent on technologies capable of amplifying "the powers of our bare brains" (Roden 15). As transhumanist Nick Bostrom puts it, transhumans can become post-human only if they acquire abilities that exceed "the maximum attainable by any current human being without recourse to new technological means" (219). In short, transhumans believe that post-humanism takes place only through unparalleled technological enhancement.

Yet anthropocentric thinking and techno-optimism, two fundamental value systems behind transhumanism, contrast with the notion of the post-human, since the latter aims to overcome anthropocentrism and its hierarchical logic. As Roden has argued, post-humanism in all its forms resists anthropocentrism because it challenges normative notions of what it means to be human and non-human. In the same vein, post-humanist thinkers like Braidotti perceive post-humanism as an opportunity to address human and non-human subjectivity from a standpoint that negates "classical Humanism and carefully avoids anthropocentrism" (56).[2] Regarding technological enhancements and identity, Hayles underlines that "even a biologically unaltered *Homo sapiens* counts as posthuman" because post-humanism is about "the construction of subjectivity, [and] not [about] the presence of nonbiological components," as transhumanists claim (4). In this chapter, the concepts *transhuman* and *transhumanism* indicate perspectives and practices that rely heavily on advanced technologies and validate anthropocentrism. *Los tiempos* presents radical transhumanism as a philosophy that never abandons anthropocentrism and espouses extending exclusive privileges of the "autonomous liberal subject … into the realm of the posthuman" (Hayles 287). Therefore, in this chapter, the terms *post-human* and *post-humanism* contrast with transhumanism and refer to viewpoints that challenge anthropocentric thinking and grant value and agency not only to non-human beings, but also to marginalized and underprivileged humans.

Radical Transhumanism in *Los tiempos del odio*

Los tiempos del odio, the third work in the series that also includes *Lágrimas en la lluvia* (*Tears in Rain*, 2011) and *El peso del corazón* (*Weight of the Heart*, 2015), continues to follow the life of detective Bruna Husky, a techno-human that lives in Madrid in the year 2110. Techno-humans are androids, a product of biotechnology using human genetic material. In the third novel, Montero inserts an intricate summary that allows newcomers to the series to learn about the creation of techno-human life and human–techno-human enmity: the destruction of earth's ecosystems, the extinction of species on a larger scale, and the dangerous impact of climate change on entire populations. Readers also discover the existence of intelligent alien life, the increasing social and economic inequality caused by advanced capitalism and biopolitics, the political and economic instability on our planet, and worldwide violence. While addressing current anthropocenic political and socio-environmental planetary issues – including access to water and clean air – and denouncing the ways by which toxic anthropocentrism endangers a future society's democratic systems and values, Montero explores the politics of death – necropolitics – and provides suggestive insight into the question of the Anthropocene within human, transhuman, and post-human paradigms.

Los tiempos revolves around the sudden disappearance of Paul Lizard, the human police inspector who is professionally and romantically involved with Bruna Husky. Paul, Bruna learns through her investigation, has been abducted by an obscure organization, Instant Justice Army (IJA), a radical group of terrorists that has committed several attacks in different locations in the United States of the Earth. Husky sets off on a desperate journey to locate and save Lizard, as the terrorists begin to execute hostages daily. With the help of other human and non-human allies, the investigating protagonist will have to fight the IJA, face the sociopolitical turmoil of a discontent world society, and dismantle a political conspiracy that threatens the onset of a civil war.

Informing the treatment of transhumanist thought in Montero's series might be the 1998 Transhumanist Declaration, crafted by the most influential transhumanist theorists of the time, whose first article indicates: "Humanity will be radically changed by technology in the future. We foresee the feasibility of redesigning the human condition, including such parameters as the inevitability of aging, limitations on human and artificial intellects, unchosen psychology, suffering, and our confinement to the planet earth" (qtd. in Roden 14). On the role of technology in reshaping the human condition, the Declaration echoes Heidegger's conception of technology as "a means to an end" and "a human activity," and highlights "the instrumental and anthropological definition of technology" but not the "essence" of technology per se, which, according to Heidegger, "is by no means anything technological" (*Question Concerning Technology* 4–5).[3] Heidegger contends that we cannot apprehend the essence of technology "so long as we merely conceive and push forward the technological, put up with it, or evade it" (4). By relying on the instrumental conception of technology alone in the road to becoming post-human, transhumanists avert addressing what Braidotti calls "the four horsemen of the posthuman apocalypse: nanotechnology, biotechnology, information technology and cognitive science" (59). She underscores the inconsistencies and socioecological disparities "engendered by our advanced technologies" (42). Furthermore, Braidotti underlines the social and ethical implications that arise due to machine autonomy and complexity, which leads directly to important questions of subjectivity and agency within post-humanist theory. Likewise, transhuman philosophy not only posits the possibility of overcoming the physical and cognitive limitations of the human condition through science and technology, but also claims that in so doing, it can solve the current environmental conundrum. Techno-optimism, or the conviction that technological progress will resolve contemporary ecological issues, can be very "seductive," notes degrowth scholar

Samuel Alexander (3). The critic argues that technological optimists firmly believe that technology can achieve economic and social equality on the planet "without destroying the necessary ecosystem services that sustain life as we know it" (2). This approach, affirms Alexander, "is profoundly flawed" (3). In Montero's novel, transhumanists' techno-scientific achievements – driven by advanced technologies that replicate human life – design powerful artificial intelligences and increase human life expectancy to an unimaginable degree but cannot decelerate the ecological catastrophe affecting all species on the planet, including enhanced transhumans.

Implicit within the language of the Transhumanist Declaration's first article are two issues relevant to the trans/post-human condition addressed in Montero's text, namely, human essence and human disconnection. A private corporation called "Transhuman," which in the novel parodies a futurist version of today's Humanity+ (the former World Transhumanist Association), represents a perverse politically and economically powerful organization that delivers the promise of creating superhumans, "los ciudadanos del futuro" ("the citizens of the future"; 167).[4] Like transhumanist proponents today, the radical transhumanists, or cyborgists, as they call themselves, of Montero's novel advocate personal freedom and zealously oppose human essentialism.[5] The latter refers to the belief that there exists an invariable and fundamental human essence, a set of required biological or mental attributes or properties "that no member of that kind can be without" (Roden 48). Roden suggests that if we were to believe in human essentialism, one could potentially "identify each path to posthumanity with the deletion of some component of the human essence" (113). If, for example, the display of moral capacities or rationality were essential to human subjectivity as essentialism claims, there would be a way to establish a distinct disconnection between human and post-human subjectivity. In *Los tiempos*, threatened by the high degree of complexity and autonomy achieved by several techno-assemblages, the government of the United States of the Earth enacts a law of human essentialism based on arbitrary biological criteria:

> Poco después de la Unificación de los EUT se promulgó una ley restrictiva, la Ley de la Integridad Humana, que establecía una complicada tabla de porcentajes de humanidad medidos en puntos Bío, dependiendo del órgano a sustituir. En total un ser humano poseía mil Bíos, escrupulosamente reflejados en su chapa civil, y la ley prohibía que se le cambiara más del sesenta por ciento; esto es, la frontera estaba en poseer cuatrocientos puntos naturales.

(Soon after the unification of the United States of the Earth, a restrictive law was enacted, the Law of Human Integrity, which established a complicated table of percentages to determine humanity, measured in Bio points, depending on the substituted organ. Overall, a human being possessed one thousand Bios, meticulously reflected in their civil tag, and the law prohibited any substitution greater than 60 per cent, that is, the limit was set at possessing four hundred natural points; 162)

This Law of Human Integrity entrenches anthropocentric hierarchical philosophy in future society. After all, as post-humanist and animality critic Christopher Peterson cleverly puts it, "Human exceptionalism is no doubt a phantasm, but phantasms have a way of persisting" (5). On the other hand, in her critical view relating to the construction of future post-human entities, Braidotti emphasizes the need to reject models of subjectivity that sanction anthropocentrism and support humanist values. She adamantly argues that "this is not time for nostalgic longings for the humanist past, but for forward-looking experiments with new forms of subjectivity" (45). In the novel, the presence of various alien species on planet earth, along with mutants, that is, humans who have suffered considerable physical alterations due to teleportation, and techno-humans like Bruna Husky, embody some progressive forms of post-human subjectivity that challenge this law and pose a threat to anthropocentrism. For radical transhumanists in the text, the Law of Human Integrity violates personal freedom and limits their aspirations towards achieving a post-human condition through unparalleled physical and mental enhancements of the human body. Some of the novel's radical transhumanists have surpassed the established biological threshold by turning into radical cyborgs referred to as "ciborrads." The most salient example of such subjectivity is Dom Lago, a 189-year-old radical cyborg who is also the owner of TriTon Corp., the company that fabricates techno-humans, and the head of a plot conspiring against the United States of the Earth's democracy.

On his way to a post-human condition, Lago distances himself from his own humanity but still displays arrogance towards techno-humans when Husky confronts him: "tú y yo somos paralelos, somos criaturas de la misma clase, Bruna ... Somos semidioses y hemos mejorado la especie. Bueno, sobre todo yo, sinceramente, porque vosotros os estropeáis enseguida con esa lata del TTT [Tumor Total Tecno] ... Sois un ensayo que no salió bien" ("You and I are parallels; we are creatures of the same category, Bruna ... We are demigods and we have improved the species. Well, especially me, to be honest, because you techno-humans break down fast with that nagging TTT [Total Techno Tumour] ... You are an experiment that did not turn out well"; 362).

Lago's contrast between his unique subjectivity and the biogenetic subjectivity that Husky embodies prompts evident signs of hierarchical thinking. Lago acknowledges that techno-humans have transcended a human condition; nevertheless, he also highlights their inability to outdo death – techno-humans have a lifespan of only ten years after activation – a transhumanist aspiration that Lago has managed to achieve thus far. Ironically, within the realm of this transitional post-human subjectivity, Lago maintains anthropocentric hierarchical views. As Hayles indicates, "[T]he posthuman need not be recuperated back into liberal humanism, nor need it be construed as antihuman" (287), which is precisely what Lago attempts in Montero's text. Therefore, the transhumanist philosophy enacted in the novel by radical transhumanists negates what Braidotti calls a post-anthropocentric approach to subjectivity within a post-human condition because it does not rise above "the sedimented habits of thought that the humanist past has institutionalized" (54). One can further assert that Montero's negotiations with trans- and post-humanism unpack the types of techno-scientific configurations that reinforce the spread of necropolitics and advanced capitalism, and cleverly reveal the persistence of rampant anthropocentric practices.

Necropolitics in *Los tiempos del odio*

To illuminate Mbembe's concept of necropolitics and its significance in the text, it is useful to examine the concepts of sovereignty, biopolitics, and biopower in Foucauldian terms. In his lecture of 17 March 1976, reprinted in *Society Must Be Defended*, Foucault asserts that the classical theory of sovereignty is the right of life and death and that the sovereign's power over life is ultimately exercised only when "the sovereign can kill" (240). In his analysis of the nineteenth century, Foucault observes a major alteration from sovereignty's "right to take life or let live" to "the right to make live and to let die" (241). He uses this change in sovereignty's power to introduce the concept of biopolitics, or positive "power's hold over life" (239), that is, the phenomenon by which "the biological came under State control" (240). For Foucault, *biopower* describes the mechanisms that support the work of biopolitics in society, not to discipline populations politically, scientifically, or biologically, but to regularize them (247). However, Foucault warns that even regulatory biopower "that guarantees life" (253) can act "in excess of sovereign right" and come "to call for deaths, to demand deaths, to give the order to kill, and to expose not only its enemies but its own citizens to the risk of death" (254). This latter version of biopower is fundamental to understanding Mbembe's necropolitics and necropower, or "contemporary forms of subjugating life to the power of death" (92).

Mbembe analyses the corrosive effects of biopower upon the principles of contemporary liberal democracy, drawing on Foucault and adding a decolonial approach to necropower founded on Frantz Fanon's political and psychiatric works. Mbembe argues that in today's world, Foucault's notion of biopower is deficient because it does not make up for "new and unique forms of social existence in which vast populations are subjected to living conditions that confer upon them the status of the *living dead*" (92; emphasis in original). In particular, he speaks of the creation of "*death-worlds*" (92; emphasis in original), structures of violence and domination that foster necropolitical practices through contemporary colonial power, like in the Palestine occupation or the establishment of refugee camps where people are turned "into objects that can be deported, stopped in their tracks – or even destroyed" (103). Since the creation of "*death-worlds*" also negatively affects animals, ecosystems, and non-human entities, manifestations of Mbembe's necropolitics in Montero's novel can likewise be seen to encompass ecosocial systems that are severely damaged or destroyed.

According to Foucault, biopower is a mechanism of all modern states and functions according to a biological break that distributes human populations into two groups: those who must remain alive and those who must perish. Such a biological gap emerges because of racism, which Foucault concludes to be "the basic mechanism of power" as it generates a "hierarchy of races" or a "human race of races" (254). As Mbembe states, "[I]n Foucault's terms, racism is above all a technology aimed at permitting the exercise of biopower" (71). In *Los tiempos*, racism, as a device of biopower, not only maintains the human biological break, but also reveals itself as speciesism within two subsequent subdivisions comprising techno-human and other non-human populations. In both cases, it is the creation of biological fragmentation, which, in the novel, also encompasses class, cultural, and ecosocial divisions, that then justifies killing or the exposure to death, as Husky underscores:

> Y las supuestas injusticias sociales de las que se quejaban *los humanos* siempre le habían parecido una bagatela comparadas con la suprema, obscena injusticia de haber sido creada, en origen y antes de las guerras rep que los liberaron, como una mano de obra esclava. De haber sido manipulada,

alterada genéticamente para aumentar su rendimiento comercial y *con-denada* a esta breve vida de mariposa y a una *muerte cruel* a fecha fija que equivalía a una *ejecución*.

(In addition, the alleged social injustices *humans* complain about seemed trivial to Husky compared to the supreme, obscene injustice of having been created, originally and before being liberated by the rep wars, as slave labour. Having been manipulated, genetically altered to increase her commercial performance, and *condemned* to this brief butterfly-like life cycle and to *a cruel death* with a fixed date, equivalent to her own *execution*; 85; emphasis added)

Bruna's gripe refers to the toxic influence of anthropocentric biological and racial distinctions, but she also underscores how the mechanisms of biopower seem more justified and more lethal when it comes to non-human species. In this way, Montero addresses the Anthropocene by highlighting multiple systems of violence and signals the devastating impact of warfare supported by death technologies on both human and non-human populations.

Relying on Fanon's insights regarding colonial occupation and violence, Mbembe argues that, at the turn of the twenty-first century, war is "the sacrament of our times" (2). He asserts that war has been transformed into a Platonic *pharmakon*, both as remedy and as poison, because war can protect against external attacks or destroy enemies – that is, war is a "legitimate defense" (31), but it can represent revengeful violence outside the law by inflicting death upon innocent beings within or outside the state apparatus. This transformation of war into a *pharmakon* undermines democratic societies because it "let[s] loose gruesome passions" that push societies "to exit democracy" and "to convert into societies of enmity" (3) and into "societies of separation" (42). Mbembe asserts that contemporary democratic states have failed to dispose of their "nocturnal body," or dark side, and continue to exercise similar violence and disciplinary practices that in the past drove their colonial and slave systems (15). *Los tiempos* not only highlights the concept of human-waged war as *pharmakon* but also examines how the "nocturnal body of democracy" exposes all human and non-human populations to the power of death. The IJA's alleged war against widespread capitalism, which, according to its urban activists, "seguía asesinando día tras día a miles de personas en el mundo con su desigualdad criminal" ("continued day after day killing thousands of people around the world with its criminal inequality"), quickly turns into a *pharmakon*, as the group's terrorist attacks inflict multiple massacres on the innocent civilian population, human and non-human, around the planet (Montero, *Los tiempos* 20). Financed and supervised by the powerful tycoon Lago and supported by technologies designed by the totalitarian Cosmos Democratic Republic, in a matter of months, the IJA has turned into a powerful global terrorist organization.

In her weekly column for *El País semanal* and other news media, Montero recurringly addresses a culture of dogmatism, fanaticism, totalitarianism, and especially terrorism to examine irrational acts of violence, brutality, and massacre against human and non-human populations in today's world. Montero has argued that the fictional world of the Bruna Husky novels emulates contemporary reality, in which dogmatic and totalitarian thinking prevails and threatens democratic credibility and legitimacy (Castro). In *Instrucciones para salvar el mundo* (*Instructions for Saving the World*, 2008), Montero examines suicide bombing, which in *Los tiempos* becomes a central theme that highlights the inescapability of extremism and the pernicious violence that these acts engender. According to Mbembe, suicide bombers embody the logic of martyrdom, in which both the will to take the life of the other and the will to take one's own life merge. Since homicide and suicide happen concurrently, this form of exercising the right to kill represents a "new semiosis of killing," one that "slam[s] shut the door on the possibility of life for everyone" and that differs from the "logic of survival," that is, killing the other "while preserving one's own life" (89). Montero's novel emphasizes that terrorism and martyrdom belong exclusively to the realm of human beings and underscores their aggressive tendencies. In the first book of the trilogy, some techno-humans commit acts of terrorism against the civilian population; however, they are forced to do so when supremacists implant them with a chip that leads them to believe that they are human beings and to commit suicide attacks against innocent human and non-human populations to protect their imaginary children. Therefore, a careful analysis of the whole Bruna Husky series not only reveals a strong connection between human destructive behaviour and necropolitical power, in which the latter is further enhanced by uncontrolled dogmatism and the persistence of violence in society, but also how the novels directly link the anthropocentric assumption of the right to kill with indiscriminate and pervasive environmental devastation and the destruction of human and non-human ecosocial systems (Montero, "Odio").

Suicide bombing intensifies when the IJA's terrorists equip themselves with more sophisticated and destructive explosives produced by the Cosmos Democratic Republic called Inferno, "*indetectable* por los métodos tradicionales y con una potencia de *destrucción aterradora*" ("*undetectable* through traditional methods and with *terrifying destructive power*"; 21; emphasis added), causing several massacres around the world. In discussing contemporary warfare within the post-human predicament, Braidotti asserts that contemporary death technologies are post-human because they are subject to "intense technological mediation" (9). The theorist accentuates the acute changes within the practices of warfare "in the direction of a more complex management of survival and of extinction" (9). Inferno fits the description of such post-human death technologies because of its intricate, specialized design, and its destructive force, and because it expands the notion and impact of necropower on all populations. Moreover, the deployment of Inferno using the body as a weapon contrasts with what Braidotti calls "post-anthropocentric weaponry" (127), a term that emphasizes the "tele-thanatological" quality and prominent autonomy given to or gained by death technologies such as military drones (126), whose "new killing techniques" redefine "contemporary necro-politics" and "human [and non-human] vulnerability" (128). The novel exposes the necropolitical power of such lethal technologies through the GAFPA machine, a Large Plasma Flux Accelerator, which Lago's private army uses to cause a massive blackout over the Iberian Peninsula, jamming electronic communications, rendering conventional weaponry useless, and producing widespread chaos and death among the human and non-human populations relying on electrical power. Incapacitating the enemy's networks and dismantling basic and complex physical and organizational eco-social structures is an example of what Mbembe calls "infrastructural warfare" (82).

Husky underscores the frightening effects of infrastructural war as she tallies the potential lethal effects on the human and non-human populations. She highlights how technological optimism and dependency, so vital for survival in today's world and in this future fictional society, suddenly turns into a *pharmakon*: "los ciegos redirigidos electrónicamente habrían dejado de ver, los cojos de andar, los paralíticos de moverse. Los diabéticos morirían sin sus páncreas artificiales y los epilépticos volverían a tener ataques" ("The blind, who were electronically guided, would lose their sight; the lame their ability to walk; the paralytic their ability to move. Diabetics would die without their artificial pancreases, and epileptics would again suffer from seizures"; 303). At first, Husky admits that this type of warfare does not differentiate "between the external and the internal enemy" (Mbembe 82), as the entire human and non-human population suffers its destructive power equally. Nevertheless, disparities re-emerge when, while searching for Lizard, the protagonist accidentally discovers the maturation plants where techno-humans undergo gestation and, in so doing, learns about the horrid effects of the blackout on the techno-human population. There, she witnesses the terrible agony suffered by hundreds of androids on the brink of death trapped in their incubation tanks: "hombres y mujeres, de expedición, de combate o cálculo, a punto de madurar, o niños de dos, de seis, de doce años. A todos se los veía descoyuntados, atormentados, enfermos. Sufriendo" ("replicant men and women – those made for expedition, combat, or computation – all about to mature; or children of just two, six, or twelve years of age. They were all disjointed, tormented, and sick. Suffering"; 357). The appalling scene of entombed techno-humans calls attention to Braidotti's point that death technologies could redefine modes of killing and reformulate the notion of necropolitics as well as human and non-human vulnerability. Still in a foetal stage of development, techno-humans are more vulnerable than humans because magnates like Lago have made them high commodities; valuable, but also disposable, individuals under the control of large corporations like TriTon Corp. that embody and sustain advanced capitalist economy. As Mbembe indicates, "the constant manufacturing of races, or species" and the exploitation of techno-humans sustain advanced capitalism, which in *Los tiempos* represents a powerful death technology that exposes underprivileged humans, and especially techno-humans and non-human minorities, to necropolitical power (Mbembe 177).

Advanced Capitalism as Necropolitics

Throughout the series, Husky constantly criticizes the ecosocial injustice suffered by underprivileged humans as well as non-human populations forced to inhabit the deadly contaminated Zone Zero, and the limitations that big corporations impose over these marginalized sectors by regulating access to clean air and water. Beyond their environmental impact on all beings, the commercialization and cruel treatment of techno-human life accentuate both human irresponsibility and the lack of ethical commitment when confronting techno-human subjectivity within the prospects of a post-human condition. A horrified Husky demands an explanation from Lago for his lack of empathy and negligence in not protecting the plant from the blackout or preventing the exposure of the techno-humans to death. Lago's cynical apology is grounded exclusively in market imperatives and averts any discussion about the worth and dignity of techno-human life: "Habría sido muy llamativo. Lo siento mucho, pero tuve que hacerlo así. Y lo siento de verdad, porque es una pérdida económica cuantiosa. Sois muy caros"

("It would have been very striking. I am very sorry, but I had to do it this way. I am truly sorry, because it is a substantial economic loss. You are very expensive"; 366).[6] Despite being a radical cyborg himself, Lago envisions techno-humans as an inferior, non-human species, meaningful only for capital gain and precluded from moral status. From the standpoint of transhumanism, Lago's own bio-technological augmentation, which he also financially quantifies, does not reduce his own worth or dignity. On the contrary, from his perspective, his bio-technological configuration intensifies his anthropocentric transhuman ego and brings him closer to his perverted notion of post-humanity. By addressing techno-human life in terms of profit, he also emphasizes the biogenetic ramifications of a capitalist economic system, which for Braidotti are fundamental for the discussion of the post-human predicament since they transform human and non-human life into goods for trading and economic gain: "In substance, advanced capitalism both invests and profits from the scientific and economic control and the commodification of *all that lives*" (59; emphasis added).[7] Through Lago's post-human quandary as a high-commodity item, *Los tiempos* emphasizes the ways in which techno-humans are more susceptible to necropolitical power because the market, governed by capital gains and losses, plays an unparalleled role in determining their fate. When opting between exercising the right to kill or to let live, the radical cyborg shows no empathy for techno-human life and does not hesitate to choose the former.

When Husky posits the damaging effects of the blackout and the years that it would take to restore a balance in the Iberian Peninsula, Lago's response aligns fundamentally with the telos of advanced capitalism: "En veinticuatro horas se puede arreglar todo. Nuestras empresas están preparadas para servir, reparar y sustituir todos los componentes eléctricos y electrónicos estropeados. Y, por otra parte, será un revulsivo económico, el dinero se moverá, la sociedad se enriquecerá. Ya sabes, la magia del mercado" ("Everything can be fixed in twenty-four hours. Our companies are ready to serve, repair, and substitute all the electrical components and malfunctioning electronics. Moreover, it will be an economic lever, money will move, society will get rich. You know, the magic of the market"; 366–7). At the text's conclusion, Husky confirms Lago's predictions about the speedy recovery of the stock market and the economy after the powerful engine that moves advanced capitalism restores all the infrastructures that anthropocentric elites destroyed in the first place. Indeed, throughout *Los tiempos*, Montero reinforces the notion that advanced capitalism relies on advanced technologies to thrive and highlights the intrinsic relationship between advanced capitalism, biopower, and "technologically mediated" life (Braidotti 61). These significant connections are fundamental to contradicting the myth within neoliberal rationale that technology is the key to reversing the ecologically damaging impacts of the Anthropocene. As carbon footprint researcher Mike Berners-Lee puts it, "Neoliberalism's free market … turns out to be unable to deliver what we need" (45). Using the example of techno-human mistreatment, Montero cleverly illustrates how advanced capitalism's reliance on biogenetic technology, rather than promoting more unbiased, safe, and harmonious sustainable societies, engenders inequality and exposes all beings to constant violence and often to death. Most importantly, her third novel evinces the ways in which neoliberal thinking and the technology that supports it exert violence, limit personal agency, and promote constant insecurity for many deprived human, techno-human, and non-human citizens, all the while stimulating a culture of prejudice and hate that mirrors contemporary society.

Human, Techno-Human, and Non-Human Enmity in the Age of the Anthropocene

Montero has always defended the suggestive realism of the Bruna Husky series. In the afterword to *Los tiempos*, the author insists that the fictional world that she fabricated in the series has become reality through many contemporary predicaments. For instance, "el populismo, la añoranza de las dictaduras de todo tipo, la pérdida de los valores democráticos, la ruptura del acuerdo social, el triunfo de la manipulación informativa, el aumento del odio y la violencia. Pues bien, me temo que en la última década todo ello no ha hecho sino empeorar" ("populism, the longing for all sorts of dictatorships, the loss of democratic values, the rupture of the social contract, the triumph of media manipulation, the rise of hatred and violence. In short, I am afraid that in the last decade all of this has only gotten worse"; 398). As the title of her novel states, "odio" ("hatred"), a synonym of enmity, becomes a powerful leitmotiv that emerges because of unequal opportunities and rights existing between those who inhabit the less contaminated and privileged Zone One and those who occupy the oppressed and heavily polluted Zone Zero. Early on in the text, during a raid against undocumented human and non-human migrants, Emma, a young refugee from Zone Zero, denounces the injustice suffered by the neglected citizens there, condemned to die at an early age solely for financial reasons.[8] In the last pages of the novel, the reader discovers that Emma, whose real name is Lorena Monfort, is commander Vengeance, the leader within the IJA ranks and one of the main accomplices in the plot against the United States of the Earth. Aware that the IJA is a corporation controlled by Lago, Emma befriends Gabi Orlov, a Russian child whom Bruna saves from a certain death due to exposure to high levels of radiation in Zone Zero. In *El peso*, Husky adopts Gabi and delegates her care to Yiannis Liberopoulos, Bruna's best human friend. Gabi, who also shares bitterness towards Zone One and its discriminatory practices, is unaware of Emma's real identity or intentions until the end of the novel.

Emma and Gabi evince how limiting inclusivity to classifications of citizenship that are determined solely by purchasing power fosters a society of enmity. Here enmity lies in the "unequal redistribution of capacities for mobility" (Mbembe 3), which restricts the chances of survival for the Zone Zero inhabitants. As Mbembe notes, borders are "no longer sites to be crossed but lines that separate" (3), so even when many of the undocumented human and non-human migrants, scornfully referred to as "polillas" ("moths"), manage to reach the cleaner sectors of the planet, they still experience a feeling of non-belonging, exacerbated by the constant fear of forced labour, jail, eviction, or death. Enmity escalates in the streets after the blackout as cyborrads begin a spree that terrorizes the human and non-human populations. It also rises due to the ruthless persecution and lynching of techno-humans carried out by Lago's private army and by the subsequent battle between the latter and the loyal forces of the United States of the Earth, who try to prevent the extreme right-wing's *coup d'état*.

Montero engages with the idea of a society of enmity by highlighting the human–non-human hierarchy that she first established in *Lágrimas* with the introduction of techno-human and other non-human subjectivity, including human mutants, non-human animals, and various alien species. Moreover, the author accentuates differences between human and techno-human life through Husky's ambivalent configuration. Biogenetic technology has fashioned the protagonist as a bright and emotional techno-human; however, it has also endowed her with enhanced physical and instinctive animal-like qualities such as amplified strength and agility, a heightened sense of smell and acuity, and more importantly, a more fierce personality. Her biological design disturbs "the laws of natural selection" and substitutes "them with the laws of intelligent design" (Harari, qtd. in Martín Galván, "Narración" 109). In the series, Husky is always grudgingly navigating those two elements of her identity. At times, she hates herself for experiencing human emotions, and at others, she loathes her primordial behaviour. The techno-human protagonist sees herself as "[una] criatura aberrante con cuerpo de androide" ("a repulsive creature with an android body"), unable to "manejar sus emociones ni su sentido de culpa ni su maldita pena y su violencia" ("manage her emotions, nor her sense of guilt, nor her damned grief or her violence"; *El peso*, qtd. in Martín Galván, "Narración" 107). She at once contrasts and bridges the two species that she embodies. Importantly, this hybridity functions in the novel to centre the question of enmity within speciesism.

Lago corroborates Husky's human genetic configuration when she confronts him at the gestation plant: "Pero quizá no sepas que vuestras células madre se fabrican a partir de las células epiteliales de un humano. Así que todos provenís de un hombre o una mujer reales" ("Perhaps you are unaware that your stem cells are manufactured from the epithelial cells of a human. Therefore, you all come from a real man or woman"; 371). However, he hastily establishes that her heightened artificiality, enhanced by her animality, excludes her from fitting within the human species. After all, supremacists consider techno-humans "una especie subsidiaria y unos ciudadanos de tercera clase" ("a subsidiary species and third-class citizens"; Montero, *Lágrimas* 61). Montero's exploration into the ambiguity of techno-human identity and its mistreatment delves into the notion of societies of separation and exposes the hatred, antagonism, and violence that they generate. Husky and her fellow techno-humans are representative of the type of surplus populations that Mbembe asserts are a part of even the most liberal democracies, "undesirables of whom one hopes to be rid" (42). As such, along with aliens and mutants, they represent for Lago "a problem of excess of presence" (Mbembe 43). In addition, their existence triggers an anxiety among the dominating anthropocentric population, that is, a "desire for an enemy" and a need of protection "from external danger" (Mbembe 43). Lago voices such supremacist apprehensions as he addresses angry demonstrators in the streets through public screens. He declares, "Porque no sabemos quiénes somos. ¿Somos androides, somos alienígenas, somos mutantes? ¡No, señor! ¡Somos humanos! ¡Humanos! Y tenemos que recuperar el orgullo del largo legado de nuestra Humanidad" ("Because we don't know who we are. Are we androids, aliens, mutants? No, sir! We are humans! Humans! And we must regain our pride in the long legacy of our Humanity"; 143). Lago's anthropocentric views discount the value and agency of the non-human other and stress the ranked character of a human-centred world view, which grants humans a "privileged status as lords of nature" (Steiner 1).[9] While Lago's speciesist discourse is a charade that will allow him to set up his extreme capitalist policies after overthrowing the government, and in spite of the fact that he is a radical android, a transhuman himself who has transcended human "biologically determined limits,"

Lago continues to reassert a hierarchical value system (Harari, qtd. in Martín Galván, "Narración" 109). Even though he loathes the Law of Human Integrity and the physical and mental limitations of the human condition, he embraces an anthropocentric liberal humanist subject's philosophy.

Excluding a few human individuals (Yiannis, Mirari, Gabi, and Lizard), Husky develops enmity toward the human species as she struggles to survive her necropolitical destiny. The creation of false memories to endow techno-humans with a random identity, the subsequent biological mechanisms inscribed on them to supervise their behaviour, and humans' exercise of the right to kill in order to dictate techno-humans' lifespan represent for the protagonist the pivotal expression of biopower over the techno-human population. While still confronting Lago at the gestation plant, Husky learns more about the mechanisms of control imbedded in techno-humans to prevent them from ever accessing their place of origin. Lago asks Husky, "¿No te extraña no haberte preguntado nunca por el lugar en donde te hicieron? Eso, esa falta de curiosidad, también ha sido implantada por nosotros" ("Does it not seem strange to you that you have never asked yourself about the place where they created you? That lack of curiosity has also been implanted by us"; 362). The lack of techno-human curiosity regarding their own ontology specifies the limitations imposed by humans over techno-human agency as well as their political and moral status.[10]

Despite the lack of techno-human autonomy and Husky's ambivalent subjectivity, Montero shows through the series' three novels that the protagonist is capable of disabling various dictates concerning her life and conduct, and her death too. In her discussion of the inscriptions of cultural codes in *Lágrimas*, environmental Hispanist Katarzyna Beilin indicates that "Bruna's effort to rewrite codes inscribed in her should be read as a metaphor of a needed transformation in human culture, one that would lead toward an alternative biopolitics that cares for all life" (251). Beilin further notes, "Bruna's refusal to follow the induced behavior algorithm implanted in her brain [one that makes her believe she is human and the mother of a child that she must protect by committing an act of terrorism] is a metaphor for contemporary humans' need to resist cultural codes that lead us to destroy nonhuman life" (252). As Husky approaches the gestation plant where Lizard and the other hostages are confined, she begins to feel horribly sick: "Todas las células de su cuerpo se negaban a entrar en ese edificio, era como si cada paso adelante la condujera a la destrucción y a un inmenso dolor" ("All the cells in her body were refusing to enter the building; it was as if each step forward were leading her to destruction and to an immense pain"; Montero, *Los tiempos* 355). Once inside the building, she feels an excruciating terror but rallies on until she finally reaches the gestation tanks where fellow techno-humans are dying. The heartbreaking scene becomes the trigger that allows her to rewrite the code that originally prevented her from being there in the first place. "Y de ese dolor salió un alarido, y una furia que la puso en pie y le dio fuerzas para avanzar por la nave a tropezones, entre los pobres cuerpos torturados, entre niños espasmódicos y jóvenes perfectos agonizando" ("And from that pain came a scream, and a fury that set her on her feet and gave her the strength to move forward through the warehouse stumbling among the poor tortured bodies, among spasmodic children, and perfect youngsters in agony"; 357–8). Beilin posits that Husky embodies the type of cyborg that ecofeminist Donna Haraway conceives in her *Cyborg Manifesto* (1991), that is, entities "capable of rewriting what has been programmed in their bodies because their posthuman nature is based on flows of information and not blood ties that are more deterministic" (Beilin 252). I agree with Beilin's analysis of Husky's resistance as a rewriting of anthropocentric cultural codes. Furthermore, via what Braidotti calls "the post-anthropocentric turn" (38), which rejects hierarchical practices within a post-human condition, I contend that the series as a whole affords us the opportunity to explore an alternative post-human vision resulting from incorporating kinship ties.

Through Haraway, Beilin writes that cyborgs are better equipped than humans "to save the world" because of their detachment from "biological connections to other bodies," which somehow provides them with a better "chance to break the vicious cycle of repeating past errors" (252). I argue that blood ties and biological connections play an important role in configuring Husky's subjectivity, in elucidating her ability to offset the effects of necropolitics, and in creating the kind of post-human subjectivity capable of bridging the conspicuous gap that in the novel and in real life divides human and non-human species. While such post-human subjectivity is not faultless, Husky's mistakes are "not based on the us-and-them principle of the anthropological machine"; nor are her faults "structured and limited by fixed taxonomy, by defensive or aggressive sovereignty" (Pettman 196). As Maryanne L. Leone cleverly points out, the first two novels of the series "present a paradigm of interdependent care that extends to the non-human realm to suggest that the rights and contributions of all beings must be considered as we address social and environmental injustices" (74). In *Los tiempos*, Montero continues to strengthen human–non-human alliance and interdependency stressing the means by which multispecies bridges materialize through trust, solidarity, and, above all, sacrifice for each other. Montero ingeniously develops such a dependable relationship between Husky and two human female characters new to the series: Barri Aznárez, Lizard's sister and a member of a human colony holding technophobic leanings, and Angela Gayo, a mathematical and computational prodigy. In fact, Gayo crosses the multispecies bridge manifestly when she pays the absolute price of dying to save Husky's life from a plasma gunshot. In so doing, her conduct contrasts starkly with Lago's sovereign behaviour; when Gayo, a human being, is faced with the biopower dilemma of exercising the right to kill or let live, she willingly commits to the latter.

Haraway postulates that cyborgs "are neither mothers nor have mothers" (Beilin 252). In the gestation plant, Lago adds fundamental details about the influence of blood ties and motherhood on Husky's conduct. Addressing her, he states, "[E]res un clon de Rosa Montero, Husky" ("You are a clone of Rosa Montero, Husky"; 371). Moreover, in *Lágrimas*, Husky's original memories – penned by Pablo Nopal, a human writer of techno-human memories based on his own traumatic childhood – neutralize the adulterated code that makes her a human mother and save her from an imminent death. Throughout Nopal's own recollections of his unsettling youth, motherhood plays a crucial role (Martín Galván, "El universo posthumano" 9–10). By reinserting her original memories, Husky becomes aware that she never had a real mother and that she is not, nor could she ever be, a biological mother. However, her maternal protective instincts, proven by Gabi's adoption and by her own longing for a mother figure, are irrefutable. In the concluding pages of the novel, while Husky is about to die, Yiannis tries to download her consciousness onto silicon discs in an attempt to preserve her identity and to transfer it to a new techno-human body. Nopal asks the protagonist if she would like him to erase her false childhood traumatic memories, but she refuses: "Pero eso era ella. Sin eso no sería" ("But that was who she was. Without them, she would not be"; 388). Husky also asks Nopal to include in her new memories a short story that her fictitious mother used to tell her in her made-up childhood. Husky's reluctance to relinquish her fake memories and her refusal to forgo blood bonds and biological connections, namely, her prosthetic nostalgia for familial ties, demonstrate her identitary agency and thus expand the post-human subjectivity that Haraway's cyborgs embody. Nevertheless, her longings for human ties and motherly connections must not be interpreted as a refusal of her own techno-human/non-human subjectivity; nor should they be conceived as favouring anthropocentric perspectives or hierarchies, which she continuously confronts and rejects throughout the series.

In *Los tiempos del odio*, Husky finally affirms a human and non-human family that she has assembled throughout the previous volumes and grants them equal value and "ontological dignity" (Bryant 246): Mirari, a human friend; Maio, an alien friend; Yiannis; Gabi; Bartolo, an alien she adopts; and "ahora también Ángela y hasta un poco la fastidiosa Emma. No podía arriesgarse a perderlos, como había perdido a Lizard" ("now Angela too, and to some extent even annoying Emma. She couldn't risk losing them, like she had lost Lizard"; 278). The kind of subjectivity that Husky personifies relates to the post-human position that Braidotti defends, one that can transcend anthropocentrism and create "new formations of subjectivity" without erasing the power of human connection (38). Montero's techno-human protagonist also manages to overcome her animosity towards human life and to embrace her own humanity, while acknowledging that her technologically mediated animality is an inherent part of the subjectivity that she must also learn to accept without falling into the trap of dual anthropocentric thinking. Husky's determination to offset her ambivalent subjectivity, forcibly inscribed on her, should encourage us, as Beilin ingeniously suggests, to analyse and change our own current biopolitical practices. We must break, as Husky does, the codes of a Cartesian duality that support anthropocentric philosophies and dispense with our current human-centric economic and cultural ways of thinking, which promote racism, enmity, and violence towards the environment, the underprivileged human, and the non-human other.

New media scholar Richard Grusin, who sees the non-human turn as a fundamental component of environmental humanities, suggests that to decentre the human, we must favour and engage with the non-human, "understood variously in terms of animals, affectivity, bodies, organic and geophysical systems, materiality, or technologies" (vii). Montero's series as a whole, along with Mbembe's necropolitical theory and Hayles's, Roden's, and Braidotti's assertions regarding a non-anthropocentric post-human condition, critically engage with the decentring of the types of human subjectivity that currently promote ecosocial inequalities, speciesism, and necropower in our contemporary society. Their originality, commitment, and critical views prove fundamental to approaching the contentious debates surrounding the Anthropocene.

NOTES

1 Contrary to other species, the technical world of humans has made us "the ultimate ecosystem engineers" responsible for dramatically "shaping biotic

communities" (Smith 1797). Environmental scientist Erle Ellis has noted that when addressing the onset of the Anthropocene, some archeologists do not focus exclusively on the impact of human activity on our planet, but also analyse the rise of unparalleled human abilities to engender "a diverse array of potent environment altering behaviours" (76). Such unique behaviours are a consequence of human niche constructions, that is, processes by which organisms, through their actions and decisions, alter their own and each other's niches.

2 In "'The Plague': Nonhuman, Posthuman, and the Environment in Spanish Science Fiction," I underscore the way post-human thinkers like Hayles, Braidotti, and new-media scholar Richard Grusin advocate for theoretical developments within the post-human and non-human turn that challenge human exceptionalism and human-centred thinking.

3 The existential conflict surrounding technological alterations of the human condition that extend beyond human intent or control include Spanish manifestations such as those studied by Óscar Iván Useche in his chapter for this collection. Through his analysis of the theories of automation developed by Regenerationist engineer and inventor Leonardo Torres Quevedo, Useche evinces the post-1898 imperative to extol human ascendancy over the non-human world by emphasizing the regenerative capacity of technology as a means by which to reinforce the metaphysical constitution of national identity.

4 All translations into English of citations from *Los tiempos del odio* are my own.

5 Article 8 of the 2009 version of the Transhumanist Declaration states: "We favor allowing individuals wide personal choice over how they enable their lives. This includes use of techniques that may be developed to assist memory, concentration, and mental energy; life extension therapies; reproductive choice technologies; cryonics procedures; and many other possible *human modification* and *enhancement technologies*" (Humanity+; emphasis added).

6 Ecocritic Katarzyna Beilin suggests in her study about *Lágrimas* that synthetic bodies are part of "the economic realm" (251). In her reading of *El peso*, co-editor of *Beyond Human* Maryanne L. Leone indicates that producing androids in sets of twelve "prioritizes monetary calculations over the ethical implications of reducing a life to a mere product" (72). In *Los tiempos*, Husky and the reader gain a deeper understanding of this pernicious economic transaction as revealed by Lago's comments.

7 For Braidotti, the biogenetic configuration associated with present-day capitalism represents "a perverse form of the posthuman" (7).

8 In his study of *El peso*, Spanish environmental humanist Luis I. Prádanos indicates that the system of borders designed by the United States of the Earth "results in the technocratic, militarized, and

neoliberal management of populations and spaces, as well as extreme segregation based on income" (118). Prádanos underlines that in the text, "new borders are determined not by nations but by the degree of pollution" (118).

9　Lago's supremacist views and lack of care towards the welfare of other non-human species contrast considerably with article 7 of the Transhumanist Declaration, which reads: "We advocate the well-being of all sentience, including humans, non-human animals, and any future artificial intellects, modified life forms, or other intelligences to which technological and scientific advance may give rise" (Humanity+). Despite the anthropocentric emphasis and the persistence of humanist values embedded within the Transhumanist Declaration, article 7 suggests that present transhumanists would reject Lago's demeaning of all non-human beings.

10　In 2015, I conducted an interview with Rosa Montero about *El peso del corazón*, in which I asked her about techno-humans' agency and their inability to end their own lives voluntarily. Montero responded that she could not resolve whether techno-humans could not self-destruct because of an inscribed code that prevents it, or if they had the free will to do so. For her, this uncertainty raises an old debate concerning human free will. She said, "Are we really free to choose or are we not? I really don't know" (Montero, interview; much of the content of this interview appears in Martín Galván, "Narración").

WORKS CITED AND CONSULTED

Alexander, Samuel. "A Critique of Techno-optimism: Efficiency without Sufficiency Is Lost." Prosperous Descent: Crisis as Opportunity in an Age of Limits. Simplicity Institute, 2015, pp. 1–28, https://samuelalexander.info/wp-content/uploads/2017/02/A-Critique-of-Techno-Optimism-Samuel-Alexander.pdf.

Beilin, Katarzyna Olga, with Sainath Suryanarayanan. "Debates on GMOs in Spain and Rosa Montero's *Lágrimas en la lluvia*." *Search of an Alternative Biopolitics: Anti-Bullfighting, Animality, and the Environment in Contemporary Spain*, by Katarzyna Olga Beilin, Ohio State UP, 2015, pp. 235–61.

Berners-Lee, Mike. *There Is No Planet B: A Handbook for the Make or Break Years.* Cambridge UP, 2019.

Bostrom, Nick. "Why I Want to Be Posthuman When I Grow Up." *Ethics and Emerging Technologies*, edited by Ronald Sandler, Palgrave Macmillan, 2014, pp. 218–34.

Braidotti, Rosi. *The Posthuman.* Polity, 2013.

Bryant, Levi R. *The Democracy of Objects.* Open Humanities Press, 2011.

Castro, Antón. "Rosa Montero: 'Me molestan los dogmas, los fanatismos de izquierdas y de derechas.'" *Heraldo*, 13 Nov. 2018, https://www.heraldo.es/noticias/ocio-cultura/2018/11/13/rosa-montero-espantan-los-dogmas-los-fanatismos-izquierdas-derechas-1277123-1361024.html.

Ellis, Erle C. *Anthropocene: A Very Short Introduction*. Oxford UP, 2018.

Foucault, Michel. *"Society Must Be Defended": Lectures at the Collège de France, 1975–76*. Edited by Mauro Bertani and Alessandro Fontana, translated by David Macey, Picador, 2003.

Graham, Elaine L. *Representations of the Post/Human: Monsters, Aliens and Others in Popular Culture*. Rutgers UP, 2002.

Grusin, Richard. "Introduction." *The Nonhuman Turn*, edited by Richard Grusin, U of Minnesota P, 2015, pp. vii–xxix.

Hayles, Katherine. *How We Became Posthuman: Virtual Bodies in Cybernetics, Literature, and Informatics*. U of Chicago P, 1999.

Heidegger, Martin. Being and Time. Translated by Joan Stambaugh, State U of New York P, 2010.

Heidegger, Martin. *The Question Concerning Technology and Other Essays*. Translated by William Lovitt, Harper and Row, 1977.

Humanity+. "The Transhumanist Declaration." *Artificial Intelligence and Transhumanism*, https://itp.uni-frankfurt.de/~gros/Mind2010/transhumanDeclaration.pdf. Accessed 17 Apr. 2023.

Leone, Maryanne L. "Trans-Species Collaborations in Response to Social, Economic, and Environmental Violence in Rosa Montero´s *Lágrimas en la lluvia* and *El peso del corazón*." *Ecozon@*, vol. 8, no. 1, 2017, pp. 61–78, https://doi.org/10.37536/ECOZONA.2017.8.1.1040.

Martín Galván, Juan Carlos. "Narración, monstruosidad y la condición poshumana en *El peso del corazón*: La segunda novela de Bruna Husky." *Hispanófila*, vol. 176, 2016, pp. 99–115. *Project MUSE*, https://doi.org/10.1353/hsf.2016.0006.

Martín Galván, Juan Carlos. "'The Plague': Nonhuman, Posthuman, and the Environment in Spanish Science Fiction." *Ometeca*, vol. 24, 2018–19, pp. 154–83.

Martín Galván, Juan Carlos. "El universo posthumano de Lágrimas en la lluvia: Memoria artificial, identidad, historia y ficción." *Alambique. Revista académica de ciencia ficción y fantasía / Jornal acadêmico de ficção científica e fantasía*, vol. 5, no. 1, 2017, https://doi.org/10.5038/2167-6577.5.1.5.

Mbembe, Achille. *Necropolitics*. Duke UP, 2019.

Montero, Rosa. *Instrucciones para salvar el mundo*. Alfaguara, 2008.

Montero, Rosa. Interview with the author, 16 Mar. 2015.

Montero, Rosa. *Lágrimas en la lluvia*. Seix Barral, 2011.

Montero, Rosa. "Odio." *El País semanal*, 9 Sept. 2017, https://elpais.com/elpais/2017/09/10/eps/1504994751_150499.html.

Montero, Rosa. *El peso del corazón*. Seix Barral, 2015.

Montero, Rosa. *Los tiempos del odio*. Seix Barral, 2018.

Peterson, Christopher. *Monkey Trouble: The Scandal of Posthumanism*. Fordham UP, 2018.

Pettman, Dominic. *Human Error: Species-Being and Media Machine*. U of Minnesota P, 2011.

Prádanos, Luis I. *Postgrowth Imaginaries: New Ecologies and Counterhegemonic Culture in Post-2008 Spain*. Liverpool UP, 2018.

Roden, David. *Posthuman Life: Philosophy at the Edge of the Human*. Routledge, 2015.

Smith, Bruce D. "The Ultimate Ecosystem Engineers." *Science*, vol. 315, no. 5820, Mar. 2007, pp. 1797–8, https://doi.org/10.1126/science.1137740.

Steiner, Gary. *Anthropocentrism and Its Discontents: The Moral Status of Animals in the History of Western Philosophy*. U of Pittsburgh P, 2005.

Chapter Ten

The Salvage Poetics of Ben Clark's *Basura*

MICAH MCKAY

To know the world that progress has left to us, we must track shifting patterns of ruination.

Anna Lowenhaupt Tsing, The Mushroom at the End of the World

As the global climate crisis continues to unfold, it becomes increasingly important to examine received ideas about the distinction between culture and nature.[1] Are those ideas useful to us, or should we be rethinking them? If such a re-examination is necessary, what tools are available to us in order to carry it out? What things should we focus on as we think about these issues? The last question – about the *things* that should occupy our thoughts – is, I think, of central importance. The intersection of the material world and our ideas about it, things and thought, is, in essence, the terrain I would like to cover in this chapter. More specifically, what I examine here is the intersection of a certain kind of thing with a certain kind of thought (or product of thought): the presence of trash in an example of contemporary Spanish poetry, the aptly titled collection *Basura*, published in 2011 by Ben Clark.[2] Clark's collection takes a broad view of waste, presenting the reader with poetic fragments that refer to trash-strewn parks, nuclear fallout, waste flows from the Global North to the Global South, hoarders, the Great Pacific Garbage Patch, and more.[3] His book is divided into five titled sections that each contain a series of brief, interrelated poetic fragments, plus a coda and a series of what he calls "Apuntes basura" ("Trash Notes"),[4] which serve to explain many of the references he makes throughout the collection. To my mind, the idea of salvage offers a useful conceptual frame for thinking through what is at stake in *Basura,* in terms of both the poetic project Clark undertakes in the book and the text's orientation toward ecological crisis and the place of the human in a more-than-human landscape that has been profoundly damaged by human activity.

In what follows, I develop the concept of salvage as it relates to *Basura* in two ways: first, building on Walter Benjamin's reading of Charles Baudelaire (as distilled by philosopher Irving Wohlfarth), I explore the way that Clark's collection can be seen as a salvage operation, a book composed of the detritus of history; second, I consider the way that Clark presents this detritus by reading it through the lens of anthropologist Anna Tsing's theorization of the relationship between salvage and capitalism. Tsing's reflections on sites for salvage, landscapes that decentre human hubris, and the possibility of political solidarity in the midst of ruination and precarity allow us to see Clark's work as a critical meditation on the possibility of cultivating life and meaning in a world full of garbage.

Trash and the Ragpicker-Poet

At face value, trash, the matter that we discard because we no longer find it useful, seems to be a relatively simple thing, a problem that transcends historical specificity because creating waste and throwing it away are activities in which human beings have always engaged. In fact, some might argue that producing trash is a natural human activity that requires less theorization than it does technical solutions. Archaeologist William Rathje and writer and editor Cullen Murphy, for instance, in a very engaging discussion of the Garbage Project, downplay the dimensions and import of the vertiginous production of trash in contemporary consumer societies by universalizing the garbage problem.[5] They note that "our species faced its first garbage crisis when human beings became sedentary animals" (33). As for how we humans have managed those "crises," Rathje and Murphy add:

> There are no ways of dealing with garbage that haven't been familiar, in essence, for thousands of years, although as the species has advanced, people have introduced refinements. The basic methods of garbage disposal are four: dumping it, burning it, turning it into something that can be useful (recycling), and minimizing the volume of material goods – future garbage – that comes into existence (this last is known technically in the garbage field as "source reduction"). Any civilization of any complexity has used all four procedures simultaneously to one degree or another. (33)

They continue by comparing modern environmental research data about rates of trash production in various places with archeological data from sites like the ancient city of Troy, asserting, for instance, that "if all of the garbage from Manhattan that is currently sent to Fresh Kills and all the construction and demolition debris from Manhattan that is currently dumped at sea were instead spread out evenly over the island, the rate of accumulation per century would be exactly the same as that of ancient Troy" (35). While I am certainly in no position to dispute the basic premise that waste disposal is an issue that all human societies have had to confront or the more specific claim regarding rates of accumulation of solid waste, I do want to emphasize that the eliding of distinct cultural and historical contexts upon which such a comparison relies only serves to obscure the problematic, slippery, historically specific quality of the objects that we call trash. The comparison between Manhattan and Troy exhibits a naïve optimism regarding the problem of trash because, regardless of similar rates of accumulation, it overlooks questions of siting, toxicity, and scale. Where garbage is stored and how it affects surrounding communities, the noxious effects of newer forms of trash (plastics and industrial waste, for example), and the ever-increasing production of solid waste complicate the rosy picture Rathje and Murphy paint.[6] For them, the information trash provides is transparent and easily classifiable, just as the trash that provides the information can be safely neutralized and contained if it is subjected to the appropriate combination of the methods of garbage disposal cited above.

Despite their view of trash as a relatively straightforward problem, Rathje and Murphy are right to point out that humans have always had to deal with waste in one way or another. In fact, we could even go so far as to say that the production and disposal of waste is, as anthropologist Joshua Reno has argued, one of the processes that all biological entities on this planet, whether human or non-human, have in common. In this seemingly universal dimension, waste is not only an index of death and decay, but also of life:

> [B]oth bodily waste and discarded artifacts … share more than symbolic relevance; they actively resemble each other because of the similar interpretive fate they face when separated from the form of life – the living process – that gave rise to them. The transience of decomposing and deteriorating matter can be seen as loss, but also as the perpetuation of life. Unless they are actively maintained and preserved under the right conditions, moreover, such objectual forms become unbound and gradually devolve into other life processes. (Reno 9)

Whereas Reno ultimately prefers to undertake a bio-semiotic reading of the trace of life that such waste communicates both before and beyond human culture by following various trails of animal scat, I am more concerned with the cultural construction of waste in all its historical specificity, particularly the types of human-made waste that are paradigmatic of the Anthropocene. Nonetheless, the inherent tension that Reno points out concerning what waste signifies – it is a sign of both life and death – is fundamental to any consideration of the way that trash works in specific cultural contexts.[7]

The specific context that interests me here is global in scale; it is marked by the growing awareness of a concept like the Anthropocene that grapples with the enormous dimensions of the crises – both cultural and natural – that human beings currently face and for which they are in large part responsible. And trash has a central role to play in thinking about the Anthropocene. It is, as waste researcher Myra Hird has claimed, "*the* signifier of the Anthropocene" (emphasis in the original) in that this new partition of geological time is defined by the traces of waste and detritus that modern industrial societies have scattered about the planet, whether it be carbon dioxide emissions from the burning of fossil fuels, plastic particles that overwhelm ocean ecosystems, nuclear waste that remains radioactive for tens of thousands of years, landfills of such enormous dimensions that they change the topography of the regions where they are located, or any number of other manifestations of trash. And the waste produced by globalized, consumer-oriented, capitalist societies threatens to engulf those societies. As Spanish philosopher José Luis Pardo has put it,

> Nosotros tendríamos que decir, hoy, que *la riqueza de las sociedades en las que domina el modo de producción capitalista se presenta como una inmensa acumulación de basuras.*[8] En efecto, ninguna otra forma de sociedad anterior o exterior a la moderna ha producido basuras en una cantidad, calidad y velocidad comparables a las de las nuestras. Ninguna otra ha llegado a alcanzar el punto que han alcanzado las nuestras, es decir, el punto en el que la basura ha llegado a convertirse en una amenaza para la propia sociedad.

> (We would have to say, today, that *the wealth of those societies in which the capitalist mode of production prevails presents itself as an immense accumulation of trash.* Indeed, no other form of society prior to or outside of modern society has produced trash in such quantities, of such quality, or with such speed as ours. No other society has reached the point that we have, that is, the point where trash has become a threat to society itself; 163; emphasis in the original)

The *nosotros* to which Pardo refers remains unclear: is he talking about Spanish society, people who live in capitalist societies, or everyone on the planet? Despite the potential pitfalls that invoking "our modern society" (in the singular) entails, I think that what Pardo is getting at is the seeming ubiquity of a brand of consumer culture that goes hand in hand with the logic of neoliberal social and economic policies. And as he implies, the flipside of the accelerated rates of production that are necessary to meet ever-increasing demands of consumption is an alarming upswing in the production of trash. Sadly, as scholar of Hispanic cultural studies Samuel Amago makes clear, "the material profligacy of a system designed to create ever-greater quantities of rubbish" is facilitated by neoliberalism's logic of externalization, which both "keep[s] lived environments clean" and "minimize[s] any real reckoning with waste" (8). Indeed, "the veiled operation of disappearance is crucial to the continued function of capitalist societies" (Amago 8). Perhaps it goes without saying that something has to be done with all the trash produced in consumer societies: it is let go, thrown away, or externalized, as Amago puts it.

Have the acts of determining that an object has lost its value and throwing it away changed somehow with the advent of contemporary consumer habits? Have the ethical parameters of that action remained the same ever since "human beings became sedentary animals" (Rathje and Murphy 33)? Social and cultural theorist Gay Hawkins sustains that, in contemporary consumer society, our relationships with things are not solely based on an instrumental logic of using goods for the convenience with which they allow us to go about our daily lives; additionally, the desire for commodities reveals a libidinal investment in the act of disposal itself (9). In other words, disposal functions as a key node in the production, maintenance, and regimentation of desire in a consumer economy. Easy disposability lubricates the machinery of production and consumption and heightens that consumer's desire for new products to consume, a desire that is never really fulfilled, but rather deferred and rearticulated as disposal clears the way for further consumption. Within this dynamic of incessant production-consumption-disposal, what are the implications for the relationships that human beings have with the material objects that pass through their lives? Hawkins suggests that

> [d]isposability constitutes waste as a technical problem, something to be administered by the most efficient and rational technologies of removal. Generally this means dumping; the bin, the local tip and the drain have become emblematic sites for the disposal of anything and everything;

these are the homes of waste. Yet, as anyone who has stood at the edge of a tip or stared down a drain and felt the wave of horror and fascination would know, this ethos of disposability is a technical and spatial fantasy. Our relations with waste cannot be so easily severed; out of sight does not necessarily mean out of mind. Disposability represents our waste relations as necessary elimination, an inevitable part of progress and consumption. This is a relation of mastery that constitutes the self that discards as whole, separate, untouched, purified. And in this relation the moral implications of our complex and shifting connections with rubbish are denied. (10)

I quote Hawkins at length because she so expertly outlines what is at stake in the ethos of disposability. What does this stuff, this material substance that we throw away, have to say to and about us, we who are also fundamentally material beings? By occluding the ontological dilemma that trash presents to human beings, the regime of disposability, with its technification of the problem of trash, spins a fantasy, as Hawkins puts it: a fantasy of human separation from and mastery over the material world. If the growing prominence of the idea of the Anthropocene can be characterized as the realization that the waste we produce is more rebellious and uncontrollable than we thought, then this fantasy deserves serious critical attention. And such attention is especially timely given the seemingly unchecked advance of the consumption of disposable commodities all across the globe.

Clark's *Basura* questions the fantasy spun by the ethos of disposability by taking up discards, cast-offs, and excess both thematically and formally. In his own study of the cultures of waste in Spain, Amago contends that the "interpenetrating activities of design, refinement, disposal, and separation – of past from present, of useable from disposable, of urban from rural, of the authoritarian from the democratic, of capitalist from socialist – are always incomplete and ongoing" in what he describes as "an unceasing process of becoming, and therein lies the value of 'remains,' discards, rubbish as objects of study" (19). There is no doubt that the theoretical, the aesthetic, the social, and the material are distinct domains, but as Amago intimates, they are inextricably tangled and shot through with the procedures and decisions that go into the production of trash, disposal, and waste management. In order to tease out Clark's formal approach to waste, which recognizes this complex entanglement of the material and the symbolic, I turn to Wohlfarth's reading of Benjamin and Baudelaire to advance the notion of the poet as a ragpicker who salvages material from the detritus produced by society. In his essay "Et Cetera? The Historian as Chiffonnier," Wohlfarth argues that, among the many metaphors Benjamin uses to invoke the "materialist historian" in his work, the figure of the ragpicker is especially potent because it is a dialectical image that usefully condenses Benjamin's vision of historical materialism (144). For Benjamin, the materialist historian reads history against the grain by seizing upon the fractured elements of history that teleological brands of historiography (what he calls "historicism") sweep aside because they do not fit into narratives of universal progress. Instead, historical materialism disrupts teleological thinking by reading the past not as the inevitable forebear of the present, but rather as a node in a constellation that is dialectically related to the present and can therefore be made to act upon the present in ways that short-circuit the forward march of progress.[9] Such a conception of historiography strikes me as particularly relevant in the current context of ecological crisis, given the amplification that discourses of inevitability seem to enjoy, whether it be inevitable doom or triumph.

A central moment in Wohlfarth's essay comes when he cites Benjamin's citation of the following passage from Baudelaire's *Du vin et du haschisch*:

> Let us descend a little lower and consider one of those mysterious creatures who live, as it were, off the leavings (*déjections*) of the big city … Here we have a man whose task is to gather the day's rubbish in the capital. Everything that the big city has cast off, everything it lost, everything it disdained, everything it broke, he catalogues and collects. He combs through the archives of debauchery, the stockpile of waste. He sorts things out and makes intelligent choices; like a miser assembling his treasure, he gathers the trash that, after being regurgitated by the goddess of Industry, will assume the shape of useful or gratifying objects. (Wohlfarth 151)

Wohlfarth notes that this passage is key to understanding both Baudelaire's poetic philosophy and Benjamin's engagement with the archive (151–2). What is more, it is a potent illustration of a ragpicker-poet like Clark, whose "useful or gratifying objects" are fed by the discursive and material detritus of consumer society. He foregrounds this poetic salvage operation in a number of ways. For example, by giving his collection the title *Basura*, he not only refers to the work's thematic engagement with garbage; he also names the contents of his book as trash. In this sense, the very title of the work echoes a fundamental fact about trash: it is a culturally constructed category, a label that can potentially adhere to almost any material object. In other words, what marks the distinction between trash and non-trash is a culturally determined consideration about the value or usefulness of an object.[10]

Beyond the title of the work itself, Clark reflects on this dynamic in the following fragment from the section "Tu basura no es basura" ("Your Trash Is Not Trash"):

Si llenamos el Nilo de desechos
seguirá todo el Nilo en la palabra
Nilo.
Pero con la basura es diferente:
será si así se llama o no será.
Y una vez bautizado, entonces sí:
el Nilo envenenado en la palabra
– y toda la basura en la palabra –
basura.

(If we fill the Nile with waste
the whole Nile will continue in the word
Nile.
But with trash it's different:
it will be if it's called by that name or it will not be.
And once baptized, then yes:
the Nile poisoned in the word
– and all the trash in the word –
trash; 66)

By imagining the Nile River full of garbage, Clark meditates on the slipperiness of the category of trash: while the Nile can take on an amount of pollution that would change its material composition and still be called the Nile, trash has to be called trash in order to be recognized as such. Beyond affirming the basic lack of essence at the heart of the definition of trash ("será si así se llama o no será"), this fragment also signals the material consequences of what might be criticized as a mere linguistic game: while *basura* is indeed a *palabra*, a linguistic label, it is, more importantly, an agent that can poison one of the world's great waterways.

Clark further signals the trash status of his collection through a number of paratextual elements that enrich the present consideration of what I am calling his salvage poetics.[11] The book's front cover and flyleaf, for instance, work in tandem to hint at both the overwhelming presence of trash in the collection and the potential ideological ends to which Clark will put it. The cover illustration is a photograph, a medium shot of a human being whose head is covered with a trash bag and who looks to be struggling mightily to remove the bag before suffocating. And the flyleaf, included at the beginning and end of the book, is not the typical blank page, but rather what looks to be a section from a block of text, since fragments of the type are abruptly cut off at the edges of the page. The text consists of the word "SPAM" repeated several dozen times (in all caps and a few times in boldface type), interrupted only by a few instances of the word "MAPA" ("MAP") and the edges of the page. While these kinds of visual cues are easy for the reader to pass over in order to arrive at the book's supposedly real content, they strike me as richly suggestive paratexts that reinforce the aesthetic and intellectual effect of the poems themselves. By invoking spam, the flyleaf hints at different manifestations of garbage and junk in contemporary society: on the one hand, the discursive detritus of unsolicited advertisements (i.e., offers to engage in consumption that always entails the production of waste) that any email or social media user has had to learn to live with, and on the other, the material waste that haunts the production of highly processed consumer goods like the form of canned ham for which electronic spam is named. And the easily missed instances of the word "mapa" mixed in with the accumulation of its near anagram "spam" seem to signal Clark's poems as a sort of guide through the trash that is filling up our conceptual and material horizons and highlight the fundamental connection between space and waste. The human consequences of all this accumulated waste receive a clear visual treatment in the cover image: we are inescapably connected with the trash we produce and, despite our efforts to attain dominance over the material world, our trash seems to be choking us out and playing the role of protagonist in the story of human experience on earth. What is more, these design elements clearly foreground the question of literature as a product that is consumed and discarded, a trashiness that Clark welcomes. However, this embracing of literature as trash should also be viewed with scavenging in mind: if Clark's poetry is garbage (as opposed to a form of expression that transcends material concerns), it also can be scavenged and put to new uses.

While the visual impact of *Basura*'s cover and flyleaf are very suggestive in terms of framing the collection as a compendium of waste, there is one other paratextual element that clearly establishes the dynamic of poetic ragpicking or salvage that I am advancing here: the "Apuntes basura" at the end of the book. Beyond the textual excess that footnotes and endnotes inevitably represent, Clark's notes show us the scavenging process in which he engaged while composing his collection of poems.[12] In the twenty notes following the poem that serves as the collection's coda, Clark signals the real-world provenance of many of the references that give shape to the book's poems.

These references range from people, like Charles Moore (credited with discovering the Great Pacific Garbage Patch) and Edmund Trebus (a hoarder who achieved minor fame after being portrayed in a BBC documentary), to places, like the Fresh Kills landfill, and concepts, such as spam and planned obsolescence. In most cases, the information in the notes is attributed to a concrete source, whether it be Wikipedia, a newspaper, a website, or a documentary film. In addition to clarifying references in the poems that might otherwise remain opaque, these "Apuntes basura" both ground Clark's work in the trashy material and social world outside of the text and make evident his procedural approach to poetic composition: like Baudelaire's *chiffonier* or Benjamin's *Lumpensammler*, he scours the information that is constantly being produced and cast off by his society (one centred on the news cycle and data) and salvages the fragments that he sees as useful kernels for poetic creation. What is more, the liminal condition of the notes (they appear at the book's end on five unnumbered pages without explicit callouts to anchor them in the text of the poems) underscores their trash-like status. Like garbage, which is "neither one thing nor another, but ... the remainder of such neatness," the "Apuntes basura" occupy the threshold zone of the paratext, a space that is neither inside nor outside the text proper and therefore troubles the neat distinction between literary creation (poems about trash) and the world (a place full of trash; Scanlan 16). It bears repeating that Clark is not, strictly speaking, scavenging literal waste, but rather conceptual waste. This conceptual work, however, cannot be fully separated from material trash for two reasons. First, the referential value of the concepts and signifiers with which Clark works in these poems points us towards material waste; when we read what he writes about litter, nuclear testing, and apartments full of hoarded junk, we cannot help but think of real garbage. And second, through both the paratextual elements I analyse and, to a lesser extent, the content of the poems themselves, Clark emphasizes his book's status as a material object that was made with tools and instruments that will one day become trash and that is itself bound to end up in the trash as well.

In his analysis of Benjamin's reading of Baudelaire's *chiffonnier*, Wohlfarth notes that real ragpickers are "so abjectly dependent on the laws of exchange-value that [they] can reproduce [their] own existence only by directly serving the reproductive needs of the capitalist economy" (152). While ragpickers could be seen to slow down capitalist production by extending the life of the goods they scavenge, Wohlfarth's point certainly signals a potential limit to the subversive capacity of recycling or reusing garbage; moreover, he underscores a key difference between real ragpickers and the materialist historian who works as a metaphorical ragpicker with the detritus of history:

> Whereas the real-life *chiffonnier* seeks to salvage his own existence by collecting debris that is to be fed back into the jaws of … Industry, thereby paying the mythical "divinity" the strange tribute of serving her own "waste" into her jaws, his literary counterpart seeks, by contrast, to save *his* "treasure" *from* the capitalist order of things in order to construct objects that will help upset its digestive system. (152; emphasis in the original)

It seems, then, that the purpose to which the ragpicker-poet's "useful or gratifying objects" are put is key. Does Clark's *Basura* feed the discourses of triumphant capitalism or upset its digestive system? In answering this question, it is helpful to keep in mind environmental Hispanist Luis I. Prádanos's concept of the political ecology of waste. For Prádanos, "[a] politically effective representation of waste must understand the deep temporalities and perverse socioecological entanglements that play out in the emergence of modern waste and attempt to track its physical as well as discursive networks," and this engagement must not "reduc[e] waste to an ahistorical, post-political, and isolated material waiting to be repurposed and revaluated by the growth economy" (171). A poem like the one about a trash-filled Nile River gives some indication of how Clark's collection is oriented with regard to the representation of waste and its social, political, and ecological ramifications, and in the final section of this chapter I will examine how his salvage poetics reflects on these issues in a way that compels us to consider what it means to live in and with disturbed environments, landscapes that have always been produced by varying forms of human and more-than-human activity.

Salvage Poetics for More-than-Human Landscapes

In *Basura*, the concept of salvage is relevant to more than just a consideration of how the work is composed. In a number of ways, Clark's geographically and thematically kaleidoscopic poems reflect what Tsing notes are the two complementary faces of contemporary precarity: the precarious fate of the earth and the surprising contradictions of post-war global development that have intensified the perilousness of many people's living conditions (3). In her effort to search for ways of "collaborative survival in precarious times," Tsing turns to spaces of ruination and abandonment, like erstwhile industrial forests where matsutake mushrooms thrive and support lively communities of pickers, spaces where she sees the potential for entanglements that could promote solidarity in and with the more-than-human world (2). For Tsing, the concept of salvage is central to understanding both the ongoing process of primitive accumulation that alienates humans and nonhumans from their lifeworlds to make them into sources of wealth and the possibility of enacting collaborative survival through coexistence with and in environmental disturbance.[13] Salvage, simply put, is the act of "taking advantage of value produced without capitalist control," and the sites in which salvage occurs are "pericapitalist," which is to say, "simultaneously inside and outside capitalism" (Tsing 63). Salvage sites are frontier zones where things that are not yet commodities (the matsutake Tsing studies) or that are no longer commodities (trash) can be gathered and introduced into systems of value.[14] In both cases, the act of salvage is essential to the capitalist cycle and, in this sense, perpetuates it. By the same token, however, salvage's liminal relationship to capitalism opens the possibility for it to interrupt that system.[15] The bits and scraps of conceptual salvage that Clark gathers into *Basura* certainly fit this description. In poems that address phenomena like rain, ocean pollution, atomic fallout, rats, feral dogs, the stuff in hoarders' apartments, or extinct languages, he translates disparate material realities into a poetic economy that opens a space of critical reflection on the stuff that humans use and discard.[16] And to return to Wohlfarth's question of to what use the ragpicker puts his scraps (and Prádanos's question of the political effectiveness of the representation of waste), it is clear that Clark does so not to celebrate trash or trumpet technical solutions to waste problems. Instead of engaging in salvage for the purpose of generating economic surplus value, Clark cultivates what we could call poetic surplus value.

Perhaps Benjamin's writing on Baudelaire can once again offer some insight. In his essay titled "On Some Motifs in Baudelaire," he argues that one of the traumatic effects of capitalist modernity is the deadening of the human perceptual apparatus and the destruction of the social conditions necessary for certain kinds of aesthetic experience, like reading lyric poetry. For Benjamin, what is remarkable about Baudelaire's poetry is not that it provides an antidote to the vicissitudes of capitalism, but rather that it is marked by the violent experience of capitalism in a way that makes present the loss of auratic experience – what he calls *Erfahrung* or "long experience" – through its investment in *Erlebnis* or "immediate experience," the jumble of ephemeral, disjointed, and meaningless states of being and material realities of capitalism (210). I sense a similar kind of translation from one mode of experience to another in *Basura*. Clark opens his poetry up to the toxicity, filth, danger, and harm of trash, the immediate experience of life in the Anthropocene, and, through the salvage operation of poetic inscription, imbues that *Erlebnis* with the weight of *Erfahrung*. The long experience that makes itself felt in *Basura*, the paradoxical lack of and potential for historical meaning or continuity, can be discerned in two aspects of the practice of salvage that Tsing underscores: first, in its presentation of disturbed landscapes, spaces of unintentional design that can be "radical tools for decentering human hubris"; and, second, in its contemplation of latent commons, spaces of solidarity and action that occur in "fugitive moments of entanglement in the midst of institutionalized alienation" (152, 255).[17]

In her consideration of landscapes – which she sees not as backdrops for historical action but as activity, entanglement, and assemblage themselves – Tsing emphasizes that they do not start "in a harmonious state before disturbance. Disturbances follow other disturbances. Thus all landscapes are disturbed; disturbance is ordinary" (160). This assertion allows for the recognition that humans are not the centre of the spaces in which we act.[18] In a surprising way, Clark meditates on this type of shift in perspective that reimagines the place of the human in the web of life by portraying the human body itself as a landscape that is not in thrall to human subjectivity. The opening poem of *Basura* makes mitosis, part of the biological process of genetic reproduction, into an agentic force that perpetuates human presence in the world. Clark calls it "mitosis hedionda / siempre garantizada, / siempre posible mientras existamos" ("foul mitosis / always guaranteed, / always possible while we exist") and notes how the spark of life it produces is a substance that fills all of us, we who are the "viejo sitio / sin tregua que se ofrece, que se entrega / en un envase nuevo cada vez" ("old site / that offers itself up without rest / each time in a new container"; 15). In this sense, from the very beginning of his collection Clark underscores that the human body is a landscape enmeshed in other landscapes, a site of salvage that is constantly mined for value by capitalism, but that reproduces itself through processes that capitalism does not control.

Decentring human hubris by positing the human body as a more-than-human assemblage sets the stage for the parade of disturbed, contaminated landscapes that Clark imagines in the rest of the collection and that are especially notable in the first section, "Historia de la lluvia" ("History of Rain"; 13–37). Over the course of twenty-three poetic fragments, the reader encounters anthropomorphized nuclear fallout, a Great Pacific Garbage Patch that bridges the Eastern and Western Hemispheres, burning tyres that poison a town in South Africa, a rat population that outnumbers the human inhabitants of London, and trash bags that become trash, among other scenes in which waste produced by humans enters their bodies and minds, enacting a dynamic in which liveliness and activity are distributed throughout the material world.[19] Even the intellectual act of composing poetry is framed as part of the assemblage of plant life and industrial products that are enrolled in the production of waste:

> Yo escribí estas palabras en papel.
> Utilicé una pluma de Kaweco
> con un cartucho Inoxcrom azul:
> yo canto a la basura con basura.

> (I wrote these words on paper.
> I used a Kaweco pen
> with a blue Inoxcrom cartridge:
> I sing to trash with trash; 29)

The repetition of the word "basura" in this poem's final line deftly draws attention to what Amago calls the real and symbolic "cultural logics of pollution" (26). This *canto a la basura*, the poetic surplus value that Clark gleans in his process of conceptual salvage, is inscribed with and on material objects – pen, ink, paper – that will become real *basura*. Writing poetry is as ineluctably enmeshed in more-than-human landscapes as any other human pursuit, and in the context of a biosphere being filled with all manner of detritus, it also performs the task of "considering livability – the possibility of common life on a human-disturbed earth" (Tsing 163).

It is precisely in the frontier zones of salvage that Tsing senses the possibility for a contingent form of solidarity, but she recognizes the limits capitalism imposes on constructing a life-affirming form of politics:

> The challenges are enormous. Salvage accumulation reveals a world of difference, where oppositional politics does not fall easily into utopian plans for solidarity. Every livelihood patch has its own history and dynamics, and there is no automatic urge to argue *together*, across the viewpoints emerging from varied patches, about the outrages of accumulation and power. Since no patch is "representative," no group's struggles, taken alone, will overturn capitalism. Yet this is not the end of capitalism. Assemblages, in their diversity, show us what I … call the "latent commons," that is, entanglements that might be mobilized in common cause. (134–5; emphasis in the original)

Tsing highlights "fugitive moments of entanglement in the midst of institutionalized alienation," a latent commons that is not universally good for everyone and everything and that cannot offer redemption or any other promises for the future because it is a non-teleological form of politics (255). The latent commons is based on paying attention to our present time and place in order to foster affective and cognitive familiarity with our surroundings and their inhabitants, which, for Tsing, can lead to a form of neighbourliness that she calls "mutuality across difference" (279).

Basura is peppered with glimpses of the latent commons that Tsing advocates as a way of acting in the indeterminacy and precarity of the present. There is a clear rejection of a form of politics that unquestioningly ties happiness, progress, and development to the kind of economic growth that has managed to turn large swaths of the planet into salvage zones and waste frontiers.[20] The second section of the collection, "El hombre de Sinope" ("The Man from Sinop"; 39–61), for instance, imagines a nameless Turkish migrant in Spain as a modern-day incarnation of Diogenes, one of the founders of Cynic philosophy and the namesake of Diogenes syndrome, one of whose characteristics is the hoarding of garbage.[21] The poems in this section recount the experiences of marginalization and violence that *un hombre de Sinope* would experience in Madrid, along with his discursive and physical proximity to waste and refuse. Clark's allusion to Diogenes allows for the fragments from this section to be read as manifestations of *parrhesia*, a form of truth-telling associated with the Cynics that flies in the face of social convention through engaging in preaching, scandalous behaviour, and provocative dialogue (Foucault 119–24). Most of the fragments in this section are directly addressed to an anonymous "usted," which gives them the air of street preaching. Provocative dialogue and scandalous behaviour are on display when the modern-day Cynic says,

> Masturbarse en el centro de un plató
> le puede parecer provocativo.
> Pero dígame ¿qué puedo hacer
> a estas alturas para provocarle?
>
> (Masturbating in the public square
> may seem provocative to you.
> But tell me, what can I do
> at this point to provoke you?; Clark 53)

This question underscores a sense of frustration at the ease with which people fail to engage in the "arts of noticing" that Tsing argues are key in the effort to cultivate social forms amid the ruins of capitalism (255). And this meditation on noticing comes into even sharper focus when the *hombre de Sinope* talks about trash:

No se engañe: yo leo los periódicos.
Somos, los vagabundos, de los pocos
que leen cada día
la prensa impresa y muerta de este nicho.
Y sí, tengo mis propias opiniones
sobre «la situación»
y sobre el paro y todo lo demás.
Pero el caso es que yo lo leo todo
sin olvidar por qué lo estoy leyendo;
porque alguien lo tiró, porque es basura.

(Make no mistake: I read the newspaper.
We bums are some of the few
who read daily
the news, printed and dead, from this tomb.
And yes, I do have my own opinions
on "the situation"
and the strike and all the rest.
But the thing is I read everything
without forgetting why I'm reading it;
because someone threw it out, because it's trash; Clark 52)

By condensing questions related to economic crisis, the invisibility of migrants and refugees, the churn of the news cycle, and disposability, Clark manages to paint the ugly truth of social exclusion and precarity that cities like Madrid have experienced in the wake of events like the financial crisis of 2008.[22]

While "El hombre de Sinope" generally keeps its gaze fixed on the crises of the present, it culminates in a poem that imagines a post-apocalyptic scene: a destroyed city where wild dogs are the dominant species and humans move about furtively through the ruins in search of meaning:

Y verán los espacios destruidos
sintiendo una nostalgia más antigua
que aquella pantomima de hormigón.
Un arrepentimiento duro y áspero
los sobrecogerá

> y por primera vez no habrá poeta
> capaz de traducir el sentimiento.
> Porque será imposible.
>
> (And they will see destroyed spaces
> and feel nostalgia more ancient
> than that concrete pantomime.
> Regret, hard and rough,
> will overtake them
> and for the first time there will be no poet
> capable of translating the feeling.
> Because it will be impossible; 60–1)

This abandonment of the sense provided by a teleological, anthropocentric frame of reference for history opens the way for another possibility: "Y empezará otra cosa para el mundo. / Y empezará otra cosa. Ya sin nombre" ("And another thing will begin for the world. / And another thing will begin. This time with no name"; 61).

While such an imagined future is full of uncertainty (and perhaps dread), it allows for the contemplation of something else, a different way of being in the world. Perhaps it could be a way of life in which human beings opt for the type of salvage that Clark models in his poetry instead of the salvage accumulation that alienates things from their lifeworlds in order to translate them into profit. Partway through *Basura*, there is a poem that suggests the benefits of caring for the things around us, trash included:

> Existe una creencia equivocada:
> es posible leer nuestra basura
> para así descubrir cualquier secreto.
> Así lo han intentado con famosos
> de todo tipo cientos de programas
> de aquello que consuela llamar «telebasura».
> Pero ignoran que nada revelan los desechos
> de quien los hizo ser. Mucho dicen
> en cambio de quien toma
> su cuerpo, devolviéndole
> sentido con su tiempo y su deseo.
>
> (There's a mistaken belief:
> it's possible to read our trash
> in order to uncover any secret.

> That's what they've tried to do with famous
> people of all kinds on hundreds of shows
> that it comforts us to call "trash TV."
> But what they don't realize is that trash reveals nothing
> about whoever made it. It does
> however say a lot about the person who takes
> its body, giving back to it
> meaning with their time and their desire; 69)

The ethic evinced here – and throughout Clark's collection – is one that cautions against instrumentalizing the things and beings with which we are enmeshed and instead advocates the forging of connections, both physical and affective, as a way of making sense of our precarious place on this planet. *Basura* is, through its aesthetic and ethical engagement with waste, a call for us to wake up to the ruination and devastation around us and to develop a greater sense of responsibility for the mess we are in.

NOTES

1 Historian and postcolonial theorist Dipesh Chakrabarty makes this point, claiming, in fact, that the idea of the Anthropocene reveals that humans do not merely have an interactive relationship with nature, but that the intertwinement of human and natural history has collapsed the distinction between the two (209).

2 Besides *Basura*, Clark (Ibiza, 1984) has published a number of poetry collections since debuting with *Secrets d'una Sargantana* in 2001, including *Los hijos de los hijos de la ira*, which was awarded the Premio Hiperión in 2006, and *La policía celeste*, winner of the thirtieth edition of the Premio Loewe in 2017 (Rodríguez). A poem Clark published in 2011, "El fin último de la (mala) poesía," has gained some notoriety due to its diffusion through social media platforms, where it has been shared up to one million times in around 250,000 different versions or formats (Fanjul). Literary critic Daniel Escandell Montiel takes up the case of Clark's poem as an example of the virality of contemporary digital poetry in his recent book *Y eso es algo terrible: Crónica de un poema viral*. Many thanks to Ksenija Bilbija for introducing me to Clark's *Basura*.

3 While the texts in Clark's collection could simply be called poems, I also employ the label *poetic fragments* for two reasons: first, in line with the reading I undertake throughout this essay, to underscore their thematic heterogeneity and seeming disjointedness; second, given their brevity, lack

of title, and typographical presentation (small blocks of text centred on the page with wide margins all the way around), the visual impression they give is one of bits or scraps of text that the reader encounters and shuffles through from page to page.

4   Unless otherwise noted, all translations are my own. Page numbers correspond to the Spanish original.

5   The Garbage Project, founded by Rathje at the University of Arizona in 1973, applied the methodologies of archeology to the municipal solid waste stream in Tucson and other cities in North America, including New York, Chicago, Toronto, and Mexico City. In addition to conducting studies in which trash from individual residences was collected, meticulously sorted and categorized, and correlated with census data in order to better understand the waste practices of various types of consumers, the Garbage Project also staged archeological digs at a variety of landfills, like Fresh Kills in Staten Island. The project operated for some thirty years. For more, see Rathje and Murphy.

6   The World Bank's most recent report on solid waste management indicates that global solid waste production increased from 1.3 billion tonnes per year in 2012 to 2.01 billion tonnes per year in 2016, and that rate is projected to reach 3.4 billion tonnes per year by 2050 (Kaza et al. 17–18).

7   While Reno's point about waste as a sign of both life and death might seem to pertain strictly to the case of organic detritus, Anthropocene scholar Nigel Clark and waste researcher Myra Hird's work on sanitary landfills as sites of proliferation of potentially unknown and unknowable forms of bacteria illustrates its relevance to human-made waste as well, and it provocatively throws into relief the way that life, death, creation, and destruction interact in human-bacteria-waste assemblages. For Clark and Hird,

> [T]he subtending relationship of the bacterial stratum to our own dominion goes beyond the challenges of negotiating coexistence in and through our mutual unfathomabilities. We have discovered enough about them to know that bacteria are the condition of our own possibility as multicellular beings: that they are at once our origin and our continuing vital support system. In an age of accelerating anthropogenic destratification, bacteria catch the fallout of our local and globalised transformation of earth systems, but we *are* the fallout of the dynamics of bacterial becomings. (50; emphasis in the original)

8   Here Pardo is modifying the opening line of the first volume of Marx's *Capital*, which reads, "The wealth of those societies in which the capitalist mode of production prevails, presents itself as 'an immense accumulation of commodities'" (41).

9 This brief sketch of historical materialism is drawn from Benjamin's "Theses on the Philosophy of History," where he famously approaches the matter in a series of non-systematic, suggestive fragments.

10 There is a strong tradition among scholars who study waste to interpret trash along these lines, which stems from anthropologist Michael Thompson's landmark study *Rubbish Theory*, in which trash is framed as a conceptual device that mediates material objects' journey back and forth between durable and transient states of value. For Thompson, determining whether or not something is rubbish is an operation that can be understood only as a socio-material process that tracks the way a certain sector of human society relates to an object.

11 Credit for these elements should also be given to Fabio de la Flor, founder and editor of Editorial Delirio, the publisher of Clark's *Basura*.

12 Regarding the general relationship of footnotes and endnotes to a body of text, historian Anthony Grafton makes the curious observation that their production "sometimes resembles less the skilled work of a professional carrying out a precise function to a higher end than the offhand production and disposal of waste products" (6). Thus, while the apparent function of such notes is to ground an author's text in some sort of authoritative discourse, they are always caught up in a relationship of excess with that text. While I am not interested in further pursuing this idea in my analysis of *Basura*, I do think it enriches the already complex dynamic of Clark's "Apuntes basura," which highlight not only the book's referential relationship to the world and the trash therein but also the relationship between trash and literature.

13 Urban and environmental anthropologist Jacob Doherty notes that, much like her approach to environmental disturbance (which gives the lie to the myth of pristine prehuman landscapes), Tsing makes the important point that "primitive accumulation is not an original sin no longer present in contemporary capitalism but an ongoing process of accumulation by dispossession" (Doherty S326n9).

14 In her approach to frontier zones and salvage, Tsing focuses on "wild" or "natural" things that are salvaged (mushrooms); however, trash is also subject to this process, as Doherty shows in his study of waste practices in Kampala, Uganda.

15 While the example on which I focus in this chapter is one of conceptual salvage, it is important to note that salvage practices that contest capitalism are not limited to poetic gestures. For a compelling example of material salvage aimed at questioning capitalist forms of value and disparity, see anthropologist David Boarder Giles's study of dumpster diving and the Food Not Bombs movement.

16 "Translation" is the term that Tsing uses to denote the process of "drawing one world-making project into another" (62).

17 Whereas the enmeshed solidarity that Tsing identifies in the latent
   commons of late capitalism is characterized by its serendipity, the chapter
   in this collection by Michael L. Martínez, Jr., studies the built-in design of
   community-determined, shared-land use for subsistence farming, fishing,
   and hunting in Spain's Albufera region and early capitalist transformation
   of these wetlands with the construction of *tancats,* or small dikes, to
   create individually farmed plots for monocrop rice cultivation. Yet, while
   Clark's poetry reveals frontier zones of enmeshment, Martínez notes that
   wetlandscapes constitute liminal spaces in defiance of the human-nature
   dualism that defines the anthropocentric paradigm and undergirds
   capitalism.

18 Shanna Lino addresses this anthropocentric, fallacious notion of a
   previously undisturbed, harmonious landscape that then becomes
   disturbed in her analysis in this collection of ecohorror in Albert Sánchez
   Piñol's *Cold Skin,* a novel in which, she explains, humans that arrive on an
   island assume that the monster inhabitants disturb their human existence
   when the reverse is true. The human arrivals cause anthropogenic
   disturbance to an ecosystem already in existence.

19 Presenting another, corresponding paradigm to salvage poetics, William
   Viestenz's post-immunology envisions enmeshment at the cellular level,
   an alternative to human-centred systems closed to other life forms. While
   Clark emphasizes in his poetic fragments the formation of assemblages
   amid capitalist-induced toxicity, the novel Viestenz studies in this
   collection foregrounds a response to precarity that affords survival through
   human and non-human hospitable hosting relationships of vulnerability
   and unconditional care.

20 See Prádanos for an explanation of the link between the growth paradigm
   of neoliberalism and the wasting of the planet, as well as a lucid analysis
   of a number of cultural responses from Spain to the ecological, economic,
   social, and political limits of growth.

21 Also of interest is the way that the (poorly named) Diogenes syndrome
   reappears elsewhere in *Basura,* for instance, in the section "Homer," which
   contains a series of fragments that explore the experience of Homer and
   Langley Collyer, brothers who were found dead among tonnes of hoarded
   items in their New York City home in 1947 (79–90).

22 In Maryanne L. Leone's chapter in *Beyond Human* about the entwined
   economic and ecological precarity that the 2008 financial crisis revealed, an
   abandoned dog and human form an affective assemblage amid the failures
   of capitalist institutions in a waste-laden city and its interspersed toxic
   waterways. As in my interpretation of Clark via Tsing, while no immediate
   revision of consumer excess is offered, relational inter-actions suggest
   some potential for attenuating anthropocentric ruin.

WORKS CITED AND CONSULTED

Amago, Samuel. *Basura: Cultures of Waste in Contemporary Spain*. U of Virginia P, 2021.

Benjamin, Walter. "On Some Motifs in Baudelaire." *The Writer of Modern Life: Essays on Charles Baudelaire*, edited by Michael W. Jennings, translated by Harry Zohn, The Belknap Press of Harvard UP, 2006, pp. 170–210.

Benjamin, Walter. "Theses on the Philosophy of History." *Illuminations*, edited by Hannah Arendt, translated by Harry Zohn, Schocken Books, 2007, pp. 253–64.

Chakrabarty, Dipesh. "The Climate of History: Four Theses." *Critical Inquiry*, vol. 35, no. 2, winter 2009, pp. 197–222. *JSTOR*, https://doi.org/10.1086/596640.

Clark, Ben. *Basura*. Delirio, 2011.

Clark, Nigel, and Myra J. Hird. "Deep Shit." *O-Zone: A Journal of Object-Oriented Studies*, vol. 1, no. 1, 2014, pp. 44–52.

Doherty, Jacob. "Filthy Flourishing: Para-sites, Animal Infrastructure, and the Waste Frontier in Kampala." *Current Anthropology*, vol. 60, no. S20, 2019, pp. S321–32. *U of Chicago P Journals*, https://doi.org/10.1086/702868.

Escandell Montiel, Daniel. *Y eso es algo terrible: Crónica de un poema viral*. Delirio, 2019.

Fanjul, Sergio C. "El poema que se hizo viral y por el camino perdió a su autor." *El País*, 3 Nov. 2019, https://www.elpais.com/cultura/2019/11/02/actualidad/1572709543_864221.html.

Foucault, Michel. *Fearless Speech*. Edited by Joseph Pearson, Semiotext(e), 2001.

Giles, David Boarder. "The Anatomy of a Dumpster: Abject Capital and the Looking Glass of Value." *Social Text*, vol. 32, no. 1, 2014, pp. 93–113. *Duke UP*, https://doi.org/10.1215/01642472-2391351.

Grafton, Anthony. *The Footnote: A Curious History*. Harvard UP, 1997.

Hawkins, Gay. "Plastic Bags: Living with Rubbish." *International Journal of Cultural Studies*, vol. 4, no. 1, 2001, pp. 5–23. *SAGE Journals*, https://doi.org/10.1177/136787790100400101.

Hird, Myra J. "Waste Flows." *Discard Studies Compendium*, https://www.discardstudies.com/discard-studies-compendium/#Wasteflows. Accessed 8 Feb. 2023.

Kaza, Silpa, et al. What a Waste 2.0: A Global Snapshot of Solid Waste Management to 2050. World Bank Group, 2018, https://doi.org/10.1596/978-1-4648-1329-0.

Marx, Karl. *Capital: A Critique of Political Economy*. Translated by Samuel Moore and Edward Aveling, Modern Library, 1936.

Pardo, José Luis. *Nunca fue tan hermosa la basura*. Galaxia Gutenberg, 2010.

Prádanos, Luis I. *Postgrowth Imaginaries: New Ecologies and Counterhegemonic Culture in Post-2008 Spain*. Liverpool UP, 2018.

Rathje, William, and Cullen Murphy. *Rubbish! The Archaeology of Garbage*. HarperCollins, 1992.

Reno, Joshua Ozias. "Toward a New Theory of Waste: From 'Matter out of Place' to Signs of Life." *Theory, Culture & Society*, vol. 31, no. 6, 2014, pp. 3–27. *SAGE Journals*, https://doi.org/10.1177/0263276413500999.

Rodríguez, Daniel J. "La mirada dorada de Ben Clark." *Zenda*, 9 Aug. 2019, https://www.zendalibros.com/la-mirada-dorada-de-ben-clark/.

Scanlan, John. *On Garbage*. Reaktion Books, 2005.

Thompson, Michael. *Rubbish Theory: The Creation and Destruction of Value*. Oxford UP, 1979.

Tsing, Anna Lowenhaupt. *The Mushroom at the End of the World: On the Possibility of Life in Capitalist Ruins*. Princeton UP, 2015.

Wohlfarth, Irving. "Et Cetera? The Historian as Chiffonier." *New German Critique*, no. 39, 1986, pp. 143–68. *JSTOR*, https://doi.org/10.2307/488123.

PART THREE

Disruptive Agentic Paradigms

Ecofeminist Materialism and Entanglements of Care in Sara Mesa's *Un incendio invisible*

MARYANNE L. LEONE

Feminist ecocriticism challenges the hierarchal dualities that structure gender- and species-based injustices, racism, classism, and the culture-nature separation at the core of environmental degradation. Ecofeminist philosopher Val Plumwood's *Environmental Culture: The Ecological Crisis of Reason* has been influential in furthering scholarship focused on understanding connections among these oppressions through a critique of arrogance-based rationality "that promote[s] human distance from, control of and ruthlessness towards the sphere of nature as the Other" (4) while "maximising [human] self-interest" (33). Within the rationalist framework is the reduction of communication to abstract, linguistic forms, which devalues alternative bodily and affective expressions along with the more-than-human and human beings who emit them (191). This model of so-called reason views non-human nature and other human lives as homogeneous, deficient, and instrumental to the centralized Western male human subject (100–9). Further, the imagined "hyper-separation" of humans from non-human nature, along with men from women or colonizer from colonized peoples, white people from people of colour, rich from poor, and so on, that structures anthropocentrism has conceived each of the latter as a resource for the former to fuel economic development (Plumwood, *Environmental* 110 and "Decolonizing" 64). It is precisely feminist ecocriticism that points to the ecosocial injustices that this patriarchal instrumental rationality engenders.

As conceptual frameworks and day-to-day practices, anthropocentrism and androcentrism fuel the environmental, social, and (sub)urban deterioration in Sara Mesa's dystopic novel *Un incendio invisible* (2011, 2017), which critiques expansionist, consumer-driven economics and real-estate speculation.[1] Alluding to Spain's housing and financial crises of the aughts, the story unfolds during the collapse of a formerly prosperous city and its suburbs, from which residents are exiting and leaving behind their domestic animals, the sick, and the elderly.[2] Some who elect to stay cling nostalgically to a pre-crisis illusion of never-ending economic growth and detachment from ecological consequences. With support from Plumwood's writings on hegemonic centralism, ecological ethics of care, and dialogical relationships; new materialist Stacy Alaimo's work on post-humanist trans-corporeality; and feminist environmental theorist Donna Haraway's discussion of interspecies response and respect, this essay argues that Mesa's novel helps the twenty-first-century reader see not only the neoliberal economic model's destructive impact on sentient and non-sentient beings but, moreover, the potential of ecological interconnectivity for realizing a collectively viable future that can emerge from those ruins.

A Crisis of Reason: Spain's Abandoned Towns and the Mistaken Ideology of Progress

Un incendio invisible opens with the self-aggrandizing Dr. Tejada en route to the fictional city Vado to direct a once luxury, now insoluble senior residence from which the previous director then precipitously departs and at which only those abandoned by their families remain: twenty-two of the former three hundred full-time residents, fifty-five day-only clients, and over five hundred persons on the waiting list (102).[3] Highlighting a crisis of care, the once extensive staff of this coveted retirement haven, called New Life, consists of just the male Tejada; three nurses, male and female, two of whom will quit; a female cook; a male launderer; and an inebriated delicensed male nurse, who ineptly serves as the gardener. In the novel, several women care for human, more-than-human others, and inorganic entities in ways that acknowledge their material presence and intra-agency, while male characters think and act individualistically and oppressively.

An ecofeminist reading of *Un incendio invisible* illuminates that this crisis of care also is a crisis of reason, a human-centred ontology of domination that devalues the non-human sphere and some human lives, a perspective embodied by Tejada. Instead of attending to the seniors' well-being and the residence's administration, the self-centred geriatric specialist sits in his office resentfully thinking about his estranged wife, has frequent sex with a female hotel owner, but cannot recall her name, and wanders about the port in search of a young girl; while the doctor's interest in her remains unexplained, the narrative hints at sexual predation. Rather than follow the custom of residing at the senior facility, Tejada distances himself by staying in another area of the city at a five-star hotel that promotes its highly regarded spa and *"el bienestar de la exclusividad"* (*"the well-being of exclusivity"*; 35; emphasis in the original).[4] In the only section in which the narrating voice shifts from the third to the first person, the doctor's reflection on why he has come to Vado evinces his hyperbolized sense of self-importance: "soy un gran hombre con una gran misión, he venido hasta aquí para libraros de la catástrofe, os sacaré de los escombros entre mis propios brazos si es preciso, etc. Basura. Me divierte hacer eso" ("I am a great man with a grand mission, I have come here to free you from the catastrophe, I will extract you from the rubble in my own arms, if necessary, etc. Rubbish. It amuses me to do that"; 227–8). The doctor's cynical heroism illustrates anthropocentric disregard for others' needs and the use of others for his own ends, in this case a distorted self-entertainment and arrogance – all practices that contribute to the pillage of the non-human environment as well.

The first sentence of the first chapter, "La llegada" ("The Arrival"), calls attention to the material vestiges of the Spanish ideology of progress that manifested in the real-estate bubble of the mid 1990s to 2008.[5] With a description of Vado's outlying neighbourhoods, the narration addresses the swaths of agricultural and undeveloped land throughout Spain on which residential developments were constructed, many never completed: "casitas adosadas, urbanizaciones a medio construir, solares roturados y, más allá, los bloques terrosos de Bocamanga y de Pozolán. Mirado desde el coche, el paisaje carecía por completo de vida" ("semi-detached houses, half-built subdivisions, turned-over plots and, beyond that, the earthy blocks of Bocamanga and Pozolán. Seen from the car, the landscape was completely devoid of life"; 13). The urbanized area consists of the following: the old city; a modern imitation on the outskirts of its commercial area, called New Vado; an industrial area; various residential developments; and a port along the river that runs through the city. The inherently paradoxical word *vado*, which means both ford, which one can easily cross by wading, and an (often gated) entrance where one cannot park and that prohibits entry to most, signals the tension between human and non-human locatedness on the one hand, and the forced migration made necessary by economic recession, toxicity, and fire on the other. As Tejada rides in a taxi along the twenty-kilometre approach, the driver notes this suburb's similarity with those of any world city, comments on its former prosperity, and parrots the capitalist notion that purchasing power brings contentment: "aquellos habían sido barrios normales, incluso más limpios y modernos de lo habitual, con gente más feliz y tranquila que en el resto de los sitios" ("those had been normal neighbourhoods, even cleaner and more modern than most, with happier and more relaxed people than in other places"; 13). His use of the pluperfect suggests a nostalgic desire to return to a seemingly idyllic time and space of economic prosperity, yet the text emphasizes the unsustainability of this suburban development model. Indeed, that past to which he alludes – grounded in economic expansion – has led to the development's economic, social, and environmental demise. As degrowth advocates argue, a growth paradigm is undesirable, unjust, and ecologically impossible; moreover, happiness does not increase with wealth once a person's needs are met.[6] The hegemony-seeking Tejada does not see this alternative perspective, however; instead, as he views the uninhabited housing from the cab's window, he focuses on the back of the driver's neck and car's dashboard, his uncritical gaze and silence an indication of his eco-ethical void.

Yet references to urban desertification and long-term environmental harm from suburban development punctuate the narration, highlighting the ecological costs of new "pueblos abandonados" ("abandoned towns") in post-crisis Spain along with the scars caused by increased energy and material use since the mid twentieth century.[7] Partially constructed buildings shift from signs of prosperity to concrete remainders and reminders of the property bust's residual effects on individuals, communities, and the land for years to come. In an industrial park, buildings lie in ruins, some have only a façade, and others are empty, while within a former factory of the business complex, semi-assembled statues of Catholic saints and other relics insinuate that consumer culture and economic growth are contemporary Spain's new religion (139–40). Indeed, a new interest in ruralism has developed in Spain in the wake of the financial crisis, including a market for the country's three thousand historic abandoned towns for the purposes of retirement, ecotourism, and ecovillages.[8] Disillusion with the city and modernity has energized a desire to learn about and conserve local knowledges and practices. This rural turn may indicate distrust in growth capitalism; at the same time, a complete escape from urban centres is not possible given the global interchange of resources, monies, and goods, as well as urban dependence on non-urban areas for food and fuel (Prádanos 141–4). Mesa's novel registers not only concrete carcasses of speculative investment but also the conversion of urban wasteland into filthy suburban pasture: "el centro comercial con su aparcamiento vacío, un polígono industrial con las naves cerradas, un desguace de coches y un rebaño de cabras pastando entre la basura –aunque no vio ni perro ni pastor" ("the mall with its empty parking lot, an industrial park with its warehouses closed, a scrapyard and a herd of goats grazing among the trash – although he saw neither dog nor shepherd"; 247). Employing an anthropocenic prism, this late-capitalist revision of the idealized (human-centred) pastoral relationship reveals in Mesa's garbage-populated scene both the toxicity of Spain's real estate development for animals, land, and humans and the abandonment of responsibility for its detritus.

Relationally Resisting Hegemonic Centralism

The hegemonic centralism inherent to the humanist diminishment of the environment devalues agency and denies dependency on human and more-than-human others who are considered subordinate (Plumwood, *Environmental Culture* 8, 19–20, 27–37; and *Feminism* 41–2, 47). In Mesa's text, the character Tejada's androcentric, racist, and colonialist interactions with women, in particular New Life's cook, its remaining nurse, and the Madison Lenox Hotel's owner, as well as his neglect of the elderly and infirm, expose the confluence of these oppressions. In one such exchange, Tejada merely feigns interest in the seniors' nutritional needs when he interrogates the cook about meal plans. With physical and verbal patronization, the doctor places his hand on her arm as he dismisses her concerns about the scarcity of provisions and unrepaired oven "sin centrar la mirada en ningún lado, como hubiese podido decir cualquier frase" ("without focusing on any particular point, as if he could have been saying anything at all"; Mesa 62). Moreover, a military metaphor suggests that Tejada's disregard for the care systems that were set in place prior to his arrival stem from an authoritative, rationalist approach to the organization's management: "recorrió la residencia como un general que pasara revista a su tropa" ("he traversed the residence like a general inspecting his troops"; 62). Viewed from an ecofeminist framework, the character projects a "rationalist imaginary" that elevates abstract reason over bodily, sensorial experiences to ascribe the domain of knowledge to an elite, male, and human subject and a utilitarian dimension onto all other human and more-than-human lives (Plumwood, *Environmental Culture* 20).

A principal attribute of mastery narratives is the "radical exclusion" that differentiates an otherized group as less-than-human to justify the privileges of some and the exploitative use of others.[9] The following three practices particularly bolster hegemonic human and male centralism: homogenization (the rendering of any one as exchangeable with another), instrumentalism (which posits another as only a means to an end), and backgrounding (the relegation of those considered to be without value to the non-essential) (Plumwood, *Environmental Culture*

100–9). In Mesa's *Un incendio invisible*, the ecofeminist reader sees this hierarchical, colonizing dimension unfold in a conversation between Tejada and the nurse Ariché. First, his uncertainty about having met her previously, even though she is one of only three nurses at New Life, makes clear his disregard for her individuality. Second, his reminder to her of his profession – a geriatric doctor – is meant to assert his distinctive social level and to dissociate himself from the responsibility for the fiscal well-being of the staff or for the continuity of care of the residents, despite his position as New Life's head administrator. Finally, Tejada qualifies her Mexican name of Tarahumara origin as "extraño" ("strange") and renames her using the Castilian Spanish translation "Atardecer" ("Dusk"), thus enacting a misogynistic colonialist power differential between himself and her (Mesa 92). Treating Ariché and the cook, as well as the elderly residents, as simple, inessential, and disposable objects, Tejada exudes a patriarchal logic of colonization that parallels the anthropocentric homogenization, backgrounding, and instrumentality of the non-human environment for human activity. Therewithin, too, lies a logic of progress that depends on an ideology of extractivism on social, political, and ecological scales.

As the introduction to this collection discusses, the Anthropocene may be described as a period in which places of refuge for humans and for the diversity of more-than-human species are disappearing and the possibility of replenishing them is ever the more diminished (Haraway, "Anthropocene" 159). While precarious conditions impact all Vado residents, the narrative of the hotel owner's loss of protection alongside the doctor's denial of her value as a living being connects vanishing safe havens to androcentrism and anthropocentrism. Tejada's contemptuous thoughts are especially cruel in the context of her physical and emotional vulnerability: "Enflaquecida, sucia, cansada, ostentaba aquella noche una especie de dignidad que hizo que Tejada sintiese ganas de abofetearla" ("Emaciated, dirty, tired, she flaunted a kind of dignity that made Tejada feel like slapping her"; 142). The two move together to a succession of empty apartments after the hotel's electricity is cut, until Tejada decides near the story's end that he has tired of her and will move to New Life: "No iba a tener ningún reparo en abandonarla; no era su problema si ella podía o no valerse por sí sola" ("He would not have any qualms about abandoning her; it was not his problem whether or not she could fend for herself"; 229). This attitude of mastery is succinctly captured in the doctor's self-designated epithet: "era un gran hombre con una gran misión" ("he was a great man with a grand mission"; 217). In this abusive relationship, the woman whom Tejada objectifyingly calls "la mujer del kimono" ("the kimono woman") and whose name he never learns acquiesces to Tejada's domineering conduct and conceives of herself within a paradigm of economic prosperity, as shown by her luxurious clothing despite her financial unravelling and the city's crumbling infrastructure (89). Seeped in ageism, sexism, and ethnic bias, Tejada exploits the hotel owner, the cook, and the nurse in what ecofeminists such as Plumwood, Carolyn Merchant, and Karen Warren recognize as relationships of instrumentality, as if the women were natural resources whose energies he extracts.[10]

Even though the culture of reason may seem inescapable and unyielding, an ecofeminist evaluation of Mesa's *Un incendio invisible* underscores the imperative to resist these hierarchical interactions of exploitation, degradation, and marginalization in order to conceive a mutually supportive ecosocial model.[11] Ariché's experience with radical exclusion not only empowers her to confront Tejada's ethnic-based misogyny but also equips her with an ability to exercise compassionate care for other vulnerable humans in a way that models ecological relationality. By insisting that she is a Vado-born Spaniard of Mexican descent, the nurse confronts the doctor's identification of her as a homogenized Latin American immigrant and asserts the need to recognize biocultural hybridity, complexity, and post-centric networks rather than dichotomic structures. Ariché meets his distanced stance and ferocious gaze with her demand that he listen, calls out his irresponsibility – the thirty-six days since his arrival without a word about the ninety-six days without compensation – and questions his motives for coming to Vado, all of which cause him to faint, which can be read as a sign of his diminished power to commodify others.

To recognize another's complexity, non-instrumental value, relational existence, and individuation – principles of Plumwood's proposal of mutuality – is to enact an ethics of care that attends to the enmeshment of all beings rather than placing only some in a supportive role (*Feminism* 158–9, 188). Any one of these principles confronts an ecologically devastating human-centredness, and yet each and every one must be enacted to fully realize an eco-ethical framework that may sustain all human and more-than-human beings. In Mesa's narration, the cook's concern for the clients' dietary requirements demonstrates her sensitivity to others' needs, but it is with the nurse Ariché that we see the most developed ethics of care. The nurse's care for one of the residents in particular, a woman with emotional trauma from sexual abuse, illustrates that ecological mutuality should not lead to negating one's own well-being. Ariché finds Clueca one night in her wheelchair, "alterada y completamente desnuda" ("agitated and completely nude"; Mesa 103), brandishing her cane, claiming to have pushed away an abusive man, and imagining Tejada was the doctor who performed a forced abortion and sterilization on her years ago. Ariché's careful stepping over the broken glass from a lamp that Clueca used for defence represents her recognition of the need of vulnerable creatures to navigate threatening patriarchal environments: "El polvo del cristal brillaba con un resplandor extraño, desasosegante. Al mirarlo, Ariché se sintió invadida por el resentimiento" ("The glass dust was sparkling with a strange, unsettling glow. Looking at it, Ariché was overcome with resentment"; 103). However, rather than allowing herself to succumb to this hierarchical dynamic, Ariché transforms her fury into compassion: she attentively listens, consoles the weeping resident, "el rostro … dibujando su sufrimiento en cada arruga" ("her face … drawing her suffering in each wrinkle"), and tucks her up in bed (104). To realize an ecologically rational society, Plumwood argues for a "relational self, which includes respect, benevolence, care, friendship and solidarity, where we not only do not place the other among our secondary or instrumental goals but treat at least the general goals of the other's wellbeing, ends or telos as among our own primary ends" (*Feminism* 155). In her relations with the elderly residents, this character attends to complex needs and values them without seeking benefit for herself, but neglects her own basic hygiene in the process; this self-abnegation does not allow for a mutuality in which each self is connected yet not absorbed by the other. Read ecocritically, Ariché is significantly closer to an ecological ethics of care than Tejada, but, nevertheless, her overcommitment forsakes her own existence and thereby impedes a mutuality of ecological sustainability.

Despite this shortcoming, Ariché's eco-ethical sensibility in her approach to community voices a counter-narrative to Spain's monetary-focused real-estate expansion, of which New Life is an example. Indeed, reflecting on families' abandonment of their relatives at the once luxury facility, this character is critical of the hyper-possession of some and dispossession of others in the seemingly perpetual expansionist, consumerist dynamic of contemporary Spain: "Familias devoradas por vuestra propia codicia, … sólo sabéis engendrar monstruos. Pero tampoco tendré un hijito; pariré otro monstruo, el monstruo de esta época" ("Families devoured by your own greed … you only know how to produce monsters. But I will not have a child either; I will give birth to another monster, the monster of this epoch"; Mesa 105). Through the nurse's characterization of monstrous progeny, Mesa's novel expresses an imperative for systemic change to growth-based global economies, which discard the weak, the poor, and the elderly. While Ariché seems to have embodied the move towards greater justice, her ethics of care – which at present is siloed from the more capitalistic and androcentric approach imposed by Tejada – has perhaps swung too far the other way; her ability to take care of others comes at the expense of her own well-being and renders it unsustainable. The dysfunction of hegemonic centralism, exposed by those humans who are more (Tejada) or less (Clueca) advantaged in an androcentric, capitalist system and whose disparity of access to care is bridged by Ariché and her hybrid relationality, is then expanded in the novel to account for non-human entwinements in a further decentring of the logic of colonization.

Material Entwinements from Human to More-than-Human

Material feminists make the case that while feminism's postmodern turn towards the discursive construction of gender has focused critical attention on dichotomous social and political hierarchies, feminists have neglected material bodies, in part to break with essentialism. Yet environmental feminists have maintained that the materiality of the more-than-human must be considered (Alaimo and Hekman 2–4). One example is Plumwood's argument "to counter radical exclusion (the first feature of anthropocentrism on the Othering model) by emphasising human continuity with non-human nature and animals" (*Environmental Culture* 111). Another is Alaimo's concept of "trans-corporeality," which underscores that "all creatures, as embodied beings, are intermeshed with the dynamic, material world, which crosses through them, transforms them, and is transformed by them" ("Trans-Corporeality" 435). To make the point that separation of humans from nature is inconceivable in the Anthropocene era and yet not all continuity is desirable, Alaimo gives the example of human-made toxins, which are absorbed by humans, soil, plants, animals, and other biotic matter in complex molecular interchanges ("Trans-Corporeal Feminisms" 260). The movement suggested via the prefix of her term ("trans") recognizes that the environment is not a mere background against which humans act, as Plumwood has already asserted, but "is, in fact, a world of fleshy beings, with their own needs, claims, and actions" (238). What is more, this reconceptualization of matter recognizes that agency occurs in other-than-anthropocentric forms, as "intra-acting phenomena"; in other words, individual entities exist *as relationships* with other organic and inorganic matter (248–9). The acknowledgment that more-than-human entities consist of processes within and with other matter facilitates environmental ethics, for non-humans are no longer inert objects to serve as resources for humans' use but rather active agents (245–50).

I situate Mesa's *Un incendio invisible* within material feminist practice as a text that foregrounds material entwinement of the environment, more-than-human beings, and humans by narratively actualizing the agency of gender. Using plants as instruments for monetary gain, New Life's developers sought to attract residents to the more than four hectares of abundantly watered gardens containing non-native species of vegetation, a variety of fountains, and so-called Bioclimatic and Microclimate Comfort zones. In the absence of capital following the market crash, however, human manipulation of the environment has diminished: plants grow at will and sprinklers resist humans' direction to provide lush gardens that offer physical comfort. These acts suggest non-human agency: "justo cuando más azotaba el calor, todos los aspersores estaban secos, o rotos, con un rumor como de agua por dentro que *nunca se decidía* brotar del todo" ("just when the heat hit the hardest, all the sprinklers were dry, or broken, with a murmur inside like water that *never quite decided* to come out"; 97; emphasis added). The anthropomorphized hose's refusal to water the humans' gardens juxtaposed with the alcoholism of the only gardener left of a twenty-five-person staff alludes to a broader contemporary addiction to consumption and overuse of resources to produce an unsustainable environment. As havens of respite from the demands and threats of everyday life, gardens are spaces for replenishment. Yet this overgrown garden managed by an inattentive alcoholic points to the inescapable consequences that result from human neglect of other-than-human sustainability, a contrast to Ariché's care for others amid her self-abnegation. In terms of (over)growth, the garden also references a stage of runaway capitalism in which progress has marched on unabated and unmediated, itself neglected by those drunk at the wheel of power.[12] A capitalist model that exploits extractivist ideologies values natural elements instrumentally for their support of economic growth; yet Mesa's text makes clear that humans can ignore neither their dependence on nor their intertwinement with other-than-human environments.

As a materially engaged text, the novel likewise calls attention to human-produced contaminants' penetration into and transformation of organic and inorganic bodies. In the river that runs through Vado, the water's movement, colour, smell, and shape make evident its toxicity: "Las aguas del río ondeaban débilmente; en algunos puntos se acumulaban pegotones de espuma de un extraño tono bilioso, con las crestas casi negras. El olor era ácido" ("The river's water faintly rippled; in some spots, patches of foam of a strange bilious hue amassed, with its crests nearly black. The smell was acidic"; 205). In another passage, the water and the fish that live in the river dismantle the fallacy of human and nature's separation: "las aguas del río – contaminadas, verdes – ondeaban con una placidez casi inquietante, sólo interrumpida por algunos peces moribundos que salían a coger su última bocada de oxígeno" ("the river's waters – contaminated, green – rippled with an almost eerie placidity, only interrupted by a few dying fish coming up to catch their last gasp of oxygen"; 161).[13] The water and fish are shown as active agents, whose materiality disputes the androcentric logic of reason expressed one sentence later, when Tejada boasts again of being a great man with a grand mission. This conspicuous textual juxtaposition recalls Alaimo's argument that "[t]rans-corporeality contests the master subject of Western humanist individualism, who imagines himself as transcendent, disembodied, and removed from the world he surveys" ("Trans-Corporeality" 435–6). As the narration suggests, ecological disconnection has facilitated an unethical absolution of human responsibility for environmental consequences.

While one might expect to find contamination in water and aquatic life in the vicinity of industrial areas, such as those on the outskirts of Vado, the novel's depiction of the ubiquity of toxins and their permeation into many different types of land and air creatures emphasizes the widespread, poisonous consequences of humans' erroneously conceived separation from the non-human. In addition to the river fish, other non-human animals materially exhibit physiological signs of environmental illness: seagulls' eyes are red and their feathers dislocated, pigeons' eyes are encircled with red excretion, and a rat has a wavy-shaped tail (137, 161–2). Illness in animals that humans often associate with trash and filth, and who have previously adapted to living among anthropogenic waste, indicates an intensification of the toxicity in their environment.[14]

Un incendio invisible also renders undeniable the shared impact of environmental toxicity and its resulting food scarcity on humans and non-human animals. Seagulls, pigeons, rats, and weasels scavenge for food in overflowing trash bins and abandoned grocery stores, while in New Life's desiccated gardens, previously indolent cats "se peleaban entre ellos, cada vez más salvajes y atigrados" ("were fighting each other, becoming more savage and tiger-like"; 38). Though it is common for non-human animals to live among humans in urban and suburban areas, what is more remarkable in this text is the reappropriation of space by non-human animals as people vacate the city of Vado, to the extent that humans seem out of place. Qualifying the cats, iguanas, weasels, foxes, lizards, and other creatures living in the city space as "animales salvajes" ("wild animals"; 190) highlights the need for a wilderness in which non-human animals are able to engage in actions consummate with their material agency (Alaimo, "Trans-Corporeal Feminisms" 249). Further, the seagulls who circle the doctor at different points in the narration, one bird grazing his head as he talks to a girl about the port's unsanitary condition, seem to blame the position of mastery that he asserts for the environment's degradation. In these ways and others, more-than-human corporal manifestations suggest intra-active agency, emphasizing unexpected and sometimes unwanted connections among material entities that call to account humans' ethical responsibility for the toxification of the environment.

Ecocritical scholar Luis I. Prádanos argues that representations of "discarded materials and degraded spaces" in post-crisis Spanish cultural production advocate for the non-human's agency to decry the ecological consequences of pairing progress with unlimited economic growth (174). In Mesa's story, seemingly inert objects transformed into enlivened agents draw attention to the neoliberal delusion that turning green spaces into suburban and urban development fosters well-being and warn of consumption's pernicious impact. Discarded human-created products that were once desirable consumer objects populate the town, fields, and waterways of the narrated city, intervening in human and non-human lives long after they have been cast aside. Along with strewn non-human detritus, the human mass exodus calls to mind sociologist and philosopher Zygmunt Bauman's term "wasted lives" – a reference to the beings that the systems of capital have deemed superfluous in order to propel economic expansion.[15] A disparate list of consumer goods in the fictional city's river highlights the incomprehensibility of contemporary consumerism, so much of which consists of acquiring and disposing of objects that serve no real need or have been rendered obsolete: "una bailarina Lladró sin brazos, un pollo de plástico, un despertador que aún funcionaba, un Ken sin Barbie, una alfombrilla para el ratón del ordenador con dibujos de osos y corazones, un bote de Pringles con su tapa" ("a Lladro ballerina missing her arms, a plastic chicken, an alarm clock that still worked, a Ken without a Barbie, a mouse pad with drawings of bears and hearts, a can of Pringles and its lid"; 20). Clearly, these myriad items show the growth paradigm's unsustainability, producing so-called disposable goods that paradoxically cannot be disposed of.[16] Their trans-corporeal depiction in the novel "resists the allure of shiny objects, considering instead the effects they have, from manufacture to disposal, while reckoning with the strange agencies that interconnect substance, flesh and place" (Alaimo, "Trans-Corporeality" 436). Through the ubiquitous presence of waste and contamination in *Un incendio invisible*, the material entwinement of human with more-than-human beings and the fallacy of human exceptionalism are undeniable.

Material Agency, Mutuality, and Interspecies Care

While the aforementioned animals, trash, and water signal that growth-oriented economics and a false human versus non-human–nature delineation have undermined ecological well-being, a character referred to as "la niña" ("the girl") provides a blueprint for enacting ecological sensibility, co-dependence, and communitarianism. Her lack of name suggests that all young people have inherited the environmental degradation caused by previous generations and alludes to the hope that their generation will enact ecologically sensitive paradigms. Moreover, the pairing of the generalized name with the character's rejection of convention in multiple manners underscores the radical re-envisioning needed to foster ecosocial well-being and environmental equity. Most patent is the character's transgender self-identification as Miguel in opposition to the third-person narrator's status quo use of referents.[17] If the narrative voice represents society's inertia and reluctance to make meaningful ecosocial change, Miguel's father's angry response to his child's gender-nonconforming self-naming and Tejada's unsurprising dismissal of it as "tonterías" ("nonsense") voice the patriarchal, binary posture. Miguel's defiant repetition of the name Miguel, "sin pestañear" ("without blinking"), followed by "Yo soy un niño" ("I am a boy"), shows their will to shift dominant practices (94).

Furthering the child's defiance of patriarchal structures, the nine-year-old creates an alternative home to the one with their father, who clings to a traditional family conception rather than adapt to a different reality. Similar to human beings' perpetuation of environmentally damaging practices despite the undeniable harm they cause, the father has placed a mannequin in a bed to feign that the child's mother, his former wife, is present but chronically ill, even though she left them years earlier. In light of the father's deceit and emotional detachment, Miguel turns an abandoned boat named *Melisa* into a matriarchal space in which to care for themself and a dog. The words "SIEMPRE CONTIGO" ("ALWAYS WITH YOU"; 51) inscribed on the boat convey their codependence. If read ironically, however, the motto points to the mother's abandonment of the family, thus debunking an essentialist pairing of women with care. In the context of Spain's market crash, the motto also paradoxically suggests pre-crisis real-estate developments' failure to provide long-term housing due to high-interest loan defaults and unfinished construction.

Building a counter-hegemonic home with a discarded boat alludes not only to the impossibility of ignoring accumulated waste, but moreover to the fact that refuges must be created within the reality of a waste-filled, toxic world. In contrast to the dominant throw-away culture, Miguel collects objects that others consider garbage (the aforementioned Ken doll, mouse pad, and other items) from the river and stores the perceived treasures in a discarded tube that the child calls a secret cave. In Miguel's view, the waste-treasures that the river's current brings to its edges are for those who first notice them; that is, for those who recognize their material presence. By safeguarding them, the child acknowledges an interconnected existence with these agentive objects and reformulates the perception of trash as a relationship of care for all things. Nonetheless, appreciating and repurposing discarded items will not solve the crisis of consumer accumulation; with so much trash beyond what we can reuse or recycle, humans must also reject the growth-based economic culture. Finally, it is worth noting that Miguel's choice to step barefooted on moss near the wharf that others fear is infectious signals the acceptance of responsibility for the effects of human actions on the environment and the recognition that the bryophyte is as much a part of the ecosystem as are humans. In these various ways, Miguel challenges established attitudes and practices related to waste, consumerism, and fear of non-human nature, yet ultimately, the child must abandon this alternative home when their father decides that the two will join a mass exodus from the environmentally damaged area.[18] By deploying mutuality, this materially conscious narration signals the little chance that small-scale alternative models of living have against the dominant paradigm of resource depletion and pollution production. In this vein, Mesa exposes the nation state's suspension of its commitment to the care of its citizens through a child who, abandoned by their mother, becomes exposed to toxins by walking on the moss and picking trash from the river. The futility of Miguel's solitary actions points to the need for systemic changes.

Not only does the young character's considerate treatment of abiotic entities acknowledge humans' undeniable intertwinement with non-humans; their care for an abandoned dog in addition proposes a pathway to realizing ethical responsibility. The dog's name Tifón ("Typhoon") refers to non-human nature's power and likewise conveys the deleterious impact that humans have had on other organisms. As with the ill seagulls, pigeons, and rats, the toxic environment pervades Tifón's hungry, flea-infested, and wounded body, which becomes increasingly sickly. His ghost-like material presence, "como una bolsa llena de huesos ligeros o de pequeñas astillas de madera" ("like a sack full of light bones or of small wood chips") signals humans' placement of their own survival over that of other species and alludes to the Anthropocene's accelerated reduction of biodiversity (216).

Plumwood acknowledges that although humans cannot detach from "human epistemic locatedness," that is, knowledge grounded in human concerns and experiences, we must undertake the ethically necessary project of decentring human interests, moral measurements, and knowledge (*Environmental Culture* 131–6). Moreover, ecological ethics should not be based on a utilitarian model that ranks species, for that only continues dualist inclusion versus exclusion by which some serve as background and instrumental value for others (147–52). Although dogs may seem more like humans than other animals, all more-than-human lives deserve equal consideration for their well-being. To this end, Plumwood recommends "openness, active invitation, attentiveness, and intentional recognition" to allow for a heterogeneity of interaction with non-human species (174, 180–2, 193). Haraway decries as well hierarchical rankings of species, noting that only about 10 per cent of the human body's cells contain human genomes, while the remaining 90 per cent consist of other organisms such as bacteria, fungi, and protists (*Species* 3–4). She traces the etymology of the word *species* to the Latin *specere* ("to look or behold") and connects it to *respecere* ("to look back again") to urge an interspecies ethics of interconnectivity that abolishes the dualistic boundaries of nature and culture, animal and human: "To hold in regard, to respond, to look back reciprocally, to notice, to pay attention, to have courteous regard for, to esteem: all of that is tied to polite greeting, to constituting the *polis*: where and when species meet. To knot companion and species together in encounter, in regard and respect, is to enter the world of becoming with" (19). Haraway and Plumwood are both suggesting that when we move away from a human-centred view of communication, we allow not only for diverse forms of expression that might encompass affect and other semiotic cues beyond the normal human understandings of language, but also for a dialogical conception of the self in relationship with others.

In *Un incendio invisible*, the child and the dog's intra-actions model a mutual development of an ethics of care founded on dialogical responsibility and more-than-human agency. The narration contrasts two different responses to the canine companion's caution towards humans, a wariness born of his likely former abuse: on the one hand, the doctor angrily orders the dog to eat, while on the other, Miguel respectfully leaves him food without looking back towards him to avoid frightening the fearful being. Actively attending to his poor health, the child also searches abandoned grocery stores for dog food and finds rags to dress the dog's wound. Seeking to understand the canine's bodily gestures, Miguel responds attentively to the dog's tense gaze, stiffened body, and shaking jaw, and looks for his intention. The child self-critically considers their unique effect on the dog, all intra-actions that acknowledge Tifón's individuality and complexity and are congruent with Plumwood's recommendations for a "counter-hegemonic stance" (*Environmental Culture* 194). Tifón eventually trusts Miguel and reciprocates: he wags his tail when the child approaches, sits with them, protects their suitcase of treasures, sleeps in the boat house, and listens to their confidences. Most broadly, the canine companion provides an interspecies alternative family to Miguel's dysfunctional patriarchal one.

Knowing a departure from Vado is imminent, the child plans for Tifón's future well-being as best they can, asking Tejada to care for the canine creature. Indicating the affective connection that the child and dog have developed, and the latter's lack of trust in the androcentric doctor, Tifón's gaze expresses a deep sadness after Miguel has left, and he appears to wish to commit suicide as he stands in the road facing Tejada's car. Ultimately, Tejada finds a caregiver for the dog and pays his veterinary bills, fulfilling his promise to Miguel. However, lest we think the androcentric doctor has changed, in the section narrated in Tejada's voice, he reveals that he is merely compensating for killing his ex-wife's dog: "perro por perro" ("a dog for a dog"; 228), a distorted ethical position that recalls his colonialist naming practice in relation to Ariché. With this additional information about the doctor's motive, the broader narrative voice condemns this misogynistic, egocentric character, with his human-centred view of other species and "disengagement from nature's contaminating elements of emotion, attachment and embodiment" (Plumwood, *Environmental Culture* 5). Through the hegemonic centralist perspective, there occurs a process of abjection that flattens both human and animal forms of life into a category of inferior ontological value. A comment focalized from Tejada about Tifón's emotions reveals this human character's failure to see that the dog need not be anything but a dog to have communicative intention, that "aquel perro no era solamente un perro" ("that dog was not simply a dog"), never mind his inability to relate to him at a basic level: "ni siquiera sabía cómo se acaricia un perro" ("he did not even know how to pet a dog"; 206). In contrast, the child develops a responsive, respectful relationship of embodied communication with Tifón, as Haraway and Plumwood urge.

Setting Fire to Expansionism to Enact Ecological Entanglement

Mesa's dystopian story links Spain's real-estate boom, bust, and economic crisis with environmental deterioration to expose the undesirability and unsustainability of a so-called good life motored by global capitalism and consumerism. By the novel's end, few residents remain, food is scarce, most buildings are without electricity or water, and fires burn throughout the city and its outskirts. The flame-induced collapse of one of the suburb's first apartment developments, named *los Diez Mandamientos* ("The Ten Commandments"), decries the corruption of foundational moral values. Other burning buildings are associated with (sub)urban development, corporate global domination, and so-called technological solutions to ecological problems, including the Vado Grand Theatre, the Hotel Carlton, the recently built Museum of Applied Sciences, and the headquarters of Ericksson and of General Motors. The fiery destruction of "la última – y polémica – ampliación de la biblioteca universitaria, obra del arquitecto tailandés Piparon Namatra" ("the latest – and controversial – expansion of the university library, designed by Thai architect Piparon Namatra"; 182) invokes the wasteful public expenditure on high-cost municipal construction projects with world-renowned architects that was prevalent during Spain's economic growth as a display of prosperity, such as Valencia's Santiago Calatrava–designed City of Arts and Sciences.[19] Theories in the novel that link responsibility for the fires to the global capitalist system – in the form of a diabolic sect, an unspecified complex organization, or people fed up with the city's decay – reflect the dramatic increase in forest fires in the Iberian Peninsula and other parts of the world in recent years not only because of climate change (heat waves, rising overall temperatures, reduced rainfall, and prolonged droughts) but also because of rural exodus, developments bordering forested areas, decreased pastoral activity, and the plantation of monocrops, such as eucalyptus. In addition to these anthropogenic acts, many large-scale, deadly fires can be linked back to unique human error (Conde; González; "Incendios").[20]

The fires that ravage Vado intimate both the destruction that hegemonic anthropocentric behaviour has wrought on ecosystems and the purifying, life-giving potential of a dialogical, relational model of human-animal-object connection. As the New Life residence burns, Tejada looks out his window and sees two terrified rats running "cada una en una dirección distinta" ("each in a different direction"; 231), each one seeking to survive on her own, illustrating Tejada's individualist framework. Everyone perishes – the elderly whose families had left them behind and the few staff who had stayed to care for them – everyone except Tejada, who runs from the burning senior residence and saves only himself. Comparing Tejada's fleeing down the path to that of a rabbit, the text affirms the intermeshing of humans and more-than-humans in materially shared environments.

Trans-corporeal entanglements of animals, humans, chemicals, plastics, microbes, water, land, and air in Mesa's *Un incendio invisible* compel contemporary readers to see the metaphorical and real fires we are creating with our anthropogenic activities and to desist from the growth-based capitalist neoliberalism that is consuming the globe. In the story's last paragraph, the constant hot winds cease and a light breeze blows for a brief moment, suggesting that we have little opportunity left to assume responsibility for the unprecedented changes to the planet's ecology or to resist the inertia of current detrimental habits of consumption. To displace the dystopic present with a future that holds promise of mutual well-being will require a major paradigm shift involving ecological respect and care about and for more-than-human others.

NOTES

1 Mesa received the Premio Málaga ("Malaga Prize") for *Un incendio invisible* in 2011, and then edited and republished the novel in 2017 to portray the characters' unfavourable traits more subtly (Mesa 11). The Madrid-born Sevillian has published five additional novels as well as two collections of short stories and one of poetry. Related to this present study, the 2019 essay "Silencio administrativo: Pobreza en el laberinto burocrático" addresses Spain's housing crisis and bureaucratic obstacles to social services. The novel *Cara de pan* (2018) addresses environmental diversity in the context of human disability (Leone).

2 Ecological exile figures as well in the fictional works that Victoria L. Ketz and William Viestenz study in their respective chapters for this collection. In these novels, and in the one studied here, the failure of adults to protect the younger characters, who must leave their respective cities or hometowns, and the young people's creation of cooperative intra- and inter-species alliances leave no doubt of the indictment of prior generations for their damage to the home of all earth species and the promise of the next to realize more ecologically responsible societies.

3 While Mesa has mentioned some inspiration in Detroit's urban blight and depopulation, the city of Vado certainly resembles many in post-crisis Spain, with rapid construction and partially built, phantom neighbourhoods (Mesa 10). While it may be mere coincidence, residents were forced to leave the Guadalajaran town of El Vado in the 1950s due to the creation of a reservoir ("El Vado"). For an analysis of the ecological exile caused by reservoir building in Spain, see Margaret Marek's chapter in this collection on the submersion of nine villages to build the Riaño Reservoir and the resulting ecotrauma. For her part, contributor Olga

Colbert observes that author Julio Llamazares captures the trauma of Spain's Civil War and the erasure of the Republican victims in the ghostliness of towns submerged by reservoir waters and the forced relocation of their residents.

4 All translations are my own. Page numbers correspond to the Spanish original.

5 The growth of Spain's construction industry was the highest in Europe between 2000 and 2012 and included not only suburban residences but urban centres, regional capitals, coastal housing complexes, commercial and industrial development, and public works, such as high-speed rail lines and bridges, often promoted by politicians to gain favour (Echevarri et al.). The country averaged 600,000 newly built dwellings annually from 2000 to 2007, often more in a given year than France, the United Kingdom, Germany, and Italy combined. Spain's soaring property market can be traced to membership of the eurozone, reduced interest rates, longer mortgage periods, loans to individuals with little savings, and the purchase of second homes by European Union citizens. Increased demand led to rising prices and more construction, also funded by loans to building companies, which drove the need for more supplies and the establishment of new factories. With unemployment low and demand for goods high, Spain attracted immigrants to work in construction and services, who also purchased homes (Garcia-Herrero and Fernández de Lis 3). This construction boom and then bust led to a precipitous fall in Spain's economic growth from 3.5 per cent in 2007 to 0.9 per cent in 2008 and turned its public account surplus of more than 2 per cent into a deficit ("Timeline").

6 The reader should consult environmental Hispanist Luis I. Prádanos's *Postgrowth Imaginaries: New Ecologies and Counterhegemonic Culture in Post-2008 Spain* for an overview of degrowth theory in the Spanish post-crisis context.

7 Inspired by Raymond Williams's literary scholarship on changing English attitudes towards the country and the city, narrative and film critic Nathan Richardson has argued that studying representations of urban-rural dynamics in Spanish cultural production since the 1950s provides insight into the nation's changing political and social concerns (17). Many towns and villages, especially in Castile, Aragon, and Extremadura, were completely or nearly abandoned when people migrated en masse despite pro-rural propaganda after the Franco regime rescinded its prohibition of permanent resettlement within Spain in 1947 (25–6). Prádanos discusses the metabolic rift that occurs when urban demand for resources and services transforms non-urban geographies and thereby extends urbanization to rural areas (96–100, 128).

8 While all but 1 per cent of buyers had been foreign a few years earlier, Spaniards accounted for 30 per cent of sales in 2019; moreover, prices at the

lower end have been rising 5 to 10 per cent annually (López Letón). In his work on new ruralism, Iberian and Catalan literature scholar Joan Ramón Resina notes the challenge posed by urban dispersion and rural exodus to modernity's hegemony of the city, and he asks whether in the context of a commodified rurality, contemporary rural experiences promoted to urban dwellers, whose interactions with local residents are generally limited to service provision, have any spatio-temporal connection to previous generations of rural life (11–12, 22–23).

9 For more on mastery attributes, see Plumwood, "Dualism: The Logic of Colonisation," in *Feminism*.

10 Merchant's notion of mechanism, which is similar to Plumwood's term "instrumentalism," expresses the scientific revolution's reconceptualization of nature as inert, available matter. For her part, Warren uses the words "logic of domination" to denote the justification of subordination on grounds of perceived superiority.

11 An analysis of Waanyi (Aboriginal Australian) author Alexis Wright's *Carpentaria* through Plumwood's ecofeminist philosophy by environmental humanities scholar Kate Rigby inspired my analysis of the (de)colonizing aspects of Mesa's novel.

12 With appreciation to contributor William Viestenz for his insightful observations about various dynamics of this chapter, including the transformation of gardens in late capitalism.

13 Mesa's vivid narration of the toxic penetration of aquatic life brings to mind the pictural revision of early twentieth-century Spanish painter Joaquín Sorolla's *Niños en la playa* in the World Wildlife Fund and Prado collaboration, which draws attention to the deathly, entwined impact of accumulated contamination on fish and boys alike, and which we analyse in the introduction to this collection.

14 Environmental education and curricular scholar Gavin P.L. Watson makes the observation in his piece on ring-gull birds in Toronto that humans project disgust on these animals for their scavenging yet fail to see that anthropogenic lifestyles produce the waste they eat.

15 With points in common to my analysis of waste in Mesa's novel, Juan Carlos Martín Galván's contribution to *Beyond Human* effectively deploys Achille Mbembe's concept of necropolitics to elucidate systemic practices of speciesism that not only qualify some lives as expendable but also subject them to violence and death, ultimately undermining the possibility of realizing democratic societies and ecojustice. For his part, contributor Micah McKay contends that while waste undoubtedly attests to the destructive capitalist stage of human history, the conceptual frame of salvage that he perceives in Ben Clark's poetic fragments facilitates readers' comprehension of the necropolitics of trash for human and more-

than-human lives, and yet also the possibility of enacting collaborative modes of survival amid the peril.

16 Prádanos points out that "the crisis of modernity is marked by the end of the utopia of a world without waste" (166). In ecocritic Samuel Amago's study of a variety of cultural media, including film, social media, comics, and narrative, he argues that discarded things reveal not only Spain's embrace of neoliberal capitalism after the dictatorship of Francisco Franco and the resulting acceleration of consumer culture, but moreover the social, political, aesthetic, and cultural values that have dominated, been marginalized, and been cast aside in contemporary Spain.

17 While the narrator uses the female pronoun *ella* to refer to Miguel, I read this as representative of society's negation of the character's gender nonconformity. Therefore, and in congruence with the ecofeminist critical position of this analysis and its proposal to eliminate andro- and anthropocentric categorizations of life, I will use the third-person plural pronouns *they* and *them* (and the adjective *their*) when speaking of Miguel.

18 Connecting with Miguel's defiance of gender conformity as a stand against hierarchies that are often buttressed by androcentric fears, including homophobia, contributor and co-editor Shanna Lino studies the irrational association of fear with the non-human environment and posits that the broader dismantling of boundaries among species in ecohorror and the ecogothic dispels myths of both andro- and anthropocentric supremacy.

19 The eighty-six-acre project, which includes a performance hall, bridge, planetarium, opera house, science museum, and park-like area, cost three times its original budget of 300 million euros and has many design flaws (Daley).

20 Relevant to this novel, the most newsworthy of the human causes of massive fires may be the increasingly popular explosions caused by the lighting of blue or pink confetti-filled cannons at binary-enforcing gender-reveal parties.

WORKS CITED AND CONSULTED

Alaimo, Stacy. *Bodily Natures: Science, Environment, and the Material Self*. Indiana UP, 2010.

Alaimo, Stacy. "Trans-Corporeal Feminisms and the Ethical Space of Nature." Alaimo and Hekman, *Material Feminisms*, pp. 237–64.

Alaimo, Stacy. "Trans-Corporeality." *Posthuman Glossary*, edited by Rosa Briadotto and Maria Hlavajova, Bloomsbury, 2018, pp. 435–8.

Alaimo, Stacy, and Susan Hekman. "Introduction: Emerging Models of Materiality in Feminist Theory." Alaimo and Hekman, *Material Feminisms*, pp. 1–19.

Alaimo, Stacy, and Susan Hekman, editors. *Material Feminisms*. Indiana UP, 2008.

Amago, Samuel. *Basura: Cultures of Waste in Contemporary Spain*. U of Virginia P, 2021.

Bauman, Zygmunt. *Wasted Lives: Modernity and Its Outcasts*. Polity, 2004.

Conde, Jesús. "El abandono de bosques y el monocultivo: Un cóctel explosivo para los incendios en Extremadura." *elDiario.es*, 23 Mar. 2016, https://www.eldiario.es/extremadura/sociedad/monocultivo-explosivo-combatir-incendios-extremadura_1_4089403.html.

Daley, Suzanne. "A Star Architect Leaves Some Clients Fuming." *New York Times*, 24 Sept. 2013, https://www.nytimes.com/2013/09/25/arts/design/santiago-calatrava-collects-critics-as-well-as-fans.html.

Echevarri, Julio Pozueta, et al. "The Spatial Dynamics of Land Use Surrounding the Spanish Property Bubble (1990–2012)." *Investigaciones Regionales*, no. 45, 2019, pp. 93–117.

Garcia-Herrero, Alicia, and Fernández de Lis, Santiago. "The Housing Boom and Bust in Spain: Impact of the Securitisation Model and Dynamic Provisioning." *BBVA Research*, 2008, https://www.bbvaresearch.com/wp-content/uploads/mult/WP_0806_tcm348-212959.pdf. PDF download, working paper.

González, Eva. "Los grandes incendios forestales dejan de ser cosa del verano." *El Confidencial*, 27 Feb. 2021, https://www.elconfidencial.com/medioambiente/clima/2021-02-27/incendios-crisis-climatica-bosques_2966576/.

Haraway, Donna. "Anthropocene, Capitalocene, Plantationocene, Chthulucene: Making Kin." *Environmental Humanities*, vol. 6, no. 1, 2015, pp. 159–65. *Duke UP*, https://doi.org/10.1215/22011919-3615934.

Haraway, Donna J. *When Species Meet*. U of Minnesota P, 2008.

"Incendios en España." *Greenpeace España*, https://es.greenpeace.org/es/trabajamos-en/bosques/incendios-forestales/. Accessed 9 Feb. 2023.

Leone, Maryanne L. "Reframing Disability through an Ecocritical Perspective in Sara Mesa's *Cara de pan*." *Journal of Gender and Sexuality Studies / Revista de Estudios de Género y Sexualidades*, vol. 45, no. 1, 2019, pp. 161–84. *Scholars Publishing Collective*, https://doi.org/10.14321/jgendsexustud.45.1.0161.

López Letón, Sandra. "Compre un pueblo abandonado en España y dese prisa porque sube de precio." *El País*, 5 Jan. 2019, https://elpais.com/economia/2019/01/04/actualidad/1546595862_297914.html.

Merchant, Carolyn. *The Death of Nature: Women, Ecology, and the Scientific Revolution*. Harper & Row, 1980.

Mesa, Sara. *Un incendio invisible*. Anagrama, 2017.

Plumwood, Val. "Decolonizing Relationships with Nature." *Decolonizing Nature: Strategies for Conservation in a Post-colonial Era*, edited by William H. Adams and Martin Mulligan, Earthscan, 2003, pp. 51–78.

Plumwood, Val. *Environmental Culture: The Ecological Crisis of Reason.* Routledge, 2002.

Plumwood, Val. *Feminism and the Mastery of Nature.* Routledge, 1994. *ProQuest Ebook Central,* https://ebookcentral.proquest.com.

Prádanos, Luis I. *Postgrowth Imaginaries: New Ecologies and Counterhegemonic Culture in Post-2008 Spain.* Liverpool UP, 2018.

Richardson, Nathan. *Postmodern Paletos: Immigration, Democracy, and Globalization in Spanish Narrative and Film, 1950–2000.* Bucknell UP, 2002.

Resina, Joan Ramón. "Introduction: The Modern Rural." *The New Ruralism: An Epistemology of Transformed Space,* edited by Joan Ramón Resina and William Viestenz, Vervuert, 2012, pp. 7–26.

Rigby, Kate. "The Poetics of Decolonization: Reading *Carpentaria* in a Feminist Ecocritical Frame." *International Perspectives in Feminist Ecocriticisms,* edited by Greta Gaard et al., Routledge, 2013, pp. 120–36.

"Timeline: Spain's Economic Crisis." *Reuters,* 29 Mar. 2012, https://www .reuters.com/article/us-spain-strike-economy/timeline-spains-economic -crisis-idUSBRE82S0L420120329.

"El Vado." *Wikipedia,* https://es.wikipedia.org/wiki/El_Vado_(Guadalajara). Accessed 14 Feb. 2023.

Warren, Karen J. "Feminism and Ecology: Making Connections." *Environmental Ethics,* vol. 9, no. 1, spring 1987, pp. 3–20. *Philosophy Documentation Center,* https://doi.org/10.5840/enviroethics19879113.

Watson, Gavin P.L. "See Gull: Cultural Blind Spots and the Disappearance of the Ring-Billed Gull in Toronto." *Trash Animals: How We Live with Nature's Filthy, Feral, Invasive, and Unwanted Species,* edited by Kelsi Nagy and Phillip David Johnson II, U of Minnesota P, 2013, pp. 31–8.

Williams, Raymond. *The Country and the City.* Oxford UP, 1973.

Chapter Twelve

Trans-Corporeal Matter Narratives in *Hierro*

Mᵃ LUZ GONZÁLEZ-RODRÍGUEZ AND
Mᵃ CONCEPCIÓN BRITO-VERA

No man is an island entire of itself; every man
Is a piece of the continent, a part of the main.

John Donne, *Devotions: Upon Emergent Occasions*

El Hierro, also called the Meridian Isle or the Island of One Thousand Volcanoes, is the youngest and most south-westerly Spanish land mass forming part of the Canary Islands archipelago. El Hierro is uniquely positioned in the Atlantic Ocean, which lends the location its distinctive character. The island sits just off the shores of Africa, and no other land mass stands between it and the American continents. This means that until the arrival of Columbus in the Americas, this location was considered by Europeans to be the last territory of the known world. According to José de Viera y Clavijo, the isle's distal position from Europe, Africa, and the rest of the Canarian archipelago induced Claudius Ptolemy to locate there the prime meridian. Thus, unfurling from this point westwards, the Atlantic Ocean, also known historically as Mare Tenebrarum or the Dark Sea, was considered a horizon of uncertainty.

El Hierro defies any preconceived ideas that one may hold about a paradise island as an oasis of palm trees, turquoise waters, and white-sand beaches: its shorelines are abrupt; its cliffs are sheer. This means the island has neither beaches nor places to sunbathe. Consequently, El Hierro has virtually no tourist industry, much unlike the other islands of the archipelago. However, this perceived commercial disadvantage has actually played an important role in the island's development as an ecologically equilibrated enclave. El Hierro covers an area of just 278 square kilometres and has a population of approximately 11,000 human inhabitants.[1] In 2000, the island was declared a World Biosphere Reserve by UNESCO, and in 2015, it was also declared a UNESCO

Global Geopark. The park itself, including both the land and the marine surface, measures a total of 595 square kilometres.[2] At this point in time, the political authorities of El Hierro, together with other organizations, aim for the island to become the first in the world to be 100 per cent sustainable.[3] As for its geology, this oceanic island was the last to emerge from the sea and is still at a relatively early stage of development. Its most recent submarine volcanic eruptions took place on 10 October 2011. Due to its relative infancy, the ground on this isle is unstable, which has led to spectacular landslides, including the one that took place 50,000 years ago and that caused the current horseshoe shape of the north face of the island. The valley that resulted from this geological cataclysm is now called El Golfo; not surprisingly, The Gulf's incredible beauty dominates the visual portrayal of the island in the television series *Hierro*.

Released in June 2019 and jointly produced by Movistar+, ARTE France, Portocabo, and Atlantique Productions, the series *Hierro* is a Franco-Spanish co-production whose first season takes the form of an eight-episode police thriller.[4] The island, with its singular traits, becomes an additional character as the drama unfolds. In this chapter, we hypothesize that by focusing on the island's distinctiveness as an agent with the capacity to affect and alter the course of events, the series, led by brothers Pepe Coira (creator, scriptwriter) and Jorge Coira (director), reflects the trans-corporeal nature of matter, a central tenet of material ecocriticism. In addition, by addressing island living in its relationship with the continent, we further demonstrate that these trans-corporeal manifestations evince a cultural ethos that is dependent not only on the island's human and non-human materiality but also on non-material global networks that contribute to the shaping of an *herreño* self-awareness.

According to new materialist Stacy Alaimo, trans-corporeality implies the "recognition that one's bodily substance is vitally connected to the broader environment" (63). Such recognition is not new, as can be inferred from the verses by the seventeenth-century English metaphysical poet John Donne quoted in the epigraph to this chapter. By showing the relational capacity of matter, trans-corporeality highlights the networks of interconnections, crossings, and assemblages that exist among all entities in the material world, be they animate or inanimate. As corporeal bodies, human beings are enmeshed in this fabric of relationships, together with immaterial domains such as culture, discourses, feelings, or emotions. In this sense, trans-corporeality blurs hierarchical boundaries between the material and the cultural or between matter and meaning, thus affirming the immanent relationality from which all entities emerge. Therefore, trans-corporeality unifies the human and the non-human, and in so doing, calls into question any human centrality.

As a product of television, the series *Hierro* displays this porous quality of matter through both its visual narrative and plot structure, finding its iconic expression in the opening credits. Here, body parts of the human characters are fused to or confused with other material elements, including a bush, a tree branch, or the island's contour, while close-up shots unravel the delicacy and intricate texture of other material elements, such as a stone or a piece of wood. As the opening sequence concludes, the contorted and tortured image of the Sabina is brought into focus. Having withstood over five hundred years of battery by the trade winds, this iconic tree has become a symbol of the island and its islanders. Today its twisted and bent limbs have found their way back to the soil from which it grows. The Sabina now takes hold of the ground not only by its roots but also by its crown; having grown full circle, its circumference affirms its willingness to live on and to survive against all odds. In its synecdochical solitude and tenacity, the Sabina tree encapsulates the island's and the islanders' long history of isolation.

While El Hierro's remoteness constitutes a recurring theme in the television series, one should refrain from interpreting the island as a passive victim of adversity. Quite the contrary: the isle is portrayed as an active agent in the thriller's investigation, one who exerts influence over the environment by altering the speed of the inquest and by assisting in the discovery of a hidden body. This fact draws attention to the interplay, connections, and relationships that arise from the material world, whose networks can be varied and wide in scope: a chemical substance reaching the bloodstream, the action of the wind on a tree, or the erosion of soil after a fire (Alaimo). By asserting matter's agentivity, trans-corporeality interrogates the traditional association of agency with intentionality and shows that matter should be studied "not in terms of what it *is* (i.e. essence) but in terms of what it *does* … in terms of its capacities to act and affect (i.e. agency)" (Monforte 380; emphasis in the original). Furthermore, focusing on matter's agency implies a repositioning of the category of human and blurs any human–non-human opposition. The television series *Hierro* demonstrates that just as the material world is not secondary to the human, so too the human cannot be considered a separate island estranged from a supposedly external world.

In tune with this re-categorization of matter, we analyse the series' ecocritical representation of El Hierro as an assemblage of earth, air, and maritime elements that together defy the conception of an island as a separate piece of land. As shall be seen, the series predicates on the tension derived from the intermingling of two potentially opposing forces: on the one hand, *Hierro* explores notions that equate island living with oppressive confinement of the type that might catalyse criminal activity; on the other hand, the series foregrounds the island's extensive connections to and communication with its surrounding environment. For instance, the diamonds that trigger the criminal investigation come from mainland Africa and the drug dealers who want to recover those same diamonds travel from the neighbouring island of Tenerife. This bidirectional emphasis on both the island's isolation and on its connectivity gives meaning to an apparent paradox: despite its seeming separateness, El Hierro's contiguity with human and non-human matter is indicative of the enmeshment that epitomizes an *herreño* ecoconscious and naturecultural identity.

Finally, we study the meeting of matter and non-material elements such as perceptions, feelings, and ideas in *Hierro*, since, as a moving-image thriller, the text exploits productively the confluence of material ecocriticism's central tenets and the conventions of crime fiction. Commonly, island detective fiction builds on both the mysterious atmosphere frequently ascribed to insular spaces and on the sense of enclosure felt by their human characters, elements also present in *Hierro*. Stereotypical island elements notwithstanding, the series' originality stems from El Hierro's agentivity, founded not simply on the pervasive presence of landscape, nor on the usual references to traditions, but rather on the dynamic character that the island acquires as a material element. In this vein, critics Ralph Crane and Lisa Fletcher have identified the power of islands not only for their function as settings, but also insofar as "they can also operate on the level of character, and influence plot" (6). What is more, extrapolating from structuralist Tzvetan Todorov's renowned assertion that crime fiction contains "not one but two stories: the story of the crime and the story of the investigation" (44), in island crime fiction, Crane and Fletcher rightly underline, there are not just those two, "but also the story of the island" (7). This singularity in the portrayal of El Hierro is better understood if we compare the series to other visual productions.

For instance, in the Anglo-French whodunnit-style detective series *Death in Paradise* (2011–), the imaginary island of St. Honorée is not depicted as an active agent taking part in the plot and affecting the denouement. If the murderer is found, it is only due to the detective's intuition and ability to decipher the clues left by the killer; if a crime is committed, its motivation is usually ascribed to prior conflicts that tourists bring to the island from their country of origin. The island serves merely as a paradisiac background against which tragic crimes occur and on which human-centred agency dominates. Virtually the same can be said of *Maltese* (2017), produced by RAI and Palomar, in which the island and the people of Sicily are just the passive victims of mafia schemes and Sicily, as an insular space, is not a necessary condition for the storyline. Both series visually and narratively centre the human.

On the official web page of the series *Hierro*, Pepe Coira observes that "[e]s bueno que el lugar donde ocurren las cosas importe, que tiña con algo de su carácter lo más sustancial, que es el carácter y la suerte de los personajes" ("it is good that the place where things happen matters, that [place] tinges the most substantial elements with some of its personality, which is the nature and the fortunes of its characters"; Movistar+ 31).[5] If it is true that the thriller is constituted "not around a method of presentation but around the milieu represented," as Todorov observes, then it is also true that the characters, their behaviour, and the space that produces and is produced by them must necessarily determine plot and structure (48). This generic predisposition to elucidate the transcorporeal relationship between the codependent agencies of the land and of its human inhabitants is reinforced by the series' disclosure of the murderer's identity at its midway point, in the fourth episode. The remaining four chapters elaborate on the murderer's personality and explore his motive for committing the crime, namely the island's lack of prospects, which he attributes to El Hierro's small size and to its distance from large urban centres. As we shall demonstrate, however, the series does not assign ethical responsibility for the human misbehaviour to El Hierro itself, but to the very real danger of human evaluations of the island territory as a remote, unproductive, or disconnected entity.

Indeed, the greatest distance between the island and the continent – one that propagates inaccurate ideas about a superior, continental life – is not only geographic but also representational, originating in social and other digital media.[6] As geographer and island researcher Jonathan Pugh rightly observes, "[E]ven if islands are not directly involved in new data production processes, in the Anthropocene it is increasingly difficult to undertake island studies in complete isolation from them" (101). The series *Hierro* offers an exceptional example of these other ways to understand island connectivity through Daniel's and other youngsters' self-perception. *Herreños* (people from El Hierro) are commonly bombarded with disempowering discourses that stem from the continent and that portray a neoliberal fantasy of individual success according to which economic affluence stands for personal improvement and comfort. This neoliberal, individualistic myth, together with the island's past of colonization and abandonment, defines the average islander's spatial self-awareness detrimentally: first, as a resident of a minuscule – and therefore devalued – island and, second, as physically and therefore symbolically distanced from continentally centred power. Recognizing the substratum of inferiority and disadvantage with which *herreños* such as those portrayed in the television series perceive themselves vis-à-vis mainlanders, *Hierro* proposes that a productive antidote to this kind of imperialistic centring of power on the continent is an ecocritical, new materialist, trans-corporeal reading of a territory that is in fact highly integrated and whose value can be perceived in proportion to its discerned material, human, and non-human interconnectivity within and beyond the island.

Hierro tells the story of examining magistrate Candela Montes (Candela Peña), who, for reasons unknown but that relate to a problem on the mainland, has been appointed to work on the island.[7] Once on El Hierro, she encounters a community in which everyone knows one another and where secrets are impossible to keep. Residents become suspicious when a young local named Fran (Alex Zacharias) is found dead, murdered on the day of his wedding. The prime suspect is Antonio Díaz Martínez (Darío Grandinetti), the bride's father and a wealthy businessman with a turbulent past. Their portrayal as oppositional characters notwithstanding, Candela and Díaz engage in a parallel investigation to discover the real killer. The viewer will eventually find out that Fran and his friend Daniel (Saulo Trujillo) had found some smuggled diamonds on a sunken ship and that the murder was motivated by Daniel's discovery that Fran planned not to share the spoils of the treasure with him. During the investigation, Daniel will also kill Reyes (Mónica López), a civil guard and the mother to one of his friends, when she accidentally uncovers the fact that he is the murderer for whom the whole island searches. The situation complicates further when Samir (Antonia San Juan), Díaz's boss in the drug-trafficking business, travels to El Hierro from Tenerife to recover those same diamonds. The climax is reached during *La Bajada*, a religious festival that takes place every four years and that brings together many *herreños*, including those living abroad. Eventually, Samir will also be killed by Daniel, who will finally get caught when trying to escape from the island.

The story of *Hierro* is told primarily from the point of view of the magistrate Candela, a fact that indicates that the series is targeted at mainland audiences. Through her eyes, the viewer is exposed critically to perceptions about the Canarian ethos: the stereotypical slowness usually confused by foreigners with laziness; the importance of *La Bajada*, which Candela reduces to a mere rural festivity; and, likewise, the absence of facilities and commodities – for instance, there are no large shopping malls on El Hierro – that consistently characterizes this place as small and distant. Díaz is also a mainlander and typifies the *godo*, a pejorative term that is used by Canarians to refer to mainlanders whose attitudes reflect those of the islands' colonial past. Individuals such as these are characterized by a sense of self-perceived superiority towards the islander; they are money-oriented and hold no regard for the land, nor concern for correctly interpreting the rhythms of the islanders. Díaz, for instance, has appropriated his Canarian wife's lands and transformed them into banana plantations. Through Candela and Díaz's portrayal, therefore, viewers are made aware of the dominance of mainland perspectives on island living and are prodded to question imperial, neoliberal, and other anthropocentric discourses that simultaneously devalue human and non-human *herreñidad*.[8]

In contrast, the civil guard Reyes epitomizes the sweetest and most amiable traits of the *herreño* people. She embodies their love for the land, as well as the know-how and patience required to confront difficult situations, whereas Daniel represents the angst experienced by islanders, especially of those who live in the remotest part of what constitutes political Spanish territory. In addition to having an abusive father and unlike most of his friends, Daniel has to work hard as a baker to earn his living. When envisioning his future, he foresees a life in which he is confined to the bakery with few other prospects. Although there exists the potential for Daniel to make the bakery more profitable, he instead becomes misguided by dreams of remote lands that would distance him from his father and from his feeling of imprisonment. In this way, Daniel personifies the long history of trials and tribulations undergone by *herreños*, which, in turn, have often precipitated a journey across the sea to begin anew elsewhere.

As living and lived matter, place produces meaning; it tells stories and can therefore be the subject of critical analysis. This vision is shared by new materialists, who, drawing on Spinoza's seventeenth-century neutral monist and epicurean materialist philosophy, defend the relentless "intra-activity" of matter in all its manifestations and argue that "matter is one" (Barad, *Meeting* 235; Braidotti 170). As one of the series' protagonists, El Hierro is much more than an innate setting; the island is a living entity that is still shaping itself and that determines the tempo of the plot.[9] Despite not being *herreños* themselves, the Galician directing duo shows great respect for the local: their cast is predominantly Canarian, as are their accents, and the creators undeniably project the idiosyncrasy of such a small place, accurately portraying popular and colloquial expressions, traditions, customs, and celebrations.

Since place links the human and non-human in equal measure, it affirms the non-hierarchical networks, relationships, and interdependencies between the two. In this sense, new material feminist Karen Barad's distinction between interaction and intra-action proves useful when reading *Hierro* ecocritically; while interaction implies the existence of pre-established bodies that later get involved in the action by primordially human intervention, intra-action entails the constant interflowing of forces working together (Barad, "Intra-actions" 77). Thus, intra-actions encompass the manifold assemblages of human and non-human matter. The Coira brothers' success in authentically evoking El Hierro's singularity through their focus on place evinces the agentive character of matter and the intra-active relationships entwining human with non-human elements. The intra-active relations between the island and its inhabitants are expressed in part through El Hierro's volcanic and climatic agentivity, which, like the series' human characters, drives the plot. In episode 1, it is a volcanic tremor that leads to the discovery of Fran's body, hidden in an undersea cave (00:10:28–00:11:25); similarly, in episode 5, the rain that extinguishes the fire that would have destroyed the traces left by the murderer on his victim's car facilitates the disclosure of the murderer's identity (00:08:15–00:09:30).

However, it is important to underline that these examples do not anthropomorphize the island as an agent intentionally helping in the human investigation. Rather, and in concrete terms, there is a volcanic tremor and it rains, and these two facts have significant consequences for the course of events plotted by the murderer and for the series' denouement. *Hierro* shows that humans merely comprise one small link in a complex network that constitutes the world of "vibrant matter" in which all manifestations of existence coexist and intra-act (Bennett). Entangled in endless ways, this "'more-than-human' materiality is a constant process of shared becoming that tells us something about the world we inhabit" (Iovino and Oppermann 1). Thus, a turn to matter enables us to listen to stories told by these phenomena and to acknowledge their agency in shaping human–non-human assemblages while asserting their ecological relevance.

Indeed, the trans-corporeal character of matter asserts place's agency as an imperative, which in turn provides a useful frame for a consideration of the material implications of island living. The sense of isolation and imprisonment expressed by the youngest characters in *Hierro* ultimately leads the series' murderer to a life of crime and reflects these humans' inability to acknowledge the extent of their interconnectivity with all human and non-human matter. For instance, when one of Fran's friends is interrogated about his possible involvement in the trafficking business, he answers, "Si llego a ser yo, con tanta pasta no me quedo aquí ni loco" ("If this were the case, I wouldn't have stayed here with all that cash, no way"; episode 6, 00:40:40). This sense of imprisonment on the island, from which Fran's friend would flee at his first opportunity, is reinforced by his human-centred focus on El Hierro's reduced dimensions and on the limited means of available transport to other territories. In the small and closed community where the *herreños* live, "[s]olo hay un barco … y varios aviones al día. Nadie sale de El Hierro sin que se sepa" ("there is only one boat … and a few planes per day. Nobody leaves El Hierro without the rest knowing it"; episode 1, 00:20:49–55). Rather than acknowledging the human–non-human interconnection that island life provides, characters like the young murderer feel watched, stifled, and surrounded by monotony. Profoundly frustrated and unsatisfied, the young baker Daniel dreams of leaving El Hierro, a desire instantiated in episode four, which opens with a general shot of a cityscape at night. This image confuses the viewer because it depicts an urban scene that would be impossible on the island. As the camera slowly pans out, the illusion is shattered: the shot reveals Daniel's eyes gazing upon beautifully lit high-rises, which the viewer then realizes are nothing more than enticing posters hanging on his bedroom wall. Dreaming of a bustling life in the metropolis, Daniel fails to recognize the material interconnectivity of his own island; instead, he seeks a more densely human-centred existence that popular imaginaries of the continent continually promote as desirable.

The islander's perception of the continent, expressed through Daniel's fantasy about urban areas, recalls the imaginative geography of Orientalism, which Edward Said has defined as an othering discourse on colonized people that empowers the colonizer. In *Hierro*, the imaginative geography works in the opposite direction to translate instead into a "continentalism" that renders islanders small and defenceless, a perception that a world of opportunities awaits outside the confines of the island, in which one could participate if only the sea did not present a seemingly infinite and insurmountable border. The television series' presentation of this imaginative geography of the continent, based on preconceived ideas about cities that appear to embody everything the island lacks, cannot be translated as an absence of involvement with the land. Rather it is reflective of the angst experienced by those who have to live on a limited set of economic or living experiences, in an example of the merging of psychological and ecological spaces.

Lamentably, Daniel is not able to view his island in a way that would transcend its traditional conception as a piece of land surrounded by water. Island cultures researcher Philip Hayward, inspired among others by political theorist Jane Bennett's notion of vibrant matter, proposes the term "aquapelago" to refer to the integrated spaces of the marine, terrestrial, and aerial environments of groups of islands, which are key to communities' senses of identity and belonging ("Aquapelagos"). As he states, "The air above the waters and land, the weather that occurs in it, the windblown seeds and species that are born by it and the birds that inhabit the air, sea and land are just as much part of the integrated space of the aquapelago" (Hayward, "Constitution" 2). Similarly, the series presents an image of the island that contrasts with the one that so derails Daniel; El Hierro is seen to be an assemblage of the land, the sea, and the air in all their manifestations, extending deeper even than Hayward's conception of the terrestrial, with its exploration of the underground depths of the island, which are of paramount importance given the centrality bestowed to its chasms and volcanism. In this context, humans "are only one of a series of actants without which the aquapelago cannot be performatively constituted" (Hayward, "Constitution" 3), while islands, as Pugh sustains, are framed as "'relational spaces' that unsettle borders of land/sea, island/mainland, and problematize static tropes of island insularity, isolation, dependency and peripherality" (94). Despite the aforementioned sense of enclosure experienced by some characters, through the coextensive visual layering of its opening and closing sequences, the series' emphasis on landscape-human entanglements, and a plot development that is dependent upon the island as a character, El Hierro is portrayed as an entity that is not only active but also in constant communication with the exterior and, as a relational space, possesses intra-active agency.

Indeed, agentivity is mediated and regulated by the ability of subjects to communicate with each other, a key characteristic of trans-corporeality. In *Hierro*, the porosity between human and non-human is again expressed through the fusion of images in the credits: human hair transforms into a bush, a branch extends until it becomes an arm, and the contour of a face is completed with the edges of the island's jagged coastline. With these visual superimpositions, the series highlights the bonding among all material elements and informs about contemporary ways of understanding the intra-connection of humanity and the environment in which nothing exists independently from the rest.

With its sustained focus on space, the landscape in *Hierro* becomes the site where the human and the non-human meet both materially and metaphorically. Indeed, the landscape is so prevailing that the series has unsurprisingly been termed "un crimen con vistas ... en clave de thriller" ("a thriller with views"; Mejino). There are scenes in which the union between human and non-human elements is most compelling, determining, as Alaimo states, "the extent to which the substance of the human is ultimately inseparable from 'the environment'" (2). For instance, during the tireless and despairing search for Reyes, powerful outdoor shots fuse the characters with the landscape: the colour of the clothes and hair worn by Candela and Reyes's son Yeray (Isaac B. Dos Santos) perfectly matches the volcanic rock, blending the landscape and human characters (episode 5, 00:41:03–00:43:55). In this scene, the identification of non-human matter that is particular to El Hierro with both a continental resident and an islander alludes to an ecological empathy with those who seek justice and those who suffer injustice regardless of origin, further suggesting that ecojustice forms an integral part of the *Hierro* series.

Through its volcanic and atmospheric behaviour, the island is revealed to be an active agent who hampers Daniel's efforts to hide the bodies and thus plays a decisive role in the plot structure. While at first Daniel benefits from the island's cooperation, the land ultimately denies him partnership as an accomplice. Hence, El Hierro's agency displaces Daniel's central position as the only actor in the course of events, suggesting, therefore, the imperative for humans to recognize their interdependency with the non-human environment.

In addition to the more predictable elements that the series associates with the island's bounded nature and its agentive quality, tension arising from the contradictory combination of the human characters' sense of enclosure and the relational properties displayed in the portrayal of the island underlines the capacity of matter to cross beyond the material in order to affect non-material domains such as emotions or perceptions. Places transcend their own materiality. They are, as environmentalist geographer Yi-Fu Tuan observes, "centers of felt value" (4). The island is presented as a "system of meaning" (Crane and Fletcher 12), which has an immeasurable impact on the spatial awareness of the islanders, especially those who have not had the opportunity to leave the tangible limits of the archipelago in pursuit of the remote geography of the continent. From the material geography of insular space marked by rugged borders, distant urban spaces are imagined through circulating discourses about city life as hubs for information, cultural life, or job opportunities and, as represented in the poster on Daniel's bedroom wall, entice some characters to go to the continent with a desire to strengthen human centredness by connecting more directly with human centres of power.

Moreover, Daniel's and other *herreño* characters' desire to migrate to continental cities, which house global corporations and centre political agendas that encourage infinite economic growth without consideration of ecological limits and where consumption of resources creates an unbalanced metabolism, contribute to extant ecologically unsustainable urban models. In her seminal *Sense of Place and Sense of Planet: The Environmental Imagination of the Global*, environmentalist Ursula Heise states, "[I]t is not just that local places have changed through increased connectivity but also the structures of perception, cognition and social expectations associated with them" (54). To put it another way, islands are in a trans-corporeal relationship with their environment beyond the level of their aquapelagic or material relational properties. In a world in which global connectedness has become all-pervasive, islanders' self-awareness is also dependent on their knowledge of other spaces propagated by media such as television or the Internet.

Viewed in this way, the absence of full camera shots of El Hierro plays a twofold purpose that reflects the paradoxical singularity that characterizes island living. In the eight episodes of the series, the viewer can see some characters moving to or from Tenerife. However, the island is never seen from afar, whether from the air or the sea (a shot could easily have shown Candela looking at the island from her plane seat, or El Hierro from the ship arriving from Tenerife). What is more, bird's-eye view shots, like those characterizing the first season of the television series *True Detective* (2014) or the Spanish-produced film *La isla mínima* (2014), are absent.[10] Instead, the camera is almost always positioned at eye level, a device that prevents the viewers from getting their bearings via a detached, superior outsider or a continentalist perspective and leads them to see the surroundings at an equal plane of the *herreños* themselves. In other words, the shots force a focus on the island from its own locality rather than its position vis-à-vis the Spanish mainland extending in this way a decentring of colonial power to a decentring of the human altogether.

In addition, the impossibility of the viewers to see the island as a whole underscores the reduced dimension of the space, and signals to the sea, to the island's borders. This camera recourse has the power to evoke Daniel's own sense of imprisonment, which will eventually trigger Fran's murder. Obviously, living on an island does not imply a certain predisposition to crime. Such a generalization would disregard the frustrating accumulation of circumstances that concur in this individual case. However, the fact that Daniel's resilience to these difficult circumstances is limited does call for an understanding of island living as the confluence of relational dimensions extending beyond the island itself. Undoubtedly, Daniel's desperation is founded on both his sense of imprisonment and his awareness of other places. Although this type of awareness, which has triggered the commission of a crime, is presented negatively in the series *Hierro*, deterritorial-izing local knowledge, as Heise states, "does not necessarily have to be detrimental for an environmental perspective, but on the contrary opens up new avenues into ecological consciousness" (55). *Hierro*'s diegetic presentation of the island in a trans-corporeal relationship with its environment does not stop at the island's materiality and agency. Rather, by highlighting Daniel's imaginative geography of the continent, the series acknowledges El Hierro's enmeshment in a vast and complex network of discursive, technological, or media-produced relations. This conceptualization has the potential to enrich our understanding of the current environmental challenges posed by new technological and digital media.

Presenting the Canarian island of El Hierro as an assemblage of enmeshed human and non-human agentive matter, the television series counters centuries-long devaluations of the isle that were grounded in its distance from the European continent and contemporary dismissal supported by market-based value calculations. Through diegetic and extradiegetic techniques of the visual medium that decentre the human and by portraying landscape and non-human agency conver-gently, the series' local perspective calls on viewers, whether from the continent or islands of Spain, to invoke an *herreño* ecoconsciousness. Ultimately, *Hierro* presents the viewer with a seemingly paradoxical combination of isolating and relational elements that together assert the trans-corporeality of matter, and in so doing, calls for a conceptual-ization of insularity as an entanglement of material and non-material intra-active relations that defy the notion of an island as a separate piece of land.

NOTES

1 Data taken in 2016 from the official web page of the Island's government ("Geografía").
2 For further information, see "Unesco Global Geopark."
3 This decision is the result of the "El Hierro 100% Renewable Project," an undertaking led by Gorona del Viento El Hierro, S.A., and including the El Hierro Island Council (65.82 per cent), the electric enterprise Endesa (23.21 per cent), the Canary Islands Institute of Technology (7.74 per cent), and the Autonomous Community of the Canary Islands (3.23 per cent). Renewable energy is obtained on the island from different natural resources such as wind, sunlight, and heat from geothermal or wave energy. For more details, see "Example of Sustainability."

4 While this chapter was in its final stage before publication, a second season was released in March 2021. All references in this chapter are to the first season.

5 All the translations from Spanish are by the authors.

6 The role of news, social, and other media in shaping environmental consciousness, sustaining the neoliberal status quo, or participating in ecological devastation beyond sensationalistic coverage of catastrophes is the subject of the recent field of ecomedia studies, which locates "media within a multiscalar resource economy of extraction, production, distribution, consumption, representation, wastage, and repurposing" that must be acknowledged and addressed in any effort to influence ecological amelioration (Starosielski and Walker 15). Along this vein, in her chapter for this collection, Carla Almanza Gálvez shows how Galician graphic fiction on the 2002 *Prestige* oil spill, for example, critiques the news media's significant role in buttressing fossil fuel dependence for economic expansion when short-lived reporting on environmental causalities ignores long-term effects.

7 Historically, both El Hierro and Fuerteventura have been utilized as places of banishment for political dissidents. The Spanish writer Miguel de Unamuno, for instance, was confined for four months in Fuerteventura during Primo de Rivera's dictatorship in 1924. Another example was that of Leandro Pérez, the first doctor in El Hierro. He came to the island as an exile in the nineteenth century ("History of El Hierro").

8 Bonnie Gasior explores the colonialist roots of this mainlander standpoint in her reading for this collection of Lope de Vega's Golden Age play about the Guanche people's integration with the Tenerife environment and critique of the Spanish conquest. Imperialist interruptions of earthly cadences are likewise explored in this volume by John Beusterien, whose chapter discusses bird caging in the sixteenth century, in order to highlight imperialist rupture of the earth's polyrhythms for the presumed purpose of enhancing human health.

9 The Coira brothers' portrayal of El Hierro as a living entity unto itself operates in contrast to recent film adaptations by Fernando González Molina of Dolores Redondo's homonymous crime novels *El guardián invisible* (2017), *Legado en los huesos* (2019), and *Ofrenda a la tormenta* (2020). Whereas these police dramas, known as the *Baztán Trilogy*, may be lauded for drawing critical attention to a long history of strong women, their depiction of the Baztán Valley remains human-centred and nature a mere extension of human emotions.

10 The similarities between the film *La isla mínima* and the first season of the television series *True Detective* are striking and point to a change in television language, which media scholar Jason Mittell has termed *complex*

TV. At first glance, and in very simple terms, complex TV involves a more novelistic or even cinematic language style, especially in serial television. For more information about the similarities between *La isla mínima* and *True Detective*, see "Review: Marshland."

WORKS CITED AND CONSULTED

Alaimo, Stacy. *Bodily Natures: Science, Environment, and the Material Self.* Indiana UP, 2010.

Barad, Karen. "Intra-actions." Interview with Adam Kleinman. *Mousse,* vol. 34, 2012, pp. 76–81, https://www.academia.edu/1857617/Intra-actions_Interview_of_Karen_Barad_by_Adam_Kleinmann.

Barad, Karen. *Meeting the Universe Halfway: Quantum Physics and the Entanglement of Matter and Meaning.* Duke UP, 2007.

Bennett, Jane. *Vibrant Matter: A Political Ecology of Things.* Duke UP, 2010.

Braidotti, Rosi. "Writing as a Nomadic Subject." *Comparative Critical Studies,* vol. 11, nos. 2–3, 2014, pp. 163–84. *Edinburgh University Press,* https://doi.org/10.3366/ccs.2014.0122.

Crane, Ralph, and Lisa Fletcher. *Island Genres, Genre Islands: Conceptualisation and Representation in Popular Fiction.* Rowman & Littlefield, 2017.

Death in Paradise. Created by Robert Thorogood, Red Planet Pictures /Atlantique Productions/Kudo/France Télévision, 2011.

Donne, John. "XVII. MEDITATION." *Devotions: Upon Emergent Occasions, Together with Death's Duel.* 1624. U of Michigan P, 1959, pp. 108–9.

"Geografía." *Portal Web de El Cabildo del Hierro,* https://www.elhierro.es/geografia. Accessed 9 Feb. 2023.

El guardián invisible. Directed by Fernando González Molina, Nostromo Pictures/Atresmedia Cine, 2017.

Hayward, Philip. "Aquapelagos and Aquapelagic Assemblages." *Shima: The International Journal of Research into Island Cultures,* vol. 6, no. 1, 2012, pp. 1–10.

Hayward, Philip. "The Constitution of Assemblages and the Aquapelagality of Haida Gwaii." *Shima: The International Journal of Research into Island Cultures,* vol. 6, no. 2, 2012, pp. 1–14.

Heise, Ursula. *Sense of Place and Sense of Planet: The Environmental Imagination of the Global.* Oxford UP, 2008.

Hierro. Created by Pepe Coira and Jorge Coira, Movistar+/Portocabo/Atlantique Productions/Arte France, 2019.

"El Hierro, an Example of Sustainability." *Endesa,* 28 Oct. 2016, https://www.endesa.com/en/projects/all-projects/energy-transition/renewable-energies/el-hierro-renewable-sustainability.

"El Hierro Unesco Global Geopark (Spain): The Island of a 1000 Volcanoes." *Unesco Global Geoparks*, 2017, https://webarchive.unesco.org/web/20180706003105/http:/www.unesco.org/new/en/natural-sciences/environment/earth-sciences/unesco-global-geoparks/list-of-unesco-global-geoparks/spain/el-hierro/.

"History of El Hierro." *El Hierro*, https://elhierro.travel/en/discover/history-el-hierro/. Accessed 9 Feb. 2023.

Iovino, Serenella, and Serpil Oppermann. "Introduction: Stories Come to Matter." *Material Ecocriticism*, edited by Serenella Iovino and Serpil Oppermann, Indiana UP, 2014, pp. 1–17.

La isla mínima. Directed by Alberto Rodríguez, Atípica Films/Sacromonte Films/Atresmedia Cine/Canal + España, 2014. DVD, Altitude Film Distribution.

Legado en los huesos. Directed by Fernando González Molina, Atresmedia Cine/Nadcon Film/Nostromo Pictures/ARTE/ZDF, 2019.

Maltese. Il Romanzo del Commissario. Directed by Gianluca Maria Tavarelli, Rai Fiction/Palomar, 2017.

Mejino, Lorenzo. "Hierro: El Magnífico 'crimen con vistas' que descubre una isla maravillosa." *El Diario Vasco*, 31 July 2019, https://blogs.diariovasco.com/series-gourmets/2019/07/31/hierro-el-magnifico-crimen-con-vistas-que-descubre-una-isla-maravillosa/.

Mittel, Jason. *Complex TV: The Poetics of Contemporary Television Storytelling*. New York UP, 2015.

Monforte, Javier. "What Is New in New Materialism for a Newcomer?" *Qualitative Research in Sport, Exercise and Health*, vol. 10, no. 3, 2018, pp. 378–90. *Taylor & Francis Online*, https://doi.org/10.1080/2159676X.2018.1428678.

Movistar+. *Hierro*. Press release. https://comunicacion.movistarplus.es/wp-content/uploads/2019/05/Hierro_dossier-small.pdf. Accessed 17 Apr. 2023.

Ofrenda a la tormenta. Directed by Fernando González Molina, Atresmedia Cine/Nadcon Film/Nostromo Pictures/ARTE/ZDF, 2020.

Pugh, Jonathan. "Relationality and Island Studies in the Anthropocene." *Island Studies Journal*, vol. 13, no. 2, 2018, pp. 93–110, https://doi.org/10.24043/isj.48.

"Review: Marshland (La isla mínima)." *Little Vittles*, 28 June 2015, https://literaryvittles.wordpress.com/2015/06/28/review-marshland-la-isla-minima/.

Said, Edward. *Orientalism*. Penguin, 1987.

Starosielski, Nicole, and Janet Walker. *Sustainable Media: Critical Approaches to Media and Environment*. Routledge, 2016.

Todorov, Tzetan. "The Typology of Detective Fiction." *The Poetics of Prose*, Blackwell, 1977, pp. 42–52.

True Detective. Created by Nic Pizzolatto, season 1, HBO, 2014.

Tuan, Yi-Fu. *Topophilia: A Study of Environmental Perception, Attitudes, and Values.* Prentice-Hall, 1974.

Viera y Clavijo, José de. *Historia de Canarias.* 1772. Biblioteca Básica Canaria, 1991.

Chapter Thirteen

¡El toro no entiende de toreo! Taurine Naturecultures, Wenceslao Fernández Flórez's Anti-Taurine Essays, and the Emergence of Post-Humanist Views of Animals in Spain

DANIEL ARES-LÓPEZ

Introduction

This essay explores the cultural history of *tauromaquia* (which can be translated as "tauromachy" or "bullfighting") in modern Spain. The concept of *tauromaquia* used here encompasses a variety of interrelated material-semiotic practices (such as writing about bullfighting, writing polemically against it, breeding fighting bulls, and performing at bullfights) that include the presence and inter-actions of living beings from different species (humans, bovines, and horses). I am specifically concerned with the ways the intellectual exploration and critique of human-animal relations in modern Spain have been overlooked or disregarded by literary critics and cultural and literary historians.[1] As we will see, the necessary rescue from oblivion of Wenceslao Fernández Flórez's (1885–1964) brilliant literary work on animals – unique in the context of twentieth-century Spain – requires not only putting aside any facile historical judgment on its author's contradictory biography and public persona (Llera 13–30; Mainer 16) but also reading it with an unprejudiced appreciation of the writer's intellectual curiosity about animals and of his post-humanist sensibilities to our historical engagements with them.

I use the terms *material-semiotic, inter-action,* and *multispecies* here because I share the materialist conviction – widely accepted in the environmental humanities and social sciences as well as in fields like biosemiotics – that all semiotic processes arise from, and are ontologically ingrained in, the materiality of the world and of the embodied, evolving, and inter-acting lifeforms that inhabit the earth (Wheeler; Haraway,

Species; Barad; DeLanda and Harman; Margulis and Sagan). If one is congruent with this materialist and relational ontological conviction, semiosis and communication cannot be considered a uniquely human trait but an attribute of all organic life and the ecosystems of which they are part. At the same time, what we call modern cultures and societies are made up not only of humans but also of agentive inorganic objects (e.g., technologies) and morphologically heterogeneous living beings (such as plants, animals, and microorganisms) who inter-act and coevolve – or go extinct – *with* people as well as among themselves in material environments (Haraway, *Species*; Latour, *Reassembling*; Law). To put it in simpler terms: we humans are animals who belong to the biosphere and, as such, we become what we are (culturally, physically, and cognitively) through constant inter-actions with many other living beings and, more broadly, the material world that surrounds and penetrates us. While the concept of the Anthropocene reminds us that humans – and especially those with political, economic, and military power – have radically transformed natural objects and processes at a global scale, it is no less true that these natural objects and processes (physical, chemical, biological, etc.) also participate in the evolving configuration of societies to the point that the conventional division between the natural and the cultural or social becomes inadequate. For that reason, I use the term natureculture to refer to *tauromaquia* in this essay to name an assemblage of cultural and biological entities (such as animal bodies, social practices, and cultural meanings and values ascribed to particular animals) that have coevolved in constant inter-action (Latour, *Reassembling*; Law; Haraway, *Species* and *Simians*; Ares-López; Latour, *Modern*).

In the first section of the essay, I introduce the intellectual figure of Fernández Flórez and provide an outline of his forgotten literary work on animals in genres such as comic journalistic essay and fiction. The second section provides an overview of *tauromaquia* as a set of material-semiotic practices aimed to produce, reproduce, and sustain aggressive behaviour in bovines and to use this behaviour (through strict regulations and in a semi-controlled way) to conjure human feelings traditionally associated with masculinity in Western patriarchal societies, such as self-control over fear, physical domination of other beings, and admiration for courage and bravery (Marvin 142; De Haro and Marvin 100). This biocultural manufacturing and exploitative use of bovine aggressiveness, termed *bravura* ("bravery"), also aims to generate excitement and aesthetic pleasure in audiences, as well as huge economic profits and social recognition for the most conspicuous bullfighters and promoters (Marvin 90, 106–10; Mitchell 85–9; De

Haro and Marvin 95–8; Shubert 17–52). To outline the historical material and discursive terrain from which Fernández Flórez's comic anti-taurine writing emerged, this section will also sketch the antagonizing discourses and imaginaries that configured *tauromaquia* as a polemical field for intellectual debates in modern Spain (Beilin 48–105; Cambria; Codina Segovia).

The third section consists of an analysis of Fernández Flórez's comic essays on bullfighting that were first published in well-known Spanish magazines from the 1920s to the 1950s and then compiled in the book *El toro, el torero y el gato* (*The Bull, the Bullfighter, and the Cat*, 1946, second edition in 1952). This interpretation situates Fernández Flórez's work within twentieth-century Spain's (*anti*)*tauromaquia* ("anti-bullfighting") traditions of thought and practice and, more generally, within modern Spain's thinking about animals and human-animal relations.[2] Fernández Flórez's comic anti-taurine essays must be taken quite seriously, not only as the most lucid and subversive anti-taurine writing in modern Spain's literary history, but also as a work that inaugurated post-humanist forms of thinking and feeling about animals and human-animal relations in Spain. These are forms of thinking-feeling (*sentipensar*) that recognize the existence, value, and dignity of non-human others who possess a corporeal morphology and ways of experiencing the world that are relatively different, but not biologically and ontologically severed, from ours.[3]

Animals, Animality, and Human-Animal Relations in the Work of Fernández Flórez

The place of Fernández Flórez in twentieth-century Spain's cultural and literary history has been complex and contradictory. During his writing career from the 1910s to the 1960s, he was one of the most popular novelists and political journalists in Spain (Mainer 16–17). In the decades before the civil war, his parliamentary chronicles for the Madrilenian conservative newspaper *ABC* were celebrated for his witty use of satirical humour (Llera 31–53). His equally successful novels, some of which became bestsellers and were highly popular among the urban middle and lower-middle classes, skilfully combine naturalist and modernist elements with dark humour to provide a sceptical and pessimistic view of Spain's urban and rural society (Mainer 97–103). Fernández Flórez's anti-communist stance and his critical views of the leftist Spanish governments in 1931–3 and 1936, advertised through his work as a political reporter for *ABC*, put him in a difficult position in Republican-controlled Madrid at the outbreak of the civil war. He was accepted as a refugee at the Dutch embassy in Madrid and, years later, wrote an unsuccessful novel chronicling the Red Terror, to which he was subjected during the war (Mainer 35–36; Llera 22–4). Because of his experience as a journalist for *ABC* and his personal troubles in wartime Madrid, he was able to comfortably resume his literary and journalist activity once Francisco Franco's reactionary nationalist-Catholic regime took absolute control of the Spanish state (Mainer 36–42).

The few scholars who have studied Fernández Flórez lament the lack of academic interest in his work and his invisibility in Spain's literary historiography, in contradiction with his lifetime success as a writer and enhanced visibility from dozens of films based on his novels (López Criado; Llera 13–30; Mainer 43–8). According to the literary critic José Antonio Llera, this absence is due to the double dismissal of Fernández Flórez's writings as both popular and reactionary. However, the writings, thought, and public persona of Fernández Flórez escape the clear-cut categorizations that literary and cultural historians often keep at hand as part of their methodological and epistemological toolbox. The writer was politically conservative and socially elitist, but he was also a freethinker with views that Spanish conservatives in the twentieth century regarded with suspicion or hostility. He was anti-militaristic, a supporter of women's rights, an adherent to Darwinian evolutionism, and, ultimately, a humorist fairly sceptical of subjecting society to any particular moral order (Llera 13–30).

There is also an important aspect of Fernández Flórez's work to which no critic seems to have paid attention: he wrote about animals and human-animal relations in many of his essays and short stories, and he did it in ways that single him out among twentieth-century Spanish writers and intellectuals. In many of his essays and stories, the presence of animal characters and voices is not laden with the task of representing symbolically or metaphorically human affairs. Rather, they manifest a genuine and empathic curiosity and concern about animal life as an independent biological and existential other, which is not ontologically separated from human animals.[4] He was probably the only well-known Spanish writer of his time who explored the possibility of writing about non-human animals as the planetary fellows and evolutionary relatives of human animals. While other Spanish writers of Fernández Flórez's generation, such as Juan Ramón Jiménez and Gabriel Miró, produced very sensible representations of animal characters, none of their works questioned the humanist and anthropocentric foundations of modern Western culture as he did in some of his fictional and journalistic works. Fernández Flórez conceived and represented non-human animals' embodied experience, as well as their relationships with humans, non-anthropocentrically, that is, by imagining what the world would be like on their own terms.

In the 1924 article "Perros y gatos" ("Dogs and Cats"), Fernández Flórez presents himself as a modern urban animal lover and pet owner: "Confesaré ante todo que amo a los animales y que procuro no hacerles mal. Mantengo a un perro y a un gato … y he conseguido, con el ejemplo de mis amabilidades, que no riñan jamás" ("I will confess that I love animals and I try not to harm them. I have a dog and a cat … and I have achieved, by setting an example with my kindness, that they don't ever fight among themselves"; *Perros* 7). In several of his pre-war articles, he also supports the precarious and underfunded activist efforts of Madrid's Sociedad Protectora de Animales ("Society for the Protection of Animals") to protect animals from human violence and denounces the senseless violence to which feral cats and some working animals were subjected in Spain's capital (*Perros* 9–13, 14–19, 53–6). These articles have historical interest because they point to the origins of modern urban middle-class identities and activism associated with the practice of living with domestic companion animals and recognize urban Spain as a multispecies society that includes vulnerable non-human inhabitants in need of institutional protection.

The significance of Fernández Flórez's best writing on animals, however, goes well beyond this historical interest. In some of his articles and short stories we find a materialist and evolutionary view of organic life derived from Darwin and his followers as well as an intellectually provocative relativist recognition of the diverse ways in which animals from different species, humans included, experience reality as embodied beings. This view is akin to, and may well have been influenced by, the groundbreaking theoretical vision of the Baltic German biologist Jakob von Uexküll, some of whose works were translated and published in Spain in the 1930s and circulated in Madrilenian intellectual circles before the civil war (Utekhin). In one of his best articles on animals, "Las redes de la araña" ("The Spider's Webs"), Fernández Flórez criticizes with witty irony the humanist – or human-chauvinist – certitudes that sustain modern Western thought:

[Y]o no figuro entre aquellos que preconizan la superioridad del hombre entre todos los seres que pueblan el mundo. Sé perfectamente que todos tenemos por ascendiente común un anélido marino, y guardo profunda consideración a mis parientes, por remotos que sean … [N]o creo que nos asista ningún derecho a ser vanidoso, porque cada especie animal tiene singularidades que no podemos aventajar … Más de una vez me he preguntado adónde llegaría nuestro orgullo si fuésemos capaces de fosforecer, como algunos animales oceánicos. ¡oh, qué cruelmente nos bur-laríamos entonces de los seres … que tuviesen que utilizar la luz eléctrica para ver en las sombras!

(I am not one of those who affirm the superiority of man above all the beings that populate the world. I know perfectly well that we all have a marine annelid as our ancestor, and I hold in high regard my relatives, no matter how remote they are … I do not think that we are entitled to be con-ceited, because each animal species possesses singularities that we cannot surpass … More than once I have asked myself how proud we would be if we possessed bioluminescence, like some oceanic animals. Oh, with what cruelty we would then deride those beings … which need to use electric light to see in the dark!; *Perros* 27–8)

In "El amigo perro" ("Our Dog Friend") a similar scorn is directed to the anthropocentric beliefs and attitudes that underpin the modernizing and colonizing project of subjecting all the earth's life forms and matter to humans' needs and to the requirements of industry and commerce:

[N]uestro egocentrismo … se resiste a admitir que ni el más pequeño detalle de cuanto ha sido creado puede tener otra finalidad que la de ser-virnos; así las abejas hacen miel para que la gustemos, y las estrellas están colgadas allá arriba, en el techo del cielo, para que los poetas las utili-cen en sus imágenes, y suponemos que la marta cibelina, en cuanto llega a cierta edad, anda muy preocupada, diciéndose: «¿Cuándo vendrán a arrancarme esta piel que ya está a punto para formar parte de un gabán de señora?»

(Our egocentrism … cannot admit that even the smallest detail of what has been created has a different aim than to serve us; thus, bees make honey for us to savour, and the stars hang up there, in the ceiling that is the sky, for poets to use as images, and we suppose that the sable, when she gets old, says to herself with concern: "When will they come to tear this fur from me, since it is already in its prime to make a women's fur coat?"; *Perros* 40)

The satirical and humorous tone of these passages must not keep us from reading them as an account of corporeal existence – both human and other-than-human – in evolutionary, non-anthropocentric, and multispecies ways; that is, in terms that recognize the interwoven evo-lutionary history of life on earth and account for the fact that inhabit-ing the world is a multifarious world-making activity grounded in the particular bodily configurations, cognitive apparatus, and interests of each species.

In his late novel *El bosque animado* (*The Animated Forest*, 1942), Fernández Flórez provides his most lyrical meditations on non-human life and the relations between humans and other life forms. In the first chapter, which can be read independently as an essay on environmental philosophy illustrated with a fable-like moral tale, we find a marvellous description of a primeval Iberian Atlantic forest ecosystem from the phenomenological perspective of a person visiting in the forest:

> Donde fijáis vuestra mirada divisáis ramas estremecidas, troncos recios, verdor; donde fijáis vuestro pie dobláis hierbas que después procuran reincorporarse con el apocado esfuerzo doloroso de hombrecillos desriñonados; donde llevéis vuestra presencia habrá un sobresalto más o menos perceptible de seres que huyen entre el follaje ... de insectos que se deslizan entre vuestros zapatos, con la prisa de todas sus patitas entorpecidas por los obstáculos de aquella selva virgen que para ellos representan los musgos, las zarzas, los brezos, los helechos.

> (Wherever you fix your gaze, you see trembling branches, sturdy trunks, greenery; wherever your foot lands, you crumple grasses that later try to unfold themselves with the slight and painful effort of little, hunched old men; wherever you carry your presence there will be a more or less perceptible commotion of beings fleeing through the foliage ... of insects that slide between your shoes, with the rush of all their little legs hindered by the obstacles of that virgin forest, which, for them, is made up of mosses, brambles, heather, and ferns; *Bosque* 39)

Significantly, this description of the lived experience of a human visiting the forest also includes some sentences that suggest how the forest's insects "that slide between [one's] shoes" would experience this environment as a virgin rainforest full of gigantic plants and obstacles. In other chapters of the novel, Fernández Flórez allows animal characters of different species to speak for themselves in a more anthropomorphic fashion. Yet this technique, typically associated with children's literature and film, is employed in a satirical and reflective way to question the anthropocentrism and contempt for animal and vegetal others that characterize the management of the national territory and its ecosystems as a stockpile of resources for economic development, which obsessed Spanish elites during and after Franco's dictatorship (Ramos Gorostiza; Swyngedouw).[5]

The qualities displayed by Fernández Flórez in his writing about animals, including his recognition of non-human animals as others who belong to our own biological kingdom, his ethical stance against cruelty to animals in Spain's cities, and his ability to see the world from diverse biological perspectives with a satirical flair, are also displayed in his comic anti-bullfighting texts with brilliantly pungent results. But before we explore those texts, we need to clarify what bullfighting is from a historical material-semiotic perspective and to which debates and traditions of thought this activity gave rise in twentieth-century Spain.

The Bravery and the Flesh: Bullfighting as Taurine Natureculture and Material Semiosis

What is bullfighting? Reading the most thoughtful and well-researched books on this topic does not provide a clear answer to this question. Because disciplinary perspectives on and groups' relationships with bullfighting vary greatly, the practice is characterized in a myriad of ways: a public performance, a religious-like ritual, an urban spectacle, part of the entertainment industry in urban Spain, a folk tradition – Spain's *fiesta nacional* ("national celebration") – a European blood sport, and more. In fact, the different groups most concerned with it (such as aficionados, animal-rights activists, and the veterinarians and politicians that side with one or the other of the first two groups) would strongly disagree on any clear-cut definition of bullfighting. To this point, many people in Spain and abroad would question the definition of *toreo* as "el arte de torear" ("the art of bullfighting") in the dictionary of the Real Academia Española and would rather consider it as a form of torture (Beilin 21–3; Viestenz 143–6).

Since its origins in the eighteenth century, bullfighting in Spain has been an object of intense governmental scrutiny and historiographical inquiry. In France and the Anglophone world it has also been an exoticized object of fascination for erudite travellers and tourists (such as Ernest Hemingway) and an alluring research topic for anthropologists. What makes bullfighting impossible to define, however, is not its complexity as a cultural practice but the fact that, at different times in modern Iberian history, it has been the subject of incensed public debates that involved cultural, ethical, and political arguments. As environmental humanist Katarzyna Beilin has suggested (45), the intents of some American anthropologists to study bullfighting objectively, from an emic ethnographic perspective and as a manifestation of the idiosyncrasy of Spanish culture, have failed because they have omitted one key consideration: its inherent polemical and contested nature within modern

Iberian culture(s) and society(ies). If Spain has developed a strong taurine culture – or, rather, subculture – around the practice of bullfighting, it has also developed an anti-taurine one (Beilin; Viestenz 143–6; Codina Segovia; Brandes). In his detailed historiographical account of Spanish anti-taurine thought, Codina Segovia shows that anti-bullfighting has been present in Spain's public sphere as a sentiment, civic discourse, and activist stance for the entirety of its modern history. In some periods, this presence of anti-taurinism has been more visible, at other times much less so, often depending on the ebbs and flows in the popularity and political support enjoyed by bullfighting. In any case, it has always been there and signals a defining tension that should inform any cultural-historical account of Spanish bullfighting.

The definition of bullfighting I will sketch here does not shy away from the difficulties of its complexity, disciplinary multi-sidedness, or polemical nature, but rather builds upon them. Yet, as a materialist who believes that any discourse or semiotic process stems from and circulates through embodied beings and material environments without ever transcending them, I will not shy away from an objective materialist definition of bullfighting either. Objectivity must be understood here, though, not in the conventional Cartesian-positivist sense that divides immaterial knowing subjects from material objects but rather as a situated knowledge that transcends those divisions (Haraway, "Game"); that is, the situated knowledge of an embodied being (myself) that belongs to the earth and, like everyone, is enmeshed in the ecological material-semiotic entanglements of the biosphere. Though this theoretical stance may at first glance seem far removed from the topic under discussion here, I consider it crucial when dealing with the topic of animal pain and physical and psychological stress in bullfighting. In this essay I talk about animals (bovines, horses, and humans) not as a disembodied rational mind but as a sentient animal myself; as one who shares the biosphere with them, who shares an evolutionary history with them, and who possesses a central nervous system that is very similar to those of other mammals.

What is bullfighting, then? Let us start with a terminological adjustment. Following the suggestion of the anthropologist Garry Marvin, I will from now on use the Spanish term *tauromaquia* because the English term bullfighting does not reflect well what the performance of *toreo* is about for its audience or its participants: not a fight but a public display of male bravery, domination over animals, and self-control (133–6). The term *tauromaquia* also more appropriately signals bullfighting as a contested discursive field in modern Spain's political and intellectual history.

As Adrian Shubert has shown in his masterful historiographical work on this subject, *tauromaquia* does not only take place in bullrings where the *toreros* ("bullfighters") tease, harass, poke, and stab unnaturally aggressive bovines before an audience. That is only the tip of the economic, social, cultural, political, and, in my view, biological and environmental iceberg. *Tauromaquia* must be considered first and foremost as a set of diverse practices that take place across multiple interconnected spaces, both rural and urban. Among them we find the large ranches of Andalucía or Castile, where *toros de lidia* ("fighting bulls") are bred and raised for years with great care and financial expense; the newsrooms of national and regional newspapers from which the specialized taurine critics emit the chronicles of the *corridas* ("bullfights") that may contribute to building or destroying bullfighters' and bull breeders' reputations; the desks of intellectuals who write passionately either about the refined aesthetic pleasures and mythic origins of bullfighting or about its degrading condition as a national social and moral ill; and the parliament's podiums, from which *tauromaquia* and the laws that regulate its practice are discussed (Shubert). Among all those places we find abundant flows of ideas, animal and human bodies, and, as Shubert makes clear, money and financial interests. Therefore, *tauromaquia* must be understood as an activity that connects Spain's rural economies with politics, with the modern urban industry of mass entertainment for locals and tourists, and with cultural production both high and low, such as literary essays, novels, poetry, popular songs, newspaper articles, and taurine chronicles (Shubert 17–52). Since the early and mid twentieth century, we must also add to this list the films, television shows, and colour features in gossip magazines about the private lives of bullfighters.

Another key aspect of *tauromaquia* is that it is not a human social or cultural activity but one that involves the closely interrelated actions of animals from diverse species: mainly humans, bovines, and horses. It is in this sense that we may use the adjectives *multispecies, naturecultural,* or *biocultural* to refer to what happens in *tauromaquia* at different stages of the production of the *toreo* as a mass spectacle; namely, during the selective breeding and technical rearing of bovine bodies to manufacture their body shape and future aggressive behaviour in the bullring, and in the bullfighters' management and exploitative use of that bioculturally manufactured aggressive behaviour (Marvin 85–105, 128–42). As is well known, this is performed through an established set of techniques, which include: placing the animal – raised in rural *dehesas* (Iberian cattle ranches) – within the enclosed space of the bullring without any previous experience of this urban built environment; adjusting the bullfighters' corporeal movements to the animal's charge; using a cape to deceive and harass the animal; and piercing and spearing him in the lower neck at various times to intensify or slow his aggressive behaviour (Marvin 85–105, 1–35). The individual bullfight typically concludes when the bull is killed with a sword thrust at his back. On very rare occasions, though, a bull that shows and sustains an exceptionally aggressive behaviour that benefited the bullfighter's performance may be pardoned and allowed to return alive to the ranch.

The horses ridden by the picadors, who lance the bulls in the back, have a much less visible role than the bulls in the *corrida*, but their bodies are equally subjected to acute stress and physical pain because they receive on their bodies the charge of fighting bulls that outweigh them. Until the 1930s, horses were exposed to the bulls' horns without any protection and very often died in the ring, disembowelled, with their intestines and other internal organs hanging from their bodies or lying on the ground, exposed to public view before they were taken away. This image of the agonizing disembowelled horse has been used with a very intense dramatic effect in some of the best Spanish anti-taurine literary works of the early twentieth century: Vicente Blasco Ibañez's masterful naturalist novel *Sangre y arena* (1908), Eugenio Noel's influential article "El caballo del picador" (Beilin 101–2), and, as we will see, Fernández Flórez's pre-war darkly comic anti-taurine essays.

Closely related to *tauromaquia* as a disputed discursive field and as a biosocial manufacturing of aggressive animal bodies is the contested biocultural process of forming material-semiotic assemblages made up of bodies and meanings. This double process attaches values or affects to supposedly natural animal bodies (e.g., attaching the qualities of bravery and nobility to the Spanish *toro de lidia*) and, simultaneously, manipulates carefully and incessantly their morphology and behaviour to make them incarnate – unwittingly and more or less convincingly – those imposed meanings (De Haro and Marvin 95–101). As Marvin has convincingly demonstrated in his research on bullfighting, the most important aim of the *corrida* is to generate human emotions traditionally associated with maleness, male values, and male bonding in Western patriarchal societies: self-control over fear at potentially life-threatening situations, admiration for male courage and bravery, and a sense of domination over supposedly wild animals (143–65). There is also an aesthetic biocultural component in the *corrida* because the control of the bull's dangerous charges and the self-control of the bullfighter's own fear needs to be performed by means of a repertoire of slow and graceful movements. Indeed, the main aim of these slow ballet-like movements as the bull charges is to exhibit not the bullfighter's skills but their fearless self-control and dominion over an animal perceived as wild and brave (Marvin 131–42; De Haro and Marvin 95–101). If the *torero* is able to do that, they will arouse enthusiastic feelings of empathy and admiration in the audience and the *corrida* will be deemed a success by the bullfighter, bull breeder, and aficionados. Conversely, if the audience notices that the bullfighter's movements or gestures show nervousness, intimidation, or fear, they may boo and heckle them, and may even throw the stands' cushions, food, or other objects at them (Marvin 141–2). The audience may proffer a similar treatment on the fighting bull who acts *manso* ("tame or domesticated") and does not show the sustained hyper-aggressive behaviour associated with the concept of *bravo* ("brave"; Marvin 99–105).

The biocultural material-semiotic construction of bodies in *tauromaquia*, therefore, attaches patriarchal meanings, values, and emotions to both human and animal bodies. The most important one is bravery, seen as a noble and male instinct of aggression in the case of the bovines, and as the ability to control emotions while facing a dangerous beast in the case of the bullfighter (De Haro and Marvin 96–8; Marvin 102, 131–9). These attachments of meanings, values, and emotions to bodies have real material consequences for bovines and humans. The first are selectively bred in the countryside to be performed and killed in cities, while the second are trained to risk their lives in a graceful and confident manner for money and social prestige. This material-semiotic construction, however, is inherently unstable and can collapse in many ways, sometimes contributing to the drama and mythology of bullfighting. This is the case, for example, when an apparently brave bullfighting star like Manolete or Paquirri becomes a perceived legend after being gored by a bull in some second-rate bullfight. Other collapses of *tauromaquia* as a material-semiotic construction are more troublesome for its continued existence and take the form of public critical interrogations or subversions of the meanings, values, and emotions that *tauromaquia* attaches to living and dying bodies. This is precisely what Spanish anti-taurine intellectuals and activists have been doing since the nineteenth century: questioning the patriarchal ethos of *tauromaquia* by representing the fighting bull as a vulnerable and suffering body (Beilin 174–85). Performances in public spaces, publicity campaigns, and detailed scientific reports have provided empirical evidence of the intense pain and stress experienced by bovines during the bullfight (Beilin 174–85).[6]

While it is doubtful that Fernández Flórez considered himself an abolitionist anti-taurine activist, his early and mid-twentieth-century comic anti-taurine essays – published during the golden age of bullfighting in terms of popularity, social influence, and political support – seem to share this movement's goal of demolishing the material-semiotic edifice of *tauromaquia* by subverting the meanings, values, and affects that it attaches to animals' and humans' bodies. In any case, his work develops within an Iberian anti-taurine intellectual tradition that dates back to the eighteenth century. In the long list of affiliates to this intellectual tradition, we find celebrated names in modern Spain's cultural history, such as the romantic painter Francisco de Goya, the nineteenth-century liberal writer Mariano José de Larra, and contemporaries of Fernández Flórez like Eugenio Noel and Miguel de Unamuno (Beilin 78–104; Codina Segovia 78–9, 84–8).

Blood, Words, and Guts: Fernández Flórez's Discursive Subversion and Materialist Reframing of *Tauromaquia*

The comic anti-taurine essays that Fernández Flórez published between the 1920s and the 1950s, mostly in the weekly art and literary magazine *Blanco y negro* but also in the monthly comic magazine *La Codorniz*, were later compiled as a parodic treatise on bullfighting in the volume *El toro, el torero y el gato* (Llera 67–8). Those essays present a calculated discursive intervention within Spain's taurine culture of the first half of the twentieth century, a period in which bullfighters such as Belmonte and, after the civil war, Manolete acquired the status of popular heroes and national myths (Shubert). Both as a mass-entertainment industry and as a public discourse, *tauromaquia* was at its peak during this period, not only in Spain but also – thanks to Hollywood bullfighting films, the opening of Spain to mass tourism, and the publicity that American celebrity aficionados gave to the *fiesta* – in the United States and Western Europe.

Fernández Flórez's comic anti-taurine essays undermine *tauromaquia* as a material-semiotic assemblage of bodies, discourse, and affects by means of rhetorical strategies that one can trace back to prominent Spanish literary and cultural traditions (such as Goya's grotesque or darkly comic representations of violence and social ills and Larra's satirical criticism of social customs) and to Spain's twentieth-century literary subculture of absurdist comic writing practised by Jardiel Poncela, Miguel Mihura, and other collaborators of the comic magazine *La Codorniz*. In his writing, these rhetorical strategies perform two actions. First, they subvert *tauromaquia* as an anthropocentric performative and discursive practice, that is, a fixed tradition or ritual that involves constantly talking about animals and inter-acting with them but that blocks any understanding of those animals beyond some fixed narrow terms. Second, they discursively reframe *tauromaquia* in order to show it not as a spiritual or aesthetic experience but as a multispecies material practice that involves the brutal piercing and evisceration of sentient animal bodies.

In the introductory chapter of *El toro, el torero y el gato*, Fernández Flórez affirms that he is not "un enemigo de las corridas de toros" ("an enemy of bullfighting"). He distances himself from the main arguments deployed against *tauromaquia* by fellow anti-taurine intellectuals such as Noel: "[no] creo que hayamos de atribuir a [las corridas] cuantas desgracias nos ocurrieron, nos ocurren y nos han de ocurrir [ni] admito que tengan relación ni congruencia con nuestra idiosincrasia [nacional]" ("[I do not] believe that we should attribute to [the bullfights] all the misfortunes that happened, happen, and will happen to us[; nor do] I admit that they are related to, or congruent with, our [national] idiosyncrasy"; 6). His main argument against *tauromaquia* is that it constitutes a boring spectacle in which cruelty is put "al servicio del tedio" ("to the service of tedium"; 6). Later in the essay, he presents himself not as an anti-taurine polemicist but as a reformer of bullfighting: "las corridas son monótonas, aburridas, fatigosas; si se las quiere conservar, ha de ser modificándolas. No nos dejemos alucinar por la rutina de un tradicionalismo que está ya reclamando su jubilación; contemplemos con ojos nuevos el viejo espectáculo" ("the bullfights are monotonous, boring, tiring; if we want to keep them, we have to modify them. Let's not be deluded by the routine of a traditionalism that is already claiming its retirement; let us contemplate with new eyes the old spectacle"; 8). In the next paragraph, he comments on his aptitudes and credentials for this task:

> Carezco de precursores y también de prejuicios … Otra de mis ventajas es que sólo aparecí por las plazas cuando las circunstancias me obligaron, lo que quiere decir que conservo íntegra mi facultad de observación, ya que es sabido que el hábito la entorpece. Este contacto mío con los tendidos duró apenas lo necesario para abastecer de motivos mis cavilaciones; fui, bostecé y me retiré a filosofar.
>
> (I lack precursors as well as prejudices … Another of my advantages is that I only showed up in the bullrings when circumstances forced me, which means that I have kept my powers of observation intact, since it is known that habit hinders them. My contact with the rows of seats lasted just long enough to supply my musings with motives; I went, I yawned, and I retired to philosophize; *El toro* 8–9)

Although these statements must be read as comic writing, or *humorismo*, Fernández Flórez also positions himself rather seriously vis-à-vis *tauromaquia* in several respects: he looks at *tauromaquia* with a reflective and critical distance from conventional anti-taurine discourses, and he does not necessarily revere national cultural traditions. In many of the book's essays, the implied author looks at bullfighting as if he were visiting Spain from another planet, irreverently parodying and satirizing *tauromaquia* as a discourse and ritual performance.

In the third chapter, "Contribución al estudio del origen de las corridas" ("Contribution to the Study of the Origins of Bullfights"), Fernández Flórez presents himself as a scholar who tries to explain what *tauromaquia* is. He approaches this question with a derisive critical distance from *tauromaquia* as an artistic practice and erudite discourse:

> Es tan extraño el fenómeno de una corrida, que casi todo el mundo pensó alguna vez en él con afán de explicárselo. Que unos hombres vestidos de colorines hostiguen a un determinado animal utilizando instrumentos diversos, parece verdaderamente estrafalario, y no se puede admitir que exista … con suficiente razón de ser en su simple apariencia. Por eso se le ha dedicado tanta atención y se hicieron tantas exégesis suyas. Y como, en verdad, nadie encontró la explicación convincente, los comentaristas se refugian en esta frase demasiado vaga: —Es que se trata de un arte. Yo estudié esta opinión, la remiré, la tomé al peso, la olfateé … y me dije … : —Arte no es; pero ¿qué es, entonces?

> (The phenomenon of a bullfight is so strange that almost everyone has thought about it sometime with the desire to explain it. That some men dressed in colours harass a certain animal using different instruments seems truly bizarre, and Its simple appearance is not a sufficient reason to justify its existence … That is why so much attention has been devoted to it and so many exegeses made of it. And since, in truth, no one has found a convincing explanation, the commentators take refuge in this too-vague phrase: "It is an art. I studied this opinion, I reviewed it, I weighed it, I sniffed it … and I said to myself: 'Art it is not; but what is it then?'"; *El toro* 32–3)

The comically absurd theory with which he tries to answer this question adopts the perspective of the bovines and reduces human bullfighters – by means of a zoomorphic rhetorical shift – to the biological condition of a virus, a parasite, or an insect that pesters the bulls: "cuando aparece la primavera, los toreros sienten un vivo deseo de clavar picas, banderillas y espadas en el cuerpo de los toros. Y creen que es por eso de la 'sangre torera' … Pues no, señor: su excitación es la misma que la de un microbio, y obedece a misteriosos motivos de la biología" ("When spring appears, the bullfighters feel a strong desire to drive pikes, flags, and swords into the body of the bulls. And they think that is because they have 'the bullfight in their veins' ... But no, sir: their excitement is the same as that of a microbe, and obeys mysterious motives of biology"; *El toro* 35).

In other essays, Fernández Flórez ridicules *tauromaquia* as a discourse and performance by proposing new rules and regulations aimed to make the bullfight less monotonous and predictable. These proposals have the obvious comic aim of generating farcical and ludicrous taurine scenes such as bullfighters persecuting graceful cats in the bullring (*El toro* 163–77) and bulls jumping the fence and running over the public in the stands as part of the excitement of the *corrida*. Those scenes also have another critical function. Substituting the bull for the cat may show the absurdity of harassing and piercing an animal (no matter what animal) in a bullring as a public performance. Similarly, allowing the bulls to jump the fence and reach the audience critiques the voyeuristic pleasure in watching a person risk their life if one is unwilling to literally share the thrill of the danger.

Chapter 5, "Donde se pueden leer sensatos conceptos acerca de los toros mansos" ("Where One Can Read Judicious Arguments about Tame Bulls"), is a lucidly comic critique of the material-semiotic construction of the physical trait and masculine moral value of *bravura*, on and through the bodies of *toros de lidia*. Fernández Flórez affirms with irony that the fighting bull, "que los aficionados aplauden[,] es un animal esencialmente estúpido [ya que] se pone frente a él un hombre con una tela extendida, y el sencillo bruto no se cansa de embestir contra la tela" ("which the fans applaud[,] is an essentially stupid animal [since] a man with an extended cloth stands in front of him, and the simple brute never tires of repeatedly ramming into the cloth"; *El toro* 52). He continues his argument praising the intelligent caution of the *toro manso*: "deberíamos haber admirado sin regateos la reserva que demostró ante los capotes, síntoma de sagacidad" ("we should have admired, without haggling, the reservation he showed before the capes, a sign of sagacity"; 53). Next, he playfully envisions a bullfighting performance in which the bull is allowed to use his intelligence and learning capacities through prior exposures to the instruments, aims, techniques, and material environment of the *corrida* – something that, paradoxically, is carefully avoided when raising fighting bulls in the countryside: "presenciaría con deliciosa sorpresa el caso de un toro que huyese de los banderilleros, que fingiese ir a acometer a un espada y se lanzase bruscamente sobre los peones que tuviese detrás ... que se tumbase patas arriba a la hora de la estocada ante el desconcierto del diestro" ("I would witness with delicious surprise a bull fleeing from the banderilleros, pretending to mount an attack on the bullfighter and throwing himself abruptly on the peons behind him, … that lay upside down at the time of the thrust, to the bewilderment of the bullfighter"; 54). The author concludes that "el que menos entiende de toreo es el toro" ("the one who least understands bullfighting is the bull") and that "debe perderse la esperanza de que comprenda todo lo que se necesita de él … las obligaciones que le impone su condición de *ente lidiable*" ("the hope that he understands everything that is needed from him should be abandoned as well as the obligations imposed by his condition as a *fightable entity*"; 59–60; my emphasis). Fernández Flórez suggests, in other words, that as a living sentient being, the fighting bull is totally alien to the roles and expectations that *tauromaquia* imposes on his body as a fightable and killable entity. Later in the article, when discussing the use of "banderillas de fuego" ("banderillas of fire") as a punishment for the perceived tameness of bulls that do not show a sufficiently aggressive behaviour, the implied author argues that "el concepto que los toros tienen de la mansedumbre no es exactamente el mismo que nosotros les atribuimos. Un toro puede ser muy toro y no tener la más mínima afición al toreo" ("the concept that bulls have of meekness is not exactly the same as the one we attribute to them. A bull can be a real bull and not have the slightest fondness for bullfighting"; 60). In this way, he further ridicules the material-semiotic attachments that *tauromaquia* establishes between male bovines' bodies and the concepts of *bravura* and tameness, suggesting that bullfighting's core patriarchal values and meanings are ultimately foreign to the species-being of bovines, to what being a bull is about.

In his best pre-war anti-taurine essays, the voice of Fernández Flórez is less playful and more emotionally charged. These essays also situate bulls' and horses' living and dying bodies more clearly centre stage as the focus of the author's feelings and concerns. The author discursively reframes and demystifies *tauromaquia* through a non-anthropocentric lens that may be described as post-humanist since it allows human observers to recognize bulls and horses as biological others and embodied sentient beings (comparable to humans, in this sense) beyond the narrow roles, meanings, and values that *tauromaquia* assigns to them.

Fernández Flórez's most gloomy, dramatic, and fierce anti-taurine essay, "Que habla del público, del torero y del bruto" ("On the Public, the Bullfighter, and the Brute"), focuses on the bovine's physical suffering, corporeal vulnerability, and mental devastation at the end of the *corrida*. In this essay, a three-part narrative chronicles a bullfight, with each part focusing on one of the participants in the *corrida*: the audience, the bulls, and the bullfighters. The second part describes a scene in which an agonizing bull refuses to lower his head when the *matador* is prepared to kill him. Next, the animal tries to retreat from the confrontation:

> Al fin, el pobre bruto dio la vuelta y se separó lentamente del grupo de sus enemigos … Atravesó toda la plaza por su diámetro … Era la renuncia a luchar, la confesión de inferioridad, de derrota. Mejor que con palabras, la actitud del toro venía a expresar: —He acometido a los caballos, he perseguido a los hombres; recibí muchas heridas. Estoy cansado y dolorido. Podéis más que yo … Dejadme … Cuando llegó a la barrera se tumbó. Era un infeliz animal aniquilado. No había en él ya ni bravura, ni afán de pelea, ni siquiera ánimos para defenderse. Tan sólo un pobre ser que sufría, exhausto

> (At last, the poor brute turned and slowly separated himself from the group of his enemies … He traversed the entire bullring along its diameter … It was the resignation to fight, the confession of inferiority, of defeat. Better than words, the bull's attitude came to express: "I have attacked the horses, I have chased the men; I have received many injuries. I am tired and sore. You have power that I do not … Let me be." … When he reached the sideline, he lay down. He was an unhappy, annihilated animal. There was no bravery left in him, no desire to fight, not even the courage to defend himself. Just a poor being who was suffering, exhausted; *El toro* 83)

This scene describes both the bull's powerlessness and his powers for the communication of affects. On one hand, we can see how the bull's expected bravery has vanished because of the feelings of pain and exhaustion that overwhelm his body, and, on the other hand, his agency and capacity to express these feelings to humans by means of gesture and movement.

The essay "¡Caballos! ¡Caballos!" ("Horses! Horses!") also aims to make visible to the readers the corporality, vulnerability, and suffering of animals who are forced to participate in the *corrida*, in this case focusing on horses. The theme of the (in)visibility of horses' suffering and their wasted lives and bodies is discussed at several points. In the first part of the essay, a horse bitterly complains through a fictitious letter sent to the author about the hypocrisy of late-1920s taurine regulations that required horses' bodies to be covered with pads:

> Lo esencial es que no nos den cornadas. Si se nos va a vestir de toreros para evitar la exhibición de nuestras tripas, pero sin evitarnos las heridas,

preferimos seguir así, porque la brutalidad de que se nos hace víctimas es más evidente y acaso alcance a conmover a los hombres. ¿Nosotros agonizando y ustedes tan tranquilos porque no se nos ven las tripas? ¡Jamás! Reclamamos el derecho de enseñarlas, de pisotearlas.

(The essential thing is that we not get gored. If we are going to be dressed as bullfighters to avoid the exhibition of our guts, but without avoiding injury, we prefer to continue like this, because the brutality of which we are made victims is more evident and may even move men. We lie in agony while you remain calm because our guts can't be seen? Never! We claim the right to show them, to trample them; *El toro* 116)

At the end of the essay, the author describes in a more naturalistic tone a harrowing scene he witnessed "en el patio de caballos de la plaza de toros de Madrid" ("in the horse yard of Madrid's bullfighting ring"):

Yo he visto a los monosabios hundir sus manos en el sangriento vientre de los jamelgos para rellenar con estopas las tremendas heridas. Un incesante temblor corría por las patas de los infelices animales, y sacudía su lomo y su cola mutilada el temblor de un sufrimiento horrible ... Después, para reanimar a la bestia moribunda, arrojaban contra ella el agua de un balde ... Y tornaba al ruedo.

(I have seen picador's assistants plunge their hands into the bloody bellies of nags to fill the tremendous wounds with tow. An incessant trembling ran down the legs of the unhappy animals, and their backs and mutilated tails shook with the trembling of horrible suffering ... Then, to revive the dying beast, they threw a bucket of water at her ... And she returned to the ring; *El toro* 125–6)

The representation of the effects of violence through the use of gruesome imagery and dark humour in Spain's cultural history can be traced back to Goya's celebrated print series *Los desastres de la Guerra* (*Disasters of War*), which exposed the inglorious atrocities of Spain's War of Independence against Napoleon's invading army. Fernández Flórez's grotesque images of horses' intestines hanging from their open belly at the bullring, and his implied denunciation of the use of sentient animal bodies as something that can be wasted and discarded beyond any moral consideration, is comparable to Goya's and it responds to the same anti-aesthetic ethical impulse. Like Goya before him, the writer considers that the moral obligation of the modern artist is to make that suffering and waste visible, no matter how uncomfortable these gruesome images may make the readers: "Ya sé que es muy fácil alarmar la sensibilidad y hasta la sensiblería de la gente narrando malos tratos a animales ... Que no se me acuse de intentarlo. Pero ese aspecto de las corridas no debía ser pasado en silencio, como si no existiese" ("I know that it is very easy to alarm the sensitivity and even the sentimentality of people by narrating the mistreatment of animals ... Let me not be accused of trying to appeal to that. But that aspect of the bullfights should not be passed over in silence, as if it did not exist"; *El toro* 125). With this article, therefore, Fernández Flórez aims to counteract the taurine aesthetic imagery and discourse – which upholds *tauromaquia* as a noble art form – with an anti-aesthetic imagery that denounces its callous misappropriation and misuse of living sentient animals.

Conclusions

I have defined *tauromaquia* not as social practice or a cultural institution but as a naturecultural material-semiotic assemblage of bodies, values, affects, and meanings – as well as of urban and rural environments, money, and financial interests. At a time when *tauromaquia* in Spain enjoyed its historical zenith of popularity, social influence, cultural prestige, and political support, the comic anti-taurine writings of the popular novelist and freethinking conservative journalist Fernández Flórez aimed to undermine *tauromaquia* as a material-semiotic construction. By means of comic-writing techniques such as absurdist humour and grotesque imagery, Fernández Flórez undermines *tauromaquia* as a humanist and nationalist discourse and reframes it non-anthropocentrically as a multispecies material event in which embodied animals from different species are pierced, stabbed, eviscerated, and discarded without any consideration for their suffering. This reframing of *tauromaquia* also includes a critical interrogation of the material-semiotic inscription of human values and sentiments in our biological others. In particular, the writer ridicules the contrived material-semiotic inscription of taurine patriarchal values and sentiments – such as bravery – on bovines' bodies. Even though *toros de lidia* are selectively bred and carefully raised to make them fulfil their biocultural role as brave, wild, fightable, and killable animals, Fernández Flórez's anti-taurine chronicles show that bovines' interests and sentient bodies exist beyond those simplistic categories. By showing this, he signals the point at which the material-semiotic edifice of bullfighting begins to crumble.

While many forms of interspecies violence – such as the ones that result from predation – are commonplace in all ecosystems, most of these are the result of the diverse strategies that the requirements of natural selection and biological adaptation demand from biotic communities to reproduce themselves. Domestic working and companion animals, such as horses and dogs, are also the result of a slow biosocial human–non-human co-adaption to practices and environments (Clutton-Brock; Haraway, *Species*). Human-animal relations in *tauromaquia*, however, are not based on any of these forms of biological or biocultural adaptation. They are based on brutal environmental displacements from the rural *dehesa* to the urban bullring, patriarchal fantasies, and ecologically unnecessary violence and suffering. As Fernández Flórez suggests, they are also based on interspecies dishonesty, deceitfulness, and disrespect for one of the defining characteristics of organic life: its open-ended adaptive potential for environmental change and for the presence and actions of other life forms. Fernández Flórez got it right: "the fighting bull doesn't know anything about bullfighting."

NOTES

1 The most important volumes in English in this area to date are the monographs of Katarzyna Beilin (contemporary cultural studies), John Beusterien (literary studies of the early modern period), and Abel Alves (history of early modern Spain), as well as the interdisciplinary volumes edited by Beilin and William Viestenz, and by Margarita Carretero-González.
2 All translations provided in this chapter are mine in collaboration with Markéta Kryslova.
3 The term *thinking-feeling* is a translation of *sentipensar*. According to the social scientist Patricia Botero, "[T]his term was originally reported by sociologist Fals-Borda as used by people on the river and marshes of the Colombian Caribbean coast region." For Botero, *sentipensar* "questions the sharp separation that capitalist modernity establishes between mind and body, reason and emotion, humans and nature, secular and sacred, life and death." I am using this term here in a more straightforward way to point to Fernández Flórez's affectively engaged reasoning about animals in his anti-taurine essays. In many of those essays, Fernández Flores's arguments about animals and *tauromaquia* need to be understood as something that emerges from the author's feelings (of compassion, indignation, distress, bitterness, etc.) and cannot be separated from them.
4 Since the publication of Peter Singer's classic *Animal Liberation* in 1975, the bibliography on the question of the human-animal divide and the ethical status of animals has grown exponentially each year. It would be impractical to even try to summarize the key debates and theories. Instead,

I will clarify my own position and its sources. The arguments of Derrida and Wolfe have shown me that humanism, based on the idea of unique human capabilities, crumbles when we consider the vulnerabilities we share with animals as embodied beings (e.g., our common mortality and capacity for suffering). Recognition of common needs then creates the possibility of interspecies empathy (Calarco; Wolfe; Derrida). Timothy Morton, on the other hand, has convinced me that animals are also "strange strangers" with which we are intimately entangled in the same ecological web. From an evolutionary perspective we are all animals, but animals are also morphological and existential strangers that cannot be reduced to any human system of thought. As such, they may incite human feelings of curiosity, hospitality, solidarity, and respect (Morton, *Ecological Thought* 38–50 and *Humankind*). I use the expression *animal other* for its simplicity. More precise and evocative terms would be perhaps *other-than-human animal* or *strange stranger*.

5 Elite and state management of natural resources to promote economic progress began well before Franco's government, as other contributions to this collection discuss. See Daniel Frost's chapter on enlightened land reform in support of a market economy in the late eighteenth and early nineteenth centuries, and Óscar Iván Useche's discussion of technological development to propel an industrial society that would regenerate the nation at the turn of the twentieth century. Likewise, Margaret Marek's chapter addresses the trauma enacted by the Franco regime's construction of dams to harness water's power without regard for environmental damage or community annihilation.

6 A similar strategy is seen in the twenty-first-century texts that William Viestenz and Maryanne L. Leone study in their respective chapters in *Beyond Human*, in which stories of human and animal precarity not only expose the vulnerable existences that patriarchal, extractive societies have generated but also allow for a mutuality grounded ethics of care (Leone) and post-immunological kinship (Viestenz).

WORKS CITED AND CONSULTED

Alves, Abel. *The Animals of Spain: An Introduction* to *Imperial Perceptions* and *Human Interaction* with *Other Animals, 1492–1826*. Brill, 2011.

Ares-López, Daniel. "Culturas de naturaleza y naturalezas-culturas: Hacia una redefinición de los estudios culturales desde el Antropoceno." *Arizona Journal of Hispanic Cultural Studies*, vol. 23, no. 1, 2019, pp. 215–34. *Project MUSE*, https://doi.org/10.1353/hcs.2019.0004.

Barad, Karen. *Meeting the Universe Halfway: Quantum Physics and the Entanglement of Matter and Meaning*. Duke UP, 2007.

Beilin, Katarzyna Olga. *In Search of an Alternative Biopolitics: Anti-bullfighting, Animality, and the Environment in Contemporary Spain.* Ohio State UP, 2015.

Beilin, Katarzyna, and William Viestenz, editors. *Ethics of Life: Contemporary Iberian Debates.* Vanderbilt UP, 2016.

Beusterien, John. Canines in Cervantes and Velázquez: An Animal Studies Reading of Early Modern Spain. Routledge, 2016.

Botero, Patricia. "Sentipensar." *Pluriverse: A Post-Development Dictionary,* edited by Ashish Kothari et al., Tulika Books, 2019, pp. 302–4.

Brandes, Stanley. "Torophiles and Torophobes: The Politics of Bulls and Bullfights in Contemporary Spain." *Anthropological Quarterly*, vol. 82, no. 3, 2009, pp. 779–94. *Project MUSE*, https://doi.org/10.1353/anq.0.0076.

Calarco, Matthew. *Zoographies: The Question of the Animal from Heidegger to Derrida.* Columbia UP, 2008.

Cambria, Rosario. *Los toros: Tema polémico en el ensayo español del siglo XX.* Gredos, 1974.

Carretero-González, Margarita, editor. *Spanish Thinking about Animals.* MSU P, 2020.

Clutton-Brock, Juliet. *Animals as Domesticates: A World View through History.* Michigan State UP, 2012.

Codina Segovia, Juan Ignacio. *Pan y toros: Breve historia del pensamiento antitaurino español.* Plaza y Valdés, 2018.

De Haro, M. Verónica, and Garry Marvin. "The Bullfight in Twenty-First-Century Spain: Polemics of Culture, Art and Ethics." *Cosmopolitan Animals,* edited by Kaori Nagai et al., Palgrave Macmillan, 2015, pp. 93–106.

DeLanda, Manuel, and Graham Harman. *The Rise of Realism.* John Wiley & Sons, 2017.

Derrida, Jacques. *The Animal That Therefore I Am.* Edited by Marie-Louise Mallet, translated by David Wills, Fordham UP, 2009.

Fernández Flórez, Wenceslao. *El bosque animado.* Edited by José-Carlos Mainer, Espasa-Calpe, 2001.

Fernández-Flórez, Wenceslao. *El toro, el torero y el gato.* Libreria General, 1952.

Fernández Flórez, Wenceslao. *Perros, gatos y otras amistades.* El Sol, 1991.

Haraway, Donna J. "A Game of Cat's Cradle: Science Studies, Feminist Theory, Cultural Studies." *Configurations*, vol. 2, no. 1, winter 1994, pp. 59–71.

Haraway, Donna J. *Simians, Cyborgs, and Women: The Reinvention of Nature.* Routledge, 1991.

Haraway, Donna J. *When Species Meet.* U of Minnesota P, 2008.

Latour, Bruno. *Reassembling the Social: An Introduction to Actor-Network-Theory.* Oxford UP, 2005.

Latour, Bruno. *We Have Never Been Modern.* Harvard UP, 1993.

Law, John. "Actor Network Theory and Material Semiotics." *The New Blackwell Companion to Social Theory*, edited by Bryan S. Turner, Wiley-Blackwell, 2009, pp. 141–58.

Llera, José Antonio. "Introducción." *Wenceslao Fernández Flórez: Artículos Selectos*, edited by José Antonio Llera, Diputación de Pontevedra, 2008, pp. 13–75.

López Criado, Fidel. "Recepción crítica de Wenceslao Fernández Flórez: El canon y la historia de la literatura." *Wenceslao Fernández Flórez y su tiempo. Evasión y compromiso en la literatura española de la 1a mitad del S. XX*, edited by Fidel López Criado, Ayuntamiento de La Coruña, 2002, pp. 19–30.

Mainer, José-Carlos. *Análisis de una insatisfacción: Las novelas de W. Fernández Flórez*. Castalia, 1975.

Margulis, Lynn, and Dorion Sagan. *What Is Life*? U of California P, 2000.

Marvin, Garry. *Bullfight*. U of Illinois P, 1994.

Mitchell, Timothy J. *Blood Sport: A Social History of Spanish Bullfighting*. U of Pennsylvania P, 1991.

Morton, Timothy. *The Ecological Thought*. Harvard UP, 2010.

Morton, Timothy. *Humankind: Solidarity with Non-human People*. Verso Books, 2017.

Ramos Gorostiza, José Luis. "Gestión ambiental y política de conservación de la naturaleza en la España de Franco." *Revista de Historia Industrial*, no. 32, 2006, pp. 99–138.

Shubert, Adrian. *Death and Money in the Afternoon: A History of the Spanish Bullfight*. Oxford UP, 1999.

Swyngedouw, Erik. *Liquid Power: Water and Contested Modernities in Spain, 1898–2010*. MIT Press, 2015.

Utekhin, Ilia. "Spanish Echoes of Jakob von Uexküll's Thought." *Semiotica*, vol. 2001, no. 134, 2006, pp. 635–42.

Viestenz, William. "Sins of the Flesh: Bullfighting as a Model of Power." *Iberian Modalities: A Relational Approach to the Study of Culture in the Iberian Peninsula*, edited by Joan Ramon Resina, Liverpool UP, 2013, pp. 143–62.

Wheeler, Wendy. *Expecting the Earth: Life, Culture, Biosemiotics*. Lawrence & Wishart, 2016.

Wolfe, Cary. *Zoontologies: The Question of the Animal*. U of Minnesota P, 2003.

Chapter Fourteen

Ecohorror as Critique of Anthropogenic (Self-)Destruction in Albert Sánchez Piñol's *Cold Skin*

SHANNA LINO

Mai no som infinitament lluny d'aquells qui odiem. Per la mateixa raó, doncs, podríem creure que mai no serem absolutament a prop d'aquells qui estimem.

(We are never very far from those we hate. For this very reason, we shall never be truly close to those we love.)

Sánchez Piñol, *La pell freda*.[1]

Ecophobia, Ecogothic, Ecohorror

In his pivotal 2009 essay, "Theorizing in a Space of Ambivalent Openness," Simon C. Estok identifies a potentially paralysing problem with contemporary ecocriticism: in an effort to avoid strict delineations as a theoretical field that might reproduce the kinds of borders, restrictions, centres, and hierarchies that it aims to dismantle, ecocriticism has become plagued by an ambivalence incapable of dealing with the theoretical or practical challenges set forth by its activist motivations and intentions (206). Estok's response to this ambivalence has been to theorize the human contempt for and fear of the agency of the non-human natural environment, what he identifies as ecocriticism's primary matter of concern, ecophobia:

> Ecophobia is an irrational and groundless hatred of the natural world, as present and subtle in our daily lives and literature as homophobia and racism and sexism. It plays out in many spheres, … it is about power and control; it is what makes looting and plundering of animal and nonanimal resources possible. Self-starvation and self-mutilation imply ecophobia no less than lynching implies racism. (Estok, "Theorizing" 208)

Since addressing ecophobia also requires that we address the question of evil – a fact that Estok finds too often overlooked in ecocriticism – the literary and cinematic genre of ecohorror is well situated for such theoretical applications. As Estok notes in his more recent book, *The Ecophobia Hypothesis* (2018), a considerable number of scholars (although no Hispanists) have applied the term when studying horror and the ecogothic, which the critic considers to be a logical extension of the notion's theorizing (5–6).

The present essay contributes to this vein of ecocriticism with an analysis of Albert Sánchez Piñol's 2002 novel *La pell freda* and its 2017 cinematic adaptation directed by Xavier Gens, titled *Cold Skin*. The texts follow an unnamed weather analyst to a remote island in the Antarctic Circle, where he engages with only one other human, a man whom he believes to be the lighthouse operator. However, the two men are not alone. Nightly, hybrid amphibian creatures with humanoid features emerge from the sea and, seemingly, attack. Whereas the lighthouse operator reacts to the beings with fear, hatred, misogyny, and murderous intent, the novel's protagonist repeatedly seeks to understand the non-humans, whose water and island the two men have colonized: "Tenen mil greuges contra nosaltres. Pensi-ho així: som invasors. Aquesta és la seva terra, l'única terra que tenen. I nosaltres l'hem ocupat amb un fortí i una guarnició armada. No li sembla prou motiu perquè ens ataquin? … Jo no puc recriminar-los que lluitin per alliberar la seva illa dels invasors! No puc!" ("They have a thousand grudges against us. Think of it this way: we are invaders. This is their land, the only land they have. And we have taken it over with a fortified garrison. Is that not enough reason to attack us? … One cannot blame them for defending their island from invaders! I most certainly cannot!"; Sánchez Piñol 221–2; Morgan 173). Yet he is ultimately unable to resist the temptation to dominate, oppress, and destroy the beings with whom he coexists, and eventually participates in the self-destructive activities of his predecessor. While the imposing presence of the humans on the hybrid creatures' island could be read allegorically as a postcolonial (sovereigntist) critique, one dually nourished by the author's Catalan heritage and his protagonist's Irish origins, material ecocritical readings of the novel point to the extinguishing repercussions of ecological attitudes that do not sufficiently destabilize human exceptionalism. Drawing on ecogothic preoccupations with the uncanny and abject, and building upon a growing corpus of criticism that identifies the catalysing potential of monster fiction, this essay illuminates Sánchez Piñol's exposé of humanity's ecologically devastating consumptive practices and its cyclical trajectory towards self-annihilation.[2]

While criticism on the Iberian ecogothic or ecohorror is largely non-existent – a gap that this chapter barely begins to fill – recent volumes on American, British, Irish, and Italian literature and cinema have brought together analyses of texts in which humans do horrific things to the non-human natural world or that employ particular gothic tropes and symbols in order to present cautionary tales of the dangerous consequences of mistreating non-human nature.[3] Some critics distinguish definitively between the often synonymously deployed *ecogothic* and *ecohorror*, seeing the first as a lens or mode and the second as genre (Smith and Hughes, Parker and Poland). In this sense, the ecogothic refers to a method of inquiry whose purpose is to elucidate the fear, anxiety, and dread that often pervade the literary and cultural relationships of humans to the non-human world and to orient us "to the more disturbing and unsettling aspects of our interactions with nonhuman ecologies" (Keetley and Sivils 1). By contrast, ecohorror can be defined as a literary and cinematic genre in which non-human nature has traditionally been presented as evidently monstrous but, notably, whose focus has shifted in recent decades from the sensationalist exploitation of human anxieties as expressed through revenge-of-nature narratives to a corpus more purposefully engaged with raising ecological awareness and deconstructing the human–non-human dichotomy (Rust and Soles 509).

Yet it is the dual prism afforded by these terms that proves to be the most fruitful when analysing the literary and cinematic versions of *La pell freda*, since the ecogothic framing complicates ecohorror's premise of a monstrous nature by spotlighting the unequivocally disturbing human attitudes towards non-human nature. At the intersection of the ecogothic and ecohorror, then, lies the struggle for and loss of human control over non-human nature, one that aligns directly with Estok's definition of ecophobia: "Control, of course, is the key word here. Ironically, the more control we seem to have over the natural environment, the less we actually have" ("Theorizing" 208). Thus, rather than narrowly depicting the apocalyptic or catastrophic dimensions of beyond-human nature and their threat to humanity as standalone phenomena, contemporary ecogothic readings of ecohorror increasingly highlight the unsettling consequences of anthropogenic activity through texts that disrupt agentic paradigms of human supremacy over an enmeshed more-than-human natural environment.

In 2001, material ecocritic Stacy Alaimo recognized that monster movies "could be the single most significant genre for ecocriticism and green cultural studies," since they "offer sometimes stunning insights into how the arguments, images, and rhetoric of environmentalism have been received; moreover, these films shape contemporary responses to environmentalism" ("Discomforting" 279–80). In her analysis of monstrous natures in films of the second half of the 1990s, Alaimo outlines the problematic, anthropocentric structures of many of these movies: for one, they employ a vertical semiotics in which humans are ultimately free to float above beasts; moreover, they are predicated on masculinity and conclude by reaffirming myths of triumphant transcendence. However, Alaimo includes in her critique a minority of films that depict monstrous nature in manners that counter the above dynamics by insisting upon horizontality, dramatizing the futility of demarcating protected human spaces, and encouraging viewers "to dwell, self-reflectively, within spaces or environments" (291). These films "can catalyze some sort of resistance to the desire to demarcate, discipline, and eradicate monstrous natures" (294). Indeed, Sánchez Piñol's novel – and, in slightly different ways, Gens's filmic adaptation – shows beyond-human nature to be "neither a benign landscape for passive contemplation nor a passive, empty resource for human consumption" (292); rather, it depicts it as an active, purposeful force that intimates human and non-human interdependency.

Hybridity, Blurred Borders, and the Nature-Culture Divide

In *La pell freda*, there is a clear move to dismantle boundaries of various sorts. While the text makes no explicit mention of *catalanitat*, it may be read as an allegory of imperialism with its multiple references to contemporary sovereignty movements, most notably that of Ireland – the protagonist's homeland – but also that of Quebec, a region about whose right to exist as an independent state the weather analyst was made to research in his youth. While the novel is of Catalan origin, the protagonist (and first-person narrator) is a British-educated Irish orphan who sails on a ship captained by a German-born Dane and whose sailors are Scottish and Senegalese. His only other human companion on the island – who he has been told is the lighthouse operator, but who, he will learn, is the previous weather analyst whom the protagonist thought he had come to replace – is Austrian and refers to the unnamed narrator for the remainder of the text simply as *kollege* ("colleague"). Despite the cast of international human characters, while they are at sea and on the island – which operates synecdochally for a vengeful earth – their nationalities matter very little. Instead, the narrative builds on the traditional bonds inherent to seafarers, whose primary goal is survival and for whom their ship becomes a referent for home more than any territory from which they may have originated. In so doing, the literary text sets the stage for post-nationalist and, by extension, post-humanist readings of anthropogenic ecological considerations. What begins as a disassembling of human allegiances to particular nations extends to a questioning of human exceptionalism and speciesism after the protagonist's encounters with the island's hybrid inhabitants. Therefore, in what might be considered a text that precedes present-day ecocritical studies that directly address our immediate ecological crises, this dismantling of borders among humans and other animals manifests a burgeoning global perspective not only on kinship, belonging, and the earthly right to exist, but also on collaborative approaches to dealing at a global scale with the negative impacts of polluted waters, species extinctions, resource extraction, and other anthropogenically driven dynamics.

In the literary and cinematic versions of Sánchez Piñol's text, the protagonist deliberately chooses his post as a climate scientist in a remote part of the world in order to flee precisely the kind of nationalist demarcations that have repeatedly made war among humans so prevalent. Whereas in the Iberian-language versions of the novel the action takes place in the 1920s, and middle chapters of the text refer analeptically to the protagonist's youth and subsequent reluctant participation in the IRA, both the novel's English-language translation and Gens's cinematic adaptation eliminate these recollections, leaving ambiguous the exact nationality of *Cold Skin*'s protagonist. In either case, what starts off as a naive, ecophilic attempt to escape from organized human violence through a non-human-nature-infused self-exile as far away from civilization as possible ends up distilling violence to its truest essence: humanity itself. It is in this context that Sánchez Piñol's narrative introduces hybridity – human/animal and beyond – as a frame through which to address and seek to overcome anthropogenic (self-)destruction.

As he disembarks on the island, the first-person narrator observes the animated comportment of the vegetation that surrounds him, employing language that endears the reader to their environment: "Els arbres creixien com un ramat de bèsties que s'estrenyen les unes amb les altres, tot buscant refugi en els cossos aliens. La molsa els abrigava. Una molsa més compacta que les bardisses dels jardins i alta fins al genoll, fenomen curiós" ("The trees grew like a herd of beasts, huddled together, seeking refuge in other bodies. Moss protected them, a moss more compact than garden hedge and knee-high"; 7; my trans.).[4] On this land, vegetation behaves in the way of sentient beings; like the human protagonist who seeks harbourage at the end of the earth from the perils of interhuman bellicosity, the seemingly more-than-vegetal bodies of the trees enmesh with the moss as their cloister. The narrator's relational description of the flora continues: "Des del vaixell m'havia semblat que era una massa boscosa molt atapeïda. La distància sovint enganya pel que fa a la densitat, humana o vegetal. Aquest cop no. Estaven tan junts els uns i els altres que, sovint, es feia difícil precisar si dos arbres sortien de la mateixa arrel o si eren independents" ("From the boat, the forest had looked extremely thick. Distance is often misleading when it comes to density, whether it is human or vegetable. Not this time. The trees grew so close together that it was often difficult to tell whether two sprang from the same root or whether they were separate"; 12; 7). The weather analyst's observation about distance, deception, and the density of humans and vegetation sets the stage for the novel's leitmotiv of reformulating limits through material entanglement. As will be seen through his interactions with the man whom he believes to be the lighthouse operator and the aforementioned analepses that recount his reticent IRA activism, interhuman physical proximity does not ensure interconnectedness, which in fact, may be more present and meaningful between plant and animal forms.[5] It is also worth noting the metaphorical function of the two trees who share a common root, an image that may be interpreted both ecocritically, as a common source of earthly life – whether vegetal or animal – and in decolonial terms, as an allusion to the arbitrary imperialist division of earthly territories.

The narrator's focus on and appreciation of vegetation is an important point that is coherent with Estok's theoretical call to move beyond speciesism. As an earlier ecocritical theorization, speciesism drew critical attention to the biases "toward the interests of members of one's own species and against those of members of other species" (Singer 15), and its articulation led to, for example, the now broadly accepted need to ban animal testing for cosmetics and the growing movement to call out human hierarchical attachments to some animals (pets) but not others (such as those produced and consumed through agro-industry). The problem with speciesism, as Estok outlines, is that it posits sentience at the border of moral consideration and therefore privileges increasingly complex organisms and, ultimately, anthropocentric ontologies ("Theorizing" 207).

In one of the recollective chapters of the Sánchez Piñol novel, the narrator reminisces affectionately about a tutor whom he was assigned as an adolescent upon release from his orphanage. Importantly, each of the enlightened mentor's lessons contributes to the narrator's ecocritical and decolonial posture as he sets forth to establish a relationship with the flora and fauna of the island. Describing one of his tutor's teachings, he explains, "[E]l meu únic deure era anotar totes les formes de vida que existissin en un petit rectangle, curosament delimitat per vetes i fils. Al principi només hi veia herba, però a poc a poc va aparèixer una gama increïble d'insectes grimpadors, voladors, i subterranis. Tot vivia, el vent també, i tot manifestava una unitat poc descriptible amb paraules" ("My only duty was to write down all the life forms that existed in a small rectangle, carefully delimited by veins and threads. At first, I only saw grass, but little by little an incredible range of climbing, flying, and underground insects appeared. Everything was alive, the wind too, and everything manifested an indescribable unity with words"; 34–5; my trans.).[6] The tutor would go on to guide the narrator beyond an appreciation of the entomological life coexisting in that small rectangle and to extend his awareness to the plant species underfoot:

> Va manar-me que destriés les males herbes de les plantes beneficioses. Com que jo no en coneixia cap, estava obligat a consultar-l'hi abans d'arrencarles. Aquesta no és una mala herba, deia d'unes, se'n poden bullir les fulles i fer-ne infusions. Aquesta tampoc, deia d'altres, són espàrrecs silvestres i per tant comestibles; encara més, exquisits. Aquesta tampoc: com s'entén que pugui ser una mala herba si al maig treu unes flores bellíssimes?

> (He ordered me to separate the weeds from the useful plants. Since I did not recognize any of them, I had to check each one before doing so. This is not a weed, he said, and the leaves can be boiled and infused. Neither is this, he said of others. This one is wild asparagus that is both edible and delicious. This one is not a weed either: how could it be if it produces beautiful flowers in May?; 35; my trans.)

After examining each of the plant species above, the tutor and pupil are left with just one. It possesses dark, pointy, and toxic leaves, as well as a hard and ugly stem; the tutor acknowledges that there is no apparent human use for such a plant, "però si l'arrenquem, quin sentit tindrien les altres? Cap, vaig dir jo. I a quina conclusió arriba doncs? Que les males herbes no existeixen" ("but if we pull it, what sense would the others make? None, I replied. So, what is the conclusion? That weeds do not exist"; 35–6; my trans.). *Males herbes*, in English *weeds* but also *lowlifes* and *scum*, do not exist according to this lesson. And even if a being, sentient or not, is observed to be nothing but a *mala herba*, it has the right to exist nevertheless.[7]

Fast-forward to the weather analyst's arrival on the island, and he not only observes vegetation that appears to possess sentient behaviours but also encounters a man who seems to be more vegetable than animal: "En moure's feia pensar en un arbre desarrelat que aprèn a caminar. ... El pit apareixia cobert per una catifa de pèls, que s'enfilaven per les dues espatlles com plantes silvestres. Al sud del melic la densitat del borrissol era de jungla" ("His movements were those of an uprooted tree learning to walk ... The man's chest was covered in a mat of hair that twined up his shoulders like wild vines. The tangle took on a jungle-like density below his navel"; 17; 11). Settled back in his cabin after his inability to communicate effectively with the vegetational human, the protagonist continues his observation of the island topography as not only sentient but artistic, further blurring the limits between animal and vegetable beings and even suggesting an advanced, ecologically aesthetic sophistication: "La ressaca havia clavat a la costa dotzenes de troncs nets i polits. Alguns eren arrels d'antics arbres abatuts. Les marees els havien treballat amb rigor d'artista, i s'hi podien admirar escultures d'una rara bellesa laberíntica. Per fragments, el cel patia una trista coloració d'argent brut o, encara més fosc, d'armadura rovellada" ("The undertow had driven dozens of cleanly polished tree trunks onto the coastline. Some were roots of old trees that had been chopped down. The tides had formed them with an artist's precision, leaving sculptures of a rare and contorted beauty. The sky was tinged a gloomy shade of tarnished silver, with the even darker tones of a rusty suit of armour"; 23; 16). This blurring of borders between forms of life, followed closely by a description of a fractured, armoured, and lamenting sky, illustrates the potential of the ecogothic lens for examining hybridity and, ultimately, for dismantling anthropocentric perspectives on ecology.

While absent of any reference to the material ecocritical implications of Sánchez Piñol's text, Brian J. Showers's reading of *Cold Skin* (the English-language translation in novelistic form) situates the text within the gothic tradition for its depiction of strange landscapes, invasions from outside, the intermingling of love and hate, and "the raging beast within" (98). The author and critic identifies in the novel the gothic sense of isolation, its emphasis on the shadowy and unknowable, and, most notably, the tradition's exploration of the darkness that lies within (humanity). For Showers, the text leaves the reader with the need to reconcile between gothic fiction's traditional dichotomies: "real versus unreal, man versus beast, passion versus apathy, civilization versus destruction, and – most importantly – how easy it is to pass from one extreme to the other" (110). If, however, one reads *Cold Skin* not merely through the gothic but through the ecogothic lens, one finds a text that points towards a myriad of avenues through which to explore not only the passing between such binaries but their demolition, moments in which hybridity manifests. In *La pell freda*, the obvious hybridity of the amphibian-humanoid creatures is extended to the humans, who at times seem more vegetal than animal, and to the landscape, whose agency includes artistry.

The notion that landscapes and vegetation possess artistic agency is further extrapolated to the artistry of monstrous nature in *Cold Skin* through a visual motif that is particularly powerful in Gens's cinematic adaptation. Throughout the film, the protagonist takes frequent contemplative daytime walks around the island and regularly happens upon circular formations that have been meticulously constructed using intentionally positioned black and white stones. While at first he and the viewer may assume the constructions to be the work of the apparent lighthouse operator or of another human who may have previously disembarked on the island, we eventually understand that these are works created by the female hybrid creature whom the lighthouse attendant keeps captive. She is the ultimate embodiment of beyond-human hybridity in the text: like the rest of her species, she is part human, part amphibian; she can live underwater but also walk and breathe on land; and as the lighthouse attendant's enslaved creature, she is mistreated as part domesticated pet and part lustful object, a body that is human enough to dominate sexually despite her non-human monstrosity. The unmistakeably gendered dynamics of this dominion, which ultimately serves to ease both male protagonists' fears, echo what Alaimo has identified in monstrous nature movies as the role of women who, "it seems, must serve as the border zone between nature and culture, keeping nature safely at bay in order that men can be fully human" ("Discomforting" 283). Indeed, the narrator cannot wrap his head around his and the lighthouse attendant's sexual attraction to the monstrous creature; while initially horrified by their mutual lust for her, he too eventually succumbs to the appeal to possess her sexually. However, and despite those apprehensions, he is motivated towards increasing compassion for and, ultimately, a desire to protect the female creature, an impulse that is fuelled in part by his appraisal of her positionality on a liminal front between nature and culture, which she exhibits artistically through her mosaic creations.

The aesthetic pleasures of installations built by and for the non-human is a subject analysed by Alaimo in her 2016 book *Exposed: Environmental Politics and Pleasures in Posthuman Times*. Through her analysis of multispecies art, Alaimo shows the corporeal experience of the unexpected when works aim "to please plants and nonhuman animals, and in the process of doing so … diverge from human aesthetic expectations" (*Exposed* 35). In *Cold Skin*, the protagonist progressively tears down his anthropocentric expectations of the hybrid creatures, artistic and otherwise, and, catalysed by artistic appreciation and engagement, he gradually communicates to them his desire for peace and cohabitation. In one such articulation, he places a small boat that he has carved out of a whale bone washed ashore in the centre of one of the aforementioned circular mosaics, thus collaborating in the creation of multispecies art. His ability to move beyond the nature-culture divide sets him apart from the lighthouse attendant, who, right when the narrator finds himself at the brink of creating some interspecies kinship, imposes his anthropocentric masculinity and destabilizes any symbiotic gestures that the narrator and the hybrid creatures may have made. The incoherence of the lighthouse attendant and his inability to dialogue despite possessing human language, coupled with his insatiable propulsion towards violence, make him far less relatable to the protagonist or to the viewer than the island's humanoid-amphibian inhabitants. As far back as Michel de Montaigne, naturalists have affirmed that there exist more differences between some humans than between humans and animals (Gutiérrez Carbajo 69), a fact upon which the narrator explicitly remarks when identifying the irrelevance of species demarcations in the quest for interconnectedness: "[ell] havia anat tan lluny en l'intent d'allunyar-se dels granotots que havia acabat convertint-se en el pitjor dels granotots imaginables: un monstre amb qui resultava impossible sostenir cap diàleg" ("[he] had gone so far in his attempts to distance himself from the beasts that he had turned into the worst toad imaginable"; Sánchez Piñol 269; Morgan 209);[8] "Aquells dies m'hauria estat infinitament més fàcil disparar contra [ell] que contra [ells]" ("On those days, I should have infinitely preferred to murder [him] than any [of them]"; 255; 197). As in the earlier sections of Sánchez Piñol's text, in which hybridity is explored through the sentient behaviour of plants and, simultaneously, the botanical appearance and movements of the lighthouse attendant, the border between monstrosity and humanity is made porous, a nebulosity that makes clear the horror narrative's significance as ecogothic fiction.

Dismantling Verticality

One important trope of gothic literature is the existence of an imposing castle or tower, a human-erected construction whose purpose is to fortress those inside from the dangers that lie without, but which ends up actually snaring protagonists in either physical or psychological capacities (Showers 103). Shortly after the ship, captain, and crew have departed – hesitantly leaving behind the protagonist on the strange island and without having been able to find the former weather analyst whom the protagonist has come to replace – Sánchez Piñol's narrator installs himself in the flimsy cabin assigned to his post to unpack his belongings. All the while, the man whom he believes to be the lighthouse attendant, but who is in fact the former weather analyst, barricades himself within the monolithic construction at the opposite end of the island. However, the narrator enjoys only a few nights of the sought-after peace for which he chose this exile. One evening, his cabin is unexpectedly surrounded by the island's hybrid creatures, and he responds to their rapping and scurrying, which at first he cannot see but only hear, with an instinctual dread. His drive to survive grows as they surround his wooden dwelling and reveal their webbed extremities through windowpanes and under doors. He manages to shelter himself in a cellar but emerges in the morning determined to take up residency in the lighthouse and, in that moment, the fight for the fortress becomes a key element in the novel's plot.

In his sophisticated analysis of *La pell freda*'s treatment of neighbourliness as an ambivalent oscillation between friendship and enmity, *Beyond Human* contributor William Viestenz argues that the Manichean origins of that divide likewise expose the problematic fault line between human and animal, which the novel then sets out to complicate through a progressive humanization of the text's amphibian creatures and a parallel animalization of the lighthouse attendant (180). In his reading, Viestenz highlights the symbolic order to which the narrator is subject, one that has been established by the lighthouse operator and which is represented phallically by the stone residence. Indeed, the price that the narrator must pay for admission to the tower is great: he must abandon his pacifist ideology, which he was able to maintain even as an IRA recruit – "mai no havia disparat una arma" ("I had never fired a weapon"; 75; my trans.) – and is forced through a kind of fraternal initiation by the Austrian to exterminate the hybrid creatures nightly.[9] If, in the absence of the lighthouse resident, the narrator might have moved more swiftly towards interspecies connection and understanding, his fear drives him to cohabitation in the edifice where he becomes infected with the Austrian's violent and misogynistic tendencies.

To be sure, the verticality of the lighthouse, which juts out imposingly from the island's rugged terrain and whose light atop might symbolize human exceptionalist values, complicates the novel's reading as a text that destabilizes hierarchies – anthropocentric, speciesist, or otherwise. And within the lighthouse, a clear verticality is in fact established, with the weather analyst eventually permitted to inhabit the middle floor and the lighthouse resident continuing to occupy the top one, along with the hybrid creature whom he has enslaved. Nevertheless, and despite the building's solid construction, to which the attendant has even added menacing protective spikes, the lighthouse is a rather ineffective shelter for the humans when, each night, large numbers of the humanoid-amphibian sea creatures aim to pierce through its walls. The hybrid beings can easily climb up the building's exterior and are able to break open most of its locks and latches. What prevents them from entering is not the fortress per se but the point-blank rifle shots and head-on hatchets that first the lighthouse attendant and eventually both men execute from the balcony. Indeed, the ineffectual verticality of the lighthouse does not seem to reaffirm any kind of anthropocentric world order but to question it by exposing its futility, and even absurdity.

The most notable incongruity is that the lighthouse attendant never sufficiently interrogates either his occupation of the island or his aggression towards and enslavement of the hybrid female as possible instigating factors for the nightly offences. The attacks by the marine creatures are always preceded by a turning on of the lighthouse lamp, the launch of a threatening flare into the water's edges, and the attendant's establishment of his post on the balcony with rifle and hatchet in hand. Shortly after this ritual, most nights, the creatures do in fact approach the lighthouse en masse. However, with the cinematic adaptation even more so than with the novel, the viewer is repeatedly left wondering if the hybrid creatures would have emerged from the waters at all if the flare had not been shot into their waters, menacingly imposing the humans' presence on the island and provoking conflict. In her analysis of Australian ecohorror movies in which animals carry out Gaia's revenge upon humans, critic Catherine Simpson astutely evinces the ways in which these films – especially those that predate climate-change awareness – do not necessarily raise new environmental issues but rather "extend old discourses about human-caused environmental destruction" (45). Central to her analysis is the argument that when humans conduct ecological and cultural trespass, they rightfully become prey to animals – especially hybridized predators – who do not passively adapt to their environment but instead go out of their way to change their environment in order to survive.

This notion of active adaptation, espoused by environmentalist and futurist James Lovelock (*Revenge* and *Vanishing Face*), problematizes straightforward theories of passive evolution and recognizes an agency in non-human animals that Darwinian perspectives undermine. Gens's film points directly to this agentic reformulation in an early scene in which the weather analyst, still naively housed in his cabin, peruses the previous climate scientist's journal, which is filled with gothically drawn images of amphibians hybridizing and in which the only legible words among paragraphs of cursive text are, in all caps, "DARWIN WAS WRONG." This ecohorror text, like those analysed by Simpson, inverts anthropocentric hierarchies of predator and prey, depicting humans as symbols of degeneracy and giving focus to animals who will exploit the opportunities that we provide (Simpson 50). If, as ecofeminist philosopher Val Plumwood has stated, the "idea of human prey threatens the dualistic vision of human mastery in which we humans manipulate nature from outside, as predator but never as prey," then the ecohorror genre functions productively to expose our dread not only of "becoming food for other forms of life" but also of acknowledging that, as ecocultural trespassers, we had it coming.

One of the ways in which *La pell freda* explores alternate paradigms of human–non-human positionality is through the introduction of hybrid children characters whom the narrator befriends but whose storyline, lamentably, is eliminated from the filmic text. At one point, dozens of baby humanoid-amphibians emerge from the waters and watch the two male humans with curiosity, inverting expected voyeuristic roles: "Feien que ens sentíssim com bèsties de zoològic. Centenars d'ulls, grossos i verds com pomes, ens espiaven hores i hores, seguint tots i cadascun dels nostres moviments" ("The creatures made us feel like animals in a menagerie. Hundreds of eyes like large green apples scrutinised our every movement and spied on us for hours on end"; 241; 186). The hybrid youth's observation of the adult humans as curious creatures reinforces a theme of bidirectional and intra-zoological analysis that pervades the text. In addition to the aforementioned botanical characteristics that the narrator notes in the lighthouse operator, he repeatedly employs similes of animal expressions in such a way that all animal (human and non-human) behaviour is seen as congruent and contiguous. Just as post-humanist ecocriticism recognizes the conclusions of pre-modern ecocentric epistemology, which situate humankind among and within animality rather than apart from or superior to it, *La pell freda* recentres the natural, animal world as referent for interhuman and interspecies understanding, thereby rearticulating classical, Renaissance, and nineteenth-century naturalist philosophies. In contrast to the perspective of monstrosity espoused by his human companion, the narrator is able to observe the hybrid creatures neutrally and, in so doing, recognizes their ability to feel fear, pain, joy, and heartbreak. Beyond externally identifiable shared physical traits, the narrator observes: "Està rient! ... Plora. Riu. A quines conclusions arriba? ... S'imagina que fossin alguna cosa més que monstres submarins? ... podríem entendre'ns amb ells" ("She is laughing! ... She cries, she laughs. What is your conclusion? ... What if they are something more than just monstrous amphibians? … We could get along with them"; 209–10; my trans.).[10] Importantly, what the humans initially interpret as acts of cannibalism when the hybrid creatures retrieve injured bodies following the beyond-human nightly encounters, the protagonist eventually understands to be acts of rescue: "Quantes vegades no havíem disparat contra individus que només volien salvar germans?" ("How many of our bullets had struck souls who were simply trying to save their companions?"; 215; 168). His horizontal view of beyond-human nature, inspired initially by his tutor's post-taxonomic teachings, allows him to perceive multiple nodes of entanglement between his existence and that of the island creatures, not the least of which through the search for refuge.

Once upon a winter storm, the narrator engages in a snowball fight with two of the young island creatures: "Jugàvem, res més, però jugàvem. I el joc, per innocent que sigui, posa al descobert igualtats i afinitats, perquè quan juguem amb algú no existeixen les fronteres, ni les jerarquies, ni les biografies; el joc és un espai de tots i per a tothom" ("We were playing, and that was all. But play, no matter how innocent, creates a sense of fellowship and equality. Borders cease to exist when people play together. There are no hierarchies, no past. The game is a space open to all"; 251; 194). The act of play, an ability shared by all animals and which takes place in a neutral space, is explored in the novel as a site for dismantling speciesist hierarchies. When the protagonist discovers the hybrid children playing in a sunken ship's bow, he describes how their playfulness cancels any previous sense of horror: "Oh Déu meu, vaig comprendre, només juguen. Jugaven, sí, havien convertit la ferralla en jardí i jo era un intrús curiós … Com si fos un llast penós, em sentia lliure de l'horror" ("Oh Lord, it dawned on me, they are just playing. Oh yes, playing. They had transformed that slag heap into a garden and I was an odd intruder … I felt free of horror, as if it were dreadful ballast"; 173; 132). Through his interactions with the young more-than-human creatures, the narrator eventually develops a true kinship with one of the youngest among them, orphaned as a result of the nightly exterminations of his species by the human intruders, whom he names El triangle. His and the weather analyst's shared experience of parental loss – also eliminated from the cinematic adaptation – does not escape the reader. Their exchanges, more so than the gendered and more problematic relations between the narrator and the female adult creature, are the most indicative of a hopeful, symbiotic interspecies cohabitation.

The narrator's physical descent from the elevation of the light-house and his side-by-side engagement with the sea creatures in the island's ponds and surrounding waters progressively contribute to a horizontality that seems far more effective as an ecological strategy than that of fortressed, top-down aggression. Likewise, the orphan El triangle embodies an alternative mapping to binarity for the relational positioning of human and more-than-human animals. His naming by the narrator, as with that of the female as Aneris (anagram of *Sirena* 'mermaid') and of the species as a whole as the Citauca (anagram of *Acuatic*), represents the playful way in which Sánchez Piñol creates opportunities for conceptualizing inversions to and reformulations of the alternative vertical structures horrifyingly predicated on dominion and extermination. The naming of the lighthouse operator is likewise a curious point for consideration. While in the English novelistic translation he is ironically named Grüner – German for "green," "greenie," or "environmentalist" – in the Iberian-language texts he goes by Batis Caffó, in reference to the deep-sea submersible bathyscaphe invented by August Piccard in the 1940s and successfully propelled by his son to the deepest known point of the earth's surface in 1960. Built with a powerful light, the vessel was able to illuminate a small fish and thereby dispelled the belief that fish could not exist at such depths in the absence of light. Whereas the novel's original Batis Caffó is able only to descend symbolically into further and further depths of self-annihilatory cruelty until ultimately luring and then throwing himself to the Citauca, his eventual replacement by the weather analyst suggests the possibility of a more productive lowering from human exceptionalism.

The circular novel concludes just over a year after the narrator is brought to the island and shortly after the suicide of Batis Caffó, whom we now know was in fact the former weather analyst meant to have been replaced by the protagonist upon the latter's arrival at the text's opening. As his predecessor did before him, the narrator installs himself permanently in the lighthouse and cohabits with Aneris. When the captain of a French ship deposits the next weather analyst and inquires about the whereabouts of the former one, the narrator does not reveal that he is in fact said former weather analyst; nor does he make any move to return to Europe, as the captain anticipates. Instead, the newly assumed Batis Caffó chooses to remain on the island, having realized that the world order as he had previously known it was irrevocably altered and that his place was now there, at the geographic and symbolic periphery: "El més devastador de tot era que, de fet, res no havia canviat. Havíem estat paisatgistes que pintaven la tempesta d'esquena a l'horitzó. Només ens calia girar el cap, res més" ("The most devastating thing about it all was how, in fact, nothing had changed. We were like landscape painters trying to depict a storm with their backs to the horizon. We simply needed to turn around, nothing more"; 213; 167).

Referring to the natural landscape and its horizon in order to invoke a horizontality of perspective, the narrator suggests that the greatest challenge to human survival is humanity's insistence on man-made order itself, and that perhaps, like the Aneristic Principle of Discordianism – to which his Citauca partner's name also alludes – humankind's acknowledgment of beyond-human nature's chaos may be the first step in avoiding self-annihilation. Likewise, Gens's ecohorror adaptation ends with neither of the representations of verticality that Alaimo identifies in most monster movies as the re-establishment of patriarchal order: there is no transcendent, masculine reaffirmation through any conclusive slaying of the beast, nor any concluding vertical, helicopter shot that suggests the salvation of human characters from monstrous nature below. Instead, the final sequence includes a shot taken horizontally from the ship that sails slowly away from the island and an underwater shot of the Citauca swimming freely alongside.

Conclusion

Through his ecophobia hypothesis, Estok outlines a theory that provides contemporary ecocriticism with a framework by which the field can be held accountable to its activist roots, thus delivering an alternative to previous nebulous analytical approaches that risk ultimately undermining present-day practical outcomes. Once humans understand our irrational fears of non-human nature and natural things, we can begin to address how these fears pattern relationships that are very destructive to our environment (*Hypothesis* 8). At the same time, as a scholar whose criticism evinces roots of ecophobia in medieval and Renaissance literature, Estok's application of ecophobia to cultural texts from all periods demonstrates the importance of historicizing ecocritically the political, cultural, economic, and psychological postures that have led us to our contemporary ecological crises.

While an ecocritical analysis of *La pell freda*, a novel published in 2002, may not lead us to conceptualize obvious or immediate proposals to address current Iberian or global anthropogenically caused crises, its reading as an intersection of the ecogothic and ecohorror offers the possibility of acknowledging "that some of the most destructive actions we have taken toward nature may be more difficult to change than we think, may have more genetic roots than we are comfortable acknowledging, and may align us more than we can bear with what we have so feverishly tried to define ourselves against," that is, of acknowledging our ecophobia (Estok, *Hypothesis* 12). And since ecophobia "is all about frustrated agency" (10), there is an important role to play for the ecocritical humanities, wherein the link between *agentism* and activism can be productively articulated. As environmental humanist and monster theorist Jeffrey Jerome Cohen argues in *Prismatic Ecology: Ecotheory beyond Green*, "*agentism* is a form of activism: only in admitting that the inhuman is not ours to control, possesses desires and even will, can we apprehend the environment disanthropocentrically" (xxiv; emphasis in original). As a manifestation of ecophobia, *La pell freda* exposes the Anthropocene's cyclical and nihilistic processes, explores the agency of non-human nature – monstrous as it may appear – and examines the challenges faced by even the best-intentioned humans when seeking to extract themselves from hierarchical anthropocentric tendencies. Its nebulous, spiraloid structure and eerie open ending combine a somewhat hopeful turn-of-the-century shift in ecological awareness with a paralysing fear that is all too recognizable: our (in)ability to ultimately negotiate with beyond-human nature.

NOTES

1 Unless otherwise noted, translations are from Cheryl Leah Morgan's 2006 Canongate edition.
2 While I read *La pell freda* as ecohorror, Sánchez Piñol's first novel is popularly associated with the genres of adventure writing and historical fiction, particularly because of his extensive intertextual references to canonical authors of seafaring enterprises such as Daniel Defoe and Joseph Conrad. The novel can likewise be read with consideration for its allusions to *The Narrative of Arthur Gordon Pym of Nantucket* by Edgar Allan Poe because of its particularly macabre exploration of shipwrecks and the southern seas. Hispanists who have paid the novel critical attention study the text for its deliberations about postcolonialism, alterity and Otherness, neighbourliness, post-essentialist community, and Iberian and Catalan xenophobic attitudes to immigration. For these, see Gómez López-Quiñones; Liminyana Vico; Pardo Fernández; Resina; Viestenz.
3 On the ecogothic, see Andrew Smith and William Hughes's 2013 collection *EcoGothic*, David Del Principe's 2014 special issue of *Gothic Studies*, and Dawn Keetley and Matthew Wynn Sivils's introduction to the volume *Ecogothic in Nineteenth-Century American Literature*. On ecohorror, see Stephen A. Rust and Carter Soles's 2014 special cluster in *Interdisciplinary Studies in Literature and Environment* (*ISLE*) and Robin L. Murray and Joseph K. Heumann's 2016 book *Monstrous Nature: Environment and Horror on the Big Screen*.
4 Here, I have provided my own translation to more closely align with the original. Morgan translates this passage as follows: "The trees grew like

a herd of huddled animals *seeking their own kind*. Moss protected them,
a moss more compact than garden hedge and knee-high" (2; emphasis
added). Her text replaces the notion of a search for "refuge" with a desire
to be with one's "own kind," a substitution that lamentably undermines
the novel's exploration of materialist permeations across all bodies and
instead emphasizes xenophobic tendencies.

5 In her study on plant consciousness, *Beyond Human* contributor Olga
Colbert similarly observes plant sentience and animated vegetal
intervention in human history, a process that decentres human
consciousness in Julio Llamazares's *Luna de lobos*. In that novel, beech trees
among whom antifascist freedom fighters take shelter in the Spanish Civil
War's immediate aftermath feel and express pain and behave as a team,
thereby augmenting their agency interrelationally.

6 This fragment, along with all flashbacks to the protagonist's youth, are
absent from the English-language translation.

7 This positive valuation of weeds differs notably from the late eighteenth-
century Enlightenment view espoused by Gaspar Melchor de Jovellanos,
former Spanish Minister of Grace and Justice, who, as contributor Daniel
Frost examines in his chapter in this collection, saw weeds as obstacles to
sought-after agricultural reformation. Driven by the goal of production
for the benefit of humans, Jovellanos appraised the natural landscape as
nothing but *maleza* ("weeds," "underbrush"), whose Latin root is, notably,
malitia ("bad," "evil").

8 Morgan's translation omits this final fragment, which I include here:
"a monster with whom it was impossible to hold any dialogue."

9 I translate this fragment since it is absent from Morgan's translation, which
omits references to the protagonist's former IRA activism.

10 I prefer my translation for the last fragment of this citation, which Morgan
translates instead as "it might be possible to negotiate" (165), thereby
eliminating the notion of conviviality or of becoming with.

WORKS CITED AND CONSULTED

Alaimo, Stacy. "Discomforting Creature: Monstrous Nature in Recent Films."
Beyond Nature Writing: Expanding the Boundaries of Ecocriticism, edited by
Karla Armbruster and Kathleen R. Wallace, UP of Virginia, 2001,
pp. 279–96.
Alaimo, Stacy. *Exposed: Environmental Politics and Pleasures in Posthuman Times*.
U of Minnesota P, 2016.
Cohen, Jeffrey Jerome. *Prismatic Ecology: Ecotheory beyond Green*. U of
Minnesota P, 2013.
Cold Skin. Directed by Xavier Gens, Babiela Films, 2017.

Del Principe, David, editor. *EcoGothic*, special issue of *Gothic Studies*, vol. 16, no. 1, May 2014.

Estok, Simon C. *The Ecophobia Hypothesis*. Routledge, 2018.

Estok, Simon C. "Theorizing in a Space of Ambivalent Openness: Ecocriticism and Ecophobia." *Interdisciplinary Studies in Literature and Environment*, vol. 16. no. 2, spring 2009, pp. 203–25. *Oxford Academic*, https://doi.org/10.1093/isle/isp010.

Gómez López-Quiñones, Antonio. *La precariedad de la forma. Lo sublime en la narrativa española contemporánea: Javier Tomeo, Enrique Vila-Matas, Albert Sánchez Piñol y Arturo Pérez-Reverte*. Biblioteca Nueva, 2011.

Gutiérrez Carbajo, Francisco. "El animal no humano en algunas obras teatrales actuales." *Anales de la Literatura Española Contemporánea*, vol. 34, no. 2, 2009, pp. 67–92.

Keetley, Dawn, and Matthew Wynn Sivils. "Introduction: Approaches to the Ecogothic." *Ecogothic in Nineteenth-Century American Literature*, edited by Dawn Keetley and Matthew Wynn Sivils, Routledge, 2018, pp. 1–20.

Liminyana Vico, Elisabet. "La alteridad en *La pell freda* de Albert Sánchez Piñol: Una lectura del monstruo desde el racismo." *Hispanet Journal*, vol. 5, 2012, pp. 1–16.

Lovelock, James. *The Revenge of Gaia: Earth's Climate Crisis and the Fate of Humanity*. Penguin, 2007.

Lovelock, James. *The Vanishing Face of Gaia: A Final Warning*. Penguin, 2009.

Morgan, Cheryl Leah, translator. *Cold Skin*. By Albert Sánchez Piñol, Canongate, 2006.

Murray, Robin L., and Joseph K. Heumann. *Monstrous Nature: Environment and Horror on the Big Screen*. U Nebraska P, 2016.

Pardo Fernández, Rodrigo. "El *limes* de la civilización en la novela *La piel fría* de Albert Sánchez Piñol." *Castilla: Estudios de Literatura*, vol. 5, 2014, pp. 444–57.

Parker, Elizabeth, and Michelle Poland. "Gothic Nature: An Introduction." *Gothic Nature: New Directions in Ecohorror and the EcoGothic*, vol. 1, 2019, pp. 1–20.

Plumwood, Val. "Prey to a Crocodile." *AISLING Magazine*, no. 30, https://www.aislingmagazine.com/aislingmagazine/articles/TAM30/Val Plumwood.html. Accessed 17 February 2020.

Resina, Joan Ramon. "Tránsito imposible: La seducción de lo abyecto en *Pell Freda* de Albert Sánchez Piñol." *El andar tierras, deseos y memorias: Homenaje a Dieter Ingenschay*, edited by Jenny Haase et al., Iberoamericana, 2008, pp. 129–43.

Rust, Stephen A., and Carter Soles. "Ecohorror Special Cluster: 'Living in Fear, Living in Dread, Pretty Soon We'll All Be Dead.'" *Interdisciplinary Studies in Literature and Environment*, vol. 21, no. 3, summer 2014, pp. 509–12. *Oxford Academic*, https://doi.org/10.1093/isle/isu085.

Rust, Stephen A., and Carter Soles, editors. Ecohorror, special cluster of *Interdisciplinary Studies in Literature and Environment*, vol. 21, no. 3, summer 2014, pp. 509–87.

Sánchez Piñol, Albert. *La pell freda*. 48th ed., La Campana, 2019.

Showers, Brian J. "What We Hide within Us: Thoughts on Albert Sánchez Piñol's *Cold Skin*." *21st-Century Gothic: Great Gothic Novels since 2000*, edited by Danel Olson, Scarecrow, 2011, pp. 98–110.

Simpson, Catherine. "Australian Eco-horror and Gaia's Revenge: Animals, Eco-nationalism and the 'New Nature.'" *Studies in Australasian Cinema*, vol. 4, no. 1, 2010, pp. 43–54. *Taylor & Francis Online*, https://doi.org/10.1386/sac.4.1.43_1.

Singer, Peter. *Animal Liberation: A New Ethics for Our Treatment of Animals*. Discus, 1975.

Smith, Andrew, and William Hughes, editors. *EcoGothic*. Manchester UP, 2013, pp. 1–14.

Viestenz, William. "Monstrous Birth: The Evolving Neighbor in Albert Sánchez Piñol's *La pell freda*." *Hispanic Issues On Line*, vol. 15, 2014, pp. 179–99, https://conservancy.umn.edu/bitstream/handle/11299/184484/hiol_15_10_viestenz_monstrous_birth.pdf?sequence=1&isAllowed=y.

PART FOUR

Medium as Activism Igniter

Monstrous Humanity: An Ecopostcolonial Reading of Laura Gallego García's Trilogy *Guardianes de la Ciudadela*

VICTORIA L. KETZ

Young adult literature (YAL) is a genre of writing that seeks to engage adolescents by presenting characters of similar ages involved in a societal or cultural challenge relatable to the reader. Since it mirrors the intended reader's range of emotions, YAL can become a vehicle for social acceptance and positive self-image by fostering understanding, empathy, and compassion, and it can do so while exploring values and critical global issues, like the environment, that warrant current attention. Though M. Daphne Kutzer, a British critical scholar, states "the role of children's texts … is to help acculturate children into society and to teach them to behave and believe in acceptable ways" (xv), many times these texts go beyond propagating mainstream perspectives and treatment of the non-human environment by leading readers to critically examine societal hierarchies and to reimagine relationships among species. This literary form, disregarded for many years and devalued among critics, has seen, since the mid 1990s, "increased viability as a body of critically lauded literature" (Cart). Cultivated by a number of well-known authors, it now includes narrative, poetry, non-fiction, picture books, comics, and graphic novels. YAL pushes the boundaries of artistic innovation by embracing experimentation.

One of the most interesting features of YAL is the importance placed on the connection between protagonists and their environment. Due to the interconnectivity between the fictional characters and nature, literary scholar Harini Das has argued that the adoption of ecocriticism when analysing children's texts is vital. The ecocritical perspective offers an acute vision, which can lead to change in the patterns of humans' inhabitation of the planet, to analysis of the representation of nature in texts, and to the reassessment of the values held by society about the environment and non-human life. This chapter employs the lens of postcolonial ecocriticism to analyse Laura Gallego García's *Guardianes de la Ciudadela* trilogy of novels, comprised of *El bestiario de Axlin* (2018), *El secreto de Xein* (2018), and *La misión de Rox* (2019). In these works, Gallego animates young readers to engage with complex environmental and social issues by revealing the dangers of striated social structures, speciesism, and dualism, while also encouraging environmental literacy and the development of an ecoconscious self-identity. Gallego's world demonstrates a systemically biased allocation of uncultivated and urban space as well as a striation of social structures. Speciesism in the text creates class distinctions and apportions specific sites for each group to inhabit. Dualisms, including urban/rural, centre/periphery, human/non-human, civilized/savage, anthropocentric/supernatural, individual/collective, self/other, and good/evil, further a binary construction of the world, which heightens the environmental crisis in the narrative. This study explores how an ecocritical postcolonial agenda in Gallego's work not only shapes the young fictional characters in their development of a self-identity but also has the potential to shape real-life young readers, thereby creating basic environmental literacy and inspiring environmental leaders for the future. The narratives' language prods readers to an ecopostcolonial sensibility by various methods. The texts explicitly delineate injustices that are perpetrated on the environment and its inhabitants and that affect sustainable life. The hierarchical cataloguing of non-humans in bestiaries and the recognition of tenuous physical and emotional differences with these beings remind the reader that humans are largely responsible for the planet's disequilibrium. The balancing of ecosystems, endorsed in YAL, is vital for sustaining all life on earth. By "reframing the text," as Kate Rigby, British environmental scholar, states, the young reader can better understand "the necessity of recalling the true cost, both to subordinate humans and to the earth, of our production processes and consumption habits" (151). Thus, Gallego's YAL work develops an ecoawareness and mobilizes the reader to take action towards healthy ecological habits.

Laura Gallego García (Valencia, 1977) is a Spanish author of teen and young adult fantasy fiction who has examined a wide range of literary themes. In the *Guardianes de la Ciudadela* triolgy, Gallego explores the relationship between humans and non-human entities. The trilogy is a *Bildungsroman* of three main characters who seek to save their world from monsters whose attacks have depopulated rural areas and threaten human existence. Axlin, one of the young protagonists, initiates a journey in order to learn more about the monsters and to catalogue their qualities in a bestiary that will help combat their attacks. In her travels, she befriends others, including Xein, Rox, and Dex, who join her quest to find the origin of the beasts. During this process, all of the characters undertake voyages, overcome challenges, learn to appreciate their talents, and confront their limitations in order to mature and find their place in the world.

Gallego's unique composition blends high fantasy with social, political, and environmental concerns. This trilogy can be classified as an environmentally oriented work as it meets the characteristics outlined by Lawrence Buell, a pioneer of ecocriticism:

1. The non-human environment is present not merely as a framing device but as a presence that begins to suggest that human history is implicated in natural history.
2. Human interest is not understood to be the only legitimate interest.
3. Human accountability to the environment is part of the text's ethical framework.
4. Some sense of the environment as a process rather than as a constant or a given is at least implicit in the text. (7–8)

In *Guardianes*, the intertwined history of human and non-human species has evolved to a point where the environmental imbalance created by a colonizing human group threatens an impending ecocatastrophe. Thus, an analysis of Gallego's trilogy is also enriched when a postcolonial approach is applied to ecocriticism. Postcolonial theory focuses on how colonial hegemony has influenced power relationships, economic diversity, language usage, and cultural identity to maintain control over the other, who struggles to reclaim their self-identity. It is clear from the onset that a dominant class in this fictional world has created an ecological disaster, as it colonized the lands and introduced new species without taking into consideration the environmental impact. Although the combination of ecocritical and postcolonial lenses for an analysis might seem disjunctive, it is possible to meld these two theories. Rob Nixon, an environmental humanist, has contended that between postcolonialism and ecocriticism lie "schisms" (235) due to their dominant diametrical concerns of hybridity/purity, displacement/place, transnationality/nationality, and marginality/privilege. However, critics such as Graham Huggan and Helen Tiffin see a commonality between the two in that both are "utopian discourses aimed at providing conceptual possibilities for a material transformation of the world" ("Green Postcolonialism" 10). While postcolonial critical practice explores the problematics posed by social, cultural, economic, and political hegemony, ecocriticism engages in the study of anthropocentric interaction and relation with the physical environment. This chapter will focus primarily on the dialectical relationship evident in ecocriticism's and postcolonialism's concern for the social constructs and material experiences of class, species, identity, interspecies encounters, and social justice. In Gallego's narratives, the dominant group controls the knowledge and the metanarrative of society, asserting superiority while categorically excluding and vilifying other entities inhabiting the ecosystem. The narrative adopts the concerns of the younger marginalized citizens and questions the choices made by the ruling class.

Spatial Allocation in Gallego's Ecopostcolonial Text

The inclusion of maps in each of the books in Gallego's trilogy highlights the cartographic designs of those in power, who seek to dominate the depicted spaces. According to geographer David Harvey, "Mapping is a discursive activity that incorporates power. The power to map the world in one way rather than another is a crucial tool in political struggles" (111–12). Cartography has long been utilized by (neo)colonial pursuits as a way to lay claim and control borders; yet the absence of prescriptive identifiers, such as cardinal directions, borders, or scaling, on diagrams that emphasize the topographical features of mountains, rivers, and vegetation suggests the novels' contention with measurements that aid in conquest. In *El secreto de Xein*, there is a cadastral map indicating the individual properties located in the Citadel. What becomes evident is that the orderliness of the old city contrasts with the outer rings of the urban centre, where the neighbourhoods become progressively more chaotic. Cartography, in this trilogy, illustrates the waning power of the elite, who struggle to control the area and impose their world view. In this series, rather than reproducing colonial-style indoctrination, the fragmented cartography relies on the reader to decode and assemble the knowledge about this world. By observing and reinterpreting the elements of the maps, the reader decolonizes the space and assigns new meaning to the information contained in them. These maps offer an ecopostcolonial view of the world, as they neither are centred on the major cities nor provide limits to the world; instead they highlight natural elements. The topographical distribution of space grants readers a symbolic window from which to view social and environmental inequities.

The geographical land distribution in the trilogy addresses ecological as well as postcolonial issues. Cheryll Glotfelty, scholar and co-founder of the Association of the Study of Literature and the Environment, argues that place should be considered a new category in addition to race, class, and gender in ecocritical studies (xix). The unnamed world of the trilogy is spatially constructed as a neocolonial place through the dualistic terminology of wilderness and civilization. The dominant power's campaign depicting the countryside as wilderness and the cities as civilization creates a binary that responds to an anthropocentric hierarchical conceptualization of the world whereby the wilderness is related to negative attributes while the cities are viewed positively. The attitudes towards these environmental spaces respond to patriarchal and ethnocentric imperialistic beliefs and behaviours in which the depiction of the natural environment "promotes a type of environmental stewardship based on … [an] interpretation … that suggests only … civilized … people are capable, rightful environmental stewards" (Echterling 100). Throughout the narration, the theme of rights in and responsibilities to the community evolves to one that engages the entire ecosystem.

In *Guardianes*, the wilderness becomes a site of conflict when two competing powers seek to impose their species's control over the land. Monster attacks depopulate the rural areas and threaten the political and environmental stability of so-called civilized lands, while also casting doubt on the founding families' legitimizing claim as regents. The human dominant group, which mirrors white hegemonic power, seeks to impose their will and ideology over other so-called uncivilized lands. The wilderness is portrayed as inhospitable, threatening, and forbidding by the dominant power, and these remote lands are given names such as the Final Frontier, the Savage Lands, and the Forgotten Lands. Ursula Heise, a prominent ecocritic, notes that "the wilderness concept makes it difficult for a political program to conceptualize desirable forms of human inhabitation, relying as it does on the categorical separation of human beings from nature" ("Hitchhiker" 507). Interestingly, banishment to remote outposts like the Final Frontier is used to punish nonconformity in individuals who threaten the society's way of life. There, at a mountain range constructed by humans to deter the colossal monsters from entering human space, soldiers know that "jamás regresaría[n] a casa. Aquel destino era el lugar reservado para aquellos que ya no eran útiles en la Ciudadela que causaban problemas o que estaban perdiendo la fuerza, la resistencia, y los reflejos de la juventud" ("they will never return home. That destination was the place reserved for those who were no longer useful in the Citadel, who caused trouble, or who were losing the strength, stamina, and reflexes of youth"; *Misión* 30–1).[1] Thus, the neocolonial desire to control paradoxically banishes human and non-human life that is considered unproductive and threatening.[2]

These remote outposts connect with the capital city through a web of enclaves, vestiges of colonial settlements meant to help populate the terrain and form a human sphere. As the colonial enterprise failed due to the humans' inability to control the flora and fauna, the inhabitants of the enclaves were left to fend for themselves and provide a safe haven along the trade routes. Unwittingly, the imperial project that established the enclaves harbours danger for the sustainability of the ecosystem, since "[t]his domination strips nature of any value other than as a material resource and commodity and leads to a gradual destruction that may in the end deprive humanity of its basis for subsistence" (Heise, "Hitchhiker's" 507). Yet the dominant power's project falls short, as the enclaves' isolation leads to a means of negotiating with nature through a communal project. The enclaves are the only setting in the trilogy that approaches sustainability and ecological balance. In the enclaves, humans cultivate their own vegetables, raise their own animals, and manufacture necessary tools, in communities that are entirely self-contained aside from occasional visits from hunting parties and itinerant peddlers. The children are raised as communal individuals so that responsibility for their survival does not fall on one family unit. Further exemplifying this fluid societal structure, people's tasks in the community are assigned by their current abilities but may be reassigned if the community's needs or their abilities change. The alternative modes of social organization existent in the enclaves provide a blueprint for readers to imagine more sustainable communities by challenging the dominant societal structures established by the Citadel. By building communities based on kinship, they establish a web of relations between households, which mobilizes them into collective actions (Chandoke 2872). This representation of interwoven human relationships suggests the possibility of extending this network to include non-human entities.[3]

Unlike these small non-hierarchic human settlements, the capital city replicates the rigid hierarchy that governs an anthropocentric world. Founded by the original eight families, the Citadel is the largest and most important urban centre in this world, housing the seat of government as well as all other important institutions and concentrating the community's resources. This urban construct is the locus of homes, markets, finances, management, and knowledge-based activities (Chandoke 2868). The city's structure provides safety for the upper classes in the centre and diminishing protection for the lesser classes in the surrounding concentric neighbourhoods. Reserved for the homes of the founding families, who have the privilege of ambulating freely throughout the city, the heavily guarded central old city is accessible only with paperwork secured through an audience with a magistrate. The first expansion of the Citadel contains the institutional headquarters and the library, where the majority of the society's knowledge is housed. Joanne Gottlieb, an American ecocritic, views cities as progressive sites defined by the flow of information, which diminishes as it approaches the peripheries (234). This is certainly reflected in the construct of the Citadel, where knowledge is concentrated in the centre and its transmission diminishes as it radiates outwards. The second expansion of the city contains the majority of dwellings for the common people, as well as several plazas. The exterior ring is where the marketplace is located, along with new housing developments for the recent influx of people arriving to the Citadel.

The cultivated urban topography of the Citadel reserves the outermost concentric ring for minority populations such as the unemployed and environmental refugees. Guided by the belief that cities are "social organizations to promote the protection of the individual from a hostile and chaotic environment" (Wolfe 87), the humans flock there, not realizing that the Citadel is not a self-sustaining ecosystem. The ecological crisis brought on by the monster attacks triggers a migration of humans to the capital, depopulating the western territories while revealing the inequity and tenuous construct of this society. The displacement of the rural population to an urban domain that is unable to accommodate them places pressure on the urban infrastructure and results in the proliferation of makeshift housing for the environmental refugees at the peripheries. This terrain becomes a site of contested space (as more humans are compressed into a small area) with insufficient alimentary resources (since the food chain originated in the now depopulated rural areas). However, the societal structure created by the ruling class reserves the best space and scarce resources for them. Ironically, the presence of the inner city's manicured park, called the Plaza de los Ocho Fundadores ("Eight Founders' Square"), represents a cultivated wilderness where the "aesthetic appreciation of nature has not only been a class-coded activity, [but also signifies] the insulation of the middle and upper classes" (Reed 151). This space is emblematic of the Founders' desire not only to control nature but also to prevent access to well-being and prosperity from outside the limited inner circle.

Social Order in Gallego's Ecopostcolonial Texts

The striated social system created in Gallego's YAL texts demonstrates the manner in which current structures abuse and misuse not only the humans but also the various other species inhabiting shared spaces. Gallego's trilogy reflects human societies that are hierarchical, with each class assuming power over others through language, knowledge, and culture. The trilogy extends this social stratification to four main categories of entities that inhabit the environment – humans, Guardians, monsters, and animals – and, in doing so, explores the ecological dimensions of expansionist and neocolonial structures. In Gallego's fictional world, the system of governance concentrates power in the hands of a select group of humans by constructing a political and legal system that inequitably benefits them. Philosopher Henri Bergson notes that humans often like to elevate themselves with respect to other living beings: "l'humanité est invitée à se placer à un niveau déterminé – plus haut qu'une société animale, où l'obligation ne serait que la force de l'instinct, mais moins haut qu'une assemblée de dieux" ("humanity is invited to place itself at a determined level – higher than an animal society, where the only obligation is the force of instinct, but lower than an assembly of gods"; 86; my trans.). The Founders' self-perceived superiority guides their actions in the text. Of particular importance are the interrelationships established between the different species, which lead to stratified social dynamics whose inequities mirror those embedded in the unequal allocation of geographical space and which suggest a society in crisis.

In *Guardianes*, the oligarchy asserts rigid social structures that threaten the peaceful coexistence of communal and environmental configurations. The Founders, composed of the eight founding families who built the Citadel, assume a dominant role in their relations with other groups, imposing upon them their beliefs and values, which results in inflexible social systems and inequitable treatment. The ruling class subscribes to a conservative ideology that fosters neocolonial morals and values. Their attitudes and behaviours towards the land and its dwellers are both paternalistic and imperialistic. As the original settlers of the land, they not only organized the city's edifices but also created the legal system that protects their interests. Adherence to their laws is mandated, and any deviance is punished by ostracism from the community or death. The Founders carefully cultivate "anthropocentric delusions of grandeur" to maintain their social structures (Alaimo 292). The power of this speciesist class is passed down from one generation to the next, and special care is taken to preserve their bloodlines through intermarriage.

Strategically exercising power over the larger group of humans by regulating the flow of knowledge and suppressing the discourse that surrounds the topic of the monsters, the Founders promote an illusion of safety and well-being for the citizens of the Citadel. As postcolonial scholar Edward Said notes, "[T]he power to narrate, or to block other narratives from forming and emerging, is very important to culture and imperialism, and constitutes one of the main connections between them" (2). In Gallego's novels, the ruling class zealously guard the cultural narrative they have constructed around the social fantasy of human superiority over other species. For this reason, Axlin's bestiary represents a challenge to the Founders, who fear that she will learn and share her knowledge of the Guardians' secret with the general public. Initially they attempt to thwart her investigation, later they try to discredit her, and finally they attempt to assassinate her. Spanish ecoliterary scholar Luis I. Prádanos has pointed out that two aspects of colonial dynamics are the dispossession of common rights and collective knowledge and "the imposition of a universal definition of the good life that is neither desirable nor viable" (53). In this trilogy there is no equity between the distinct groups, as each has been assigned different values and rules by the Founders. The Guardians and non-human beings, deemed inferior, see their freedoms and behaviours restricted by the Founders' nonsensical laws to preserve the human society's purported good life.

The narrative promoted by the Founders fosters a teraphobic attitude towards the non-human entities due to the latter's constant invasion of the enclaves, which disrupts the humans' way of life and poses a cultural threat. To best understand the discourse of speciesism and the alienation of non-human beings in ecocritical contexts, Heise asserts that one must consider

> how the nonhuman interacts with human culture: how ecological conditions shape cultural expression and conversely how culture shapes the perception and uses of natural environments; how cultural communities structure and give meaning to human's relations with other species; and how risk scenarios, crises, and disasters amplify or reduce sociocultural differences, define community boundaries, and change cultural practices. The question of difference in ecocriticism, in other words, is never purely human. Alterity is always also defined by the nonhuman other. ("Globality" 638)

The Founders, who only focus negatively on alterity, ignore the productive interrelationship that could exist between humans and non-human entities. The anthropogenic ecocatastrophe elicits terror among the humans, while also nurturing a deep-seated hatred of the monsters. By highlighting their non-humanness, the ruling class provokes fear and anxiety in the population. Huggan and Tiffan have highlighted "[t]he history of western racism and its imbrication with discourses of speciesism; the use of animals as a basis for human social division; and, above all perhaps, the metaphorisation and deployment of 'animal' as a derogatory term in genocidal and marginalizing discourses" (*Postcolonial Ecocriticism* 135). The Founders similarly promote a beast fable, which enables them to mistreat the other entities that coexist with them due to a misguided sense of their own superiority. As Huggan argues, such attitudes can be described as an "arrogant belief in sovereign reason, a belief that has historically been used to legitimize dominion over the entire animal kingdom, as well as over large numbers of allegedly 'inferior' members of the human race" (710). To justify the extermination of non-human creatures, the Founders foster the idea that monsters are repulsive and vilify their nature (Alaimo 280). And as postmodernist Donna Haraway notes, "Monsters have always defined the limits of community in Western imaginations" (180). This long-standing limit in Western imaginaries often means that humans insist on implementing a firm division between humans and non-human entities. Hence, the Founders frame a cultural narrative that spatially and ideologically isolates each of the different species.[4]

A paradoxical relationship emerges between the Founders and the non-humans. On the one hand, these entities are believed by the humans to pose an existential threat, so the deliberate erasure of their species is seen as a means of guaranteeing victory in the neocolonial project. On the other hand, the Founders rely on the non-humans' existence to secure their position of power. By purporting to guarantee safety to the human stratum in the Citadel, the Founders are able to assert their laws over the human population and remain in power. Human oppression of the other relies on animal metaphors and categorization to justify exploitation, objectification, and enslavement. Many of the captured unmentionable monsters are incarcerated in the Bastion. There, they employ methods to assert dominance over the other through physical punishment, torture, and ritual (Huggan and Tiffin, *Postcolonial Ecocriticism* 163). Thus, by controlling the discourse, the Founders label these entities as monsters and play on their infamy as predators to legitimize their imperial rule. However, the propagation of the notion of the non-human entities' savagery causes the human world, which supports a delicate network of organic alliances, to enter into crisis.

The unbalanced power dynamics between the dominant group and the monsters is repeated with other species in the trilogy. With their physical enhancements and favoured genetic origins, the Guardians serve as an alter ego of humanity, representing that which is admirable yet feared. This division of human/non-human and familiar/foreign serves as a metonym for the speciesist divisions in this world. As Jessica Langer, a postcolonial theorist, notes, "[T]he distinction between the self and the other has functioned as a method of control in colonial societies, creating a power hierarchy predicated both on physical and cultural difference and on enforced Foucaldian differentials of knowledge" (82). Foucault's history of thought relies on three axes – knowledge, power, and ethics – which in Gallego's trilogy manifest as the Founders' suppression of how they created non-human entities, their use of the Guardians to eradicate those non-human entities, and their justification of this extermination. These neocolonial practices have ecological implications, since the Founders' creation of the non-human species to assert their own power causes an imbalance in the environment.

Through speciesism, the relationship between the Founders and the Guardians mirrors a master-slave relationship, as is evident when Raxni points out, "Los guardianes se han convertido en esclavos de los humanos a los que protegían" ("The Guardians have become slaves to the humans whom they protected"; *Misión* 131). Heise has noted that the presence of non-human species in environmental texts serves a very specific function: "The otherness, the exploitation, and the oppression of the animal are sometimes a transparent metaphor, double, or proxy for humans' oppression of humans, as frequent assimilation of indigenous peoples, colonized populations, or more generally racial others with animal existence highlights" ("Globality" 640). Oppression is achieved through the systematic inculcation of the Guardians with the Founders' values (neocolonial power) as a means of inducing them to kill the unmentionable monsters (colonized). The Guardians' hybrid nature undercuts the colonial ideology, as it challenges the dominant knowledge and stereotypical representation of what is considered monstrous. Postcolonial scholar Homi Bhabha asserts that stereotypes create the illusion of safety for the group in power since they grant them superiority over the other (37). The revelation that the Guardians are the results of a genetic cross of human and monster lays bare the reason for the severe repression by the Founders as well as their fear of the Guardians. More concretely, "[I]n hybridity lies the potential for humanity to be either subsumed or enhanced, or perhaps both" (Langer 108). This hybridity results in a superior being that surpasses the capabilities of either of its progenitors.

Rather than accept the Founders' cultural construct of an anthropocentric world, the young protagonists espouse a biocentric perspective of their surroundings. Gallego's main adolescent characters recognize that living organisms exist only in relation to other entities as well as to the inorganic material world, giving rise to a complex web of interactions between the different organisms and their environment (Vital 92). Axlin is the first to promote biocentrism by conceiving a more equitable world. She views her bestiary as a positive way to promulgate information to avoid attacks by different non-human entities, subverting the compendium's original function as a colonial tool of knowledge. Traditionally, bestiaries have contained detailed descriptions of animals' physical characteristics, along with their behaviours in their material environments, and they were first written by the ancient Greeks, including Aristotle, Herodotus, and Pliny the Elder. When recreated in medieval times, these catalogues of beasts were also accompanied by a moral lesson. This desire to categorize animals re-emerged in the Enlightenment and beyond with the works of Linnaeus and Darwin. As cultural theorist Shehla Burney states, "[T]he power to use one's language – the license to name, to express, to speak, to represent oneself – has belonged to the colonial oppressor, not to the oppressed" (52). Bestiaries manifest the colonial desire to quantify, qualify, and control biological life as well as land by claiming, studying, mapping, and renaming environmental features for the sake of human knowledge (Adams and Mulligan 24). Therefore, this attempted organization of the environment in a hierarchical system promotes the binary oppositions of human/non-human, civilized/savage, and superior/inferior. Yet Axlin's purpose for writing the bestiary poses a challenge to the dominant power in that she seeks to reveal the role played by the Founders in contributing to the rise of the monsters and their subsequent desire to eradicate this species. Throughout the trilogy, the protagonists believe that humans have in some fashion provoked the unwanted attacks by the non-humans. Therefore, the search for information about the monsters is brought about by the desire to lessen this harm and reset the balance in the world. Literary critic Philippe Merlo suggests that in the works of Gallego the pursuit of an equilibrium is paramount: "este equilibrio es sinónimo de libertad y sobre todo es la síntesis entre lo mejor de cada parte constituyente de su ser" ("This balance is synonymous with freedom, and above all it is the synthesis between the best of each being's constituent parts"; 291; my trans.). James Mandrell, a Spanish studies scholar, also points to the importance of equilibrium in Gallego's fiction, whether it be physical, emotional, psychological, political, or ideological (25–8). Hence, the youths' quest is guided by a desire to restore the ecological balance of their world.

In response to the need for equilibrium, Gallego presents alternative modes of social organization, communities that challenge the dominant power's notion of a civil society. The first is one encountered by the adolescent Rox when she returns to the enclave where she spent her childhood. There, she discovers a social system that is the inverse of the Founders' world. The colony of silver-eyed Guardians, who refer to themselves as the Blessed, live in an arrangement where the human inhabitants serve them: "Ellas realizaban la mayor parte de las tareas domésticas, preparaban la comida para todos, limpiaban las casas, y se encargaban de cuidar el huerto y de los animales" ("They did most of the housework, prepared food for everyone, cleaned the houses, and took care of the garden and the animals"; *Misión* 132). When Rox tries to convince the residents of the enclave to return with her to the Citadel for their own safety, Raxni, her sister, points out that they are better off in their village: "¿Acaso no es verdad que en la Ciudadela mandan las personas comunes, y vosotros, los Guardianes, obedecéis sin rechistar? … Entonces, vuestro líder … ¿tiene ojos plateados? ¿O dorados … ?" ("Isn't it true that ordinary people rule the Citadel, and you, the Guardians, obey without question? … So your leader … does he have silver eyes? Or gold … ?"; *Misión* 109). Rox has never considered the lack of equity among the species of her society or the powerless state of the Guardians, who, ironically, are physically superior to the humans. This visit leads her to question the validity of the value system promoted by the Founders, who have convinced others "to embrace the reasoning of their oppressors" (Prádanos 51). Despite this newly acquired knowledge, Rox succumbs to her training and instinctively kills the unmentionable monster, whom the villagers consider their god (*Misión* 161). In contrast to the hierarchical system of Rox's childhood enclave, which is presented as unsustainable because it subjugates other species just like that of the Founders, Romixa's enclave situated in La tierra civilizada ("The Civilized Land") emerges as a more viable social structure. This village functions as a communal project where all members and their talents are valued equitably. The communal living arrangement attracts the young protagonists, who decide to settle in this enclave at the dénouement of the trilogy.

The presentation of the varieties of species in the *Guardianes* forces young readers to rethink their perceptions of the other. By endowing its non-human species with anthropomorphic traits and illustrating the crises caused by speciesism, the trilogy encourages readers to experience empathy for the non-humans and to question the Founders' views of them. Alberto Martos García, a literature professor, remarks on the ability of fantasy "de construir imaginarios, fundar reinos, relacionar razas y seres de todas clases, en suma ampliar horizontes" ("to build imaginaries, found kingdoms, link races and beings of all kinds, in short, expand horizons"; 18; my trans.). By functioning in a fictional world, the protagonists are able to work together to rectify the ecological error that was committed by the humans in the past and assume responsibility for the future. This responds to comparitivist Katrina Dodson's call for a "reframing [of] human-animal relationships in more symmetrical or two-way terms; here, mutual dependence, vulnerability, and drive for life are crucial factors that connect human and nonhuman animals" (15). It is worth noting, however, that Gallego's narrative's championing of an ecocitizenry falters at the trilogy's conclusion. The final novel ends on a celebratory note, as the protagonists accomplish their quest and return the world to a supposed ecological equilibrium. What is not addressed is that now that the metaphysical portal is closed, the propagation of the non-humans will cease, dooming two species, the monsters and the Guardians, to extinction.

Ecopostcolonial Identities: New World Order

The impact that societies have on the natural environment cannot be overstated, and in Gallego's novel, the consequences are hopeful. The young protagonists champion more equitable and sustainable ways to inhabit their world. Their conceptualization of the environment is quite different from that of the Founders and deeply affects the formation of their self-identity. Due to their concern for nature, they take cues from the environment, and their identities are forged in relationship to non-humans instead of in opposition to them. Thus, the protagonists are able to appreciate non-human entities in a way that previous generations did not due to the Founders' ideology. Axlin exhibits wonderment and interest in trying to understand better the life forms that co-inhabit her world (*Bestiario* 102). Even Xein notes that in the Founders' battle with the non-human life forms, "había algo absurdo en todo aquello" ("there was something absurd in all of that"; *Bestiario* 387). By valuing the non-humans on their own terms, the protagonists in Gallego's trilogy seek to foster an interspecies kinship, whereby ecological crisis can be mitigated and the world re-envisioned from a biocentrist perspective.

The journey to self-actualization is more problematic for Guardians like Xein and Rox due to their hybrid lineage, compounded by the fact that they are separated from their families at a crucial developmental stage. According to pedagogy specialist Lois Stover, adolescents need to delineate themselves in order to "determine an individual set of moral, ethical, religious or political principles; come to terms with developing sexuality and with physiological changes brought on by puberty; develop positive relationships with peers; think about the future; and forge a niche in the larger society" (108). The Guardians are denied this self-identification and self-authentication, since their training fosters a unified collective identity. Stripped of their individuality, all cadets wear the same grey uniform and sport identical haircuts. Suppression of human emotions is necessary for them to execute their duties. Yet when Xein kills a metamorph in front of Axlin, he thinks, "Piensa que soy un monstruo. Peor que un monstruo" ("She thinks I am a monster. Worse than a monster"; *Secreto* 181). This self-doubt only increases as he begins to realize that the Guardians may themselves be the children of monsters (*Secreto* 249). In order to mitigate his fears, Xein decides to return to visit his mother to ask about his origins, and he learns that "su padre había sido un monstruo innombrable. Que él mismo era también, por tanto, un monstruo en cierto modo" ("his father had been an unmentionable monster. That he himself was also, therefore, a monster to a certain extent"; *Secreto* 319). The realization that he is what his society detests the most, a monster, fills him with self-loathing. Xein has internalized the Founders' neocolonial ideology, which relegates the monsters to an inferior status. As the concept of mimicry explains, those in power construct an identity for their subordinates based on the dominant class's philosophical system rather than the self-proclaimed identity of the individual. Postcolonial theorist Franz Fanon has demonstrated that colonialism creates a loss of identity in the other when they internalize the dominant culture's values and attitudes (51). This generates feelings of inferiority, negativity, and self-hatred in the subordinate. Xein has to overcome "the spectre of the stranger, the other, who is both self and not-self, who is human and dismissed as 'animal'" (Langer 107). Similar to the experiences of the YAL readers, Xein must forge an identity by understanding all the components that constitute his existence.

While establishing his identity, Xein goes through a process of self-acceptance throughout the *Guardianes* trilogy, rejecting the characteristics ingrained in him by the dominant power. His journey for self-definition is as perilous and difficult as the unsurmountable tasks in the missions upon which he embarks. Similar to the development that Merlo has noted in Gallego's *Alas de fuego*, the hero goes through a three-step process (286–8). In the trilogy, Xein must first come to terms with his special abilities, then realize that he is a hybrid being, and finally accept his dual nature. According to Anabel Sáiz Ripoll, a Spanish children's literature specialist, these feelings, and the way in which they are represented, "hacen que los personajes de Laura Gallego sean reales, ya que se emocionan, lloran y sufren, ríen y aman, aunque no siempre tengan una naturaleza del todo humana. El amor es el sentimiento rey, aunque a menudo confundido con la amistad … y en ocasiones desvirtuado por el odio" ("make Laura Gallego's characters real, since they get emotional, cry and suffer, laugh and love, although they do not always have a fully human nature. Love is the main sentiment, although it is often confused with friendship ... and sometimes distorted by hatred"; 15; my trans.). By learning to accept and celebrate his hybridity, Xein begins to be able to use it as a strategy for challenging the dominant culture. In this manner, Xein and the other protagonists learn to re-delineate the societal limits placed upon them by the Founders and demarcate new boundaries that value all beings in this world.

Conclusion

The ecopostcolonialist critique of the environmental imbalances caused by humans, the extinction of non-human species, and the lack of sustainability of systems in crisis in Gallego's *Guardianes* trilogy draws attention to the webbed structures and conservationist attitudes proposed by the younger generation of characters to replace the detrimental anthropocentric and hierarchical structures that control knowledge. The attitudes towards the environment and the non-human species depicted in this work challenge the ideologies surrounding speciesism and imperialism. Since YAL establishes connections between the fictional events and the real world, this genre has the capacity to encourage readers to internalize the possibility of new values and attitudes. Michael Cart, a literary historian, notes that YAL "equips readers for dealing with the realities of impending adulthood and for assuming the rights and responsibilities of citizenship." Rashna Singh, a children's literature specialist, points to the intentionality of the elements included in a YAL text: "political and ideological dimensions of children's literature are not just an accident or a harmless by-product but an integral part of its purpose" (7). As evident from the work of these theorists, and from Gallego's novels, YAL can serve as a vehicle for change, as it breaks with established norms and embraces imagination to find solutions to critical current problems. Many urgent social topics are addressed in Gallego's trilogy in an open and creative manner, such as environmental concerns, communal projects, class divisions, fear of immigration, the fallibility of those in power, and acceptance of same-sex coupling. The protagonists defy social rules that hierarchize human and non-human lives when they learn to accept those who differ from them, a development that highlights the value of all types of beings on the ecological spectrum.

Like the genre of science fiction, fantasy attracts readers during their adolescence because it is "devoted to the principle that change is continuous, inevitable, and even desirable" (Asimov 264). The fact that the stories occur in worlds that are able to transform for the better is very appealing to young readers, as it diminishes the frustration that they feel in the world in which they live. Laura Gallego has opined that YAL provides readers with hope: "no se trata de pintarlo todo de color de rosa, sino de hacer ver a los niños y a los jóvenes que hay cosas que se pueden cambiar; que tenemos el poder de la acción y la fuerza del futuro; que juntos podemos hacer un mundo mejor, pero no conseguiremos nada si nos quedamos en un rincón lamentándonos de lo mal que va todo" ("It is not about seeing everything through rose-coloured glasses, but about making children and young people see that there are things that can be changed; that we have the power of action and the strength of the future; that together we can make a better world, but we will achieve nothing if we remain in the corner lamenting how badly everything is going"; qtd. in Sáiz Ripoll 10; my trans.). It is this hope that will allow a younger generation to mitigate human-generated ecological catastrophes. The dystopic world found in the novels provides a cautionary tale for readers, who can see how poor guardianship of the earth can have long-term ramifications. The new perspectives explored within the pages of the trilogy help to cultivate future ecocitizens who will be better equipped to create sustainable futures. Throughout the three volumes of the *Guardianes* series, ecological stances empower the protagonists to champion the environment. By reading the texts' social and environmental impacts with postcolonialist underpinnings, readers of YAL have the opportunity to interrogate dominant ideological and environmental perspectives in order to address the multitude of global ecological problems and create a more equitable ecocitizenry.

NOTES

1 Translations of Gallego's trilogy are my own.
2 In her chapter for this collection dealing with Spain's colonial incursions on the island of Tenerife, Bonnie L. Gasior coins the neologism "ecolonial," uniting "ecology" and "colonialism." "Ecolonial," as she states, emphasizes "the inescapability yet vulnerability of nature in recorded New World literary contexts," a complexity that is fruitful for my reading of the paradoxical human and more-than-human destruction in Gallego's trilogy.
3 While cooperative interspecies enclaves and shared living spaces remain unrealized in Gallego's trilogy, other chapters in this collection study texts in which multispecies kinships do form. William Viestenz delves into human and animal kinship in situations of personal and collective insecurity to propose unreserved generosity as a necessary foundation for surviving capitalist-driven environmental and economic crises and as a means to reveal the illusoriness of protective boundaries between self

and environmental other. Also focused on a twenty-first-century novel, Maryanne L. Leone's chapter explores compassionate responses of care and the assistance of women and a dog amid environmental contamination, scarce food and energy, patriarchal dominance, and consumer-based greed.

4 Ecocritic Simon Estok proposes that the desire to separate human from non-human stems from a fear of the environment that drives "the ethical position that humanity is outside of and exempt from the laws of nature" (217). For a study on the ecocritical utility of studying ecophobia in fictional encounters between human and hybrid creatures in order to consider the environmental fallout from manifestations of human supremacism, see Shanna Lino's chapter in this collection.

WORKS CITED AND CONSULTED

Adams, William M., and Martin Mulligan. "Nature and the Colonial Mind." *Decolonizing Nature Strategies for Conservation in a Post-colonial Era*, edited by William M. Adams and Martin Mulligan, Earthscan Publications, 2003, pp. 16–50.

Alaimo, Stacy. "Discomforting Creatures: Monstrous Natures in Recent Films." *Beyond Nature Writing: Expanding the Boundaries of Ecocriticism*, edited by Karla Armbruster and Kathleen R. Wallace, UP of Virginia, 2013, pp. 279–96.

Asimov, Isaac. "Social Science Fiction." *Science Fiction: The Future*, edited by Dick Allen, Harcourt Brace Jovanovich, 1971, pp. 263–90.

Bergson, Henri. *Les deux sources de la morale et de la religion*. Presses Universitaires de France, 2003.

Bhabha, Homi K. *The Location of Culture*. Routledge, 1994.

Buell, Lawrence. *The Environmental Imagination: Thoreau, Nature Writing, and the Formation of American Culture*. The Belknap Press of Harvard UP, 1995.

Burney, Shehla. "Edward Said and Postcolonial Theory: Disjunctured Identities and the Subaltern Voice." *Pedagogy of the Other: Edward Said, Postcolonial Theory, and Strategies for Critique*, Peter Lang, 2012, pp. 41–60.

Cart, Michael. "The Value of Young Adult Literature" *Young Adult Library Services Association*, 8 May 2008, https://www.ala.org/yalsa/guidelines/whitepapers/yalit.

Chandoke, Neera. "The Post-colonial City." *Economic and Political Weekly*, vol. 26, no. 50, 14 Dec. 1991, pp. 2868–73.

Das, Harini Patowary. "Ecocriticism: A Review and Study of Its Relevance to Children's Literature." https://www.academia.edu/8389927/ECOCRITICISM-A_REVIEW_AND_STUDY_OF_ITS_RELEVANCE_TO_CHILDREN_S_LITERATURE. PDF download, working paper.

Dodson, Katrina. "Eco/critical Entanglements." *Qui Parle*, vol. 19, no. 2, spring/summer 2011, pp. 5–21.

Echterling, Clare. "Postcolonial Ecocriticism, Classic Children's Literature, and the Imperial-Environmental Imagination in *The Chronicles of Narnia*." *Journal of the Midwest Modern Language Association*, vol. 49, no. 1, spring 2016, pp. 93–117. *Project MUSE*, https://doi.org/10.1353/mml.2016.0016.

Estok, Simon C. "Theorizing in a Space of Ambivalent Openness: Ecocriticism and Ecophobia." *ISLE: Interdisciplinary Studies in Literature and the Environment*, vol. 16, no. 2, spring 2009, pp. 203–25. *Oxford Academic*, https://doi.org/10.1093/isle/isp010.

Fanon, Franz. *Wretched of the Earth*. Translated by Richard Philcox, Grove Paperback, 2005.

Gallego García, Laura. *El bestiario de Axlin*. Penguin Random House, 2018. Vol. 1 of *Guardianes de la Ciudadela*.

Gallego García, Laura. *El secreto de Xein*. Penguin Random House, 2018. Vol. 2 of *Guardianes de la Ciudadela*.

Gallego García, Laura. *La misión de Rox*. Penguin Random House, 2019. Vol. 3 of *Guardianes de la Ciudadela*.

Glotfelty, Cheryll. "Introduction: Literary Studies in an Age of Environmental Crisis." *Ecocriticism Reader: Landmarks in Literary Ecology*, edited by Cheryll Glotfelty and Harold Fromm, U of Georgia P, 1996, pp. xv–xxxvii.

Gottlieb, Joanne. "Darwin's City, or Life Underground: Evolution, Progress, and the Shapes of Things to Come." *The Nature of Cities: Ecocriticism and Urban Environments*, edited by Michael Bennett and David W. Teague, U of Arizona P, 1999, pp. 233–54.

Haraway, Donna J. *Simians, Cyborgs, and Women: The Reinvention of Nature*. Routledge, 1991.

Harvey, David. *Justice, Nature and the Geography Difference*. Blackwell, 1996.

Heise, Ursula K. "Globality, Difference, and the International Turn in Ecocriticism." *PMLA*, vol. 128, no. 3, May 2013, pp. 636–43.

Heise, Ursula K. "The Hitchhiker's Guide to Ecocriticism." *PMLA*, vol. 121, no. 2, Mar. 2006, pp. 503–16.

Huggan, Graham. "'Greening' Postcolonialism: Ecocritical Perspectives." *Modern Fiction Studies*, vol. 50, no. 3, autumn 2004, pp. 701–33. *Project MUSE*, https://doi.org/10.1353/mfs.2004.0067.

Huggan, Graham, and Helen Tiffin. "Green Postcolonialism." *Interventions*, vol. 9, no. 1, 2007, pp. 1–11. *Taylor & Francis Online*, https://doi.org/10.1080/13698010601173783.

Huggan, Graham, and Helen Tiffin. *Postcolonial Ecocriticism: Literature, Animals, Environment*. Routledge, 2010.

Kutzer, M. Daphne. *Empire's Children: Empire and Imperialism in Classic British Children's Books*. Garland, 2000.

Langer, Jessica. *Postcolonialism and Science Fiction*. Palgrave Macmillan, 2011.

Mandrell, James. "Fantasy and Equilibrium in Laura Gallego García's *Alas de fuego* [*Wings of Fire*]." *The Lion and the Unicorn*, vol. 36, no. 1, Jan. 2012, pp. 20–34. *Project MUSE*, https://doi.org/10.1353/uni.2012.0009.

Martos García, Alberto E. *Introducción al mundo de las sagas*. Universidad de Extremadura, 2009.

Merlo, Philippe. "La ejemplaridad en la literatura infantil: El caso de la obra de Laura Gallego García." *La ejemplaridad en la narrativa española contemporánea, 1950–2020*, edited by Amélie Florenchie and Isabelle Touton, Iberoamericana/Vervuert, 2011, pp. 279–98.

Nixon, Rob. "Environmentalism and Postcolonialism." *Postcolonial Studies and Beyond*, edited by Ania Loomba et al., Duke UP, 2005, pp. 233–51.

Prádanos, Luis I. "Toward an Ecocritical Approach to the Spanish Neoliberal Crisis." *Postgrowth Imaginaries: New Ecologies and Counterhegemonic Culture in Post-2008 Spain*, Liverpool UP, 2018, pp. 37–87.

Reed, T.V. "Toward an Environmental Justice Ecocriticism." *The Environmental Justice Reader: Politics, Poetics, and Pedagogy*, edited by Joni Adamson et al., U of Arizona P, 2002, pp. 145–62.

Rigby, Kate. "Ecocriticism." *Literary and Cultural Criticism of the Twenty-First Century*, edited by Julian Wolfrey, Edinburg UP, pp. 151–78.

Said, Edward W. *Culture and Imperialism*. Vintage, 1993.

Sáiz Ripoll, Anabel. "'Todo puede ser real o no serlo': Análisis de la obra de Laura Gallego." *Cuadernos de literatura infantil y juvenil*, vol. 18, no. 188, 2005, pp. 7–25.

Singh, Rashna B. *Goodly Is Our Heritage: Children's Literature, Empire, and the Certitude of Character*. Scarecrow, 2004.

Stover, Lois T. "Who Am I? Who Are You? Diversity and Identity in the Young Adult Novel." *Reading Their World: The Young Adult Novel in the Classroom*, edited by Virginia R. Monseau and Gary M. Salvner, Boyton/Cook, 2000, pp. 100–20.

Vital, Anthony. "Toward an African Ecocriticism: Postcolonialism, Ecology and *Life & Times of Michael K*." *Research in African Literatures*, vol. 39, no. 1, spring 2008, pp. 87–106.

Wolfe, Gary K. *The Known and the Unknown: The Iconography of Science Fiction*. Kent State UP, 1979.

Chapter Sixteen

La cuenta atrás: An Ecodystopian Graphic Novel on Spain's Greatest Ecological Disaster

CARLA ALMANZA-GÁLVEZ

Introduction

On 13 November 2002, one of Europe's worst ecological disasters took place off the coast of Galicia in north-western Spain: the oil spill caused by the sinking of the Greek-owned and Bahamas-operated tanker *Prestige*. Resulting in profound damage to the marine environment not only of Spain but also of Portugal and France, this tragedy inspired the creation of *La cuenta atrás* (*The Countdown*),[1] a two-volume graphic novel written by Carlos Portela, a Galician comics and television series scriptwriter, and drawn by Sergi San Julián, a Catalan comic book artist and illustrator. In light of environmentally themed dystopian fiction and ecological ethics, the present study explores how *La cuenta atrás* addresses a significant socio-environmental issue through the formal properties of graphic narrative, especially through the use of visually expressive and detailed images as a vehicle for ecosocial criticism, defined as a critique based on the premise that an environmental crisis is always a crisis for the most vulnerable members of a society (Matthies and Närhi 4). The analysis also draws significance from the fact that Portela and San Julián do not focus much on the accidental causes of the disaster, but rather on the social actors and their responsibility for the tragic consequences.

The first part of *La cuenta atrás* was published in both Galician (*A conta atrás*) and Castilian in 2008. In 2014, the authors resorted to crowdfunding to publish the second part of the story, but the fundraising target was not reached. As a consequence, the release of the second volume could not be realized, despite the fact that, in the same year, this unpublished material was the second recipient of the Social Graphic Novel Prize, awarded by the Divina Pastora Foundation, a Spanish organization dedicated to promoting culture, social inclusion, and community welfare. This international prize recognized *La cuenta atrás* as a social graphic novel whose role was concerned with civic and environmental awareness. Although the award was to have included the publication of the new material, Portela explained in a 2014 interview that even then a combination of personal, financial, and logistical factors hampered the project's materialization (Fajardo). Happily, in August 2022, both parts of the graphic novel were finally published, as a single volume, to commemorate the 20th anniversary of the catastrophe (Portela and San Julián, *A conta atrás/La cuenta atrás*). The present analysis focuses on the material that was available when this chapter was written in 2020.

Graphic Fiction as Critical Inquiry

More than a hybrid genre that is both visual and verbal, comics and graphic novels are media that convey information and emotions through images, words, and sequences, the three fundamental communicative components of graphic narrative. What distinguishes graphic novels from comics, caricatures, or newspaper political cartooning is their primary storytelling motivation (Baetens and Frey 7). The panel is the essential unit of graphic storytelling and is usually composed of an image and words that appear in captions or speech bubbles, which are also used to represent sound effects. The reader must engage in connecting text and images to understand the narrative. Graphic stories are told in sequences of panels, during which "closure," or the reader's mental process of filling the narrative gaps between panels, occurs (McCloud 63). The gutter, or the blank space between two panels, creates a transition that moves the story along while demanding the reader's active interpretation.

Generally targeted at mature readers, graphic novels tackle complex and sophisticated topics through powerful narratives that combine non-fiction and fiction, "going far beyond the previous newspaper comics' light entertainment, superhero adventures, and children's stories" (Tabachnick 1).[2] In Spain, comic books and graphic novels encompass themes ranging from the Spanish Civil War and the Francoist period – Jorge García and Fidel Martínez's *Cuerda de presas* (*String of Prisoners*, 2005), Carlos Giménez's *36–39: Malos tiempos* (*36–39: Bad Times*, 2007–8), Paul Preston and José Pablo García's *La Guerra Civil española* (*The Spanish Civil War*, 2016) – to the economic crisis and the post-2008 recession – Aleix Saló's *Simiocracia: Crónica de la gran resaca económica* (*Simiocracy: Chronicle of the Great Economic Hangover*, 2012), Óscar Ibáñez's *Leaving Spain* (2015). The object of this study, *La cuenta atrás*, was produced during the 2008 world financial crisis that framed the Great Spanish

Recession. The parallel publication of *La cuenta atrás* in Galician and Castilian speaks both to the regional audience most affected by the environmental disaster and to a broader national public about government mismanagement and community response.

Although the term *graphic novel* appeared in Spain in the 1940s, the Spanish market for the genre developed more slowly than in other European countries (García 21; Gil González 2; McKinney and Richter, "Graphic Spain" 11). During the final years of Franco's regime, there emerged in Galicia an artistic ambition that accompanied a purposeful, industry-driven impetus for the creation of graphic fiction. According to Galician comics specialist Xulio Carballo Dopico, far from being a subcultural or marginal form of expression, from the 1970s onwards, the graphic format has become an important element of the cultural landscape (720). Not only has graphic narrative in Galicia been influenced by artistic disciplines such as painting, engraving, and photography, but it has also been characterized by (1) an experimental style defying that of conventional comic books, (2) a spirit of vindication and anti-authoritarianism in response to Francoism and censorship, and (3) a critical engagement with socio-economic issues such as migration, labour revolts, and ecological defence (Carballo Dopico 720, 722).

Similar to *La cuenta atrás*'s critical view of the impact of environmental issues on humanity, there are a number of Spanish graphic novels that equally react to ecological threats and dangers caused by human agents. *Wáluk* (2011) and its sequel *Wáluk: La gran travesía* (*Waluk: The Great Journey*, 2017), written by Emilio Ruiz, illustrated by Ana Miralles, and published in Spanish, Basque, English, and French, address the consequences of global warming and pollution for the environment and for polar bear cubs. With an approach similar to that of Portela and San Julián, and a similar focus on a particular environmental event, *Chernóbil: La Zona* (*Chernobyl: The Zone*, 2011), published in both Spanish and English with a script by Francisco Sánchez and drawings by Natacha Bustos, addresses the consequences, rather than the causes, of the nuclear accident for three generations.

Environmentally focused graphic novels reveal the power of the visual format to address ecocritical concerns about humans and non-human animals in the Anthropocene. Following animal studies scholar Laura Perry's understanding of graphic novels in light of the representational challenges of the anthropogenic world view and discourse, "[T]he Anthropocene acts as a visual phenomenon even in exclusively written texts and becomes an aesthetic quandary as well as an environmental and narratological one" (6). The critical focus of both graphic narrative and ecocritical thought is channelled through acts of representation:

"the graphic novel provides its creators with a medium for conceptual expression, while ecocriticism critically analyzes and evaluates the representational strategies of multiple media" (Bealer 1). Graphic novels that recreate mass trauma events, such as ecological disasters, employ different visual design techniques – ink washes, watercolours, sepias, or monochromes – to depict distressing memories. Thus, graphic fiction becomes "a rich field from which to shape, process, and 'materialise' trauma narratives because of the medium's ability to hold and represent narrative complexity" (Nabizadeh 21). It is precisely such a collective trauma that the town of Caldelas experiences in *La cuenta atrás*.

Environmental discourse also finds in the graphic narrative format an ideal vehicle for ecocultural analysis, since the visual tensions created by sequence composition, layout, and colour constitute an effective instrument of socio-environmental criticism. Moreover, the reader's closure process constructs a sense of continuous reality that mirrors the fluidity of boundaries between humans and non-human nature: "Sequential art introduces new dimensions for imagining environments … When comics take up environmental themes and questions, the act of closure further involves readers in the relationship between characters, settings, and conflicts. Reading color, line art, and iconicity contributes to a comic's environmental imagination" (Vold 69–70). Through the techniques deployed by Portela and San Julián in their imagined re-enactment of the *Prestige* tragedy, *La cuenta atrás* channels the reader to denounce the sociopolitical and environmental consequences of the oil spill, with particular attention paid to the repercussions on beyond-human ecosystems.

The Countdown to the Disaster

According to cognitive psychologist Steven Pinker, "The epitome of environmental insults is the oil spill from tanker ships, which coats pristine beaches with toxic black sludge and fouls the plumage of seabirds and the fur of otters and seals" (131). Among the most destructive oil spills have been those involving the *Exxon Valdez* (Alaska, 1989), the Gulf War (Kuwait, 1991), and the *Deepwater Horizon* (Gulf of Mexico, 2010).[3] After a 2002 winter storm caused one of the *Prestige*'s fuel tanks to burst, the sinking of the vessel resulted in a massive spill of about 67,000 tons of bunker oil that polluted more than 1,000 beaches on the Spanish, French, and Portuguese coastline, especially along the region of Galicia, where the damage was most extensive and severe. The black tide affected coral reefs, sharks, whales, fish, and other marine fauna. It also killed about 200,000 birds from seventy-one species. Galicia's government was forced to ban fishing activities for one year, paralysing one of the region's main industries. The disaster had a significant impact not only on Galicia's natural resources and economy but also on Spain's collective consciousness about ecological culture and environmental education.

La cuenta atrás attempts to keep the memory of the *Prestige* disaster alive in order to raise awareness about the lack of involvement of government authorities and society in emergency planning and environmental protection operations. In this sense, Portela and San Julián's work can be seen as representative of a generation of comics and graphic novels that have had "a clear impact on Spanish society in recent decades, not only as a means of recovering historical memory – and thus doing justice to a large part of society that has gone underrepresented in art –, but also in the recognition of unhealed traumas" (Simón Abad 47). In fact, the high sales rate of *La cuenta atrás* – over 3,000 copies sold, one-third of them in Galician – reveals its favourable reception by a readership that approached the text hoping to find "no un cuento de niños, sino una investigación política" ("not a children's tale, but a political investigation"), as defined by Portela himself (Fajardo).[4] In an interview with Spanish comics expert Álvaro Pons, Portela also claimed that, because strip cartoonists have a strong commitment to social responsibility, employing that format was the best way to convey all the aspects of the tragic event, even better than producing a feature film (Portela and San Julián, Interview 90).[5]

The story of *La cuenta atrás* begins in a fictitious maritime area called Caldelas one year after the occurrence of a disaster that bears striking similarities to the *Prestige* oil spill. This imaginary town can be identified with the fishing village of Muxía, one of the most exposed and affected areas on the Galician coast. According to San Julián, "Caldelas podría verse como un trasunto de Muxía, pero nuestra intención es trascender el ámbito local. Intentábamos mostrar que [el desastre] puede pasar en más países. Es más, puede tener mucha fuerza en otros países donde ha pasado algo similar" ("Caldelas could be seen as a copy of Muxía, but our intention is to transcend the local sphere. We were trying to show that it [the disaster] can happen in other countries. Moreover, it can be very meaningful in other countries where something similar has happened"; Portela and San Julián, Interview 90). Unfolding the story in reverse chronological order rules out the possibility of a better future for Caldelas (or for its non-fictional counterparts). Instead of advancing towards a future resolution, the text presents the characters' past decisions and the events that led to the current circumstances in the fictional town. Spanning six months, the polyphonic text is narrated from the perspective of journalists, politicians, and average citizens. By telling the story backwards, month by month, a narrative technique to which the title alludes, the text enables the characters to reflect on how their lives have been impacted by the tragedy. After an introductory set of panels visually foregrounds the machinations of corrupt local government administrators, five titled sections retrospectively give an account of the political strategies and action plans implemented by the regional authorities in order to win the municipal elections the year after the environmental disaster.

The opening set of strips of *La cuenta atrás* shows a discussion between Sonia Saavedra, a television news presenter, and Miguel Otero, the influential regional government's councillor with whom she is having an affair, about the choice of image for a government-sponsored advertising campaign to convince the people of Caldelas that their coast has completely recovered from the black tide and that their town has been restored to its pre-disaster state. While Sonia criticizes the simplicity of the picture, Otero believes that "[e]sa imagen significa que todo está bien ... que la vida sigue como siempre" ("that image means that everything is fine ... that life goes on as usual"; 11). The political ad is presented at a press conference and features a fisherman with a smiling and optimistic facial expression against a background consisting of a beach with crystal-clear water and blue skies. The slogan that accompanies the poster's image reads, "La cuenta atrás ha terminado ... estamos de nuevo en marcha" ("The countdown is over ... we are back on track"; 14). By juxtaposing the diegetic text on the poster with the corrupt politician's speech bubbles, the graphic novel not only exposes the government's intention to trivialize the community's shared trauma but also denounces any attempt to hide or erase the memory of the ecological disaster. The whole story develops around this controversial political and media campaign (fig. 16.1). Furthermore, the campaign's image points to the resignation of the people of Caldelas to government hypocrisy due to their need to survive financially.

Although the affected residents receive government subsidies that help them face the consequences of the ecological incident, they are aware that this compensation comes at an ethical cost. Otero bribes the population with generous financial contributions with the intention of gaining votes for the governing party's candidate, Fidel, who is running for the mayorship of Caldelas. As Emilio González, the fisherman chosen for the ad campaign, admits to his wife during an argument, "Ese es el problema, que vivimos de favores en vez de exigir lo que es nuestro" ("That is the problem, we live on favours instead of demanding what is ours"; 75). In the case of the actual crisis, even though the *Prestige*

Fig. 16.1. Miguel Otero at a press conference presenting the supposed
progress in the recovery of the coast

Source: Portela and San Julián, *La cuenta atrás* 14, page detail.

shipwreck represented a catastrophic event for the Galician population,
some Muxía victims sought to profit from the tragedy and the government's bribery. Not only did they indeed receive generous subsidies,
around 6,000 euros per month, but some also tried to fool the authorities
in order to continue to benefit from government funding: "when the
ban on fishing ended, some fishermen stained the fish they caught with
oil to try and deceive the regional government and stretch out the aid
for another month or two" (Carretero). A few affected residents even
bought apartments and cars, exactly as the guilt-ridden Emilio does
in *La cuenta atrás*. The image of Emilio and his friends taking a look at
expensive cars at a dealership shows that the dirty money that Caldelas
receives engenders greed in them: "en la vida se vio semejante riada de
dinero en el pueblo. Y si [la situación] se complica, que manden más
[dinero]" ("such a flood of money has not been seen in this town before.
And if it [the situation] gets complicated, let them send more [money]";
69). The fishermen emulate the self-serving actions of local officials, who
are concerned with their own well-being rather than with the ecological health of the sea or its non-human animals; and yet, the fishermen's
future income will depend on those very same contaminated waters.

Contrary to the objective of the government's campaign, the townspeople of Caldelas cannot pretend that the disaster never took place,
or that its inhabitants can return to their pre-disaster lives. Having
looked back with nostalgia at a picture from when he helped out with
the clean-up efforts after the oil spill, a friend of Emilio's, a social activist known as Moncho, explains that the aftermath of the tragedy has
destroyed the essence of Caldelas (fig. 16.2): "El problema es que a mí lo
que ha pasado me ha cambiado y no puedo volver a lo de antes como si

Fig. 16.2. Moncho and Emilio talking about the impact of the environmental tragedy on their lives

Source: Portela and San Julián, *La cuenta atrás* 43.

no hubiera pasado nada … Para mí, este pueblo murió" ("The problem is that what has happened has changed me, and I cannot go back to the past as if nothing happened … This town is dead to me"; 43). The oil spill represents a turning point in the history of Caldelas and marks a dividing line between the old and the new life of Moncho and that of the other residents. Further, the new, post-disaster reality entails an eco-social traumatic experience that most of them are unable to overcome.

An Ecological Dystopia

In concert with Portela's assertion that the graphic format fits the *Prestige* story better than any other form of fiction, social and political philosopher Clint Jones contends in his analysis of environmental crises and post-apocalyptic societies that "the environment is often more than just the backdrop against which the human drama unfolds but is itself the stage upon which the human drama plays out. Thus, each graphic novel is capable of conjuring creative space to think about the problems humans would face" (2). Through technical aspects of graphic fiction such as colour contrast, motion, foreground effects, and panel layout, graphic novels endow the representation of the environment with a centrality that is more patent than in other genres. Indeed, the environment acts as a character rather than a passive setting for the story, especially when the plot concerns an ecological catastrophe. Particularly relevant to *La cuenta atrás* is Jones's observation that the apocalyptic "environment is usually treated as an antagonist to humanity throughout the narrative, presented as an entity still to be controlled and dominated through ingenuity and the sheer force of the human spirit" (3). Yet the hostile relationship that develops between the residents of Caldelas and their natural environment predicates on the false hope created by their regional government through the manipulative misrepresentation of the ecological impact of massive oil pollution. The antagonism in the novel, therefore, functions to decentre humans through an ethical incrimination that, inversely, centres the abused and agentic environment ecocritically.

More than a perception of nature as an uncontrollable force to be subdued by human civilization, what prevails in *La cuenta atrás* is a strong sense of nostalgia for the pristine environment that pre-existed the human-induced ecological trauma. The longing for a past that promised a better future creates a dystopian atmosphere, which is expressed through silent pages – full-page sequential panels devoid of speech bubbles – that transmit feelings of apprehension and fear. Some panels use dull colours to portray the polluted condition of the sea and to depict the gloomy reality of Caldelas's life, thus prefiguring the dystopian

Fig. 16.3. A sequence of silent panels of Emilio smoking and putting out the cigarette on a dead starfish washed ashore in black oil

Source: Portela and San Julián, *La cuenta atrás* 44.

future of the town. One emotional, silent, three-panel sequence darkened with muted colours shows Emilio sitting on the shoreline and putting out a cigarette on a starfish covered in sludgy black oil (fig. 16.3). Images like these reproduce Caldelas's state of melancholy after the oil spill and suggest a broader ecosocial despair. Notably produced during the 2008 financial crisis, *La cuenta atrás* links environmental devastation with economic dystopia and implicates carbon-fuelled market capitalism in ecological deterioration.[6]

While "the human relationship to the natural world has long been central to the dystopian imagination," the exponential progression and devastating impact of climate change of the last two decades have increasingly inspired ecodystopias (Hughes and Wheeler 2). Distinct from apocalyptic fiction, in which an ecological cataclysm typically leads to the collapse of society, the overall tone of *La cuenta atrás* corresponds more closely to the essence of (eco)dystopian narratives, in which a human social order is still present even if intolerable for those who live within it (Trotta and Sadri 4–5). If dystopias generally depict imagined societies that readers judge to be worse than the society in which they live, these texts also function as warnings that things could worsen unless humans act and make better choices (Sargent 9, 26). In Portela and San Julián's novel, the financial incentive to maintain the status quo leads some residents to be sceptical about any reform of ecologically damaging social and political structures: "Aquí no cambia nada así caiga un meteorito y nos parta en dos" ("Nothing will change here, even if a meteorite falls and breaks us in two"; 75). This negative and despondent attitude towards their adverse circumstances exposes the dystopian dimension of *La cuenta atrás* and reminds the reader that humans' failure to act ecosocially is an act of stubborn anthropocentricity that not only ignores ecosystemic balance but also self-inflicts human hardship.

Media Coverage and Environmental Accountability

Human awareness and evaluation of issues such as oppressive political control, the manipulation of information, and ecosystem-mismanagement practices are largely framed by the mass media. In her study of the influence of this powerful force on public perceptions of environmental issues, sociologist Alison Anderson characterizes the media politics of oil spills as follows:

> Dramatic oil spills make for vivid images of oil-drenched wildlife that can often strongly resonate with emotional attachments to the environment.

> Large oil spills often fulfil a number of news values including conflict, drama, shock and scandal. However, most oil spills go unreported or fail to attract much media attention. Not all major oil spills receive significant publicity and media coverage is often disproportionate to the total amount of damage incurred. It is common for large oil spills to attract a relatively short period of intense nationwide (and sometimes international) coverage, following which it rapidly subsides. (98)

In contrast to the press coverage of previous oil spills, the *Prestige* disaster has continued to attract significant national and international media attention. Several articles reporting the event and its subsequent developments have appeared in Galicia's main newspapers, *La Voz de Galicia* and *Faro de Vigo*, but also in Spain's most important national newspapers, *El País* and *El Mundo*. In 2004, *La Voz de Galicia*'s outstanding coverage of the catastrophe was recognized with the Prize for the Freedom and Future of the Media, sponsored by the Media Foundation of Sparkasse Leipzig in Germany. Since its occurrence, the tragedy has similarly been covered by major French and British newspapers such as *Libération* and the *Guardian*.

The media's coverage also focused heavily on the concerted effort to identify both the technical causes of the disaster and the people responsible for it. Investigators from the Spanish National Research Council (Consejo Superior de Investigaciones Científicas) and from other Spanish public research centres helped the state administration formulate proper measures to tackle the impact of the disaster (Tintoré 45). In December 2018, the Supreme Court in Madrid issued the final ruling that the *Prestige*'s insurance company should pay the Spanish state 1.6 billion euros in compensation for the environmental damages caused by the sinking of the oil tanker (Rincón). The court also attributed direct civil liability for an ecological crime to the *Prestige*'s Greek captain, Apostolos Mangouras, sentencing him to two years in prison. Despite the *Prestige* complying with safety regulations, Mangouras was aware that the tanker was significantly old, had technical issues, and was overloaded with oil. His reckless managerial decision ignored the vessel's conditions and the structural defects of the cargo tanks, a risk that carried with it the obvious potential of causing oil pollution with devastating consequences (Pérez).

Demonstrating a similar incompetence, the regional government represented in the novel does not have a contingency plan to properly manage an ecological emergency and reassures the population that the oil will not reach the shorelines of the village, that it is only a stain on the water. In a series of panels depicting the coast and the sea in the background through the predominance of pale blue and light brown tones (fig. 16.4), Moncho complains during an interview with a journalist

Fig. 16.4. An assemblage of panoramic and close-up views of Moncho and Molina discussing the poor political response to the spillage

Source: Portela and San Julián, *La cuenta atrás* 67.

named Molina that "[l]o primero que tenían que haber hecho era no mentir, intentar solucionar el problema y, después, ya se vería de quién es la culpa" ("the first thing they should have done was not to lie, to try to solve the problem, and they could have argued about whose fault it was afterwards"; 68). In fact, Spanish deputy prime minister Mariano Rajoy and other federal government officials at the time of the *Prestige* incident were criticized for minimizing the severity of the disaster and for their inability to effectively manage the emergency response to the crisis (Blanco). However, none of the political actors involved in the management of the *Prestige* catastrophe was found guilty by the Supreme Court.

Portela acknowledges that government accountability and transparency is a key aspect in *La cuenta atrás*, but he also emphasizes the human fallibility underlying the complexity of the *Prestige* disaster:

> Yo no creo que haya culpables. Se rompió un petrolero y eso le puede pasar a cualquier gobierno … El problema es cómo se gestiona el asunto … Vayamos a las causas y, sobre todo, … a seguir el tejido de los actores de esta tragedia … Es verdad que no sabíamos qué pasaba; que hubo mucha desinformación; pero yo lo atribuyo más a la incapacidad humana. Yo tengo una gran fe en la incapacidad humana, creo en ella como motor de la historia … Yo intentaba esa fotografía de todo el proceso, el análisis de causas … [E]l lector debe sacar sus propias conclusiones. Con la historia hacia atrás busqué ese efecto.

> (I do not believe that there are people to blame. An oil tanker broke down, and that can happen to any government … The problem is how the situation is handled … Let's go to the causes and, above all, … let's follow the web of actors in this tragedy … It is true that we did not know what was happening, that there was a lot of misinformation, but I mostly attribute that to human incompetence. I have great faith in human ineptitude, I believe it to be the engine of history … I attempted to portray the picture of the whole process, the analysis of the causes … The reader must draw their own conclusions. I looked for that effect by telling the story backwards; Portela and San Julián, Interview 88)

The novel does not identify any guilty parties, but all the humans involved in the situation can be deemed responsible in one way or another. The ecocritical role played by readers of *La cuenta atrás* fulfils the critical function of this graphic novel and brings forth answerability and truthfulness.

Whereas the mass media have played an important role since 2002 in filling in the information gaps left by the petrol company's ineptitude, by the Spanish government's downplaying of the severity of the disaster, and by the self-serving attitudes of some local Galician residents, their ability to represent the truth has nevertheless been limited by political influence. This vulnerability is made evident in Portela and San Julián's novel when Salvador, the deputy editor of the local newspaper, is forced by Otero to block the publication of a detailed article about the black tide and to publish instead the advertisement of his optimistic publicity campaign because "lo que nosotros [Otero y su partido político] no podemos hacer es lanzar una campaña informando sobre la recuperación del mar en un medio de comunicación que opina todo lo contrario" ("what we [Otero and his political party] cannot do is launch a campaign informing about the recovery of the sea in a media outlet that believes the opposite"; 51). In an attempt to disguise his capitulation to political manipulation, Salvador explains to Molina, the journalist who has been working on the article for months, that "[s]implemente, no vamos a publicar nada más sobre la marea negra. Es un tema del pasado y ahora tenemos que centrarnos en la actualidad" ("we are simply not going to publish anything else about the black tide. It is a thing of the past, and now we have to focus on the present"; 57). This section of the text points to the gaps in knowledge created by human exceptionalist greed that prevents the media from identifying truth and accountability and, therefore, exposes the value of the graphic genre, whose active reader fills in these lacunae. Rather than obstructing knowledge, the visual and narrative spaces, as well as the story's development in reverse, lead readers to the root causes of the disaster: environmentally destructive anthropocentric attitudes, policies, and (in)action.

Indeed, the manipulation and concealment of reality serve as leitmotivs throughout the story, and their impact is explored visually. The most obvious example is the misrepresentation of Caldelas's current circumstances through the publicity image that distorts the emotional reaction of the people to the disaster. The photographer asks Emilio to smile enthusiastically (fig. 16.5): "tienes que sonreír mejor, ... no sonríes. Tuerces la boca, que es distinto. Piensa en cosas alegres, ¿vale?" ("you have to smile better, ... you don't smile. You twist your mouth, which is different. Think about happy things, okay?"; 26). Not only does the photographer request that Emilio fake a smile, but Otero demands that the final photograph for the campaign be retouched: "el color ... es un poco fúnebre. Que la hagan más luminosa. No quiero nada negro ni grises. Nada que recuerde a la marea negra" ("the colour ... is a bit gloomy. Have them make it brighter. I don't want anything black or grey, anything that recalls the black tide"; 24). The tension between the

Fig. 16.5. The photo shoot for the advertising campaign

Source: Portela and San Julián, *La cuenta atrás* 30, page detail.

novel's treatment of the diegetic, human manipulation of images and the extra-diegetic deployment of that same process of visual storytelling by the graphic genre to represent anthropocentric formulations of the environment is a dynamic feature of the text that engages the reader in ecocritical interpretation at every turn.

Another instance of masking the ecologically devastated reality occurs when Sonia gives full coverage to Otero's press conference, in which the politician deceptively announces the near-complete recovery of the coast and the emergence from the crisis. As with Molina before, whose newspaper report on the black tide is replaced by Salvador with the deceptive ad campaign, Sonia fails to fulfil her ethical commitment to promote the authenticity of information. The temptation to alter or mask reality is overtly expressed when a cameraman reassures Sonia that he managed to take a close-up shot of her giving a report on the victory of Otero's party in the municipal elections: "recuerda que lo que no ves, no existe: ese es el truco … Ya sabes el dicho: que la realidad no te estropee un buen encuadre" ("remember that what you don't see doesn't exist: that's the trick … You know the saying: don't let reality ruin a well-framed shot"; 79–80). Depicting the journalist standing on a suitcase to look taller, the paradoxical graphic calls attention not only diegetically to the media's manipulation of reality but also extra-diegetically to the potential of the graphic form to reveal the truth.

Economic Impact, Civic Engagement, and Social Responsibility

The area most severely affected by the *Prestige* oil spill was West Coruña, a region that "has the highest percentage of homes living on incomes below poverty level" (Surís Regueiro and Garza Gil 319). Homes in Galicia are normally composed of two to four people, and most family units correspond to couples with children. Additionally, more than 30 per cent of homes rely solely on pensions or benefits for their income. Galicia is, therefore, "a zone that is highly sensitive, in socio-economic terms, to incidents of significant impact on its economy" (Surís Regueiro and Garza Gil 317). Expressing their frustration about systemic economic distress, victims of the tragedy such as Emilio, Moncho, and Mateo challenge the government's official stance through ironic counter-discourse: "En casa no se gana el sueldo. Y fuera tampoco. Esto es la ruina de todos … pero aquí deben los de siempre. Con marea negra o sin ella" ("You neither earn a salary at home nor outside. This is everyone's ruin … but the usual crowd is always in debt here, with the black tide or without it"; 34). In this respect, *La cuenta atrás* makes the point that, although the government periodically provides the people of Caldelas with financial aid to compensate for the environmental pollution that resulted in profound damage to wildlife and the local fishing industry, the ecological disaster has compounded an already ongoing economic struggle for the community.

La cuenta atrás highlights the value of place-based economies that (1) support local businesses, (2) allow for an equitable allocation of profits within small communities, (3) promote social cohesion, and (4) are unlikely to provoke the negative ecological impacts of global commerce (Prádanos, "Decrecimiento o barbarie" 79–80). In a set of panels that use close-ups to emphasize the facial reactions of the characters, a group of locals in a bar is discussing the amount and duration of the government subsidies that they have received as well as the best way to invest them. Mateo claims that he used the money to start a business that will benefit the community, namely a convenience store in Caldelas: "a mí me han dado el dinero, pero lo he gastado en el pueblo, que es donde hay que gastarlo, ¿o no?" ("I was given the money, but I have spent it on the town, which is where it ought to be spent, right?"; 35). The importance of localized economies is studied by Spanish degrowth scholar Luis I. Prádanos in his analysis of cultural responses that battle ecological deterioration in post-2008 Spain. He reflects on how "emerging cultural sensibilities," such as graphic novels, "are actively detaching themselves from the dominant imaginary of economic growth and, in some cases, even articulating counterhegemonic postgrowth narratives" (*Postgrowth Imaginaries* 1–2). Prádanos's concept of "postgrowth imaginaries" exposes "the socially and ecologically harmful dominant cultural imaginary that celebrates economic growth as an object of social desire and explores how an ecologically oriented criticism could play a significant role in both understanding and promoting the ongoing emergence of more desirable economic cultures in the aftermath of the neoliberal crisis" (2). What ultimately becomes apparent in *La cuenta atrás* is that an integrated model of environmental sustainability and social justice is at the centre of the project devised by Portela and San Julián. As journalist and environmental humanist Julia B. Corbett asserts, "Those with less social and economic power ... face greater environmental harm and often have less of a voice" (144). The voiceless victims in Caldelas become the developers of their community's own emerging economic system.

In addition to showcasing the low financial risk and high pay-off of a communal vision for the economic system, *La cuenta atrás* condemns the state of counternature, or the extent of human intervention in nature, caused by the oil spill's ecological disaster (Burke 181–3; Wess 86). Alternative visions of the relationship between humans and their environmental contexts entail not only an understanding of our ontological space in the natural world but also an acknowledgment of our role and responsibility in the control and domestication of nature, because "[t]o address nature is always to address counternature, and thereby ourselves" (Hartman 5). In this graphic novel, the reciprocal determination between human subjects and non-human nature foregrounds the development of an ecosocially committed civil society that, although unable to fight successfully against systemic corruption and injustice, is directly involved in rescuing its natural environment through newly established collaborative networks. This aspect can especially be observed in the work that local fishermen and volunteers from different communities do to clean up Caldelas's coast. Portela and San Julián draw on the fact that more than 300,000 volunteers from across Europe helped with the clean-up of the *Prestige* oil spill, many thousands of whom ended up suffering from health problems due to the inadequate protection provided by the face masks that were used during the clean-up activities (Rodríguez-Trigo et al. 489–90).

Voluntary work is an element that receives special emphasis in *La cuenta atrás*, not only because it was a prominent feature in the aftermath of the *Prestige* ecological disaster, but more importantly because it juxtaposes the lack of transparency and ambition for power of the government administration with the ecosocial, altruistic actions of the volunteers. This tension is reflected in the graphic juxtaposition of Otero's speech at a rally with Moncho's simultaneous rant at a public meeting, in which the social activist urges Caldelas's residents not to support Otero's party in the elections: "cuando vayáis a votar tengáis presente quién se preocupó por el pueblo. Fuimos nosotros los que limpiamos la playa; no ellos" ("when you go to vote, keep in mind who cared for the townspeople. It was us who cleaned up the beach, not them"; 71). Moncho reasserts the same statement during the interview with Molina: "Aquí lo ha hecho todo la gente. Los de aquí y los que vinieron de fuera. El gobierno mintió, reaccionó tarde" ("The people have been the ones to do it all, those from here and those who came from abroad. The government lied, it reacted late"; 68). Iberian studies scholar and ecocritic John Trevathan argues that the Nunca Máis (Never Again) platform, the environmental movement that organized the mobilizations in Galicia after the *Prestige* spill, "galvanized Galicia's human and nonhuman inhabitants in a bid to re-evaluate the region's local identity in the midst of a crisis truly brought on by the global forces surrounding the *Prestige*" (42). This action group thus conceives of Galician cultural identity as resulting from the ecological interconnection between human and non-human elements, a collaboration in which the sea plays a major role.

In his analysis of the globalization and technification of popular resistance, Spanish anthropologist Luis Díaz González-Viana connects the ecosocial response to the *Prestige* disaster with the subsequent collective response to the 2004 terrorist attack in Madrid:

> Rather than a reaction from the crowds, who would not be able to organize "from the bottom up," what occurred was a mobilization encouraged by an elaborate network of small groups, by a complex constellation of "confidence networks." These groups had previously been consolidated by the angry reactions to the *Prestige* oil spill and the Spanish government's active participation in the preliminaries of the Iraq war. (569)

However, the Nunca Máis ecosocial protest movement can be associated not only with the response to the 2004 Madrid train bombings but also with the 2008 social protests put together by civic platforms during the Great Spanish Recession and with the 2011 anti-austerity movement of the *Indignados* ("the Outraged") in Spain.[7] The logistical strategy of the majority of these movements consisted of recruiting protesters from previous activist networks by contacting them through digital channels, such as text messages, listservs, and social media sites.[8]

In his prologue to *La cuenta atrás*, renowned Galician writer and Nunca Máis spokesperson Manuel Rivas conceives of the ecosocial response to the environmental crisis as a phenomenon with biblical resonances: "El fuerte simbolismo mundial del caso *Prestige* tiene que ver con las dimensiones del daño, pero también con la extraordinaria reacción cívica (afectados y voluntariado) que compusieron un 'poema' liberador a la manera de Jonás ... Fue grito. Fue denuncia. Fue catarsis. Fue creación. Solidaridad y re-existencia" ("The strong global symbolism of the *Prestige* case has to do with the dimensions of the damage, but also with the extraordinary civic reaction (of victims and volunteers) that composed a liberating 'poem' in the manner of Jonah ... It was a scream. It was a complaint. It was catharsis. It was creation. Solidarity and re-existence"; 6). Rivas continues, stating that the enemy or threatening force is not nature, more specifically the sea, but the inaction of those who have the power to implement solutions to a very human problem. Rivas further notes the ecosocial quality of the literary response to the disaster in his qualification of *La cuenta atrás* as "un gran salto adelante ... [e]se espacio de lo imprevisible humano" ("a great leap forward ... that space of the unpredictably human"; 7). In his view, the story explores "los mecanismos de control y dominio en los ámbitos públicos, pero también ... los códigos éticos individuales, donde pueden cohabitar, de forma contradictoria, el coraje y la servidumbre" ("the mechanisms of control and domination in the public sphere, but also ... individual ethical codes, in which courage and servitude can cohabit in contradictory ways"; 7). Thus, while exploring the ecologically devastating human interventions of the political macrostructure, the graphic novel counters with the fruitful potential of network as an ecosocial human response.

La cuenta atrás stresses not only the importance of social engagement that foregrounds ecological restoration, but also that acting ecosocially requires collective action rather than spontaneous personal responses: "Todo el mundo salió a la calle a protestar" ("Everyone took to the streets to protest"; 42). As Corbett explains, "Environmental problems ... cannot be 'solved' by voluntary individual actions, and instead require various forms of 'coercion' ... along with communication ... to move the collective to action that benefits all" (145). Volunteerism or unpaid labour can also be regarded as in line with an alternative economy (Prádanos, "Decrecimiento o barbarie" 78). In *La cuenta atrás*, the collective work carried out by the volunteers emerges as a contending force against the immorality and greed of the political leaders. Portela himself acknowledges that the volunteer movement in Galicia can be understood as "[u]na cosa de la gente, que salió del corazón del pueblo, aunque algunos partidos [políticos] intentaran aprovecharlo" ("born of the people, something that came from the heart of the populace, although some [political] parties tried to take advantage of it"; Portela and San Julián, Interview 89). Network-driven volunteerism arises, then, as a response to the emotional impact of the environmental accident, but also as an ecosocial alternative to the political mismanagement of the disaster. For Caldelas's people, interconnecting human and non-human nature through the ecological rescue operation doubles the effort's impact by also helping the residents address their collective trauma from the catastrophic event.

Conclusion

La cuenta atrás is a graphic novel that represents a human-induced ecological crisis by juxtaposing the detrimental human inaction and anthropocentric political and individual responses to that tragedy with the potential for ecosocial and collaborative interrogations and recovery. The final sequence of the story consists of a set of silent panels that show the social activist character manifesting his dissent by spray-painting the wall of a building with expletives aimed at the corrupt government. This image reveals that it is popular discontent that triggers the preceding story, for which the active interpretation of the reader is required in order to produce the meaning of the text in reverse. The narrative countdown leads the reader to think about the factors that shape the current sociopolitical and environmental context in Caldelas, as well as to reflect on how to go about changing the systemic configurations that lead to human-induced ecological disasters of the type that devastated this community and the lives of its residents.

Portela and San Julián productively reimagine the implications of an emblematic environmental disaster from a critical ecodystopian perspective that examines the interactions between human and non-human agents. In this sense, their graphic novel can be seen as an act of resistance against an anthropocentric conception of ecological systems. More importantly, their textual production is also a good example of collaborative, distributed work, which traditional anthropocentric narratives typically do not model. *La cuenta atrás* visualizes the future, present, and past – in that order – of a small town hit by a major human-induced catastrophe and contaminated not only by an enormous oil spill but, more dramatically, by the very human corruption and selfishness of the political system. The fictionalized visual story of the *Prestige* tragedy is ultimately the exploration of the ecosocial, political, and media controversies surrounding the ecodystopia that this environmental disaster represents, as well as of the crisis of a society whose members are portrayed as anti-heroes fighting for a collective cause fuelled by their own personal battles.[9]

NOTES

1 All translations of quotations in this chapter are my own.
2 In the Spanish context, it is important to distinguish between, on the one hand, comic strips intended for younger audiences, such as Manuel Gago García's *El Guerrero del Antifaz* (*The Warrior with the Mask*, 1944) and Víctor Mora's *El Capitán Trueno* (*Captain Thunder*, 1956) – as well as comic strip series published in the popular children's magazine *TBO* (1917–98) – and, on the other, cartoons such as those of *viñetistas* Miguel Brieva, Andrés Rábago, and Ramón Rodríguez, whose illustrated political satire has drawn attention to the contradictions and inequities inherent in such processes as maritime migration, post-Franco consumerism, and European politics. As Christine M. Martínez shows in her chapter in this collection, recent newspaper cartoons powerfully critique Spanish and global behaviours that have led to contemporary ecological devastation.
3 The explosion of the oil rig in the Gulf of Mexico inspired the creation of two graphic novels, *Oil and Water* (2011) and *The Deepwater Horizon Oil Spill* (2014). *La cuenta atrás*'s ecocritical perspective is more in line with the first than with the chronicle-like style of the second.
4 The sales rate of *La cuenta atrás* can be regarded as high for an environmental graphic novel. In 2008, the year of *La cuenta atrás*'s publication, Valencian cartoonist Paco Roca's *Arrugas* (*Wrinkles*), a celebrated Spanish graphic novel originally written in French and translated into several languages, sold over 17,000 copies in Spain, and Carlos Ruiz Zafón's *El juego del ángel* (*The Angel's Game*) was the best-selling Spanish fiction book, with 1.2 million copies sold.
5 By the same token, in her analysis of Jorge Carrión and Sagar Forniés's *Barcelona: Los vagabundos de la chatarra* (*Barcelona: The Scrap Metal Vagabonds*, 2015), environmental humanities scholar Christine M. Martínez argues that "the comics form better enables Carrión and Sagar to engage with the complexities of Barcelona as an urban ecosystem and represent the competing interests of the city's struggles over space. Their engagement

is mainly accomplished through the form's construction of an 'ecological understanding' of the problems at hand" ("Urban Ecology" 165). Both *La cuenta atrás* and *Barcelona: Los vagabundos de la chatarra* have been used as didactic materials for the debate in Spanish higher education classrooms about current socio-economic and socioecological issues through the study of graphic novels (Gallardo and García-Reyes).

6 As Hispanist Diana Palardy has observed, "[M]any of the Spanish dystopias produced since 2008 are either a direct or indirect reaction to the financial crisis" (109).

7 For a study of environmental activism and degrowth in Spanish cartoonist Miguel Brieva's 2012 graphic narrative *Memorias de la tierra* (*Memories of Earth*), see Martínez, "Affirmative Politics."

8 A particular characteristic of the *Prestige* spill is that the Internet had a significant influence on news coverage and the organization of protest activities from the beginning of the environmental crisis (Anderson and Marhadour 100). For the role of the Internet in the flash-mob protests following the 2004 terrorist bombings in Madrid, see Flesher Fominaya 297.

9 Special thanks must be given to Carlos Portela and Sergi San Julián for their support of this research and their permission to reproduce material from *La cuenta atrás* in this chapter.

WORKS CITED AND CONSULTED

Anderson, Alison G. *Media, Environment and the Network Society*. Palgrave Macmillan, 2014.

Anderson, Alison, and Agnès Marhadour. "Slick PR? The Media Politics of the *Prestige* Oil Spill." *Science Communication*, vol. 29, no. 1, 2007, pp. 96–115. *SAGE Journals*, https://doi.org/10.1177/1075547007305543.

Baetens, Jan, and Hugo Frey. *The Graphic Novel: An Introduction*. Cambridge UP, 2015.

Bealer, Adele Haverty. *Graphic Environments: Performing Ecocriticism at the Confluence of Image and Text*. 2014. U of Utah, PhD thesis.

Blanco, Patricia R. "El Gobierno ya 'inventó' la posverdad en la crisis del 'Prestige': Cinco bulos que lo demuestran." *El País*, 19 Nov. 2017, https://elpais.com/elpais/2017/11/17/hechos/1510926474_571278.html.

Burke, Kenneth. "Variations on 'Providence.'" *Notre Dame English Journal*, vol. 13, no. 3, summer 1981, pp. 155–83.

Carballo Dopico, Xulio. *Para unha historia da Banda Deseñada Galega: A narración a través da linguaxe gráfico-textual*. 2015. Universidade da Coruña, PhD thesis.

Carretero, Nacho. "Many of Us Lined Our Pockets with the Prestige Oil Spill." *El País*, 21 Nov. 2017, https://english.elpais.com/elpais/2017/11/20/inenglish/1511186498_158426.html.

Corbett, Julia B. "Reconceptualizing the Individual as a Social Actor in Environmental Communication." *Routledge Handbook of Ecocriticism and Environmental Communication*, edited by Scott Slovic et al., Routledge, 2019, pp. 143–52.

Díaz González-Viana, Luis. "Literature and New Forms of Orality: Invisible Realities." *A Comparative History of Literatures in the Iberian Peninsula*, edited by Fernando Cabo Aseguinolaza et al., vol. 1, John Benjamins, 2010, pp. 562–73.

Fajardo, José. "Hilillos de plastilina." *El Mundo*, 18 Apr. 2014, https://www.elmundo.es/cultura/2014/04/17/534e8ba4ca474143408b4571.html.

Flesher Fominaya, Cristina. "The Madrid Bombings and Popular Protest: Misinformation, Counter-Information, Mobilisation and Elections after '11-M.'" *Contemporary Social Science*, vol. 6, no. 3, 2011, pp. 289–307. *Taylor & Francis Online*, https://doi.org/10.1080/21582041.2011.603910.

Gallardo, Marta, and David García-Reyes. "Los objetivos de desarrollo sostenible a través de la novela gráfica en la educación superior." *REIDICS: Revista de Investigación en Didáctica de las Ciencias Sociales*, no. 9, 2021, pp. 97–114, https://doi.org/10.17398/2531-0968.09.97.

García, Santiago. *On the Graphic Novel*. Translated by Bruce Campbell, UP of Mississippi, 2015.

Gil González, Antonio J. "Comics and the Graphic Novel in Spain and Iberian Galicia." Translated by Manus O'Dwyer, New Trends in Iberian Galician Comparative Literature, special issue of CLCWeb: Comparative Literature and Culture, edited by María Teresa Vilariño Picos and Anxo Abuín González, vol. 13, no. 5, 2011, https://docs.lib.purdue.edu/clcweb/vol13/iss5/17.

Hartman, Steven. "Introduction: Naturalizing Culture and Countering Nature in Discourses of the Environment." *Contesting Environmental Imaginaries: Nature and Counternature in a Time of Global Change*, edited by Steven Hartman, Brill/Rodopi, 2017, pp. 1–10.

Hughes, Rowland, and Pat Wheeler. "Introduction. Eco-dystopias: Nature and the Dystopian Imagination." *Eco-dystopias: Nature and the Dystopian Imagination*, special issue of *Critical Survey*, edited by Rowland Hughes and Pat Wheeler, vol. 25, no. 2, 2013, pp. 1–6. *Berghahn Journals*, https://doi.org/10.3167/cs.2013.250201.

Jones, Clint. *Apocalyptic Ecology in the Graphic Novel: Life and the Environment after Societal Collapse*. McFarland, 2020.

Martínez, Christine M. "The Affirmative Politics of Degrowth: Miguel Brieva's Graphic Narrative *Memorias de la Tierra*." *Journal of Spanish Cultural Studies*, vol. 18, no. 2, 2017, pp. 191–212. *Taylor & Francis Online*, https://doi.org/10.1080/14636204.2017.1308631.

Martínez, Christine M. "Urban Ecology and Comics Journalism in Jorge Carrión and Sagar Forniés's *Barcelona: Los vagabundos de la chatarra* (2015)."

Consequential Art: Comics Culture in Contemporary Spain, edited by Samuel Amago and Matthew J. Marr, U of Toronto P, 2019, pp. 164–91. *De Gruyter*, https://doi.org/10.3138/9781487531386-008.

Matthies, Aila-Leena, and Kati Närhi. "Introduction: It Is the Time for Social Work and Social Policy Research on the Ecosocial Transition." *The Ecosocial Transition of Societies: The Contribution of Social Work and Social Policy*, edited by Aila-Leena Matthies and Kati Närhi, Routledge, 2017, pp. 1–13.

McCloud, Scott. *Understanding Comics: The Invisible Art*. Tundra, 1993.

McKinney, Collin, and David F. Richter. "Graphic Spain: From Aleluyas to the 'Second Boom.'" McKinney and Richter, pp. 3–25.

McKinney, Collin, and David F. Richter, eds. *Spanish Graphic Narratives: Recent Developments in Sequential Art*. Palgrave Macmillan, 2020.

Nabizadeh, Golnar. "Introduction: Comics, Memory, and the Visual Archive." *Representation and Memory in Graphic Novels*, edited by Golnar Nabizadeh, Routledge, 2019, pp. 1–26.

Palardy, Diana Q. *The Dystopian Imagination in Contemporary Spanish Literature and Film*. Palgrave Macmillan, 2018.

Pérez, Fernando J. "El Supremo condena al capitán del 'Prestige' por daño ambiental." *El País*, 26 Jan. 2016, https://elpais.com/politica/2016/01/26/actualidad/1453809050_900584.html.

Perry, Laura. "Anthroposcenes: Towards an Environmental Graphic Novel." *C21 Literature: Journal of 21st-Century Writings*, vol. 6, no. 5, 2018, pp. 1–24, https://doi.org/10.16995/C21.37.

Pinker, Steven. *Enlightenment Now: The Case for Reason, Science, Humanism and Progress*. Allen Lane, 2018.

Portela, Carlos, and Sergi San Julián. *A conta atrás / La cuenta atrás*. ECC Ediciones, 2022.

Portela, Carlos, and Sergi San Julián. *La cuenta atrás. Parte I*. Faktoría K de Libros, 2008.

Portela, Carlos, and Sergi San Julián. Interview. Conducted by Álvaro Pons, Portela and San Julián, *La cuenta atrás*, pp. 87–91.

Prádanos, Luis I. "Decrecimiento o barbarie: Ecocrítica y capitalismo global en la novela futurista española reciente." *Ecozon@: European Journal of Literature, Culture and Environment*, vol. 3, no. 2, 2012, pp. 74–92, https://doi.org/10.37536/ECOZONA.2012.3.2.473.

Prádanos, Luis I. *Postgrowth Imaginaries: New Ecologies and Counterhegemonic Culture in Post-2008 Spain*. Liverpool UP, 2018.

Rincón, Reyes. "El Supremo fija en más de 1.500 millones las indemnizaciones por el 'Prestige.'" *El País*, 20 Dec. 2018, https://elpais.com/politica/2018/12/20/actualidad/1545300528_440878.html.

Rivas, Manuel. "El descubrimiento de las sombras." Portela and San Julián, *La cuenta atrás*, pp. 5–7.

Rodríguez-Trigo, Gema, et al. "Health Changes in Fishermen 2 Years after Clean-Up of the Prestige Oil Spill." *Annals of Internal Medicine*, vol. 153, no. 8, 2010, pp. 489–98. *ACP Journals*, https://doi.org/10.7326/0003-4819-153-8-201010190-00279.

Sargent, Lyman Tower. "The Three Faces of Utopianism Revisited." *Utopian Studies*, vol. 5, no. 1, 1994, pp. 1–37.

Simón Abad, Fernando. "Memory, Amnesia, and Forgetting: Graphic Representations of a Chronic Disease in Twentieth- and Twenty-First-Century Spain." McKinney and Richter, pp. 47–65.

Surís Regueiro, Juan C., and María Dolores Garza Gil. "Evaluation of Direct and Indirect Damages. Methodology and Work Programme for the Prestige Case." *Economic, Social and Environmental Effects of the "Prestige" Oil Spill*, edited by Albino Prada Blanco and María Xosé Vázquez Rodríguez, Consello da Cultura Galega, 2004, pp. 311–51.

Tabachnick, Stephen E. "Introduction." *The Cambridge Companion to the Graphic Novel*, edited by Stephen E. Tabachnick, Cambridge UP, 2017, pp. 1–7.

Tintoré, Joaquín. "La investigación, un elemento clave del futuro económico y social: El papel del CSIC ante el vertido del buque Prestige." *Las lecciones de la catástrofe del* Prestige, edited by Antonio Figueras et al., Consejo Superior de Investigaciones Científicas, 2005, pp. 45–53.

Trevathan, John H. "*Nunca Máis*: Ecological Collectivism and the *Prestige* Disaster." *Ethics of Life: Contemporary Iberian Debates*, edited by Katarzyna Beilin and William Viestenz, Vanderbilt UP, 2016, pp. 35–55.

Trotta, Joe, and Houman Sadri. "Introduction: Welcome to the Beginning of the End of Everything." *Broken Mirrors: Representations of Apocalypses and Dystopias in Popular Culture*, edited by Joe Trotta et al., Routledge, 2020, pp. 1–14.

Vold, Veronica. "The Aesthetics of Environmental Equity in American Newspaper Strips." *Ecomedia: Key Issues*, edited by Stephen Rust et al., Routledge, 2016, pp. 66–84.

Wess, Robert. "Burke's Counter-Nature: Posthumanism in the Anthropocene." *Kenneth Burke + The Posthuman*, edited by Chris Mays et al., Pennsylvania State UP, 2017, pp. 80–97.

Chapter Seventeen

Drawing Ecological Thought: Anthropomorphism and Satire as Critique of Capitalism in the Twenty-First-Century Spanish Comic

CHRISTINE M. MARTÍNEZ

Memorias de la tierra (2012), a graphic narrative by the Spanish illustrator and cartoonist Miguel Brieva, offers an unusual format; the text gathers many of Brieva's previously published cartoons from the Spanish daily *El País*'s monthly supplement *Tierra* alongside annexes of collected quotations within a narrative framework that recounts these items as the memories of an extraterrestrial observer, Zuth Egbedius Mö. Zuth visits earth on the brink of mankind's self-destruction due to "la explotación indiscriminada de sus recursos planetarios" ("the indiscriminate exploitation of planetary resources"; 6).[1] The collected quotations – which Zuth presents as the words of exceptional humans with "la lucidez suficiente para comprender y anticiparse a su inminente declive" ("sufficient lucidity to understand and anticipate their imminent decline") – are eclectic, spanning from the likes of Lao Tse to Stanley Kubrick, and foreground ideas and names associated with degrowth, postcolonial and feminist critiques of capitalism, alterglobalization, and Marxist critiques of consumer society. As I have argued previously ("Affirmative Politics" 196), this unusual combination of annexes, cartoons, and narratives creates a relational matrix and multiplicity of voices that not only undermine the myths decried by Zuth's narrative and Brieva's vignettes but also engage the reader in the dialogical and participatory thinking advocated throughout *Memorias*. The book thus presents a notion of environmentalism profoundly involved in questioning fundamental values of late-capitalist society, economy, and politics and in the imagination of just and desirable social alternatives. Building on this network analysis, I study here how Brieva and two contemporary Spanish comics artists, Andrés Rábago (pseudonym El Roto) and Ramón Rodríguez (Ramón), employ the comics form to engage ecological thought, a mode of thinking that extends beyond

Fig. 17.1. Miguel Brieva, *Memorias de la tierra* 126

This image is licensed under the CC BY-NC 4.0 licence.

embedded capitalist and anthropocentric notions of value, humanity, and nature.[2]

Published at the height of Spain's neoliberal economic crisis (2008–14), at a time when social and political debate in Spain was dominated by pressing questions of debt, political representation, austerity, unemployment, and financial and political corruption, *Memorias* placed ecological (and specifically degrowth) critiques of capitalism at the centre of a host of societal ills, reminding readers that the most critical concerns of the day formed part of a much deeper and long-developing commodification of life and of the material world within modern society. During Spain's preceding economic bonanza, cartoonists like Brieva, El Roto, and Ramón published vignettes and/or comic strips that foregrounded the invisibilized damage and externalized costs of so-called economic progress, as measured in terms of GDP growth, the proliferation of ambitious construction and infrastructure projects, and the expansion of multinational corporations and consumer markets. The work of these artists decried global consumer society's reliance upon the systemic destruction of ecosystems, biodiversity loss, and the commodification and depletion of planetary resources.[3] Spain's prolonged economic recession coincided with the early years of renewed global climate activism and legislation, galvanized in the decade following the 2009 UN Climate Change Conference. While this coincidence brought new challenges to prioritizing ecological and global climate concerns within Spain, this period also saw a greater public appetite for critiques of global capitalism and interest in climate and environmental sustainability. Both El Roto and Brieva's previous environmentally themed work was re-edited and published at this time. From 2006 to 2014, Ramón's comic strip *Hipo, Popo, Pota y Tamo* brought to the funnies section of *El País* warnings of planetary overheating and biodiversity loss, pedagogical illustrations of endangered species, and lamentations of the irrational and irresponsible behaviour of twenty-first-century humankind from the imagined perspective of zoomorphic characters. In 2014, Rábago collected five years of previously published cartoons dealing with the destruction of ecosystems and the hypocrisies of late-capitalist anthropocentrism in *El libro verde*, consciously emphasizing the importance of contemporary ecological devastation at a time of deep social, political, and economic turmoil. In relation to his other texts published throughout the Recession years – *A cada uno lo suyo* (2013), *Camarón que se duerme* (2012), *Viñetas para una crisis* (2011) – Rábago describes the issues treated in *El libro verde* as "preocupaciones más íntimas" ("more intimate concerns") and "asuntos de más largo recorrido" ("longer-term issues"; Vincent). Interviews with both Rábago and Brieva show their understanding of consumer society's unsustainable ecological metabolism as central to the numerous social, democratic, and economic crises that define the twenty-first century.[4]

In this context, I argue that cartoonists within Spain have been some of the most persistent advocates for critically engaged ecological thinking, especially at times when the longer-term and larger-scale issues highlighted by such perspectives have been pushed to the margins as peripheral concerns. Furthermore, I show that the comics form is particularly adept at communicating ecological modes of thought given its use of: graphic satire to dismantle hegemonic narratives and convey complex critiques to expanded audiences; graphic images to present network relations, such as those that compose ecological networks or material flows within globalized capitalism; and the combination of image and text to present non-human beings for ethical consideration, ultimately challenging the anthropocentrism of late capitalism.

Ecological Thinking and the Comics Page

By the terms *ecological thinking* and *ecological thought* I refer to thought that is radically different from the so-called green politics of contemporary capitalist democracies and from the pigeonholed environmentalist discourses of mainstream mass media.[5] Rather than referring to complex networks of human and non-human interdependence over varying and coexisting scales of time and space, terms like "environmental impact" and "ecology" are often employed by conventional discourses in a reductionist manner. The categorical limitations of the capitalist imaginary often demarcate green politics as a focus upon primarily non-human entities, usually at the exclusion of social concerns and racialized and precarized human communities. Brieva describes this limited discourse while reflecting upon his own reasons for publishing *Memorias*:

> Encuentro que a menudo el discurso que reclama el respeto al medioambiente se queda corto, y por tanto ineficaz, cuando se reduce a una serie de consignas bienintencionadas y por otra parte bastante de cajón (la madre naturaleza es buena, salvemos al lince, reciclo mi basura, los domingos coge la bici, etc.) que se esgrimen aisladamente, al margen de un discurso más ambicioso y englobador, más realista, que inevitablemente adquiriría contenidos económicos y políticos contrapuestos a los generalmente establecidos ... Procuremos, pues, huir de los tópicos y los simplismos acerca de esta cuestión.

(I find that often the discourse that demands respect for the environment falls short, and is therefore ineffective, when it is reduced to a series of well-intentioned but stereotypical slogans (mother nature is good, save the lynx, I recycle my waste, ride bikes on Sundays, etc.) that are wielded in isolation, apart from a more ambitious and encompassing discourse that would inevitably acquire economic and political content opposed to that which is generally established … Let's try then to avoid the usual clichés and simplistic approaches that frame this question; "El secuestro de la imaginación" 300–1)

Ecological thinking opposes the "clichés" and "simplistic approaches" of this official, intentionally naive, and purposely inefficient environmental discourse and exposes the commodification of persons, labour, and material flows required by contemporary capitalism and its short-term, ever more rapid cycles of production, profit, and obsolescence.[6] Ecological thinking engages an enhanced awareness of multiple human and non-human entities and phenomena. It includes the ability to think within the spatial or temporal scales required by the "hyperobjects" of global overheating or ocean acidification (Morton, *Hyperobjects* and *Ecological Thought* 19), to narrate the history of industry and capitalist markets within ecological systems and their temporal cycles (Moore), and to consider the span of human life within the aeons that compose planetary life (fig. 17.1).[7]

While there is variation in the extent to which the cartoonists discussed in this chapter develop this critically engaged form of ecological thinking, their work has allowed for deeper and more sustained debate, especially throughout the first decades of the twenty-first century, a period of growing interest in sustainability and mitigation of environmental catastrophe among mainstream advocates of market economies. Corporations and growth-oriented politicians have long struggled to control and adapt popular environmental concerns and discourse to short-sighted, market-driven, and anthropocentric priorities. Examples include the practice of greenwashing, critiqued by Brieva in *Memorias* (85) and El Roto in *El libro verde* (78); renewable retrofitting, motivated by calculated economic opportunity; and the proposal of large-scale climate-mitigation tactics, such as geoengineering and carbon capture. Ramón critiques the latter in a cartoon that personifies the overheated earth and its moon, imagining the moon's cynical reaction to geoengineering projects through a comparison with the privatization of medicine. Witnessing the planet's feverish suffering, the moon claims, "[L]o que pretenden con la geoingeniería es dejar que revientes para luego enviarte a la privada" ("Their intention with geoengineering is to let you get so sick that you will go to the private hospital"). For the personified planet, of course, "la medicina natural y pública" ("natural and public health care") would imply a simple cessation of contemporary habits of ecosystem disruption and contamination (Ramón, 30 June 2014).

Art critic and cartoonist Nick Sousanis argues in *Unflattening* (2015) that the comic's "expansive way of seeing corresponds to an understanding of ecosystems" (45). As he makes this statement, he juxtaposes a mosaic of drawn scenes, rendering visible a diversity of spatial scales related to the flow of water: a hand reaching to turn on a faucet, steam evaporating from a kettle, torrential rain falling from clouds and into puddles, the course of a stream, rivulets of liquid beneath a microscopic cellular view, a tangle of metallic pipes, the aerial view of the map of a reservoir … (fig. 17.2). In the depiction of cellular and bird's-eye views, his illustration decentres the human perspective heading the page. Sousanis's ecological understanding of the comics form is composed of an ability to view from multiple perspectives and viewpoints (similar to James Joyce's use of literary parallax) and to rhizomatically bind visual boundaries, rendering perceptible their often obscured connectedness. This presentation works differently than the narration made possible by video images or written narrative (progressing in linear time), though it finds some parallels with the plastic arts and multimedia installation.[8] For graphic narratives and vignettes, the image offers the potential to embed verbal narrative into a visual ecology of relations that, while illustrating or resonating with that narrative, also opens up multiple lines of flight.[9]

This capacity to redraw and juxtapose multiple relations that develop across time and space has been frequently employed by Brieva in his critiques of the externalized social and environmental costs of consumer capitalism. Take, for example, his illustration of the networks of exploitation required by a typical holiday celebration in the Global North. In fig. 17.3, Brieva decentres the hegemonic white-Christmas narrative of Western twentieth- and twenty-first-century consumer culture by dispersing it within various imagined perspectives of the externalized social and material effects of such consumerism. Via the consumption of unethically made toys and fossil fuels, the Sistemez family's holiday celebration is connected to scenes depicting ecological devastation (smokestacks encircling the city centre, the bulldozing of forests), climate change (a polar bear on diminishing ice caps), and human rights abuses (child labour in squalid conditions, the displacement of native populations). Brieva often employs an exaggerated, self-mocking aesthetic as he illustrates the socioecological effects of petro-dependent and consumer capitalism. As seen

Fig. 17.2. Nick Sousanis, *Unflattening* 45

Copyright © 2015 by Nick Sousanis. Used by permission from Harvard University Press. All rights reserved.

Fig. 17.3. Miguel Brieva, "Los Sistemez en ¡Oh blanca Navidad!"; *Memorias de la tierra* 61

This image is licensed under the CC BY-NC 4.0 licence.

in fig. 17.3, he either visually exaggerates situations or re-employs the overused tropes of conventional environmentalist and human rights discourses transmitted by mainstream media and NGO advertising campaigns (the polar bear, shanty-town children). Such tactics allow Brieva's socioecological critique to avoid a self-righteous and pedantic tone and to mobilize a playful re-employment of scrutinized cultural aesthetics: for example, thanks to its rapid succession of images, fig. 17.3 is also legible as the simultaneous broadcasting of multiple television channels, such as viewed by the Sistemez family members at the close of the vignette. The comics form thus provides a particular set of tools for cartoonists, like Brieva, to develop critiques of capitalism whereby ecological thinking is shown to be inseparable from questions of consumer culture, contemporary politics, or social justice.

Ecology, Satire, and the Critique of Capitalist Realism

"La letra con risa entra" ("Spare the laughter, spoil the child"), writes Brieva, explaining his own pedagogical tactics in *Memorias*. A play on the adage "La letra con sangre entra" ("Spare the rod, spoil the child"), the statement highlights the cartoon's power to make otherwise complex and detailed arguments more appealing and accessible. As Brieva argues, his own praxis combines the use of satirical laughter as *denuncia* ("denunciation") alongside the pedagogical and imaginative potential of the graphic form ("El secuestro de la imaginación" 339–40). Many of the concepts illustrated and satirized by Brieva, El Roto, and Ramón distill the ideas of influential thinkers that, for decades, have criticized hegemonic global capitalism and its society of spectacle and commodification of life, especially as articulated in Spain and Southern Europe.[10] Visual-cultures critic Daniel Mourenza describes the satirical cartoons of El Roto as engaging in what poet and playwright Bertolt Brecht called "crude thinking," a way of referring theory to reality by means of the proverbs and idioms of everyday language instead of by means of highly theoretical vocabulary (92). At the same time, Spanish studies scholar Isabelle Touton mentions how the simple and austere aesthetic of El Roto's images and satire stands out from mass media's constant flow of information (209–10). The visual interplay of drawing with accessible and popular expressions has been highly effective in engaging Spanish audiences experiencing the accumulated exhaustion of compound crises. It also clearly communicates the consumerist source of the country's interrelated economic and ecological difficulties and thus offers a palpable alternative to the path of least resistance:

industry-driven greenwashing and the short-term mitigation tactics of economic and political elites.

In his analysis of El Roto's economic cartoons, Mourenza mentions the cartoonist's ability to depict with succinct facility, in a single austere graphic image, Marx's concept of commodity fetishism. In the simple juxtaposition of dissonant image and text, El Roto illustrates the means by which people and their relations take the form of objects (Mourenza 88). Take, for example, fig. 17.4, in which objects become known only by their ascribed number in a catalogue: bicycle, cherries, mountain, and hat are placed side by side, extracted from their imagined surroundings, subjected to the same system of commodification and the same visual scale of the catalogue page, and given seemingly arbitrary numbers according to the unknown demands of the system processing their sale. The cartoon depicts this commodification of objects as a memory loss and cultural oblivion of biblical proportions ("Olvidaron los nombres de las cosas" 'They forgot the names of things'). Thus, Rábago provides a reworked citation, updated for his contemporary audience ("y las llamaban por sus números en los catálogos de venta" 'and they called them by their numbers in shopping catalogues'), as a passage from the Book of Revelation (Apocalipsis). Mimicking the layout of late nineteenth- to early twenty-first-century mail-order catalogues, the cartoon recalls the origins of mass consumption and their corollary, societal amnesia.

While this vignette is published in Rábago's ecologically themed book, *El libro verde*, other cartoons illustrate how contemporary capitalism (especially during times of recession) commodifies and devalues persons just like objects for sale at a discount in shop windows (El Roto, *Viñetas* 61) or like money (14) and reduces people and interpersonal relationships to numbers and statistics ("Detrás de los números hay personas," *El País*, 1 March 2012). The depiction of the commodification and devaluing of various forms of life – human and non-human – is a common theme throughout El Roto's work in the 2000s and 2010s. As the cartoonist states in an interview with *El País* about the launch of *El libro verde*, "Hay que recuperar los valores de la vida frente a los valores de la economía" ("We must recover the values of life versus the values of the economy"; Vincent). Given the anthropocentrism implicit in modern capitalist notions of life and value, re-evaluating definitions of "human" and "nature," therefore, is pivotal in this task.

As in the case of theatre, the destabilizing and didactic ends of satire in the graphic cartoon are achieved through the juxtaposition of unexpected elements. El Roto is a master of this form of montage, frequently combining dissonant text and imagery (Mourenza 93; Touton 212). The

Fig. 17.4. El Roto, *El libro verde* 13

© 2023 Artists Rights Society (ARS), New York/VEGAP, Madrid.

succinctness of his technique is seen in fig. 17.5, in which the caption "Paseo por el bosque" ("A walk in the woods") accompanies the illustration of a man walking over several piles of neatly cut logs. While a simple change in caption, such as "Paseo por un mes de labor" ("A walk through a month of labour") or "Paseo por los salones del futuro barrio" ("A walk through the living rooms of the future neighbourhood"), could emphasize these logs through the positivity of a capitalist lens – that is, their relation to human labour or their identity as raw material for construction – Rábago's choice of words forces the reader to consider above all the destruction required by such processes. The caption codes the timber as negativity and absence, focusing the reader's attention to what has been destroyed in the lumber's creation (the forest) and

Fig. 17.5. El Roto, "Paseo por el bosque"; *El libro verde* 52

© 2023 Artists Rights Society (ARS), New York/VEGAP, Madrid.

stirring up feelings of irreparable loss. The linguistically conjured but visually inaccessible forest implies a far richer concept than that which is visible in fig. 17.5's pile of logs: an entire ecosystem composed of bird calls, ground cover, moss, lichens, streams, rotting plants, communities of insects … all flattened, silent, and absent. Brieva's "Los Sistemez" draws connections between the production of consumer objects and the destruction of ecosystems through the juxtaposition of multiple images, mimicking the visual excess of consumer society; "Paseo," however, achieves similar ends by mere suggestion and by the combination of text and image. Austere, echoing the desertified and stripped land-scapes of late capitalism's extractive sites, El Roto's approach is argu-ably even more disquieting than that of Brieva.

For El Roto, satire cuts deep, deeper than conventional pedagogy, for example. Paraphrasing and quoting the artist, Vincent writes,

"[P]rofundiza más en aquello que uno quiere llamar la atención y 'lo deja dentro, en un lugar del que es difícil escapar'" ("It cuts deeper into that to which one wants to call attention and 'plants the message within, in a place that is difficult to escape'"). By allowing the reader to arrive at their own conclusions or feel disquieted by the contradictions staged in the satirical image, these techniques powerfully contest the naturalized beliefs of contemporary capitalism. Mourenza describes how El Roto's deployment of satire, whose essence lies in revealing the contrast between reality and pretence (Feinberg 3), breaks up the ideological narratives that support economic consensus. The satirical function of El Roto's cartoons is particularly interesting as the venue for his daily vignettes, *El País*, has also been one of the most influential public organs in consolidating late-capitalist economic consensus within democratic Spain (Mourenza 84). This observation not only evinces *El País* as a powerful platform for the work of the cartoonists discussed in this chapter but also points to how their satire coexists with or even depends upon such organs of consensus. Nonetheless, the power of El Roto's graphic satire in challenging Spain's economic and political hegemony is made patent by the informal circulation of his work during the Spanish *indignados* movement, reproduced in social media or as placards during the 15M anti-austerity protests (Mourenza 95; Touton 212–13; Mate 15–16).[11]

Graphic satire helps Spanish cartoonists approach the environmental question in ways that are deeply critical of late-capitalist society and its co-opting of environmentalist discourse, precisely through its ability to reveal fundamental inconsistencies in the ideological structure that justifies the commodification of ecosystems and life forms. El Roto's cartoons on the economy reveal the falsity of arguments that maintain wealth for elites and the contradictions of narratives that naturalize the economic status quo (Mourenza). In the same vein, El Roto's cartoons of rivers, exploited forests and animals, landscapes marked by climate change, and contaminated coastlines expose the contradictory claims of green capitalism, demonstrating the incompatibility between growth-oriented and free-market economic logics and the sustainable reproduction of ecosystems and human society. In one cartoon, a thistle speaks, "[S]oñé que me hacía rico y me convertía en una urbanización" ("I dreamt that I became rich and turned into a housing development"; El Roto, *El libro verde* 44); in another, a razed forest proclaims, "[A]l campo no le vemos futuro, nos hemos trasladado a la industria" ("We don't see a future in the country, we've switched to industry"; 38); while in another, a technician comments before a pair of water runoff pipes, "[E]stas aguas llevan mercurio, cemento petróleo y plomo" ("These waters bring mercury, cement, petroleum, and lead"), as the other responds, "¡[C]uánta riqueza!" ("So much wealth!"; 80). Rábago's cartoons expose the falsity and temporal myopia of late-capitalist society's perception of wealth and good living: we know the thistle will be ploughed over by the coming urbanization, the forest's future iteration has required its destruction, and the wealth of the technicians' waters is one that intoxicates and acidifies.

Other cartoons from El Roto satirize short-term fixes and market responses to the effects of climate change: a man waters a desertified field as he shouts, "¡[T]anta tontería con el cambio climático!, ¡pues si no llueve se riega y ya está!" ("So much nonsense with climate change! If it doesn't rain, just water and problem solved!"; *El País*, 21 July 2015); a polar bear swimming in open water mentions to another, "[M]e han dicho los desarrollistas, que si queremos hielo nos compremos un congelador" ("The developmentalists have told me that if we want ice we just need to buy a freezer"; *El País*, 25 Dec. 2014); a fallow field is accompanied by the title "[L]a sequía es falta de riego, dijo el experto" ("The drought is because of a lack of watering, said the expert"; *El País*, 17 July 2017). Such cartoons render visible the absurdity of palliative logics based upon the maintenance or acceleration of present habits of consumption often advocated by neoliberal elites and so-called experts. Ramón's previously mentioned vignette, in which a personified moon complains about geoengineering, functions in a similar way, arguing that the proposed solutions of neoliberal capitalism are part and parcel of the problem itself.

While often illustrating the same conventional and conservationist environmentalist themes decried by Brieva earlier, Ramón's comic strip also employs similar tactics of satirical montage to stage the superficiality of climate accords and environmental ministries, breaking through rhetorical façades to reveal their service to the maintenance of industry and petro-dependent economic growth. Recurrent figures of attack in Ramón's comic strip include Spanish ministries with competencies for environmental regulation, International Climate Conferences, and the particularly contentious figure of European Commissioner Miguel Arias Cañete, elected in 2014 to represent European citizens in the development of climate policy despite his multiple conflicts of interest and familial connections to the oil industry.

Fig. 17.6 presents the no-longer-extant Spanish "Ministerio de Medio Ambiente," housed within the Palacio de Fomento, as a ministry of petroleum extraction. While the ministries responsible for the health of Spanish ecosystems have been constantly renamed and reconfigured throughout modern history, their frequent articulation within the

Fig. 17.6. Ramón, "Ministerio de medio ambiente," *El País*, 30 May 2014

Reprinted with the artist's permission.

Fig. 17.7. Ramón, *El País*, 3 Oct. 2014

Reprinted with the artist's permission.

context of development, agriculture, fishing, conservation, and rural spaces makes evident a long-standing tendency to approach environmental concerns within the context of industry and commodifiable resources separated from urban metabolisms. While the cartoon makes no mention of this history, it denounces the management of environmental policy by fossil fuel interests through a juxtaposition that is meant to surprise. Conjured by the textual header, expectations of what an environmental ministry should be clash with the illustration of one that appears crowned by an oil rig. The contamination produced by the rig is accentuated when placed within the context of the urban landscape of the Spanish capital.

Fig. 17.7, though published in October of 2014, forecasts the outcome of the 2014 United Nations Climate Change Conference in Lima (December 2014) by depicting the EU representative Arias Cañete. Before receiving his post in September of that year, Arias Cañete had been forced to sell his shareholdings in Petrolífera Dúcar and Petrologis

Canarias due to protestations of conflict of interest from fellow EU parliamentarians. Fig. 17.7 illustrates the disquieting contradiction that the man responsible for climate policy – he literally holds climate policy in his hands by way of a briefcase labelled "CLIMA" – has the hose of a gas pump and an envelope filled with pay-offs trailing from his pocket. These satirical cartoons foreground the corrupt and self-interested fabric of Spanish and European institutions, illustrating the impossibility of producing meaningful climate policy while being steered by the very industries responsible for the climate's accelerated alteration.

Anthropomorphism: Challenging Anthropocentrism and the Commodification of Life

The personification of non-human animals and elements is a common feature of El Roto's and Brieva's cartoons and an essential feature of Ramón's comic strip, whose name is derived from its four baby hippopotamus protagonists (Hipo, Popo, Pota, and Tamo), each of which is given a unique human personality trait ("*ELPAÍS.es* presenta"). In their illustration of non-human animals, these artists engage in one of the oldest and most varied tropes of comics and satirical forms. They do so, however, in ways that specifically counter the commodification of life under late capitalism and consider the inherent value and experience of what progressive columnist Nathan Robinson has called "the other proletariat." Robinson writes that under global neoliberalism "animals are granted permission to live solely to the extent that they are capable of generating benefit for humans" and concludes that "[w]ild animals are therefore a kind of massive global proletariat, being exploited and destroyed by the merciless human bourgeoisie." El Roto's vignettes giving voice to animals subjected to industrial meat and dairy industries and Ramón's cartoons condemning zoos and the keeping of pets add domesticated, farmed, and captive animals to this "other proletariat," in resonance with the ideas of the animal abolitionist movement.[12]

The illustration of animals throughout the history of comics has not typically been deployed with the purpose of creating empathy or challenging the capitalist commodification of life forms. As media studies critic Daniel Yezbick explains, from early print media onwards, illustrated animals have appeared as metaphors for human vices and virtues or as more acceptable conduits for political satire. While a number of texts throughout the history of the graphic animal contest capitalist logics, decry animal mistreatment, or advocate awareness of environmental issues, the vast majority of illustrated animals in comics speak more about the human condition than that of the non-human animal or of interspecies relations.[13] As Yezbick mentions, the twenty-first century has seen an increasing number of cartoonists and illustrators engaging the graphic image in order to promote greater awareness and appreciation of non-human experience. Rather than employing the graphic and sequential image to create zoomorphs (human behaviour presented in non-human form), work by such creators imagines and translates animal subjectivity and experience, whether through wordless illustration of that experience, didactic explanation of communal organization and habits, the partial transcription of animal minds mediated by digital technology, or the anthropomorphic attribution of thoughts and emotions.[14]

As zoomorphs, Ramón's hippopotami and their friends embody a particular set of human values and experiences that arguably reflects those of the environmentally concerned reader of *El País*. Among other uses, they serve as conduits for political satire and guide emotional responses to the information presented in the comic strip. A cartoonish frog, for example, frequently mocks and mimics conservative politicians such as Arias Cañete (*El País*, 8 Oct. 2014) or Spanish ex-president José María Aznar (*El País*, 24 May 2013), while Pota is illustrated expressing stupefaction or passing judgment before graphs of increasing CO_2 levels (*El País*, 17 May 2013 and 7 Oct. 2008). Though Ramón's zoomorphs also reveal the double standards of ecologically devastating discourses, as discussed later in this section, these characters often advance simplistic environmentalist agendas that are easily capitalized by corporate interests. For example, the comic strip uncritically praises renewable energy technologies, presented as the Manichean opposites of demonized fossil fuel and nuclear power industries (*El País*, 22 Feb. 2007, 3 Feb. 2010; 2 Oct. 2012, and 24 July 2013). Popo, in their characteristic optimism, is drawn soaring high on a bicycle (another technology universally praised by the comic strip) shouting, "¡¡¡Todo va a cambiar!!!" ("Everything is going to change!!!"; *El País*, 10 Oct. 2014), or projecting the shadow of wind turbines while imagining the future (*El País*, 25 May 2010). Though purportedly living in a reserve at the foot of Mount Kilimanjaro, these zoomorphs universalize a particularly urbanite and Global North set of priorities.[15]

The illustrated animals of the cartoonists discussed in this chapter are all, however, instrumentalized to challenge the capitalist commodification and mistreatment of non-human life. At times, and especially in the work of El Roto and Brieva, this challenge extends to anthropocentric notions of ethics, value, and vulnerability. As political theorist Jane Bennett argues in *Vibrant Matter* (2010), anthropomorphism is an effective tool in dismantling anthropocentrism, making visible the system of subjectivities and

Fig. 17.8. El Roto, *El País*, 12 Mar. 2018

© 2023 Artists Rights Society (ARS), New York/VEGAP, Madrid.

capitalist values that codifies and defines the rights (or lack thereof) of the non-human. She writes, "A touch of anthropomorphism, then, can catalyze a sensibility that finds a world filled not with ontologically distinct categories of beings (subjects and objects) but with variously composed materialities that form confederations" (99). The anthropomorphism encouraged by Bennett and present throughout the non-human animal cartoons of Brieva and El Roto, and several cartoons of Ramón, questions ontological divisions that have structured modern understandings of humanity, suffering, subjectivity, value, and ethical identification. Challenging central categories of Western modernity, such as nature/culture and human/non-human, opens up the possibility of taking seriously the personhood and sentience of non-human beings, which could result in a change of legal frameworks and human behaviour. As seen in the vignettes of these cartoonists that foreground non-human experience, the inability to perceive or take seriously the suffering and inherent value of non-human life is a major barrier to the development of meaningful environmental politics and a more just and resilient society. Thus, El Roto's animal cartoons often challenge the ontological categories that foreclose or render irrelevant the suffering of non-human life.

Figs. 17.8 and 17.9 are part of a series of cartoons by El Roto that illustrate key concepts of animal ethics: the relevance of the suffering of the

Fig. 17.9. El Roto, *El País*, 7 Apr. 2017

© 2023 Artists Rights Society (ARS), New York/VEGAP, Madrid.

non-human other and the ways in which anthropocentric definitions of humanity preclude the non-human animal from ethical and moral consideration. Rábago's cartoon of what appears to be a suffocating fish in fig. 17.8 attributes the accompanying caption, "You don't know our suffering because we don't shout," to Corine Pelluchon, a French philosopher and ethicist who considers the struggle for animal liberation and human equity within late capitalism to be one and the same (35).[16] The silence of the fish is piercing – it appears as if attempting to scream – while its open eye directly confronts the reader. In a simple montage of image and text, the human audience is invited to approach the fish no longer as a consumable item (neither as commodity nor food) but as a being capable of suffering and of feeling pain.

Fig. 17.9 anthropomorphically attributes text to challenge conventional definitions of personhood and humanity to a stag, who comments, "Many men believe themselves to be humans because they look like [humans] on the outside." Appearances are likely important for such a stag, coveted by trophy hunters for its antlers. Because of the gaps in meaning between image and text (i.e., a stag speaking of humanity?) and within the caption itself (i.e., humans are not human?), the stag's statement elicits various questions in the mind of the reader (i.e., *What is humanity?* and *What is the stag beyond its initial appearance?*). This line of questioning, while not immediately explicit, has a host of moral, ethical, and political implications. The consideration of what constitutes "humanity" points to numerous associated concepts, such as intelligence, ingenuity, and emotional complexity, that have supported not only narratives of human exceptionalism but also colonialist ideologies that have denied rights to and justified the exploitation of subjugated communities for centuries. A reconsideration of the human and associated concepts within ecological networks and beyond colonialist frameworks has thus been pivotal to numerous initiatives (the Rights of Nature movement) and fields (environmental humanities) working to generate political tools and cultural narratives to confront twenty-first-century social and ecological challenges.[17]

Mariana Pestana, co-curator of the 2018–19 Lisbon iteration of *Eco-visionaries*, argues that confronting the ecological issues of the current century requires the recognition of the co-constitution and interdependence of the human being as a part of planetary ecosystems (80). El Roto's, Brieva's, and Ramón's vignettes highlight the extent to which humans and non-humans share the burdens of contemporary capitalism, insofar as they are similarly exploited, objectified, and made precarious. In Ramón's zoomorphic cartoon depicting two polar bears seated on receding ice reading the daily news report about surges in human climate refugees, one reads, "145 millones de personas desplazadas en cinco años por el calentamiento global" ("145 million displaced people in five years because of climate change"), while the other replies, "[R]ecuerdo a los negacionistas riéndose de 'esos pobres ositos.' Bien: parece que, desplazados, no somos los únicos" ("I remember those climate deniers laughing at 'those poor bears.' Well: it seems like we aren't the only ones displaced"; *El País*, 24 May 2014). Not only does the cartoon encourage readers to consider the similarities between human and non-human experience beneath the disruptions wrought by climate change, but it also interrogates the hierarchies according to which life is given value and, thus, is worthy of protection in contemporary political discourse.[18]

El Roto extends his anthropomorphizing to ecological confederations and to forms of plant life in order to point out anthropocentrism and to ridicule both the commodification of complex systems of life and the hypocrisies of nationalist rhetoric. In his depiction of rivers, the cartoonist decries the containment and alteration of water sources and narratives of so-called progress used to justify the market's reduction of complex ecosystems into electricity or concrete-paved water sources for urban centres (El Roto, *El libro verde* 23, 25, 27, 29). In his depiction of trees and forests, the artist stages the hypocrisy of human valorization of place-based origins. Alluding to the contemporary resurgence of nationalist discourse within Spain, Rábago illustrates the indiscriminate uprooting of trees and forests, which provide raw material for industry or clear space for urban development. A hillside of razed stumps speaks, "[N]os ha dicho el leñador que lo importante es conservar las raíces" ("The logger told us that what matters is conserving our roots"; *El País*, 19 Jan. 2017). Echoing the exercise in empathy conducted in fig. 17.8, a caption is attributed to a felled tree: "no parece un asesinato porque no se ve la sangre" ("it doesn't look like murder because there is no blood"; *El País*, 8 May 2016). In another cartoon, the trunks on a loaded truck are given a voice that claims, "[L]os hombres matan por conservar sus raíces pero nos amputan las nuestras" ("Men kill to protect their roots while amputating ours"; *El País*, 12 Dec. 2016). In revealing the disconnect within rhetoric that holds roots as sacred while simultaneously and indiscriminately violating the roots of the very life forms from which such rhetoric stems, these vignettes also indict the hypocrisies of nationalist movements that promulgate the exploitative practices of consumer capitalism.

A final, recurrent anthropomorphized and zoomorphed figure in the work of Spanish cartoonists is the globe itself, the image par excellence of what has now become mainstream global environmental consciousness. Visual culture theorist Nicholas Mirzoeff begins his book *How to See the World* (2016) with a description of how the first photograph of planet earth as a visible whole, taken from the *Apollo 17* spacecraft in 1972, galvanized global consciousness and approximated a deep spiritual experience for contemporary audiences (2–3). Fifty years later, *The Blue Marble*, including its narcissistically edited version that foregrounds North America, has become one of the most reproduced photographs in history and a commonplace visual stand-in for the shallow and commodified environmentalism critiqued by Brieva, Rábago, and Ramón. In their representations of a personified planet, Ramón and Rábago ironically reproduce many of these anthropocentric commonplaces, such as the notion of a sick or destroyed planet. *El libro verde* opens with an image of a zoomorphic globe with a thermometer in its mouth (10), and Ramón frequently depicts one suffering from fever (*El País*, 10 Sept. 2014) or lamenting mankind's failure to implement meaningful climate change policy (*El País*, 7 Dec. 2014, 14 Dec. 2014, and 23 Sept.

2014). Another cartoon by Ramón juxtaposes three images of this zoomorphic globe, strikingly similar to cellphone emojis: a jubilant smiling planet ("la que recibimos" 'the planet we receive'), an ill and feverish planet ("la que vivimos" 'the planet we experience'), and a pungent pile of excrement ("la que dejamos" 'the planet we leave behind'; *El País*, 30 Sept. 2014).

Perhaps one of the most stubborn anthropocentric conceits of contemporary environmental discourse is the idea that mankind can and should save the planet. Ecological thinking, however, subjects the understanding of mankind's current dilemma to deep geological scales of time and finds complexity and new strangeness in what has been taken for granted as known and familiar. As seen in the cover image to *Memorias*, Brieva's anthropomorphized version of the earth illustrates not the massive totality of the globe but rather the very confederation of ecologies beneath the viewer's feet (soil, plants, earthworms …). In a version of this image reproduced within the book, the earth is given speech bubbles that prophetically dismantle human exceptionalism (fig. 17.1):

Y NO OS SINTÁIS ABATIDOS TAMPOCO … QUE SI BIEN VUESTRO DESVANECIMIENTO AUTOINDUCIDO ES SIN DUDA ALGO TRISTE, PENSAD QUE EN APENAS UNOS CIENTOS DE MILLONES DE AÑOS DE NADA … ALGUNA NUEVA ESPECIE, TAN BELLA E INTELIGENTE COMO LA VUESTRA, VOLVERÁ A TENER LA OPORTUNIDAD DE HACER LAS COSAS BIEN …

(And don't feel despondent either … Even if your self-induced disappearance is without a doubt a sad thing, keep in mind that in a mere few hundred million years … some new species, as beautiful and intelligent as yours, will once again have the opportunity to do things right …)

Fig. 17.1 not only encourages identification with the abstract "Tierra" ("sois una ínfima parte de mí. Sois yo misma" 'you are a miniscule part of me. You are me') but decentres the human through the reminder that the human race is but a blip in hundreds of millions of years of terranean history.[19] The drawn perspective of the cartoon places the reader in Brieva's own shoes, contemplating the earth as both same and other, looking straight into the speaking and seeing eye of a living and never fully knowable ecological confederation that returns the reader's gaze. In such an ecological vision, the environmental question is revealed as profoundly human after all.[20]

NOTES

1 All translations throughout the chapter are my own.
2 What are now embedded capitalist and anthropocentric notions of value, humanity, and nature were not always so. For more on modern capitalism's disruption of more symbiotic relationships between humans and non-human nature in the context of Spain, see the chapter by Michael L. Martínez, Jr., in this collection, which deals with the turn from small-scale farming, fishing, and hunting in the Albufera region to larger-scale rice cultivation to support capital accumulation. Whereas I explore the contemporary comic form's propensity for ecocritical commentary, his study shows that the nineteenth- to early twentieth-century naturalist novel's human-nature binary mirrors the foundation of capitalist-centred economic and social progress.
3 Earlier examples of graphic representations of environmental concerns within Spain include illustrations for counterculture and environmentalist magazines – notably, *Ajoblanco* (1974–80), *Alfalfa* (1977–8), and *Bicicleta* (1977–82) – and Max's comic book *Gustavo: Contra la actividad del radio* (1993). There are numerous examples beyond Spain, which include the underground comix anthology *Slow Death Funnies* (1970–92), various graphic narratives, including work by Sue Coe, and comic strips, such as Quino's *Mafalda* (1964–73). The ability of Rábago and Brieva to illustrate ecological issues within contexts deeply critical of consumer culture and capitalist ideology should also be understood within wider artistic and comics traditions. Pablo García, for example, traces conceptual and aesthetic similarities between Rábago's early cartoons in the Spanish satirical magazine *Hermano Lobo* (1972–6) and artistic works by the Valencian duo Equipo Realidad and American underground comics artists, among others.
4 Reporter Mauricio Vincent writes of Rábago's interest in ecological critiques of capitalism that the cartoonist "[c]ree que la crisis [económica] pasará, pero no la vigencia de los problemas medioambientales" ("believes that the [economic] crisis will pass, but not the relevance of environmental problems"). Similarly, Brieva has also stated, "En nuestra actualidad coexisten varias crisis en paralelo" ("Presently, various parallel crises coexist"), adding that "la ecológica ... sin duda es la más grave de todas" ("the ecological crisis ... is, without a doubt, the most serious of all"; Olcina).
5 The terms *ecological thinking* and *ecological thought* have been employed across a wide variety of academic fields for decades (e.g., the humanities, education, anthropology, architecture) and mostly to refer to forms of human thought that reflect the multiple scales of interconnectedness that compose systems of planetary life. In its consideration of the human as

inextricably enmeshed within ecosystems, ecological thought is at times offered as an alternative to "environmental thought" (which expresses concern for what is perceived as external to human activity). In his 2010 monograph, *The Ecological Thought*, Timothy Morton proposes "the ecological thought" as a mode of thinking the interconnectedness of planetary life that extends specifically beyond limited, idealized, and anthropocentric discourses of nature and environment characteristic of modern society and mainstream environmentalisms. For Morton, the ecological thought is profoundly political and, like a virus that heals, "infects all other areas of thinking," undoing the damage that modernity has done not only to ecosystems, species, and the global climate but to thinking itself (2–3). I do not engage with Morton's text here, but my critique of global thinking developed at the end of this chapter diverges from Morton's criticism of the local and praise for thinking big and planetarily. The ecological thought I propose considers the strangeness, complexity, and deep timescales of the very soil beneath one's feet, as seen in the vignette by Brieva that opens and closes this chapter (fig. 17.1). Ecocritic Colleen Culleton traces ecological thinking in techniques of networked literary storytelling, especially those that give equal weight to human and more-than-human forces. For Culleton, ecological thinking perceives the interactions between different systems and is "alert to how causes can be separated from their (intended or unintended) effects by distance and complex networks," especially when considered on a global scale (194).

6 For a more detailed critique of mainstream environmental discourses, see Spanish ecocritic Luis I. Prádanos's description of EU corporate environmentalism ("Toward"), British green political theorist Andrew Dobson's discussion of "light green" and "shallow" environmentalism in *Green Political Thought* (1990), American literary critic Lisa Lebduska's critique of green advertising ("How Green Was My Advertising." *ISLE*, vol. 1, no. 1, 1993, pp. 5–17), and Giacamo D'Alisa et al.'s *Decrecimiento: Un vocabulario para una nueva era* (2015).

7 The "political ecology of waste" and "post-growth imaginaries" described by Prádanos (*Postgrowth Imaginaries*) are types of ecological thought specifically directed to the critique of late-capitalist growth ideology and its processes of consumption and externalization of social and environmental costs. In this chapter, the term *ecological thinking* functions more broadly to refer to the capacity of comics and other art and literary forms to illustrate interspecies relations and the complex networks that compose ecosystems. This capacity often leads to appreciation of the political ecology of waste or post-growth representations of places and events. For example, Carrión and Sagar's *Barcelona: Los vagabundos de la*

chatarra (2015) illustrates "political ecologies of waste" in Barcelona during Spain's Great Recession through the comic's illustration and narration of the material flows of scrap metal. Brieva's illustration of resilient post-capitalist Spanish cities in *Memorias* and *La gran aventura humana* (2017) imagine "post-growth" futures.

8 One example of my comparison between the simultaneity of the image in comics and that of the plastic arts is Argentinian sculptor Adrián Villar Rojas's *Theater of Disappearance*, on display at the Geffen Contemporary at Los Angeles' MOCA from 22 October 2017 to 13 May 2018. Villar Rojas's installation placed objects, such as fruits, metal, stone, flowers, plastic, flesh, and taxidermy animals, together in industrial freezer displays and columns, conjuring reflections on the interconnectedness and ephemerality of contemporary life forms, despite their varying rates of decay.

9 Beyond vignettes and cartoons, graphic illustration allows the presence of material objects and histories to be maintained throughout the linear and long-form narratives of graphic novels (Martínez, "Urban Ecology" 173). Examples of graphic illustration that highlights the presence of environmental devastation in narratives detailing social neglect under twenty-first-century capitalism can be found in the journalistic comic by Carrión and Sagar, *Barcelona: Los vagabundos de la chatarra* (2015), and Joe Sacco's illustrations for Chris Hedges's 2012 non-fiction book *Days of Destruction: Days of Revolt*. For further discussion about the narrative possibilities afforded by visual cultural production, see Carla Almanza-Gálvez's chapter in this collection on *La cuenta atrás*, a graphic novel that details in reverse time the aftermath of the *Prestige* oil spill disaster. In her contribution, Almanza-Gálvez evinces the unique storytelling opportunity afforded by the graphic novel's fundamental unit, the panel, and its counterpart, the gutter, which together engage readers in a verbal and visual ecology of relations as they are required to provide narrative closure to or interpretation of the relational gaps.

10 Brieva and Rábago channel ideas from a number of thinkers. Brieva's corpus includes thought from Austrian philosopher and polymath Ivan Illich on conviviality and technology; Marxist thinkers on hegemony and consumer culture, such as French philosopher Guy Debord and Spanish essayists Santiago Alba Rico and Jorge Reichmann; Spanish economists José Luis Sampedro and Joan Martinez-Alier, who highlight the externalized social and environmental costs of free-market capitalism; ecofeminists, such as Argentinian Spanish philosopher Alicia Puleo and Indian activist Vandana Shiva, who decry the commodification of life under patriarchal capitalism; and Spanish researchers that critique the hegemony of neoliberal capitalism within Spanish democracy, such as sociologist Isidro López and urbanist and activist Ramón Fernández Durán.

11 Cartoons – especially single-panel vignettes that combine simple image and brief text – have a long history of being used to prove a point. Eliot Borenstein notes how, with the growing prevalence of social media, such cartoons are employed and circulated, at times virally, much like memes. Beyond their use as protest images for 15M, El Roto's vignettes have been widely circulated within such a social media context and employed to accompany publications such as the *Última llamada* manifesto (2014). In his description of the re-employment of El Roto's vignettes during 15M protests, philosopher Reyes Mate also mentions how the style of the cartoonist's punchy and acidic language is likewise reproduced in popular 15M slogans, such as "Tu botín, mi crisis" ("Your loot, my crisis") and "Si no nos dejáis soñar, no os dejaremos dormir" ("If you don't let us dream, we won't let you sleep"; qtd. in Touton 212). The circulation of vignettes in social media is often dislocated from the date and context of initial publication, thus favouring constantly updated readings and uses (Touton 212).

12 Rábago's cartoons touching on animal rights give voice to farm animals who proclaim, hanging slaughtered and bleeding from the mouth, "Recordad que os coméis el maltrato que nos dais" ("Remember that you swallow the same abuse that you give to us"; El Roto, *El libro verde* 65; *El País*, 29 June 2014). Two dairy cows remind readers of commodity fetishism, which externalizes their suffering, stating, "En el precio de la leche no incluyen nuestro sufrimiento" ("Our suffering is not included in the price of milk"; *El País*, 30 Sept. 2015). In another vignette, a pig to slaughter looks out from a tiny hole, declaring, "¡En los mataderos también debería intervenir la ONU!" ("The United Nations should intervene in slaughterhouses as well!"; *El País*, 1 Apr. 2016).

13 The history of employing the illustrated animal as a proxy of the human condition spans nineteenth-century political satire; early twentieth-century childhood fictions of morals, friendship, and manners (e.g., *Beatrix Potter*, *Winnie the Pooh*); mid-twentieth-century American comic strips (e.g, *Snoopy*, *Garfield*); massively reproduced characters of 1950s and 1960s American "funny farms" (e.g., Mickey Mouse, Daffy Duck); and the politically subversive or sexually charged figures of underground comics (e.g., Robert Crumb's fetishized ostrich women or Fritz the Cat).

14 Other twenty-first-century comics that employ the graphic image to imagine and translate animal subjectivity and experience include the insect books of entomologist and comics artist Carly Tribull and author and illustrator of science-oriented comics Jay Hosler; author Frédéric Brrémaud and artist Federico Bertolucci's multispecies *LOVE* series (2011–15); writer Grant Morrison, illustrator Frank Quitely, and colourist Jamie Grant's *We3* series (2004); and author Matt Dembicki and illustrator Evan Keeling's graphic novel *Xoc: The Journey of a Great White* (2012).

15 Ramón's comic strip also includes several series of cartoons that illustrate – in more realistic detail – the faces of endangered, trafficked, or caged animals and of various humans from Amazonian and sub-Saharan tribes. These cartoons are drawn in marked contrast to the comic strip's cute and iconic zoomorphs and often face the reader as if making a direct appeal, much in the style of mediatized animal rights and human rights campaigns of the 1990s. In a clear attempt to inspire a pathetic response to information on current events, Ramón anthropomorphically draws a single tear falling from the eyes of illustrated animals (*El País*, 30 Sept. 2014 and 13 Oct. 2013). While one series of cartoons highlights the situation of domestic animals, Ramón's illustrated animals appeal to urbanite sensibilities of conservation and wilderness, prioritizing big game and exotic species. Most of Ramón's zoomorphs and illustrated animals are more aptly understood as didactic and pedagogical tools meant to introduce trending topics in species conservation to a wide age range of readers ("*ELPAÍS.es* presenta"). These cartoons provide information regarding exotic species, extinction trends, CO_2 increases, and so on but do little to challenge the central categories structuring environmentalist and conservationist discourse.

16 Rábago's non-human animal vignettes reflect a long tradition of animal ethics predicated upon consideration of the sentience of non-human animals (Gary Francione) and their capacity to suffer (Peter Singer) or the re-evaluation of conceptual categories dividing humans and non-human animals (Jacques Derrida and Donna Haraway). In contrast to rights-based (Tom Regan) or feminist (Kathy Rudy) approaches, which develop frameworks for the custodianship and care of the so-called animal "other," Pelluchon considers "la causa animal" ("the animal cause") as "también nuestra causa" ("our cause as well"). As a result, she calls for an "animalism" that is at the same time a profoundly rethought humanism, which breaks from anthropocentric frameworks of Enlightenment philosophy (42).

17 The legal attribution of personhood and enforceable rights to nature and ecosystems was first written into the Ecuadorian constitution of 2008, an innovation made possible by engaging with Indigenous frameworks for personhood and nature as Pachamama. The ability of humans to bring legal cases against the abuse of ecosystems has been central to international projects such as the Universal Declaration of the Rights of Mother Earth, signed in 2010 in Cochabamba (Bolivia) and the International Rights of Nature Tribunals (2014–present). Anthropomorphism is central in such legal tasks as humans speak on behalf of violated ecosystems. Similarly, the development of notions of "humanism" and "the human" that shed anthropocentric and colonialist foundations has been fundamental in the emergent field of the environmental humanities. These legal and philosophical notions

aim to better reflect the place of humans within complex ecosystems and consider the intelligence of other forms of life.

18 Rábago's anthropomorphism further exposes such hierarchies and highlights the double standards of denying rights to sentient and autonomous beings in a society that supposedly values justice and the rule of law. One vignette gives posthumous words to a felled stag, who asks, "¿Por qué nos matáis sin juicio?" ("Why do you kill us without a trial?"; El Roto, *El libro verde* 55). Another cartoon features a caged ape, who inquires, "¿Puede alguien explicarme por qué estoy entre rejas y de qué se me acusa?" ("Can someone explain to me why I am behind bars and of what crime I am accused?"; *El País*, 5 June 2015). While Ramón's anthropomorphically attributed captions most often take the form of accusations, commands, and statements (e.g., in *El País*, 27 Oct. 2012, a grey wolf exclaims, "¡Vosotros sí que sois dañinos!" 'You are the harmful ones!'), El Roto's technique of posing questions gives more room for the reader to work through the deeply embedded anthropocentric foundations of culturally normalized practices.

19 Perhaps one of the next frontiers for comics and ecological thinking lies in addressing the challenges of perceiving the non-human scales of time that make up contemporary ecosystems, climate crises, and ecologies of "waste." This task has been taken up already by Brieva in *La gran aventura humana: Pasado, presente y futuro del mono desnudo* (2017), Richard McGuire's graphic novel *Here* (2014), and shorter pieces of comics journalism, such as American journalist and editorial cartoonist Susie Cagle's comics illustration of plastics waste research ("Humans Have Made 8.3bn Tons of Plastic since 1950," *Guardian*, 23 June 2019).

20 *Human*, in this statement, no longer assumes speciesism; nor does it refer to scientific definitions of *Homo sapiens* or Western colonial assumptions of humankind as an isolated, superior species. My use of the term is deeply revised to recognize the human as a confederation of living and non-living things, including gut bacteria and minerals, for example, inextricable from the ecologies in which it is embedded. *Human* also refers to the capacity for personhood, subjectivity, and will among sentient life and the potential for identification and communication between these life forms.

WORKS CITED AND CONSULTED

Bennett, Jane. *Vibrant Matter: A Political Ecology of Things*. Duke UP, 2010.
Borenstein, Eliot. "Re: proofreading." Email to the author. 27 Jan. 2020.
Brieva, Miguel. La gran aventura humana. Reservoir, 2017.
Brieva, Miguel. *Memorias de la tierra: El otro mundo*. Vol. 2, Random House Mondadori, 2012.

Brieva, Miguel. "El secuestro de la imaginación como freno crucial al cambio social." *Revista de ALCES XXI*, vol. 1, 2013, pp. 297–353.

Cagle, Susie. "Humans Have Made 8.3bn Tons of Plastic since 1950. This Is the Illustrated Story of Where It's Gone." *Guardian*, 24 June 2019, https://www.theguardian.com/us-news/2019/jun/23/all-the-plastic-ever-made-study-comic.

Carrión, Jorge, and Sagar. *Barcelona: Los vagabundos de la chatarra*. Norma, 2015.

Culleton, Colleen P. "The Force of Nature: Learning to Think Ecologically from Rúben Abella's *El libro del amor esquivo*." *Letras Hispanas*, vol. 13, 2017, pp. 194–206.

D'Alisa, Giacomo, et al. *Decrecimiento: Un vocabulario para una nueva era*. Icaria, 2015.

Dobson, Andrew. *Green Political Thought*. 2nd ed., Routledge, 1995.

"*ELPAIS.es* presenta un tira cómica ecológica sobre las aventuras de cuatro hipopótamos en África." *El País*, 10 Feb. 2006, https://elpais.com/elpais/2006/01/23/opinion/1138009139_850215.html.

Feinberg, Leonard. *Introduction to Satire*. Iowa State UP, 1967.

García, Pablo. "OPS y El Roto en *Hermano Lobo*: Radiografías de una sociedad." *Tebeosfera*, vol. 2, no. 12, 28 Jan. 2014, https://www.tebeosfera.com/documentos/ops_y_el_roto_en_hermano_lobo._radiografias_de_una_sociedad.html.

Hedges, Chris, and Joe Sacco. *Days of Destruction, Days of Revolt*. Nation Books, 2012.

Lebduska, Lisa. "How Green Was My Advertising: American Ecoconsumerism." *Interdisciplinary Studies in Literature and Environment*, vol. 1, no. 1, spring 1993, pp. 5–17.

Martínez, Christine M. "The Affirmative Politics of Degrowth: Miguel Brieva's Graphic Narrative *Memorias de la Tierra*." *Journal of Spanish Cultural Studies*, vol. 18, no. 2, 2017, pp. 191–212. *Taylor & Francis Online*, https://doi.org/10.1080/14636204.2017.1308631.

Martínez, Christine M. "Urban Ecology and Comics Journalism in Jorge Carrión and Sagar Forniés' *Barcelona: Los vagabundos de la chatarra* (2015)." *Consequential Art: Comics Culture in Contemporary Spain*, edited by Samuel Amago and Matthew J. Marr, Toronto UP, 2019, pp. 164–91. *De Gruyter*, https://doi.org/10.3138/9781487531386-008.

Mate, Reyes. "El Roto, au secours d'une réalité occultée." *Le cahier électrique*, by El Roto, Les Cahiers Dessinés, 2013, pp. 7–17.

McGuire, Richard. *Here*. Pantheon, 2014.

Mirzoeff, Nicholas. *How to See the World*. Basic Books, 2016.

Moore, Jason W. *Capitalism in the Web of Life: Ecology and the Accumulation of Capital*. Verso, 2015.

Morton, Timothy. *The Ecological Thought*. Harvard UP, 2010.

Morton, Timothy. *Hyperobjects: Philosophy and Ecology after the End of the World*. Minnesota UP, 2013.

Mourenza, Daniel. "El Roto: A Political Cartoonist in Late Capitalist Spain." *Romance Quarterly*, vol. 63, no. 2, 2016, pp. 83–96. *Taylor & Francis Online*, https://doi.org/10.1080/08831157.2016.1146019.

Olcina Alvarado, Mariola. "Entrevista a Miguel Brieva, autor de *Memorias de la Tierra*." *El Ecologista (Ecologistas en Acción)*, no. 72, 2012, pp. 40–1.

Pelluchon, Corine. *Manifiesto animalista: Politizar la causa animal*. Translated by Juan Vivanco, Penguin Random House, 2018.

Pestana, Mariana. "Eco-visionaries: Art and Architecture after the Anthropocene." *Eco-visionaries: Art, Architecture and New Media after the Anthropocene*, edited by Pedro Gadanho, Hatje Cantz Verlag, 2018, pp. 72–91.

Prádanos, Luis I. *Postgrowth Imaginaries: New Ecologies and Counterhegemonic Culture in Post-2008 Spain*. Liverpool UP, 2018.

Prádanos, Luis I. "Toward a Euro-Mediterranean Socioenvironmental Perspective: The Case for a Spanish Ecocriticism." *Ecozon@*, vol. 4, no. 2, 2013, pp. 30–48, https://doi.org/10.37536/ECOZONA.2013.4.2.527.

Ramón [Ramón Rodríguez]. Cartoon. El País, 7 Dec. [6 Dec.] 2014, https://elpais.com/elpais/2014/12/06/vinetas/1417884318_584480.html.

Ramón [Ramón Rodríguez]. Cartoon. El País, 10 Oct. [9 Oct.] 2014, https://elpais.com/elpais/2014/10/09/vinetas/1412874202_710574.html.

Ramón [Ramón Rodríguez]. Cartoon. El País, 8 Oct. [7 Oct.] 2014, https://elpais.com/elpais/2014/10/07/vinetas/1412678067_378412.html.

Ramón [Ramón Rodríguez]. Cartoon. El País, 3 Oct. [2 Oct.] 2014, https://elpais.com/elpais/2014/10/02/vinetas/1412268575_630583.html.

Ramón [Ramón Rodríguez]. Cartoon. El País, 30 Sept. [29 Sept.] 2014, https://elpais.com/elpais/2014/09/29/vinetas/1412009190_822931.html.

Ramón [Ramón Rodríguez]. Cartoon. El País, 23 Sept. [22 Sept.] 2014, https://elpais.com/elpais/2014/09/22/vinetas/1411398362_133620.html.

Ramón [Ramón Rodríguez]. Cartoon. El País, 10 Sept. [9 Sept.] 2014, https://elpais.com/elpais/2014/09/09/vinetas/1410282233_923519.html.

Ramón [Ramón Rodríguez]. Cartoon. El País, 30 June [29 June] 2014, https://elpais.com/elpais/2014/06/29/vinetas/1404058870_896784.html.

Ramón [Ramón Rodríguez]. Cartoon. El País, 24 July [23 July] 2013, https://elpais.com/elpais/2013/07/23/vinetas/1374593373_140228.html.

Ramón [Ramón Rodríguez]. Cartoon. El País, 24 May [23 May] 2013, https://elpais.com/elpais/2014/05/23/vinetas/1400864720_409673.html.

Ramón [Ramón Rodríguez]. Cartoon. El País, 17 May [16 May] 2013, https://elpais.com/elpais/2014/05/16/vinetas/1400256747_072552.html.

Ramón [Ramón Rodríguez]. Cartoon. El País, 2 Oct. [1 Oct.] 2012, https://elpais.com/elpais/2012/10/02/vinetas/1349129157_370801.html.

Ramón [Ramón Rodríguez]. Cartoon. El País, 25 May 2010, https://elpais
    .com/elpais/2010/05/26/actualidad/1274867105_850215.html.
Ramón [Ramón Rodríguez]. Cartoon. El País, 3 Feb. 2010, https://elpais.com
    /elpais/2010/02/04/actualidad/1265280305_850215.html.
Ramón [Ramón Rodríguez]. Cartoon. El País, 7 Oct. 2008, https://elpais.com
    /elpais/2008/10/08/actualidad/1223459106_850215.html.
Ramón [Ramón Rodríguez]. Cartoon. El País, 22 Feb. 2007, https://elpais
    .com/elpais/2007/02/23/actualidad/1172227505_850215.html.
Robinson, Nathan J. "How Wild Animals Became the Proletariat." *Current
    Affairs*, 7 May 2019, https://www.currentaffairs.org/2019/05/how
    -wild-animals-became-the-proletariat.
El Roto [Andrés Rábago]. Cartoon. El País, 12 Mar. [11 Mar.] 2018, https://
    elpais.com/elpais/2018/03/11/opinion/1520793333_598936.html.
El Roto [Andrés Rábago]. Cartoon. El País, 17 July [16 July] 2017, https://
    elpais.com/elpais/2017/07/15/opinion/1500132039_263713.html.
El Roto [Andrés Rábago]. Cartoon. El País, 7 Apr. [6 Apr.] 2017, https://elpais
    .com/elpais/2017/04/06/opinion/1491491925_495577.html.
El Roto [Andrés Rábago]. Cartoon. El País, 19 Jan. [18 Jan.] 2017, https://
    elpais.com/elpais/2017/01/18/opinion/1484755315_502072.html.
El Roto [Andrés Rábago]. Cartoon. El País, 12 Dec. 2016, https://elpais.com
    /elpais/2016/12/12/opinion/1481557513_456398.html.
El Roto [Andrés Rábago]. Cartoon. El País, 8 May [7 May] 2016, https://
    elpais.com/elpais/2016/05/07/opinion/1462636307_705323.html.
El Roto [Andrés Rábago]. Cartoon. El País, 21 July 2015, https://elpais.com
    /elpais/2015/07/21/vinetas/1437498421_895542.html.
El Roto [Andrés Rábago]. Cartoon. El País, 25 Dec. [24 Dec.] 2014, https://
    elpais.com/elpais/2014/12/24/vinetas/1419429235_524676.html.
El Roto [Andrés Rábago]. Cartoon. El País, 24 May [23 May] 2014, https://
    elpais.com/elpais/2014/05/23/vinetas/1400864544_636390.html.
El Roto [Andrés Rábago]. Cartoon. El País, 1 Mar. [2 Mar.] 2012, https://
    elpais.com/elpais/2012/03/01/vinetas/1330627159_835395.html.
El Roto [Andrés Rábago]. *El libro verde*. Random House, 2014.
El Roto [Andrés Rábago]. *Viñetas para una crisis*. Random House, 2011.
Sousanis, Nick. *Unflattening*. Harvard UP, 2015.
Touton, Isabelle. "Los chistes gráficos de El Roto y J. R. Mora como 'arma de
    destrucción pasiva' antineoliberal." *Revista de ALCES XXI*, vol. 1, 2013,
    pp. 205–47.
Villar Rojas, Adrián. *Theater of Disappearance*. 22 Oct. 2017–13 May 2018, Geffen
    Contemporary at MOCA, Los Angeles.
Vincent, Mauricio. "El Roto: 'La naturaleza tiene tiempo, el hombre no.'" *El
    País*, 21 Nov. 2014, https://elpais.com/cultura/2014/11/21/actualidad
    /1416571162_957753.html.

Yezbick, Daniel F. "Lions and Tigers and Fears: A Natural History of the Sequential Animal." *Animal Comics: Multispecies Storyworlds in Graphic Narratives*, edited by David Herman, Bloomsbury, 2017, pp. 29–52. *Bloomsbury Collections*, https://doi.org/10.5040/9781350015340.ch-001.

Contributors

Carla Almanza-Gálvez teaches Hispanic studies at the University of Limerick (Ireland), where she is an affiliated member of the Ralahine Centre for Utopian Studies and the Centre for Early Modern Studies. Her research interests include urban and environmental fiction, graphic narrative, utopianism, and the Enlightenment. She is the author of *Form and Reform in Eighteenth-Century Spain: Utopian Narratives and Sociopolitical Debate* (Legenda, 2019). She has also contributed chapters and articles to a number of edited volumes and scholarly journals.

Daniel Ares-López is assistant professor of Spanish at San Diego State University. His main areas of specialization are Iberian cultural studies, environmental cultural studies, literary and film ecocriticism, and creative environmental writing. His first book project (under contract at U of Toronto P) is titled *Cultures of Nature and Iberian Wildlife in Francoist Spain (1940–1980)*. It investigates the ways capitalist modernization processes during the Francoist period transformed historical relations between human communities and wildlife, generating new productivist and biopolitical understandings of wild animals and plants. This project also proposes a theoretical revision of cultural studies and cultural history using a material-semiotic and socio-environmental approach. As a creative writer, Daniel has published the ecopoetry book *El cuaderno mundano* (Valparaíso, 2021).

John Beusterien is professor of Spanish at Texas Tech University and has published *Transoceanic Animals as Spectacle in Early Modern Spain* (Amsterdam UP, 2020), *Canines in Cervantes and Velázquez: An Animal Studies Reading of Early Modern Spain* (Routledge, 2013), and *An Eye on Race: Perspectives from Theater in Imperial Spain* (Bucknell UP, 2006). He has also co-edited *Goodbye Eros: Recasting Forms and Norms of Love in the*

Age of Cervantes (U of Toronto P, 2020), *Death and Afterlife: The Case of the Early Modern Hispanic World* (special issue of *Hispanic Issues On Line*, 2010), *Sustaining Ecocriticism: Comparative Perspectives* (special issue of *Comparative Literature Studies*, 2013), and *Touching the Ground: Female Footwear in the Early Modern Hispanic World* (special issue of the *Journal of Spanish Cultural Studies*, 2013), which won the Collaborative Project Award from the Society for the Study of Early Modern Women.

Mᵃ Concepción Brito-Vera is an associate professor at the University of La Laguna, Canary Islands, Spain. Her research focuses on South and South-East Asian literature from a spatial perspective and on material ecocriticism, environmental justice, and crime fiction. She was a jury member for the IX Premio Ciudad de Santa Cruz de Novela Criminal (City of Santa Cruz Prize for Crime Fiction) in 2023. Her publications include "Life out of Balance and Its Aftermath. Paradoxes in Arundhati Roy's *The Ministry of Utmost Happiness*: A Material Ecocritical Reading," with Mᵃ Luz González-Rodríguez, in the edited volume *Aftermath: The Fall and the Rise after the Event* (Jagiellonian UP, 2019); "Absolute and Abstract Spaces: The Sea, the City and Class Divisions in Thrity Umrigar's *The Space between Us*" (*Annales Universitatis Paedagogicae Cracoviensis*, 2016); "A Spatial Reading of Fiona Cheong's 'Shadow Theatre': The Production of Subversive Female Spaces," in the edited volume *English and American Studies in Spain: New Developments and Trends* (Universidad de Alcalá, 2015); and "Science and Discourse, Acculturation and Schizophrenia in the Literary Work of Singaporean Author Catherine Lim" (*Via Panoramica*, 2014).

Olga Colbert is associate professor of Spanish at Southern Methodist University in Dallas. She received her PhD from Stanford University in 1999. Her book *The Gaze on the Past: History and Popular Culture in the Novels of Antonio Muñoz Molina* was published by Bucknell UP in 2007. Her work has appeared in journals such as *España Contemporánea*, *Romance Language Notes*, *Ojáncano*, *Revista Hispánica Moderna*, and numerous anthologies. Her research interests include contemporary Spanish literature and culture, ecocriticism, historical discourses, and cognitive approaches to literature. She has contributed to the ecocritical anthology *Energy in Literature: Essays on Energy and Its Social and Environmental Implications in Twentieth-Century Literary Texts*, edited by Paula Farca ("In the Shadow of the Mine: Life and Death in Julio Llamazares' *Escenas de cine mudo*"). Her most recent work examines the representation of states of consciousness in literature, such as her chapters in Leslie Marsh's edited anthology *Theology and Geometry: Essays on John Kennedy Toole's* A Confederacy of Dunces ("Ignatius' Brain") and

Grzegorz Maziarczyk's edited volume *Novelistic Inquiries into the Mind* ("Apocalypse and A-bomb: States of Consciousness in John Kennedy Toole's *A Confederacy of Dunces*").

Daniel Frost is professor and former chair of Spanish at the College of the Holy Cross in Worcester, MA, where he teaches language, literature, and culture. He is author of *Cultivating Madrid: Public Space and Middle-Class Culture in Madrid, 1833–1890* (Bucknell UP, 2008) and has published articles in the *International Journal of Iberian Studies*, the *Journal of Spanish Cultural Studies*, *Modern Language Notes*, and the *Revista de Estudios Hispánicos* on how public landscapes and emerging technologies such as the phantasmagoria and *diligencia* figure in eighteenth- and nineteenth-century literary representation in Spain.

Bonnie L. Gasior is professor of transatlantic literary studies of the early modern period (Spain and Latin America). She is also a Faculty Fellow with Innovative Teaching and Future Faculty Development at the CSU Chancellor's Office (2020–) and a mental health first aid instructor. Dr. Gasior has co-edited three volumes: with Mindy Badía, *Crosscurrents: Transatlantic Perspectives on Early Modern Hispanic Drama* (Bucknell UP, 2006) and *Reconsidering Early Modern Spanish Literature through Mass and Pop Culture: Contemporizing the Classics in the Classroom* (Juan de la Cuesta, 2021); and, with Yolanda Gamboa, *Making Sense of the Senses: Current Approaches in Spanish* Comedia *Criticism* (Juan de la Cuesta, 2017), which earned the 2020 Vern Williamsen Comedia Book Prize. Her textbook, also with Badía – *Redes literarias: Antología del texto hispánico en su contexto histórico-cultural* (McFarland, 2018) – was recently reviewed in *Hispania*. Her most recent book project, a co-authored manuscript under contract with Routledge, is titled *Internships, High-Impact Practices and Provocative Praxis in Higher Education: A Social Justice Framework Based on Diversity, Equity, and Inclusion*.

Mª Luz González-Rodríguez is an associate professor at the University of La Laguna, Canary Islands, Spain. Her research focuses on Anglo-Canadian literature, cultural studies, and Anglo-Indian literature belonging to the American and Canadian diaspora. Her publications deal with women's studies and the search for identity from both an individual and a national point of view through symbology, Jungian psychoanalysis, ecocriticism, and affect studies. Among her latest publications are "El cuerpo de la mujer como trofeo nacional en *Cracking India* de Bapsi Sidhwa: Historias de vergüenza y culpa" (*Philologica Canariensia*, 2023); "The Overflow of Contained Emotions in Anita Rau Badami's *The Hero's Walk*: An Analysis of Affects through the Imagery of Water" (*Indialogs*, 2022); "'Cultural Schizophrenia' in Some Diasporic Indian Women Writers," with Juan Ignacio Oliva, in the edited volume *Revolving around India(s): Alternative Images, Emerging Perspectives* (Cambridge Scholars, 2020); and "Life out of Balance and Its Aftermath," with Mᵃ Concepción Brito-Vera, in the edited volume *Aftermath: The Fall and the Rise after the Event* (Jagiellonian UP, 2019).

Victoria L. Ketz is professor of Spanish, chairperson of Foreign Languages and Literatures, and director of the Central and Eastern European Studies Program at La Salle University in Philadelphia, PA. Dr. Ketz publishes on curricular innovation and new classroom technologies, as well as on historical memory, immigration, violence against women, and urban studies in the context of twentieth- and twenty-first-century Spanish literature. In 2015, she co-edited with Debra Faszer McMahon *African Immigrants in Contemporary Spanish Texts: Crossing the Strait* (Ashgate). In 2019, she co-edited with Esther Fernández a special edition on disability studies for the *Revista de Estudios de Género y Sexualidades*. In 2021, she published the collection of essays *A Laboratory of Her Own: Women and Science in Spanish Contemporary Cultural Productions*, co-edited with Debra Faszer McMahon and Dawn Smith Sherwood (Vanderbilt UP). Her current book project examines the representation of gender-based violence and the usurpation of the female voice in contemporary Spanish writings.

Maryanne L. Leone is professor of Spanish and chairperson of the Department of Modern and Classical Languages and Cultures at Assumption University in Worcester, MA. Her ecocritical work includes studies of feminist ethics of care and synergies between environmental and disability studies, with publications in *Ecozon@* and the *Revista de Estudios de Género y Sexualidades*; her entry on ecofeminism for the *Companion to Spanish Environmental Cultural Studies* (Tamesis, 2023), co-written with Shanna Lino; and this book. Dr. Leone has also published on gender and migration in contemporary Spanish narrative in *Anales de la Literatura Contemporánea Española*, *Letras Hispanas*, the *Revista Canadiense de Estudios Hispánicos*, and the edited volumes *A Laboratory of Her Own: Women and Science in Spanish Culture* (Vanderbilt UP, 2020) and *Toward a Multicultural Configuration of Spain: Local Cities, Global Spaces* (Farleigh Dickinson UP, 2015).

Shanna Lino is associate professor of Spanish and Latin American Cultures & Societies at York University's Collège universitaire Glendon. She has published on the representation of immigration to Spain in short fiction by women writers, the *novela negra*, and Basque and Catalan crime fiction. Her articles have appeared in *Studies in 20th and 21st Century Literature*, *L'édudit franco-espagnol*, and the *Revista Canadiense de Estudios Hispánicos*, for which she co-edited with Luis Molina Lora the special issue *Tráfico y producción cultural: Trazas de una globalización fragmentada* (2013). She has chapters in *Fronteras de la memoria: Cartografías de género en artes visuales, cine y literatura en las Américas y España* (Cuarto Propio, 2012) and *African Immigrants in Contemporary Spanish Texts: Crossing the Straits* (Ashgate, 2015). Her more recent focus on ecocriticism and ecohorror is reflected in her chapter in *Spanish and Latin American Women's Crime Fiction in the New Millennium: From Noir to Gris* (Cambridge Scholars, 2017); her entry on ecofeminism for the *Companion to Spanish Environmental Cultural Studies* (Tamesis, 2023), co-written with Maryanne L. Leone; and this book.

Margaret Marek is professor of Spanish at Illinois College in Jacksonville, IL. She has published on Cervantes and on the *libro de pastores*. She is particularly interested in the intersection of these books and the booming Merino wool trade, which drove the early modern Spanish economy. She studies herding practices, both early modern and present-day, and has spent time with Merino flock owners in León and Extremadura.

Juan Carlos Martín Galván is professor of Spanish at Stonehill College in Easton, MA. His research interests include the study of historical memory in Spanish narrative and feminist approaches to science fiction, ecocriticism, and post-human/non-human identities. He is the author of *Voces silenciadas: La memoria histórica en el realismo documental de la narrativa española del siglo XXI* (Libertarias Prodhufi, 2009). Other publications include "Narración, monstruosidad y la condición poshumana en *El peso del corazón*: La segunda novela de Bruna Husky" (*Hispanófila*, 2016), "Hacia una identidad poshumana: El Planeta hembra de Gabriela Bustelo" (*Millars. Espai i Historia*, 2016), "El universo posthumano de *Lágrimas en la lluvia*: La memoria artificial como constructora de la identidad, la historia y la ficción" (*Alambique*, 2017), and "'The Plague:' Nonhuman, Posthuman, and the Environment in Spanish Science Fiction" (*Ometeca*, 2018–19).

Christine M. Martínez is a postdoctoral fellow in the Department of Spanish and Portuguese Languages and Literatures at New York University. Her research and teaching develop ecofeminist and ecocritical readings of film, comics, literature, and photography that critique neoliberal capitalism and consumer society in Spain and beyond. She is particularly interested in communities and creators that imagine socially desirable and ecologically sustainable alternatives through decolonizing and re-localizing practices of economy, community engagement, and agroecology. She is an active member of the Ecopedagogy Working Group with ALCESXXI and has published various articles and book chapters on ecological thought and Spanish comics in the *Journal of Spanish Cultural Studies*; in *Consequential Art: Comics Culture in Contemporary Spain*, edited by Samuel Amago and Matthew Marr (U of Toronto P, 2019); and with co-author Jorge Catalá in the *Companion to Spanish Environmental Cultural Studies*, edited by Luis I. Prádanos (Tamesis, 2023).

Michael L. Martínez, Jr., is assistant professor of Spanish at Georgia State University-Perimeter College. His research interests include urban studies, ecocriticism, critical geography, and contemporary Spanish literature and culture. He has published articles in the *Bulletin of Spanish Studies*, the *Journal of Urban Cultural Studies*, and the *Arizona Journal of Hispanic Cultural Studies*. His current book project examines neoliberal capital's co-production of urban spaces and cultural imaginaries in Madrid during Spain's Transition and early democratic periods.

Micah McKay is assistant professor of Spanish at the University of Alabama. His first book, *Beyond the Dump: Trash and Limits in Contemporary Latin American Culture* (under contract with U of Florida P), is a study of the representation of trash in contemporary Latin American cultural production and attempts to consider the ecological, political, and aesthetic stakes of waste. He is the co-editor of *Environmental Cultural Studies through Time: The Luso-Hispanic World* (special issue of *Hispanic Issues On Line*, 2019), and his work has appeared in *Chasqui*, the *Latin American Literary Review*, the *Luso-Brazilian Review*, the *Revista Canadiense de Estudios Hispánicos*, and *Romance Notes*.

Luis I. Prádanos (Iñaki) is professor of Hispanic contemporary studies at Miami University. His research focuses on political ecology and the environmental humanities in relation to contemporary Iberian cultures. Iñaki is the author of *Postgrowth Imaginaries: New Ecologies and Counterhegemonic Culture in Post-2008 Spain* (Liverpool UP, 2018). In recent years, he has guest-edited four special issues related to ecocriticism and the environmental humanities for different academic journals: *Contemporary Iberian Ecocriticism and New Materialisms* (*Letras Hispanas*, 2017); *South Atlantic Ecocriticism*, with Mark Anderson (*Ecozon@*, 2017); *Humanidades ambientales: Ecocrítica y descolonización cultural* (*Revista de*

Teoría de la Literatura y Literatura Comparada, 2019); and *Culture and Ecology in Contemporary Iberian Cultural Studies* (*Arizona Journal of Hispanic Cultural Studies*, 2019). Iñaki is the editor of the *Companion to Spanish Environmental Cultural Studies* (Tamesis, 2023).

Óscar Iván Useche is a lecturer in culture and writing at the University of Wisconsin-Madison. As a specialist in modern peninsular studies, he focuses on exploring the interaction between industrial modernization and cultural production in *fin-de-siglo* Spain. He is the author of *Founders of the Future: The Science and Industry of Spanish Modernization* (Bucknell UP, 2022). His work has also appeared in a variety of academic publications, including the *Journal of Spanish Cultural Studies*, *Decimonónica*, and *Siglodiecinueve*. Currently he is at work on a new book project about failed inventions, scientific hoaxes, and literary forgery at the turn of the twentieth century.

William Viestenz is associate professor of Spanish in the Department of Spanish and Portuguese Studies at the University of Minnesota, Twin Cities, where he holds a joint appointment at the Institute for Global Studies. He graduated from Stanford University with a PhD in Iberian and Latin American cultures in 2011. Prof. Viestenz specializes in modern Iberian literature and culture, with an emphasis on the intersection of Catalan studies and political theory. He is the author of *By the Grace of God: Franco's Spain and the Sacred Roots of Political Imagination* (U of Toronto P, 2014) and has co-edited *The New Ruralism: An Epistemology of Transformed Space* (Iberoamericana/Vervuert, 2013), *Ethics of Life: Contemporary Iberian Debates* (Vanderbilt UP, 2016), and *A Polemical Companion to* Ethics of Life: Contemporary Iberian Debates (special issue of *Hispanic Issues On Line*, 2016). He has published multiple articles in specialized journals and contributed to a number of edited volumes.

Index

Note: The letter *f* following a page number denotes a figure and the letter *m*, a map.

Toronto Iberic

CO-EDITORS: Robert Davidson (Toronto) and Frederick A. de Armas (Chicago)

EDITORIAL BOARD: Josiah Blackmore (Harvard); Marina Brownlee (Princeton); Anthony J. Cascardi (Berkeley); Justin Crumbaugh (Mt Holyoke); Emily Francomano (Georgetown); Jordana Mendelson (NYU); Joan Ramon Resina (Stanford); Enrique García Santo-Tomás (U Michigan); H. Rosi Song (Durham); Kathleen Vernon (SUNY Stony Brook)

1 Anthony J. Cascardi, *Cervantes, Literature, and the Discourse of Politics*
2 Jessica A. Boon, *The Mystical Science of the Soul: Medieval Cognition in Bernardino de Laredo's Recollection Method*
3 Susan Byrne, *Law and History in Cervantes'* Don Quixote
4 Mary E. Barnard and Frederick A. de Armas (eds.), *Objects of Culture in the Literature of Imperial Spain*
5 Nil Santiáñez, *Topographies of Fascism: Habitus, Space, and Writing in Twentieth-Century Spain*
6 Nelson Orringer, *Lorca in Tune with Falla: Literary and Musical Interludes*
7 Ana M. Gómez-Bravo, *Textual Agency: Writing Culture and Social Networks in Fifteenth-Century Spain*
8 Javier Irigoyen-García, *The Spanish Arcadia: Sheep Herding, Pastoral Discourse, and Ethnicity in Early Modern Spain*
9 Stephanie Sieburth, *Survival Songs: Conchita Piquer's* Coplas *and Franco's Regime of Terror*
10 Christine Arkinstall, *Spanish Female Writers and the Freethinking Press, 1879–1926*
11 Margaret E. Boyle, *Unruly Women: Performance, Penitence, and Punishment in Early Modern Spain*